America in Our Time

America in Our Time

1896 - 1946

Dwight Lowell Dumond

PROFESSOR OF HISTORY—UNIVERSITY OF MICHIGAN

Henry Holt and Company

PRINTED IN THE UNITED STATES OF AMERICA

Preface

THE first half of the twentieth century constitutes a distinct epoch in American history. The Square Deal of Theodore Roosevelt, the New Freedom of Woodrow Wilson, and the New Deal of Franklin D. Roosevelt were but stages in the progress of one great reform movement. World War I and World War II were but episodes in one great contest of armies and ideas. Both the reform movement and the wars produced an intellectual ferment, a conflict of ideas, and a revolution in concepts and attitudes which taxed our faith and democratic processes, the flexibility of our institutions, and our adaptability to changing environment.

It has been a turbulent half-century, in many ways more dynamic, complex, and romantic than any comparable period of American life. Gigantic forces have altered our physical and social environment with bewildering swiftness. Since we are a democracy, and our democracy has not withered with age, it is essential to know something of these changes in our social and economic life. The author has tried diligently to avoid overemphasizing one aspect of activities at the expense of others. Economic, social, and political developments and foreign affairs are all given the space warranted by their delicate interrelationship.

Writing a history of the recent past is extremely difficult. It must be done, however, because our young people today were Depression offspring. They know nothing from experience about World War I, the rampaging twenties, or the Great Depression. Yet, knowledge of those years, as a minimum, is essential to intelligent citizenship today; and only *intelligent* citizenship can provide the stability and the courage essential to progress, even to survival, in an atomic age.

Much has happened in this old world of ours since *Roosevelt to Roosevelt* was published in 1937. *America in Our Time, 1896–1946,* is a revision of that pioneer effort in the field of Recent American History. The book has been completely reorganized, the history of the last decade has been added, and greater emphasis has been placed upon the role of the United States in world affairs.

The author has not shirked his responsibility to interpret as well as to record, knowing full well that it is difficult to interpret correctly the events of one's own generation. We are a people of many minds, and the views of other men will not always coincide with these interpretations. That is as it should be. There is nothing more stimulating to thought than the knowledge that scholars disagree.

DWIGHT L. DUMOND

Ann Arbor, Mich.
January 15, 1947

Contents

vii

CONTENTS

CONTENTS

CONTENTS

CONTENTS

America in Our Time

1

The Heritage of
Twentieth-Century Americans

THE SOUTH

THE turn of the century opened a new era in the history of the United States. The westward movement was complete. The spirit of imperialism had been satiated, finally, by the acquisition of our island possessions in the Caribbean and the Pacific. Boundary disputes with Canada and Mexico, the interminable search for a satisfactory land policy, the herding of Indians into reservations, the fratricidal contest over human bondage—all these problems of national expansion had been disposed of, however unsatisfactory the disposition might have been in many respects. The people of the United States were a nation, smugly satisfied with their achievements, glorying in their strength, and for the most part, tragically unaware of the unsolved problems created by the blunderings of past generations.

The veterans of the Union armies of the Civil War had finally come into their own and were wielding a power in the nation far beyond their numerical strength. They were enjoying the reward of earlier sacrifice at the expense of the public treasury, and the glory that was theirs shone too brightly for most people to see the stark realities of a great national tragedy. We had freed the slaves, given them civil equality with the whites, and saved the Union from dismemberment; but the superficial attempt to elevate the Negro in the South to social and political equality with the whites

1

had been abandoned amid a wreckage of social disorganization and economic chaos. Slavery had provided a fixed relationship between the two races. Its merits and deficiencies are fairly well established but not germane to our present problems. It may be that a slow transition from the status of slavery to that of freedom could have been arranged, had reason rather than emotion prevailed; but emancipation did not come as the consequence of natural evolution or of social planning. It was violent, forced, and without regard to the creation of new and difficult problems. The shock of the social upheaval produced by this forced rearrangement of status, both of groups and individuals, continued to reverberate for generations. The twentieth-century South was free from the odious sin of slavery only to bear the curse of social and racial cleavages with their hideous consequences of lynchings, political demagogues, and blind party allegiance. Reconstruction did not end in 1876. It did not, in fact, begin until the nineties.

The Old South had excelled in facilities for higher education. It had made exceptional progress in establishing a common school system under the handicap of sparsity of population. The war had wiped out endowments, dispersed faculties, impoverished state and local governments. Carpet-bag rule had added the threat of mixed schools, and a generation of whites had grown up with precious little formal education, combining ignorance, poverty, and indifference in resistance to human progress. The great contributions of men like J. L. M. Curry, Charles B. Aycock, and Booker T. Washington to the establishment of correct social attitudes and of the George Peabody and John F. Slater funds in training a corps of teachers cannot be ignored; but years passed and the new century was well under way before the task of building a dual school system was begun in earnest. Poverty still casts a blight over wide areas. Illiteracy and near illiteracy remain to plague us in the solution of new social problems.

The Civil War had disrupted the plantation system, had dispossessed many old families of their estates, and had put an end to the system of forced labor in agriculture. New owners of large land holdings had replaced the old. Forced labor had given way to the crop rental system. The expensive factorage system by which slave owners had financed their operations had been diffused into a new crop *lien* system. The country merchant had replaced the merchant prince of exporting centers; but the laborer in the cotton fields continued to pay his annual tribute to one-crop culture, a vicious credit system, and absentee landlords. His standard of living scarcely equalled that of the former slave. His very existence required the combined labors of his entire family.

The emancipation philosophy that every man was entitled to the products of his own labor fared little better with the march of time than the great delusion of "forty acres and a mule." Child labor was a sorry substitute for the prewar promise of a better day. It fastened its ugly tentacles deep in the soil of the great agricultural states of the South and West, and under the protecting mantle of agrarian individualism spread to the new industrial units of the Piedmont Crescent. There it remained to take its annual toll of stunted bodies and blighted souls, a direct challenge to twentieth-century America's scale of human values.

The Old South had enjoyed the benefits of a vigorous two-party rivalry. Blessed with an economic system which encouraged participation in public affairs either as a profession or as an avocation, that section had furnished the nation with a succession of distinguished statesmen. Thomas Jefferson, James Monroe, John Taylor, and Spencer Roane of Virginia, John C. Calhoun of South Carolina, Henry Clay of Kentucky, Andrew Jackson of Tennessee, Alexander Stephens, Howell Cobb, and Robert Toombs of Georgia, and Jefferson Davis of Mississippi, are names to conjure with in that long space of agrarian control in national affairs. Staunch defenders, for the most part, of their own section's peculiar institutions, they also had furnished intellectual leadership for parties and political coalitions national in scope. If there had been questions of national interest which gave them national and international prominence, it is also true that they had reached that high estate by the rough road of the local hustings. Each state had its own peculiar social and economic problems aligning men one against another into parties for control of state and local governments. There had been a healthy interest in public affairs which sent men of ability to governorships and the state legislatures. The Civil War period had changed the entire pattern of political organization. William H. Seward and others had hoped to seize the opportunity offered by the disruption of the Whig party after 1852 to extend the Republican party organization throughout the South. It was a golden opportunity for abolitionists to reach into the southern states with their anti-slavery agitation. Fear of that had been at least a contributory factor to the South's stroke for independence. The first steps in the reorganization of state governments under Lincoln's and Johnson's proclamations had given promise of continuing the two-party system along the lines of former cleavages in the white population. It was then that Congressional leaders of the Republican party, through ignorance of the human elements involved or ineptitude, had thrown precedents to the winds and had sought to extend and perpetuate their control of the South, and through it, of the nation by enfranchising the former slaves and corralling them into the fold. Honest fear in the North that the Negro could be protected in his new civil liberties in no other way had been an important factor in the decision. Slowly at first and then more rapidly as the Klan and Union League swung into action, the southern whites had withdrawn from the Republican party, closed their ranks, and thereafter scorned everything and everybody tainted with Republicanism. There had been threats, at times serious, to the Solid South thus created; but the century closed, with that section, as Congressional Reconstruction had left it, cursed with blind allegiance to a one-party system and a perfect breeding ground for political demagoguery of every sort. Political preferment fell to those who questioned not or, questioning, remained discreetly silent. Deprived of their natural allies in the great agricultural states of the Middle West, who just as blindly voted for the opposing party on the basis of ancient prejudices, southern agrarians had to be content within a minority party and seldom sat at the council table of the nation.

Neither was the nation's loss the Negro's gain. One device after another had been perfected in most of the southern states to thwart the plain intentions of the Fifteenth Amendment and the enforcing act. Southerners had felt there was no choice if even a semblance of honest government was to be maintained. The Supreme Court had decided that neither the Amendment nor the enforcing act contained a positive grant of the franchise, and that federal courts could not intervene unless disfranchisement arose by action of a state, and then only if the disfranchising action were based on race, color, or previous conditions of servitude. Deprived of recourse except in state courts, faced with the administration of literacy tests by hostile election judges, poll tax hurdles, and long lists of disqualifying crimes, and unwilling to endanger personal connections by impolitic action, the natural leaders of the Negro race had abandoned the thankless task of arousing their people from lethargy and despair. Individuals voted occasionally in urban communities, seldom in the rural districts and for the most part only when dragged into the political picture by the importunities of unscrupulous whites engaged in factional strife. The hierarchy of politicians in the national Republican party, however, continued to maintain skeleton organizations even in the Black Belt as a convenience in the distribution of patronage, and because Black and Tan delegations to national conventions were always an asset to those in control of the party machinery.

THE WEST

The Civil War era likewise left its scar upon the agricultural area of the North Central states. The contest between an agrarian economy and an industrial economy is as old as civilization. The two systems and the political philosophies they produce scarcely can be reconciled. The agrarian interests of the South and West had largely controlled the legislative and executive departments of the national government before the Civil War. They had suffered some defeats in the early years of the Republic but had recovered and were in command of the situation when the slavery controversy disrupted their party in 1860. The war had not progressed very far when Congress came under the control of the old Whig element of the Republican party, which revived, as war measures, its pet tariff and banking policies. Tariff walls, erected for the protection of new war industries, remained and were increased and extended until the country became, if not a closed market, certainly a very privileged one for all classes of manufacturing enterprise. The farmers of the Great Plains, unlike those of the Ohio Valley, became producers of staple crops. They learned by experience the nature of the cotton planter's grievances. Wheat was not as sensitive to world price fluctuations as was cotton, but an exportable surplus—and there always has been one—destroyed the efficacy of tariffs and depressed prices in the domestic market to world price levels.

The Banking Act of 1863 had its inception in the desire to facilitate the sale of government bonds. It established a national banking system, designed to promote commerce and industry, but with little to offer agrarians in the way of easy, long-term credits or flexible currency. Congress followed with the 1865 act taxing note emissions of state banks out of existence. State banks did not recover from the blow thus dealt until the widespread use of personal checks gave them a new lease on life. Meanwhile, the agrarians, whose money income depended upon the prices received for what they produced, suffered from a contracting per capita volume of currency. They had assumed heavy obligations during the period of war inflation, only to find those same obligations increased relative to their ability to pay. Finally, in the sphere of fiscal policies, the wartime Congresses had authorized the issue of greenbacks to the amount of nearly $500,000,000. Retirement of this fiat money meant further price deflation. The West had opposed it with some success, but had failed in an effort to secure additional amounts of greenbacks or the free coinage of silver. Forced, therefore, to sell in the world market and buy in a closed market, to adjust his financial necessities to a new banking system, and to yield to the usurious interest rates of eastern money lenders, the western farmer had little cause to rejoice over the changed government policies. Nevertheless, voting the Republican ticket had become a habit. The great anti-slavery impulse had come out of the Ohio Valley. A Republican Congress had passed a free homestead law in 1862. Thus was the original strength of the party in that section created. It survived by tradition.

Free homesteads, the long-cherished hope of frontiersmen, had not been an unmixed blessing. The liberal land donation policy which had made possible free homesteads, also had bequeathed imperial tracts to the railroad promoters and had eased the path of the land speculator and exploiter of natural resources. State and local governments had made their contributions, in cash and accumulated debts to railroad building, and in zealous encouragement to prospective immigrants. Expansion and exploitation had been unrestrained. Hundreds of millions of dollars of public funds had been poured, directly or indirectly, into the building of the railroads, without a single safeguard for the public interest. The government had not even received a minority share in their ownership, much less a recognition of the principle of regulation or control. Unscrupulous promoters levied ruinous tribute upon communities the railroads were built to serve. They corrupted legislatures and courts. They wrecked the financial structure of their own far-flung enterprises in the mad, competitive struggle for private gain.

Equal lack of foresight had prevailed in the disposition of the great national forest areas. Settlers had long been notoriously destructive of timber resources in their haste to bring the soil under cultivation, and the timber barons had exploited remaining areas on an industrial basis for profit with little protest from anyone. The devastation was complete in the upper Mississippi Valley and Great Lakes region by the turn of the century. Millions of acres of marginal and submarginal agricultural land had been abandoned to forest fires, soil erosion, and the jetsam population of the lumber camps—wreckage left behind by an impulsive people, heedless of their children's heritage.

More far-reaching in its ultimate consequences perhaps than any other public policy was the startling rapidity with which the public lands had been transferred to private ownership. The Homestead Act of 1862, the encouragement of foreign immigration, and the postwar depression had combined to promote the final and most extensive phase of the westward movement. Within the space of one generation the Great Plains had passed from Indian and buffalo country to range-cattle country, to sod-house frontier, to homestead farms, towns, and little cities. Four and one-half million acres of land had been entered under the Homestead Act within three years after the close of the war, and more than nineteen million acres before 1880. The homesteader's frontier had passed into history by 1900, and by 1910 most of the area suitable to farming had been occupied.

INDUSTRIAL EAST

How many millions of people, weary of the restraints and inequalities of older sections or revolting against the numerous tyrannies of Europe, had found a haven in the boundless West will never be known. We shall never be able, probably, to assign to each of the impelling motives in migration of people its relative importance. Certain it is, however, that the lure of the West had offered an amazingly simple solution to many of life's problems. It had carried the nation through periods of unemployment and economic distress. It had drained away from the industrial East both the incompetents and the natural leaders of labor. It had made possible an uncritical development of industrial life, and the solution of social problems had not kept pace with material and technical progress. Discontented laborers had escaped to the frontier and their places had been filled by immigrants. Thus industry had not paid the cost either of rearing its labor or supporting its derelicts. Little wonder, therefore, that industry, wealth, and population should have shown such phenomenal growth in the period following the Civil War. No government ever dispensed its wealth of natural resources more liberally, no people ever exploited them more recklessly, and no nation ever received a more generous gift of mature men and women for industrial exploitation.

Those who had raised their voices in defense of human bondage as well as some who had inveighed against it, notably Wendell Phillips, had hurled severe indictments against the northern industrial system. There was one remarkable difference between the plantation, which was the unit of industrialized agriculture, and the factory, which was the unit of production in manufacturing. The southern slaveholder could not discharge his laborers when the cotton crop failed or could not be sold at a profit and then take them back again when profitable operations could be resumed. Nor could he turn them out to starve when injury, sickness, or old age made them unfit for productive labor. The maintenance of his laborers at all times and under all conditions had been a fixed charge against the owner. That was not true in the northern industrial system. Child labor, sweatshops, hazardous and unhealthy working conditions, a competitive labor market, constantly recurring and sudden periods of unemployment, long hours, and distress in sickness and old age combined to form an unsavory social pattern. These were the things from which men had fled to the frontier. They continued throughout the nineteenth century because the moral force of the nation was exhausted in the contest over bond slavery, because the acquisitive instinct was so universally predominant after the war, and because such a large proportion of the laboring class was of foreign origin. It was not until the twentieth century that there appeared in the nation a group of men who, in social consciousness, moral enthusiasm, and intelligence, were comparable to those who had initiated and carried through the crusade against slavery. Laboring men were unable to organize effectively or, having organized, to accomplish much in the way of reform for a variety of reasons. Individual independence was still a prominent characteristic of American life. The most aggressive and capable among them were able to rise from the ranks into supervisory or managerial positions. A diversity of racial origins, languages, and living standards militated against group solidarity. Lacking intelligent leadership, influenced by foreign radicalism, and faced by employer-controlled governmental agencies, they struck out blindly against intolerable conditions in a riot of mob violence, death, and destruction.

The Haymarket Riot of 1886, the Homestead Strike of 1892, and the Pullman Strike of 1894 had left a legacy of ill will, bitterness, and misunderstanding in industrial relationships. There could be no rational approach to the correction of economic maladjustment while the public regarded strikes as evil and strikers as evildoers. The public still did so at the turn of the century.

Decades had come and gone and we had become the greatest industrial nation in the world without a single achievement in the direction of economic security for the laboring classes or machinery for the elimination of industrial conflicts. Corporations had their technical laboratories and their expensive research departments designed to maintain and increase profits; but they had no sense of social responsibility, much less established formulas for adjusting their business to human relationships. Labor had succeeded in forming craft organizations, a part of which were loosely joined in the American Federation of Labor; but that organization had become progressively more representative of labor's aristocracy. Non-technical laborers, especially the Negroes, the agricultural laborers, and the servant groups, remained unorganized and unrepresented. Nor did organized labor display any inclination or ability to assume responsibilities with the rights and privileges it sought to establish. Warfare continued year after year and was viewed by society as the inescapable growing pains of an industrial system. There was no general acceptance of the theory that strikes were but surface indications of underlying maladjustments in the economic and social system. Society was content, therefore, to see each violent outbreak adjusted as quickly as possible or summarily suppressed, seeking only to keep the total inconvenience and property loss at a minimum.

We were rapidly becoming a highly complex, industrialized society with a government designed by a decentralized, agrarian people. In the realm of government it is pertinent to remember that our chief concern from the time of founding of the Republic had been to protect minorities against the unrestrained will of majorities. John Adams and the Federalists generally had arranged an elaborate system of checks and balances in the federal system. The Jeffersonians had preached the doctrine of decentralization on the theory that the happiness of the greatest number could best be secured by retaining wide powers in local and state governments. John C. Calhoun, cognizant of the power of a permanent majority to control the judicial as well as the legislative and administrative branches of the government, had devised a scheme for placing restraining powers in the hands of minorities for whose benefit limitations had been imposed. The Federalists had been willing to trust their fortunes to the judgment of the Supreme Court. The Civil War had closed the half-century struggle between these contending political philosophies. It left us with the written Constitution as a fundamental law and the Supreme Court as the final judge of the powers of Congress and the several state legislatures. The ultimate recourse of a majority checked by the Court remained, as always, in constitutional amendments. The power of amendment, however, was not exercised again for nearly a half century.

Meanwhile, the Fourteenth Amendment turned out to be something quite different from what it was intended to be at the time of its adoption. Instead of being a safeguard for the rights of the Negro it became, by virtue of successive Supreme Court decisions, a charter of liberties for a new creature of the law: corporations. The point is that this Amendment to the fundamental law did not transfer powers from the state governments to the Congress of the United States. It circumscribed and narrowed the powers of the state legislatures without adding to the powers of Congress, thus creating for corporations a broad immunity from regulation by either agency. The federal government having no police powers could not go beyond the regulation of interstate commerce in its effort to remedy abuses in production. The states retained the power to charter corporations engaged in interstate commerce, and certain states were willing to enact extremely lax corporation laws for the sake of revenue. On the other hand, the states could not interfere with interstate commerce, nor go beyond definite limits in regulating corporate practices because of the "due process" clause of the Fourteenth Amendment. Thus it was that when society became conscious of its responsibilities for protecting human rights in our new industrial society, it found property rights firmly entrenched behind a clause written into the fundamental law to protect the rescued victims of an earlier exploitation. The Amendment could not have been adopted had not southern states been compelled to ratify it in order to regain representation in Congress; and it is safe to assume that the agrarian West and South would never have approved it had the purpose of its framers been known and the Negro question been absent. The men who framed the Amendment purposely concealed their objective. The revelation of how and why it was done was not made by Roscoe Conkling until 1882. The Supreme Court did not accept all of its implications as a basis for reinterpretation of the Fourteenth Amendment until 1889. The full effects of the change did not appear until the twentieth century.

Many things, therefore, contributed to the unprecedented industrial development of the country during this period: (1) the expansion of agriculture into the region west of the Mississippi, affording a rich market for all kinds of artifacts; (2) the rich reservoir of previously untouched natural resources suddenly brought into use by technical improvements and scientific discoveries; (3) a superabundance of labor provided by unrestricted immigration and by the release of agricultural laborers by improved farm machinery; (4) freedom from restrictive legislation due to the prevailing doctrine of laissez faire and the protecting mantle of the Constitution as interpreted by a friendly judiciary.

This combination of forces was destined to present twentieth-century America with a magnificent accumulation of material wealth and an appalling array of social and economic perplexities. Agriculture expanded more rapidly than our ability to provide adequate means for consumption, and was forced to rely upon foreign markets which were neither stable nor permanent. Immigrants flowed in faster than the nation could assimilate them, until businessmen and agrarians alike mistrusted the safety of our Anglo-Saxon traditions. Technical progress opened new fields of employment; but it likewise lessened the necessity for human labor, destroyed the ancient skills, and shortened the life span of productive endeavor. Laissez faire brought us to the low estate of an industrial feudalism which in some respects was less compatible with the liberties of men than the landed feudalism of the Middle Ages. Industrial expansion created a surplus of manufactured goods for sale in world markets at a time when there was a surfeit of agricultural products for export and a firmly established system of protective tariffs. It drew men and women from the soil into great metropolitan districts, increasing the hazards of economic depressions; it also created such a multitude of material comforts that the accumulation of wealth became a major objective in life. Industrial expansion likewise increased production to the point where the literacy and intelligence of the masses were essential to the functioning of our economic system.

PARTIES AND PUBLIC POLICIES

Many forces in operation during this period tended to produce a marked change in the administration of public affairs. That the government has never been as faithfully administered in all departments as honorable men desire is a simple historical fact. We are prone to forget, however, that the term "the people" is a historical fiction. Society is made up of individuals with diverse interests, ideas, and ideals. They group themselves into political parties seeking control of the agencies of government in order to direct its policies along the lines of their own peculiar philosophies; or they form organizations for the purpose of influencing governmental policies through pressure politics and propaganda. Retention of wide powers in local and state governments tends to minimize the clash of such rival groups. Centralization of powers in the federal government tends to increase it, and centralization went on at a terrific rate after the close of the Civil War. Pressure groups likewise increased in number and influence, notably the Grange, the Grand Army of the Republic, and the American Federation of Labor. This combination of circumstances made it increasingly difficult for political parties to write their platforms and choose their candidates. They cultivated the art of ambiguity, wrote platforms of meaningless generalities, spoke the sort of platitudes that sounded well in country stores and barber shops, and chose candidates who had never been identified with public questions in such a way as to make enemies. They raised false issues to confuse the voter and act as a smoke screen for the deficiencies of their candidates and the corruption of their administration. The strength and stability of the government built upon the affection of the people and a widespread appreciation of the justice and righteousness of its acts was slowly undermined. Hatreds engendered by the Civil War created a blind party allegiance which lived on in families for generations. Political parties paid tribute to it by drafting men for public office whose sole qualification was an honorable record of service in the army of their section. The power of accumulated wealth increased until it could influence legislatures; the United

States Senate was spoken of as a millionaires' club; and extra-legal or *liaison* officials known as bosses came into power. The free-lance newspaper editor who knew no superior all but disappeared, abandoning public opinion to the mercies of unintelligent, and ofttimes intellectually dishonest, editorial hack writers. Official corruption, spreading through all branches of the public service, was condoned by many, regarded with helpless alarm by others, and utterly disregarded by the public at large. Individuals who betrayed the public trust were seldom punished. Parties suffered no more than temporary embarrassment. Nothing was done to strike at the roots of a system which was destined to threaten the very existence of popular government itself. The mere misappropriation of public funds, bad as it was, belongs to the history of that period and is of little concern to us here; but the forces which alter civilizations are very subtle and very deep. The roots of impulses which give character to national life reach back through many generations. The fact that men should seek high official positions fifty years ago for no other purpose than to be able to sell the prestige thus gained for private gain, and do so without fear of condemnation and disgrace, is evidence of a diseased body politic pregnant with meaning to the twentieth century.

The incompetence of Congress to deal with social and economic questions on any other basis than that of political expediency was clearly demonstrated. Reconstruction legislation took its character from the desire to insure Republican electoral votes from the southern states and congressional interference was terminated only because of the growing displeasure of northern voters. It was politics which reduced the House of Representatives to an inferior position in the government and which forestalled the adoption of an adequate civil service system. But overshadowing all else was the brazen fashion in which Congress built up an elaborate system of Civil War pensions, whereby thousands who had no honest claim against the government for support and thousands more who had no need of it received their monthly government dole. Pension agents infested the land, and aging veterans became choice meal tickets for thousands of young women who were destined to constitute a formidable list of pensioners after most veterans had answered the final roll call. Patriotism was thus tainted with materialism and an unwise precedent was established for future generations. It would have required a courageous Congress, indeed, to have restricted financial aid to those suffering from service disabilities; but Congress had no desire to be courageous. War veterans and their families represented such a considerable group as to hold the balance of power in all closely contested elections. The Republican party could hardly have won a presidential election during the period against a hostile G.A.R. Pensions for veterans, their widows, and dependents carried on the war tradition after waving the bloody shirt lost its appeal. Moreover, liberal pensions relieved that party of the embarrassing treasury surpluses accruing from high tariff rates. Tariffs represented everything but a scientific adjustment of the cost of production at home and abroad. They probably did little to protect the American workingman's standard of living because immigration always provided a surplus of cheap, competitive labor; but they were defended on that ground. They did, however, afford the manufacturer a wide margin of profit and the Republican party made high tariffs its own special province. The Democratic party ceased to be a unit for free trade and repudiated Grover Cleveland when he advocated lower tariff rates and correction of pension abuses. The tariff and pensions, therefore, supplemented each other as a source of profit to two powerful groups. Never before had the government so openly taken money from the consumer for the benefit of favored classes in society. It presaged the day when the taxing power was to be used frankly for the purpose of redistributing wealth as a new form of social control.

The large industrialists were not the only privileged group which directed governmental policies through the agency of the Republican party, with enough support from Bourbon Democrats to offset agrarian defections in the West. The financiers—bankers, brokers, commission men—were their faithful allies. They stood for "sound money," meaning a circulating medium which retained a fixed value in terms of gold irrespective of how much havoc it wrought by a fluctuating purchasing power. Specifically, they stood for the gold standard as opposed to bimetallism and for the retirement of all fiat money. They were not as consistently successful in their battles with the agrarian West, but had little cause for complaint. They prevented the issuance of more greenbacks at the expense of retaining permanently, as a part of the currency, $346,681,000 of those already in circulation. They passed the Resumption Act in 1875 establishing the value of greenbacks at a parity with gold. They established the national banking system, with government bonds as the basis for bank note issues, and drove the bank notes of state banks out of circulation. They prevented the restoration of free coinage of silver, but not the limited purchase of silver for coinage by the treasury department. They did nothing themselves, and prevented others from doing anything to establish a flexible or adequate currency system, to provide agricultural credits at manageable rates, or to safeguard prices and values against periods of ruinous deflation.

Associated with these two groups were the railway builders and promoters. Sharing abundantly in the reckless generosity of the government, they resisted every effort at regulation or control. Billions in watered stock were added needlessly to the capital structure of the railway systems necessitating exorbitant rates to the public and seriously handicapping the roads later in their struggle with automotive competition. Roads were built in regions for no other reason than the profits of construction. Parallel lines were built between distant terminals, and the losses occurring from competitive rates on through traffic were balanced by discrimination against helpless shippers, mostly farmers, from intermediate points. These and other abuses indicate the extent to which railroads were built and operated for decades purely as private enterprises for profit. Money extorted from the public was used to corrupt state and national governments in resistance to regulation. The operators suffered a temporary reverse with the enactment of the state Granger laws in the seventies, but recovered their independence when the Supreme Court, in 1886, reversed its former principle and limited the state legislatures to control of intrastate commerce. They suffered an apparent defeat with the enactment by Congress in 1887 of the Interstate Commerce Act, but again the Supreme Court came to their rescue, and the century came to a close without a really worthwhile accomplishment in the direction of railroad regulation. The questions of determining valuations as a basis for rate fixing, of top-heavy financial structures, of speculative banker control, of consolidations in the interest of economy and public service, and of possible government ownership, were passed on for a later generation to ponder over at a time when new economic developments tremendously complicated the whole question of transportation. Leaders in finance, manufacturing, and transportation were closely knit together by economic forces and controlled by interlocking directorates. They created billions of intangible wealth based upon nothing more secure than probable earning power; they exploited the nation's natural resources, built the nation's highways, controlled its circulating medium, and dictated its fiscal policies. All this they did in the interest of private gain and to the end of a vast concentration of accumulated wealth more powerful than political parties, more powerful in its indirect influences than Congress. All this was the great American achievement of the late nineteenth century—the achievement of the Republican party by its own admission. Thus did the party's philosophy and interests change. It had risen to power as the party of protest. In its inception, it was the party of youth and idealism. It ventured greatly, even war, in its crusade against property rights, established privilege and class, then serenely secure in the strength of the Democratic party and the majesty of the fundamental law. It had championed the cause of human rights in the name of the "higher law," threatening Court and Constitution alike. Three decades later the situation was completely reversed, and the party both represented and defended accumulated wealth, established privilege, government by precedent rather than impulse, the sacredness of the Constitution, and the infallibility of Supreme Court decisions.

Opposition to this composite edifice of economic and political power did not come from the Democratic party as such. That party had its Tildens, its Clevelands, and its Gormans, conservative by instinct and association. Bourbons were in control, for the most part, in the southern states and the party was, even more than the Republican, a congeries of contradictions. The only opposition which succeeded in organizing and seriously threatening the capitalistic control of the government came from the agrarian West and it also represented a propertied interest. Populism did not offer much except the substitution of the principles of an agrarian economy for those of an industrial economy in the formulation of governmental policies. It would certainly have utilized its power to aid the farmers as the industrialists had used theirs to aid business and manufacturing. It would have lowered the tariff rates, brought the railroads under strict supervision or public ownership, revised the currency and banking systems, and perhaps have instituted governmental interference in business to the end of eliminating monopolies. That would have constituted a real revolution in our economic life, and might have restored agriculture to its previous high estate; but it would not necessarily have led to the solution of the many social and economic problems peculiar to our industrial civilization. The Populists had no program for that and their individualism and decentralizing philosophy would certainly have restrained them from investing the central government with the power to carry through such reform measures. The West's great contribution in these closing years of the nineteenth century arose from its frontier characteristics more than from its agrarianism. Men had been moving into new regions beyond the limits of established authority continuously for more than a century. They had never hesitated to establish their own governments in such cases, drawing upon the experiences of the older sections and upon their inherent creative abilities, applying both to the task of meeting the exigencies of their new environment. Territorial organization and state-making had followed in due time. This constant process of state-making had been the rich reservoir from which flowed new ideas, democratizing tendencies, and leveling influences into the expanding structure of American life. Much that had been initiated had been discarded by the test of time. Much, also, had become an established part of our national system. True to precedent, this last great experience of American state-making made its contribution to creative political thought. It did not come in time to alter materially the course of nineteenth-century development; but it did give to twentieth-century America most of its leading statesmen and much of its new governmental machinery. We shall see its influence in the careers of men like Borah, Walsh, Norris, Clark, and Johnson, and through such innovations as woman's suffrage, the popular election of United States Senators, the Initiative and Referendum, and Preferential Primaries.

It must be remembered, however, that this last concerted effort of the agrarians to wrest control of the federal government from the industrialists was so narrow in vision as to be almost naïve. Its tragedy lay in its utter futility. America was already industrialized and was becoming more so. The agrarians did not see the inadequacy of their program for shaping the destiny of an industrial people, nor did the industrialists quite realize the importance of restoring agricultural prosperity. It remained for our generation to seek, perhaps in vain, for the correct formula—not for reconciling the two philosophies, for they cannot be reconciled—by which the two economic systems can be maintained under the same government to their mutual benefit.

THE INTELLECTUAL WORLD

Entirely aside from this contest which resulted in a submerged agricultural population was the effort to free a rapidly changing social and economic state from a static social philosophy. Surviving inhibitions of agrarianism complicated the task in many ways. The test of any civilization is the degree to which it applies intelligence to the solution of problems created by its own development. Answers to its problems are not given, nor do they spring spontaneously from the brain of any man. The wisdom of the ages is not thus concentrated. The rapidly developing industrialism created an unbalanced economic system and hopelessly deranged the equitable adjustment between the rights of property and the rights of man; but it also paved the way for the corrections of its evils by making possible a degree of widespread literacy and intelligence never before known to mankind.

Wealth flowed in endless streams to those who organized the corporations, built the railroad, telephone, and telegraph lines, and exploited the natural resources of the new industrial empire. Many of them happily believed with Andrew Carnegie that they had a moral obligation to dispense their wealth for the benefit of humanity, and they did so in generous fashion. Their philosophy, that superior intelligence had given them wealth and the same superior intelligence enabled them to spend it more wisely than their less fortunate brethren, belonged to a passing age; but their benefactions were for the most part wisely chosen and hastened the progress of sweeping reforms.

Universities like Cornell, Chicago, Leland Stanford, and Johns Hopkins were established, free from political and sectarian control. Hundreds of colleges and universities received large endowments for buildings, libraries, research laboratories, and professorships. Public libraries and museums were erected in every city of any size in the country. Foreign missions, public education, welfare agencies, hospitals for handicapped children, medical research centers, and educational foundations were established and richly endowed. Finally priceless collections of paintings, porcelains, tapestries, books, and other treasures were collected and permanently preserved for future generations.

The richest inheritance of twentieth-century America was the foundation of its school system, combined with academic freedom and the freedom of the press. Industry and science produced wealth, and only a wealthy people could have established an educational system extending from the kindergarten through the universities available to every child. Joseph Pulitzer could reach the minds and hearts of millions with his forthright denunciation of injustice and corruption, and his defense of the lives and fortunes of the masses against privilege, demagoguery, and plutocracy because the press was free and the people literate. Thorstein Veblen's merciless criticism of the unsocial consequences of the accumulation of wealth became a vital, moving force because young men and women sat at his feet and learned the way to a better life. Countless thousands entered the universities and colleges during these three decades to drink deeply of the humanities and learn something of new social and economic theories.

Faith in the scriptures as the source of all knowledge slowly gave way before the advance of natural science; and the application of scientific principles to the study of social, economic, and political problems gave mankind new hope for happiness and security. The net result was a twentieth-century environment unparalleled in history for health, comfort, and cultural advancement, and an ability to make personal adjustments to greater environmental changes in one generation than had occurred in many centuries.

Every civilization produces its men and women to whom life offers no other value so incomparably rich as constructive service. There were many whose historic statures loom large in this period of transition from an agricultural to an industrial civilization. Jane Addams established the first settlement house in Chicago, from which have developed our modern social centers, employment agencies, child nurseries, and clinics. Jacob A. Riis devoted his life to rescuing the child victims of disease, crime, and poverty in New York City's slums, and to securing for them an opportunity to grow up in normal, healthful surroundings. Robert G. Ingersoll argued relentlessly for controls by which science and invention would operate to free rather than enslave mankind. Washington Gladden awakened the churches to a new social consciousness and urged the application of Christian ethics to business enterprise. Charles M. Sheldon emphasized the need for a new code of personal conduct in a changing world where every opportunity for personal gain was matched by a possibility of irreparable injury to countless thousands. Lincoln Steffens labored to arouse civic pride and establish honorable and efficient city governments. Henry D. Lloyd exposed the evils of monopolies and pled for the rights of small businessmen, consumers, and industrial workers. Henry George urged the elimination of poverty by a reform of the tax system which would prevent land speculation. These, and countless others, were steeped in the venerable American tradition of progress and took steps as best they could to save it from the impact of the new industrialism.

2

A Restless People

IMMIGRATIONS

IT is difficult to realize now the extent to which people in the United States were moving about at the turn of the century. Foreign immigration was at its peak. Young men and women were deserting the rural sections for the more attractive life of the cities. Negroes were abandoning the inhospitable surroundings of the rural South for the more secure haven of northern cities. Rural folk were still seeking better soil and more elbow room in the West. A spirit of restlessness, born of insecurity and the inherent desire to better one's economic situation, pervaded the land.

Immigration had always occupied a foremost place in the changing character of the population. The flow of people from Europe for two centuries, and the evolution of both the American race and its way of life are inseparable. They had represented nearly every nationality, every class, and every religious belief when they came. Here in the United States they had found a deep-rooted conviction that every individual derives from nature certain inalienable rights which the government must respect. The basic one was the right of the individual to his own beliefs, to make contacts with the great minds of the past and present, to impress his beliefs upon his fellow men—in short, the right of free inquiry and discussion. They had found a nation of people who looked upon progress as the natural way of life. The degree of progress for the individual was determined by his own ability and enterprise; and the institutions of the people, from a Bill of Rights and judicial review to free schools and cheap land, were designed to keep the individual free from restraints and aid him in the improvement of his mental, moral, and economic progress. They had found a democratic society, characterized by strong individualism, self-reliance, and equality. Those who came late in the nineteenth century had found a people born of an amalgamation of races, and a way of life created from the cross fertilization of ideas brought from Europe and those of indigenous growth. Above all, they had found a nation with the highest standard of living in the world, the greatest diffusion of material comfort among the masses of the people, the greatest array of technological and scientific equipment, the greatest industrial empire, and the greatest degree of intellectual, spiritual, and cultural freedom the world had ever known.

More than twenty million of these Europeans had come to this country during the nineteenth century. Economic opportunity had been the lodestar of this restless mass of humanity. Freedom from religious and political oppression, and to some degree from military service, had contributed heavily to the movement in pre-Civil War days; but it was America as the land of opportunity that figured most prominently in our advertisements and their response in the last three decades of the century. Western states, railroads, steamship lines, employment agencies, real estate speculators, and industrialists joined forces in selling America abroad. Lowly folk of every land were told that America offered free land for home-stead farms, limitless opportunity to work for wages, and above all else equality, dignity, and self-respect. They read it in the news-papers, heard it from public lecturers and from house-to-house canvassers. What need had they to hesitate when railroads and steamships would carry them to Iowa or to Minnesota more quickly and more cheaply than their fathers could have reached Berlin or London! They came between 1860 and 1900 in almost mass migra-tion, largely from those countries of northern Europe which had made great progress in industry, education, and political freedom: 3,364,000 Germans, 1,913,000 Irish, 1,207,000 Norwegians and Swedes, and 1,519,000 Englishmen.

Meanwhile, however, there were signs of repentance among a

people who had for so long and so confidently offered to share America's bounty with the oppressed of other lands, and signs of a demand for selection, for restriction, ultimately for exclusion. It had originated with the labor unions. Organized labor, composed of American-born artisans, early recognized the advantage accruing to capital from the plentiful supply of foreign immigrants. They were a handicap to labor organizations, a threat to American standards of living, and a dual menace at times of industrial strife. Immigrants were used as strike breakers, and alien radicals welcomed every incident of industrial unrest as an opportunity for violent agitation. Thus their presence had rendered ineffective labor's only weapon and had cost it the valuable support of public opinion.

Radical agitation, moreover, reversed the attitude of industrialists. They had recruited labor abroad for the process of industrial expansion. Latins and Slavs had built the railroads, laid the pipe lines, operated the stone quarries and mines, and furnished the constantly increasing percentage of unskilled labor required for mass production. Not all of them, however, had proved strong and docile. Many were intelligent, radical refugees from the espionage systems of European autocracies. They brought the beneficent ideas of European liberalism, also, much that was extremely radical, and a desperation born of despair. Socialism and anarchy were equally abhorrent to the dominant class in America. They were synonymous terms to most people, and evoked abject fear for the safety of American institutions. Conservative opinion, therefore, began to demand some restrictive measures to exclude the undesirable aliens.

A third source of dissent was the new social consciousness. For decades, immigrants had come from Northern Europe and settled in agricultural areas. Industrial expansion and the exhaustion of free lands drew an increasing number from Southern Europe to our own industrial centers. The transition had occurred before 1900. Earlier immigrants were of the same racial origins and cultural backgrounds as native Americans. They had tarried briefly or not at all at the ports of entry, hastening on to the rural frontier to merge their blood and their cultures with those of native stock.

Assimilation had never been a problem. The new immigrants were of many racial origins, largely from Italy and the submerged nationalities of Russia and Austria-Hungary. There were Bulgarians, Bohemians, Bosnians, Croats, Czechs, Poles, Moravians, Ruthenians, Serbians, Ukrainians, and Jews. They left Europe by way of Palermo, Naples, Vienna, Prague, Warsaw, and Bucharest. They landed at Boston, New York, or Baltimore. They went to the cities and industrial centers of the East and remained there.

These new immigrants came to escape persecution and military service; to find relief from heavy taxation; to get away from the rising tide of anti-Semitism in Europe. They were part of a world-wide migration from rural to urban centers, who came to American cities instead of going to those of their own countries. Free land, even cheap land, in America was gone. Homestead farming as a way of life had given way to farming as a capitalistic enterprise. Few of the immigrants possessed the means to buy land, much less expensive machinery. They were a lowly people, content to enter American economy as household servants and unskilled laborers; but they were a colorful people, too, of rich and varied cultural heritages, customs, and folkways.

Native Americans, long accustomed to think of our land as a "melting pot," failed to realize that the rural frontier had been replaced by a city frontier. These two frontiers were alike in many ways, but exactly opposite in two important respects. They were alike in the sense that those who came had to adjust themselves to an entirely different environment from the one which they had left. People went to both to lose themselves, or to be free from restraints, or to rid themselves from interference by others in their private affairs. The city was even superior to the rural frontier in this respect. They were alike in offering new opportunities to the disheartened and discouraged. In this, too, the city was superior because of its many diverse trades and services. But city environment did not nurture either social and economic equality or amalgamation of racial groups. Americans were bewildered to see these newcomers living in their own sections of the cities, preserving their own racial customs and morals, establishing their own economy, and finding it unnecessary to speak the English language. Pauperism, crime, and immorality—old evils, but new problems—were charged to the account of racial origins. The idea that an unbalanced economic system might be partially responsible received little attention because people lacked the benefit of modern sociological research. We know, of course, that they have taken advantage of every opportunity for cultural advancement, that they have contributed many leaders in science, industry, and government, and that they are loyal citizens in time of peace and highly patriotic in times of crisis; but we have the advantage of a half century of experience on which to base our judgments.

All of the objections to foreigners were accentuated in the case of Orientals. It was against them that legislation was directed first. Chinese laborers were excluded for ten years by Congressional action in 1882. The act was renewed in 1892, extended in perpetuity in 1902, and made applicable to Chinese in Hawaii and in the Philippines. Contract labor was excluded after 1885. Control of immigration was assumed by the federal government in 1891, and restrictions were applied on the principle of individual selectivity. The list of types of undesirable individuals was steadily increased, without, however, lessening the numbers who came. Agitation began to exclude persons who could not read some language. The purpose, of course, was to exclude large numbers, to reduce immigration, but to do it by retaining the principle of individual selectivity. An act of Congress providing for a literacy test was vetoed by Cleveland in 1897. For some strange reason the literacy test as a basis of selection gained in popularity. Taft vetoed such a bill in 1913 and Wilson in 1915, but an act excluding everyone unable to read some language was passed over Wilson's veto in 1917. Meantime waves of immigrants continued to roll in, reaching an annual volume of more than one million in 1905 and a grand total for the twentieth century of more than 13,000,000 before our entry into World War I. The outbreak of World War I in 1914 served to stop the flood of immigration. Thus it dropped from 1,218,000 in 1914 to 326,700 in 1915, and to 110,618 in 1918. Imminence of renewed immigration on an unprecedented scale when war restraints were removed led to abandonment of the principle of individual selectivity by Congress and the assignment of

quotas to each foreign country. All of the early attempts to place
some restriction on immigration aimed to set up selective machinery
for the exclusion of undesirables: paupers, criminals, mentally deficient, prostitutes, and polygamists. The quota system was a definite effort to reduce the numbers of immigrants.

THE NEGRO

Less spectacular than this addition of foreign millions to our
urban populations, but equally significant, was the first trek of
Negroes from the rural South. The disintegration of the Black Belt
—the most historic section of the country—had begun. The reason
for it cannot be stated with finality. The abuses of the tenant
system—crop *liens*, one crop tillage, falsified accounts—and myriad
other links in the chain of economic slavery no doubt were a factor.
The increasing difficulty of wresting a living from exhausted lands,
or of restoring their fertility without cash resources; the desire to
escape from a pattern of rural life in which competing economic
groups of the white race wielded their power ruthlessly to preserve
racial inequality; the alluring legends of urban freedom; the certain
benefits of an independent racial economy; the influence of educational opportunities—all these, and other influences, no doubt,
contributed to the movement. In any case Negroes had been
moving from the farms to the small towns of the South for many
years. The urban Negro population increased 489,000 in the South
and 193,000 elsewhere during the first decade. At the same time,
the Negro rural population in the South increased only 336,000
and decreased 27,000 elsewhere. Foreign immigration kept them
out of the North until World War I. The sharp decline in immigration at that time, coupled with the withdrawal of many men
from industrial pursuits for military service and the pressure for
increased production, accelerated the migration and turned it
northward. During the second decade of the century, Negro urban
population increased 397,000 in the South, while the rural population decreased 233,000. It increased 479,000 in the North during
the same period. The movement was both northward and to industrial centers. The non-industrial, southern city of Nashville, for

example, had 30,000 Negroes in 1900 and only 47,000 in 1940, whereas the Negro populations of the more industrialized cities of Memphis and Atlanta increased from 49,000 and 35,000 to 121,000 and 104,000, respectively, during the same period. Increase of Negroes in northern cities, however, was amazing. New York had 60,000 in 1900 and 458,000 in 1940; Philadelphia, 62,000 and 250,-000; Chicago, 30,000 and 277,000. These cities offered relatively good homes, modern schools, and an established Negro economy of stores, theaters, banks, lawyers, and physicians. Above all else, they provided a greater degree of individual freedom and less frequent racial conflicts.

The repercussions from this second great shifting of population almost defy description. The threatened depletion of the South's agricultural labor supply became an actuality in many sections. Productive cotton plantations became abandoned lands. The aged, the infirm, and the children were left behind, increasing the percentage of population in unproductive ages with far-reaching effects upon taxation and relief. Those who migrated, because they began at the bottom of the industrial ladder, crowded into the least desirable residential sections of the cities; but, flowing into the cities faster than the whites could or would make way for them, they overflowed the segregated districts, precipitating race riots and innumerable court battles. They were excluded from labor unions, and served as strike-breakers. They competed with whites under a dual wage standard, profiting by depressions and being thrown back upon relief when recovery began. But, year after year, the Negro press of the North, particularly the Chicago *Defender*, urged them to hasten to the section of economic equality, and, in the new environment, they steadily increased their contribution to the composite civilization that was America: Bert Williams, of Ziegfeld Follies, said by W. C. Fields to have been the funniest and saddest man in the world, star of *Under the Bamboo Tree*; Charles Gilpin, star of Eugene O'Neill's *The Emperor Jones* and recipient of the Spingarn Medal; Paul Robeson, affectionately known among his people as "King of Harlem," graduate of Rutgers University, member of Phi Beta Kappa, and forever associated in the minds of those who love artistry with the productions of *Porgy* and *Show Boat*; Jules Bledsoe, internationally known singer and actor in *In Abraham's Bosom*; Frank Wilson, who rose from the status of a Harlem mail carrier to enduring fame as a foremost actor in *Porgy*; and Richard B. Harrison, the "Lawd" in Marc Connelly's *The Green Pastures*. They also entered the field of productive literature: Paul Lawrence Dunbar, known to most people for his *Ships That Pass in the Night* and *Lyrics of Lowly Life*, but with an established reputation in the fields of short stories, classic English poems, and dialect verse; William E. B. Du Bois, poet, novelist, historian and essayist, successor to Booker T. Washington as the outstanding leader of his race, and author of *The Souls of Black Folk*, *Dark Princess* and *The Quest of the Silver Fleece*; William Stanley Braithwaite, prominent poet and critic, contributor to the Boston *Evening Transcript*, *The Forum*, *Century* and the *Atlantic*, author of *Lyrics of Life and Love* and *The House of Falling Leaves*; James Weldon Johnson, sometime Secretary of the National Association for the Advancement of Colored People, author of the anthems "Lift Ev'ry Voice and Sing" and "The Young Warrior"; and a younger generation of poets including Claude McKay, Countee Cullen, Jean Toomer, and Richard Wright.

SOUTHERN WHITES

The South was the scene, also, of the most pronounced population shift from rural to industrial life—this in the Piedmont Crescent. Universal demand for the bright-leaf pipe tobacco of North Carolina and invention of a cigarette machine in 1876 gave the region its first great industry. The demand for cigarettes was constant and unaffected by depressions or seasonal variations. Virginia, North Carolina, Tennessee, Georgia, and Alabama also had rich resources of iron, coal, water power, and timber. Textile manufacturing in the Piedmont began in the late eighties and early nineties and southern mills were using 70 percent of all the raw cotton being manufactured in the country by 1927. Iron manufacturing developed in Alabama and the furniture industry in North Carolina, Virginia, and Tennessee. The existence of a tremendous reservoir of cheap labor, as well as proximity to raw materials, was responsible for this industrial development. The first factories were established by intrepid Southerners as community enterprises. They were followed by branch factories of northern companies, and later by large investments of foreign capital, particularly in the rayon industry. The labor for these enterprises was drawn from the hinterland—simple upland folk and mountain people, tenant-farmers, and small landowners. They were the descendants of early Scotch-Irish and German immigrants. Their standard of living had never been high, but they were almost entirely native Americans, conservatives, and strongly individualistic. The movement of these peoples does not show heavily in population statistics by states; and, because water power and then electric power made decentralization possible, it does not show in the growth of large cities. Nevertheless, it was one of the most important developments at the turn of the century, pregnant with meaning for future generations.

Nowhere else in the country did the attitudes and inhibitions of an agricultural philosophy carry over so completely or survive so tenaciously in the new industrial system. An agricultural people were becoming a part of an industrial economy while retaining all of the traditions and social attitudes of their rural background. This was happening, moreover, in a section where there were few labor unions, a great deal of child labor, poorly developed schools, and almost no laws regarding working conditions, or welfare agencies, or industrial commissions. Paternalism and patronage, honest attitudes in the first generation, instruments of exploitation in the second; child labor, regrettable perhaps though not wholly bad under parental control in simple rural life, but an atrocious robbery of body and soul in a factory system; individualism, the strength of a sturdy yeomanry, but a fatal weakness in an industrial laborer—these were agricultural and frontier survivals. Society reveled at the prospect of increased wealth and an opportunity for honest work for a ne'er-do-well segment of population. It was slow in developing a critical attitude toward the new industrial process. The prevailing racial cleavage served to distract attention from economic grievances. Fear of radical influences upon the Negro population and prevailing resentment against outside interference, both survivals of Reconstruction days, militated against organized labor movements.

All of these things were destined to exert a mighty influence in the history of the nation within a generation. He who owned the mill and mine, and also owned the houses in which his workers lived, the church in which they worshipped, the school in which their children sat, and whose money directly or indirectly supported the preacher, the teacher, the doctor, the sheriff, and perchance the judge—that person, be it man or corporation, owned the workers, body and soul. Even the generous, Christian humanitarianism which had conditioned the slaveholding planter's control of his slaves was lacking in the management of a soulless corporation. Had it been otherwise, the nation might have been spared one of its blackest pages in the history of industrial relations.

THE NEW FRONTIER

The shifting fortunes of country towns and villages cannot be gleaned from statistical tables. They had served, for more than a century, as the shopping and amusement centers for surrounding farming populations. Here were located the hardware and dry-goods stores, the barber shops and drug stores, the blacksmith shops, the post offices, the banks, the elevators, the railway stations, and the express offices. Here, too, were the doctors and lawyers, the circuit preachers, the secondary schools, the newspapers, the justice courts, the taverns, and bar-rooms. Hamlets, villages, and county seats alike, they served as the hubs about which rural economy revolved. They not only served a rural population, but were rural themselves. A large proportion of their population consisted of retired farmers. Few of them were wealthy, although many, deceived by increasing land values, thought they were. Tenantry increased, the value of farm mortgages soared, and all the evils of absentee ownership appeared as more and more moved into the towns.

The children of these retired farmers, their ranks swelled by their more countrified cousins, turned eagerly toward the cities, again leaving behind the less capable and the aged. It is safe to say that almost every family in the small towns and rural sections of the North and Midwest contributed at least one member to city populations during the first two decades of the century. Improved farm machinery released labor from the farms, made large-scale production possible, stopped the subdivision of homestead farms, even dispossessed whole families from the soil. Young people could no longer look forward to married life on the farm, except as tenants, unless perchance inheritance gave them capital for land and equipment. Money economy and technology had relieved farm life of much of its drudgery, but had robbed it of its variety of tasks. Young people fled from rural monotony to the pleasant associations of the city. Automobiles and good roads hurried the social and economic transformation begun by electric and steam railways. Business decayed and all but disappeared from the majority of the small towns. Blacksmith shops and rural churches alike lost their patronage, and the little red schoolhouse, most colorful of American institutions, became little more than a memory. Improved roads and consolidated schools added their burden of bonded indebtedness to a drooping rural economy. County seats and larger industrial centers grew in wealth and importance, serving larger areas, and exercising a city influence upon those areas in the same way that the rural areas had formerly influenced the small towns.

In view of these facts, it is not strange that the urban population of the country should have increased from 40 percent to more than 65 percent of the whole in thirty years; that the percentage of our foreign born in the populations of states like Massachusetts, Rhode Island, Connecticut, New York and New Jersey should have steadily increased; that persons of voting age should constitute a larger percentage of the population in urban than in rural areas; and that the combined population of Massachusetts, New York, New Jersey, Illinois and Michigan should have increased from 19,200,000 to 33,351,000 in thirty years as compared to an increase from 8,388,000 to 10,678,000 in the strictly agricultural states of Wisconsin, Iowa, Nebraska, Kansas and Mississippi. Cities not only grew in size, but overflowed their boundaries so that today comparisons, to be of any value, must be made between metropolitan districts.

This rapid urbanization, already in progress in 1900, presented some interesting developments and many vexatious problems. The relatively rapid transportation provided by street railways permitted unlimited expansion of metropolitan districts. Residential suburbs established their own governments, utility services and schools, resisted consolidation, and thus aggravated the evils of extravagance, corruption and crime. Fortunes were made in real estate. Bonded indebtedness for streets, lights, waterworks, garbage disposal plants, municipal buildings and schools was lightly assumed. An outmoded county government system superimposed on an expanded town government, both political in character, produced mediocrity at best and more often appalling corruption in the discharge of public affairs.

The individual citizens, making the transition from rural to urban economy, were forced to adjust themselves to intensified nervous strains, new food habits, new forms of relaxation and amusement. They were forced to adjust themselves entirely to a money-making and money-spending basis, modified by the insecurity of unemployment. Apartments, with their bathrooms, improved heating and lighting systems, and close proximity to one's neighbors, were not always a fair exchange for the gardens and flowers and fresh air of yesterdays. Some people made the change easily and gracefully; others faltered before the glittering allurements of vice and crime; still others suffered varying degrees of discomfort from the inevitable derangement of bodily functions and mental habits. The birth rate declined. Cities came to have a much higher percentage of voting population than rural sections. Women deserted the home for remunerative labor in the shops and factories. Family income rather than that of the husband and father came to determine the standard of living; and, eventually, 11,000,000 women were working, 15,000,000 men were idle, and millions of young people approached maturity without prospect of honest labor.

The disadvantages of urban life were felt most by the immigrants, the Negroes, the native rural whites who should have remained close to the soil. These were the low-income groups. They contributed most heavily to the sweatshop systems, to child labor, and to female employment. Two hundred and six out of every 1000 women over sixteen were gainfully employed in 1900, including 769,000 married women. In 1910 these figures were 243 of every 1000 and 1,891,000 married women. Percentages varied only slightly thereafter, but the total number of women employed in 1930 was 10,500,000 and of married women slightly more than 3,000,000. The greatest gains were in domestic service, manufacturing, and clerical occupations. In domestic service and manufacturing, immigrant and Negro women predominated. Living conditions for these low-income groups were deplorable. Slums and tenement houses, unbalanced diets, lack of sunshine, fresh air and recreation facilities, inadequate medical attention and impure water supplies contributed to a death rate among women and children as appalling as that on the early frontier.

THE WESTWARD MOVEMENT

The westward movement, about which so much has been written in American history, continued for a time after the turn of the century. The population of North Dakota increased from 319,000 in 1900 to 646,000 in 1920. Comparable increases occurred in South Dakota, Colorado, Idaho, Montana, Utah, and Wyoming. This was a continuation of the century-old westward trek of homestead farmers. It carried on into the Pacific Northwest where Washington and Oregon, with a temperate climate, abundant rainfall, rich lands, and virgin timber, increased in combined population from 833,000 in 1900 to 3,633,000 in 1940.

The movement was even more pronounced in Texas, Oklahoma, New Mexico, and Arizona. These four states were in many respects a distinct regional area of 568,000 square miles. Most of the region was wild Indian country when the rest of the nation experienced the first impact of the industrial revolution, but it was rich in mineral resources, timber, and agricultural lands. Oklahoma was admitted into the Union in 1907, Arizona and New Mexico in 1912. Exploitation was not long delayed, as is shown by the increase in population through four decades, and the region became a new industrial section of the country after World War I.

	1900	1940
Texas	3,048,000	6,414,000
Oklahoma	790,000	2,336,000
New Mexico	195,000	531,000
Arizona	122,000	499,000

Arid lands were irrigated in Arizona, New Mexico, and Texas. Texas soon became the leading cotton-growing state of the nation. Texas and Oklahoma were producing petroleum equal to two-thirds of the nation's production and 40 percent of the world's production by 1930, with substantial amounts of other mineral products such as coal, sulphur, zinc, and lead.

Vast as the westward movement had been, only a small part of the population in any generation had ever set forth on a flatboat or in a covered wagon. Once on their way, few had ever returned; and once settled in new homes, few had ventured forth a second time. Accumulated wealth and technology combined to give twentieth-century Americans new opportunities to see something of the world beyond the limits of their own communities. The automobile put the whole nation on wheels, carrying thousands each year to far-distant states for short vacations. Florida and California soon became winter playgrounds. California, in addition to a mild climate and scenic beauty, had vast stores of mineral wealth, an extensive irrigation system, rich agricultural lands, fine schools and colleges, and it became the fastest growing state in the Union with 1,485,000 people in 1900 and 6,907,000 in 1940.

These western states also absorbed the foreign people who came into the United States after immigration from Europe was cut off by World War I and the quota laws of the 1920's. Mexicans, Puerto Ricans, Hawaiians, and Filipinos came to the United States in increasing numbers. There were only 400,000 Mexicans, for example, in the United States in 1910, and more than 1,500,000 in 1930. They came during the 1920's because of revolutions in

Mexico, returned in large numbers after the panic of 1929, and came back again to the United States during World War II. They went largely to Texas, Arizona, and California, then on into Colorado, Kansas, and Minnesota. They took the place of Negroes in the cotton fields, and became migratory laborers in the fruit, vegetable, and sugar-beet areas. They went to work on the western railroads, and then took over the least desirable jobs in the steel, meat-packing, and automobile plants of the industrial states.

About the turn of the century there developed in the West a proletarian class of migratory laborers, who had no developed culture, lived close to the poverty level, and were both exploited and restless. They worked in industrialized agriculture, not on homestead farms, and moved about, like gypsies, as seasonal laborers. The wheat harvest after 1900 required about 250,000 migratory workers, who started in Texas in June, reached North Dakota by the middle of August, and then went on into Canada. Some of these men worked only within the limits of a single state, some only in the winter wheat belt from Texas to Nebraska, and some only in the spring wheat belt of the Dakotas, Minnesota, and Canada. This type of migratory labor disappeared when wheat harvesting became fully mechanized after World War I.

It was entire families, however, who moved about, working in the orchards, beet fields, vegetable fields, and packing sheds. There ultimately were about 1,000,000 of these, of whom 300,000 were in Texas, 200,000 in California, and 100,000 in the Pacific Northwest. The West had most of these people because fruit and vegetables were grown commercially from the Imperial Valley on the Mexican border to the Hood River Valley in Oregon; and in Arizona, Colorado, Idaho, and Montana. In the East, however, Italians worked in the berry crops from Philadelphia and Camden to southern New Jersey; Poles and Indians in the cranberry bogs of Wisconsin; and all sorts of racial groups in the grape, peach, cherry, and apple orchards of Michigan, the strawberry beds of Louisiana, Arkansas, and Missouri, the citrus fruit orchards of Florida, and the peach orchards of Georgia. There were few states, in fact, but ultimately had contact with migratory laborers; but little thought was given to their low incomes, their haphazard family life, the almost total lack of education for the child laborers, and their inadequate housing, until after the great depression of the early 1930's.

PEOPLE OF DEPRESSED AREAS

Finally, there developed in the United States, as the twentieth century progressed, certain depressed areas. The more important of these were the Southern Appalachian Highland, the Cotton Belt, the cut-over timber lands of Michigan, Wisconsin, and Minnesota, and the Great Plains. In the Appalachian Highland, farm incomes were very low, and there were few automobiles, telephones, or bathrooms, no electric lights or power, poor medical service, and a wholly inadequate diet. The people were a hardy race living in frontier agricultural circumstances, and possessing the characteristics of a frontier civilization. They were self-reliant, hospitable, honest, devoted to family, and religious. The birth rate was high.

There were no railroads into the region until 1906, no paved roads until 1926, and no bus lines until 1927; but, once people could get out of the region, the population began to decline. Young men and women went to work in cities like Pittsburgh, Cincinnati, Detroit, and Chicago. They came back again during the depression, as young people usually do at times of adversity, and they left once more when the demand for industrial labor increased during World War II.

The Cotton Belt began to feel economic adversity at an early date, first because of the boll weevil and then because of the collapse of world markets. Nearly two million tenant, share-cropping families lived in this area extending for 1600 miles from the Carolinas to Texas and embracing 125,000,000 acres. These eight million people were poverty stricken even in prosperous times in spite of the almost universal labor of women and children in the cotton fields. The cotton crop of 1921 was only half as large as it had been in 1914. Twenty-seven percent of all cotton-growing farm units stopped operations between 1920 and 1925. Some of these people went into the mills of the Piedmont, some went north to the industrial cities, some remained on the land to eke out a miserable existence. Like the highlanders, they went home again in large numbers during the depression to conditions that were worse than before.

The cut-over timber lands of the northern region embraced almost half the area of the three states. People lived in isolation, on submarginal lands, where once there had been magnificent forests and sawmills. They were a poor, stranded lumbering population trying to live on land that should never have been touched by a plow. They went to the automobile plants in the 1920's, home again during the depression, and back into industry during World War II.

The Great Plains, extending from Canada to Mexico, and embracing no less than ten states, had once been covered with sod and roving herds of buffalo. The plowing of this sod in a region of uncertain rainfall and constant winds ultimately resulted in drought, crop failures, and dust storms. The soil began to blow away and the settlers to move away. Crop failures began in 1890; but the great crisis came about the same time as the depression of 1929; and, when it had ended, 65 percent of the land area of these states lay damaged or totally destroyed. One hundred fifty thousand people had moved to other regions.

It was these depressed areas that felt most severely all the fluctuations in national prosperity. In them was a population of sturdy people who lived as best they could until driven by desperation to go elsewhere, or until the demand for labor in war industries drew them to the cities of the Pacific Coast and the North Central States. Some stayed permanently in their new homes where they had acquired property and formed new community ties; some formed the habit of moving about in search of better jobs and increased the ranks of migratory laborers.

3

The Spirit of the People

THE EVE OF SOCIAL REVOLUTION

THE railroads, the telegraph, and daily mail deliveries had done much to break down the cultural isolation of rural America by 1900; but they had not altered in any important respect the institutional life of the people. The family, the church, and the schools, the newspapers, lyceum lectures, and local governments, the county poor farms, the prisons, and the hickory stick, the general merchandise store, the traveling salesman, and the fringe-topped surrey—in short, the institutions and instruments for social control, for communication, and for exchange of goods—were fundamentally what they had been for generations, yet America was about to become as unique in these respects as it had long been in the matter of personal freedom.

In the intellectual world, distinctly American literature began to be popular in the late nineties. In 1899, for the first time, the six most widely read books were all by American authors: *To Have and to Hold, Janice Meredith, Richard Carvel, When Knighthood Was in Flower, David Harum,* and *Mr. Dooley in the Hearts of His Countrymen.* Americans had their Mr. Dooley, as twenty years later they had Will Rogers, combining homespun philosophy, common sense, satire, and good humor. They had their dime novels, frowned upon by parents but a model of rectitude compared with the best sellers of the 1920's. Most American homes had their traditional organ and hymnal, and some were wont to sing such favorite songs of their day as "The Sidewalks of New

39

York," "Little Annie Rooney," "I Don't Want to Play in Your Yard," "Sweet Marie," "When You and I Were Young, Maggie," "After the Ball," "She Was Bred in Old Kentucky," and "A Bird in a Gilded Cage." Some families had the more modern piano; and most communities had their local brass bands featuring the stirring marches of John Philip Sousa of the United States Marine Band: "Washington Post," "Liberty Bell," "El Capitan," and "Stars and Stripes Forever."

The circulation of daily newspapers was increasing rapidly as the cities grew, largely because advertising by the city merchants gave to the owners the money with which to add a constantly expanding list of feature articles to their papers. They lacked the brilliant editorials of an earlier day, and some of them emphasized sensational news; but some, too, notably the New York *World* and St. Louis *Post Dispatch* of Joseph Pulitzer, were emerging as powerful agencies for reform in social and political life.

Some children were expected to read and follow the precepts of *Goops and How to Be Them* (a manual of manners for polite infants). Some had their *Master Skylark*, *Mrs. Wiggs of the Cabbage Patch*, and the *Jungle Book*, perchance one of the three children's magazines: *Harper's Round Table*, *St. Nicholas*, and the *Youths' Companion*. They got their weekly lesson sheet and tiny picture card portraying some Biblical scene at Sunday School. The first great mass production genius, Horatio Alger, steeped in the tradition that anyone might rise from obscure origins to high positions in fabulous America, was schooling its youth in the simple virtues with his fanciful stories of *Ragged Dick* and *Tattered Tom*. No comic strip or radio hero has the hold on boyhood imagination today that Alger had at the turn of the century.

G. L. White and his 13 choir members of Fiske University had returned from a tour of Europe in 1874 to awaken America to the indigenous, unique, and unexploited art treasure of the Negro spirituals. Minstrel shows were still popular, and *Uncle Tom's Cabin* was still the best money-maker in New York. Ellen Terry was starring in *Merchant of Venice*, Minnie Maddern Fiske in Ibsen's *A Doll's House*, Richard Mansfield in *Arms and the Man*, Julia Marlowe in *As You Like It*, Maude Adams in *The Little*

Minister, and Ethel Barrymore in *Trelawny of the Wells*. Stoddard's travel talks and lantern slides were tremendously popular with some people; the comic supplement with its Yellow Kid, Happy Hooligan, Mutt and Jeff, and Barney Google were even more so with others.

In this brief panorama of less material things of life, one sees much of the old and something of the new, faint indications that romance was giving way to realism, the first glimpse of a new generation of genuine, gay, courageous boys and girls. The aristocracy of newly rich factory, mine, railway, and city property owners—there were only three millionaires in 1860 and 3800 in 1899 —had no repressions and were unchecked by classical traditions. They loved color, glitter, pomp, display; they erected palaces, bought jewels, and hired European tutors; they bought the services of genealogists to prove their ancestry, private libraries of set editions in rich bindings to prove their learning, and titled Europeans to prove their daughters' charms. But this aristocracy had quickly run its course. There was no more place for it in twentieth-century America than there had been for bewigged aristocrats in the America of Andrew Jackson.

Twenty years later Edith Wharton's *The Age of Innocence*, portraying society in the 1870's, Hamlin Garland's *A Daughter of the Middle Border*, and *The Americanization of Edward Bok* were being awarded Pulitzer prizes. H. G. Wells' *The Outline of History*, Sinclair Lewis' *Main Street*, and John Dos Passos' *Three Soldiers* were best sellers. Leo Tolstoy's *The Power of Darkness*, a gloomy tragedy of Russian peasant life, and Eugene O'Neill's *Beyond the Horizon*, a tragedy of American farm life, were top-flight attractions in the theaters of New York. Thus did the interests of Americans change from romance to realism, and from the glamour to the stark tragedy of life.

EXPANDING HORIZONS

Never before in the history of man did such a bewildering array of technical inventions alter human life so completely within the span of a single generation. The nineteenth century had been an age of steam power. The steam engine had taken manufacturing out of the home and put it into factories. It had deprived communities with waterfalls of their monopoly on manufacturing and food processing. It had enabled every community to develop its own local industries. Then the railroads had destroyed local industries and created large industrial centers. Finally, just before the turn of the century the dynamo and motor had introduced the age of electric energy. Electric power made every region within 300 miles of a waterfall a potentially great manufacturing center. It spread industry once more to the edges of the cities and to the small towns. It lighted homes and factories, and obliterated the last vestiges of drudgery from housekeeping. It did all of these things for the American people after 1900.

The combined horsepower of electric motors in industry was 475,000 in 1900. Forty years later it was 45,291,000 and was steadily increasing. General use of electric household appliances did not come until the 1920's. Meanwhile the era of electric street railways had come and gone. They had reached a total mileage of 43,000 and an investment of $5,000,000,000, only to disappear as if by magic before the impact of the most revolutionary change of all times in the use of energy: the internal combustion engine and its application to moving vehicles. There were 8000 automobiles and 144 miles of paved highway in the United States in 1900. The speed limit was fixed by law at 15 miles an hour in Connecticut, and one was required publicly to advertise his intention of going upon the highway with an automobile one week in advance in the State of Tennessee. Thirty years later there were 25,000,000 automobiles, 750,000 miles of hard-surfaced roads, and speeds ranging upward to 80 miles an hour with safety. Automobile manufacturing was the third largest industry in the United States. Curves had been eliminated from the main highways, obstructions to vision removed, dangerous crossings and embankments protected, and many grade crossings eliminated. A trip of 25 miles in one day by horse and buggy had been unusual. Passenger automobiles are now driven more than 300,000,000,000 miles annually. The vast automobile manufacturing plants and distributing agencies, garages and service stations, tourist camps, highway markets and paying-guest homes suggest something of the economic change. Social changes represented by the closer contact between cities and rural areas, and between citizens of widely separated regions through tourist travel, by the effect of increased mobility upon education, crime, and the amusements and recreations of the people, can hardly be estimated.

The automobile enabled people to live in the city or in the country as personal tastes required, to enjoy the conveniences and cultural advantages of both, and to recapture the invigorating, soul-inspiring contact with nature so many had lost by the rise of the cities. Men and women could now live thirty or forty miles from their place of business or employment and drive back and forth each day. They could drive even longer distances on occasion to patronize the better stores of the large cities, and they could drive hundreds of miles for week end visits or for short vacations in nature's wonderland.

Cities became the shopping centers of ever larger areas. City stores and city newspapers began to make regular deliveries to nearby towns and rural homes. City streets and parking lots could no longer carry the burden of traffic. Business and service establishments began to spread out along the highways. City people began to move outside the city limits, where they met more remote country people moving in, and soon great metropolitan areas came into existence. Boston, for example, in 1940 had a city population of 769,000, but a population of 1,579,000 in outlying areas for a total of 2,348,000 in the Boston Metropolitan District. There were 92 such districts by 1930 containing 45 percent of the population of the United States.

The motion picture made its appearance in 1895. Thomas A. Edison was primarily responsible for its development, with his original peep-show machine. Thomas Armat added a projector to produce the vitascope. The first successful showing of a picture was that of *The Great Train Robbery* in 1903. Several theaters were opened in the eastern cities in 1905 on the basis of a five-cent admission charge. Biograph Studios engaged the services of D. W. Griffith in that year, and presented Mary Pickford in 1909 in *The New York Hat*. Between the appearances of these two films

was an era of experimentation. There were other films showing the
national interest in crime, with distinct emphasis upon the spark
of goodness in every bad man: *Bandit King, Raffles,* and *Hold-up
of the Leadville Stage.* There were films portraying poverty and the
struggle for existence such as *The Need of Gold,* showing a miner
dying from lack of food and medicine; films expressing sympathy
for the poor and distrust of bankers and politicians such as *Crooked
Bankers* and *The Grafters;* and films making sport of racial minorities such as the *Wooing and Wedding of a Coon* and *Fights of
Nations.* Finally, there was some attempt at reenacting history for
the benefit of recent immigrants: *Paul Revere, The Boston Tea
Party,* and *Saving His Country's Flag.* Mary Pickford was quickly
followed on the screen by other stars, including Mabel Normand,
Norma Talmadge, and Anita Stewart. Adolph Zukor turned
the attention of actors from the legitimate stage to pictures with
his production of *Queen Elizabeth,* made famous by Sarah Bern-
hardt. Serials became popular in 1913. These were the years of
the great crusade for social and moral reform, and movie directors
became enthusiastic preachers. They insisted that wealth alone
does not bring happiness, in *Gold Is Not All;* that the possession of
wealth leads to selfishness and immorality, in *Secrets of a Miner's
Cave and The Usurer;* that sin is always punished, in *The Sorrows
of the Unfaithful;* that every cloud has a silver lining, in *Watches
of the Night.* The simple virtues of charity, tolerance, and kind-
ness were taught in *Wife's Devotion, Tempered with Mercy,* and
Judge Not that Ye Be Not Judged. In addition to the morality
dramas, there were many films glorifying America as a land of
opportunity, rugged individualism, and stalwart virtue: *From Cabin
Boy to King* and *The Best Man Wins.* The long series of Western
pictures began which were to star through the years such actors
as William S. Hart, Hoot Gibson, Ken Maynard, and Gene Autry.
Every phase of the Progressive Movement was emphasized in a
dozen films: woman's suffrage in *Her Duty,* prostitution in *Damaged Goods,* graft and corruption in *How They Got the Vote,*
labor problems in *Pete Wants a Job,* the status of minorities in
*Solomon's Son, An Eye for an Eye, The Mayor of Ireland, The
Seminole's Trust,* and *A Persistent Suitor.*

44

Then came World War I, and the movies really reached top rank as a propaganda agency. Few more powerful films for arousing prejudice, sympathy, and hate have ever been produced than *The Birth of a Nation*, *Lest We Forget*, and *The Battle Cry of Liberty*. Following World War I, the industry reached maturity, lost much of its crudeness, and emerged as a finely conceived art. There were films serving as powerful agents for the reform of social evils: *Grapes of Wrath*, *The Moon Is Down*, and *The Lost Weekend*; films which were entertaining and educational for children: *Five Little Peppers*, *Wizard of Oz*, *Snow White*, *Peter Pan*, *Alice in Wonderland*, and the many animated cartoons like *Mickey Mouse*; films of historical value: *Union Pacific*, *Cimarron*, *Cavalcade*, and *Catherine the Great*; films encouraging an appreciation of music: *Desert Song*, *Rhapsody in Blue*, and *Showboat*; and films dealing in a subtle fashion with foreign affairs: *The Good Earth*, *Mission to Moscow*, and *A Bell for Adano*.

By 1930, the motion picture houses of the country were able to seat one tenth of the population at one time, and an estimated 100,-000,000 people paid admissions each week. Sound motion pictures were introduced in 1927 as a result of long and patient research by the Bell Telephone Laboratories and the General Electric Company. They have become tremendously popular both as an agency for amusement and for education in the schools and churches. The influence of motion pictures upon habits of dress, diction, etc., is not easily determined; but their combined utility in the field of advertising, scientific research, and education is enormously large.

There were no radios or airplane travel in 1900, although the radio was in process of development and flying already an accomplished fact. The first permanent radio broadcasting station, KDKA, was established by the Westinghouse Electric and Manufacturing Company in 1920. Its first program announced the election returns of that year. In 1921, the company opened stations WBZ at Newark, New Jersey, and KYW at Chicago, and the Detroit *News* opened station WWJ. Thereafter, the opening of new stations proceeded rapidly and the radio has, within two decades, influenced the lives of the people in a great diversity of

45

ways. In 1921, the first sports broadcast was given over the air; and, the following year, the first stage show—Ed Wynn's "The Perfect Fool"—the first prize fight, the first band concert, the first bedtime stories for children, the first world-series baseball games, grand opera, and the New York Philharmonic. Gimbel Brothers sponsored the first hour-long commercial-musical program in 1923; and, in 1924, Calvin Coolidge spoke over the radio in the presidential campaign, the broadcasting of crop and weather reports and news began, and newspapers introduced radio departments.

The objective of the broadcasting companies at first was the development of good will and markets for radio equipment, until the American Telephone and Telegraph Company, operating station WEAF, hit upon the idea of toll broadcasting in 1924. The public desire for entertainment soon altered programs from sales talks to music, drama, and other forms of entertainment. The Red and Blue Networks were organized in 1926. The operation of broadcasting stations became a major industry, selling time to commercial broadcasters who, in their effort to please the masses, introduced cheap entertainment, jazz, inferior monologues, and drama.

Lessons in accounting were broadcast by WJZ as early as 1923. The Smithsonian Institution began weekly scientific talks in 1924. Lectures on Greek and Roman classics were broadcast by New York University in 1925. Courses in philosophy, psychology, and physics were soon added, and other universities took up the work with ever-expanding curricula. A Public School of the Air was established in Atlanta, Georgia, in 1926. The Standard Oil Company supplied an educational program for the schools in 1928. The Columbia Broadcasting System started the American School of the Air in February, 1930, with programs including history dramas, literature, art, travelogues, foreign news and music. Walter Damrosch began educational music concerts for the schools on Friday mornings of each week. These and dozens of other programs of superior quality carried the finest music, drama and public lectures into the farthest corners of the world and most remote sections of our own country. They emancipated our rural and mountain people from the blighting influence of ignorant and incompetent leadership. The radio's use in transportation, especially in the air and marine service, in industry and business, and in government and politics, is almost without limit.

Radio broadcasting brought its problems. Commercial advertisers were reluctant to sponsor educational programs because of the limited audiences. The pressure to popularize university broadcasts was great. The University of California lost its radio time to *True Story Magazine*. The air was filled with programs deemed unfit and actually detrimental to children. All of this created a new problem of public policy and led to the demand by prominent educators like Robert G. Sproul, President of the University of California, and Professor Grace Abbott of the University of Chicago that entire wave channels be withdrawn from commercial use and turned over to educational institutions; or that all radio broadcasting be government owned and operated. Opposed to these demands was the ever-present fear of political influence, bureaucratic control, and the much greater obstacle to cultural programs of getting the people to listen to them. The news of the day, sports of all kinds, farm programs, and religious services did not encounter these same difficulties. The National Farm and Home Hour, presented by the United States Department of Agriculture, became one of the most popular programs of the air, and the inspiring talks of Drs. S. Parkes Cadman, Harry Emerson Fosdick, and Daniel Poling were brought to the homes of all who cared to listen. Year by year, the radio became more important in national life, in the promotion of social solidarity, the apprehension of criminals, the relief of suffering and distress, the dissemination of accurate news, the education and entertainment of the people, the encouragement of wide interest in public affairs, and the development of skills, vocations, and habits. No other invention has so extended the environment, broadened the cultural interests, and provided the mental stimulation of so many people.

Finally, there came the development of the airplane. Work began on heavier-than-air machines in the late nineties, and short flights were made by Wilbur and Orville Wright in 1903. Then came public exhibitions in 1908, air-mail service in 1918, and commercial passenger service in 1926. By 1940 air lines totaled 40,000 miles and commercial planes were flying one billion passenger miles annually. Various government units were supplying most of the landing fields. Ownership and operation was a private enterprise, but few planes were used as privately owned means of conveyance and fewer still for carrying freight.

THE FAMILY

It was inevitable, of course, that such a dynamic civilization should modify severely ancient institutions like the family, the schools, the church, and the government.

Life's activities ceased to revolve about the home as rural isolation was broken down. Commercial amusement such as motion pictures, and increasing facilities for outdoor recreation in public playgrounds, parks, and golf courses, demanded more of the time of more and more people. Large-scale commercial canning, meat-packing and baking, laundry and cleaning services, and the wearing of custom-made clothing by everyone relieved the home of its function as a unit of production. Youth's new freedom not only lessened the restraints of parental control, but robbed the night of its terrors and increased the day's activities by many hours. Seldom, indeed, are all the members of a modern family together except at mealtime, and frequently not even then. Children ceased to be cherished as an economic asset whose labor in youth supplemented the family income and whose contributions would alleviate the privations of old age. The size of the family came to be regulated to conform with the ability of the parents properly to rear and educate them rather than by accident and God's providence. Young people married at an earlier age; divorces increased; families decreased in size; but the rearing of children became more of a conscious privilege and responsibility. Family relationships are anything but uniform even in the same community, and they vary greatly between city, village and rural environments; but what has been said above indicates discernible trends during the past three decades.

Urbanization and technical progress combined steadily to broaden the horizon of life's activities for young men and women after the turn of the century. It is pertinent to remember that not every one who moved to the city entered into the factories. As a city grows, it builds its own diversified economy, including institutions and services non-existent except in dense populations. This, in turn, multiplies manyfold the special fields of productive enterprise open to young people and creates new requirements of specialized training, opportunity for the development of special talents, and a sharper division into groups and classes on the basis of intelligence and inherent ability. This process became so rapid and continuous after the turn of the century that life's possibilities were vastly broader for each maturing generation. It steadily lengthened the period of education, increased the percentage of people, both men and women, gainfully employed, and enlarged their productive capacity. It altered our norms of conduct and our social philosophy, creating a really serious crisis in the lives of millions who found difficulty in making the adjustment. That was particularly true where parental authority, religious sanctions, and the rights of private property were involved.

Life's basic pattern changed as completely for women as it did for young people. The feminist movement had begun before the Civil War. By the turn of the century, women were enjoying the franchise in several states, equal educational opportunities, and some privileges in business and public life. Nothing had been done, however, to relieve them of the inevitable drudgery of rearing large families. The gains of the nineteenth century, therefore, were relatively small, and limited to a small portion of their sex. Since then household electrical appliances have done more to emancipate women than all the generations of agitation by militant suffragettes. Add to their benefits those of new methods in the care of children, the eradication of many children's diseases, and the assumption by the schools of responsibilities formerly resting upon mothers, and it is not difficult to realize that women were living in a new and happier world. Leisure time became a reality. Women's clubs of all kinds sprang up like mushrooms. The joy of homemaking replaced the drudgery of housekeeping, and even

5277

the tyranny of servants could be dispensed with by those who were financially able to employ them.

Youth was given recognition. The universal longing of parents to give their children advantages they, themselves, had never enjoyed assumed a new importance. America became child conscious. Not only did parents make untold sacrifices to provide their children with a college education, but society spent enormous sums for new school plants and equipment, children's playgrounds, and parks. Each new advantage brought corresponding responsibilities for child welfare. Rearing children in the isolation of a rural homestead had been simplicity itself compared to rearing them in the new economic age. Parental control was no longer sufficient. Only society through government agencies could cope with the new environment, and so there emerged an ever-increasing demand for rigid censorship of the movies, radio, and magazines, for the regulation of milk and food supplies, for the suppression of gambling and prostitution, and for the prohibition of the sale of alcoholic beverages. This urge for reform legislation did not arise entirely from the circumstances of the new environment. It was, in part, a revival of the great reform and benevolent movements of pre-Civil War days, which had been submerged by that conflict. It was, also, the result of a new interest in childhood. It can not be separated from the new attitude toward child delinquency, the crusade against child labor, or the establishment of public health nursing, and children's aid societies. It was a severe blow to a nation which had, for thirty years, shown a progressive interest in its children to be told by the White House Conference of 1930 that more than one fifth of the 47,608,000 children in this country were suffering from blindness, deafness, tuberculosis, heart disease, or were crippled or mentally deficient.

THE SCHOOLS

The influence of an earlier day and the new economic order are both readily discernible in the modern school system. Free public schools for all children, with no distinction of wealth or social position, have always been one of the most unique and cherished of our social institutions. From kindergarten to university, no barriers have ever existed for any child except the tests of ability provided within the system itself. Our school system, moreover, has always been decentralized and largely under local control. Both of these fundamental characteristics survived the tests of a new order; but industrialism and urbanization forced important modifications in other equally fundamental features. Reduction of child labor, new cultural standards, and the demands for a more intelligent citizenship increased school enrollment rapidly. The number of students in institutions of higher learning increased from 284,000 in 1900 to 1,178,000 in 1930, in secondary schools from 630,000 to 4,740,000, and the total school population to 29,500,000. The curriculum also changed to meet more adequately the needs of a diverse civilization. In 1890, most high school pupils were studying Latin, geometry, algebra, and history. By 1900, physical geography, physiology, English literature, and civil government had been added. During the next decade, German was added, only to be discarded during the hysteria of World War I. Zoology and botany were introduced, but lost favor after a few years. Physical geography almost disappeared before 1920. The percentage of pupils studying algebra, geometry, physics, and chemistry declined sharply after the beginning of the second decade. English literature and rhetoric assumed a leading position as required subjects, and enormous gains were made by general science, community civics, home economics, manual arts, music, art, bookkeeping, and typewriting. These changes were largely due to the influence of the educational philosopher John Dewey, whose School and Society (1899) popularized the theory of experimentation in educational processes to the end of properly equipping the child as a useful member of society.

Not only did enrollment increase and curricula change, but the organization and administration of the several units of the school system were radically revised. The rural school of one room, one teacher, and eight grades predominated at the turn of the century. Certification of teachers was under the control of county examining boards. Village and city schools retained the eight elementary grades, with four-year secondary schools over which the colleges and universities exercised strong indirect influence. All of this rapidly changed. Consolidated schools replaced the old type rural school. Junior high schools were introduced. Senior high schools ceased to serve primarily as college preparatory schools. The junior college and normal schools took over the work of the first two years of university training, with strong indications that the junior college and senior high school would ultimately become a single unit, the four-year college disappear, and the university be devoted increasingly to preparation for graduate work and research. The field of education, also, was extended by the establishment of nursery schools, extension departments, and adult education classes.

Finally, there was the unique development of a dual school system in the southern states. The South was confronted with the twofold problem of restoring the shattered school system for the whites and formulating a policy with respect to Negro education. After the close of Congressional Reconstruction, the idea of destroying race prejudice by forced association of Negro and white children in mixed schools was repudiated. The principle of a dual system was generally agreed upon, and slightly more than $100,000,000 had been spent for Negro education by southern states before 1900. That represented real progress in view of the handicap to be overcome: widespread poverty and prevailing prejudices against mass education, particularly of the Negro. The most serious threat was an attempt to base school appropriations for each system on the ratio of taxes paid by each race. The greatest problems were to secure adequately trained Negro teachers and overcome the reluctance of Negro parents to educate their children.

The work of Samuel C. Armstrong at Hampton Institute and of his pupil, Booker T. Washington, at Tuskegee Institute, did much to build up correct attitudes among the Negro race toward both education and labor, to break down prejudice against Negro education among the whites, and to promote mutual understanding and cooperation between the two races to the end of sectional betterment. The George Peabody Fund (1867) and the John F. Slater Fund (1883) were so administered as to promote the training of Negro teachers and the appropriation of public funds for the establishment of elementary schools for both races. By 1927 more than 300 accredited high schools had been established by these foundations. Building slowly upon the basic achievements of these pioneering efforts, great things were accomplished after the turn of the century. The Anna T. Jeans Fund (1908), the donations from the General Education Board (1902), the Caroline Phelps Stokes Fund (1913), and the Julius Rosenwald Fund (1914) made possible the establishment of adequate supervision, fellowships and scholarships for teachers' training and research, comprehensive surveys and the erection of modern school buildings in every rural community.

There are still many discouraging aspects of the situation, principally inadequate enforcement of attendance laws, the lingering apathy of the Negroes themselves and the inequality of public expenditures in the lower South; but the trend is unmistakable and the accomplishment of three decades far from negligible. Low property valuations, low density of population, a high percentage of children, the gravitation of the better teachers to regions of higher salaries, and the predominantly rural nature of the section must always be considered in making comparisons between the South and other sections of the country.

No institution could expand so rapidly and adjust its functional structure so quickly to the changing needs of society without encountering difficulties. It was difficult to secure an adequately trained corps of teachers and keep them from being drawn away from the profession by more lucrative returns in other fields of employment. Local control too often introduced personal prejudices and politics into the schools at the expense of efficiency. The burden of increased taxes to meet bonded indebtedness and current expenses aroused severe criticism of each new addition to the curriculum. It was often difficult to reconcile the demands of the universities and the needs of the community. The promotion of extracurricular activities, play and recreation, the new training for social life, and the teaching of new natural and social scientific principles too frequently clashed with the political, religious, and economic prejudices of parents, produced tension in family circles, and brought a storm of protest down upon the

53

heads of the teachers. One might go on to fill a volume with the symptoms of progress. The annual expenditures for public elementary and secondary schools increased from a paltry $215,000,-000 in 1900 to more than $2,000,000,000 in 1930. The value of school property increased from less than $1,000,000,000 to more than $7,000,000,000 in the same period. The number of people who doubt the wisdom of educating the masses gradually lessened. Many were fretful over the huge outlay of public funds and, at times of economic depression, lost no opportunity to bring about a retrenchment. But the faith of the people, generally, has deepened in the one institution which, more than any other, has served to teach men how to live happily and harmoniously together and thus given solidarity to the nation. That such material prosperity as the nation came to enjoy could never have been possible with an illiterate people has become an accepted truth.

THE CHURCH

The church yielded less, perhaps, to the pressure of changing conditions than either the family or the schools. Nevertheless its social attitudes and its influence in the lives of its members depend largely upon the degree of cultural and economic isolation of the people. Many aspects of religious institutions were swept away beyond recovery with the breakdown of rural isolation. At the turn of the century, liberalism in large urban communities and in institutions of higher learning was heresy elsewhere. People in the small towns and country still went to church, zealously supported church enterprises, reveled in the spirit of denominational rivalry, and believed explicitly in the orthodox faith. Every community had its several denominational church groups, served by resident or circuit preachers who, as a rule, were more dogmatic than intelligent.

Slowly but surely, the church lost its viselike grip upon the more essential customs of the people. Marriage and divorce came to be regarded as far too important to be controlled by religious sanctions. The clergy, along with teachers, lost much of their commanding position as authorities on all matters, temporal as

well as spiritual. The great advance in higher education placed in
every church congregation men and women whose education was
equal, if not superior to that of the pastor. The solution of social
problems now required a technical knowledge he did not possess.
Psychiatrists and social workers, highly trained and maintained
for a particular type of work invaded two of the fields formerly
dominated almost exclusively by pastors of the churches. The
newspapers, magazines, and radio began comprehensive discussions of science, morals, and religion, which were formerly the
almost exclusive province of ministerial sermons. Whether they
turned to an interest in social and economic reform, or made
their churches into agencies for social activities and public welfare, the pastors met increasing competition.

Small, struggling churches were abandoned, denominational
rivalry lost its appeal, and community churches made their appearance. Less emphasis was placed upon individual salvation and
religious dogma, more upon social reform and economic justice.
The camp meeting and mid-winter revival disappeared almost entirely from large sections of the country. Billy Sunday marched
through the land in the early years of the century, lambasting
sinners and successfully appealing to hundreds of thousands to hit
the sawdust trail; but in the last years of his life audiences were
amazingly small and his picturesque language had lost its flavor.
Family worship and familiarity with the Bible were rare in the
new generation, and religious inhibitions no longer controlled sex
relations, birth control, marriage, and divorce. There was no uniformity in these matters between denominations, of course, and
even within single denominations there came to be fundamentalists, modernists, and cynics. Naturally, in an age when science
became a household word and anything called scientific was accepted without question, increasing numbers of churchmen tried
to reconcile science and Christianity. Naturally, too, those who
clung to the fundamentals of orthodoxy resisted to the point of
open conflict within the church and to heresy hunts without. The
brunt of the battle fell upon the public schools, colleges, and universities and upon that portion of the population which regarded
Sunday as a day for recreation in sports and movie houses.

About 50 percent of the people belonged to a church at the turn of the century and about the same proportion belong today. It is pretty generally agreed that an increasing number render only lip service to their professed faith and regard the obligation of membership lightly. On the other hand, many who do not care to affiliate with church organizations contribute liberally to their support, attend religious services, and utilize the services of ordained ministers for marriage and burial ceremonies in much the same way as those of a public notary transacting legal business. The churches have more women members than men, and a higher percentage of the population in the cities than in rural communities. Of the 212 independent denominations, more than half have only a few thousand members.

4

The Bonds of Union

REGIONAL AGRICULTURE

EARLY in the nineteenth century Henry Clay had won lasting fame by advocating a program of national policy to make the nation strong and all its sections prosperous by promoting their interdependence. Clay's dream became a reality fifty years after his death, but by virtue of technology rather than congressional legislation.

First the railroads, then automobiles, trucks, tractors, and other power-driven machines revolutionized agriculture. Farming, for generations, had been a way of life. Every farm homestead had produced food for the family, fuel, and much of the clothing. Houses and barns were built from the surrounding stands of timber. Fuel was cut as needed in the farm wood-lot. Fruit from the orchard was preserved or buried for winter use. Meat was slaughtered in autumn. Eggs, butter, and milk were constantly fresh items in the family diet. Horses and mules, fed from the pasture and corn and oat fields, supplied the power. The few items needed from the outside world were purchased in the rural towns, and a wide variety of products not needed for family use were sold in the local market. Now farming ceased to be a way of life and became a commercial enterprise. Every city became a market for the products of every agricultural community and every agricultural community entered into competition with every other one for these markets. Farmers could no longer grow a variety of products for a local market. They had to specialize on the par-

57

ticular grain, fruit, or vegetable best suited to their soil and climate. Ever higher prices for land and expensive machinery increased the pressure to do so. Soon every fertile region became identified with a particular money crop—rice, beet sugar, cantaloupes, onions, berries, celery, etc.—with its large markets in the cities along the coast and the Great Lakes. Likewise, factories were clustered in particular regions close to needed raw materials, power, and labor; and regions of specialized agriculture, specialized manufacture, and cities were tied together by the railroads, by trucks, and in late years by airplanes. The daily needs of every community, however small, were supplied by the products of far distant places.

Farmers did not make the transition easily. Farm machinery cost money, and its use led to overexpansion of production. Rapid transport brought them into competition with farmers the world over, and particularly with those who operated on an industrial basis and exploited cheap labor. The sugar producers of Louisiana, for example, had to meet competition not only from the Philippines, Hawaii, and Cuba, but from the beet-sugar industry of Colorado, California, and Michigan. Fruits and vegetables for the winter markets of northern cities came from the South and the Pacific Coast. Meat and dairy products came from Canada and South America, fruit from the tropical countries, and a wide variety of products from far distant countries of the Orient and the Near East.

Life in the cities necessitated a change in the food habits of the people. Not the least of a variety of reasons for this was the fact that women who worked for wages and lived in cramped apartments had neither the energy to prepare food nor the space to store it. They began buying prepared foods, and there was a tremendous increase in packaging and distribution of breakfast foods, baked goods, canned fruits and vegetables, soups and condensed milk, fish and pressed meats, and frozen meats, vegetables, and fruits. This development also promoted specialization in agriculture, the interdependence of widely separated farming and urban communities, and the almost complete dependence of millions of people for their daily food supply upon the smooth and continuous functioning of many processing and distributing enterprises, not to mention highly integrated methods of transportation and communication.

INTEGRATION IN INDUSTRY

One of the most revolutionary changes of the period, a change which began before the turn of the century but increased progressively thereafter, was the development of large-scale operations in manufacturing, in finance, and in distribution. Many volumes have been written about combinations, corporations, trusts, and holding companies, but the whole story has not yet been told. Stability and security from the uncertainties of unrestricted competition were largely responsible. The desire for greater profits by increasing efficiency and establishing monopolies; the desire to create wealth through stock issues against future earning power; the influence of banking interests which got to gambling with the people's money in investment trusts; and the demands of the public for new fields of investment—all these entered into the mergers of independent companies, stores, and banks, and the creation of holding companies.

The movement began near the end of the nineteenth century. It was, therefore, a survival about which nothing had been done —a development which was to evoke more public discussion, consume more of the energies of men in public life and arouse more bitterness than any other subject in the next three decades. This was true for three principal reasons: (1) consolidation did not lead to economic stability; (2) the profit motive predominated with little regard to social responsibilities; and (3) the concentration of wealth and economic control gave to a few men extraordinary power over the lives of the people and the government itself.

The history of this mobilization of property interests is too complicated to be described adequately by illustration. It is best to designate the nature of what was accomplished in every field of production and distribution. Until near the close of the nineteenth century business was conducted under the competitive system, with each of the units owned and operated by one man or a small group of men. The small neighborhood retail store, the small local bank, and the little factory, were characteristic of the several units. Capital and management were combined in the same hands and there was close contact between the employer and the employee. Then began the process of integration. Improved communication broadened the markets of the producer. Mechanization made possible large-scale production. A surplus of fluid capital became available for huge financing operations and facilitated the sale of stock to the public.

Soon after the Civil War, intrepid manufacturers began to add coal and iron mines, railroad and steamship lines, and innumerable factory units all along the line of production to their holdings. Only occasionally did such tremendous corporations remain under the ownership and control of the men who created them. The Henry Ford and Andrew Mellon corporations are such exceptions. More often monopolies were created by bringing competitive industries under the same management through trusts or holding companies. The banking interests who financed and arranged for consolidations received enormous commissions in the form of common or preferred stock which they disposed of as rapidly as possible to the investing public through the medium of stock exchanges. The owners of the constituent companies received fabulous amounts of stock in the new companies in exchange for their properties. The total amount of stock issued, most of which was eventually purchased by thousands of small investors, invariably exceeded the actual value of the physical property involved. It had no par value and sold for whatever it would bring on the stock exchange, which was whatever the investing public thought it was worth on the basis of probable dividends or for resale at a profit. The stock sold to the public did not always carry voting power, that stock being retained by a small group who manipulated the organization. The same procedure was followed in the organization of banking trusts and retail chain stores.

The social and economic implications of this whole development were startling. Management was thus separated from ownership. The thousands of owners had no direct interest in the manufacturing process, being concerned only with the size of their dividend checks and the stable or increased resale value of their holdings. The savings of the people who would never venture to purchase stock directly were inevitably drawn into the system as directors of insurance companies, banks, and trust companies invested the funds under their control in stocks and bonds. A greater cleavage exists between the employee and the manager than was ever possible between employees and owner control. Thus management became independent of ownership and the needs of labor, ruthless in its dealings with smaller competitors, reckless in its handling of the people's savings—in short, economic freedom and rugged individualism were severely modified. Every individual in the nation, whether or not he owned stock or was employed by these huge corporations, came directly under their influence through his use of public utility services, his purchase of the necessities of life, his quest for amusement, and the disposition of his savings.

Consolidation of business and industrial enterprises was at its height at the turn of the century. Transactions on the New York stock exchange involved the transfer of 266,000,000 shares in 1901, nearly five times the volume of 1896. The country was prosperous and the national economy was well balanced. Businessmen had confidence in the government, now firmly under control of the Republicans. That party was pledged to maintain a high protective tariff, the gold standard, and a hands-off policy with respect to business. The supply of gold from new fields in Alaska and South Africa was adequate to produce a continuous rise in the level of prices until World War I. Food prices increased 50 percent. The demand for farm products was greater than the supply despite the plowing of almost 100,000,000 acres of new land in the West. The annual output of manufactured goods increased from $13,000,000,000 in 1900 to $65,000,000,000 in 1920. Steel production increased from 5,000,000 tons in 1890 to 32,000,000 in 1920.

The reason for this unbounded prosperity was clearly apparent. The millions of immigrants and native Americans passing into the cities needed food, clothing, shelter, and household furnishings. Skyscrapers, new factories, automobiles, household appliances, steel rolling stock for the railroads, farm machinery, power plants, transmission lines, machine tools—all of these things required steel, copper, and other metals, and all of them required an enormous labor force. More and more, however, the sale of these products of industry depended upon the continued prosperity of the farmers and the industrial wage earners; and consolidation placed upon ever fewer men the power and responsibility of maintaining stability in this complex economy.

INTEGRATION IN GOVERNMENT

The governmental system of the country, both state and national, was essentially the same in 1900 as it had been at the close of the Civil War. The Supreme Court had recovered much of the prestige that it had lost during the war period, and was about to enter upon the most stormy period of its existence. The social and economic trends of the period created many problems in government and led to many legislative experiments. Time after time, the people were to find difficulty in regulating their affairs within the limits of a written constitution and the delegation of powers belonging to the federal government. Due process, equal protection of the laws, the obligations of contracts, and interstate commerce proved to be havens of refuge for minority property interests and a source of unending labor for the Justices of the Supreme Court.

In its outward appearances, the government changed but little during the first three decades of the twentieth century. One amendment was adopted giving the franchise to women and another providing for the popular election of United States Senators. A law prohibiting the manufacture and sale of intoxicating liquors was written into the Constitution and afterwards removed. Otherwise there was no change in the fundamental law. Nevertheless, the functions and powers of the several departments of the federal government no less than those of the state governments increased tremendously.

The most interesting innovations involved the division of

power between the federal and state governments: the reserved rights of the states, and the limitations placed upon the power of Congress by the Constitution as interpreted by the Supreme Court. The people of the United States, finding it impossible to cope with modern social and economic conditions through the agencies of forty-eight independent state governments, were yet reluctant to surrender local autonomy by conferring larger powers upon the central government by constitutional amendment. It was not the difficulty of amendment but the faith in state rights and fear of a federal bureaucracy surviving from an earlier day that were responsible. They chose rather to test the limits of the Constitution under liberal interpretation, and then to rely upon previously unexplored fields of experimentation.

The concentration of wealth and income within a relatively small section of the country placed them beyond the reach of most state governments and made the tax on individual and corporate incomes the particular province of the federal government. This wealth, in a way, took the place of the public domain as a rich resource from which the federal government could make grants-in-aid to the several states. The power of Congress to tax and spend for the general welfare had never been questioned. The practice of making unconditional grants to the states for education and internal improvements was based on ample precedent extending back to the early nineteenth century. The device of making conditional grants-in-aid to the states from the federal treasury followed as a natural sequence. Congress, in 1911, inaugurated the policy of requiring the states to match its subsidies with an equal amount of money. Later, it began to set up boards and commissions to approve and exercise supervision over the projects for which appropriations were made in the fields of agricultural and vocational education, highway construction, conservation, etc. Much of the legislation of the Roosevelt recovery program was based on these precedents, especially the public works and social security acts.

This sort of federal appropriation increased to $37,000,000 annually by 1920 and to more than $2,000,000,000 annually during the early thirties. How far Congress may be allowed to go in this direction depends upon the willingness of the several states to surrender their special prerogatives in return for financial assistance and upon the degree of regulation the Supreme Court will allow the federal government to exercise by compulsion. The whole experiment was somewhat shaken by the Court's invalidation of the AAA (*Hoosac Mills Corporation v. United States*, 1936). In any case, it represents one method by which the legislative branch of the government has sought to overcome the handicap of a decentralized governmental system in a nation whose economic and social institutions demand an ever-increasing uniformity of regulation.

The second innovation along new lines was stimulated by the desire to preserve the sovereignty of the states. The pleas for state rights so eloquently advanced by one party or the other throughout American history are more than a fetish of professional politics. There can be no question that adherence to the principle has promoted domestic tranquility, served the peculiar interests of widely separated sections, and fostered a rich variety of social institutions. The submergence of the state governments within a highly centralized system would deprive the nation of their use as experimental laboratories. Yet, in large measure, that was the trend at the turn of the century. The remedy lay in closer cooperation between governors and state legislatures within natural sectional areas to the end of uniform state legislation and administration. The need for cooperative action in handling the liquor traffic, automobile traffic, and the suppression of crime are cases in point. Out of those very problems came the urge for action. Theodore Roosevelt called the first Governors' Conference at Washington in 1908 and such conferences were held with increasing frequency thereafter. A legislators' association was organized in 1925. The organization, however, which ultimately gave indications of taking the lead was the American Bar Association, which organized committees for drafting uniform legislation to be passed upon by the Association and then presented to state legislatures for adoption. The success of the scheme is still problematical in view of the general inefficiency and provincial viewpoints of most state officials.

Returning to the expansion of federal power during the period, we find that much of it arose out of control of interstate commerce. It began with the revolutionary Interstate Commerce Act of 1887, designed to regulate the railroads. Subsequent changes to strengthen the government's control were made by the Hepburn Act (1906) and the Esch-Cummins Act (1920). In 1912, Congress passed an Interstate Commerce Act for the control of wireless communication; in 1926, the Air Commerce Act for the control of aviation; and in 1927, the Radio Control Act for the control of radio. All of these measures established commissions modeled after the Interstate Commerce Commission of 1887. In 1914, Congress created the Federal Reserve Board, the Tariff Commission, and the Federal Trade Commission; in 1920, the Federal Power Commission and the Federal Farm Board. The host of boards and commissions established under the recovery acts of Franklin D. Roosevelt's Administration beginning in 1933 will be mentioned later.

The attempt of Congress to expand federal authority by using the taxing power to destroy was curbed by the Supreme Court in the case of *Bailey v. Drexel Furniture Company* (1922). This act placed a prohibitive tax upon the products of child labor and was based upon the precedent established in 1865 when Congress drove state bank notes out of circulation by a 10 percent tax on all such issues.

Finally, the powers and duties of the federal enforcement agencies were increasingly taxed by legislation designed to drive out of existence certain social evils: the white slave traffic, stolen automobiles, narcotics and liquor. By 1930, such cases were occupying most of the time of the federal courts. The evasion of income taxes by those engaged in these professions enabled the Treasury Department to lend its assistance and the combination gave the federal government, indirectly, important police powers in the breaking up of numerous rackets and criminal syndicates. Demands for more effective control of trusts, public utilities, stock and security exchanges, and banking increased as centralization of control was established in these several fields.

EXPANSION OF GOVERNMENT SERVICE

More important than the expansion of government control was the expansion of government service. The nature of the demands for federal service in the new machine age are clearly shown by the history of rural postal service. The breaking down of rural isolation, carried swiftly along by the automobiles, the radio and improved highways, was first begun by the telephone. Its development and influence are too familiar to need repetition except to say that between 1900 and 1930 the number of telephones increased from 1,355,000 to 20,201,000. In 1896, however, the federal government took an important step in this direction by inaugurating rural free delivery mail service. The mileage of these routes increased steadily from 29,000 in 1900 to 1,354,000 in 1930. This service multiplied contacts with the outside world, increased the circulation of newspapers, and made possible the development of the great mail-order houses such as Sears, Roebuck and Company and Montgomery Ward & Co., Inc., which depend largely upon a rural patronage. Not more than 800 cities had free delivery service in 1900. By 1930, the service had been extended to nearly 3000 cities.

Other demands for service in the collection of information and its distribution to businessmen, manufacturers, consumers, and the public at large were met by the creation of the Department of Commerce, the Public Health Service in the Treasury Department, and the Bureau of Home Economics and Food and Drug Administration in the Department of Agriculture. The popularity of these services is indicated by the increase in the cost of the federal Public Health Service from $42,000 in 1910 to $13,000,-000 in 1930.

State governments no less than the federal government responded to the demands of the new age by extending the scope of their services and the exercise of police powers. The rapid extension of the school system required funds for operation which could be provided only by the states. State legislation was necessary to permit consolidation of school districts. State normal schools and universities required ever larger appropriations to train the teachers and accommodate the thousands of young people who were no longer satisfied with a high school education. State superintendents of schools and state certification supplanted the old township boards and county teachers' examinations. State old-age pensions and mothers' pensions replaced the old county poor farms. The number of child health centers increased from 20 in 1900 to 1500 in 1930. Schools introduced free lunches for undernourished children, and added physicians, dentists, nurses, and physical training teachers to their staffs. New facilities were provided for handling the mentally ill and criminally insane. Fifteen hundred institutions for dependent, neglected, and handicapped children were established by 1930. The use of new serums in combating contagious diseases required the distribution of numerous biologicals. The growth of corporations, particularly of great utility holding companies, called for state utility commissions and legislation to regulate stock sales. The automobile rendered obsolete the former dirt and gravel roads, required the construction of new highways, and the hard surfacing of all. New interest in recreation led to the building of state parks, the conservation of game, and protection of forest areas. Summer camps to provide for 3,000,000 children were established by public and private agencies. Public playgrounds were built in every city. Municipal park acreage increased to 350,000 by 1930 with an annual maintenance cost of $100,000,000. The number of people visiting state and national parks annually increased from 199,000 in 1910 to 31,000,-000 in 1940. Commercial amusements failed to function in conformity with modern moral standards without regulation. The ease with which automobiles could be stolen and transported long distances, the dangers to public safety from irresponsible drivers, and the increased mobility of criminals resulted in state automobile license systems for cars and drivers and the establishment of state constabularies. State tax commissions, law-drafting bureaus, welfare departments, and public employment agencies were created. The courts failed to administer properly the new workmen's compensation laws and state industrial relations boards came into existence. There was legislation for the regulation of chain stores, small-loan companies, farmers' cooperatives, and licensing for the practice of law, medicine, and dentistry, and for the operation of hotels, restaurants, and barber shops.

Much of this new legislation came at the insistence of organized labor. Mechanization increased the productive capacity of labor, but the laboring man had no control over the unit of production, and lived in an atmosphere of insecurity. His inability to secure a guaranteed return from his labor sufficient to provide what once were luxuries but now were necessities led to his dependence upon the state for them. Every new free social service added to the real income of the laboring man. It enabled him to get indirectly by taxation what he was unable to gain directly in wages. In a very real sense the machines of the new industrial era funneled money from the entire nation into the pockets of those who owned them. The income tax took it away from them and government services redistributed it for the benefit of all the people. Some of the new control legislation was enacted to appease the reform groups who capitalize upon the supreme faith of the American people in their ability to effect changes in the habits and customs of the people by compulsion. Some of the new services were created to satisfy politically powerful minority groups. Most of them, however, were the inevitable result of the inability of local government agencies to function in the new social and economic order.

Yet there was remarkably little progress toward eliminating obsolete units of government. Township and small county organizations, with their host of minor officials, contribute little in the way of efficiency and much in the nature of extravagance and annoyance. They continue to exist because our entire political spoils system depends upon them. They constitute the most serious obstacles to the efficiency of taxation and crime control and to civil service reform. The power of all state legislatures was restricted by taking away from them the election of United States Senators. The powers of many of them were curbed by the adoption of elaborate state constitutions and the Initiative and Referendum. Responsibility was transferred from legislatures to governors by the adoption of state budgets and the creation of state administrative boards. Bicameral city councils disappeared. Mayors were replaced by city managers. An increasing number of cities adopted the civil service reform.

CULTURAL INTEGRATION

The one fact which stands out above all else about this period of American life is the increasing cultural unity of the people. Millions of people ate the same breakfast foods, used the same household appliances, and rode in automobiles. They patronized the chain stores, relied upon the same public utilities, and looked at the same advertisements. They listened to the same speeches, music, and sermons on the radio, saw the same moving pictures, and laughed or cried over the same comic strips. They worried over the same income tax blanks, gambled on the same stock market, and bought the same life insurance policies. They read the same articles and received the same government literature on problems of health, the care of babies, and the rearing of children. The result was that their emotions, their attitudes toward public questions, and their standards of social conduct and morality became more uniform. Mass impression followed mass production and large-scale distribution as inevitably as day follows the night.

The first important aspect of this change was the tremendous power for good or evil which it placed into the hands of a few people. Centralized control of newspapers, the motion pictures, and the radio increased the control of a relatively few people over public opinion. Mass impression became as significant a term as mass production and had vastly greater implications. It is one thing for millions of people to wear the same kind of clothes and drive the same make of automobile, but quite another thing altogether for them to read the same newspaper, see the same picture shows, and hear the same radio programs. It is something else, again, if the men who control these powerful agencies permit them to be used for purposes of propaganda and for the promotion of selfish interests, or deny their use to those whose opinions and ideas are distasteful to their own social philosophy. Would interests which were powerful enough to exclude the writings of abolitionists from the mails also have been able to keep their voices off the air? If the showing of a single film, *The Birth of a Nation*, was in large part responsible, as we think it was, for the subsequent revival of racial hatreds, what vast possibilities for social change rest in the control of such an instrument? The fact is that the creation of large corporations for the control of manufacturing, of banking and credit, of the press, of radio, of motion pictures, of public utilities and services, gradually gave to their directorships the character of positions of great public trust and responsibility. In so far as events of the period showed them to have been used for selfish rather than for social purposes, we shall see demands arising for governmental ownership and control.

The second important consequence was the manner in which it threw into sharp relief the substandard cultural areas of the country, and created a demand for remedial action by the federal government. Leisure time for cultural activities and active participation in public affairs by women depended so wholly upon electric household appliances that the distribution of electricity and the cost of electric appliances became matters of acute public interest. When millions of men and women, reared in an area of poor school and library facilities, where there were few child clinics and no child labor laws, and where superstition, ignorance, and starved emotions regulated social conduct, began moving into areas of high cultural levels, then such matters as education, medical facilities, and family income became national problems.

Finally, the rapidity with which masses of people could be swayed by the emotional appeal of demagogues, the positive proof that men of superior intellectual attainments will use their talents for selfish and devilish purposes, and the universal craving for money with which to buy the material comforts and pleasures of the machine age—all of these things cast grave doubts upon an educational system which emphasized rational criticism, and upon a political system which relied so heavily upon the inherent morality of man.

5

Resurgence of Jeffersonian Liberalism

PHILOSOPHY OF REFORM

THE years between the close of the Spanish-American War and our entry into World War I may well be designated the flowering period of reform. This twentieth-century reform movement was identical with that of the Jacksonian period in the sense that it rested upon the same Jeffersonian philosophy: that institutions, and the concepts and attitudes of the people which sustain them, must change with changing times. It had the same elements of our spiritual heritage sometimes called humanitarianism and benevolence, sometimes generosity and good will; the same diversity of ideas and tolerance of dissent; the same belief in the dignity and worth of the individual; the same sense of sharing in a common destiny. In two respects it differed widely from the earlier reform movement. It went much farther in the directions of reform by law and of financial aid to individuals from public funds.

A widespread revolt against the prevailing philosophy of government and its relation to human rights and property was already brewing when Theodore Roosevelt stepped upon the stage of national politics in 1900. It was, in the first instance, a demand that the individual be accorded a larger, more effective share in the processes of government from the nomination of candidates for office to the enactment of one's favorite ideas into law. It was, also, a demand for more honesty and efficiency in government

71

service, and for more consideration of the public interest at the expense of accumulated wealth both in the selection of public officials and in the discharge of their duties. This movement for more direct democracy and more responsible government began many years before.

The Liberal Republican movement of 1872 centered in the civil service reform. The Pendleton Act of 1883 had established a United States Civil Service Commission and had placed on the classified list certain employees of the Treasury and Post Office Departments. Presidents Harrison and Cleveland both had made some additions to the service; but, at the turn of the century, public officials were the political sublieutenants of their party's chief officer to whom, as President of the United States, they also were responsible for honest public service. The question was to remain as troublesome in 1936 as it had been in 1872. Meanwhile, much emphasis was being placed upon the need for purifying elections by the use of secret ballots and voting machines, for extending the franchise, and for making public opinion a potent force in public affairs. These reforms, which required action by the states, were accomplished in the early years of the century.

The second source of discontent with the way politicians were running the country was the agrarian West. The great agricultural states had made their bid for control of the national government under the banner of William Jennings Bryan in 1896 and had lost; but Bryan had not faltered in his crusade to educate the country to a realization of the actual grievances of his section. That ringing challenge of 1896 could not so easily be thrust aside:

We say to you that you have made the definition of a business man too limited in its application. The man who is employed for wages is as much a business man as his employer. The attorney in a country town is as much a business man as the corporation counsel in a great metropolis. The merchant at the crossroads store is as much a business man as the merchant of New York. The farmer who goes forth in the morning and toils all summer—and who, by the application of brain and muscle to the natural resources of the country, creates wealth, is as much a business man as the man who goes upon the board of trade and bets on the price of wheat. You come to us and tell us that the great cities are in favor of the gold standard. We reply that the great cities rest upon our broad and fertile prairies. Burn down your cities and leave our farms, and your cities will spring up again as if by magic; but destroy our farms, and the grass will grow in the streets of every city in the country.

Bryan was destined to be the candidate of his party in 1900 and again in 1908, and four years later to place his mantle upon the shoulders of one, who, still unidentified with unpopular causes, was to lead the forces of reform to victory in an era of unprecedented progressive legislation. The reform of banking, currency, and credit, and of the tariff system could be accomplished only by the Congress of the United States. These things were delayed until the forces of reform were politically strong enough to get control of the federal government. That was to come, however, only as the result of a revolt within the Republican party.

These states of the Upper Mississippi Valley and Great Lakes region were Republican by tradition. There is no escaping the fact that "gentlemen" voted the Republican ticket here just as they voted the Democratic ticket in the southern states. In no other way can the survival of the two old parties, each embracing industrial and agrarian groups, be explained. Republicans followed their progressive leaders in the enactment of state reform legislation, returned them to Congress in spite of their violent disagreements with the party leadership, but would not follow them in support of Democratic presidential candidates. Robert La Follette of Wisconsin bolted his party in the campaign of 1924 and polled 5,000,000 votes; but he carried only his own state. George Norris of Nebraska, whose career represents the most resplendent nonpartisanship of the century, was returned to Congress over his own protests in 1928, but could not carry his state for the Democratic candidate, Alfred E. Smith. William E. Borah of Idaho often opposed his party's policies in Congress, but never opposed its candidate in presidential elections. This situation accentuated the cleavage between the two sections of the Republican party. Year after year, the gulf between the agrarian West and the industrial East widened. Year after year, the position of the western Republicans became more difficult. They disagreed generally with the economic fundamentalism of their party and particularly with its refusal to alter government policies which were enriching the industrialists at the expense of the farmers. They carried their disagreement to the point of open insurgency in Congress during Taft's Administration, and secured the legislation they had so long desired when Woodrow Wilson entered the White House.

The political reformers and the western agrarians were not alone in their demand for a new concept of government. Not all of the abuses of the new industrial system had appeared at the turn of the century, but the trend was plainly visible. The first great question was whether wealth should be allowed to gravitate into the hands of the few and control over all the instruments of production be concentrated unhampered by restrictive legislation, or whether some effort should be made to regulate economic processes in the interest of the people at large.

The reform movement was increasingly directed, therefore, toward checking the gross inequalities of wealth developing from limited ownership of productive enterprises. Society was viewing with increasing apprehension the waste of human life and natural resources in the industrial process. It was groping for a philosophy which would justify public regulation of industry, and for formulae which would establish and maintain standards sufficiently high to relieve society of the presence of so much human wreckage. It was a matter of simple justice to some, conscience to others, and dollars and cents to many. More and more, then, it became a movement to curb the excesses of economic individualism; to protect groups and classes from exploitation by their fellow men; and to make the machine an instrument for lightening the burdens and enriching the lives of all. The efficacy of the doctrine of *laissez faire* came under indictment, as man learned that our new industrial society, so deeply involved in exchange of goods and services, was based upon coercion with a multitude of individuals and groups exercising it. The negative conception of liberty no longer sufficed. The government must coerce and restrain some men to protect the freedom and rights of many men.

There was general dissatisfaction with the system of taxation which fell heaviest upon the home owner and touched but lightly or not at all the vast resources of intangible wealth. Henry George sought to correct the inequality by advocating in his *Progress and Poverty* a single tax upon the economic rent of land. Others demanded the simpler method of income, estate, and corporation taxes.

⌐ Closely allied to the reform of taxes was the principle of using the total resources of the nation to raise the cultural level of depressed areas, to extend government aid to the unfortunate and underprivileged, and to extend government services in those fields which private enterprise could not or would not enter. The workers were in revolt against the barbarism of a common law which threw upon helpless widows and orphans the entire burden of industrial accidents by relieving employers of all financial responsibility. Forward-looking intellectuals were regarding with dismay the operation of rugged individualism in the employment of women and children for long hours and ofttimes at wages little higher than those of a coolie.

APOSTLES OF REFORM

It is important to re-emphasize that the Progressive Movement was a *liberal* reform movement. It had no central direction, no fixed goals, no scheme of a perfect society. It did have principles and ideals as stated above, and public-spirited men and women sought to direct the reforms accordingly, but the confusion of ideas is positive proof of a general intellectual ferment rather than a skillfully directed propaganda campaign. Progress came slowly, first in one direction, then in another, but always after widespread discussion and by democratic processes. The movement was beset by an entrenched economic individualism on the one hand, and by an emerging collectivist ideal embraced in socialism, then communism, then fascism on the other.

Thousands of people took part in the reform movement, discussing conditions in newspapers and magazines, on the lecture platforms, in women's clubs and churches, and in state legislatures and Congress. Many of the early reforms were in city and local government, and were achievements of a few pioneer reformers.

The city of Boston, for example, established a juvenile court in 1906; but not until 1917, after years of experience by its first judge, Harvey H. Baker, was the machinery of the court supplemented by a child clinic. Jacob A. Riis waged relentless war against the vice, crime, and filth of tenement house districts for years before New York City added a tenement house department to its city government in 1902. This was the type of pioneering effort which resulted in a gradual shifting of emphasis from aiding unfortunate individuals to correcting social maladjustments, and to the evolution of charities and corrections into social service and public welfare.

By 1908, the Protestant Episcopal, Congregational, Presbyterian, and Methodist churches had established industrial commissions and were advocating protection of workers from dangerous machinery, abolition of child labor and sweatshops, shorter hours, social insurance, and a more equitable distribution of the returns from production. They then formed the Federal Council of Churches of Christ in America, which soon became one of the most powerful agencies for reform in the country.

The General Federation of Women's Clubs was organized in 1890 with Charlotte Emerson Brown as its first president. The Federation had 20,000 members by the end of its second year, and had increased its membership to 500,000 by 1905. It had its committees on education, pure food, forestry conservation, and a legislative committee pressing for juvenile court laws and general security legislation for women and children. A group of reform mayors had attracted wide attention with their crusades against public utilities: Samuel M. Jones of Toledo, Tom L. Johnson of Cleveland, and Max Fagan of Jersey City. Johnson, who was best known for his advocacy of the single tax, believed in an informed and interested electorate. He bought a circus tent which would hold 5000 people and moved it from place to place in the city for meetings to discuss public affairs. Governor Franklin Murphy in New Jersey, beginning in 1902, established a state tenement house commission and a state sanatorium for tuberculosis patients, and introduced such reforms as an audit of all state financial records and compelling banks to pay interest on state deposits. State legislatures gradually enacted legislation requiring factories to install fire escapes, devices for the removal of dust, and guards on exposed machinery, and forbidding the use of explosive oils, cleaning of machinery in motion, and the fining of employees for defective work. Laxity of enforcement, however, indicates that much of this legislation was passed to still the clamors of reformers without any serious intention of enforcement.

Then came the journalists. Frank Norris published his *Octopus* in 1901 and *The Pit* in 1902. The third of his proposed trilogy of wheat was never finished; but in these volumes dealing with the growing and marketing of the West's staple crop, he revealed the havoc wrought by the railroads and the grain markets in the lives of those who till the soil. Upton Sinclair, more frankly hostile to the capitalistic system, struck viciously at the profit motive and its social effects in his *The Jungle* (1906)—a story of immigrant exploitation in the famous stockyards and packing houses of Chicago. William Allen White added his protest against economic centralization in *A Certain Rich Man* (1909). Ida M. Tarbell, Lincoln Steffens, and Ray Stannard Baker contributed to *McClure's Magazine* in the short space of three years (1903–1905) the *History of the Standard Oil Company, Shame of the Cities*, and *Railroads on Trial*, respectively. Lincoln Steffens, like Tom L. Johnson of Cleveland, believed that all the evils of graft and corruption were due to a lack of interest by the people; and he worked indefatigably to arouse civic pride. Jane Addams, Ernst Freund, Roscoe Pound, Walter Lippmann, and Herbert Croly re-examined, in a series of brilliant monographs, many of our social and economic doctrines and found them inadequate. Not every one accepted these exposés of unpleasant realities with graceful complacency. Men and women motivated by a desire for preferment and notoriety were inevitably drawn into the movement. Convinced of their own righteousness and possessing few qualifications except the use of invective, they resorted to sensational denunciations generally spoken of as yellow journalism. Their activities injured the cause established by the careful and painstaking research of earlier writers. Finally, in the spring of 1906, President Theodore Roosevelt called attention to the excesses in these words:

Gross and reckless assaults on character, whether on stump or in newspaper, magazine or both, create a marked and vicious public sentiment, and at the same time act as a professed detriment to noble men of normal sensitiveness and tend to prevent them from entering the public service at any price. . . . It is because I feel that there should be no rest in the endless war against the forces of evil that I ask that the war be conducted with sanity as well as with resolution.

POLITICAL REFORM

There followed a full decade of state reform legislation. Its first objective was to break down the restraints upon the will of the majority provided by undemocratic governmental machinery. It involved the changing of parts of the system, the adding of new devices and, ultimately, an attack upon the written constitution and the power of judicial review. Oregon introduced more of these innovations than any other state: the initiative and referendum (1902), the direct election of United States Senators (1904), the recall of all elected officials (1908), and the preferential primaries for presidential nominations (1910). Wisconsin enacted the first direct primary law (1903). Arizona succeeded in gaining admission to the Union in 1911 only after promising to remove from her constitution a provision for the recall of judges. Colorado provided for the recall of judicial decisions (1912). Woman's suffrage, the most difficult of all the reforms to secure, had its beginning in the Territory of Wyoming in 1869. Not all of these changes were widely accepted. The Seventeenth Amendment to the Constitution, providing for the popular election of United States Senators, was ratified and became a part of the Constitution in 1913. Its wisdom had been discussed for many years. The power of accumulated wealth in the legislatures, the urge to undemocratic gerrymandering of states, and the unresponsiveness of Senators to popular will under the old system were responsible for the change. The Senate itself, however, under the leadership of conservatives like George F. Hoar of Massachusetts, had delayed the change for many years. The House of Representatives had passed resolutions in 1894, 1898, 1900, and 1902, but the Senate was adamant. The change was advocated by such men as William Jennings Bryan and Senator Cullom of Illinois, opposed by prominent men like Chauncey M. Depew. Finally, Senators William E. Borah of Idaho and Joseph L. Bristow of Kansas forced the amending resolution through the Senate in January, 1911. Woman's suffrage encountered such widespread hostility from prominent men like William H. Taft and Henry Watterson, editor of the Louisville *Courier Journal*, that it required an intensive campaign in legislatures, party conventions and Congress before the Nineteenth Amendment was fully ratified and declared a part of the Constitution in 1920. No one, aside from their overenthusiastic sponsors, expected these two changes to bring immediate results in the correction of political abuses. Women showed a disposition to work within the party system instead of maintaining an independent position to bring united pressure to bear upon both parties for the enactment of legislation they desired. In the early twenties, however, the Women's Joint Congressional Committee, representing a score of national women's organizations, was formed. It succeeded in getting the Maternity and Infancy Law (1921) enacted and the Cable Act (1922) granting to married women the right of independent citizenship. Their success in securing state legislation for child welfare, women's legal rights, social hygiene, and education has been little less than phenomenal. More money was spent, because more was required, on occasion to buy senatorial seats from the voters than had ever been spent in the state legislatures; but it could not be concealed so easily, and most attempts have ended disastrously because of an aroused public opinion.

The direct primary, the initiative, the referendum, and the recall were all devised to encourage a wider popular participation in public affairs, break up the evils of machine politics, and create responsible party government. The direct primary system was adopted by thirty-seven states, the preferential primary system by thirteen, and the initiative and referendum by twenty before the first phase of the movement came to an end. The use of the recall was confined largely to city administration. None of these changes accomplished what its sponsors had expected. The preferential primary, devised by Senator Jonathan Bourne of Oregon to give every voter an opportunity to register his choice among candidates, failed to work from the beginning. President Wilson and Charles Evans Hughes failed to enter the direct primaries in 1916. As a result, Alabama, Indiana, Iowa, Michigan, Minnesota, Montana, North Carolina, and Vermont repealed their laws. The next presidential campaign introduced the obnoxious practice of entering favorite sons in the primaries. Men who were handling the preconvention campaigns of certain candidates refused to enter their candidates in doubtful states. Instead, by previous arrangement, a favorite son would be entered against opponents in each such state with the understanding that after a courtesy ballot in the convention the state delegation would shift its ballot to the machine candidate. The initiative and referendum failed almost as completely and fell into disuse. Three decades later another movement was started to make government more responsive to popular opinion. Regular referendums of public opinion were taken by the *Literary Digest* and a new Institute of Public Opinion was launched by a bipartisan group of newspapers. Congress fell into line by specifying that a popular referendum must be taken on the question of prohibition repeal, and a constitutional amendment was adopted eliminating the "lame duck" sessions of Congress and the long period between the election of a President and his inauguration. Senator George W. Norris of Nebraska, whose political career extends from the early reform period till his death in 1944, sponsored the latter reform as well as the establishment of a unicameral legislature in Nebraska (1935). The trend may point to the ultimate introduction of a parliamentary system in one of the states and its acceptance by all. Laws to prevent the election of state officials by minority votes and to give proportional representation to minorities were adopted in Michigan (1889), Pennsylvania (1895), New Jersey (1901), and at various times in Ohio and Rhode Island. All were invalidated by the courts. Finally, there has been vigorous agitation from time to time for the direct election of President and Vice-President, and several attempts to secure provision for a popular referendum before going to war.

SOCIAL LEGISLATION ~ *stop*

The second phase of the movement, that to provide social and economic security, was the most important. Most of this legislation was by the states, and included social insurance legislation, the regulation of child labor, and safety and health codes. Social insurance legislation began with workmen's compensation laws. The old rule of the common law had enabled employers to evade the cost of industrial accidents unless the injured employee could prove that the employer had been unduly careless in some respect, that a fellow servant had not caused the accident by carelessness, that he himself had not contributed in any way to the cause, and that he had been compelled to assume an unusual risk. Needless to say, under such a system of jurisprudence, the cases in which an injured employee could recover damages were few and far between. Long hours, unprotected machinery, and the urge to profit took their annual toll of dead and injured, leaving behind an appalling wreckage of broken homes, destitute widows, and orphans.

By the turn of the century, there was a growing conviction that accidents with their resulting loss of time, medical care, burial fees, and support of minor dependents were as much a part of the cost of production as raw materials and should be borne by the consumer of the products. Congress passed an Employers' Liability Act in 1906, relieving railway employees from the operation of the contributory negligence and fellow servant rules of the common law. A revision was made two years later limiting it specifically to employees engaged in interstate commerce in conformity with a Supreme Court ruling. Five states adopted workmen's compensation laws in 1911. Twenty-five more followed their example before 1916, and all but Florida, Mississippi, South Carolina, and Arkansas by 1929. Steady progress was made in transferring jurisdiction from the courts to special administrative boards, in increasing the amounts payable to the injured employee or his estate, and in extending the benefits to a wider range of occupations.

Other types of social security legislation did not fare so well. Labor unions, completely dominated by men, were on the whole opposed to regulation of hours and wages. Women, not being organized, were peculiarly subject to exploitation in the form of long hours, low wages, unsatisfactory and indecent working conditions. The census of 1900 had shown that more than 2,500,000 girls under 25 years of age were employed as wage earners and that most of them were under 21 years of age. The dangers to health and morality, particularly of those employed in factories at night and for low wages, did not need to be argued. Only four states prohibited the employment of women at night in 1900: Indiana, New York, Massachusetts and Nebraska. Not more than 20 states prohibited night employment of children, and, in some of those, regulations were little short of criminal. South Carolina, for instance, forbade the employment of "women" at night who were under 12 years of age. Thirty-three states had no legal restrictions upon the number of hours per day or week that women might be gainfully employed; and there were no restrictions upon tenement-house work of the cities where all sorts of clothing, cigars, cigarettes, and other artifacts were made during long hours at starvation wages. The humanitarian desire to throw the protecting mantle of the law over the defenseless victim of economic distress, as well as the desire to protect the future of the social state from the physiological damages visited upon its wives and mothers by ruthless exploitation, led to corrective legislation. Acting under the police powers of the state, Massachusetts had inaugurated a maximum ten-hour day for women employees as early as 1875, and the state courts had held the act to be constitutional (*Hamilton Manufacturing Co. v. Massachusetts*). A similar law passed by Oregon in 1908 was upheld by the United States Supreme Court (*Muller v. Oregon*). The decision in this case stands as a permanent monument to the brilliant labors of Louis D. Brandeis who prepared the arguments for the Oregon case before being appointed to the Supreme Court. From that point there was a succession of such laws until, by 1930, all but four states had regulated hours of work and a considerable number had provided commissions with wide discretionary powers to deal with the conditions of employment of both women and children. A companion movement to establish minimum wage laws was completely thwarted when the Supreme Court in 1923 held such laws to be a violation of the Fifth Amendment of the Constitution (*Children's Hospital v. Adkins*). This decision dealt with an act of Congress requiring that the wages of women in the District of Columbia be sufficient to "maintain them in health and to protect their morals." Justice Brandeis did not join in the decision because his daughter was a member of the minimum wage commission of the District. The decision was 5 to 3—Holmes and Taft writing as vigorous dissenting opinions as had ever appeared. Later events gave this case far greater significance than it appeared to have at the time. The Court said:

We cannot accept the doctrine that women of mature age require or may be subjected to restrictions upon their liberty of contract which would not lawfully be imposed in the case of men under similar circumstances. To do so would be to ignore all the implications to be drawn from the present day trend of legislation, as well as that of common thought and usage, by which woman is accorded emancipation from the old doctrine that she must be given special protection or be subjected to special restraint in her contractual and civil relationships. Enough has been said to show that the authority to fix hours of labor cannot be exercised except in respect to those occupations where work of long continued duration is detrimental to health. This court has been careful in every case where the question has been raised, to place its decision upon this limited authority of the Legislature to regulate hours of labor and to disclaim any purpose to uphold the legislation as fixing wages, thus recognizing an essential difference between the two.

Those words might well have ended the attempts of state legislatures to fix minimum wages; but the Court also said: "A statute requiring an employer to pay in money, to pay at prescribed and regular intervals, to pay the value of the services rendered, even to pay with fair relation to the extent of the benefit obtained from the service, would be understandable." Taking these words at face value, the legislature of New York passed a statute in 1933 fixing minimum wages for women in laundries. The law was carefully drawn. No attempt was made at broad social reform, and the regulation was limited to one industry. The case came before the Court in 1936 and, on June 1, it left no further doubt of its position, holding that state legislatures are "without power by any form of legislation to prohibit, change or nullify contracts between employers and adult woman workers as to the amount of wages to be paid" (*Morehead v. People of State of New York*). This was a 5 to 4 decision with Justices Hughes, Brandeis, Stone, and Cardozo dissenting. Justices McReynolds, Butler, Sutherland, and Van Devanter were opposed to both the act of Congress in 1923 and the act of New York in 1936. Their decisions designated a field into which neither the federal nor state governments might enter with regulatory legislation and limited the scope of the states in their most valuable function: social experimentation. The state of Washington went on enforcing its law without regard to the New York decision, and when a new case (*West Coast Hotel Co. v. Parrish*, 1937) came before the court Justice Roberts changed his position and the law was upheld.

Child labor, strangely, has been very difficult to control by state legislation. It was one of the earliest recognized evils of our modern industrial system, but after thirty years of agitation for reform it remained to plague the nation at the time of the last great depression. Statistics show that in 1900 one of every five children between the ages of ten and fifteen was gainfully employed. By 1930, it had decreased to one in twenty. Nevertheless, the census of 1930 showed 2,145,000 employed children between the ages of ten and seventeen, and the census figures were far from complete. They included no children under ten, although thousands below that age are employed in agriculture, in the street trades, etc., and there is some doubt if all types of agricultural employment were included even for those above the age of ten. A nation with two million juvenile employees at a time when millions of men were idle and on the relief rolls had not progressed far in that type of social reform.

The difficulty lay in securing effective uniform legislation in the several states and in the constitutional restraints upon action by Congress. The Supreme Court did not question the power of state legislatures, but cheap child labor gave states with low standards a tremendous advantage in competition for new industries. Senator Albert J. Beveridge introduced a bill in Congress in 1906 which was so designed as to exclude from interstate commerce the products of factories and mines employing children less than fourteen years of age. The bill did not pass and nothing more was accomplished for ten years. Then the Keating-Owen bill was sponsored by President Wilson and enacted into law. This Act excluded from interstate commerce the products of any factory employing children under fourteen years of age, or children between the ages of fourteen and sixteen at night or for longer than an eight-hour day. Mines were forbidden to employ children under sixteen years of age. The Act was contested in the courts and declared unconstitutional by a 5 to 4 decision as an improper use of Congress' control over interstate commerce and an invasion of state rights (*Hammer v. Dagenhart*, 1918). The decision was bitterly assailed because in previous decisions Congress had been allowed to exclude from interstate commerce such commodities as lottery tickets, impure foods and drugs, obscene literature, women for immoral purposes, etc. Congress then passed an act (1919) taxing out of existence the products of child labor. It was carelessly drawn and, as was freely predicted at the time, the Supreme Court in a decision written by Chief Justice Taft declared it an unwarranted extension of the power to tax (*Bailey v. Drexel Furniture Co.*, 1922).

In 1924, therefore, Congress passed a Constitutional Amendment giving to Congress "the power to limit, regulate and prohibit the labor of persons under eighteen years of age." Only six states ratified before the depression, eighteen more under the pressure of that calamity. Meanwhile, the legislatures of more than thirteen states had rejected the Amendment, making ratification extremely doubtful. Opposition to the Amendment was cleverly concealed in an organization known as the National Committee for the Protection of Child, Family, School and Church. It was opposed as an impairment of the freedom of contract, as a threat to parental control, and as an invasion of state rights. Communism, the regimentation of children in concentration camps, and bureaucratic interference with schools and non-religious children's organizations were mentioned as probable consequences of its adoption. The American Legion and the American Federation of

Labor both endorsed the Amendment. Elihu Root effectively answered the state rights argument when he said: "It is useless for the advocates of state rights to inveigh against the supremacy of the constitutional law of the United States, or against the extension of national authority in the fields of necessary control, where the states themselves fail in the performance of their duty." It was pointed out that Congress no less than the state legislatures was under popular control, and that children as well as adults were protected by the Bill of Rights, but to no avail. The only real progress came through compulsory school attendance laws. States gradually increased the minimum age at which children could leave school, raised the degree of proficiency required, and lengthened the school year. The more advanced states required attendance until eighteen years of age unless high school had been completed, and placed the employment of all children who have not completed the educational requirements under the supervision of school superintendents. Other laws requiring physical examinations before securing employment, and excluding minors from certain types of employment altogether had done something to correct the situation.

A further extension of social legislation had to do with the care of dependent children. Illinois established a juvenile court system in 1899, and the plan had spread to all but two of the states by 1930. Mothers' pensions, established to preserve the home influence over children whose fathers were dead, in prison, or had deserted, were first established in 1911. Eighteen states enacted some form of assistance to mothers during the next two years and, by 1930, all but four had done so. The White House Conference of 1930 reported that during the previous year 220,000 children were thus cared for at a cost of $30,000,000. Old-age pensions and unemployment insurance lagged definitely behind in the movement. They occupy such a prominent part in the revival of reform legislation during the early 1930s that it is better to deal with them later.

The most dilatory states in the enactment of social legislation were in the South. They made up the stronghold of economic as well as religious fundamentalism. They were the great agricultural

86

states, whose cotton crop depended so heavily upon the labor of women and children. They were the states in which industry was still in its growing pains, where parental authority and individual liberty still made a strong appeal, and where the Negro question still hampered the development of a critical attitude toward social and economic reform. Mississippi, South Carolina, Florida, and Arkansas have no workmen's compensation laws. Alabama, Louisiana and Tennessee have compensation laws but no industrial commissions for their administration. South Carolina, Mississippi, Georgia, and Alabama have more than 25 percent of their women employed. Eighty-four percent of the children employed in agriculture in the country are in the cotton states. Georgia and South Carolina are the only two states without mothers' pension laws.

6

The National Scene

THE reform movement made its first progress in the organization of state and municipal governments and the control of their policies as recorded in the preceding chapter. This was true because the movement grew from small beginnings, and not until 1913 were there enough Progressives in Congress to accomplish much in the way of legislation. It was true because state and local governments possess the powers by which to regulate conduct and to influence the moral and intellectual development of the people. The influence of the movement, however, was early evidenced in the political history of the federal government, which exercises control over the more material aspects of life and may greatly alter the rights of private property and contracts respecting such valuable things as land, factories, mines, labor, and services by tariffs, by banking, currency, and tax laws, and by regulation of interstate commerce. Three developments of the late nineteenth century had aroused wide discussion of the entire question of business regulation. These were the railroads, trusts, and labor unions.

THE RAILROADS

The railroads had always been a vital part of our national life. They were absolutely essential to industrial development and to the life of any business enterprise. In their haste to promote the development of transportation, the people had recklessly granted charters and bestowed favors upon railroad promoters. The mighty railway system, embracing a total of 160,000 miles when federal regulation began and 240,000 miles in 1930, could not have been built on any such scale without the government's generous donations of land and loans of public money. Land grants by the federal government and several states amounted to more than 200,000,000 acres, and money grants to more than $1,000,000,000. Eventually, the people came to realize that the roads were public highways, and demanded that they no longer be operated as private enterprises. The railroad owners, particularly where large blocks of stock were held by industrial corporations, insisted upon the same freedom as was accorded other businesses under the prevailing doctrine of *laissez faire*. The period of rapid railway building between 1850 and 1890 witnessed the unique situation of governmental units, even down to towns and counties, straining their credit to furnish the nation transportation facilities while promoters of the roads stretched moral and legal restraints to the limit in a mad scramble for private gain. There were rate discriminations between communities, and between farmers and manufacturers, partial repayment or rebates to large shippers, preferential treatment in the supply of cars, and favors of all kinds to influential people. It was this excessive will to profit, rather than to serve communities through which the roads passed, that eventually led to government regulation; and it was the original public investment in the system which finally broke down the resistance of the roads to public control of rates and services.

Rhode Island, Connecticut, and Massachusetts in the East established railroad commissions before 1870. Minnesota, Illinois, Iowa, Wisconsin, and Michigan followed with state commissions to regulate railroads and grain elevators. State control of rates and services was contested in the courts as a violation of the due process clause of the Fourteenth Amendment, but the principle that states had the power to regulate corporations rendering a public service was confirmed by the Supreme Court (see *Munn v. Illinois*, 1876). The Court also ruled that a state might regulate the railroads even to the extent of affecting interstate commerce since Congress had not acted in the matter. Ten years later, the Court reversed its position on this point and greatly restricted the powers of the state. Congress promptly passed the Interstate Commerce Act of 1887.

The Interstate Commerce Commission created by the Act of 1887 was little more than a fact-finding agency for many years. Congress had not intended it to be merely that, but the appointments of Presidents Cleveland and McKinley and several Supreme Court decisions stripped it of both the will and the power to regulate rates or exercise judicial functions. The Act stated that all rates "shall be reasonable and just." The Supreme Court held in 1897 that this did not give to the Interstate Commerce Commission the power to require a reduction of rates nor to set maximum rates. The statement of the Court in *Smyth v. Ames* (1898) contains the fundamentals of the rate-making problem. Said the Court:

We hold—that the basis of all calculations as to the reasonableness of rates to be charged by a corporation maintaining a highway under legislative sanction must be the fair value of the property being used by it for the convenience of the public. And, in order to ascertain that value, the original cost of construction, the amount expended in permanent improvements, the amount and market value of its bonds and stock, the present as compared with the original cost of construction, the probable earning capacity of the property under particular rates prescribed by statute, and the sum required to meet operating expenses, are all matters for consideration, and are to be given such weight as may be just and right in each case.

The items here listed by the Court as a basis for determining reasonable rates contained such a medley of contradictions as to render their use as a formula impossible. The original cost of constructing the roads bore no relation to the amount of stocks and bonds outstanding because of the tremendous amount of water that had been pumped into the latter. The original cost of constructing the Erie Railroad had been $15,000,000, but when Daniel Drew and Jay Gould finished their fight for its control by manipulating the market, bribing legislatures, and printing stock, its capitalization was $60,000,000. The Union Pacific had cost $50,000,000 to build, but because of the exorbitant profits taken by its promoters through the medium of the Credit Mobilier, its stocks and bonds amounted to $94,000,000. The New York Central alone had nearly $50,000,000 of watered stock before the Interstate Commerce Act was passed. By 1930, there was an estimated $8,000,000,000 of watered stock in the capital structure of the roads. Likewise, there was no relation between the market value of stocks and bonds and any other item except probable earning power or probable bankruptcy. Indeed the roads were wrecked by irresponsible management so frequently as to ruin thousands of small investors throughout the country.

The question of railway regulation, therefore, was very much under discussion when Theodore Roosevelt became President, and we shall follow the programs of regulation in the Hepburn Act (1906), the Mann-Elkins Act (1910), the Physical Valuation Act (1913), the Transportation Act (1920), and the Emergency Railroad Transportation Act (1933). For the most part, these acts dealt with the regulation of rates and services, capital structures, the sale of securities, consolidations, and the extension of the jurisdiction of the Interstate Commerce Commission over other, but not necessarily competing, communication.

TRUSTS AND MONOPOLIES

The second development was the growth of corporations and new corporate practices. These creatures of the law possessed the qualities of permanence, impersonality, limited liability, and a division of interest among many owners. The people at large became both the owners of and money lenders to them, the former being the stockholders, the latter the bondholders. Their capitalization was based not upon original investment nor upon replacement valuation, but upon probable earning power. They were so constituted that the officers and directors exercised control without personal responsibility, and they came more and more under the power of banking interests. Most of them held their charters from a state, although a few were incorporated by act of Congress. In the decade of the seventies, there developed large industrial combinations based upon agreements between otherwise independent companies to fix prices, divide sales territory, limit production, or share profits. These were followed by trusts, in which the controlling company exchanged its trust certificates for the stock of the several constituent corporations. These, in turn, were followed by the holding companies: corporations whose property consisted of shares of stock in other corporations. This evolution resulted in the strangulation of small competitive enterprises, in the establishment of monopolies, in overcapitalization, and in tremendous amounts of watered stock; and the public at large insisted upon intervention by the government to protect stockholders, employees, the consumers, and the government itself from the tremendous pressure of accumulated wealth.

The first step toward federal regulation of industrial relations was taken by Congress in 1887 when it passed the Interstate Commerce Act. Its primary purpose was to require equitable service to all patrons of the railroads by outlawing rebates and pools; but it was also an indirect blow at the trusts. Three years later Congress passed the Sherman Anti-Trust Law, designed to prohibit contracts in restraint of trade and monopolies. It declared "every contract, combination in the form of trust or otherwise, or conspiracy, in restraint of trade or commerce among the several states, or with foreign nations," to be illegal. It imposed upon district attorneys the duty of instituting proceedings against such combinations; and it permitted those injured by such illegal acts to recover threefold damages.

The Sherman Anti-Trust Law, like all such laws, depended for its effectiveness upon vigorous action and eternal vigilance on the part of the Department of Justice for its enforcement. So far as the trusts were concerned, it was allowed to languish by the Attorney-Generals until Theodore Roosevelt became President. Furthermore, the Supreme Court (*U. S. v. E. C. Knight Co.,* 1895) said that the Act did not apply to manufacturing monopolies.

The meaning of the Sherman Act with respect to industry and trade was still a disputed question at the turn of the century. Moreover, this was the one phase of the reform movement in which the reformers themselves disagreed both as to objectives and methods not only in 1900 but later. There were men who would have been satisfied to remove the influence of industrial corporations from legislative bodies, believing such activities to be outside their legitimate sphere of action and inimical to the public welfare. There were others who believed that full publicity of financial and trading practices would make the corporations honest in their relations with competitors and the public. Some authorities regarded industrial combinations as indispensable to modern economic life, and asked that they be preserved under regulation. They took the realistic view that the nation could never return to the era of small individual business, but that competition must not give way to monopoly. There were others who insisted that the trusts must be destroyed with despatch and great fanfare. It was a question of the relative merits of combination as opposed to unrestricted competition. There was a question of whether competition could be restored by any sort of legislation. James M. Beck held that the Sherman Act had "not altered the underlying basis of any industry, and it never will, because you cannot compel men to compete if they do not want to compete." Senator Francis G. Newlands of Nevada, a member of the Interstate Commerce Committee, found men from all types of business and professions demanding either a federal incorporation law or an amendment to the Sherman Act clearly defining the words "reasonable or unreasonable" as used by the Supreme Court and specifically stating what should be considered evidence of conspiracy in restraint of trade. Louis D. Brandeis and Senator Robert M. La Follette favored such an amendment. Beck took much the same position when he said: "If the Supreme Court of the United States, after two years of deliberation and the use of sixteen thousand words, cannot give a plain definition of what a business man may do or may not do, then business men ought not to be charged with violation of law if they mistake their way in this jungle of legal terms." Attorney-General George W. Wickersham, who believed that 50 percent of evil corporate practices arose from lax incorporation laws of the several states, and President Taft favored federal incorporations. Senator John Sharp Williams of Mississippi favored a national law barring from interstate commerce all corporations operating under charters from states whose incorporation laws did not meet requirements laid down by Congress. The trouble, as he saw it, was in "charter-enacted legislation," but he opposed federal incorporation as likely to result in "government and industrial centralization . . . more laws and more offices." The final suggestion was embodied in a bill introduced shortly after the decision of the Supreme Court in the Standard Oil Case. It provided for a federal administrative agency similar to the Interstate Commerce Commission, which would gradually build up through administrative procedure a body of law for the conduct of industry and trade. When men like William H. Taft, George W. Wickersham, Robert M. La Follette, James M. Beck and John Sharp Williams could not agree on the remedial legislation required, it is conclusive evidence that there was no well-defined program among the reform elements of the country.

ORGANIZED LABOR

The third development was that of organized labor. The modern history of organized labor in the United States may be divided roughly into three periods. The first began with a series of events between 1886 and 1894, and gradually terminated between 1914 and 1917. The second period came to an end in 1933. Within these dates occurred certain definite trends with respect to the type and degree of organization among wage earners, the attitude of government toward labor and of organized labor toward government, and general aspects of American life vitally affecting the status and conditions of wage earners though not directly pertaining to labor.

The Noble Order of the Knights of Labor was organized in 1869. It was a secret order under the control of Uriah S. Stephens until 1879 when it dropped the cloak of secrecy and passed under the direction of Terence V. Powderly. It reached a peak membership of 700,000 in 1886, almost disappeared by 1890, and was absorbed by the Populist movement in 1892–1893. Previous to the Knights of Labor, in the Civil War period, labor had been organized on the basis of crafts. These early trade unions were at a serious disadvantage in the contest with capital. Composed of skilled workmen, their membership was peculiarly vulnerable to the black list and their organization to prosecution under the state conspiracy laws. The Knights of Labor, therefore, was organized along radically different lines. It was secret; it admitted everyone to membership who gained a living by honest toil; and the membership of each chapter included everyone living in the locality who belonged to the organization. Legislatures and courts generally had legalized unionization by the time it ceased to regard secrecy as a virtue. Its chief attribute, however, and its greatest weakness lay in its type of organization. Craft distinctions were ignored, and three classes of labor were brought into the organization whose relative importance in the labor market steadily increased through the years, becoming paramount in the modern machine age: women, Negroes, and unskilled laborers. The order deprecated strikes though it did not outlaw them. Failing to develop the technique of conducting strikes, the Knights nevertheless supported the May Day strike of 1886, called to gain the eight-hour day in industry, and their failure marked the beginning of a new era in labor history.

The second aspect of this short but highly dynamic period of labor history was the organization of the American Federation of Labor on the ruins of the Knights of Labor. The Federation was first organized as the Federation of Organized Trades and Labor Unions of the United States and Canada in 1881 and assumed its present form in 1886. It was under the presidency of Samuel Gompers from the date of its organization until his death in 1924 and then of William Green. It had 550,000 members in 1900, 2,000,000 in 1914, 2,725,000 in 1918, and about 3,500,000 in 1929. It was never able to bring the Railway Brotherhoods into membership, but was not seriously threatened by competitive organizations until after World War I when the Communist party sought to gain control of it by boring from within. Again, in 1933, capital sought to thwart its growing prestige under the National Industrial Recovery Act by organizing a host of company unions.

With the founding of the Federation, organized labor purged

its ranks of all but skilled craftsmen and started the way of becoming the most conservative labor body in the world. All schemes for the socialization of industry were repudiated. The Federation was composed of labor's aristocracy. It fought bitterly to maintain its privileged position: against capital with the strike and boycott; against alien radicals by supporting restrictions on immigration; against unskilled labor with apprenticeship rules and the closed shop; against foreign competition with a protective tariff. Its officers and those of the affiliated unions drew salaries comparable to the salaries of United States Senators. The operating unit of the organization was the local craft union. In a given locality, there were unions of teamsters, bricklayers, stonecutters, stationary engineers, etc., with no common interest or contact except that each was part of state and national unions, all of which were loosely joined in the Federation. The representation of each of the national craft unions in the Federation was based on its membership.

The disastrous Haymarket riot of 1886 and the Pullman strike of 1894, both in Chicago, precipitated a sharp divergence in the attitude of the public and of government toward organized labor. The Haymarket riot introduced into labor controversies the most persistent feature of all such tests of strength since that time: the confusion of rational consideration of issues involved with alien radicalism. In this instance, violence followed police interference with an orderly assemblage of labor sympathizers. Someone threw a bomb, killing one policeman; in the ensuing riot several more policemen were killed. Unable to find the guilty parties, they rounded up the leaders of the Black International, an anarchists' organization of some two thousand persons. The court ruling, that it was only necessary to show that their teachings were of such nature as to have provoked the violence, led to the hanging of four, the suicide of the fifth, and imprisonment of three others. Seven of the eight were of foreign birth. From that time until the present, radicalism has been dragged into so many cases involving the struggle for social and economic justice that the historian cannot ignore its significance if he would. It inflamed the public mind against Illinois' humanitarian governor, John P.

Altgeld, and weakened his position in the controversy with President Cleveland on a really vital constitutional question. It silenced popular resistance to equally fundamental violations of the safeguards of personal liberty by the Department of Justice's raids upon aliens in 1920. It deprived the textile workers of Elizabethton, Tennessee, and Gastonia, North Carolina, in 1929, of the public support needed to win their strike against atrocious conditions in the mills of those towns. It deprived the defendants in the famous Scottsboro Case of an impartial consideration of guilt. It was harped upon continuously by the defense in the Tampa flogging cases in 1936. Back of all these and many other specific cases was the psychological effect upon general public opinion when labor disturbances ensued and the cry of radicalism was raised.

Even more important than the question of radicalism, however, was the realization that labor unions could be just as destructive of individual freedom and initiative of the laboring man as industrial combinations were of the small businessman, and that strikes were as injurious, even more annoying, to the peace, safety, and good order of the community. The Pullman strike of 1894 marked a significant step in labor history. When the American Railway Union refused to handle trains carrying Pullman coaches, Attorney General Richard Olney directed its prosecution under the Sherman Act of 1890. This Act declared illegal "every contract, combination in the form of trust or otherwise, or conspiracy, in restraint of trade or commerce among the several states or with foreign nations." An injunction was issued against the union's head, Eugene V. Debs, and he was given a six-months' sentence for contempt of court. The Supreme Court upheld the sentence, May 27, 1895 (*In Re Debs*). Injunctions had been used against the Knights of Labor in the eighties; but they became very prevalent after the Debs decision. Their scope was broadened gradually until they were issued finally against the attempted organization of unions, picketing, strikes, the payment of strike benefits, boycotts, and even the assembling of strikers or members of their families. Almost all the damage done to organized labor was through temporary injunctions which required neither hearing nor trial, but violations of which were punishable as contempt of court. Strikes were broken ordinarily by temporary injunctions before the time arrived for a hearing on the question of making the injunction permanent. The Supreme Court had based its decision upholding injunctions in the Debs Case on broader grounds than the Sherman Act. As a consequence, both the rights of labor under the Sherman Act and the scope of injunction became political questions.

The situation, then, when Theodore Roosevelt became President, may be summarized as follows. Congress had done little to assist labor except to enact a high protective tariff and to create a Bureau of Labor in the Department of Interior in 1884. Labor's battle to form unions and engage in collective bargaining was hampered by severe restrictions on the effectiveness of strikes. These restrictions were imposed by the government through the use of troops, prosecution under the Sherman Act, and interference by injunction. We shall trace the steps by which the government recognized the new status of labor in modern economic society through the creation of the Department of Commerce and Labor (1903), and the passage of the Clayton Act (1914), the Norris-La Guardia Act (1932), the National Industrial Recovery Act (1933), and the National Labor Relations Act (1935).

THE TERRITORIES

The historic policy of the United States with respect to the acquisition and government of territory outside the limits of the several states was first established in the Ordinance of 1787 and was developed gradually in the several treaties of cession, the acts of the President as Commander in Chief of the Army and Navy, the legislation of Congress, and the decisions of the Supreme Court. Without exception, all previous accessions of territory had consisted of regions contiguous to the several states of the United States. They were regions sparsely inhabited by Indian tribes and a few thousand people of European extraction, and already known to be attractive for settlement. Indeed, in most cases, it was the previous infiltration of hunters, traders, and even settlers, which constituted the pressure for their acquisition. They were opened to settlement as rapidly as land surveys and Indian relations would* permit. None of the fundamental principles of Americanism: freedom of speech, the press, assembly, religion, etc., were denied the people. The full measure of self-government was extended to them as rapidly as circumstances allowed. The government facilitated, in every possible way, the early incorporation of these new possessions into the Union of States on a basis of perfect equality with the rest. So long as they remained under the jurisdiction of Congress, the best interest of the dependent people, regardless of expense or inconvenience to the people of the states, was the determining factor in all legislation. To that end, the people were expected to manage their domestic affairs and administer their local governments to the limit of their capacity for self-government as determined by Congress. In only one respect may this traditional policy be said to have been modified at the close of the Spanish-American War: ultimate incorporation into the Union of States.

The territorial possessions of the United States as the twentieth century opened were not contiguous to the states. Some of them were already densely populated with foreign peoples. None of them proved attractive to settlers. American penetration was commercial in character. Even Alaska, the only possession approaching the traditional character of our territorial domain, was some distance away and thought to be undesirable as a haven for surplus population. There were, therefore, no such disturbing problems as land surveys and sales, the status of slavery, or the admission of states, which had consumed so much of the energy of government and aroused such tempestuous strife during the decades before 1860. The fact that precedents in territorial government were not wholly applicable, however, created many questions of national policy for Congress to determine, questions of constitutional law to tax the ingenuity of the Supreme Court, problems of administration for executives to ponder, and arguments for political campaigns.

The subject of much of the contemporary discussion was whether, as the Supreme Court said, some of these lands had been incorporated as a part of the United States by treaty and congressional legislation, while others were merely owned by and under the jurisdiction of the United States. The question was of immediate importance as determining the status of children born in the Philippines and Puerto Rico. The inhabitants of these islands had not been accorded United States citizenship either by treaty or act of Congress. Their children, however, would be citizens under the provisions of the Fourteenth Amendment if the opinion of Justice John M. Harlan prevailed. His opinion had held that (1) the Constitution of the United States became the supreme law for any and all peoples immediately upon their coming under the jurisdiction of the United States, and (2) that Congress, a creature of the Constitution, could not suspend the Constitution in any particular, in any place, or for any length of time.

The distinction between what the Supreme Court chose to call incorporated and unincorporated territories seems, in reality, to have been made by the treaty-making power and to have been confirmed as a national policy by Congress. Its endorsement by the Supreme Court was by a 5 to 4 decision. The interpretation of the Constitution with respect to territorial government as made by the combined action of Congress and the Court included the following pertinent points:

1. Incorporation into the United States of acquired territory had been left to the discretion of Congress, though the treaty-making power, at times, may have committed the government to such ultimate action.

2. The Constitution did not extend to acquired territories except by congressional action. "The liberality of Congress in legislating the Constitution into all our contiguous territories has undoubtedly fostered the impression that it went there by its own force, but there is nothing in the Constitution itself, and little in the interpretation put upon it, to confirm that impression" (*Downes v. Bidwell*, 1901).

3. The legislative power of Congress over the territories was complete. It might establish, change, or abolish territorial governments; legislate directly for the people of a territory; supple-

ment or set aside acts of the territorial government provided for in its organic act.

4. The executive and legislative departments of the government, in administering territorial affairs, were restrained by certain constitutional limitations. "The guaranties of certain fundamental personal rights declared in the Constitution, as for instance that no person could be deprived of life, liberty or property without due process of law, had from the beginning full application in the Philippines and Porto Rico . . ." (*Balzac v. People of Porto Rico*, 1922).

5. It was locality and not the status of people living in it which determined the application of constitutional provisions. Thus, a citizen of the United States and of a state, enjoying the right of trial by jury, did not carry this right with him in removing to Puerto Rico. A citizen of the United States and of Puerto Rico, denied the right of trial by jury at home, possessed it while residing in one of the several states. It was within the province of Congress to extend to the people of the territorial possessions, at its own pleasure, United States citizenship; to levy tariff duties· upon their products shipped into the states; to establish civil government for them or to retain them under arbitrary rule; to elevate them through successive stages to statehood or to grant them their independence.

Congress was thus given a free hand to work out a colonial policy, if it so desired, distinct from the traditional territorial policy of the nation. The two possessions which Congress chose to incorporate and organize into territories in the traditional manner, as if contemplating eventual statehood for them, were Alaska and Hawaii. Between 1898 and 1903, Congress legislated directly for Alaska, enacting civil and criminal codes, transportation and homestead laws. The most important of these acts was the Civil Code of June 6, 1900, which provided for a new taxation system, a surveyor-general, and municipal incorporation. This was the period in which exploiters of natural resources were reaching beyond the limits of the United States for the buried riches of Alaska. It was also the period of an awakening national consciousness of the need for conservation. The result was a bitter contest in Congress, with the financial interests represented in the Alaskan Syndicate able to prevent the organization of the Territory of Alaska until 1912.

The Hawaiian Islands, lying in mid-Pacific, have an area of 6449 square miles and, at the time of annexation, had 154,000 inhabitants, about 30,000 of whom were native Hawaiians, a slightly smaller number Americans, and the remainder Asiatics. The Islands were brought under the possession of the United States by the same slow process of penetration as western territory had been. The treaty of annexation (1898) placed every department of government in the hands of the President until Congress should take further action.

Congress passed the organic Act Creating the Territory of Hawaii, April 30, 1900. This Act conferred United States citizenship upon citizens of Hawaii resident there on that date. It provided for an elected legislature of two houses and for a governor and secretary to be appointed by the President and Senate of the United States. Other administrative officials were to be appointed by the governor with the approval of the Hawaiian Senate. The franchise was granted to all male citizens at least 21 years of age who could speak, read, and write Hawaiian or English. The territorial legislature was given a delegate to Congress and the responsibility of organizing a system of local government. It could not pass legislation with less than a majority vote of all members, and appropriation laws were to continue in effect if a legislature failed to act. All public lands were placed under the control of the territorial government.

THE COLONIES

The two most important Spanish possessions obtained by the Treaty of Paris, 1898, were Puerto Rico and the Philippine Islands. Public opinion was sharply divided over the advisability of acquiring them, and it remained so over the problems of their administration and ultimate status. Alaska and Hawaii had been acquired with very little opposition and largely without public agitation. There was some discussion about the methods employed in Hawaii and doubts on the part of President Cleveland as to whether the proposed annexation really was the expressed will of the people in the islands. The case of the Philippines, however, was quite different. The islands were gained by purchase and conquest. Spain was paid $20,000,000 to relinquish her claim to them, and a three-year military campaign was required to subjugate the natives who were fighting for independence. Few people in the United States knew anything about the Philippines when the Spanish-American War began. The peace commission was divided on the question of retaining them. Mid-Western Democrats and New England Republicans joined forces to oppose the terms of the treaty, and only the insistence of William Jennings Bryan that it be ratified and imperialism be made the ensuing campaign issue secured its ratification. The opposition insisted that the entire procedure was contrary to the fundamental principles of Americanism and would lead to nothing but disastrous foreign complications. Those who favored the purchase—Alfred T. Mahan, John Hay, Theodore Roosevelt, Henry Cabot Lodge, President McKinley, and others—variously based their position upon the needs of national defense and Asiatic trading centers, and the responsibility of extending the blessings of American civilization to a benighted and oppressed people. Their position was strengthened by the support of American missionaries, the difficulty of withdrawal under pressure from a native insurrection, and the desire of Great Britain to encourage our expansion as a restriction upon German imperialism. The determining factor was our unwillingness to shirk a responsibility created by the destruction of Spanish authority and prestige. Having joined forces with the native Filipinos in driving the Spanish out of the islands, we could not, with honor, do less than protect them against the imperialistic ambitions of other nations, and we were not disposed to assume a position of responsibility without authority.

Both Puerto Rico and the Philippines were governed for some time by the President as Commander in Chief of the Army. The Foraker Act, establishing civil government in Puerto Rico, was passed by Congress on April 12, 1900. Actually, army rule extended from July 25, 1898, to May 1, 1900. The army took over the administration of the Philippines on August 13, 1898. The revolt of the Filipinos, under the leadership of Aguinaldo, began on February 4, 1899, and continued until early in 1902. It was not until then that Congress passed an organic act for the islands (July 1, 1902). Meanwhile, in December, 1898, President McKinley ordered the Secretary of War, Elihu Root, to establish civil government in the islands under army administration. The First Philippine Commission, under the chairmanship of President Jacob G. Schurman of Cornell University, was sent out on January 20, 1899. This Commission, the other members of which were Rear Admiral George Dewey, Major General Elwell S. Otis, Charles Denby, and Dean C. Worcester, made its final report on December 31, 1900. It was a lengthy description of the islands, of the attitude of the people, and of the Commissioners' opinions with respect to their government. The Second Philippine Commission, under the chairmanship of Judge William H. Taft, was sent to the islands on March 16, 1900. It was given authority to enact legislation, to create a court system, and to appoint administrative officials. Its authority was derived from the war powers of the President until March 2, 1901, when Congress passed the Spooner Amendment to the Army appropriation bill, authorizing President McKinley to continue to govern the islands as a civil official until Congress should pass additional legislation. Acting under this authorization, the President gave Taft the position of Civil Governor of the Philippines and, September 1, 1901, ordered three Filipinos added to the Commission and four executive departments created: interior, commerce and police, finance and justice, and education.

The new colonial policy gradually took shape from the investigations of the Commission, the experience of administration under the War Department, and the discussions during the Presidential campaign of 1900. Colonial policy was a major issue in that campaign. Few people in the country, Republicans or Democrats, would have endorsed as a deliberate policy the expansion incident to the war. The purchase or conquest of distant territory, inhabited by a foreign race, was denounced as hostile to the spirit of Americanism as expressed in the Declaration of Independence and as likely to foster militarism, entail enormous expense, and involve the country in foreign complications. The Administration's defense of its action as a solemn duty arising from the destruction of Spanish authority in the Islands was ridiculed as a pretense. The Democrats, under the leadership of Bryan, promised to grant independence to the Philippines, and condemned the war of subjugation in strong terms. There were also anti-imperialists in the Republican party, particularly Senator George F. Hoar and Speaker Thomas B. Reed, but they did not desert their party to support Bryan. Likewise, there were Democrats who supported the Administration's Philippine policy. The Populists, who ultimately supported Bryan, spoke of the Philippine policy as "in conflict with all the precedents of our national life; at war with the Declaration of Independence, the Constitution, and the plain precepts of humanity." They endorsed the addition of Puerto Rico to the United States, but insisted that the Constitution followed the flag. The Democratic platform held that "no nation can long endure half republic and half empire." It said further: "The Filipinos cannot be citizens without endangering our civilization; they cannot be subjects without imperilling our form of government; and as we are not willing to surrender our civilization, or to convert the Republic into an empire, we favor an immediate declaration of the Nation's purpose to give the Filipinos, first, a stable form of government; second, independence; and third, protection from outside interference such as has been given for nearly a century to the republics of Central and South America." The Republican platform endorsed the war record of the Administration as having given "to ten millions of the human race . . . a new birth of freedom, and to the American people a new and noble responsibility." It merely promised to extend to the Filipinos "the largest measure of self-government consistent with their welfare and our duties. . . ." The question of colonial policy cannot be said to have exercised a determining influence in the re-election of President McKinley, but it did leave the Republican party free to continue the organization of governments in Puerto Rico and the Philippines along lines established by the Foraker Act and the Taft Commission.

Puerto Rico had a population of 953,000 of whom 589,000 were whites. They were a civilized people with Spanish institutions. The Philippine Islands had a population of 11,000,000 of whom about 9,000,000 belonged to the principal cultural group of Christian Filipinos. The government of both Puerto Rico and the Philippines, under Spanish rule, was highly centralized. In each, the important administrative officials held office at the pleasure of the governor general, and the judiciary, public works, transportation, education, and police were under the control of this representative of royal prerogative. Their legal systems were based on the Roman law. The Catholic Church was the established church. The basic problem, therefore, was to bring the institutions of these people into harmony with those of the United States; to extend to them the American system of decentralization and self-government with freedom of speech and press, the jury system, habeas corpus, etc. The greatest administrative problem was to maintain efficient government while training the native people to govern themselves. The question of incorporation or independence was postponed to some future date, when the people should have demonstrated the extent of their ability to adapt themselves to American institutions.

Preliminary steps in the establishment of a new regime were taken by the Army officers both in the Philippines and in Puerto Rico. The most important work in Puerto Rico was done by the medical, engineer, and paymaster departments of the Army of Occupation in introducing new methods of sanitation, road building, and public finance. Administrative costs were reduced drastically and a new provisional court system was installed. The same procedure was followed in the Philippines. Army rule there extended over a longer period and, in addition to the reforms mentioned above, preliminary steps were taken toward establishing an educational system, civil marriages, public trials, and popular elections with a limited suffrage. When President McKinley first sent the Taft Commission to the Philippines, it was with instructions to be guided in all matters by the best interests of the native people; to grant them as much autonomy as was consistent with good government; and to place the responsibility for local government upon them. Congress then passed the Foraker Act (April 12, 1900) for the government of Puerto Rico. It was to the new colonial policy what the Ordinance of 1787 had been to the territorial policy, containing the basic principles of government for the new dependencies.

The Foraker Act provided that the President, with the approval of the Senate, should appoint for Puerto Rico a Governor and Commission of six administrative officers: Secretary, Attorney-General, Treasurer, Auditor, Commissioner of Interior, and Commissioner of Education. These Commissioners might be either Americans or Puerto Ricans. To this group of administrative officers, the Puerto Rican government added (1904) a Commissioner of Public Health and a Commissioner of Charities and Corrections. Each Commissioner had full discretionary power to administer the affairs of his own department and was responsible to the several Cabinet members in Washington rather than to the Governor. The House of Delegates, consisting of thirty-five members, was to be elected bi-annually. The Delegates were to be not less than twenty-five years of age, be able to read and write Spanish, and own taxable property, but they need not live in the districts from which they were elected and franchise qualifications were left to the determination of the legislature. The six Commissioners and five others to be named by the President were to serve as an Executive Council. Not less than five of the eleven members must be Puerto Ricans. The Executive Council was to serve as the upper house of the legislature and was to sit permanently as a supervisory body for the granting of franchises, determining the salaries of all officials not appointed by the President, and approving municipal ordinances. Thus, the House of Delegates was, from the first, controlled by native Puerto Ricans, and they were given a majority in the Executive Council during President Wilson's Administration.

The Spanish court system was abolished and the American legal system, both criminal and civil, was introduced by the territorial legislature. Justices of the seven district courts received their appointments from the Governor and Executive Council and the five Justices of the Supreme Court at San Juan from the President and Senate. The Justices of the municipal courts were made elective. The Island was given a Resident Commissioner at Washington rather than a Delegate to Congress.

The Foraker Act also gave Puerto Rico control of its own customs duties. It levied a duty equal to 15 percent of normal tariffs on all commerce to and from the United States. These duties were to be assessed only until the Puerto Ricans had established a sound revenue system, when free trade was to prevail. In no case was the collection of tariff duties to extend beyond March 1, 1902. Actually, none were collected after July 25, 1901. The money which had been collected at the ports of the United States was placed in a trust fund and used for the construction of highways and schools in the Island. The monetary system of the United States was extended to Puerto Rico. The territorial legislature was given control of its own revenue system, but borrowings were limited to 7 percent of assessed property valuations. Inhabitants of the Island were declared citizens of Puerto Rico. They were not given United States citizenship until 1917.

The Philippine Act of July 1, 1902, was passed before the conquest of the Islands had been completed. This Act approved and continued in force the work already accomplished under the governorship of Taft, which included the establishment of a Philippine constabulary, bureaus of agriculture and forestry, a rigid civil service, a highway department, and a public school system. The Act made provision for a census after the conclusion of peace, to be followed by an election of representatives to the Philippine Assembly. Meanwhile, until 1907, the government of the Islands was the Philippine Commission, consisting of the civil governor (governor general after 1905) and seven other members, four Americans and three Filipinos. This Commission was to serve as the upper house of the legislature. The justices of the supreme court were to be appointed by the President and Senate. Local government was to be created by the territorial legislature. There were to be two resident commissioners in Washington. The Act, also, specifically extended to the Philippine people such fundamental rights as due process of law and freedom of speech and assembly. Municipal indebtedness was lim-ited to 5 percent of assessed property valuations. A Philippine currency system was created, but it was tied to the currency of the United States by giving the peso one half the value of the gold dollar. Tariff duties of 75 percent of those on commerce with foreign nations were levied on trade with the United States. During the interval before the election of an Assembly, the Commission created a complete administrative system of bureaus, including agriculture, public lands, biologicals, statistics, forestry, mines, archives, public buildings, ethnology, printing, coast guard, prisons, and education. The most important part of this work was accomplished before Taft returned to the United States in 1903 and during his Presidency when William Cameron Forbes was Governor General of the Islands.

FOREIGN POLICY

The one important possession wrested from Spain which was not retained by the United States was Cuba. It was under the governorship of Major General John R. Brooke until December, 1899, and then of Major General Leonard Wood. Wood's appointment was due to the efficiency with which he cleaned up the filthy and disease-ridden city of Santiago after its capture. His administration of Cuba was equally efficient. The government was completely reorganized in every department. The greatest and most-needed reforms were in the administration of justice, in education, and in the fiscal system; but in addition, differences between the state and the church were eliminated, the railroads were modernized and regulated, and complete sanitation was introduced in the cities. Dr. Walter Reed headed a commission for the study of yellow fever in the Island and proved that it was carried by the mosquito. Eradication of the disease was then easily accomplished. There had been 1400 cases in Havana alone in 1900. There were but 37 cases in all of Cuba in 1901 and none in 1902. General Wood took over the administration of Cuba with the native population hostile and suspicious. He left Cuba at the end of three years with the respect, indeed the affection, of the people.

Reorganization of the government of Cuba began with municipal elections in June, 1900. The franchise was restricted to persons who could read and write, or who possessed $250 in property, or who had fought for Cuban independence. A constitutional convention met in February, 1901, and framed a constitution similar to that of the United States. The United States was reluctant to turn the new republic loose without some form of acknowledged relationship, and so Congress passed the Platt amendment to the Army Appropriation Bill of March 2, 1901. This amendment provided (1) that Cuba should never permit a foreign power to gain control of the Island; (2) that Cuba should not incur a public debt beyond the ability to liquidate from ordinary revenues; (3) that the United States might intervene to maintain order and Cuban independence; (4) that Cuba should sell or lease naval bases to the United States; (5) that the program of sanitation initiated by the United States should be adhered to by Cuba for the protection of Cubans and of the southern ports of the United States; and (6) that ownership of the Isle of Pines should be left to future determination. This amendment was the work of Secretary of War Root. The Cubans reluctantly wrote its provisions into their constitution, and it was confirmed by treaty in 1903. The United States was forced to send troops to restore order in 1906, much to the disgust of President Theodore Roosevelt, who feared an unfavorable reaction in South America. Military occupation continued for two years and was followed by a threat that Cuba would lose her independence completely unless order was maintained. Cuba was a protectorate and remained a dependency of the United States, though nominally independent.

Events of far-reaching importance had occurred, meanwhile, in the Far East. The strength of Japan and the impotence of China had been demonstrated in a war between the two nations in 1894–1895. The war grew out of a dispute between China, Japan, and Russia for control of Korea. Japan won the war easily and forced China to sign the Treaty of Shimonoseki, acknowledging the independence of Korea, surrendering the island of Formosa and Liaotung (with the naval base of Port Arthur) to Japan, and providing for a heavy war indemnity. This was the first factor in upsetting the *status quo* in the Far East. Germany and France joined Russia in a protest and forced Japan to give up Liaotung, which Russia secured for herself. Germany, taking advantage of the killing of two missionaries in 1898, forced China to give her a 99-year lease on Kiaochow. Russia then demanded a lease of Port Arthur; France, a lease of Kwang-chow; and Great Britain, a lease of Weihaiwei. The intrusion of European power politics into the Far East, and the acquisition of Hawaii and the Philippines by the United States further upset the balance of power. Nobody knew quite all that a leasehold involved. It was a clever device for avoiding the consequences of colonial expansion while gaining its benefits. Leaseholds of ports were opening wedges for spheres of influence in which the foreign power would have a monopoly of mining, railway, transportation, banking, and commerce.

Traditional American foreign policy had included the principles of (1) no foreign alliances; (2) non-interference in European affairs; (3) non-aggression by European nations in the Western Hemisphere; and (4) equal commercial privileges for all nations in the Far East. The mad scramble for concessions in China, from which the United States remained aloof, seriously threatened the principle of equal trading privileges, if not the very existence of China as an independent state. National monopolies, recognized by international treaties, of the right to exploit natural resources, transportation, and opportunities for investment were recognized as inimical to American interests. The British were equally concerned, and the British minister to Washington, Sir Julian Pauncefote, suggested joint action by the two nations to maintain the Open Door in China.

Opposition to joint action as inconsistent with traditional foreign policy, and fear of the wrath of the anti-British element in the United States, resulted in Secretary John Hay deciding upon independent action by the United States. He invited the governments in Berlin, London, St. Petersburg, Tokyo, Rome, and Paris, in September, 1899, to agree to certain principles of action in China. They were requested to respect the control by China of tariffs and customs duties within all spheres of influence, and not to use their control of leaseholds, spheres of influence, or treaty ports to discriminate in favor of their own nationals. This policy was laid down in a series of notes which meant that the United States would not back up its doctrines with armed force. Hay's request placed the nations in an awkward position. Most of them, in some fashion, not entirely graceful in all cases, made the self-denying pledge, but with little intention of keeping it.

This Open Door policy, or equal commercial opportunity for all nations in China, was nothing more than a reaffirmation of the traditional policy of the United States in the Far East. The restatement was the work of William W. Rockhill, an adviser to Hay and an expert in Far Eastern affairs. The exchange of notes was scarcely completed when a nationalist secret society in China, known as the Boxers, undertook to stop the spoliation of their country by killing all foreigners. The German minister was murdered and the foreign legations at Peking were besieged. The several nations, including the United States, joined in a military expedition for relief of their besieged nationals. Secretary Hay used every effort to prevent the dismemberment of China. The Peking government disavowed the acts of the Boxers, and paid heavy indemnities to the several powers. Those due the United States were remitted and the money was used to educate Chinese youth in American universities. The insistence upon equal commercial opportunity in the Open Door notes, and upon the territorial integrity of China in the notes of July 3, 1900, constituted the full statement of American policy to which the other nations paid some deference. Russia and Japan, knowing that the United States would not go to war to maintain that policy, continued their expansion at the expense of China and to the inevitable conclusion of a Russo-Japanese War in 1904–1905.

The new situation created by the events of the late eighteen-nineties made the construction of an Isthmian canal an absolute necessity. It was highly desirable from a commercial point of view, and it was the only alternative to a rapid and costly construction of a two-ocean navy by the United States. The first obstacle to its construction was the Clayton--Bulwer Treaty, which the State Department had not been able to modify by negotiations with Great Britain in days of less friendly relations.

Congress, in January, 1900, showed a disposition to proceed with the building of a canal in utter disregard of the treaty. Great Britain, involved in the Boer War, and apprehensive of conditions in Europe, instructed Lord Pauncefote to arrange a new treaty. The first effort in this direction proved highly unsatisfactory to the American public because it pledged the United States not to fortify a canal. The Senate amended the treaty so drastically that Great Britain refused to ratify in March, 1901. Six months later, the British government, completely reversed its policy, and agreed to a new treaty (November 18, 1901). This treaty was ratified on February 21, 1902, and gave the United States complete freedom to construct and fortify a canal, with the single requirement that it was to be open for use by all nations on terms of equality. Britain also reduced her fleet in the West Indies.

7

Liberal in the White House

ROOSEVELT: AN EVALUATION

POLITICAL parties have long served as the cement of the nation. Men seeking public office must not only go upon the hustings and satisfy their constituents of their soundness on particular questions, but must meet in national convention, compose their differences, and agree upon a platform satisfactory to all sections. The system operates neither perfectly nor smoothly at all times, and in seasons of great reform agitation there is a tendency toward evasion and subtle deception in many quarters. Practically, it means that many men in a party are far in advance of its published principles, many lagging behind. That is why the final test on any question cuts across party lines. It gives meaning to party regularity, to party leadership, to political independence. It makes men's records their own platforms. It nullifies sweeping claims of partisan achievement. It enhances the worth of a minority party and gives victory to its principles though it languish and die.

The success of a national administration depends upon the degree to which it fulfills the mandates of public opinion and meets the exigencies of the times while in power. The need for social and economic security makes and breaks political parties. The disposition of the people to hold the government responsible for that security is one of the soundest virtues of democratic institutions. It teaches men in public life the responsibility of their positions. It teaches them to remain responsive to the changing needs of society during their tenure of office. Men who falter in that respect are thrust aside, regardless of past achievements or intellectual brilliance.

The accession of Theodore Roosevelt to the presidency in 1901 ushered in the twilight of Republican party solidarity. No longer were the stalwarts to rule their party with an iron hand or shape the policies of the government with selfish impunity. Not that Roosevelt himself was to pioneer in the realm of non-partisanship. He was a career politician. He rose to the heights of popular acclaim, but he rode the crest of the great reform movement initiated and carried along by countless other men. He bore the same relation to Robert M. La Follette, William Jennings Bryan, John Peter Altgeld, and others, in that respect, that Lincoln had borne to Theodore D. Weld, William Lloyd Garrison, and Wendell Phillips, or Andrew Jackson to John Taylor of Caroline. How much the philosophy of any one man in public life creates the prevailing attitudes of a people and how much it indicates his recognition of the people's desires and obedience to them, is difficult to determine. In the case of Roosevelt, it is still a matter of conjecture.

William McKinley, whose assassination enabled Roosevelt to escape from the political graveyard of the vice-presidency, and Marcus A. Hanna, whose death fortuitously opened the way to Roosevelt's leadership in the party, both represented Republican stalwartism. McKinley was the foremost champion of a high protective tariff. Hanna was a businessman, manufacturer, banker, and promoter of public utilities who preached and practised the faith of rugged individualism. He was willing to assist men into office, to pay them on occasion for what he wanted, and he wanting reform less than anything else. Thomas A. Platt, who had placed Roosevelt in the governorship of New York at a time when he was a resident of Washington, D. C., represented the party boss—that class of men who seldom sought public office but wielded tremendous power as directors of machine politics and liaison with big business. Henry Cabot Lodge of Massachusetts, a close personal friend and confidential adviser of Roosevelt, represented the social and economic aristocracy of the East.

Roosevelt, himself, was the scion of an old, aristocratic family and was rated a wealthy man. His party was the party of big business, of wealth, of economic fundamentalism; the champion of rugged individualism and laissez faire, of government by precedent rather than by impulse, by tradition rather than by experiment, and of senatorial dignity and superiority. It was thoroughly institutionalized, conforming to the established procedure of holding local, state, and national conventions, but controlled by a closed corporation of machine politicians rather than by the rank and file of Republican voters. In the Senate was a group of "elder statesmen" who formed a sort of privy council of the Republican party: Nelson W. Aldrich of Rhode Island, Orville H. Platt of Connecticut, William B. Allison of Iowa, and John C. Spooner of Wisconsin. Aldrich had come into the Senate in 1881, Platt in 1879, Allison in 1872, and Spooner in 1885. They were the close advisers of McKinley, and, except for a brief interval, of Roosevelt.

Roosevelt knew the system from first-hand experience. He entered the legislature of New York state within two years after graduating from Harvard, served for three terms, and then retired to his Dakota ranch. For three years he rode the range, delved into the history of the westward movement, perfectly identified himself with the spirit of the West, and formed many lasting friendships. In 1886, he was back again in New York City, contesting with Henry George and Abram S. Hewitt for the mayoralty. He lost to Hewitt and traveled abroad. From 1889 to 1895, he served as a member of the federal Civil Service Commission, then for two years as Police Commissioner of New York City, and for a short time as Assistant Secretary of the Navy. He resigned from that position to lead a famous company, known as the Rough Riders, through the Spanish-American War, and emerged from the war a national figure. He was chosen by Boss Platt for the governorship, because the party stood in need of his popularity in the election. As governor, however, he made himself so obnoxious to the machine politicians that they pushed him into the vice-presidency to get him out of the way.

Roosevelt knew how to win and hold the confidence of other

men. He enjoyed life to the full—a bundle of nervous energy which sought and found expression in the restless spirit of the age. He was impulsive, too much so for the conservative men of his party, but it gave to his official acts and utterances a dramatic touch that caught the fancy of the people. He knew how to speak in vigorous generalities that exactly satisfied the imperious longing for reform without committing himself to a definite program impossible of fulfillment; he capitalized on the achievements of La Follette and Bryan and all those who had borne the burden of reform when to champion the cause of human rights was to drink the poison hemlock of political ostracism. He knew his people, but he knew his party, too, and for four years he scrupulously followed the rules of a first-term presidency, feeling his way into the leadership of his party and the hearts of the people.

He did nothing and said very little until after his re-election which would alienate the industrialists and financiers. It was not until the closing day of his presidency that anything was attempted in the way of monetary reform and then nothing more than the appointment of a National Monetary Commission to study the question. He urged Congress, in his first message, to extend the powers of the Interstate Commerce Commission and bring corporations under stricter regulation, but did not push the issue beyond the Elkins Act of 1903; and, in 1906, he did not throw his support back of La Follette to write a physical valuations clause into the Hepburn Act. He pushed the prosecution of trusts under the Sherman Act, settled the anthracite coal strike, and concluded the preliminary steps for the building of a Panama Canal, all in dramatic fashion. He vigorously supported the conservation program, being peculiarly suited to the role as a devotee of outdoor life and being closer to the soil than most men of his inheritance. That subject, too, was free from political heresy, being opposed only by certain elements in the Far West and viewed with askance as a prospective danger by the power interests. He endorsed the pension policy of his party, avoided any controversy over the protective tariff, and remained on intimate terms with the oligarchy of party conservatives. His renomination was by acclamation and his re-election a foregone conclusion. No man before him had ever received a 2,000,000 majority of all the popular votes nor as many as 336 electoral votes. Whatever doubts were expressed as to the welfare of the country in the ensuing four years arose from the fear that Roosevelt's impulsiveness would lead to his accidental death and the elevation of Charles W. Fairbanks to the presidency.

His real service to the cause of reform came during his second administration, not in the form of congressional legislation, but through his influence over public opinion. No President since Lincoln had spoken so often and intimately to the people. None cherished popular acclaim more, nor received it so generously. We must remember that the great reform movement gathered momentum throughout the eight years of his presidency, and reached its crest in a flood of liberal state legislation during Taft's Administration and of national legislation during Wilson's Administration. Conservative wealth was firmly entrenched when he came into office. It controlled the economic life of the nation and, consequently, the state itself. It wielded tremendous influence in legislative assemblies, and too often influenced judicial decisions, silenced the press, and closed the mouths of its critics. What he could or would have accomplished with the more liberal Congress following the 1910 elections must remain a matter of speculation. He had no such forward-looking legislators. His life-long intimacy with reactionary stalwarts, his occasional petulance toward the more outspoken reformers, and his failure to press reform legislation in Congress more energetically might have been due to inheritance and association; but it is not likely. His wholehearted denunciation of selfish greed, of judicial conservatism, and machine politics, and his endorsement of income and inheritance taxes toward the end of his second administration belie that interpretation. The fact is, that his tremendous popularity and the confidence placed in his judgment by the common man counted heavily for reform at a time when they were most needed to convert those unmoved by the appeals of extremists.

ROOSEVELT AND LABOR

When Roosevelt became President in September, 1901, in consequence of the assassination of McKinley, he assured the public of his intention to continue "absolutely unbroken" the policies of his departed chief. Looking back from the vantage point of 1946, however, the manner in which he handled the first difficult problem of his administration represented a revolutionary departure from traditional governmental policies.

John Mitchell, president of the United Mine Workers, led the anthracite coal miners of Pennsylvania into a strike in the summer of 1902. Conditions in the mine fields closely resembled the type of industrial feudalism so common in the mill villages of the Southern Piedmont; with company houses, stores, physicians, etc., imposed upon the workers at exorbitant rates. Wages were low, working conditions were hazardous, and there were none of the modern securities of workmen's compensation, unemployment insurance, or old-age pensions. Moreover, the real issue was not hours and wages, but collective bargaining which the mine operators were determined not to recognize. They had refused to meet the representatives of the United Mine Workers in conference; and they had refused Mitchell's offer to submit the dispute to arbitration. George F. Baer went so far as to say that the "rights and interests of the laboring man will be protected and cared for not by labor agitators, but by the Christian men to whom God in His infinite wisdom has given the control of the property interests of the country, and upon the successful management of which so much depends."

Industrial disputes, at this time, were governed almost entirely by the common law. Intimidation or coercion by strikes, picketing during strikes, and attempts to gain the closed shop were generally held to be illegal. The individual workingman was secure in his right to quit work at will by virtue of the Thirteenth Amendment of the Constitution, but often in danger of losing all semblance of personal liberty through punishment for contempt of court in violation of injunctions. Strikers had been prosecuted under the Sherman Anti-Trust Act, and they had been intimidated by the use of federal troops. The public, however, was beginning to demand legislation which would eliminate industrial warfare. It was suggested that the Interstate Commerce Commission and the state public service commissions be given power to investigate controversies and enforce their studied decisions; that emphasis be placed upon forestalling violence by eliminating the cause of strikes rather than upon the suppression of rioting; that machinery for conciliation and compromise be substituted for strong-arm police activity. Slason Thompson published in *The Outlook*, December 17, 1904, statistics showing that, during the previous two and one half years, 180 persons had been killed, 1651 injured, and 5533 arrested in industrial warfare in the United States. Concerning the Pennsylvania coal strike of 1902, he said:

From beginning to end it was attended by every conceivable description and degree of human fiendishness. Malicious and criminal mischief held carnival in many districts. Outbreaks of minor deviltry did not spare the mother bearing her infant in her arms, or innocent children on their way to school. Clergymen were notified not to bury dead non-unionists, and union men refused to worship at the same altar with the industrious "scab" who preferred to work rather than see his family starve.

In this particular case, the striking miners numbered no less than 150,000, and they had succeeded in completely suspending operations for more than five months. Winter was approaching and the public was becoming restless. Early in October Roosevelt called representatives of both sides to Washington, reminded them of approaching winter and the needs of the public, and suggested that it was time for conciliation. The operators scorned the offer of mediation and asked that Roosevelt suppress the strike by using the Army and prosecuting the miners' union for violation of the Sherman Anti-Trust Law. The miners agreed to resume operations while an arbitration board sat, and to abide by its decision. Roosevelt arbitrarily, and contrary to all precedents made arrangements to appoint an investigating commission, and to seize the mines and operate them with army labor. J. P. Morgan hastened to bring the operators to terms while there was still time, and they suddenly petitioned Roosevelt to undertake mediation. The miners resumed operations and the Commission awarded them the nine-hour day and a 10 percent increase in wages. Nothing was accomplished, however, in the way of establishing labor courts, compulsory arbitration, or even relief for the workers from the widespread use of the injunction during Roosevelt's and Taft's Administrations. For the first time, however, the federal government had thrown its tremendous power and prestige into an industrial dispute, not against the strikers under the guise of protecting persons and property, but in favor of a just settlement based upon the findings of an impartial commission of experts. Roosevelt had established the principle that the public interest was superior to the rights of property. Never again could employers count upon the use of federal troops in peacetime to break a strike of their employees.

RAILROADS

In his first message to Congress, December 3, 1901, Roosevelt demanded increased attention to corporate practices and an increase in the powers of the Interstate Commerce Commission. Shortly thereafter he suggested, in a series of public addresses, that the Sherman Anti-Trust Law would be enforced and that legislation should be passed providing protection to the public through publicity of corporate affairs and a prohibition of overcapitalization. This meant, as a minimum, that the Sherman Anti-Trust Law would be given an interpretation by the Supreme Court with respect to corporations as it had been with respect to labor unions in 1894. Congress had, in 1893, passed a law compelling witnesses to testify before the Interstate Commerce Commission, and another providing for the installation of safety appliances on all railroad equipment. In 1901, they ordered the roads to make monthly reports to the Commission. These slight gains in regulation, however, were more than balanced by the Supreme Court decision in the case of *Smyth v. Ames* (1897) which stripped the Commission of most of its power to adjust rates. The powerful influence of Roosevelt and of the Senate progressives under La Follette's leadership secured some decidedly important legislation in 1903 and again in 1906. In the former year a Bureau of Corporations was set up in the Department of Commerce and Labor. James R. Garfield was appointed Commissioner with the power to investigate corporations engaged in interstate commerce. His duties were those of a fact-finding agent whose reports were to be the basis of presidential recommendations to Congress and a contribution to an enlightened public opinion. The Elkins Act (1903) was passed primarily as anti-trust legislation although it applied specifically to railroads. In addition to giving the Department of Commerce and Labor the power to inquire into corporate practices, it provided punishment for the receiver as well as the giver of railway rebates. The purpose was to eliminate rate discriminations and thus deprive large corporations of their most potent weapon for stifling competition. At the same time, it was provided that in all cases in which the government was the complainant, either under the Interstate Commerce Act or the Sherman Act, a direct appeal could be taken to the Supreme Court of the United States. This eliminated the long period of time which usually elapsed before a case, originating in one of the lower courts, reached the Supreme Court.

In 1906, Congress passed the Hepburn Act, regarded at the time as the greatest achievement of the Roosevelt Administration because it gave renewed vigor to the Interstate Commerce Commission. It gave that body the power to compel uniform bookkeeping practices by all railroads, and the power to establish maximum rates after complaints and investigations had been made; but it was not a general grant of rate-making authority. Senator La Follette insisted, when the Hepburn Act was under consideration, that to give the Commission power only to fix rates high enough to give the railroads a reasonable return on their own valuations was little more than a pretense at rate regulation. He demanded that the roads be given no more than a fair return on their investment, the physical valuations to be determined by the Interstate Commerce Commission. Roosevelt would not support him and the rate-making power of the Commission remained paralyzed, although the Act did outlaw discriminations, abolish passes, and separate railway management from that of other productive enterprises such as mining. It also extended the jurisdiction of the Interstate Commerce Commission over express companies, sleeping car companies, and pipe lines.

ROOSEVELT AND BUSINESS

Businessmen always insisted that Roosevelt lacked an understanding of economic processes and problems. Conservative statesmen said he lacked respect for the authority of the legislative and judicial branches of the government in our system of checks and balances. Actually, the industrial revolution was remaking society. Liberals were seeking controls for a gigantic industrial and financial system in which free enterprise had run riot. Roosevelt was a liberal; and liberals, because they believe in progress, in experimentation, in slow but continuous reform, are anathema to conservatives and radicals alike. He became steadily more liberal throughout his entire public career. The conservatives were without leadership after Marcus A. Hanna died in 1904, and as they became disorganized the growing strength of the progressives gave more power to such leaders as Roosevelt and La Follette.

Roosevelt's attitude on the tariff was eminently satisfactory to the conservatives of his party. The tariff was under discussion as a part of the reform movement. Tariff rates had been raised to the highest levels in the nation's history during McKinley's Administration. The primary object of our tariff laws had always been to safeguard home industries with incidental revenue to the government. They represented an exercise of the taxing power beyond its normal purpose. The Dingley tariff rates, established in 1897, had gone beyond the point of taxation for public purposes and had come dangerously close to establishing an embargo—thus creating a partnership between the government and certain industries for the exclusion from the country of relief from oppressively high prices. The demand for tariff reform, therefore, did not emanate entirely from the agrarians as it largely had at other times. It arose from a more scientific approach to the problem, with a definite claim that excessive rates were helping to create and perpetuate monopolies, fostering an inequitable distribution of wealth, restricting foreign markets, undermining the normal functions of our political institutions, and imposing excessive prices on all consumers, agrarians, and others alike. Roosevelt was a protectionist, and so was Taft. Roosevelt said with regard to protection:

Conditions change, and the laws must be modified from time to time to fit new exigencies. But the genuine underlying principle of protection, as it has been embodied in all but one of the American tariff laws for the last forty years, has worked out results so beneficial, so evenly and widely spread . . . that the American people, if they show their usual practical business sense, will insist when these laws are modified that they shall be modified with the utmost care and conservatism, and by the friends and not the enemies of the protective system.

Nothing was done, therefore, about revision during his administration.

Unwilling to move against the tariff which westerners insisted was the "mother of trusts," Roosevelt, nevertheless, was willing to move against the trusts. In fact, he soon became known as the "trust-buster." Once the coal strike was settled, he pressed Congress for anti-trust legislation. It passed the Expedition Act (February 11, 1903) giving precedence to suits filed in the Circuit Courts under the Sherman Anti-Trust Act and the Interstate Commerce Act. It established a Department of Commerce and Labor (February 14, 1903), including a Bureau of Corporations with the special function of investigating corporate practices. It then passed the Elkins Act (February 19, 1903). This act forbade any variations from the published rates of the railroads, and provided fines from $1000 to $20,000 upon corporations which gave or received rebates. The purpose was to eliminate rate discriminations and thus deprive large corporations of their most potent weapons for stifling competition, as well as to relieve railroads from pressure by these corporations. It was, therefore, anti-trust legislation although it applied specifically to railroads.

In March, 1903, Attorney-General Knox entered suit against the Northern Securities Company under the Sherman Act. This was a radical reversal of the policy of the government under the two previous administrations. The case arose out of a contest between James J. Hill, backed by J. P. Morgan, and Edward H. Harriman for control of the Burlington Railroad. Hill controlled the Great Northern and Northern Pacific. Harriman controlled the Union Pacific. Each wanted the Burlington as a Chicago connection. Harriman lost in the stock market contest, but later attempted to gain control of the Northern Pacific. Hill and Morgan then organized the Northern Securities Company, a holding company, to insure permanence and stability to their management. The government sought to restore competition between the two transcontinental roads, and to check the use of the holding company device for establishing monopolies. Since the operations of the company clearly involved interstate commerce, it was hoped that a better test of the Sherman Act could be made than had been possible in the case of *United States v. E. C. Knight Company*.

The Supreme Court handed down its decision in 1904 (*Northern Securities Co. v. United States*). It was a 5 to 4 decision against the Northern Securities Company, but Justice Holmes dissented on the ground that if control of two railroads in the same hands were a penal offense "then a partnership between two stage drivers who have been competitors in driving across a state line, or two merchants once engaged in rival commerce among the States, whether made after or before the Act, if now continued, is a crime." He continued:

I am happy to know that only a minority of my brethren adopt an interpretation of the law which in my opinion would . . . disintegrate society so far as it could into individual atoms. If that were its intent, I should regard calling such a law a regulation of commerce as a mere pretense. It would be an attempt to reconstruct society. I am not concerned with the wisdom of such an attempt, but I believe that Congress was not entrusted by the Constitution with the power to make it and I am deeply persuaded that it has not tried.

This minority opinion of Holmes, that the words of the Sherman Act must be interpreted by their meaning in the common law and that there must be an attempt to restrain trade for a combination in restraint of trade to exist (actual monopoly instead of power to monopolize), became the opinion of the majority in 1911 (*Standard Oil Co. v. United States* and *American Tobacco Co. v. United States*) and was clearly sustained in 1920 (*United States v. United States Steel Corporation*).

Meanwhile, the Commissioner of Corporations had made extensive investigations of other trusts preparatory to prosecutions under the Sherman Act. Forty-four proceedings in all were brought during Roosevelt's administration and ninety during the succeeding administration of President Taft. Many of them were against outstanding corporations such as Standard Oil Company, the American Tobacco Company, the United States Steel Corporation, the International Harvester Company, the National Cash Register Company, and the General Electric Company. Roosevelt, in addition, advocated federal charters for all corporations engaged in interstate commerce; and both he and Taft urged that specific practices such as holding companies and stock watering be outlawed. Yet, in spite of all the public agitation, Congress refused to enact further legislation, being content to test to the limit the possibilities of restoring competition by action under the Sherman Act. The government won many of its cases, but somehow the old monopolies that were ordered to be dissolved reappeared in a different form and it became apparent that competition was not being restored or monopolistic growth retarded. Near the end of his second administration, Roosevelt began to make a distinction in his public utterances between "good" trusts and "bad" trusts. The Supreme Court recognized the same distinction in 1911 in the American Tobacco and Standard Oil cases, when it said that the sweeping language of the Sherman Act required the application of the "rule of reason," and that only combinations in unreasonable restraint of trade could be held in violation of the law.

Roosevelt's first real break with the conservatives in the Senate came early in his second term. He had a great deal to say about the railroads in his speeches of 1904 and 1905, following the government victory in the Northern Securities Case, and specifically urged that the Interstate Commerce Commission be given the power to fix rates. The railroads mustered all of their power in Congress to prevent such legislation. The Hepburn Act, sponsored by Roosevelt and Senator Robert La Follette of Wisconsin, was finally enacted and approved on June 29, 1906. La Follette wanted two provisions in the act which were not included. He objected strenuously to allowing the roads to determine the physical valuation of their own properties as a basis for rate making. That power, he insisted, should be lodged in the Interstate Commerce Commission, which should be bound only to allow the roads a fair return on their investment. He also insisted that rates ordered by the Commission should go into effect at once, pending review by the courts, without any provision for recovery of losses by the roads if the courts should reverse the Commission's order. Senator Aldrich led the fight against these two provisions, and they were finally eliminated from the act.

Roosevelt was not satisfied, but he accepted the compromise in preference to no legislation at all. The act did revitalize the Interstate Commerce Commission, deprive giant industrial companies of one method of crushing smaller competitors, and firmly establish the old Populist principle of public control over common carriers. It extended the jurisdiction of the Commission over express companies, sleeping car companies, terminals, and pipe lines. It outlawed rate discriminations, abolished the granting of passes, and separated railway management from that of other productive enterprises such as mining. These provisions were designed to wipe out one source of political corruption and to prevent roads which owned coal mines from using their position to crush competition. It empowered the Commission to hear complaints about rates, to determine reasonable rates, and to order the new rates into effect. The railway company might appeal such orders to the courts for review, and the old rates were to remain in effect pending the decision of the court. The burden of proof, however, was upon the roads rather than upon the Commission.

CONSERVATION

Conservation of natural resources, particularly coal and timber lands, soil, and water power sites, was an integral part of the general reform program. Its purpose was to withhold from exploitation for private gain the exhaustible resources such as public coal lands, to place restrictions in the public interest upon the development of inexhaustible resources such as water power, and to restore to normality those resources already partially destroyed such as forests and soils. It was a movement close to the hearts of men like Theodore Roosevelt and Gifford Pinchot (Director of the United States Forestry Service), heartily endorsed by William H. Taft, and supported by all lovers of wild life and outdoor recreation, opponents of monopolistic tendencies, and those interested in the future prosperity and economic democracy of the nation. In its broader aspects, it marked the period of transition from the exploitive philosophy of pioneering days to the conservative philosophy of a mature people concerned over the adequacy of its original inheritance to meet the needs of present and future generations.

The demand for action by the federal government arose from (1) a realization that private enterprise would not engage in a general plan of conservation for the public good at the expense of private gain, (2) the close interrelation between forest areas, the flow of water in navigable streams, flood control, and soil erosion by wind and water in regions far beyond the limits of one or even a group of states, (3) the riparian rights of the federal government along navigable streams and its control over the transmission of power across the state lines in the realm of interstate commerce, and (4) the proved ineffectiveness of state control over large corporations. It was opposed by special interests engaged in lumbering, mining, and water-power development, by individualists who feared the stifling of individual enterprise, and by state-rights devotees, particularly in the new western states, who resented radical departure from traditional policies by the federal government while they were in the stage of early development.

The general policy of the government throughout the nineteenth century had been to encourage settlement by rapidly disposing of public lands to individuals or corporations. The Homestead Act (1862), however, had failed to benefit urban workers, largely because they were far distant, and in no small measure because companies and individual speculators contrived ways to gain and hold choice areas. The Homestead Act had benefited the homesteaders least of all. Beginning with the Reclamation Act of 1902, greater emphasis was placed upon reclaiming arid lands, preventing soil erosion, conserving mineral resources, and preventing land monopoly.

Irrigation projects on the public lands began with the Reclamation Act and continued without intermission to the present time. The Act provided for the building of irrigation projects by the federal government from the proceeds of public land sales. A new reclamation service was established, and from this beginning emerged the recent Roosevelt Dam in Arizona, the Boulder Dam on the Colorado River, and the Grand Coulee project on the Columbia River. The program succeeded in restoring to cultivation millions of acres of productive soil; and eventually evolved into gigantic enterprises for the production of hydroelectric power and still greater projects for reforestation and flood control. By 1940 about 20,000,000 acres of land were under cultivation. No progress was made toward flood control, however, until after the disastrous flood of 1913, and none in the direction of government power production, except as a World War I activity, until after 1932. It is a mistake to think that agitation over the power trust and for the control of public utilities began in the late twenties. The whole question was thoroughly discussed during the first decade of the century, leaving little to be added except the aggravation of then existing evils by the rapid increase in power production and the perfection of an intricate system of holding companies.

Finally in 1908 Roosevelt called a White House Conference of governors, members of Congress, justices of the courts, and technical authorities for the purpose of formulating a national conservation program. It made two important recommendations: (1) that timber lands on the headwaters of all navigable streams be preserved, lumbering operations on all other lands, public and private, be placed under strict regulation, and vigorous measures for the control of forest fires be adopted; (2) that the government should retain all lands containing deposits of phosphates, natural gas, oil, and coal, and retain title to all mineral deposits in other lands that it might sell. The establishment of state and national conservation commissions dates from this conference. Roosevelt, acting with his characteristic vigor and impulsiveness, had closed 64,000,000 acres of public lands in 1906. Following the establishment of the National Conservation Commission in 1908, he closed to entry over 140,000,000 acres, including valuable forest areas, water-power sites, and mineral deposits; and requested Congress to enact the necessary legislation to fulfill the second recommendation of the White House Conference, namely, the retention by the government of all mineral and water-power sites and their development under lease. Congress refused to do this, and Taft took up the burden where Roosevelt left off. He succeeded in getting legislation for the Roosevelt withdrawals, for the right to separate titles to land and mineral deposits, and to withhold permanently water-power sites and some mineral lands. By 1940 there were 176,000,000 acres in the national forests, and the government retained the mineral, water power, and oil rights to another 47,000,000 acres.

ROOSEVELT THE STATESMAN

Roosevelt took over the presidency with two vital foreign problems in process of readjustment. The Hay-Pauncefote treaty, which was concluded shortly after his accession, cleared the diplomatic obstacles to construction of an Isthmian canal out of the way, but left much to be done before actual construction could start. In the Far East, China was in disorder, Japan had emerged as a world power, and the conflict of interests of the United States as an insular power and of Japan as a continental power was becoming increasingly apparent. Roosevelt approached the solution of both problems with his usual vigorous and direct methods, and although he achieved immediate results, they were not entirely happy results over the long view.

McKinley had appointed a commission in 1899 to study the relative merits of the Panama and Nicaraguan routes for a canal. The commission, after the New Panama Canal Company had reduced the demands for its holdings of the original de Lesseps property from $109,000,000 to $40,000,000, reported in favor of the Panama route. The desire of the company to salvage as much as possible from its ill-starred venture, however, introduced intrigue into the negotiations with the Republic of Colombia. Its chief lobbyists in the United States were William H. Cromwell, an attorney in New York, and Philippe Bunau-Varilla, chief engineer of the de Lesseps company. Congress, on June 28, 1902, authorized President Roosevelt to proceed with the undertaking in Panama if satisfactory agreements could be reached with the French company and with Panama "within a reasonable time and upon reasonable terms." Otherwise, the canal was to be constructed through Nicaragua. Secretary Hay then negotiated a treaty with Thomas Herran, the Colombian chargé in Washington (January 22, 1903) which gave the United States a canal zone six miles wide in return for a cash payment of $10,000,000 and an annual payment of $250,000. This treaty was ratified by the Senate on March 17, 1903; but Colombia refused to ratify, probably because the French company's concession, for which it was to receive $40,000,000 from the United States, would expire late in 1904, and its properties would revert to Colombia.

The failure of Colombia to ratify was directly contrary to the interests of the French company, of the United States, and of the people of Panama, though she was clearly within her rights in the action she took. Roosevelt, impatient over the delay and not of a nature to brook opposition, used exceedingly strong language in his public utterances about Colombia and contemplated seizure of the canal zone. There was little opposition in the United States to construction of a canal, and public opinion no doubt favored strong measures. Roosevelt, in fact, seldom misjudged the moods of the people.

The combined resentment of the three interested parties, finding expression in the acts of President Roosevelt, William K. Cromwell, attorney for the French company, and Manuel Amador of Panama, provoked a revolution in Panama. The United States government did not instigate the revolution, but the full details for it were worked out in New York City. The United States government prevented its suppression when it occurred, and President Roosevelt departed radically from the traditional policies of the nation in recognizing the new Republic of Panama within a few hours after it came into existence.

The United States battleship *Nashville* arrived at Colon, Panama, on November 2, 1903, as the revolutionists had been informed by Bunau-Varilla that it would. The revolution, amounting to little more than a good-sized riot, occurred November 3, 1903, and the *Nashville* prevented Colombian troops from landing to suppress it. The Republic of Panama was organized on November 4, 1903. Roosevelt recognized it two days later. Bunau-Varilla was appointed to represent the new republic in Washington. On November 18, fifteen days after the revolution occurred, the Hay-Bunau-Varilla Treaty was signed, by which the United States formally recognized the Republic of Panama and guaranteed its independence. Panama received $10,000,000 in cash and $250,000 annually in return for a canal zone ten miles wide. The Senate approved the treaty on February 23, 1904.

There was considerable criticism both in the United States and abroad of the high-handed methods by which results had been attained, but majority sentiment in the United States was favorable. Roosevelt defended his action as "justified by the interests of collective civilization," which, although it won the approval of a majority of the people, did not alter the fact that his precipitate action represented full-blown imperialism and seriously impaired the development of good relations with South America. Once the action had been taken, the United States was in a position of being unable to make restitution to Colombia. Colombia insisted that she had a grievance and wished to arbitrate, but not until Wilson's Administration was any real consideration given to the question. The Republicans in Congress, led by Senator Henry Cabot Lodge, blocked an effort at that time to pay Colombia $25,000,000 and to express sincere regret for what had occurred. On April 20, 1920, however, the Senate agreed to pay the $25,000,000 without an expression of regret.

The long-brewing conflict between Japan and Russia over Korea and Manchuria broke into open warfare on February 8, 1904. Japan revealed unsuspected strength in the war, winning every battle on land and sea. Port Arthur was captured in January, 1905, and the Russian fleet was destroyed soon afterward. Russia, by the spring of 1905, was desperately in need of peace to prevent a threatened revolution. Japan was reaching the end of her financial resources. The United States, at the outbreak of war, promptly circularized the belligerents and then interested neutral powers to secure respect for the integrity of China. On May 31, 1905, the Japanese secretly asked President Roosevelt to mediate.

The United States was anxious to preserve the balance of power in the Far East and received assurances from Japan that Manchuria would be restored to China and the principle of the Open Door respected. Roosevelt then arranged a peace conference which met at Portsmouth, New Hampshire, in August, 1905. The Japanese wanted the Island of Sakhalin and a large money indemnity, both of which Russia refused to give. Finally, Japan abandoned her demand for a money payment, under pressure from Roosevelt, and accepted one half of Sakhalin; but she got the Liaotung leasehold and the South Manchuria Railway. She also emerged from the war as the dominant nation in the Far East. The United States inherited considerable ill will from the Japanese people because Roosevelt had insisted upon the abandonment of the demand for an indemnity.

On July 29, 1905, the Roosevelt Administration, acting through Secretary of War Taft, who was then in Tokyo, recognized Japan's control of Korea in return for a promise to refrain from aggressive action against the Philippines. Japan then took control of the foreign affairs of Korea and the United States withdrew its diplomatic officials from the kingdom. This exchange of courtesies, however, did not lead to permanent understanding between the two countries. Japan's control of Manchuria soon led to friction with commercial interests of the United States. Japanese began to emigrate to the United States. The Californians objected to their presence, and the school board of San Francisco decreed that Japanese children must be segregated in the schools. Japan protested against what was regarded as an insult to the Japanese nation. The federal government was without authority, but Roosevelt partially appeased Japan by sending the Secretary of Commerce and Labor to San Francisco to make an investigation. The school board, however, refused to rescind its order. Roosevelt then called the members of the board to Washington for a conference where it was agreed that the discriminatory rule would be revoked and Roosevelt would undertake to prevent further immigration of Japanese. He then secured by a series of diplomatic exchanges an agreement by which Japan herself undertook to keep Japanese laborers from coming to this country.

The upsurge of intense nationalism throughout the world had reached a dangerous point by this time. This was especially true in Japan and Germany, which the people of the United States now regarded as most unfriendly, the one in the Far East and the other in South America. Roosevelt therefore decided upon a show of strength. The entire fleet of new battleships was sent to the Pacific Coast, then to Japan, and then on around the world. It left Hampton Roads in December, 1907, and returned in February, 1909. The Japanese, alarmed by the growing tension between the two countries, approached the United States with a proposal for expanding the Taft-Katsura memorandum of 1905. On November 30, 1908, the Root-Takahira agreement was concluded by which both nations agreed to maintain the status quo in the Pacific, to respect each other's territorial possessions in that ocean, to uphold the Open Door policy in China, and to support the independence and integrity of China.

Two other important but not serious controversies occurred in the Western Hemisphere during Roosevelt's Administrations. Canada, as early as 1896, began to insist that the Canadian-Alaskan boundary along the panhandle should run in a straight line from mountain peak to mountain peak instead of paralleling the sinuosities of the coast. This interpretation of the treaties of 1824 and 1825 would give Canada some access to the Pacific on the deep inlets. The question became acute in 1903 due to the discovery of gold, and a convention was signed on January 24, 1903, by which the dispute was referred to a commission of three persons from the United States, two from Canada, and one from Great Britain. The tribunal met in London on September 3, 1903. Lord Alverstone, Lord Chief Justice of England, supported the position of the United States, perhaps, though not certainly, because Roosevelt let it be known that he would resort to force if the decision of the tribunal were not a correct one.

The second controversy concerned the finances of Santo Domingo, which reached a disordered state in 1904. Revolutions and unsound fiscal policies had put the Republic in debt to European nations, and had raised the question of how far those creditors might go in forcing payment without violating the Monroe Doctrine. Great Britain and Germany previously had resorted to a blockade of Venezuela to force payment of claims, but had been scrupulously careful at all times to keep the United States informed and to prevent any unpleasant situation from developing over the Monroe Doctrine. It was certain, however, that if the procedure were repeated often enough something would happen to involve the United States in trouble with other nations.

In his message to Congress on December 2, 1904, President Roosevelt placed an interpretation upon the Monroe Doctrine which remained the official interpretation until 1928. He said:

Chronic wrongdoing, or an impotence which results in a general loosening of the ties of civilized society, may in America, as elsewhere, ultimately require intervention by some civilized nation, and in the Western Hemisphere the adherence of the United States to the Monroe Doctrine may force the United States, however reluctantly, in flagrant cases of such wrongdoing or impotence, to the exercise of an international police power.

Congress refused to approve an agreement negotiated by Roosevelt under which an official representative of the United States would be placed in control of the Republic's finances. Nevertheless, Roosevelt kept naval vessels in Dominican waters, marines on the island, and secured the appointment of an acceptable financial dictator who succeeded in reducing the claims of the European nations by nearly 50 percent and in placing the Republic's finances on a sound basis. Finally, on February 25, 1907, the Senate approved a treaty which included the principles of this working agreement.

8

Republican Insurgency

TAFT AND THE PROGRESSIVES

ROOSEVELT named William Howard Taft, his Secretary of War and former Governor General of the Philippines, as his successor, and that was sufficient to elect him. The Democrats, after their miserable failure under conservative leadership in the previous campaign, entrusted their fortunes again to Bryan. Taft did not receive the votes of those independent Democrats who had voted, four years earlier, for Roosevelt. He did, however, receive the votes of many conservative Democrats who refused to endorse Bryan. His popular vote of 7,677,000 was slightly larger than Roosevelt's had been four years before. Bryan's, on the contrary, was 6,407,000, more than 1,323,000 greater than Alton B. Parker's had been in 1904. Moreover, the Democrats elected governors in five states which gave their electoral votes to Taft, and Taft's popular vote was greater in most Republican states than that cast for the state tickets. Roosevelt was tremendously popular. People voted for Taft because he had the confidence and endorsement of Roosevelt. Certain that Taft would continue the policies of his own Administration, Roosevelt left for an extensive hunting trip in Africa.

The forward surge of progressivism, the final stand of conservatism, and the practical politics of the Democrats in the House of Representatives combined to make Taft's Administration anything but an era of good feeling. The Progressive movement was reaching maturity. Progressive Republicans in Congress were strong enough to oppose party policies without fear of being disciplined. Democrats were ever ready to unite with them in any move which would embarrass the Administration. Roosevelt had been roundly assailed as a radical by conservative Republicans, but the one failure of his Administration had been his compromising attitude toward the old conservative leadership of the party. They were still in control, and Taft did not have the power, even if he had the will, to force a continuation of the progressive program initiated by his predecessor and sponsor.

Taft was an embodiment of the spirit of deliberation in government. He was instinctively opposed to all reform measures designed to introduce quick and impulsive action: the initiative and referendum, the recall, the direct primary. He believed implicitly in the party system and in party discipline. He opposed all tendencies toward socialism and toward excessive regulation of individual conduct. He was, in short, unsympathetic to the prevailing spirit of the times, constitutionally ill-adapted to the task of leadership bestowed upon him by Roosevelt. His life of public service, begun soon after graduation from law school, had been spent in appointive positions. His election to the presidency, the one-time advancement dependent upon popular support, was in no sense a test of his ability as a practical politician. He was conservative, congenial, intellectually able, and an unusually skillful public speaker; but his judicial mind, his too great readiness to trust executive responsibilities to other men, his unwillingness to encroach upon congressional independence, and his simple faith in the virtue of individualism and self-reliance unfitted him for the presidency at a time of political and social turmoil. Roosevelt left him to his own resources, and by the time he returned from Africa Taft's political fortunes were beyond salvaging. Meanwhile, a group of able Progressives undertook to wrest control of the party from the conservatives.

The three outstanding leaders of Republican insurgency were George W. Norris of Nebraska, Robert M. La Follette of Wisconsin, and William E. Borah of Idaho. Norris, a native of Ohio, was an adopted son of Nebraska. He entered the national House of Representatives in 1904 and the Senate in 1913. For more than thirty years he continued in public life as an outstanding progressive, always fighting machine politics, always opposing special interests, always confident of the ultimate survival of democratic institutions. His victory against Speaker Joseph Cannon was followed subsequently by three other equally significant ones. The greatest battle of his career centered about the disposal of Muscle Shoals. For years he studied the question from every angle: the needs of the Tennessee Valley, the effect of cheaper power upon the manufacturing industry, the utility of government ownership and operation. His interest in the labor question, particularly the use of the injunction in labor disputes, was equally great. Finally, he took the lead in carrying on that phase of the reform movement having to do with political machinery. The Tennessee Valley Authority established in 1933, the Norris-La Guardia Anti-Injunction Act of 1932, the Twentieth Amendment abolishing the lame-duck session of Congress, and the unicameral legislature of Nebraska were to represent the achievements of three decades of public service. His non-partisanship was as distinctive as his record of public service. He followed Roosevelt out of the Republican party in 1912, supported Robert M. La Follette in 1924, Alfred E. Smith in 1928, and Franklin D. Roosevelt in 1932 and again in 1936. Senator Arthur Capper of Kansas once spoke of him as "a perambulating Declaration of Independence." Nominally a Republican, he remained through the years consistently opposed to the demands for party regularity, and consistently in favor of whatever public policies he believed would promote political and economic democracy.

Robert M. La Follette, regarded by many as the greatest of the three outstanding political leaders of the reform movement, was not a showman in the way of Roosevelt. He was as democratic as had been John P. Altgeld of Illinois, with great faith in the common man. He was, moreover, a man of action, not impulsive but patient, indomitably courageous, indefatigable in labor. As governor of Wisconsin, he had learned to rely upon the faculty of that state's great university for the facts and theories upon which he based all his political action, for he was not a career politician nor an opportunist. He thoroughly understood the economic basis of politics. All the great battles he waged in his own state and in Congress were against monopolies and the influence of organized wealth in government, and unlike Roosevelt he never compromised. His first battle in Wisconsin was with the railroads. He succeeded in breaking their hold upon the state and in writing into the statutes a law which gave them rates sufficient only to provide a fair return on their physical valuation. That was his objective in Congress. He bitterly denounced Roosevelt's acceptance of the Hepburn compromise because, without a physical valuations clause, it was little more than a pretense at rate regulation. He continued his campaign until the Interstate Commerce Commission was authorized to make a thorough study of railroad valuations and then went on to advocate public ownership. He was responsible for the first state primary law (1903), a progressive inheritance tax, a state civil service commission, and a workmen's compensation law. The Department of Labor, the Federal Trade Commission, the Employers' Liability Act, and the initiation of the naval oil lease investigations were in large measure his handiwork. Damned, in later years, because of his opposition to our entry into World War I and to the Versailles Peace Treaty, he carried on to poll 5,000,000 votes without a party organization on a platform of hostility to the Supreme Court's power of judicial review. Hated, loved, and feared; denounced as a fanatic, a demagogue, and a dangerous radical; discourteously treated and his cause betrayed by the friends of Roosevelt; denounced by Wilson—all this notwithstanding, he stands out as the foremost leader of those forces which were seeking to make democracy function, and his high place in history is unalterably secure.

The third of the leading western insurgents was William E. Borah of Idaho. Like Roosevelt, La Follette, and Norris, he believed that the special interests must be curbed, that corporate wealth was becoming too powerful in the political and economic life of the nation. His hostility to concentration of economic power, however, was matched by an equal hostility to concentration of governmental power. It was this which gave his career a flavor of inconsistency and made him the despair of conservatives and liberals alike. All of these men—from Roosevelt to Wilson and from Brandeis to Borah—believed in the efficacy of competition to keep wealth widely distributed and economic opportunity a living force in American life; but while other Progressives, for the most part, moved in the direction of socialism, Borah instinctively moved away from governmental control in the direction of individualism. Virtually all of the others, Roosevelt included, advocated curtailment of the Supreme Court at one time or another. Borah became the staunchest defender of the Court, the most able expounder of the Constitution, and probably the leading debater in the Senate.

THE GATHERING STORM

Roosevelt had steered clear of the tariff issue, and his Administration had closed without anything being attempted in the way of revision. Taft was in favor of a protective tariff, having said very bluntly: "The present business system of the country rests on the protective tariff and any attempt to change it to a free trade basis will certainly lead to disaster." The public, however, was demanding that rates be revised downward to the point where cost of production at home and abroad would be equalized. The Republican platform of 1908 promised as much, declaring "unequivocally for a revision of the tariff by a special session of Congress," and for duties which would "equal the difference between the cost of production at home and abroad, together with a reasonable profit to American industries." This was understood to mean a reduction in tariff rates and was so interpreted by Taft in his inaugural address. He called a special session of Congress to deal with the question and the greatest tariff debate in three quarters of a century ensued. He had not invited any representative of the insurgent Republicans into his Cabinet; and it was the insurgent Republicans and Democrats from the Midwest who were demanding revision as a move against the trusts. The House of Representatives, after an exhaustive study by the Ways and Means Committee, passed a bill which not only met the requirement but provided for free trade with the Philippines, and for a progressive inheritance tax. The reactionary Senate, however, under the leadership of Nelson

W. Aldrich, went all the way in catering to the demands of special interests, revised the House bill beyond recognition with 847 amendments, restored rates to their old levels, and repudiated the inheritance tax. The Progressives, who were by this time numerous enough to make their presence in the Senate felt, denounced the bill as a repudiation of party pledges and a reversion to unadulterated class legislation. The issue was fairly joined in the greatest of our public forums, and while the Progressives failed to defeat the bill, they materially advanced their cause in the country at large. The debate marked the beginning of party schism, with Taft failing to rise to the occasion as the leader of his party. The bill passed both Houses by narrow margins, substantially as the Senate had written it. The inheritance tax was not included; but there was a 1 percent tax upon the annual net incomes of corporations earning more than $5000. The conservatives had opposed this provision strenuously because it was an entering wedge, however slight, to publicity for corporate profits and practices. It was also a recognition of the principle that Congress could tax corporations. Taft was largely responsible for its inclusion. The law also provided for a customs court of five judges and for a tariff commission. The commission was instructed to obtain precise information as to sources of supply, costs of production, and uses of every item on the tariff schedule; to gather statistics on the relative cost of production at home and abroad; and to investigate the relation between tariff rates and the degree of competition in each industry. In these respects, the act was an improvement over previous ones, as President Taft insisted, because it provided a basis, for the first time, for a scientific revision at a later date.

The insurgents were angered not only by their failure to secure a reduction of rates in the interest of western farmers, but by their failure to secure an income tax provision in the law. Taft believed that an income tax was constitutional, but the Supreme Court had said otherwise (1895) and he was unwilling to "resubmit the question to the Supreme Court." He said: "I am opposed to this method of securing an income tax or the power to pass one. I think it exposes the court to very severe criticism whatever it does, and the best thing to do is to accept the opinion

of the Court and submit to the people the question of a Constitutional Amendment." Taft, therefore, went along with Aldrich
who, for purposes of strategy wished to divorce the income tax
from the tariff. Following a special recommendation from Taft,
Congress passed an income tax amendment later in his Administration which was ratified by the states and proclaimed a part of the
Constitution on February 25, 1913.

The enactment of the Payne-Aldrich Tariff Bill was the final
victory of reaction in the Senate. Taft signed the bill and publicly
praised it as a great achievement, thus assuming an unnecessary
burden of popular resentment in much the same fashion as
Hoover was to do many years later. Public opinion made no allowance for his known preference for reduced rates and his support of
the measure because of its administrative features: the introduction
of maximum and minimum rates, and the establishment of a tariff
commission. La Follette had succeeded in organizing a western
bloc of Insurgents, among whom were Albert B. Cummins of Iowa,
William E. Borah of Idaho, and Albert J. Beveridge of Indiana,
who were determined to gain control of the party organization.

Roosevelt, in launching his conservation program, had relied
heavily upon the advice of the Secretary of the Interior, J. R. Garfield, and Gifford Pinchot, Chief of the Bureau of Forestry in the
Department of Agriculture. Taft did not retain Garfield in his
Cabinet but instead appointed Richard A. Ballinger, a former commissioner of the General Land Office. Roosevelt, by executive
order and without authority from Congress, had withdrawn about
1,500,000 acres of land from entry in Montana and Utah. These
lands contained valuable timber and water-power sites, and a storm
of protest broke when Ballinger restored them to sale on the
grounds that they had been withdrawn by Roosevelt without authority in law. Roosevelt had also withdrawn valuable coal lands
of Alaska from entry in 1906. Now, when interests which had
been exploiting transportation, fishing, and copper, attempted to
patent the coal lands, a major scandal broke over the actions of
Secretary Ballinger. Investigations were under way into coal land
claims that were suspected of being fraudulent.

Louis R. Glavis, a field man for the Land Office, after a conference with Pinchot, reported that Ballinger was impeding the investigation. Taft authorized Ballinger to dismiss Glavis, who then reported his side of the controversy to the public through the columns of *Collier's Weekly*. A joint committee of Congress conducted an investigation which cleared Ballinger of all charges which had been brought against him. Pinchot was then dismissed and Ballinger resigned. The Progressives now insisted that Taft was betraying the Roosevelt policies with respect to conservation, and the rift between the two sections of the party, begun by the tariff contest, was considerably widened.

It was an embarrassing situation for President Taft with the Roosevelt-Pinchot forces gaining much the better of the argument so far as public opinion was concerned. More recent historical investigations have shown that Ballinger was not guilty of wrong-doing, but at the time the Roosevelt adherents in the country at large believed both Taft and Ballinger were sacrificing the public interest to enrich a group of businessmen. The final result was the advancement of Alaska to the status of an organized Territory on August 24, 1912. This Act provided for a two-house legislature: a senate of eight members and a house of representatives of sixteen members, both elective as in the case of Wisconsin, 1836. The franchise was given to all male citizens of the United States who were twenty-one years of age and who had resided in Alaska for one year. The legislature was authorized to extend the suffrage to women at its discretion and to elect a delegate to Congress. Provision was made for the building of a government railroad, and coal lands were placed under the leasing system. Oil lands and water power sites were brought under the same system during Wilson's Administration. The several departments of the President's Cabinet were given the responsibility of administering timber lands, homesteads, water power (agriculture), coaling and wireless stations (Navy), roads (War), customs and taxes (Treasury), and mails (Post Office).

Meanwhile, Ballinger proposed and Taft recommended to Congress a body of legislation in the interest of conservation. Laws were passed providing for the separation of surface rights from mineral (coal and oil) rights in agricultural lands opened for entry; for the withdrawal from entry of lands containing water-power sites; and for withdrawal of lands from entry by Presidential proclamation without special authorization from Congress.

The tariff and conservation battles had enabled the Progressives to register important gains in the sphere of politics. A major revolution was in the making. The first skirmish of the forces which were to make the campaign of 1912 memorable in history occurred in the House of Representatives. On March 18, 1910, George W. Norris of Nebraska offered a resolution to make the Committee on Rules elective and deprive the Speaker of membership on the Committee. The Speaker was Joseph Cannon of Illinois, one of the most popular men, personally, who had ever held that position. The insurgency was not against Cannon but against the system—a system which had developed by precedent to the point where the Speaker was the most powerful man in the government next to the President. He appointed committees, and the House operated on the basis of a committee system. He was chairman of the Committee on Rules. He held the power to deny recognition to a member in debate; and he could, as a member of the House, thwart any resort to unanimous consent. All of this was particularly bad because Cannon believed, as few men, in party discipline, in the infallibility of the Republican party, and in the maintenance of the *status quo*. He never hesitated to use his power to silence opposition. The group of insurgent Republicans, assisted by the Democrats, carried the resolution; and, in Wilson's first Congress, the Speaker was deprived of all power to appoint committees, that function being assigned to the elected Ways and Means Committee in conjunction with the leader of the minority party.

PROGRESSIVE–DEMOCRATIC COALITION

The growing power of the Progressive-Democratic combination in Congress was a substitute, to some degree, for the lack of dramatic and forceful leadership in the White House. Taft never sought to thwart Progressive legislation. He simply could not furnish the driving force necessary to whip conservatives into line in Congress. This partial defeat in the House of Representatives resulted in a large volume of legislation sponsored by the insurgents.

In June, 1910, Congress passed the Mann-Elkins Act. It was recommended by Taft and was forced through Congress by the Progressives against stiff opposition. It brought telephone, telegraph, cable, and wireless companies under the jurisdiction of the Interstate Commerce Commission, gave the Commission power to initiate investigations as well as to hear complaints and to suspend new rates during the period of investigation, created a special commission to investigate the marketing of railway securities, and established a special commerce court of five circuit judges to deal only with cases arising out of the activities of the Interstate Commerce Commission.

In June, 1910, also, upon recommendation of President Taft, a postal savings system was established by Congress, providing 2 percent interest on all money, not to exceed $500, deposited at designated post offices, and for the redeposit of such funds in state and national banks. The struggle for such a system had been going on for forty years. Eight postmaster-generals had recommended such a system, most European countries had them, and Taft pointed out that recent immigrants had sent $90,000,000 abroad during the preceding year. Advocates of the system insisted that it would encourage economy and thrift, would provide places of deposit in which the people would have confidence at times of financial uncertainty, and would prevent hoarding in small communities. Yet, it was with great difficulty that the Act was passed over the opposition of the American Bankers' Association. More than $20,000,000 was on deposit in 12,000 offices within the space of two years, $43,000,000 by 1914, and $1,180,000,000 by 1933. Taft also recommended establishment of a parcel post system, but opposition of express companies and of country merchants who feared the competition of mail-order houses delayed enactment of the law until August, 1912.

The first steps in two important governmental reforms, also, were taken early in 1910. The first was an act requiring publicity of expenses in connection with elections to Congress. The names of all persons contributing to campaign funds in national elections, the amount of money which they contributed, and an itemized account of all expenditures by campaign committees were required to be published. The second was an act establishing an Economy and Efficiency Commission to study the business methods of the government's administrative units to the end of eliminating extravagance. Its work was to constitute the preliminary steps in establishing a national budgetary system.

Taft also recommended at this time a law to provide for voluntary federal incorporation of corporations engaged in interstate commerce. Such a measure would have meant federal supervision of stock issues and operational reports to the Department of Commerce and Labor. Taft believed, too, that corporations engaged in ethical business practices would welcome the opportunity for federal incorporation, and all which did not would automatically fall under suspicion. Thus "good" and "bad" trusts would automatically be classified and the problem of enforcing the Sherman Anti-Trust Law be greatly simplified. Congress failed to pass the requested legislation; but Taft's Attorney-General, Wickersham, prosecuted the trusts vigorously, initiating 22 civil suits and 45 indictments under the criminal provisions of the law. In 1911, the Supreme Court enunciated the "Rule of Reason" (p. 126) and the public was convinced by the end of Taft's Administration that further legislation was essential if competition were to be restored.

During the summer of 1910, Roosevelt returned from Europe and made an extended speaking tour through the West—not the West of his earlier campaigns, but a new West in which the tariff was now a great moral issue, in which the fight was not against rates nor based primarily upon agrarian economy, but against the industrialists and financiers who were using the government to enrich themselves at the expense of everyone else. It turned out to be one of the most amazing performances ever seen in the country. The economic and political philosophy revealed in his public utterances was more socialistic than ever before advanced by either Democrat or Republican, Bryan included. At Osawatomie, he said:

We grudge no man a fortune which represents his own power and sagacity, when exercised with entire regard to the welfare of his fellows. But the fortune must be honorably obtained and well used. It is not even enough that it should have been gained without doing damage to the community. We should permit it to be gained only so long as the gaining represents benefit to the community. This, I know, implies a policy of a far more active governmental interference with social and economic conditions in this country than we have yet had, but I think we have got to face the fact that such an increase in governmental control is now necessary.

The implications of such a philosophy practically applied were tremendous, involving as they necessarily would a radical departure from fundamental principles of government and an explicit faith in the efficacy of law to remedy social and economic maladjustments. Returning to New York, he dominated the Republican state convention without so much as lifting his voice against a strong endorsement of the Payne-Aldrich Tariff Act. His speeches in the West crystallized, for the first time, the ultraconservative forces in the East against him. His action in New York, designed to allay their fears, only brought chagrin and resentment in the West. Fundamentally, however, the consequences were much more far reaching. His following among the rank and file voters was a personal one. He recovered it sufficiently to impair seriously La Follette's chances of capturing control of the Republican convention. At the same time, he revealed, in the East, his fatal weakness for compromise of principles in order, as a practical politician, once more to place himself at the head of the Administration forces. No one saw more clearly what had happened than La Follette.

The elections of 1910 revealed the amazing strength of progressive forces throughout the nation, represented by Democratic victories in some instances and by insurgent Republican victories in others. It was a situation in which the Democratic party and the minority seeking control of the Republican party were fighting for substantially the same principles. In Kansas, Senator Joseph L. Bristow and the Congressmen who had been prominent in the fight against the Aldrich tariff interests, captured control of the Republican party. In Wisconsin, Democrats again rallied to the support of insurgent La Follette and returned him to the Senate. Hiram Johnson, insurgent candidate for the governorship of California, captured his party and won the election on a platform of hostility to the Southern Pacific Railway and boss-ridden politics in the state. In Nebraska, the Democrats administered a smashing blow to the prestige of Bryanism by defeating his candidates in the primaries and opened the way to new leadership in the presidential campaign. The people of Ohio did likewise, re-electing Judson Harmon, Democratic governor of that state, by a large majority. In New Jersey the people elected Woodrow Wilson, previously unknown in politics, who had based his campaign upon an appeal to the intelligence of the voters. In New Hampshire, the novelist Winston Churchill won his fight to purify the Republican party by electing Robert P. Bass as governor. The Democrats also elected governors in Maine, Massachusetts, Connecticut, North Dakota, Colorado, and Oregon, normally Republican states, and captured control of the national House of Representatives, 223 to 168. Eighteen Republican Senators saw the legislatures which had elected them replaced by Democratic legislatures.

The result of the 1910 elections placed the Democratic party in the strongest position it had occupied for years. Bryanism was no longer an issue, the party was united. It was not in power, and therefore not responsible for the administration of the government during the ensuing two years. Its close agreement with the insurgent Republicans, particularly on the tariff question, gave it an opportunity to make a vigorous assault upon the conservatives in Congress.

The Democratic House of Representatives, according to custom, took up the question of tariff revision in 1911 in order to embarrass the administration as the presidential election approached. Three tariff measures, placing such items as agricultural implements, shoes, and lumber upon the free list and greatly reducing rates on cotton goods, paints, metals, and other items, were passed but were vetoed by the President because no use had been made of the information provided by the recently created Tariff Commission. Taft was on sound ground in his veto because the new rates, while more satisfactory to farmers than previous ones had been, were no nearer to a scientific tariff.

In January, 1911, the administration negotiated a reciprocity agreement with Canada which provided for a free list of more than 100 items and greatly reduced tariff rates on more than 400 others. This agreement had to be submitted to the legislative bodies of both countries for enactment into law. The insurgents opposed it because the farmers feared competition from Canadian agricultural products. The Democrats supported the measure, and it was finally approved by a Democratic and eastern Republican vote; but the Liberal government in Canada was overthrown and the new government rejected the measure, probably because the insurgents in the United States spoke of it as a first step toward annexation.

Near the close of Taft's Administration, New Mexico and Arizona were admitted to the Union; Alaska was given full territorial status; and the Amendment providing for the popular election of United States Senators (p. 78) was passed and submitted to the states for ratification. It was a fitting conclusion to a remarkable record of achievement. In addition to the above record, Taft had advanced the cause of civil service by transferring second- and third-class postmasters to the classified lists; had appointed a Chief Justice and five Associate Justices to the Supreme Court; and had established a federal Children's Bureau and a separate Department of Labor. Roosevelt no doubt would have publicized these achievements in such manner as to have derived much favorable publicity; Taft succeeded only in dividing his party and in being widely regarded as a rank conservative.

ELECTION OF 1912

Few presidential elections in our history compare with that of 1912 in importance, in the personal attainments of candidates—Roosevelt, Taft, Wilson, Debs—and in the scope and exposition of party principles. Never before had a candidate been selected by a decidedly minority vote who yet represented the philosophy of an overwhelming majority of the people. Seldom has a President, standing for re-election after four years of real achievement, been so abused by men in his own party and so utterly repudiated by the voters. Only three times previously in the history of the country, however, had reform movements developed such a crescendo of enthusiasm, hatred, and confident expectation as that which reached its peak between 1913 and 1917.

Roosevelt and Taft drifted apart rapidly after the former's return from Europe in the summer of 1910. No one thing caused the break in their long-standing friendship. It was due in part to their political philosophy, Roosevelt being impetuous in his judgments, careless of constitutional restraints, and ever ready to do what needed to be done unless it was specifically prohibited by law; Taft being an administrator, having great respect for government by law, and being restrained always by his judicial mind and intellectual integrity. It was due in part to the insistent charge that Taft had betrayed the Roosevelt policies. His restoration to entry of a million and one-half acres of public lands in Montana and Wyoming, upon the advice of Secretary Ballinger, alienated the conservation enthusiasts. His dismissal of Gifford Pinchot from the office of Chief Forester for insubordination aggravated his offense in the judgment of Roosevelt's followers. His refusal to approve the admission of Arizona until a provision for recall of judges had been eliminated from her constitution antagonized the more extreme advocates of governmental reform. The effort of his Postmaster-General, Frank H. Hitchcock, to increase postage rates was interpreted as an attempt to silence cheap magazines, particularly Collier's Weekly and Everybody's, conspicuous for their attacks upon vested interests. His failure to veto the Payne-Aldrich Tariff, his refusal to support the revolt against Cannon, and his oft-repeated praise of men like Aldrich led to the charge that he had deserted the Progressives who elected him for the camp of their enemies. The attention which all such potentially unfortunate episodes received to the exclusion of a vast amount of constructive legislation serves to indicate how completely the spirit of reform dominated the changing scene. A President who adhered so strongly to a strict construction of executive power could hardly have been popular with reform enthusiasts who frequently had little regard for legal procedures so long as what they wanted was justified in their own minds by moral principles.

On the other side, there was the rapid drift of Roosevelt toward "radicalism" in his public speeches. Mention has already been made of his speech at Osawatomie in the summer of 1910. In that speech, much as he may have regretted it later, Roosevelt came closer to grasping and expressing the fundamental issue of the reform movement than at any other time. Said he: "we are face to face with new conceptions of the relations of property to human welfare . . . The man who wrongly holds that every human right is secondary to his profit must now give way to the advocate of human welfare, who rightly maintains that every man holds his property subject to the general right of the community to regulate its use to whatever degree the public welfare may require it." Finally, on February 21, 1912, before the Ohio constitutional convention, he made his attack upon reactionary courts and advocated the recall of judicial decisions, saying, in part, that "either the recall will have to be adopted or else it will have to be made much easier than it now is to get rid, not merely of a bad judge, but of a judge who, however virtuous, has grown so out of touch with social needs and facts that he is unfit longer to render good service on the bench." Utterances such as these were anathema to a man like Taft who believed "we have a government of limited powers under the Constitution and have got to work out our problem on the basis of law." They also alienated men like Henry L. Stimson, Elihu Root, and Henry Cabot Lodge who finally were convinced that Roosevelt was hostile to the Supreme Court and the Constitution, that is, to judicial review.

Early in January, 1911, the National Republican Progressive League was formed by the insurgent Congressmen and a group of western governors. It was the beginning of organized opposition to Taft's renomination and the initial step in La Follette's campaign which was formally announced in the early summer. What happened between that time and the nominating convention one year later is a tangled maze of contradictions. By successive stages, Roosevelt informed the country that he was not a candidate, that he would support no one, that he would not consider himself bound by his previous renunciation of a third term, that he would accept the nomination if the people demanded it, and, finally, that he was a candidate. An attempt was made to read La Follette out of the race by the announcement that he had suffered a nervous breakdown, but he refused to be sidetracked and bitterly denounced Roosevelt for his betrayal. He never had believed that Roosevelt was a genuine reformer, and he was now convinced that Roosevelt had used him as a stalking horse until certain that there was a real possibility of defeating Taft for the nomination. La Follette, doubtful of wresting the nomination from Taft and certain that Taft could not be re-elected, had hoped to emerge from defeat with a strong Progressive leadership in control of the Republican party. Roosevelt wanted the presidency, and conservatives who thought him safer than any Democrat who might be elected, gave him their support.

The weight of precedent demanded Taft's renomination. Being a Republican President, and therefore in control of southern delegations to the convention, he was in a strong position to secure a renomination; but there was only slight enthusiasm for him in the pre-convention contest or in the convention itself. His greatest handicap, from first to last, was having permitted Roosevelt to place him in the presidency four years before. It left him under a great personal obligation, which he fulfilled with such dignity as becomes a gentleman, replying in the most restrained language to Roosevelt's rancorous assaults. He had, moreover, no personal enthusiasm for another term. Roosevelt never succeeded in presenting specific indictments of Taft's Administration which did not apply with equal severity to his own. There is no longer any question but that Roosevelt did misrepresent him in the campaign, deliberately and repeatedly. He exaggerated Taft's weaknesses and belittled his accomplishments. He even questioned his personal character. There is no question, also, but that Roosevelt's strength in the preferential primaries was not a test of his progressivism but of his availability. He won too easily in states like Illinois and Pennsylvania. Illinois gave him 266,000 in the primary to Taft's 127,000, but in the election Roosevelt received 437,000 and Taft 631,000. In Pennsylvania, Roosevelt received 298,000 and Taft received 193,000 in the primary, while in the November election they received, respectively, 492,000 and 720,000. Moreover, it is extremely improbable that a man, even Roosevelt, could have secured the backing of an estimated $3,000,000 in a primary campaign and the support of the arch monopolist and former Morgan banker, George W. Perkins, on the basis of his liberalism. There were not enough contested seats in the convention to have given Roosevelt the nomination had all of the contests been decided in his favor. He did not wait for the nomination, however, choosing to make the issue upon the election of Elihu Root as temporary chairman. He issued a statement which said in part: "Under the direction, and with the encouragement of Mr. Taft, the majority of the National Committee . . . with scandalous disregard of every principle of elementary honesty and decency, stole eighty or ninety delegates. . . . The Convention as now composed has no claims to represent the voters of the Republican party. . . . It would be deeply discreditable to any man to accept the Convention nomination under these circumstances, and any man thus accepting it would have no claim to the support of any Republican on party grounds, and would have forfeited the right to ask the support of any honest man of any party on moral grounds." The Roosevelt faction took little part, thereafter, in the proceedings of the convention, but organized a convention of its own and made plans for a third-party movement with Roosevelt as its candidate. Its call for a convention at Chicago, on August 5, was addressed to all persons who "realize that today the power of the crooked political bosses and of the privileged classes behind them is so strong in the two old party organizations that no helpful movement in the real interest of our country can come out of either."

This convention was unique in three respects: (1) It was not a true convention, because Roosevelt had already been tendered the nomination and had accepted. (2) That circumstance and the irregularity of choosing delegates made of it, in reality, an emotional mass meeting, a political resuscitation of the several reform elements. (3) It was the first attempt at a lily-white movement, Negroes from the South being excluded from the convention in the hope of breaking the Democratic ranks within the Solid South. Albert J. Beveridge of Indiana presided over the convention. The platform endorsed such reform measures as the direct primary, short ballot, and initiative, referendum and recall. It promised an easier method of amending the Constitution, without specifying details. It endorsed woman suffrage, publicity for campaign contributions and expenditures, registration of lobbyists, jury trial for contempt cases arising out of labor disputes, safety and health codes, prohibition of child labor, the eight-hour day, a Department of Labor, a federal administrative commission for the supervision of corporations, a revised currency system, downward revision of the tariff, a graduated inheritance tax, etc. Roosevelt and Hiram W. Johnson of California were nominated by acclamation for President and Vice-President.

Woodrow Wilson, reform governor of New Jersey, was recognized, from the very first, as the strongest potential candidate for the nomination the Democratic party possessed. He was attacked by Tom Watson of Georgia as a tool of the Papacy because his secretary, Joseph Tumulty, was a Catholic. So, too, was Taft indicted by Watson for having completed negotiations for the purchase of the church lands in the Philippines. Wilson, having been president of the oldest Presbyterian university in the country, probably did not suffer much loss from Watson's demagoguery. Governor Harmon, of Ohio, was Wilson's most prominent opponent for the nomination during the early months of the campaign, but Bryan attacked him as a reactionary because he would not endorse the initiative and referendum and supposedly had the backing of Tammany Hall. Champ Clark, Joseph Cannon's successor as Speaker of the House of Representatives, finally forged to the front as Wilson's most formidable opponent, but his great weakness was his purported alliance with William Randolph Hearst and his suspected opportunism. Oscar Underwood of Alabama, Chairman of the Ways and Means Committee of the House of Representatives and leading exponent of lower tariff rates, would have been a strong contender except for a personal feud with Bryan. Bryan was still a power to be reckoned with, and in the end he threw his support to Wilson, thus breaking a deadlock in the convention and giving Wilson the nomination on the fifty-sixth ballot. Wilson's nomination, however, was in response to the wishes of the rank and file of his party to a much greater degree than is ordinarily true. His nomination was accomplished without previous pledges or promises of the sort that so frequently prove embarrassing later.

The Socialists, whose party was first organized in 1900 and was growing rapidly, had held their convention at Indianapolis, May 12–18. Their platform advocated public ownership of "all grain elevators, stockyards, warehouses, and other distributing agencies," mines, quarries, oil wells, forests, water power, land, banking, and currency. It demanded the relief of unemployment by public works; adjustment of hours of labor to increased productiveness of machinery; abolition of child labor and prison contract labor; minimum wage laws, unemployment insurance, workmen's compensation laws, and old-age pensions; income and inheritance taxes, the proceeds to be used for the socialization of industry; woman's suffrage; the initiative, referendum, recall, and proportional representation; abolition of the Senate, and of the presidential veto; direct election of the President and Vice-President; abolition of judicial review; amendment of the Constitution by majority vote in a majority of the states; and vocational education. Eugene V. Debs of Indiana and Emil Seidel of Wisconsin were chosen as the party's candidates.

Not all of the Progressive Republicans supported Roosevelt. William E. Borah of Idaho had sought to secure his nomination instead of Taft's, but refused to desert the party. Governor Herbert S. Hadley of Missouri, who had led the Roosevelt forces in the Republican Convention, did likewise. Roosevelt lost heavily from the incontrovertible fact that parties are born, not made, and his was got together without previous impulse and under the spell of a magnetic personality. Many discerning men saw more promise for the future in a blistering defeat for the Republican party than in the temporary success of an incongruous expedient. More, too, than is commonly supposed, realized how completely the cause of reform had been sold out to the special interests when it embraced the patron saint of the system, George W. Perkins, who financed the movement. On the other hand, Roosevelt got many votes which otherwise would have gone to the Socialist candidate. He devoted the greater part of his campaign to denouncing Taft as a reactionary. Taft took very little part in the controversy and refused to meet Roosevelt on the plane of personal abuse.

Wilson, seeing clearly how the greatest modern resurgence of Jeffersonian liberalism was being compromised, assumed the responsibility of leadership. He conducted his campaign with dignity and good judgment. He was not a practical politician and his mental processes were pitched far above the economic basis upon which politics so largely rest; but circumstances permitted a superior quality of appeal. He did not talk about opponents but about the system the nation had permitted to develop. Fundamentally, there was not a great deal of difference between Roosevelt's New Nationalism and Wilson's New Freedom, except the method of approach. Wilson's campaign addresses constituted a really stimulating discipline in the science of government. Not since Calhoun's day had any man contributed so freely to political thinking. It was the first step by which he ascended to a position never before occupied by an American and equalled probably not at all by any statesman anywhere: ambassador of human rights in the Court of World Opinion and trustee by faith of humanity's hopes for justice and liberty throughout the world. Active campaigning was cut short on October 14, when a fanatic in Milwaukee shot, but did not seriously injure, Roosevelt. Taft and Wilson promptly canceled their speaking engagements during Roosevelt's convalescence.

Wilson received 435 electoral votes as compared to 88 for Roosevelt and 8 for Taft. It was the largest electoral vote any man had received up to that time. The combined popular vote for Roosevelt and Taft, however, was 1,300,000 greater than that received by Wilson. His election by a strict party vote and a minority vote as well, placed in the presidency a man who was far more progressive than a large segment of his own party. His leadership, extending far beyond the limits of his own party, produced a flood of legislation in the ensuing five years more sweeping in its objectives than the country had witnessed since the days of Andrew Jackson. The Progressives were seeking to establish some system of control over the new plutocracy in order to restore the economic freedom of an earlier day. They aimed to free the people from economic

slavery, to humanize the industrial process through control legislation, not to change the underlying principles of the system itself.
They were individualists rather than collectivists, striving to save
the democratic system somewhere short of socialism, and at the
same time promote the common welfare. The system they were
seeking to displace had been disposed to extend to business a
maximum of freedom and a minimum of interference aside from
gratuities in the form of tariffs and special subsidies. That system
had used the government to serve vested interests. The Progressives sought to use the government to control vested interests and
thus rescue freedom of economic opportunity from the threat of
oligarchic monopolies. Radically different from these two concepts
of government, was that of the Socialists.

The Socialists, unlike the Progressives, did not approach the
problem from the standpoint of restoring and preserving competition in order to save the small businessman from extinction.
They had no faith in the ability of the government either to control the trusts or to force their disintegration, but looked to the
collective ownership and democratic control of all the instruments
of production as the only escape from industrial feudalism. They
polled 897,000 votes in the election. How many more votes Debs
would have received had Roosevelt not been in the race is purely
a matter of conjecture, but probably a great many. Socialism
reached its peak in 1912 and declined steadily thereafter. It is
true that eight years later Debs received over 919,000 votes. But
he was then a prisoner in the Atlanta penitentiary and probably
much of his vote was in the nature of protest against his persecution. Twenty years after the 1912 campaign, Norman Thomas, an
able and respected candidate, received little more than a quarter
of a million votes and the electorate was almost double what it
was in 1912. Widespread fear of radicalism, hostility to a centralized dictatorship of boards and bureaus, and the inherent individualism of the people account for the Socialist party's decline. On
the other hand, its platform of 1912 remained through the years
a veritable fountainhead of ideas and the party's activity provoked
an intellectual ferment which men in public life could not ignore.
Socialism preceded communism and regimentation as the night-

mare of those people who evinced apprehension for the safety of American institutions. It furnished convenient copy for the conservative press and abundant inspiration for timorous politicians, who dragged its ghastly terrors into every political campaign to the confusion of real and important issues. Many of the specific demands of socialism have been adopted into the platforms of the two major parties and have been written into law. One has only to look at the platform of 1912, with its demands of federal loans to states, public work for the relief of unemployment, old-age pensions, workmen's compensation laws, income and inheritance taxes, reforestation, and woman's suffrage or to the Socialist platform of 1932 to realize how much the needs of modern industrial society have promoted a modified program of socialism. On the other hand, one has only to look at the Progressive platform of 1912 to realize that virtually every demand of the Socialists which has been adopted was also on the agenda of the Progressives at that time, and that it is the fundamental principle of the Progressives, of men like La Follette, Wilson, and Brandeis rather than that of Socialists like Debs that remains the basis of present-day objectives.

9

The New Freedom

WOODROW WILSON

IN the realm of moral and political philosophy, Wilson belonged to that select group, small in number, whose intellectual achievements taken together have created civilization. He fought strenuously for principles, as a basis for individual conduct, for party action, and for international relationship. The search for truth and its application to rules of conduct was the consuming passion of his life. He was a thorough student of American history, and had delved deeply into the impelling forces of human progress. He stepped upon the stage of politics at the very moment when the United States had completed its national growth, when the intricacies of modern commerce and our adventures in imperialism had inevitably destroyed the possibility of continued isolation, and when traditional methods of international relationship had broken down. As the war clouds gathered, he saw beyond the narrowing horizon the greatest opportunity for service in the century and a half of our national existence, and his vision gave him immortality. Service based on character as the motive of all human action was the secret of his ideals. It was not to him a thing of limitations, nor the peculiar province of professional men. His ideal was service of the individual to the common interest of the nation, and of the nation to the world of humanity. He believed that political parties existed to serve the nation; and, in the spirit of the reform movement, he would have the material wealth, the boundless energies, and the enterprise of individual men placed

159

at the service of the whole people, that waste of natural resources and human life might be eliminated.

Wilson has often been spoken of derisively as a preacher. He was that, in the sense that he believed the essence of national life to be moral power, drawn from the whole of the people. It was not genius but character which made him the great leader he was, and he looked not to genius but to character to sustain the nation. This wholesome faith in the ultimate judgment of the common man is revealed in his efforts to encourage public discussion of domestic issues, open transactions in the field of foreign diplomacy, and the application of the principle of self-determination, that in every important issue the verdict of an enlightened public opinion might be registered.

In keeping with his ideal that governments exist for service to the people, Wilson advocated such changes in our political system as to provide for a more responsible government: resistance to further separation of powers, and the fixation of responsibility upon individuals. He suggested the abolition of the committee system with its attendant evils of secrecy and control by special interests, and a return to free and unlimited debate in the House of Representatives. He suggested the advisability of giving Cabinet members seats in the Congress with the responsibility of defending their executive action and directing legislation. The principle was that somehow responsibility be fixed. At no time did he indicate sympathy for the idea that credits government with omnipotent power and seeks in legislation the corrective for all social evils. He was a conservative in the sense of realizing that the character of national life cannot rise above its source; that as the individual citizen thinks and lives so will the national character take shape. Certainly, as no other man in public life, he sought to impress that idea upon the people. He believed in the right of a people to establish or alter on occasion their own form of government. Self-determination is an indefinite thing; it presents difficult problems in application; but the principle of a people's responsibility for its own destiny and perfect freedom of choice are present. This principle he advocated for our territorial administration. He regarded it as inevitable that the welfare of subject people would be forgotten if profits were the aim of business enterprise and the government controlled by special interests. He advocated, therefore, administration by the United States of Hawaii and Puerto Rico in the interest of the native people, that sympathy born of understanding and kindred institutions might form the basis of lasting unity. He advocated administration of the Philippines in such manner as to develop a sense of responsibility on their part for their own destiny, looking to ultimate independence.

The years between 1910 and 1917 witnessed the culmination of the economic reform movement. They were the years in which the generalities of reform oratory were translated into constructive legislative realities and subjected to the test of constitutionality. The broader aspects of this intensely human drama were too obscured from view to attract general attention. The enactment of the several legislative measures in Wilson's Administration, climaxing a decade of such activity, was simplicity itself compared to the tremendous battle being waged between the ideas of economic fundamentalism, firmly entrenched in constitutional and judicial precedent on the one hand, and the ideas of social reform arising out of the economic revolution on the other.

We are accustomed to speak of the "New Freedom" of Wilson's Administration. It was new only in the sense that for the first time a man occupied the presidency whose social philosophy envisaged the hope of preserving economic as well as political freedom for the individual, and whose political philosophy embraced the responsibility of government for the social security of the people. The task of harnessing the new economic institutions, depriving them of their anti-social tendencies, and forcing them to accept responsibilities to society as well as to property interests— all this was not begun, but was carried farther than ever before, under Wilson's guidance.

In his inaugural address, he said:

We have itemized with some degree of particularity the things that ought to be altered and here are some of the chief items: a tariff which cuts us off from our proper part in the commerce of the world, violates the just principles of taxation, and makes the Government a facile instrument in the hands of private interests; a banking and currency system based upon the necessity of the Government to sell its bonds fifty years ago and perfectly adapted to concentrating cash and restricting credits; an industrial system which, take it on all its sides, financial as well as administrative, holds capital in leading strings, restricts the liberties and limits the opportunities of labor and exploits without renewing or conserving the natural resources of the country; a body of agricultural activities never yet given the efficiency of great business undertakings . . . or afforded the facilities of credit best suited to its practical needs; water-courses undeveloped, waste places unreclaimed, forests untended, fast disappearing without plan or prospect of renewal, unregarded waste heaps at every mine. We have studied as perhaps no other nation has the most effective means of production, but we have not studied cost or economy as we should either as organizers of industry, as statesmen, or as individuals.

Nor have we studied and perfected the means by which government may be put at the service of humanity, in safeguarding the health of the Nation, the health of its men and its women and its children, as well as their rights in the struggle for existence.

The program here set forth was carried through by a series of sweeping legislative enactments among which were the Underwood Tariff (1913), the Federal Reserve Act (1913), the Federal Trade Commission Act (1914), the Clayton Anti-Trust Act (1914), the Federal Farm Loan Act (1916), and the Seamen's Act (1915).

THE TARIFF

Congress had adhered steadily to the protective tariff policy begun with the Morrill Act of 1862. Tariff revenues furnished the bulk of the money for federal expenditures, but surpluses had uniformly resulted in increased spending rather than decreased rates. Cleveland had pressed for a downward revision in response to a fairly clear popular demand, but had gained nothing from Congress but a momentary pause in the general upward trend in rates. Taft had ventured to follow the dictates of public opinion rather than the advice of his party stalwarts only to encounter the same sort of congressional rebuff as Cleveland with even more disastrous political consequences. It remained for Wilson, under most unusual circumstances, to make the third direct assault upon the protective system in a half century—and with more success.

The Ways and Means Committee of the House of Representatives under the leadership of Oscar Underwood of Alabama had spent the interval between 1910 and Wilson's first Congress studying the tariff. The Payne-Aldrich Tariff (1909) was a frank subsidy to industry, the Republican platform of 1908 having guaranteed a "reasonable profit" to American manufacturers. The Democratic House and combined Democratic-Insurgent majority in the Senate had passed bills lowering many rates and setting up a new free list during Taft's last Congress only to be met with the presidential veto. There was no question as to the desire of the country at large in the 1912 canvass, and Wilson called Congress into special session in April following his inauguration. On April 8, he delivered his tariff message in person; but it was more than a tariff message. In its broad implications, as may be seen from the following passages, it charted the path Wilson was to follow in his entire attitude toward economic reform.

Consciously or unconsciously, we have built up a set of privileges and exemptions from competition behind which it was easy by any, even the crudest, forms of combination to organize monopoly; until at last nothing is normal, nothing is obliged to stand the tests of efficiency and economy, in our world of big business, but everything thrives by concerted arrangement. Only new principles of action will save us from a final hard crystallization of monopoly and a complete loss of the influences that quicken enterprise and keep independent energy alive.

It is plain what those principles must be. We must abolish everything that bears even the semblance of privilege or of any kind of artificial advantage, and put our business men and producers under the stimulation of a constant necessity to be efficient, economical, and enterprising, masters of competitive supremacy, better workers and merchants than any in the world. . . . It is best, indeed it is necessary to begin with the tariff. . . .

The House of Representatives, shortly thereafter, passed the new tariff measure which had been prepared in advance by the Ways and Means Committee and was the work of Oscar Underwood, Claude Kitchin, and Cordell Hull. The Senate debated the measure until early in September before passing it substantially as it had come from the House. Special interests descended upon the Senate in hopes of emasculating the House bill as was done in the case of the Payne-Aldrich Tariff, but the power of Wilson and Bryan was too great. They won by simply starting a back-fire of lobbying investigations. Party discipline played an important part in the proceedings, and the new act was strictly a Democratic measure, the division in each House being along party lines to a larger degree than usual on tariff measures. Four Democrats in the House of Representatives voted against it; Edwin S. Broussard, John T. Morgan and Ladislas Lazaro of Louisiana and Michael Donohoe of Pennsylvania. Republicans William J. Cary and William H. Stafford of Wisconsin and James Manahan of Minnesota voted for the act. Fourteen Republican Senators were absent when the vote was taken. The remainder, with the exception of Robert M. La Follette of Wisconsin and Miles Poindexter of Washington, voted against the bill as did the two Democratic Senators from Louisiana. Wilson had not asked for a strict adherence to the revenue principle, having been careful to caution against sudden and ruinous reductions without allowing time for business to adjust itself to the new principle of action. The Republican principle of equalizing costs of production at home and abroad, however, was abandoned, for that of a revenue tariff without injury to business. In all cases where it could be shown that American products were occupying a dominant position in world trade, rates were reduced. There were more than nine hundred reductions as against eighty-six increases and some three hundred unchanged rates. The average reduction was approximately one-fourth of the former rates, and there was an extended list of free articles. The free list included such foodstuffs as sugar (after May 1, 1916), wheat, cattle, swine, eggs, milk and cream, potatoes, rye, and cornmeal. Rates were reduced on butter from 6 cents a pound to 2½ cents, on rice from 2 cents to 1 cent, on beans from 45 cents a bushel to 25 cents, on chocolate from 21½ percent to 8 percent, and on onions from 40 cents a bushel to 20 cents. Wool, flax, boots, shoes, leather, and lumber were placed on the free list. Woolen and cotton fabric goods were reduced from a high of 99 percent to a low of 20 percent. Steel rails, iron ore, agricultural machinery, cash registers, typesetting machinery, sewing machines, typewriters, and shoe machinery were placed on the free list as a definite stroke at monopolies. In addition to all types of machinery necessary to agriculture, there was placed on the free list for farmers: cotton and burlap bagging, band iron, harness, horseshoes, and barbed wire. Phosphorus matches, cigarettes, and the plumes and feathers of wild birds were excluded entirely.

Ratification of the Income Tax Amendment in February, 1913, after four years of intensive controversy made possible the inclusion of an income tax in the Underwood Tariff Act to provide for any revenue losses from reduced import duties. The contest over the adoption of the Amendment had been extremely bitter. It was not intended to be simply a revenue measure. Tax laws had ceased to be simply fiscal measures and had become measures of social control. This principle, inaugurated in the levying of special taxes upon amusements, liquors, tobaccos, etc., and, in the protective tariff, was amplified and given new meaning after the advent of the reform movement. The income tax was regarded as the most just of all forms of taxation when graduated on the principle of ability to pay. It was advanced as the easiest way for society to recapture for use in the new governmental services a portion of the wealth which the new industrial processes were converging into a relatively few hands. Organized wealth opposed the principle then, and never ceased thereafter its efforts to substitute excise or sales taxes for it. It was urged that income taxes should be reserved for special use at times of great national emergency; that any effective program of enforcement would lead to bureaucratic spying into private affairs; that, being class legislation, it would lead to demagogic appeals to the voting masses; that it would retard the development of industrial enterprise; and that, unlike import duties, rational rates could not be maintained because the point of diminishing returns was not so readily discernible. These arguments were of little avail until World War I reaction had reduced the once powerful progressive bloc in Congress to a mere remnant.

The difficult part of writing an income tax into the Underwood Tariff was to reach agreement upon the basic exemption and method of collection. It was finally agreed to exempt all incomes

under $3000 for single men and $4000 for the joint incomes of
husband and wife and to impose a progressive tax of from 1 to
6 percent on all incomes above these amounts. There was a
further exemption of $600 for each dependent child, not exceeding
two. The rate of taxation was extremely low, amounting to 1
percent below $50,000, 2 percent between $50,000 and $75,000,
3 percent between $75,000 and $100,000, 4 percent between
$100,000 and $250,000, 5 percent between $250,000 and $500,-
000 and 6 percent above $500,000. Deductions were allowed for
interest on indebtedness, taxes, business losses, worthless debts,
depreciation, and interest on federal, state, city, or county bonds.
The salaries of all state and local employees and those of the
President and United States Judges then in office were exempt.
The importance of the adoption of the income tax in 1913 cannot
be overestimated. World War I, coming soon afterward, placed
enormous burdens upon the federal fiscal system. The need for
additional revenue was met in large measure by increased income
taxes on individuals and corporations. The corporations tax of 1
percent imposed upon incomes in excess of $5000 in 1909
amounted to slightly more than $35,000,000 in the year the new
income tax was imposed. In 1916, Congress raised the basic income
tax to 2 percent; in 1917, to 4 percent; and, in 1918, to 12
percent. Surtaxes were increased to a maximum of 50 percent in
1917, corporation taxes to 6 percent, and an excess profits tax
imposed. In 1918, surtaxes were raised to a maximum of 65 percent
on all incomes in excess of $500,000. From 1913 on, the country
became increasingly concerned not only with financing the war
and paying the war debt, but with the problem of how to care for
its paupers and discipline its wealth. Income taxes supplied the
controversial formula for unending strife over every proposal for
increased governmental expenditures, public debts, and redistribu-
tion of wealth. They provided a liberal patronage to members of
the legal profession and taught the country new finesse in tax evasion and tax collection.

Finally, the Underwood Tariff gave the Secretary of the Treasury
authority to levy additional duties upon goods produced under
subsidies in foreign nations. It gave the President authority to

negotiate reciprocity agreements, subject to final Congressional approval, and established free trade with the Philippines. It also placed all rates upon an *ad valorem* basis instead of the previous arrangement of specific rates on some individual items and *ad valorem* rates on others. The first two of these provisions were in line with the effort to reduce the whole tariff system to a realistic basis. Foreign trade had remained fairly stationary at about $3,000,000,000 annually from 1906 to 1910, but had increased to more than $4,000,000,000 in 1912. Manufacturers were reaching out for foreign markets. The day when nations were to revert to intense nationalism and seek self-sufficiency behind high tariff walls was still in the future; but men were beginning to recognize that tariffs erected by legislative action could only be reduced successfully by negotiation; and that dumping of foreign goods in our markets could be prevented also by executive action alone. These provisions, too, were congenial to Wilson's dictation of the tariff program. He had thrown his full force back of the Underwood bill,. had, in fact, dictated many of its provisions, to prevent a recurrence of what had happened in Taft's Administration to the Payne-Aldrich Tariff bill and Canadian reciprocity. The President was no longer suggesting a legislative program to Congress; he was dictating it.

THE FEDERAL RESERVE ACT

The second part of the Wilson reform program dealt with the banking and monetary system. The National Bank Act of 1863 had been devised to serve two purposes: the sale of government bonds, and the erection of a uniform banking system under federal control. That Act had been followed by another placing a prohibitive tax upon the note issues of state banks in order to establish a uniform currency system. In 1787, the circulating medium of the country, what there was of it, consisted of specie. State banks emerged during the early part of the nineteenth century-and eventually put into circulation some six thousand varieties of bank notes. These notes were good, bad, or indifferent according to the life of the bank and the distance from it that its notes were circulated. They gave rise to many losses and great inconvenience. Their destruction forced most banks into the national banking system, created a uniform currency based upon the national debt, and made that currency inflexible and rigid. The advent of personal checks toward the end of the century reversed the process, gave state banks a new lease on life, and restored the old evil of lax state banking laws without remedying the rigidity of the monetary system or supplying long-term credits to the agrarian interests. The deflation of 1907 leveled off without precipitating an economic disaster similar to that of the 1870s and 1890s; but discerning men, finally freed from the emotional insanity of the free silver controversy, began to comprehend the need for revision.

Congress passed the Aldrich-Vreeland Act in 1908, the most important feature of which was provision for a monetary commission. This commission carried on a four-year research into foreign fiscal systems. Aldrich had retired from the Senate to devote his entire time to revision of the banking and currency system. Conferences were held with leading bankers and a plan was drawn up and published in 1911. Presented to Congress near the end of Taft's administration, it was completely ignored; but the commission's report, consisting of many volumes, furnished much valuable data for the Committee on Banking and Currency to use in drafting the new Federal Reserve Act. The Aldrich plan called for a system of currency based upon rediscounting of commercial paper, a national reserve association, and 15 regional banks. Its principal feature was a flexible currency. It was endorsed by the American Bankers' Association and by leading economists throughout the country.

There was a recognized need for some system by which banking reserves could be brought together for rediscount purposes, for a safe and elastic circulating medium, and for strict supervision of rediscount rates. As the banking system then operated, the volume of currency in circulation was limited by the something less than $1,000,000,000 bonded indebtedness of the United States. The amount of currency any national bank could issue was limited by the amount of its government bonds on deposit with the Comptroller of the Currency and bore no relation to the commercial needs of its community which might at times greatly exceed the bank's liquid assets. Moreover, banks throughout the entire country became so integrated that available reserves were sent to the money centers where they were used as "call money" for speculation purposes, and were not readily available to meet urgent demands for local credit.

The country, however, was in no mood to let the bankers revise the system. Fear of industrial monopolies had merged into fear of money monopolies. Wilson, as Governor of New Jersey, had said in 1911: "The great monopoly in this country is the money monopoly. So long as that exists, our old variety and freedom and individual energy of development are out of the question." On February 28, 1913, a Committee of the House, under the chairmanship of Arsène P. Pujo of Louisiana, had published a sensational report revealing that J. P. Morgan and Co. held 63 directorships in 39 corporations; the First National Bank of New York, 89 directorships in 49 corporations; the Guaranty Trust Co. of New York, 160 directorships in 76 corporations; the Bankers' Trust Co. of New York, 113 directorships in 55 corporations; the National City Bank of New York, 86 directorships in 47 corporations; the National Bank of Commerce of New York, 149 directorships in 82 corporations; the Chase National Bank of New York, 67 directorships in 48 corporations; the Astor Trust Co., 144 directorships in 63 corporations; the New York Trust Co., 74 directorships in 47 corporations; and similar control of banks, insurance companies, transportation systems, producing and trading corporations, and public utilities by numerous other banking houses in New York, Boston, and Chicago. Concerning this situation the Pujo Committee reported: "Far more dangerous than all that has happened to us in the past in the way of elimination of competition in industry is the control of credit through the domination of these groups over our banks and industries." This report was followed by Louis D. Brandeis' *Other People's Money*, which showed how the large profits to be gleaned from promoting corporate mergers had revolutionized banking, combining investment and commercial banking in the same hands, and subjecting industries, railroads, and public utilities to ever-increasing banking control.

There was no disagreement, therefore, on the need for some

new system of banking and currency; but there was wide difference of opinion on the form it should take. The conservatives, even in Wilson's own party, wanted to follow the Aldrich plan, with a central bank, a currency based upon commercial paper, and credit all under the control of private banking interests. Bryan and his followers were determined that the system should be completely under governmental control. Wilson insisted that the currency must be elastic, that the money reserves should furnish credit where needed for normal business and not be monopolized for speculative purposes, and that the system must be under the supervision of the government. Wilson and Bryan had their way after prolonged debate.

Wilson proposed, in a special message to Congress, that the desired features be provided by basing the currency upon commercial paper instead of government bonds and by placing the new banking system under government control. The Federal Reserve Act as first introduced in the House of Representatives by Carter Glass of Virginia, modified in the Senate and finally passed in December, 1913, completely remodeled the banking and currency system of the nation. National banks, state banks, and trust companies continued to serve the public as before; but the national banks were compelled and others permitted to purchase stock in new federal reserve banks to the amount of 6 percent of their capital and surplus. Twelve such banks were provided, one in each of twelve districts. The function of these new banks in no way touched directly the commercial life of the nation. They were to serve their stockholding banks by rediscounting their commercial paper and granting loans on government securities with new federal reserve bank notes. These new bank notes were to replace the former national bank notes, and were limited in amount only by a required 40 percent gold reserve. Thus every bank belonging to the system was placed under uniform regulation with respect to loans and cash reserves, but was assured sufficient liquid assets at all times to meet the needs of its community. The volume of currency in circulation was expected to rise and fall in each locality and in the nation as a whole in response to seasonal demands and business fluctuations.

Supervision of this new banking structure in the public interest was assured by placing it under a Federal Reserve Board of seven members, including the Secretary of the Treasury and the Comptroller of the Currency. District banks were likewise controlled by a board, consisting of nine members, three of whom were to be appointed by the Federal Reserve Board and six elected by the stockholding banks. The five (six after 1922) members of the Federal Reserve Board were to be appointed by the President with the approval of the Senate. The federal bonds, bearing 2 percent interest, which had been the basis for the old bank notes, were to be retired at the rate of $25,000,000 each year. Speculative inflation was guarded against by prohibiting rediscounting of loans for speculative purposes, by requiring 35 percent reserves in the Federal Reserve banks and 18 percent reserves in member banks, by requiring the issuing bank to retire all rediscounted paper, and by limiting rediscounts to a period of three months for commercial paper and six months for agricultural paper.

The system thus established was designed to serve the needs of agriculture better than the old national banking system had done. It was expected to provide a uniform, flexible currency, to prevent financial panics, and to lessen the influence of private banking monopolies over the commercial life of the nation and the fiscal policies of the government. In spite of its excellence, however, it proved to be deficient in two respects: participation in the Federal Reserve System was not required of state banks, and commercial banking was not divorced from investment banking.

It was assumed at the time that the merits of the Federal Reserve System would prove too attractive for state banks to resist, but events proved otherwise. Not more than one third of the country's banks ever joined, although those that did join controlled more than 80 percent of the combined banking resources. Outstanding leaders in the financial and commercial world urged from time to time that all banks be brought under the system. Action was opposed by others on the ground that it would be an unwarranted assumption of federal power and nothing was done until the banking crisis of 1933 forced Congress to take further steps to strengthen the banking structure.

INDUSTRIAL RELATIONS

Great emphasis had been placed upon destroying the huge industrial corporations during the administrations of Roosevelt and Taft. Roosevelt had won popular acclaim by prosecuting the Northern Securities Company and winning a verdict of dissolution from the Supreme Court in 1904. There had followed during the next eight years, more than one hundred suits against such outstanding corporations as the Standard Oil Company, the American Tobacco Company, the United States Steel Corporation, the International Harvester Company, the National Cash Register Company and the General Electric Company. Roosevelt had, in addition, advocated federal charters for all corporations engaged in interstate commerce; and both he and Taft had urged that specific practices such as holding companies, stock watering, etc., be outlawed. In spite of all the public agitation and government activity, it was clearly evident by 1913 that competition had not been restored nor monopolistic growth retarded. There was a definite trend, therefore, of sentiment in favor of regulation of trusts instead of attempted dissolution. Congress responded to that sentiment with the Federal Trade Commission Act. There was also a clearer conception of how the huge corporations were formed, and popular attention shifted from the corporations themselves to the financiers who controlled them. The Pujo report had showed an amazing interlocking control among the several great banking houses through directorships held by such men as J. P. Morgan, Thomas S. Lamont, Henry P. Davidson, and William H. Porter. *Other People's Money* had shown the profits of promotion. For the first time, the public at large learned how J. P. Morgan and Company received the major portion of $62,500,-000 for promoting the U. S. Steel Corporation and equally large commissions for their services in organizing other corporations including the International Harvester Company, the American Telephone and Telegraph Company and the General Electric Company. Brandeis' principal admonition was that "the Sherman Law should be supplemented both by providing more efficient judicial machinery, and by creating a commission with administrative functions to aid in enforcing the law."

In writing the Federal Reserve Act, Congress made an honest effort to reach the roots of the evil by impounding the reserve funds of the nation's banks in the twelve Federal Reserve banks and by forbidding the rediscounting of "notes, drafts, or bills covering merely investments or issued or drawn for the purpose of carrying or trading in stock, bonds, or other investment securities, except bonds and notes of the Government of the United States." At that time there was less than $100,000,000 in government bonds available for rediscount purposes. The reluctance of many banks to enter the Federal Reserve System and the tremendous increase in government bonds during the World War made available to the investment banker and to the gambling public tremendous sums for the sale and purchase of securities which those who drafted the Federal Reserve Act never intended the new system to provide.

Congress followed this Act with the Federal Trade Commission Act and the Clayton Act. The Sherman Act had attempted to regulate the relationships of business enterprise and preserve competition by outlawing combinations in restraint of trade. The broad language of the Act was purposely used in order to prevent corporations from evading the law and to enable the Department of Justice to bring them before the Court for a wide range of offenses. In actual practice, however, that purpose was defeated. Juries had shown an indisposition to convict; the government had emphasized disintegration of trusts rather than punishment for violations of the law; and the Supreme Court (1911) had decided that the law prohibited only unreasonable restraints of trade. It was obvious that public opinion was no longer disturbed by the mere size of a business organization, and that it now regarded the money power rather than the corporation directors as the invisible force behind government and the "enemy of the people." Public opinion was also turning from the idea of destroying to the idea of regulation. The Senate Interstate Commerce Committee recommended in March, 1913, that the Sherman Anti-Trust Act be amended so as to prescribe certain conditions under which persons and corporations might engage in commerce and that a commission be created to supervise corporations in the same manner as the Interstate Commerce Commission supervised the railroads. Wilson, in his trust message to Congress on January 20, 1914, more definitely requested a commission with wider powers than those enjoyed by the Bureau of Corporations.

The Clayton Act (October 15, 1914) outlawed price discriminations, which tended to lessen competition or create monopolies; tying contracts, which prohibited purchasers from handling the products of competitors; intercorporate stock holdings by which one corporation acquired participation in the conduct of its competitors; interlocking directorates of banks having capital revenues aggregating more than $5,000,000; and interlocking directorates of competing corporations capitalized at more than $1,000,000, and of corporations and common carriers. The provision of the Sherman Act allowing threefold damages to persons injured by violations of the law was continued; officers of corporations were made personally responsible for violations of the law; and complaints could be taken directly to the Federal Trade Commission for relief through cease and desist orders. The act also stated that "the labor of a human being is not a commodity or article of commerce" and that nothing in the anti-trust laws should be construed "to forbid the existence and operation of labor, agricultural, or horticultural organizations."

The Federal Trade Commission Act (September 26, 1914) set up an administrative agency to search out and eliminate abuses in business life. It was designed for a dual purpose; to compel business enterprises to be fair to each other, and to serve the public interest. It was to be composed of five members, appointed by the President with the consent of the Senate for a period of seven years. The Act declared "unfair methods of competition in commerce" to be unlawful. It gave to the Commission the power to investigate all corporations engaged in commerce, to require reports from such corporations, and to issue cease and desist orders against specific practices. It charged the Commission specifically with the duty of following up all court decrees obtained under the anti-trust laws and reporting its findings to the Attorney-

General. Thus the Commission was charged with performing the duties of the former Bureau of Corporations, was made the special agent of the Department of Justice, and was given the independent and primary responsibility of purging business of the dishonest practices. The expectation that the Commission would succeed in restoring the competition which the Sherman Act had failed to preserve was never realized, partly because economic security rather than economic opportunity became the aspiration of most people in society and partly because purging business of dishonest practices was a herculean task as revealed by the experience of the NRA in later years. The Commission did, however, through its fact-finding activities, become one of the most valuable departments of the government in the service of the people. In fact, for some time, it seemed to be the only government commission interested in protecting the consumer. During Wilson's Administration it received more than two thousand complaints and issued 379 cease and desist orders against specific unfair practices, including false advertising, false statements about competitors, bribery, adulteration of goods, misbranding of fabrics, etc. Cooperating with the Department of Justice, it secured the dissolution of the International Harvester Company (1918), and the Corn Products Refining Company (1919), and an agreement from the five great meat-packing companies (Swift, Armour, Morris, Wilson, and Cudahy) not to operate stockyards, terminal railways, market newspapers, retail meat or grocery markets, or to sell milk and cream.

Little was accomplished in the way of consent decrees during the next twelve years. It was a period in which business was given a free hand by the government. Economic pathology was distinctly foreign to the prevailing philosophy. In 1933, however, the Commission scored its greatest victory since the meat packers' consent decree of 1920. The General Electric and Westinghouse companies surrendered their stock holdings in the Radio Corporation and the radio industry was purged of its interlocking control. The monopoly of radio patents which had so seriously restricted competition and maintained discriminatory prices was eliminated. Meanwhile, however, an investigation of the power and light industry had such far-reaching consequences as alone to have justified the Commission's existence. Senator Thomas Walsh of Montana introduced a resolution in the Senate in 1928 designed to set up a Senate Committee to investigate that industry. Power interests, fearful of Walsh who had been instrumental in pushing the oil lease fraud cases to a conclusion, succeeded in having the task assigned to the Federal Trade Commission. The Commission, after a long and searching scrutiny of financial and propaganda practices of the power interests, presented a monumental report to the Senate. That report was so widely quoted and furnished the data for such an amazing number of books, magazine articles, and newspaper editorials, that it actually reversed the entire nation's attitude toward the question of government regulation of public utilities. It served, more than any other factor, to purge the educational system of subtle propaganda which was beginning to creep in. It altered the course of the prevailing economic thought in the nation at large. It forced the utilities themselves to make some gesture in the direction of better business practices.

LABOR

The feature of the Clayton Act which provoked more comment at the time than the anti-trust provisions was Section 20, relating to labor.

The open hostility toward labor shown by President Cleveland when he sent federal troops to Chicago during the Pullman strike and authorized the railway operators to deputize 5000 private guards as United States marshals, was not repeated in the twentieth century. The first evidence of a changed attitude by the two major parties was in the Democratic platform of 1896 which denounced the black list and government by injunction, and advocated both arbitration in industrial disputes and the establishment of a Department of Labor. The party did not deviate from this attitude during its minority position and some action was certain following Wilson's election. Labor had suffered a severe handicap from the widespread use of injunctions and from the common law doctrine of "malicious combination" which placed it at the mercy of the social and economic ideas of the judges and left it at a loss as to what action was or was not lawful.

Roosevelt denied the coal operators the use of federal troops to break the strike of 1902. Instead, he indicated a willingness to seize and operate the mines to the extent of supplying public needs unless operation were resumed while the issues involved were being studied by a commission of his choice. In his message to Congress, December 5, 1905, he said: "There has been a demand for depriving the courts of the power to issue injunctions in labor disputes. Such special limitations of the equity powers of our courts would be most unwise. It is true that some judges have misused this power; but this does not justify a denial of the power any more than an improper exercise of the power to call a strike by a labor leader would justify the denial of the right to strike." One year later, he said: "It is at least doubtful whether a law abolishing altogether the use of injunctions in such cases would stand the test of courts." He did advocate, however, a required hearing after due notice before the issuance of an injunction, and (April 27, 1908) trials for contempt before another judge. His position with respect to the question was admirably stated in his message of December 3, 1907, when he said:

Instances of abuse in the granting of injunctions in labor disputes continue to occur. . . . The question is becoming more and more one of prime importance and unless the courts themselves deal with it in effective manner, it is certain ultimately to demand some form of legislative action. It would be most unfortunate for our social welfare if we should permit many honest and law-abiding citizens to feel that they had just cause for regarding our courts with hostility.

In the election of 1908, violent attacks upon the judiciary were made by labor leaders. They demanded that all injunctions should be prohibited except for the protection of property rights and that jury trials should be required in all contempt cases. Roosevelt disapproved most heartily of these suggested remedies and President Taft (March 4, 1909) said:

Take away from the Courts, if it could be taken away, the power to issue injunctions in labor disputes, and it would create a privileged class among the laborers and save the lawless among their number from a most needful remedy available for all men for the protection of their business against lawless invasion. The proposition that business is not a property or pecuniary right which can be protected by equitable injunction is utterly without foundation in precedent or reason.

Congress failed to act concerning the Sherman Act or injunctions during Roosevelt's Administration. Meanwhile, in *Gompers v. Bucks Stove and Range Co.* (1911), the Supreme Court gave a sweeping interpretation to the Sherman Act with respect to labor unions in these words:

It covered any illegal means by which interstate commerce is restrained, whether by unlawful combinations of capital, or . . . of labor; and we think also whether the restraint be occasioned by unlawful contracts, trusts, pooling arrangements, black lists, boycotts, coercion, threats, intimidation, and whether these be made effective, in whole or in part, by acts, words or printed matter.

In Taft's Administration, however, Congress added a provision to the appropriation bill prohibiting the use of any funds for the prosecution of labor unions under the Sherman Act. President Taft vetoed the measure, but a similar one was signed by President Wilson under protest. Each succeeding appropriation bill contained the same restraint without protest from any executive after Wilson. Organized labor would have benefited greatly had Congress refrained from further action, because only the government could prosecute unions under the Sherman Act; but the Clayton Act was passed and approved on October 14, 1914.

Section 20 forbade any judge to issue injunctions in labor disputes "unless necessary to prevent irreparable injury to property, or to a property right." It legalized strikes and strike benefits. It forbade injunctions prohibiting strikers from "recommending, advising, or persuading others by peaceful means" to cease work; "or from attending at any place where any such person or persons may lawfully be, for the purpose of peacefully obtaining or communicating information . . . or from ceasing to patronize or to employ any party to such dispute . . . or from peaceable assembling in a lawful manner, and for lawful purposes; or from doing any act or thing which might lawfully be done in the absence of such dispute by any party thereto." This statute marked the culmination of two decades of agitation to place workingmen and their employers on the same plane in industrial warfare. It appeared to be and the public was led to believe that it was an assertion of the principle that the legislative and not the judicial branch of the government should define public policy toward industrial warfare. It appeared to the layman that certain acts had been made legal at all times and under all circumstances. Every act specified in the law had previously been held unlawful by the courts to some degree. It was the aim of the progressives in Congress to apply to relations between capital and labor the same principle of competition that was regarded so essential in industrial and business life. They recognized the value of competitive economic strength between capital and labor and sought to justify whatever damages might result from testing that strength according to certain rules. In that respect, it stands out in sharp contrast to the principle of compulsory arbitration of industrial disputes then being widely discussed throughout the country. It was the last attempt of Congress to deal with the fundamental aspects of the labor problem until Section 7a of the National Recovery Act, based upon an entirely different principle, was written in 1933.

The Clayton Act was hailed, prematurely, as the Magna Charta of labor. It was in line with the philosophy of Samuel Gompers, President of the American Federation of Labor from 1886 to 1924. Gompers always insisted that labor should remain unhampered by government interference to pit its economic strength against that of capital. He said, over and over again, that compulsory arbitration would lead to the establishment of labor courts and bitter strife between capital and labor for control of the government in order to control those courts. He stood, therefore, for absolute freedom of labor to organize its strength and thus increase its bargaining power in its relations with capital. There had been no agreement in Congress, however, as to whether the Act as finally passed merely legalized unions or went further and relieved them from injunctions against their activities. It was another case of Congress, unable to agree upon the terms of an act, writing it in ambiguous language and dumping the dispute into the lap of the Supreme Court for settlement by interpretation of the law. The Court decided that the words "lawfully" and "legitimate" gave meaning to the Act and merely legalized the past practices of the Courts with respect to injunctions (*Duplex Printing Press Co.* v. *Deering,* 1921). Even more important, however, was the fact that the Clayton Act opened the federal courts to direct suits for injunctions by corporations as well as by the government. But the failure of the Clayton Act to relieve labor organizations fully from the handicaps of the common law and the failure of labor to utilize its potential strength advantageously are two separate and distinct things. Labor's failure, as we shall see later, was largely due to its own incompetence and is not chargeable to the Courts or to the failure of the Clayton Act.

In addition to the labor provisions of the Clayton Act, Congress passed the Seaman's Act (1915) and the Adamson Act (1916). The Seaman's Act was sponsored by Senator Robert M. La Follette for the purpose of bringing some order and decency into labor relations in the merchant marine. Seamen were relieved by the Act from imprisonment for desertion and from corporal punishment. They were given the right to one half of all back pay when their ship reached port; and they were protected from incompetent fellow crewmen by a requirement that 65 percent of all deckhands must be able seamen. Minimum standards were established also for food, living quarters, and life-saving equipment.

The Adamson Act was passed to avert a threatened tie-up of the nation's transportation facilities. The Railway Brotherhoods were asking for a standard eight- instead of a ten-hour day, and for time-and-one-half for overtime. Wilson was unable to bring about a settlement by mediation. The foreign situation was too delicate to permit a stoppage of railroad transportation. Wilson asked Congress for legislation establishing the eight-hour day, and for authority to seize the railroads and to draft all employees and executives into the national service in event of military necessity. Congress passed the Adamson Act, establishing the eight-hour day for railway employees and a fact-finding commission preparatory to future railway legislation.

The next important change in government attitude toward labor was validation by the Supreme Court of "yellow-dog" contracts. The simplest form of yellow-dog contracts consisted of an agreement dictated by the employer and signed by the worker that he would not join a union so long as he remained in the employ of the company. There were many variations from this simple form but, for the most part, they were anti-union contracts, open-shop contracts, or company-union contracts. They made their appearance in the West Virginia coal fields in 1907, spread into the Pennsylvania coal fields in the early twenties, to the Lynn, Massachusetts, shoe industry in 1923, and then to the Union Pacific and the Chicago, Rock Island and Pacific railroads. They possessed few of the fundamental elements of a contract at law because coercion of the worst sort entered into the signing of the agreement. Few laborers ever signed them except through fear of losing their jobs, back of which, of course, was the cruel certainty of starvation or worse for their families. They were given sanctity by the courts, however, and added significance by the granting of injunctions for their enforcement. They became the favorite non-union weapon of capital after the *Hitchman Coal Company v. Mitchell* decision (1917) legalized them, and forbade union organizers from proselytizing among workers who were bound by them. The broader economic significance of the combination of yellow-dog contracts and injunctions was clearly revealed in the Hitchman case. The coal fields of Ohio, Pennsylvania, Indiana, and Illinois were already unionized and hours and wages fairly stabilized before the coal fields of West Virginia were opened with non-union labor working under yellow-dog contracts. The United Mine Workers of America set out to unionize the West Virginia fields as the only possible way to save their existing security from the devastating effects of cheap coal mined by non-union labor. They were enjoined from doing so by the Circuit Court in 1907, and the injunction was sustained by the Supreme Court in the Hitchman case. The result was chaos in the coal industry and the most deplorable exploitation of labor in southern coal mines of any industrial section of the United States. State legislatures, meanwhile, in large industrial states like Massachusetts, Connecticut, New York, Pennsylvania, Ohio, and Illinois, had passed laws outlawing yellow-dog contracts; but the Supreme Court in *Coppage v. Kansas* (1915) had invalidated such laws as a denial of the freedom of contract.

The Clayton Act and Hitchman decision were followed closely by World War I. Little progress was made during the period of postwar reaction toward finding a more satisfactory formula for solving the problems of capital and labor than the traditional trial of economic strength within the limits set by the courts. The next action by Congress was the Norris-La Guardia Act of March 20, 1932.

AGRICULTURE

The farming population of the country received its share of attention from the Wilson Administration. The farmers' simple agrarian economy of earlier days had disappeared. As a producer of staple crops for sale abroad and in the eastern industrial centers, his fortunes were closely linked to the management of the great railway systems and the protective tariff. The Interstate Commerce Act, the Sherman Anti-Trust Act, the Elkins Act, and the Hepburn Act had sought to free him from the tyranny of the railroads by eliminating rate discriminations and rebates. The Underwood Tariff Act removed import duties from a greatly expanded list of commodities he purchased as a consumer. The rapid introduction of farm machinery had placed the farmer at the mercy of the manufacturing monopolies. The new tariff act aimed to correct that, indirectly, by reducing the tariff rates behind which monopolies were sustained; and the Clayton and Federal Trade Commission Acts, directly, by challenging the fundamental structure and trade practices of such industrial combinations. The Clayton Act went still farther and exempted agricultural cooperatives from the operation of the anti-trust laws. In 1918, Congress passed the Webb-Pomerene Act permitting the organization of export trade associations, a distinct concession to agriculture as well as to those manufacturers selling in the world markets. The farmer had found difficulty in financing his operations even to the extent of obtaining short-term loans for seed, fertilizer, and new farm machinery. The Federal Reserve Act removed the restrictions of the National Bank Act against loans by national banks on farm mortgages and permitted such loans for five-year periods to the amount of 50 percent of the valuation. It allowed the new Federal Reserve banks to rediscount agricultural paper for periods up to six months; and it impounded reserves in the regional banks in order to keep them available for local needs of agriculture and business.

The most distressing aspect of the farm problem, however, was the increase in farm mortgages. A long period of small profits or operating deficits coupled with the increase of land values through extraneous forces (immigration and the westward movement), larger initial costs, and ultimate replacement expenses had placed mortgages on 31 percent of the farms in the United States before 1900. These were fixed charges against the returns of a better day which never came. The worst situation in this respect was in the agricultural region of the North Central States. Congress debated the situation for nearly two years and then, in May, 1916, passed the Federal Farm Loan Act. The purpose of the Act was to create banking machinery suited to the farmers' needs for long-term credits at reduced interest rates and to place farm finances upon a sound and stable basis sufficient to make them an attractive field of investment for conservative private capital.

The Federal Farm Loan Act created twelve Federal Land banks. Their initial capital had to be secured in a different way from that of the Federal Reserve banks because there were no existing land banks similar to the commercial banks which could be brought into the system. The federal government, therefore, undertook to subscribe for all stock not taken by private capital. Each of the banks was capitalized at $750,000 and of the $9,000,-000 required, the government supplied all but $200,000. There was a steady reduction thereafter until, by 1930, the government had withdrawn almost entirely from the system. The banks were under the supervision of a board of five members, including the Secretary of the Treasury. There were no subsidiary banks, but farm loan associations instead. The membership of these farm loan associations was made up of farmers who wished to borrow from the land banks and who bought stock in the associations to the amount of 5 percent of their loans. Loans, as in the Federal Reserve System, were restricted to 50 percent of valuation, but an additional 20 percent of the value of buildings and other improvements could be secured. The farm loan associations were to recommend the loans, the land banks to furnish the money. The banks were authorized to sell bonds secured by the mortgages and such bonds bore the tax exempt privileges of government bonds. Loans were to be amortized over a period of thirty-three years, interest rates not to exceed 6 percent, and profits distributed to the members of the loan associations. There were 4659 farm loan associations by 1930 and about $1,000,000,000 of farm mortgages owned by the twelve land banks. That sum represented little more than the total annual interest payment on the total indebtedness of the American farmer. The combined holdings of the Federal Land banks and the Joint Stock Land banks in that year were not more than one fifth of the total value of farm mortgages. Insurance companies held 23 percent of the total, commercial banks 10 percent, farmers and other individuals in rural communities 30 percent. The land bank system did much to set uniform, reasonable standards in agricultural financing; but it did not fulfill the complete expectations of its sponsors.

Then other laws, greatly expanding federal power and services directly affecting agriculture, were also passed by Congress. The Smith-Lever Act (1914) made available federal money, to be matched by the states, for county farm-demonstration work. The Smith-Hughes Act (1917) created a Federal Board of Vocational Education and appropriated funds for teachers of agriculture, and domestic science in the schools. The Federal Road Aid Act inaugurated the appropriations of funds for highway improvement. These latter acts were passed under the constitutional authority of Congress to tax and spend for the general welfare. The practice of making unconditional grants to the states for education and internal improvements was based on ample precedent. The device of making conditional grants followed as a natural sequence. By 1917, Congress was requiring the states to match its subsidies with an equal amount of money. Later it began to set up boards and commissions to fix standards and to approve and exercise supervision over the projects for which appropriations were made. It represents one way by which Congress sought to meet the demands of a changing social and economic life in spite of constitutional limitations.

THE NEW COLONIAL POLICY

The platforms of the Democratic party, adopted at Denver, July 10, 1908, and at Baltimore, June 27, 1912, condemned in identical language "the experiment in imperialism as an inexcusable blunder which has involved us in enormous expense, brought us weakness instead of strength, and laid our nation open to the charge of abandoning a fundamental doctrine of self-government." Both platforms favored independence for the Philippines "as soon as a stable government" could be established and the "full enjoyment of the rights and privileges of a territorial form of government" for Alaska and Puerto Rico. The Progressive party, meeting at Chicago, August 5, 1912, promised "the people of the Territory of Alaska the same measure of local self-government that was given to other American Territories." Shortly afterward (August 24) the Democrats and Republican Insurgents forced through Congress the act organizing territorial government in Alaska, and Wilson's election assured a definite change of policy in Puerto Rico and the Philippines. Congress passed the Jones Act, reorganizing the government of the Philippines on August 29, 1916; an Organic Act for Puerto Rico on March 2, 1917; and, the following day, an Act for the Government of the Virgin Islands which had been purchased from Denmark on January 25, 1917.

From 1901 to 1907, the governing body in the Philippines was the Philippine Commission, consisting of seven members, only three of whom were Filipinos. It was both a legislative and administrative body. The first Philippine Assembly was elected in 1907 and, thereafter, the Commission served as the upper house of the legislature. The Filipinos were given a fourth member of the Commission by Act of Congress in 1908. President Wilson's first action was to appoint a fifth Filipino to the Commission, thus giving the native people control of both houses of the legislature. He appointed Francis B. Harrison Governor General with instructions to allow the legislature wide latitude in the exercise of their new power of self-government. The most significant feature of the new regime was an experiment in state socialism including government enterprises in the fields of transportation, banking, mining, and manufacturing. The Jones Act definitely committed the United States to Philippine independence as soon as they had demonstrated their ability to maintain a stable government under the new policy of self-government. It abolished the Philippine Commission and the Assembly, replacing them with a Senate and House of Representatives, both elective. Senators and Representatives were required to be able to read and write English or Spanish and reside in the district from which they were elected. The legislature was given control of the franchise, power to override the veto of the Governor General by a two thirds vote of each house, and complete authority to organize all executive departments except the Department of the Interior and that of Instruction. The latter was placed under the control of a newly created executive official: the vice-governor. The Governor General and the vice-governor were the only officials appointed by the President and Senate of the United States. Governor General Harrison, by executive order, created a Council of State (1918) consisting of the Governor General, the President of the Senate, the Speaker of the House of Representatives, and the Secretaries of the six executive departments. Its purpose was to promote cooperation between the executive and legislative branches of the government, but it actually determined the policies of the government until abolished by executive order of Governor General Leonard Wood, Harrison's successor.

The Organic Act for the government of Puerto Rico gave that dependency the same measure of self-government accorded to territories in their final stage without, however, incorporating it as a territory preparatory to statehood. United States citizenship and virtually all of the fundamental rights guaranteed to the individual in the Constitution were extended to the citizens of Puerto Rico.

The legislature was to consist of a Senate and a House of Representatives, both elective. It was given power to override the Governor's veto by a two thirds vote of each house. Only the Governor, the Commissioner of Education, the Attorney-General and the Justices of the Supreme Court were to be appointed by the President of the United States. The Secretaries of the other executive departments were to be appointed by the Governor with the approval of the Puerto Rican Senate. A Delegate to Congress replaced the resident Commissioner at Washington.

Negotiations for the purchase of the Virgin Islands were begun in 1901 as a part of the Isthmian policy. They were of no value except as outer defenses for the proposed Panama and Nicaraguan Canals, having an area of only 132 square miles and a population of only 25,000, most of whom were illiterate and poverty-stricken Negroes and half-breeds. They were not finally secured from Denmark until 1917. Framing a government, March 3, 1917, Congress retained the Danish Code of Laws, allowed Danish citizens either to retain their citizenship or to become citizens of the United States and gave all others the status of nationals. The President was authorized to appoint a governor with the approval of the Senate. Jurisdiction was given to the Secretary of the Navy, as was the case with Samoa and Guam. The latter Island had been seized by the United States during the Spanish-American War. American Samoa, important for the harbor of Pago Pago on the island of Tutuila, was acquired in a tripartite agreement with Great Britain and Germany in 1900. Congress did not make provision for their government and they continued under the absolute authority of the President as Commander in Chief of the Navy.

Congress placed the government of the Canal Zone in the hands of the President on April 28, 1904, having previously provided for the appointment of an Isthmian Canal Commission. The Commission, appointed March 6, 1904, consisted of the Governor of the Canal Zone and six other members. It was given complete legislative and administrative powers. It established several departments of administration, including Public Health, Justice and Education. The Zone was divided into four administrative districts, each with a district court. A Supreme Court of three Justices was provided and both Civil and Criminal Codes enacted. The Commission continued to govern until the Panama Canal Act was passed by Congress August 24, 1912. By this Act, Congress resumed direct legislative authority over the Zone, provided for the eventual removal of all persons except government employees, and gave the President administrative authority only over it. Governors thereafter were appointed from the Engineers Corps of the Army. The Act also created the Zone into a judicial district with appeals to the Fifth Circuit Court of the United States.

10

Law Administration
and the Courts

W E have seen how the period under discussion was pre-
eminently a period of social and economic change; how the individual no less than society as a whole was compelled by forces
entirely beyond his control to alter his mode of living, his habits
of thought, his attitudes toward old and strange, new institutions.
It was a bewildering age; an age of intellectual as well as social
ferment; an age in which men and women were groping, often
ignorantly and blindly, for new values in life. The legislative program discussed in the preceding chapters represents their effort to
solve their problems and crystallize their experiences by experimental legislation; but from the enactment of legislation to the fulfillment of its objectives is a long and difficult process. It involves the
support of public opinion, the vigilance and capacity of enforcement agencies, the development of administrative procedure, and
the process of judicial review. It is essential for the student of history to remember that the individual citizen lives under the protection of a formidable list of safeguards provided in the common
law and the constitutions of both state and nation; that, in recognition of the diverse social and economic interests of widely separated sections, specific powers only are delegated to the federal
government; that, because legislators represent the people and are
directly responsible to their ever-changing moods, the protection

of legislative prerogatives is of vital importance; and that society functions under the rules of the common law in every case where it has not been modified or superseded by statute law. The subsequent history of reform legislation is of more historical importance than its enactment.

Every reform movement spawns its demagogues. Change and progress are not synonymous terms; but it is not always possible to know where statesmanship ends and politics begin. Moreover, the purging of political parties is ofttimes an indispensable preliminary step to legitimate reform; but when party discipline weakens, pressure politics flourishes. The result is sumptuary laws which remain unenforced because they invade the accepted limits of personal judgment or are invalidated by the courts because they violate the constitutional guarantees of individual liberty. In the first instance, their overzealous sponsors denounce the non-conformists, seek to destroy them, and succeed only in weakening the majesty of the law in general. In the second instance, they denounce the courts as reactionary and demand that they be shorn of the power of judicial review. Laws against the dissemination of birth control information, the teaching of evolution, the sale of cigarettes, amusements on Sunday, etc., proved unenforceable and were gradually abandoned or modified. They reached their climax in the momentous contest over prohibition. Another type of reform legislation was that which was clearly experimental in character or arose out of social conditions peculiar to a limited geographical section. Either because they proved to be unsatisfactory where tried or had a limited appeal, such laws were confined to a relatively few states. Direct primary, preferential primary, initiative, referendum and recall legislation belonged to this class. It included the Jim Crow laws of the southern states, the peculiar divorce laws of Nevada and South Carolina, and the farmers' co-operative laws of Nebraska and Wisconsin. Laws which failed to accomplish fully the purpose for which they were enacted because of lax or inefficient efforts at enforcement include the school attendance laws, the anti-trust laws, safety and health codes, and anti-lynching laws. The purposes of the Federal Reserve Act were thwarted, in part, by the inefficiency of the Federal Reserve Board.

The same may be said of the subsequent history of the Interstate Commerce Act and the several state utility laws. Finally, the test of constitutionality upset the plans of those who sought by state legislation to abolish private schools and restrict the freedom of the press; of states which attempted to regulate interstate commerce; of Congress when it attempted to reach behind interstate commerce and control child labor in the factories, or when it delegated legislative prerogatives to the executive or to administrative agencies. Obviously, space does not permit nor does relative historical importance justify a detailed treatment of much of this administrative and judicial history. There are, however, certain laws in the enactment and subsequent history of which are revealed all the surging impulsiveness of reform, the effective use of pressure politics by minority groups, the conflict of opposing philosophies, the problems of law enforcement and the human frailties of judicial bodies.

PUBLIC OPINION AND REFORM

Back in the winter of 1873, Congress was prevailed upon by Anthony Comstock to pass the first of a series of laws known as the "Comstock Laws." Comstock was a fanatic on the subject of moral reform. He believed that the salvation of the human race depended upon driving out of existence every reference to sex life with which young people might come into contact. He therefore took advantage of the prevailing sentiment against obscenity to write into the national statutes the most drastic prohibitions ever attempted before the Volstead Act. These Laws excluded from the mails, on penalty of five thousand dollars' fine and five years' imprisonment "every obscene, lewd, or lascivious, and every filthy book, pamphlet, picture, paper, letter, writing, print, or other publication of an indecent character, and every article or thing designed, adapted, or intended for preventing conception . . . and every written or printed card, letter, circular, book, pamphlet, advertisement, or notice of any kind giving information directly or indirectly . . . by what means conception may be prevented . . ." There followed a series of laws in all but two states, some directly forbidding the dissemination of birth-control information and others directed against obscenity which required definition by the courts; and, because the two terms were definitely linked in the federal statute, they proved to be as effective as the direct prohibition itself.

Comstock was then made a special agent by Postmaster-General Marshall Jewell, with authorization from Congress to enforce the postal laws. He held the position without salary until Taft's Postmaster-General G. B. Cortelyou forced him to become a regularly appointed postal inspector in 1906. His salary was paid meanwhile by the Y.M.C.A. At the same time he was Secretary of the Society for the Suppression of Vice. The society was incorporated in New York, authorized by the state to enforce its law, make arrests and receive one half of all fines imposed by the courts. No more typical example exists in the history of the country of the evils of conferring law enforcement powers upon private individuals and associations. Comstock's career was a dreary succession of 3873 arrests and 2911 convictions, the hounding of physicians and social hygienists, and the persecution of liberals everywhere.

Few people have been arrested and convicted under the federal statute in spite of its widespread violation; but it, and the several state laws, remained upon the statute books as insidious implements for the persecution of individuals who could not otherwise be reached. They deterred honorable physicians, hospitals, and clinics from applying scientific methods in individual cases, stimulated surreptitious circulation of harmful or worthless contraceptives, and denied information to the class of people who needed it most. Soon after the federal law was enacted a petition for its repeal signed by several thousand people was presented to Congress. The petition said in part: "That mental, moral and physical health and safety are better secured and preserved by virtue resting upon liberty and knowledge, than upon ignorance enforced by governmental supervision. That even error may be safely let free, where truth is free to combat it. That the greatest danger to a republic is the insidious repression of the liberties of the people." Nothing was accomplished and little more attempted toward repeal until Margaret Sanger was arrested in 1914. Her indictment led to the organization of the National Birth Control League. Thereafter, there was ever-increasing agitation of the subject with the opposition to repeal both of national and state statutes coming principally from the National Council of Catholic Women. It is interesting to note that the Methodist Church came out strongly for birth control; and that, on another phase of the reform movement, prohibition of the liquor traffic, the two groups should have taken exactly opposite positions. The religious aspects of the alignment, however, can easily be overemphasized. Far more significant in the reluctance of Congress and state legislatures to repeal these laws was the deeply ingrained inhibition against discussion of matters pertaining to sex and fear of the consequences of repeal upon the moral life of young people. They preferred to allow the laws to remain upon the statute books and gradually fall into disuse and be forgotten.

The history of the prohibition of the liquor traffic is quite different. The Eighteenth Amendment became a part of the Constitution of the United States on January 29, 1919. It was the crowning achievement of the temperance and prohibition forces. It was the beginning, also, of a disastrous experiment: that of writing a prohibitory statute into the fundamental law. The prohibition appeal was not dependent upon the agitation of a small reform group. It flourished because of the persistent lawlessness of the liquor interests, the reeking vileness of the saloon, and the inability of state and local governments to control effectually the liquor traffic. The saloon was a colorful institution. It served a useful social function as the chummery of the proletariat. It fostered intemperance; but that was its least objectionable feature. It sheltered vice and crime, maintained a consortium with politics, and resisted all efforts at control in the interest of decency and respectability. It was an open defiance of good government, clean living, and social security. Its relation to the prohibition movement is clearly shown by the platforms of the political parties in 1932 which pledged the Democrats to "effectively prevent the return of the saloon" and the Republicans to "safeguard our citizens everywhere from the return of the saloon."

The second factor was the inability of state governments to

control the liquor traffic. New Hampshire and Massachusetts established state liquor license systems in the 1840s. The laws were reviewed by the Supreme Court in 1847. The decision of the Court, written by Chief Justice Roger B. Taney, held that liquor shipments into a state were under the control of Congress by virtue of the interstate commerce clause of the Constitution; but, since Congress had not assumed control, a state might do so under its police powers. In 1886, Iowa placed restrictions on importations of liquor into the state and the subject again came before the Supreme Court in the case of *Bowman v. Chicago & N. W. Railway Company* (1888). This time the Court pronounced the Iowa statute unconstitutional in a new doctrine: that when Congress failed to legislate on a particular phase of interstate commerce, the presumption was that Congress desired it to remain unregulated. This decision rendered state governments impotent to prevent liquor shipments into dry territory and Congress failed to supply the deficiency.

Congress then passed the Wilson Law (1890) delegating the power over the liquor traffic in interstate commerce to the states; but the Supreme Court (*Rhodes v. Iowa*, 1898) held that a commodity remained in interstate commerce until delivered to the consignee. The Wilson Act was then amended by the Webb-Kenyon Act (1913). This Act regulated interstate commerce by removing all immunities of liquors in interstate commerce. The Supreme Court upheld its constitutionality by a 5 to 4 decision; but President Taft, afterward Chief Justice of the Supreme Court, had vetoed the Act as being unconstitutional, Attorney-General George W. Wickersham held it to be unconstitutional, so did George Sutherland, later a Supreme Court Justice, and Elihu Root, a distinguished authority on constitutional law. This fear of a future reversal by the Court in a new case which might arise accounts for the provision in the Twenty-first Amendment giving Congress authority to protect dry states.

It was the southern states with their heavy Negro population and the agricultural states of the Middle West that fostered the national prohibition movement. The industrial states of the East were opposed to it. The Constitution could be amended, however, against the wishes of the twelve states having more than a majority of the total population of the country; and such an amendment could only be removed by another amendment which twelve of the smaller states, with a combined population of less than 6,000,-000 in a total of more than 100,000,000, could prevent. The full possibilities of this minority rule system were not applied to the prohibition question, but approximately that is what happened. The Methodist Church fostered the Women's Christian Temperance Union, the Board of Temperance, Prohibition and Public Morals, and the Anti-Saloon League. The stronghold of the movement was in the Middle West and South. Skillfully organized independently of political parties, the prohibition forces represented a minority in most governmental units, but were able to control both parties by pressure politics. State prohibition laws were forced through legislatures contrary to the wishes of a majority of the people. The fight was carried into Congress on the eve of the World War, conducted under the direction of Wayne B. Wheeler, General Counsel of the Anti-Saloon League, and through the agency of the most powerful lobby ever established at Washington.

The resolution submitting the Eighteenth Amendment to the states was passed in December, 1917, when the country was in a mood to make any sacrifices congenial to a successful prosecution of the war. Patriotism was added to the already strong appeal. A seven-year limit on ratification was engineered by Senator Boise Penrose with the confident expectation that the Amendment would go by default. To the surprise of many, however, the Amendment was quickly ratified by all the states except Connecticut and Rhode Island. It was a unique amendment in the sense that it did not transfer power from the states to Congress but wrote an inflexible police regulation into the Constitution. Congress then passed the National Prohibition Act (Volstead Act) over Wilson's veto on October 28, 1919. The Amendment prohibited the manufacture, transportation, import, and sale of intoxicating liquors, and the Prohibition Act defined intoxicating liquors as those containing more than one half of 1 percent alcohol.

The subsequent history of the movement belongs to a later

chapter, but certain aspects of it are important at this point. The prohibition was in the fundamental law and not subject to change either by state legislatures or by Congress. It was a regulation of the customs and habits of the people in the interest of uniform standards of conduct. It took no account of the widely diverse social environments of the rural and urban communities or of the industrial East and rural South. It did not have sufficient public opinion back of it to make it effective in spite of the fanatical zeal of its sponsors. The ensuing years present a tragic record of death, of decreasing respect for law, and of a corrupting alliance between government officials and the criminal underworld. Bootlegging, smuggling, and moonshining flourished through the patronage of all classes of society. Enforcement agencies broke down. The fiction that the federal government could always enforce its laws irrespective of state and local impotence was disproved. The entire system of safeguards for individual liberty was seriously impaired. A half million persons were convicted for violating the law. Thirty thousand intoxicants were arrested in Cleveland alone in one year and their average age was only 25 years. The federal government spent nearly five hundred million dollars annually for enforcement over a twelve-year period. The net result was the most dismal failure in the history of the republic.

A third aspect of the intricate interrelationship between law, law enforcement, and the complexities of human impulses is furnished in the record of lynchings. A lynching is not a secret, premeditated murder; it is a bold and open defiance of the law by any number of people, ranging into the thousands, in which the victim is subjected to variable punishments between the extremes of instant death and all the tortures and indignities unrestrained sadism can devise. There were 1958 people lynched in United States between 1889 and 1900; 885 during the first decade of the century; 606 during the second decade; and 275 between 1920 and 1930. Seven hundred and sixty-eight of the victims were whites, the remaining Negroes. This appalling record of barbarism in twentieth-century America is of no small historical importance. It stands in sharp contrast to the humanitarian solicitude for the victims of industrial exploitation, organized vice, and demon rum. Lynchings occurred most frequently in the rural South, in localities of economic and cultural decadence, where the religious emotionalism of the Baptist and Methodist churches still prevailed. They arose out of widespread inferiority complexes on the part of the ignorant, depraved whites who lived on the margin of civilization and found satisfaction in sudden assertions of racial superiority. Lynchings were not all in the southern states nor were the victims always Negroes; but 90 percent of them were in the South, in the very sections which most actively supported the prohibition, fundamentalist, and Ku Klux Klan movements. The surviving heritage of earlier days—lawlessness of the frontier, low value placed on human life during slavery, and the need for self-preservation during reconstruction—contributed to the basic pattern. Economic rivalry between competing racial groups; the craving for emotional excitement, stimulated by the lurid publicity of mob scenes; distrust of legal process; and the indifference of the general public to the situation, all were in part responsible for the continued lawlessness. The essential facts are (1) that lynchings were always in open defiance of the law; (2) that they variously occurred before arrests were made, after arrests but before trial, while trials were in progress, after conviction but before sentence was executed, and after commutation of sentence by executive clemency; (3) that only rarely was there more than a feeble effort to punish these violations of the law; and (4) that public sentiment, through inaction or perversion, condoned lynchings, elevated men to public office who capitalized on racial prejudices, and resisted all efforts to secure federal or effective state anti-lynching laws. They had become a system of racial control.

The same people who championed federal legislation to solve the local problem of keeping liquor away from the Negro, became ardent defenders of state rights when the Dyer bill, and later the Wagner-Costigan bill, were before Congress. This proposed legislation would have given the federal courts jurisdiction where state courts failed to act against persons suspected of participating in lynchings. There were serious doubts as to the constitutionality of both; there were doubts as to whether juries would be any more disposed to convict in federal courts than in state courts;

but, of all the states, Virginia was the only one really to make an effort to devise an effective state statute. Its success, with a law defining participation in a lynching as murder and authorizing the governor to use state prosecutors and state funds to convict, stands as clear proof that the continued record of barbarism was directly chargeable to the attitude of the public. Thus was the theory of law modified in practice by the elusive factors in human behavior.

ADMINISTRATION OF THE LAW

Equally enigmatic was the administration of the law. Every extension of government in the direction of social control or of social service added to the total responsibilities of administrative personnel. The expansion of administrative units in local, state, and national governments, together with the evolution of administrative procedure, grew so rapidly as to constitute a revolutionary change in government at a time when training for government service was almost wholly lacking and the spoils system was rampant. The more capable men were, the less likely they were to enter public service, not only because the vulgarity of practical politics was distasteful to them but because service to private interests was more remunerative than service to the public interest. Nor did the public welcome the intrusion of specially trained men into public life. The explosive thrusts at the "Brain Trust" of Franklin D. Roosevelt were only repetitions of the widespread derision of the professor in the White House of Wilson's day—contemptuous expressions that were so frequent as to be nauseating in the whispering campaigns of presidential elections. This willingness of the people to permit politicians to run the country for them was a fundamental cause of the prevailing disrespect for law and order. It was cumulative and deep-rooted in the lives of the people. One only needs a cursory glance at the panorama of national life to see its ultimate results. Millions of traffic tickets torn up with a shrug of the shoulders because the offenders knew some one who could "fix" the matter with the enforcement officers, until the whole business became a national disgrace and the annual toll of traffic deaths alone reached more than thirty-six thousand. Hundreds of helpless men and women hunted like beasts, torn from the custody of officers and courts, tortured and burned by howling mobs of men, women and children without semblance of trial or effort to determine guilt, not only because of the lack of laws, but because of a complete break-down in their proper administration. The federal prohibition enforcement machinery included the Bureau of Internal Revenue in the Treasury Department and the Department of Justice which conducted prosecutions. They had at their service all the combined resources of internal revenue officers, customs inspectors, postal inspectors, and the coast guard. The federal enforcement was reinforced by prohibitory laws in all but two states and the combined activities of state and local police, deputies, and law courts. Never in history did such a horde of public officials infest the land for the enforcement of a single law. Never were they assisted so assiduously by self-appointed spies among the people. Never was conformity to the requirements of the law enforced with such utter disregard of human life and the sanctity of the rights and liberties of the individual. Yet enforcement broke down completely, partly because the combined sentiment of the majority of the people in the most densely populated sections of the country was hostile to the spirit of the law; but, in larger measure, because the tyranny of enforcement was directed at only a portion of the people. Too many enforcement officers turned out to be bootleggers who replenished their stock in trade from seizures made in the course of arrests. Too many justices of the peace and judges sentenced men to prison in the afternoon and enjoyed their cocktails at home in the evening. Thousands of barrels of alcohol were illegally withdrawn from government warehouses with the connivance of Department of Justice agents. Government officials, in short, not only considered themselves and their friends above the law but did not hesitate, in the enforcement of a single law, to violate others equally sacred.

The same situation prevailed with little variation in other fields of enforcement. School attendance laws became a vital adjunct to the control of child labor, but they might as well never have been placed upon the statute books so far as Negro children were concerned in some sections of the rural South, because little effort was made to enforce them. Presidents Benjamin Harrison, Grover Cleveland, and William McKinley made little effort to enforce the Sherman Anti-Trust Act, which was so vigorously sustained by Attorney-Generals Philander C. Knox, Charles J. Bonaparte, and George W. Wickersham during the Administrations of Theodore Roosevelt and William Howard Taft. Zealous enforcement from the beginning might not have accomplished the objectives for which the law was designed; but that is of little importance. The historical fact is, that so long as it remained on the statute books with no attention from the executive departments of the government, the representatives of the people in Congress were unaware of the necessity of approaching the problem in a different and more realistic way. The Federal Reserve Act was intended and confidently expected to establish a sound banking system. The President and Senate were given the responsibility of appointing the governing board which was to include the Secretary of the Treasury and the Comptroller of the Currency, but Senator Carter Glass could say in the Senate, May 10, 1932:

While we intended to preclude all idea of central banking, we designed that the Government, through its agencies, should keep a strict supervisory control of the system, and we appointed a Government agent, one of three of the Government directors at the Federal Reserve bank, who should be the presiding officer, and whom we intended to be the head officer of the bank. He has been literally brushed aside. He is a mere custodian of evidence of credit. They have set up in each of these banks a government of their own.

For a while this "board of governors" came well-nigh usurping important functions of the Federal Reserve Board here in Washington. They would have their meetings at their pleasure and convenience, resolve this, that, or the other things, and graciously let the supervising authority here know what they had done.

The Fordney-McCumber Tariff Act of 1922, although it established the highest rates in American history, set up a tariff commission to make a study of the differences in costs of production in foreign countries and in the United States. This commission was to make reports to the President who was given power to raise or lower rates by as much as 50 percent. In March, 1928, Edward

P. Costigan resigned from the commission, and in a letter to Senator Joseph T. Robinson charged President Calvin Coolidge with having packed the Commission, overruled its recommendations, and thwarted its every effort to accomplish what Congress intended it to do. Whatever the truth of his charges may be, and the evidence seems convincing, the President did, over a six-year period, lower rates on millfeed, bobwhite quail, paint-brush handles, phenol and cresylic acid, raise them the maximum amount on eighteen items including iron ore, and refuse to lower them in accordance with the Commission's recommendation on many items, including sugar.

On the other hand, there were important developments in the direction of improved administration of public affairs. President Taft appointed a Commission on Economy and Efficiency in 1911. The most important result of its report was the Budget and Accounting Act of 1921 and the Classification Act of 1923. These two acts created the Bureau of the Budget and the Personnel Classification Board. In 1930, the two agencies were brought into coordination by making the Director of the Budget the Chairman of the Personnel Board. Budget systems were also established in all of the states except Arkansas between 1912 and 1933. The concerted effort to improve public service by bringing into it highly trained and specialized employees and by placing them under the civil service made steady progress for many years. As administrative boards and bureaus multiplied, the task of appointing competent men to the many new posts placed a heavy responsibility upon the President. There was always pressure from partisans, "lame-duck" Congressmen, and special interests to have these agencies manned by other than specially qualified persons. This was particularly true when the government passed from the control of one party to the other. The number of federal employees under civil service reached a high point of approximately 80 percent by the close of Herbert Hoover's Administration; but the percentage dropped rapidly as new boards and bureaus were created in Franklin D. Roosevelt's Administration, and low administrative efficiency due to the spoils system was accentuated by conflicting views of desirable policies within the administration.

CONGRESSIONAL DECADENCE

In writing its reform legislation, Congress in general sought to express the policy of society on a given question. Public opinion was frequently so divided as to what that policy should be that Congress was unable to agree upon any legislation. It was frequently only a general demand for action which the intelligence of Congress was incapable of meeting. Congress ofttimes refused to be specific, framing legislation in broad terms in order (1) to exercise the full limits of legislative power under the Constitution, and (2) to relieve itself of the onerous task of specifically saying what the rules of competition should be in industrial relations. This practice forced the Court to give meaning to the law by its decisions and directed criticism away from Congress and upon the Court when one side to a controversy failed to get from the Court the full returns to which it felt entitled under the laws. Later Congress went even farther in its failure to define legislative policies in intelligible language and delegated more and more power to the President and to administrative agencies. This was particularly true in the history of legislation touching industrial relations. Economic conditions changed so rapidly that they were years ahead of public policy at all times which complicated the problem. If we would understand this relationship between public opinion and the three coordinate branches of the federal government, we must go, not to the tirades of disgruntled reformers, but to the great minds of those upon whom the responsibility of applying the nation's policies devolved: to men like William Howard Taft, George W. Wickersham, Charles Evans Hughes, Oliver Wendell Holmes, and Louis D. Brandeis, of whose intellectual integrity there can be no question.

Public opinion in the United States throughout this period was concerned with a minimum of four things: (1) the conservation of natural resources; (2) the freedom of the individual, whether laborer, producer, or trader, to rise in the economic scale; (3) a well-balanced economic system which should function smoothly through the years; and (4) protection for the consumer, the laborer, and the producer of raw materials from exploitation. With respect to the policies which should be pursued to accomplish these things there was disagreement. Complete inaction by the government (*laissez faire*) and complete public ownership and control (socialism) were both rejected except by an insignificant minority. Enforced competition by action of the Congress and the Courts was the first experiment. This was the period of the Sherman Act before 1913, of the inaction by Presidents Cleveland and McKinley, and of "trust-busting" by Presidents Roosevelt and Taft. The second period was that of regulation by law and supervision by administrative agencies. This was the period of the Clayton Act and the Federal Trade Commission Act of President Wilson's Administration. The third period was that in which concentration was regarded as inevitable and desirable. In Presidents Coolidge's and Hoover's administrations, it was undisturbed except by advice. In President Franklin D. Roosevelt's Administration, it was legalized to the full extent of price and wage regulation with restraints upon excesses attempted through administrative machinery.

Congress made three notable failures during the period in dealing with the problem. Public opinion was aroused first by revelations concerning rebates received by the Standard Oil Company from the railroads. It was thought that corporations were growing to enormous size by destroying their competitors through unfair practices. Congress was forced to act and passed the Sherman Anti-Trust Act (1890). This declaration of public policy outlawed all "combinations in restraint of trade." It made such combinations a criminal offense. It gave the Department of Justice a mandate to destroy them, and private individuals were encouraged to assist by allowing suits for threefold damages. Here was a case, however, where Congress was unable to agree and wrote the law in indefinite terms. Senator John Sherman said in debate: "It is difficult to define in legal language the precise line between lawful and unlawful combinations. This must be left for the Courts to determine in each particular case. All that we, as lawmakers, can do is to declare general principles. . . ." The burden thus thrust upon the Supreme Court by Congress may be judged from the words of Justice Brandeis (*American Column & Lumber Co. v. United States,* 1921):

Restraint of trade may be exerted upon rivals; upon buyers or upon sellers; upon employers or upon employed. Restraint may be exerted through force or fraud or agreement. It may be exerted through moral or through legal obligation; through fear or through hope. It may exist, although it is not manifested in any overt act, and even though there is no intent to restrain. Words of advice, seemingly innocent and perhaps benevolent, may restrain, when uttered under circumstances that make advice equivalent to command. For the essence of restraint is power; and power may arise merely out of position. Wherever a dominant position has been attained, restraint necessarily arises. And when dominance is attained, or is sought, through combination—however good the motives or the manners of those participating—the Sherman law is violated; provided, of course, that the restraint be what is called unreasonable.

It was generally believed, at first, that the language of the Act was so sweeping as to ruin business; but the Supreme Court adopted the attitude that Congress must bear the responsibility (*United States v. Trans-Missouri Freight Association,* 1897). In 1895, however, the Court had refused to allow the contention of the government that the American Sugar Refining Company was illegally restraining commerce among the states by bringing under its control 98 percent of the sugar-refining industry (*United States v. E. C. Knight Company*). President McKinley and Attorney-General Harmon used this decision as an excuse to say that the Act was unenforceable. President Taft later contended that the case had been presented very inadequately by the government. In 1898, the government won its case by a unanimous decision of the Court, against a division of sales territory (*United States v. Addystone Pipe and Steel Company*). These two cases were clear indication to producers that they could not enter into agreements for the elimination of competition, but that they could accomplish the same purpose by bringing their productive enterprises into one large corporation. New Jersey offered them attractive corporation laws, and the legal profession generally advised them that the federal government had no authority under the commerce clause over ownership, investments, and form of corporate organization. There had been no decision concerning this because of the inactivity of the Department of Justice. There followed several years of very active combinations of corporations into trusts, and a revival of popular agitation.

President Theodore Roosevelt took cognizance of the popular unrest and began his anti-trust prosecutions with proceedings against the Northern Securities Company. As already stated (p. 124), the case pertained to the struggle between the railroad magnates James J. Hill, backed by J. P. Morgan, and Edward H. Harriman for control of the Burlington Railroad, which each wanted as a Chicago connection. Harriman lost out and the Northern Securities Company was organized. The government brought suit to restore competition between the two transcontinental railroads, and the Supreme Court handed down its decision in 1904 (*Northern Securities Co. v. United States*).

Meanwhile, investigations by the newly created Bureau of Corporations into the oil, tobacco, steel, and farm implements industries, and of a special congressional committee into the steel industry, revealed that the Sherman Anti-Trust Law had not checked the process of industrial integration. Juries had shown an indisposition to convict, and the government had emphasized disintegration of the trust rather than punishment for violations of the law. The decision of the Court, in 1911, that the law prohibited only unreasonable restraints of trade, precipitated the third period of violent public agitation and resulted in the legislation of President Wilson's Administration. There was, however, still no unanimity of opinion as to what public policy should be. President Taft's attitude toward the trusts was realistic and in line with actual achievements under the Sherman Act. He said: "We are not engaged in trying to strike down the business of this country. Where combinations of this sort show themselves willing to come within the law, the Attorney-General is only too willing to enter a decree by consent, if need be, enforcing the law and dividing up the great combinations into lesser combinations." Attorney-General George W. Wickersham, however, pointed out that there were those who "were disappointed because, as with the wave of a wand, conditions that had existed twenty years ago were not restored . . . who regretted greatly that the national administration should have succeeded in working out a problem of this character without the embarrassment which would have attended upon a ruin of vast interests and the destruction of great businesses."

In 1913, Congress again placed the question under discussion. They put into legislative form the "rule of reason" enunciated by the Supreme Court, defined "combinations in restraint of trade," and enumerated the unfair methods of competition which public opinion condemned. It was a far more definite statement of policy than the Sherman Act had been and it remedied, by the creation of the Federal Trade Commission, the error of shifting responsibility to the Courts. The importance of creating these industrial commissions was well stated by Charles Evans Hughes, Governor of New York, in 1907, in defense of his proposal for a state public utilities commission:

We are under a Constitution, but the Constitution is what the Judges say it is, and the judiciary is the safeguard of our liberty and of our property under the Constitution. I do not want to see any direct assault upon the Courts, nor do I want to see any indirect assault upon the Courts. And I tell you, ladies and gentlemen, no more insidious assault could be made upon the independence and esteem of the judiciary than to burden it with these questions of administration—questions which lie close to the public impatience, and in regard to which the people are going to insist on having administration by officers directly accountable to them.

In establishing such administrative agencies as the Federal Trade Commission, however, there were certain fundamental principles so self-evident that it never should have been necessary for the Supreme Court to restate them. Congress, as the legislative branch of the government, could not divest itself of the legislative function. It must lay down policies and establish standards, although it might leave to "selected instrumentalities the making of subordinate rules within prescribed limits and the determination of facts to which the policy as declared" was to apply. Gradually, in practice, the Commission worked out an administrative procedure. It received complaints of unfair trade practices, elicited

answers from the accused, and examined and cross-examined witnesses. It submitted its proposed findings to the contestants with
opportunity to file exceptions. It concluded its case in each instance
with a hearing before the full Commission, a finding of facts, and
the issuance of an order. The Commission might appeal to the
Circuit Courts to have its orders enforced. In either case, it remained the duty of the Supreme Court to determine if the evidence in the case justified the findings of facts and if the facts
were sufficient under the law to justify the cease and desist order.
In no case could the Commission usurp the legislative function of
declaring policies or deprive the individual of his constitutional
right of appealing to the Courts. Furthermore, the Federal Trade
Commission was independent of the executive department. Congress limited the reasons for removal to "inefficiency, neglect of
duty or malfeasance in office" and, when President Franklin D.
Roosevelt sought to remove Commissioner William E. Humphrey
because "the aims and purposes of the Administration with respect
to the work of the Commission can be carried out most effectually
with personnel of my own selection," he was restrained from
doing so.

The second important phase of industrial control in which Congress found itself unable or unwilling to define a policy, thus shifting the burden to the Courts, was in the matter of utility valuations.
Through the entire history of rate regulations, Congress has refused
to say what basis for fixing valuations shall be followed. Public
opinion, at times of property depreciation and in order to protect
society against watered stocks, urged the rule of reproduction cost
new. A considerable minority, however, including the state of
Massachusetts, a majority of the Interstate Commerce Commission,
and a majority of the Supreme Court including Justices Oliver
Wendell Holmes, Harlan F. Stone, and Louis D. Brandeis, endorsed
the principle of honest and prudent investment. The majority of
the Court in the St. Louis and O'Fallon Railway Case endorsed
the principle of reproduction cost new, but only because it believed
Congress had stated that to be its policy in the Transportation
Act of 1920. That Congress openly shrank from the duty of
enunciating a definite policy is clearly revealed by its order to the

Commission to capture one half of all earnings above 6 percent and to give "due consideration to all the elements of value recognized by the law of the land for rate making purposes."

In addition to writing its laws in language which required definition by the Courts, and to shifting responsibility to the new administrative agencies, Congress showed an increasing unconcern about the constitutionality of its acts. The practice is not of recent origin. President Taft was constrained to say:

It is said that it should be left to the Supreme Court to say whether this proposed act violates the Constitution. I dissent utterly from this proposition. The oath that the chief executive takes, and which each member of Congress takes, does not bind him any less sacredly to observe the Constitution than the oaths which Justices of the Supreme Court take.

THE CONSTITUTION AND THE LAW

Public agitation about social and economic questions receded into the background when the United States entered World World I. It remained in abeyance during the greater part of the 1920s but reappeared with a vengeance during the depression. Meanwhile, the flood of state and federal legislation designed to meet the problems of the new economic order continued to come before the Supreme Court. Most of the congressional legislation had been passed under the constitutional power of Congress to control interstate commerce and to tax and spend. Most of the state legislation was passed under the police powers. Since it was impossible to draw the line between interstate and intrastate commerce or to define the guaranteed rights of freedom of contract, due process, and equal protection except as individual cases arose, legislative action and judicial interpretation combined through the years to give them meaning. Even so, they did not admit of non-contradictory interpretation, and the members of the Supreme Court, of Congress, and of society generally often disagreed over the constitutionality of legislative acts. Except for a few cases, however, the Supreme Court displayed a remarkable unanimity in its interpretations of the fundamental law.

In fixing the limits of the powers of Congress over interstate commerce, the Court defined regulation very liberally to mean foster, protect, and promote (*Austin v. Tennessee*, 1911), but it limited the extent of interstate commerce to the movement of goods from the point of origin to its destination (*United States v. E. C. Knight Co.*, 1895). Within those limits, Congress could keep the channels of commerce free from shipments of goods considered harmful to the health and morals of recipients. The first of these cases was *Champion v. Ames* (1903), in which the Court upheld a law of 1895 prohibiting the shipment of lottery tickets. This decision came just as the reform movement was getting well started, and Congress made full use of the newly discovered power. The Court sustained the Pure Food Act of 1906 (*Hipolite Egg Co. v. United States*, 1921), the Narcotics Acts of 1909 and 1914 (*United States v. Jim Fuey Moy*, 1916), the Mann Act of 1910 for the suppression of the white-slave traffic (*Hoke v. United States*, 1913) and the exclusion of prize-fight films (*Weber v. Freed*, 1915). The decision in the E. C. Knight case contained this interesting observation:

If it be held that the term (commerce) includes the regulation of all such manufactures as are intended to be the subject of commercial transactions in the future, it is impossible to deny that it would also include all productive industries that contemplate the same thing. The result would be that Congress would be invested, to the exclusion of the states, with the power to regulate, not only manufactures, but also agriculture, horticulture, stock raising, domestic fisheries, mining . . . interests which in their nature are and must be local in all the details of their successful management.

Changing economic conditions through three decades destroyed the validity of the statement. Production ceased to be local in all its details, and the state governments found difficulty in meeting the requirements of regulation. Public opinion condemned child labor no less than it had condemned the white-slave traffic, and Congress, acting under the same constitutional power of regulating commerce, decreed that the channels of trade should remain free of the products of child labor. But the decision that Congress could not reach back of interstate commerce to regulate production rendered their efforts futile (*Hammer v. Dagenhart*, 1918). It was another 5 to 4 decision, Justices Oliver Wendell Holmes, Joseph McKenna, Louis D. Brandeis, and John H. Clarke dissenting. Justice Holmes said in his dissent: "The act does not meddle with anything belonging to the States. They may regulate their internal affairs and their domestic commerce as they like. But when they seek to send their products across the state line they are no longer within their rights. If there were no Constitution and no Congress their power to cross the line would depend upon their neighbors. Under the Constitution such commerce belongs not to the States but to Congress to regulate. It may carry out its views of public policy whatever indirect effect they may have upon the activities of the States. Instead of being encountered by a prohibitive tariff at her boundaries the State encounters the public policy of the United States which it is for Congress to express." In addition to defining the limits of the power of Congress to control interstate and foreign commerce, the Court was called upon to restrain the states from invading that field. It said that, if Congress did not legislate in a particular case, the presumption was it wished no regulation and the states might not intrude (*Di Santo v. Pennsylvania*, 1927). The states might not interfere with things sent in interstate commerce so long as they remained in the original package (*Schollenberger v. Pennsylvania*, 1898; *Austin v. Tennessee*, 1900; *Cook v. Marshall Co.*, 1905).

The Supreme Court also reduced to a minimum the constitutional limitations on the taxing power of Congress; but, again, the cases in which it was impelled to restrain dealt with questions about which there were violent prejudices rather than unanimity of public opinion. Having failed in its efforts to reach back of the point where goods entered interstate commerce and eliminate conditions in production which were contrary to public policy, Congress turned to the taxing power and, February 24, 1919, imposed a 10 percent excise tax on all products of mines and factories employing children under fourteen years of age. The case came before the Supreme Court in *Bailey v. Drexel Furniture Co.* (1922) and was declared unconstitutional with but one dissent, that of Justice John H. Clarke. Regulation of the conduct of manufacturing and production was again held to belong to the states, and therefore beyond control by a tax imposed by the federal government. Two years previously, the Court had held that stock dividends were not subject to the income tax (*Eisner v. Macomber*, 1920). This, also, was a 5 to 4 decision, with Justices Oliver Wendell Holmes, William R. Day, Louis D. Brandeis, and John H. Clarke dissenting.

In the matter of state legislation, the Supreme Court was called upon to decide many cases under the Fourteenth Amendment which were cases of degree and could not be decided on point of law, because the terms "due process" and "equal protection" did not permit exact definition. The eternal problem was to protect the rights of the individual without seriously restricting the right of the states to legislate for the general welfare. The states were allowed wide latitude in the imposition of taxes, the one general limitation being that they must not reach the point of confiscation of property. They were allowed to use their power of taxation to curb the operations of chain stores (*Indiana v. Jackson*, 1931) and to tax out of existence business thought to be undesirable (*McCray v. United States*, 1904; *State of Washington v. Magnano Co.*, 1934). They were allowed to regulate hours of labor for both men and women (*Muller v. Oregon*, 1908; *Bunting v. Oregon*, 1916). They were allowed to license and supervise small loan companies. But neither the state nor the federal government was allowed to regulate the wages of women in industry.

This brief survey is sufficient to show how Congress and the several state legislatures sought to cope with changing social and economic conditions; and how the Supreme Court attempted to keep them within their respective fields, protect the individual's rights of person and property, and still keep the Constitution a living instrument for progress. There were people, however, who felt that the necessity of keeping legislation within the limits of the Constitution made it difficult, if not impossible, to translate public policy into legislation. They urged that the Court be deprived of the power of judicial review. There were those who made much of the occasional 5 to 4 decisions, and advocated the requirement of a 6 to 3 majority or even a 7 to 2 majority of the Court for invalidation of an act of Congress. There were those who felt that changing economic conditions rendered futile the attempts of the states to regulate production. They urged that the limits of the powers of Congress be expanded either by Constitutional Amendment or by appointment of more liberals to the Supreme Court.

THE SUPREME COURT

The relationship between the personnel of the Court, the Constitution, and the laws was never absent from public discussion after the turn of the century. When President Theodore Roosevelt was faced with the task of appointing a successor to Justice Horace Gray in 1902, he wrote that "the majority of the present Court who have, although without satisfactory unanimity, upheld the policies of President McKinley and the Republican party in Congress, have rendered a great service to mankind and to this nation." And he added: "I should hold myself guilty of an irreparable wrong to the nation if I should put in his place any man who was not absolutely sane and sound on the great national policies for which we stand in public life." After satisfying himself that Oliver Wendell Holmes could be trusted in that respect, Roosevelt gave him the appointment. Holmes was then sixty-one years old, a veteran of the Civil War, a graduate of Harvard, Chief Justice of the Supreme Court of Massachusetts. He was destined to serve upon the Supreme Bench for nearly thirty years, to retire in 1932, and to live until he reached the age of ninety-four. During those thirty years, he exercised a greater influence upon legal thought in the country than any other living man. Chief Justice Hughes spoke of him as having been "the apostle of the latest generation. . . . More modern than the modernist, for he knows what is not modern; truer to the old than many a conservative, for he is more likely to know how the old became such and what in it is worth conserving." One year before his appointment by Roosevelt, the Northern Securities holding company had been incorporated in New Jersey to bring control of the Northern Pacific Railroad and the Great Northern Railroad into the same hands. The government moved against the Northern Securities trust as a combination in restraint of trade and won a 5 to 4 decision from the Supreme Court; but Holmes wrote the dissenting opinion.

President Wilson elevated his Attorney-General, James C. McReynolds, to the Supreme Court and also appointed Louis D. Brandeis. Roosevelt had been favorably inclined to Holmes because in his labor decisions he had "been able to preserve his aloofness of mind so as to keep his broad humanity of feeling and his sympathy for the class from which he has not drawn his clients." Brandeis' whole career had been devoted to the interests of the masses, so much so that only a Wilson in the White House and the overwhelming predominance of liberal sentiment by 1916 could have secured his appointment. He was the outstanding social pathologist of his day, the champion of individuals caught in the bewildering growth of institutions, the foe of monopolistic exploitation whether by public utilities, industrial combinations, or labor unions. Ratification of his appointment was opposed by the legal profession and by businessmen in general. His social and economic views, of which his entire legal career was an expression, did not coincide with the long prevailing and accepted principles under which economic life had been allowed to develop. It was feared that the reform movement was about to invade the sacred chambers of the Supreme Court. Specifically, his ability was not questioned; but his fitness for judicial service was thought to have been impaired by his uncompromising advocacy of reform measures which were still to be brought within the purview of the Court. The Senate ratified his appointment after an extensive investigation, and there came to sit upon the bench one who looked beyond the rigidity of the fundamental law to the changing needs of the social order.

In 1930, President Hoover nominated Charles Evans Hughes to succeed Chief Justice Taft. This time the opposition came from the liberal and progressive elements throughout the country. Hughes had resigned from the Court to be the Republican candidate for the presidency in 1916 to the utter chagrin of those who believed the Justices superior to the allurements of politics. He had been a member of Harding's Cabinet during the years of disgraceful malfeasance on the part of so many public servants. He had served as attorney for many of the vested interests. His previous record upon the Supreme Bench was regarded by many as evidence of an inherent narrow vision and obstinacy. He was, in short, regarded as wholly unfit by temperament and previous record for judicial service; but his nomination was confirmed and his record for guidance of the Court during the trying period of the depression may well give him a place in history among the greatest of Chief Justices. Shortly thereafter, President Hoover was called upon to fill another vacancy and nominated John J. Parker of North Carolina. The Senate refused to confirm the nomination. Opposition to Parker was based on two facts: (1) that, as a member of the Circuit Court for the Fourth District, he had supported an injunction restraining the United Mine Workers from soliciting members who were working under yellow-dog contracts; and (2) that he was sympathetic to the Lily White movement—an effort to purge the Republican party in the South of its Negro membership. The attitude of the nominee on two great social questions, race and labor, therefore, stamped him as a reactionary and deprived him of a place on the Supreme Bench. Later on, another vacancy occurred and President Hoover nominated Benjamin N. Cardozo of New York. There was severe criticism in many quarters because the membership of the Court was tending to be drawn too much from one section of the country, a criticism which was directed at the industrial East and indicative of the increasing cleavage between the agricultural and industrial sections.

Subsequently, Franklin D. Roosevelt, Democratic candidate for the presidency, remarked that the opposition party had been in complete control of the Supreme Court. This statement was denounced by Silas Strawn, sometime President of the American Bar Association, as destructive of fundamental principles of the government and contrary to the established historical fact that there had never been "any politics in our Supreme Court and that no political party could control the actions of the Court." Two years later, three laws of singular importance came before the Court for review. One was the Agricultural Adjustment Act, representing the latest effort of Congress to solve the perplexing agricultural problem. It was strongly supported in the West and opposed in the industrial East. The second was the Tennessee Valley

Authority Act involving the controversial question of public utilities and a government project of incalculable benefit to Tennessee Valley states. The third was the National Industrial Recovery Act designed to legalize trade and industrial associations, eliminate vicious trade practices, child labor, and starvation wages. It was supported alike by the United States Chamber of Commerce and the labor unions, but opposed by the consuming public. Justices Pierce Butler, Willis Van Devanter, and George Sutherland were of the majority against the constitutionality of the AAA, and Justices Harlan Stone, Louis D. Brandeis, and Benjamin N. Cardozo of the minority supporting it. Justice James C. McReynolds of Tennessee disagreed with every other Justice of the Court and rendered a minority opinion against the constitutionality of the TVA. Every Justice of the Court united in one of the most strongly worded opinions of the century to invalidate the NIRA.

The above record is very revealing because, and only because, it does not vary in any important respect from the history of Supreme Court appointments and Supreme Court decisions since the founding of the Republic. Justices of the Court do not render decisions on the basis of previous party affiliations or sectional origins—but not because the judicial process of reasoning is susceptible to mathematical precision nor because elevation to the Court obliterates the human addiction to the social and economic philosophy of earlier days. The point is that Presidents and Presidents-to-be, Senators, and political parties generally believe that the future welfare of the country depends upon their principles being written into the law of the land and are rightfully concerned about securing a Supreme Court which will not hold their acts to be contrary to the fundamental law. History proves the futility of their efforts. They are never certain what the fundamental convictions of their appointees are with respect to government and its relation to social and economic questions, nor are they certain what the principles of their own party will be in relation to all situations which may arise. The dynamic social changes of the twentieth century greatly compounded the difficulty. It would have required a greater omniscience than any President from Theodore Roosevelt to Franklin D. Roosevelt possessed to have predicted how his appointees to the Supreme Bench would react to the perplexing problems of the thirties.

In spite of all these facts, criticism of the Court because of its adverse decisions on economic and social legislation continued unabated. Politicians and students of political science, reformers and organized labor, special interests and disinterested intellectuals joined in the chorus. The Court was frequently referred to as a House of Lords, a usurper of legislative powers, a reactionary barrier to majority will. Theodore Roosevelt was particularly incensed at the state courts as a result of the invalidation by the New York Court of Appeals of laws prohibiting the processing of tobacco in tenement houses, limiting hours of labor of women in factories, and working men's Compensation Acts. He publicly endorsed a statement by a British newspaper that the Court's determination of the legality of income taxes and factory legislation constituted "one of the most galling of all possible tyrannies." Senator Robert M. La Follette denounced the Court as a bulwark of special privilege and conducted his presidential campaign of 1924 on a demand for abolition of judicial review. Said he: "By a process of gradual encroachments now confident and aggressive, sovereignty has been wrested from the people and usurped by the Court." Among the many changes suggested from time to time were (1) limiting the term of office of the justices; (2) giving Congress the power to remove them; (3) allowing the Court only a suspensory veto, Congress being empowered to enact finally a measure after an intervening election; (4) transferring the Court's functions to the United States Senate; (5) requiring more than a mere majority vote of the Court to render an act of Congress invalid; (6) depriving inferior courts of the power to pass upon the constitutionality of acts of Congress. Resolutions embodying one or more of these provisions were introduced in Congress from time to time by such prominent men as Senators William E. Borah of Idaho, Simeon D. Fess of Ohio, and George W. Norris of Nebraska. Criticism of the Court died down during the 1920s only to burst forth with renewed vigor, as we shall see, when the legislation passed by the first Congress of Roosevelt's Administration came up for review.

11

Morality in Diplomacy

T┐ BIG STICK AND DOLLAR DIPLOMACY

HEODORE ROOSEVELT closed an era in foreign affairs,
Woodrow Wilson opened another. Roosevelt had taken over the
conduct of foreign affairs in the midst of readjustments in foreign
policy made necessary by the war with Spain. The Hay-Pauncefote
Treaty was nearly completed when he took office; a basis had been
established for cordial relations with Great Britain. The Open
Door policy had already been defined, and some measure of success
attained for its maintenance by moral force rather than by military
might. The Monroe Doctrine had become a protective mantle for
Latin America against European aggression.

Roosevelt had acted summarily to get the Panama Canal started,
paying scant heed to traditional policies in his hasty recognition
of Panama, and justifying his impatience on the "interests of collective civilization." He intervened in Dominican affairs, to safeguard both the Monroe Doctrine and the approaches to the Canal
Zone, ignoring the disapproval of the Senate, and laying the ground-
work for later large-scale interventions in Central America. He
settled the Alaskan boundary dispute by arbitration, but with
reservations as to future action should the award be unsatisfactory.
He assumed the responsibility of mediation in the Russian-Japanese
conflict, seeking to maintain the Open Door policy by maintaining
the balance of power in the Far East. He displayed the armed might
of the United States by sending its fleet on a tour of the world.
He gave to the conduct of foreign affairs something of its old-time

flavor, without quite reaching the limits of European imperialism. In short, he greatly strengthened the military and naval establishments; relied upon the nation's might to strengthen its diplomatic ventures; yet stopped short of pressing for more than could be attained with peace. His methods were popularly known as "big stick" diplomacy.

President Taft and his Secretary of State, Philander C. Knox, attempted to carry out an equally vigorous foreign policy, substituting foreign investments for military and naval power as the strong arm of diplomacy. His policy came to be known as dollar diplomacy. Their idea was to encourage private capital to seek investments in China and in Latin America in support of the Open Door policy and the Roosevelt corollary to the Monroe Doctrine. Explaining that policy, Taft said in December, 1912: "The diplomacy of the present administration has sought to respond to modern ideas of commercial intercourse. This policy has been characterized as substituting dollars for bullets. It is one that appeals alike to idealistic humanitarian sentiments, to the dictates of sound policy and strategy, and to legitimate commercial aims."

Since export trade was expanding and capital was seeking investments abroad, and traditional policy decreed government protection for American property in foreign lands, Taft's objective was to make government and foreign investments mutually helpful. The government would encourage the quest for profit, even to the extent of strong pressure, in those fields where investments would support American foreign policy. American bankers should buy heavily into the railroads and other enterprises of China to justify American insistence upon the Open Door policy and to lessen the stake of the commercial interests of other countries. Knox used diplomatic pressure to secure for American bankers a share with those of Great Britain, France, and Germany in the Hukuang railway project, and to promote huge loans to China with which that government might purchase the interests of Japan and Russia in the Manchurian railways. He succeeded only in offending Japan and Russia and in weakening rather than strengthening the integrity of China.

The objective of Taft's policies in Latin America was to safeguard the Isthmian Canal and its approaches by stabilizing the finances of Central American countries with capital investments from the United States and thus remove a primary factor in possible extension of foreign influence in the region. American investments would give financial stability and internal peace to the Central American countries, safeguard the nation's lifeline, and afford profit to American investors.

Bankers, under strong pressure from the State Department, invested large sums in the National Bank of Haiti and made large loans to the governments of Nicaragua and Honduras. Secretary Knox negotiated conventions with the two countries by which such loans were to be protected by the appointment of American Customs collectors. Private financial interests in the United States took over the Nicaraguan national bank and undertook to develop the country. Eventually their investments amounted to $15,648,700. Meanwhile, marines were kept in the country to protect these investments, but officially to protect our canal rights, at a cost of $6,076,000 before 1932. In line with this policy of safeguarding the nation's lifeline, the United States Senate, disturbed by rumors that a Japanese company was about to purchase a large tract of land in Lower California, passed a resolution (August 2, 1912) to the effect that the United States would view with displeasure any transfer of strategic areas in the American Hemisphere to private foreign companies who might be serving the interests of a foreign nation. The resolution was presented by Henry Cabot Lodge and is known as the Lodge Corollary to the Monroe Doctrine. Near the close of Taft's Administration, a treaty was negotiated with Nicaragua by which, in return for $3,000,000, the United States was to secure 99-year leases on the Corn Islands, the right to establish a naval base on the Gulf of Fonseca, and the right, in perpetuity, to build a canal across the country.

Woodrow Wilson inherited the Platt Amendment regarding Cuba, the Roosevelt Corollary to the Monroe Doctrine, and ample precedents for intervention established by Roosevelt and Taft. Secretary Root had given assurance that intervention in Cuba would not occur except in cases of anarchy or foreign invasion. The first occupation, under Roosevelt, resulted from disorders growing out of the 1906 elections. The second, under Taft in 1912, was on the pretense of suppressing race riots. Roosevelt had kept naval vessels in Dominican waters, marines in the Island, and had secured the appointment of an acceptable financial dictator to place the Republic on a sound financial basis. Taft had sent marines to Nicaragua.

Wilson continued the Roosevelt policies in Cuba and Santo Domingo and the Taft policies in Nicaragua, and extended them to Haiti. The third intervention in Cuba, in 1917, resulted from a minor revolution growing out of an election. The fourth, in 1920, was clearly at the behest of financial interests to protect their investments. The Nicaraguan treaty which Taft's Administration had negotiated was taken up by Wilson and ratified by the Senate in 1916. Meanwhile, marines were landed in Haiti in 1915 where they remained for nearly twenty years. A dictated treaty of May 3, 1916, gave the United States virtual control of the government. The same year marines landed in Santo Domingo following an insurrection and established a virtual dictatorship.

These interventions, impelled by a desire to protect the Panama Canal as well as American lives, property, and financial interests, produced many unfortunate consequences. There can be no question that the readiness of the United States government to interfere in the internal affairs of Cuba retarded political development there. The very existence of the Platt Amendment stood as an expression of skepticism as to the Cubans' capacity for self-government and fostered irresponsibility on the part of her public officials. A minority in the Republic, opposed to independence from the first, remained ever ready to create situations which would lead to intervention. The reserved right of intervention, therefore, defeated its purpose of establishing responsible government; tempted the exercise of dollar diplomacy, and engendered uneasiness among other Latin American republics. It was abrogated by the Senate during the first administration of Franklin D. Roosevelt. Occupation of Nicaragua, as in Cuba, led to instability, with the United States attempting to supervise elections and patriots engaging the marines in constant guerilla warfare. The evacuation of the country, begun in 1932, closed what was regarded by many people as a disgraceful episode, and placed relations between the two countries once more on a civilized basis. In Santo Domingo, under United States occupation, popular government ceased to exist. Elections were controlled by the armed forces of the United States. Roads were built by forced labor. Natives who rebelled were subdued in what was little else than official slaughter. Under pressure of growing criticism in the United States, President Hoover sent the Forbes Commission to investigate in 1930 and a policy of gradual withdrawal was adopted.

QUESTION OF ETHICS

Congress, in passing an act for the operation of the Panama Canal, in 1912, had exempted coastwise trading vessels of the United States from the payment of tolls. Great Britain protested the exemption as a violation of the Hay-Pauncefote Treaty, and finally suggested that the question be submitted to arbitration. President Taft and Secretary Knox rejected her claims. The Treaty had specifically stated that the ships of all nations should pay the same rates. Taft and Knox insisted this meant all other nations. Elihu Root, who had participated in the treaty negotiations, said they were wrong. Walter Hines Page, Ambassador to Great Britain, insisted we had broken our agreement—it mattered not whether it had been a wise or foolish bargain in the first place. Wilson insisted that the United States was "too big, too powerful, too self-respecting a nation to interpret with too strained or refined a reading the words of our own promises just because we have power enough to give us leave to read them as we please." This was, in short, a question of good faith, of morality in international relations, and Wilson was thinking in terms of moral force rather than physical power. He also wanted a free hand in Mexico and was willing to make concessions on Panama Canal tolls in return for British support of his Mexican policies. Congress, after much bitter debate, repealed the tolls exemption in June, 1914.

Wilson took the same attitude in the determination of his Mexican policy, and the abandonment of intervention in the internal affairs of the other republics to the south of the United States began with his handling of the Mexican situation. He insisted that the Mexican people, like all peoples, must determine the nature of their own cultural and institutional development; and the United States could "afford to exercise the self-restraint of a really great nation which realizes its own strength and scorns to misuse it."

The dictatorship of Porfirio Diaz in Mexico, extending from 1877 to 1911, had reduced the population of that country to the status of agricultural peonage; had given foreign capital control of transportation, mining, oil lands, and rubber production; and had destroyed all semblance of popular government. Revolution broke out in 1911 under the leadership of Francisco Madero, who was unable to retain power after gaining it and was overthrown by the counter-revolution of Victoriano Huerta in February, 1913. Fifty thousand Americans were living in Mexico and American investments had reached a staggering total of almost $1,000,000,000. There had been considerable loss of American property and some lives during the revolution, but Taft had refrained from intervention in order not to embarrass his successor. Huerta's methods not only were savage, but his regime gave every indication of continued oppression after the manner of Diaz.

Soon after Wilson's inauguration, he announced his Mexican policy in a speech at Mobile, Alabama (October 27, 1913). It was (1) that the United States would not recognize governments founded by force; (2) that it would assist, in every way possible, the establishment of democratic government; (3) that the armed forces of the United States would not be used to protect capital investments; and (4) that the United States would tolerate no interference with its leadership in Latin-American affairs. He said, further, that the United States never again would seek territory by conquest. Other nations, as a matter of expediency, recognized Huerta's government. Wilson refused to do so because Huerta's regime rested upon a brutal suppression of the masses, saying: "We dare not turn from the principle that morality and not expediency is the thing that must guide us and that we will never condone iniquity because it is most convenient to do so."

In November, 1913, Wilson insisted that Huerta should resign, and inaugurated a policy of permitting arms to reach Carranza, who was leading the struggle against Huerta's dictatorship. He was severely criticized, both in Europe and at home, most of the criticism coming from the representatives of vested interests and from devotees of Roosevelt's "big stick" methods in the conduct of foreign affairs. Finally an incident in the harbor at Tampico, where a subordinate Mexican official arrested American sailors without cause, precipitated a crisis. Wilson asked for, and received from Congress (April 20, 1914), authority to intervene by force of arms in Mexico. Vera Cruz was seized, April 21, to prevent landing of arms from a German merchant ship. Diplomatic relations were broken; and war fever swept over the United States. Argentina, Brazil, and Chile (ABC powers) offered their services in mediation. Wilson had said, at Mobile, October 27, 1913, that the United States was not interested in acquiring another foot of soil in Latin America, and he gladly accepted the offer. The conference was held at Niagara Falls in May, 1914, without much in the way of practical results, except that it enabled the United States to avoid war with Mexico. Huerta voluntarily went into exile in July, 1914, and Wilson threw his support back of Carranza. The latter, once in power, failed to initiate the reforms for which the revolutionists had been fighting against Huerta. Francisco Villa promptly initiated a struggle against the new dictator, but made the mistake of permitting his followers to cross the border and massacre American citizens at Columbus, New Mexico. Wilson sent a punitive expedition into Mexico after the rebel Villa in 1916, but firmly resisted all efforts of the oil and mining interests to precipitate a war. Villa was not captured, and as war approached in Europe, Wilson withdrew the Pershing expedition (February, 1917).

The demand for full-scale intervention increased after the adoption of a new constitution by Mexico in May, 1917, which included provisions for protection of labor against capitalistic exploitation, nationalized church property, secularized the schools, and prohibited further acquisition of land and water rights by foreign capital. It further declared all land, water, and mineral deposits to be the property of the state. Oil interests in the United States brought pressure in Congress and upon the Department of State, at the close of World War I and during Wilson's illness, to intervene. We shall see how only the timely action of Wilson prevented war.

CONFLICT OF IDEAS

Wilson was not alone in his ideal of introducing more probity into the conduct of foreign affairs. The same forces within the nation that had striven mightily to counteract the drift toward imperialism now sought to direct national policy toward international cooperation and world peace. It was a short twenty years from the day that the United States embarked upon its crusade to liberate the Cubans from tyranny to the day it threw its strength into a world cataclysm with the avowed purpose of bringing liberty, freedom, and justice to all peoples, everywhere. A cursory glance at the powerful forces which struggled for supremacy during those years shows the futility of any effort to explain our entry into World War I on economic factors alone. There were Americans—Jane Addams and Eugene V. Debs certainly were two—who believed in, preached, and practiced the principles of human brotherhood irrespective of nationality, race, or creed. The idea cannot be said, however, to have penetrated very far into the consciousness of the American colony in the Philippines, the champions of white supremacy in the southern states, the immigrants from the Emerald Isle, or the readers of the anti-Catholic *Menace*. There were men like Speaker Thomas B. Reed who believed that the dispute with Spain should have been submitted to arbitration, but not William Randolph Hearst, Joseph Pulitzer, Henry Cabot Lodge, or Theodore Roosevelt. There were men like Gamaliel Bradford, William Jennings Bryan, and William James who believed that Americanism and "imperialism" were incompatible; that government should rest always upon the consent of the governed; but not Senator Albert J. Beveridge, Major General Leonard Wood, or William Howard Taft. There were businessmen like Edward A. Filene of Boston who insisted that no profit was to be gained by our ventures into imperialism, but not the Wall Street bankers. There were those like Washington

Gladden who insisted that armaments create fear and distrust and provoke wars rather than prevent them, but not the Navy League founded in 1902 and sponsored by Captain Richmond P. Hobson and Theodore Roosevelt. Those who refused to look upon other nations as the presumptive enemies of our own, to agree that armaments were an insurance against war, to regard tariff barriers as the key to general prosperity, to become deliriously intoxicated by the victory over Spain, a third-rate power, or by the spectacle of the Navy passing in review—all such were but lonely souls in an atmosphere of glorified patriotism. The paramount idea in the minds of the people was that the American way of life was the best way. They supported unquestioningly the activities of their missionaries in the Far East. They brushed aside as irrelevant the methods by which the Philippine people were pacified. They never questioned the righteousness of uprooting the Latin culture of dependent peoples to make way for their own. They dug down in their pockets for billions of dollars to vindicate the theory that the way to preserve peace was to prepare for war. They displayed an amazing simplicity of thought in lauding the agreements to humanize war—as if war could ever be humanized.

Underlying all these conflicts of ideas, however, was a very real spirit of humanitarianism and love of peace; but there was an unfortunate lack of realism in both. Most people were deeply concerned over the plight of oppressed peoples in foreign lands and perfectly oblivious to conditions at home. They did not want war, but failed to understand the part that economic rivalry, national bigotry, and irresponsible governments play in creating wars. They were too absorbed in making a living and in carrying through the program of domestic reform to be aware of the destiny toward which subtle forces were leading them. The Spanish-American War and Theodore Roosevelt made the United States a world power. The war in Europe, which broke out in August, 1914, set the stage for the assumption of world leadership. Whether the United States could have attained a position of leadership without entering the war, and whether it would have been more willing to assume that responsibility had it remained neutral are now academic questions. Failure to anticipate the problems of neutrality drew the nation inevitably into the conflict. The peace movement, sympathy for oppressed peoples, and cultural affinity with Great Britain made rationalization of our decision less difficult. The intellectual brilliance and emotional fervor of Woodrow Wilson inspired a crusading zeal not equalled since the French Revolution and almost, but not quite, made justice for all men the guiding principle in international relationships.

An organized peace movement had been in progress in the United States since the founding of the American Peace Society in 1828, but the peace movement cannot be used as a criterion by which to measure the degree of repugnance for war. Isolation and opposition to large military establishments were deep-rooted and ingrained characteristics of the American temperament. They cannot be interpreted in any other way than a desire to remain out of European embroilments and to refrain from setting up any instruments even remotely threatening to democratic institutions. The desire of the American people was freedom to carry on the ordinary peaceful pursuits of life. It must not be forgotten that, at the turn of the century, the world was in an extraordinarily belligerent mood, while governments were protesting peace and peoples everywhere were bankrupting themselves to pay for armaments, not for the purpose of making war but to keep the peace. That one man believed in the efficacy of arbitration treaties and another in the efficacy of larger navies and armies does not make one less desirous of peace, though perhaps more naïve, than the other. There is no evidence that the vast majority of Americans desired anything else than international peace and good will as a permanent condition. At the same time, they did not rush to the support of the programs advanced by the devotees of peace, nor lend financial aid to their organizations. Nor did pacifists succeed in securing the aid of those powerful agencies of propaganda—the press, the churches, and the schools—to the same degree as the advocates of abolition and temperance had done. The fourth agency—the political forums—was all but closed to them because politicians too often were compelled to cater to minority groups such as the Irish-Americans. There was, also, a pronounced strain of emotionalism and humanitarianism in the American temperament. It militated against the continuity of the peace movement, and neutralized its appeal. Men were willing to forget their ideals of peace and wage war to abolish slavery. They supported the war against Spain in order to free the Spanish colonies from the iron hand of tyranny. Few outstanding pacifists were able to remain true to their convictions in either case. Each war revived the martial spirit, temporarily stimulated business, and created new vested interests, none of them helpful to the cause of peace. World War I was without precedent in that it was waged in the name of permanent peace; it was presented as a war to end wars. The real significance of the peace movement in the twentieth century lies in the effort to set up political machinery to prevent wars. Nothing was attempted in the way of disarmament.

PEACE BY ARBITRATION

The idea of a World Court for the adjudication of international disputes was first advanced by William Ladd in 1840. No practical steps were taken to establish such a court until 1899 when twenty-six nations, at the invitation of the Czar of Russia, sent representatives to a conference at The Hague. There was some suggestion that the conference might undertake to deal with the question of disarmament, but its only practical accomplishment was the creation of a Permanent Court at The Hague for the voluntary arbitration of international disputes. President Theodore Roosevelt, after much persuasion by D'Estournelles de Constant, Andrew Carnegie, and Richard Bartholdt, called a second conference at The Hague in 1907. Its most important action was an agreement of the leading naval powers to meet at London in 1908. This conference drew up what came to be known as the Declaration of London in 1909. It included, among other things, the agreement that a blockade should not discriminate between nations, nor bar ships from non-blockaded or neutral ports, and that it must be effective to be legal. It classified articles of commerce as contraband and non-contraband, including in the latter things essential to the life of non-combatants. Ratifications of this treaty were never exchanged between the signatories because the British House of Lords refused to agree to many of its commitments. Meanwhile, an effort was made to secure permanent treaties of arbitration between the United States and other nations. This was the particular objective of the Universal Peace Union, founded in 1866. Many men in public life, including President Ulysses S. Grant, had spoken in favor of compulsory arbitration of international disputes, without the usual reservation of those involving national honor.

The United States and Great Britain had long been interested in promoting the settlement of international disputes by arbitration. They began the practice with Jay's Treaty in 1794, turned to it again after the War of 1812, and thereafter relied upon it, when crises came, as readily as other nations threatened war. Yet there was always the danger that some fortuitous circumstances might lead to hostilities before arbitration machinery could be arranged. The two countries, for example, came dangerously close to war over the Venezuelan boundary dispute in Grover Cleveland's Administration; and, in consequence, Secretary Richard Olney and Sir Julian Pauncefote negotiated a general arbitration treaty in January, 1897. The support of President Cleveland, and then of President William McKinley, however, was not enough to force its ratification by the Senate over the combined opposition of the Irish-Americans, armament manufacturers, western silver advocates, and the jealous champions of the Monroe Doctrine and Senate prestige.

In 1904, the Senate again refused to approve the principle of arbitration. Secretary of State John Hay had negotiated agreements with several nations, including Great Britain, Germany, and France, by which the several nations agreed to submit to The Hague Court all disputes between themselves and the United States except when vital interests, independence, or national honor were involved. The Senate so amended the treaties as to cause President Theodore Roosevelt to regard them as lowering standards of international relations already established by the State Department and he refused to exchange ratifications. They were revived and approved by the several nations at the instance of Secretary of State Elihu Root in President Taft's Administration.

In 1910, President Taft announced that he was in favor of submitting to arbitration even those questions which were regarded as involving national honor. This was the vital point in the whole program of arbitration. To advocate less was to evade the principle, and Taft's pronouncement was a shining example of intellectual honesty and forthrightness so sadly lacking in public discussions of foreign relations. Following Taft's pronouncement, Secretary of State Knox negotiated treaties with Great Britain and France providing for arbitration of all questions, except that those about which there was delicacy, at the request of either nation, should first be surveyed by a commission. By unanimous consent of its membership, the commission could invoke arbitration. In case of disagreement, it could recommend a settlement. Taft favored a treaty of this kind with Japan. The treaties were supported by leading European statesmen and by men and women from all walks of life in the United States. Taft's political fortunes were at low ebb at the time and all his efforts to secure ratification of the treaties in their original form by the Senate were in vain against the combined hostility of Henry Cabot Lodge, the German- and Irish-Americans, and the midwestern isolationists. The Senate finally ratified the treaties but only after exempting most things about which there was likely to be disputes. President Taft, therefore, refused to conclude ratification. He did secure a treaty with Russia, Japan, and Great Britain, however, by which pelagic sealing was ended; and the ever-present fisheries dispute between Canada and the United States was finally and permanently settled by reference to The Hague Tribunal.

The inauguration of Woodrow Wilson in 1913 gave new life to the peace movement. In the first place, he led the forces of domestic reform to new achievements in social and economic change. The emotional fervor of the reform movement, which placed new values on human life, reached its peak between 1913 and 1917, and we entered the war at a time when it was at a point of hypertension. In the second place, Wilson himself was a member of the American Peace Society and he appointed a devotee of peace, William Jennings Bryan, to the position of Secretary of State. Bryan was the leading champion of the idea that international disputes could be settled without war if a crisis could be delayed until a thorough investigation by an impartial commission had been made and the force of public opinion allowed to operate. He proceeded, with the full knowledge and approval of the Senate Foreign Relations Committee, to negotiate treaties with thirty nations, not including Germany, Austria, Mexico, and Japan, which provided for the submission of all questions in dispute, without exceptions, to investigating commissions. There was to be no resort to war nor increase in armaments during the deliberations of a commission. The nations involved in the dispute might then reject the recommendations of the commission, but the theory was that by that time passions would have cooled and peace forces marshaled. The treaties were ratified by the Senate without opposition. Congress went still further in the direction of international good will when it repealed (1914) the Panama Canal Tolls Act of 1912. On the other hand, Congress refused to ratify a treaty negotiated by Bryan with Colombia because it included an expression of "regret that anything should have occurred to interrupt or mar" friendly relations between the two nations. This language was thought to be a reflection upon the procedure of President Theodore Roosevelt, and it was not until 1921 that a somewhat differently worded treaty was ratified. Entry of the United States into World War I and the subsequent effort to initiate collective security through the League of Nations pushed the idea of arbitration treaties into the background until Secretary Frank B. Kellogg revived it in the late twenties.

NARROWING HORIZONS

A crisis in world affairs came on June 28, 1914, when the heir to the throne of Austria-Hungary, Francis Ferdinand, was killed by a Serbian at Sarajevo. Austria seized upon the incident to make demands upon Serbia which were inconsistent with that country's independent sovereignty; and the German Kaiser, exalted champion of the divine right of kings, promised Austria unlimited and unqualified support. Russia mobilized for the defense of Serbia; France refused to promise neutrality; and Germany declared war on both countries at the beginning of August. She then launched an offensive through Belgium, whose neutrality the great powers previously had pledged themselves to respect. This brought Great Britain into the war, which rapidly became a war of attrition and almost world-wide in its scope. The nations involved resorted to conscription and to unprecedented regimentation of civilian life.

President Wilson issued the usual neutrality proclamation, saying on August 20, 1914, "We must be impartial in thought as well as in action, must put a curb upon our sentiments as well as upon every transaction that might be construed as a preference of one party to the struggle before another." This admonition was inspired by the presence in the United States of 32,000,000 people who were not American-born of American-born parents, by the desire to avoid involvement in the conflict, and by the hope of using the power and prestige of the nation most effectually in a peace settlement; but it was impossible of fulfillment.

The search by historians for the causes of the war and our entry into it probably will continue for many decades. The important point is not what historians believe now or will come to believe were its causes, but what the people of the United States believed at the time. No people could have made the ultimate decision to enter the war without deep convictions. Four stand out most prominently: (1) that the war represented a failure of political institutions, particularly of secret diplomacy; (2) that the piling up of armaments had created mutual distrust, powerful interests with a stake in war, arrogance, and sharp practices in foreign relations; (3) that the success of the central powers—Germany, Austria and Turkey—would constitute a threat to democratic institutions everywhere; and (4) that the liberation of millions of oppressed peoples in Central and Eastern Europe depended upon an Allied victory. There was wide discussion of the struggle for colonies, markets, and world trade. The latent devotion of millions of people to the land of their birth was aroused by the conflict. But there never was a remote possibility that the United States would go into the war on the side of the Central Powers. The question was not between assistance to one side or the other, but (1) between the two strong traditions of isolation and humanitarianism and (2) between the theory that the United States could best aid in achieving a lasting peace for all nations by isolation and that it could best do so by international cooperation.]

In cultural and institutional life, the people of the United States were closely bound to those of France and of the British Empire. We could discuss impartially the struggle for colonies, markets, and world trade; but not the invasion of Belgium, nor the statement of German statesmen that treaties are scraps of paper. These things struck at two fundamental principles of our philosophy: the right of small peoples to live their own lives, and the rule of law in international relationships. Promptly at the beginning of the war, Germany displayed a ruthlessness which foreshadowed the total war of later days. Its continuance, in her dealings with us, deepened our distrust of her ultimate ambitions, which had been growing since the nineties. At the same time, isolation soon became an impossibility, because little thought had been given to the problems of neutrality created by modern warfare.

The United States was forced to rely upon the established principles of international law because Great Britain refused to abide by the Declaration of London which had never been ratified, and in several important instances the old rules were inapplicable to new conditions. The severity of the conflict led to the establishment of what amounted to totalitarian states by all of the belligerents. Distinctions between combatants and non-combatants were narrowly restricted. Conscription of man power and material resources shattered the old conceptions of contraband of war. Blockades of enemy ports were rendered ineffective by the rapid transportation of supplies through neutral countries. The old rules of search and seizure were rendered obsolete by the advent of submarines. Great Britain established her supremacy on the high seas and then, March 11, 1915, announced a blockade of German ports. Unwilling to risk patrolling the North Sea ports and unable to control the Baltic Sea, she closed the North Sea to normal traffic by establishing a patrol between Scotland and Norway and in the English Channel. She then rationed the neutral countries of Northern Europe on the basis of peacetime imports, and licensed neutral traders with these nations to prevent supplies from reaching Germany. Successive Orders in Council extended the list of contraband until virtually all commodities were included. Unable to stop vessels and search them on the high seas because of submarines, she forced them to call at British ports for inspection. She interfered with the mails. She forbade export from Germany to the United States of items essential to industry and even to health. In short, freedom of the seas as that term was understood in the United States and used in international law succumbed to the stern necessities of a war for national survival.

The United States government protested vigorously against these annoyances to trade and violation of neutral rights, but without avail. The natural sympathies of the people were with the Allied cause. They certainly would not have supported a war against Great Britain to protect trading rights, and it is doubtful if they would have supported an embargo. War against France was likewise impossible. From the very beginning of the conflict, the Carnegie Endowment had taken the attitude that there could be no permanent peace in the world until Germany was defeated. Secretary of State William Jennings Bryan was unwilling to risk war with either side by too vigorous defense of neutral rights. His successor, Robert Lansing, was convinced that the Allied cause was the cause of democracy. Walter Hines Page, Ambassador to Great Britain, and Colonel Edward M. House, Wilson's roving ambassador to Europe, were both engaged in softening the force of the State Department's protests. Ambassador Robert Herrick had endeared himself to the French people at the outbreak of the war. However much the Allied governments might have interfered with trade and modified the rules of international law to fit the new conditions, they never needlessly endangered the lives of American citizens. Nor did Great Britain engage in acrimonious debate with the State Department, being content with a categorical statement of her position or preferring to delay answering our protests until new situations relieved the tension. The natural sympathies of the American people were re-enforced by their economic interests. Foreign trade grew rapidly as the warring nations, marshaling all resources for war, relinquished their foreign markets and the Allies turned to the United States for still greater supplies of war materials and foodstuffs. Losses incurred by American traders because of the blockade and new rules of search were small indeed compared to the profits from Allied trade, a situation which did much to ease the demands for redress. American securities held abroad and then gold were used for purchases in this country. On August 15, 1914, a group of bankers, who had inquired about the attitude of the government toward loans to the belligerents, were told that while loans could be made legally, the government frowned upon them as inconsistent with our neutral position. In October, 1914, however, the government informed the banking institutions that extension of credits was sanctioned, and outright loans were approved in August, 1916. Private loans, foreign bond flotations, and, after we entered the war, government loans made possible a demand for goods which taxed the productive capacity of the United States and gave it the greatest peacetime prosperity in history. Foreign trade reached such proportions that Congress set up a United States Shipping Board in September, 1916, and embarked upon a program of acquiring a government-owned merchant marine. J. P. Morgan and Company acted as the agent for Great Britain, France, and Russia, purchasing their supplies, selling their bonds and short-term notes and furnishing needed private credits. Bonds worth more than $1,500,000,000 were sold by the Allied governments in this country before we entered the war. The Federal Reserve Board finally became concerned about the supply of available credit for domestic use, and on November 27, 1916, cautioned member banks against further purchases. Their supply of credit for further purchases was dangerously low when the United States entered the war.

A DIPLOMATIC VICTORY

Germany protested against our sale of munitions to Great Britain. Congress had the power to place an embargo on such sales. To do so, however, would have been to penalize those nations that relied upon naval power for defense to the advantage of nations which had built up huge armies and munitions factories; and the government insisted that enaction of an embargo, after war began and without previous notice, would constitute an unneutral act. Germany, reluctant to risk a decisive naval battle, permitted her merchant marine to be swept from the seas and then sought to cut the British lifeline by unrestricted submarine warfare. She established a war zone around the British Isles (February 4, 1915) and threatened to destroy all merchant vessels entering this zone. This raised the problem of the use of submarines as commerce destroyers. The United States informed Germany (February 10, 1915) that she would be held to "strict accountability" if American lives or vessels were lost.

Secretary of State Bryan always insisted that we should have protested in similar manner when Great Britain mined the North Sea. The submarine, however, as Germany insisted upon using it was in a class with the tomahawk and stiletto, a fit companion weapon to poison gas which the Germans also introduced into the war. International law did not recognize the mode of warfare required by the very nature of the submarines. It would not have made much difference in any case. They had to strike without warning. They could not remove crews or passengers from the vessels they destroyed. They could make no distinction between combatants and non-combatants. The people of the United States simply refused to condone such barbarism. At a time when the reform movement was placing increasing emphasis upon human rights as opposed to property rights, they made a sharp distinction between British and German violations of the rules of international law. Property losses could be presented to a court of law for settlement. There could be no restitution of human life. The submarine warfare was not conducive, either, to a critical examination of reported German atrocities. British propaganda, including lies manufactured out of whole cloth, continued unchecked and unchallenged.

Germany's submarine campaign began on February 18, 1915, with the announcement that the waters about the British Isles were a war zone in which all enemy merchant vessels would be subject to destruction at sight. Citizens and vessels of neutral nations were to enter this zone at their own risk. President Wilson warned Germany, February 24, that she would be held to "strict accountability" for any losses of American vessels or lives. Some

American lives were lost when the British vessel *Falaba* was sunk on March 28 and the American vessel *Gulflight* was torpedoed on May 1. Secretary Bryan urged that citizens of the United States be refused permission to enter the submarine zone, but Wilson correctly insisted that they had a right to travel on the merchant vessels of belligerent nations.

Before the government could take action in the cases of the above vessels, the Germans, through the New York newspapers, warned Americans not to travel on vessels of the Allied nations. The Cunard liner *Lusitania* sailed from New York the same day, with many Americans on board. She was sunk off the Irish coast on May 7, with a loss of 1198 persons, including 128 Americans. It was a deliberate act, and an inhuman one which turned the world against Germany. *The Nation* expressed American sentiment accurately with the words: "She has affronted the moral sense of the world and sacrificed her standing among the nations." There would have been very little opposition to a declaration of war at that moment, in spite of the fact that the *Lusitania* was carrying contraband. President Wilson, however, was determined to win a diplomatic victory and keep the nation at peace. His position was stated on May 10, 1915, with the words: "There is such a thing as a man being too proud to fight. There is such a thing as a nation being so right that it does not need to convince others by force that it is right."

On May 13, 1915, he sent his first *Lusitania* note to the German government. He called its attention to the stupidly irregular pro-cedure of warning the American people through the newspapers that the vessel would be sunk, and announced as unacceptable the idea that warning of an "unlawful and inhumane act" about to be committed was an excuse or "abatement of the responsibility" for it. Speaking of the use of submarines, he said:

Objection to their present method of attack against the trade of their enemies lies in the practical impossibility of employing sub-marines in the destruction of commerce without disregarding those rules of fairness, reason, justice, and humanity which all modern opinion regards as imperative. . . . Manifestly submarines can not be used against merchantmen, as the last few weeks have shown, without an inevitable violation of many sacred principles of justice and humanity.

A series of notes followed the first [to Germany] without any admission by Germany that the sinking had been an illegal act; but she promised to sink no more vessels without warning and providing for the safety of non-combatants. Secretary of State Bryan resigned rather than sign the second note and was replaced by Robert Lansing. Bryan then threw his support to those Congressmen who were attempting to preserve the neutrality of the United States in a different way, chief among them being Horace Towner of Iowa, Charles A. Lindbergh of Minnesota, and Senators Robert M. La Follette of Wisconsin, Gilbert M. Hitchcock of Nebraska, and Richard Bartholdt of Missouri. They insisted (1) that continued trade with and loans to the Allies would inevitably drag us into the war; and (2) that citizens of the United States should be refused permission to travel on armed merchant or passenger vessels. The latter thesis was presented to Congress in the form of the Gore-McLemore resolution. The administration forces were thrown against its adoption. President Wilson's position, as announced in a letter to Senator William J. Stone, February 24, 1916, was that neither Germany nor any other nation was justified in setting aside the restraints agreed upon by civilized nations in mitigation of the horrors of war; that the United States could not maintain her dignity among the nations of the world much less her position as a sovereign power if she failed to protect the rights of her citizens; and that, if she receded from her position in this instance, all the principles of international law would be weakened, perhaps destroyed.

Conversations with Germany were renewed again when the French liner Sussex was sunk on March 24, 1916. President Wilson's note of April 19 stated very plainly that the United States had accepted previous explanations in good faith in the hope that it would "be possible for the German government so to order and control the acts of its naval Commanders as to square its policy with the principles of humanity, as embodied in the law of nations." Since the German government had failed to accomplish this, the United States must revert to its former conclusions "that the use of submarines for the destruction of an enemy's commerce is, of necessity, because of the very methods of attack which their employment of course involves, incompatible with the principles of humanity, the long-established and incontrovertible rights of neutrals, and the sacred immunities of non-combatants." He further threatened immediate severance of diplomatic relations unless Germany abandoned unrestricted submarine warfare. She promised to do so, May 4, but reserved to herself "complete liberty of decision" unless Great Britain were compelled to observe the rules of international law. Meanwhile, the Austrian ambassador, Constantin Dumba, had become involved in sabotage in munitions factories, and his recall had been requested in September, 1915. The German attachés, Captains von Papen and Boy-Ed, were found to be implicated, and their recall was requested in December, 1915. The promise of Germany, May 4, 1916, though not wholly satisfactory to the government, was regarded in the United States as a great diplomatic victory.

12

The First World War

1916 INTERLUDE

WILSON'S diplomatic victory on the question of unrestricted submarine warfare came at the beginning of a presidential-election campaign—at a time, too, when steps were being taken to strengthen the armed forces of the nation and a new peace program was being launched.

Wilson had not advocated any increase in armaments in his early messages to Congress; nor had he indicated in his public speeches other than complete agreement with the tradition that the United States was immune from aggression and could safely ignore the armament race of European nations. He hoped to marshal public opinion in support of the principals of moral responsibility and good faith in international relationships. Increase in armaments would have run counter to that ideal. The agitation for a stronger army and navy was supported by men like Theodore Roosevelt, Major General Leonard Wood and Samuel Gompers, and there were ample subsidies for the National Security League from the munitions interests and financiers. Fear of a victorious Germany, increasing concern over radical labor activities, and a desire to discipline the youth of the country were advanced as arguments by the sponsors. The National Security League and the Navy League carried out an intensive campaign for preparedness during 1915 and 1916 which reached its climax in a huge preparedness parade in New York City, May 13, 1916. Wilson began to advocate moderate preparedness in a series of public speeches in February, 1916; but his recommendations to Congress were so moderate that Secretary of War, Lindley M. Garrison, resigned and was replaced by Newton D. Baker. Congress debated the question of compulsory military training for months before passing the National Defense Act of June 3, 1916. The Act made provision for increases in the regular army over a period of five years to a maximum of 220,000; brought the state militia under national control and increased its size to 425,000; and provided for civilian training camps and for military training in colleges and universities. A Council of National Defense for the mobilization of wartime industry, consisting of six Cabinet officers and seven civilian experts, was authorized late in August. A Naval Appropriation Bill (August 29) made provision for the construction of ten battleships, six battle cruisers, and 140 lesser craft at a cost of $500,000,000.

William Jennings Bryan, Henry Ford, and Jane Addams, the Debs Socialists, and the Industrial Workers of the World were most prominent in opposition to increased armaments. Numerous organizations appeared, including the American League to Limit Armaments and the Woman's Peace Party, but those persons who were honestly interested in the ideal of permanent peace soon gravitated to the support of the League to Enforce Peace. That organization was formed at Independence Hall in Philadelphia, June 17, 1915, and embraced the plan of Anna B. Eckstein of Boston for a League of Nations to enforce peace with economic boycotts and a court of arbitration. It provided also for an international police force. The idea was supported from the beginning by Andrew Carnegie, Theodore Roosevelt, Hamilton Holt, A. Lawrence Lowell, and William Howard Taft. President Wilson appropriated the idea in May, 1916, and by broad resolution of Congress in August of that year the President was authorized to call an international conference at the conclusion of the war for its consideration. There was a general discussion of what should constitute a just peace at this time, and eventually the plan won the support of Bryan. Bryan and Wilson had parted company over the question of keeping Americans out of the war zone. Bryan was, at that time, in favor of resorting to a popular referendum before entering the war. The great question in the late summer of 1916 and the following winter was whether permanent peace could better be secured by our going into the war or remaining out of it. Germany, herself, left the country little choice in the end.

The Progressives were the uncertain factor in the presidential campaign because of this prominence of the question of war. Many of them had gone over to the support of President Wilson, though not into the Democratic party in 1912. Some hoped that the Republican breach of 1912 might be repaired by the nomination of former President Theodore Roosevelt; others insisted upon maintaining their own party organization. Few of them, indeed, could quarrel with Wilson's domestic policies, but many were disturbed by his foreign policy and for various reasons. Some wanted war, others a more rigorous neutrality.

The Republican National Committee had made one mild concession to the Progressives by modifying their system of representation in the national convention. Each state had previously been entitled to two convention delegates for each of its electoral votes. They were now allowed four delegates at large, one for each congressional district, and one for each district in which the popular vote of the Republicans was at least 7500 in the congressional elections of 1914.

The Progressives and Republicans met in separate conventions in Chicago on June 7, 1916. The Progressives nominated Roosevelt; the Republicans nominated Justice Charles Evans Hughes of the United States Supreme Court, former Governor of New York. Roosevelt then went over to the support of Hughes, refusing to run as a candidate, and the great adventure of 1912 came to an end. The Republicans adopted a purely negative policy—denouncing Wilson's foreign and domestic policies but offering no substitute.

The Democrats, meeting in St. Louis on June 14, renominated Wilson by acclamation, endorsed his domestic record, and paid particular tribute to his diplomatic triumph which had "preserved the vital interests of our government and its citizens and kept us out of war." The phrase "He kept us Out of War" was used as a campaign slogan; but Wilson rose above the cheapness of an appeal to foreign racial groups by repudiating their support and condemning all such as hyphenated Americans of questionable loyalty. Hughes, on the contrary, by the advice of his campaign managers, carefully avoided giving offense to foreign-born voters which seemed only to create an impression of indecision on his part toward grave public questions. Wilson defeated Hughes by a popular vote of 9,128,000 to 8,536,000 and an electoral vote of 277 to 254. The election did not hinge on the war issue. Hughes was defeated because neither he nor his party would endorse or offer a substitute for the social and economic reform program. The independent voters, therefore, supported Wilson. The Republicans' disparagements of Wilson's speeches as "shifty expedients" may have won some votes and lost others. If Wilson received votes in the Middle West because "he kept us out of war," he lost the German-American vote because of the manner in which he had accomplished it. But the German government incorrectly interpreted the re-election of Wilson as a mandate from the people for continuing the neutrality of the United States.

LAST MONTHS OF NEUTRALITY

While Americans were discussing the wisdom of strengthening their military forces, the best road to permanent peace, and the merits of Wilson's foreign policy, European belligerents were sacrificing the flower of their manhood in desperate efforts for victory. The Germans launched a great offensive at Verdun on February 21, 1916. Verdun held, but in seven months the French and Germans lost 1,000,000 men. The Russians struck the Austro-Hungarians in Galicia on June 4, 1916, and in six weeks of the famous Brusilov offensive 2,200,000 men were lost by the two contending armies. The British hurled the incomparable volunteer army of Kitchener against the Germans on the Somme on July 1, 1916, and lost 400,000 men in five months. Yet the net result of this tremendous sacrifice was continued stalemate; nowhere was there a sign of an early end to the slaughter.

President Wilson had twice sent his personal representative, Colonel Edward M. House, on peace missions to the governments of belligerent powers without success. He now decided, following his re-election, to make one more effort to end the war on the basis of a negotiated peace, and asked all belligerents, December 18, 1916, for a statement of their war aims. None of the Allied nations could foresee at this moment the Russian revolution, the suffering in Britain, the crushing defeat of Italy's armies, the demoralization in France that 1917 was to bring. No one could foresee these things, in part at least, because no one knew the degree to which German manpower had been depleted, the demands of her generals that unrestricted submarine warfare be resumed, and the length to which she would go in a desperate bid for victory. Those in Germany who made the decision to resume submarine warfare took no account of international law or humanity. They counted upon America's aversion to war to keep the United States neutral—or upon her unpreparedness, should they be in error—and upon an early capitulation by a starving Britain. First, however, the Central Powers in a moment of victory—having defeated the Rumanian armies and entered the capital of Bucharest, on December 6, 1916—indicated a willingness to discuss peace. This announcement was given out on December 12, 1916, while Wilson's note was in course of preparation. It gave an outward appearance of collusion between the United States and Germany to bring pressure upon the Allies and militated against a successful conclusion to Wilson's diplomatic venture.

Having canvassed the several warring nations as to their war aims, President Wilson appeared before the Senate, January 22, 1917, with his Peace without Victory address. Beginning with the thesis that the United States was directly concerned with the problems of ultimate and permanent peace, he stated the conditions on which the United States would participate in the postwar deliberations and "add their authority and their power to the authority and force of other nations to guarantee peace and justice throughout the world . . . the conditions upon which it (the government) would feel justified in asking our people to approve its formal and solemn adherence to a League for Peace." He mentioned specifically equality of rights between nations irrespective of size; independence for subject peoples such as Poland; an outlet to the seas, the highways of world commerce, for all large nations;

absolute freedom of the seas; and limitation of armaments. In general terms, he implied that responsible governments must be established and non-aggression policies must be adopted. That part of the address which caused the most comment was his statement that the peace must be without victory: "Victory would mean peace forced upon the loser, a victor's terms imposed upon the vanquished. It would be accepted in humiliation, under duress, at an intolerable sacrifice, and would leave a sting, a resentment, a bitter memory upon which terms of peace would rest, not permanently, but only as upon quicksand. Only a peace between equals can last." These were, substantially, the objectives of the American people when they finally entered the war. That they were to be lost sight of, bartered away, and rise again as a bitter memory, of course no one could then perceive.

Some days previously, the German Foreign Minister had written to the German Minister in Mexico that the German government would resume unrestricted submarine warfare on February 1. Germany proposed, if the United States entered the war, an alliance with Mexico by which that nation was to receive as compensation her lost provinces of New Mexico, Texas, and Arizona. The German Minister was also instructed to promote an alliance with Japan. The contents of the dispatch were delivered to the American government by the British Intelligence Service on February 26 and promptly published. The German government had notified the United States government on January 31, 1917, of its intention to resume submarine activities and Ambassador Bernstorff had been given his passports on February 3. Three American ships were sunk shortly afterward. Meanwhile the Russian people had overthrown the Czarist regime in their first stroke for freedom. Congress was called into extraordinary session, and President Wilson delivered his war message in person on April 2, 1917. The message belongs among the greatest of our state papers. Careful to make a distinction between the German people and the German government, he spoke of the latter as "an irresponsible government which has thrown aside all considerations of humanity and of right and is running amuck." Speaking of the war aims of the United States, he said:

The world must be made safe for democracy. Its peace must be planted upon the tested foundations of political liberty. We have no selfish ends to serve. We desire no conquests, no dominion. We seek no indemnities for ourselves, no material compensation for the sacrifices we shall freely make. We are but one of the champions of the rights of mankind. We shall be satisfied when those rights have been made as secure as the faith and the freedom of nations can make them.

Touching briefly on the possibilities of a just peace, he said, "We shall fight for the things which we have always carried nearest our hearts,—for democracy, for the right of those who submit to authority to have a voice in their own Governments, for the rights and liberties of small nations, for a universal dominion of right by such a concert of free peoples as shall bring peace and safety to all nations and make the world itself at last free." It is no exaggeration to say that these words lifted Wilson to a position of moral leadership among the war-weary peoples of the earth. No nation had ever before undertaken such an enterprise as the United States entered upon when, four days later, Congress declared war upon Germany: a war to end wars. The time is past when we can longer afford to ignore the fact that in winning the war we lost the peace, and the peace—a lasting, enduring peace of justice for all peoples—was the reason for our appeal to arms. It has been customary to blame the failure to achieve a lasting peace settlement upon the secret treaties, grasping selfishness, and vindictiveness of the European powers. They were contributing factors, of course, but that explanation is too self-satisfying, too much of a rationalization of our own action. The war had brought more people in the world into a receptive mood for the sort of program we had conceived than probably will be true again for generations. We had the power to dictate a peace in 1917, but not two years later and the fault was our own. We proved incapable of going to war and retaining the dispassionate attitude which the Wilson peace program demanded. Moreover, we ignored too many fundamental principles of Americanism in our haste to throw the full force of the nation's strength into the contest. The declaration of war was followed immediately by an unprecedented regimentation of manpower, industry, transportation, and public opinion. The resulting distrust, hatred, and fear destroyed the fine idealism in which the crusade was conceived.

THE SINEWS OF WAR

The United States never had prepared for war until war began, and this was no exception; but, having made the decision, the nation willingly centered its entire interest upon attaining a victory. President Wilson, by a skillful diplomatic offensive and by the formulation of a clear statement of war aims and peace objectives, gave to the war the character of a great crusade for freedom, justice, and security for all mankind. He also selected capable men for administrative posts, and gave them authority and his undeviating support. He refused to accept the status of an Ally for the nation; and, by merely associating with the Allies in a common cause, reserved to the United States complete freedom in the matter of policies.

The Administration insisted upon conscription of manpower and Congress passed a Selective Service Act which went into effect on May 18, 1917. It was the first radical departure from precedent in that it empowered the President to select for military service one million men between the ages of 21 and 30, with exemptions for clergymen, objectors on religious grounds, and defectives, and with deferred status for persons engaged in public service and in industries essential to war, including agriculture. The Act also increased the strength of the National Guard and the Regular Army to 750,000. Young men to the number of 9,586,000 were enrolled on June 5, 1917, approximately 1,000,000 more on June 5, 1918, and 13,000,000 between the ages of 18 and 45 in September, 1918. Five hundred thousand of the first registrants were called into service on July 20, 1917, and nearly 3,000,000 before the close of the war. The three units of the military forces were kept separate, consisting of (1) seventeen divisions of National Guard (26–42); (2) eighteen divisions of conscripts, known as the National Army (76–93); and (3) twenty divisions of the Regular Army (1–20). All of the National Guard divisions, all but one division of the

National Army, and eight divisions of the Regular Army were sent to France. They were trained in thirty-two hastily constructed camps, each equipped to accommodate between 40,000 and 50,000 men. Many veteran French and British officers were sent to assist in the training. Five hundred thousand troops were in France at the end of the first year and about four times that number before the Armistice was signed in November, 1918.

No one who went up the Seine with the first handful of untrained men on May 25, 1917, could fail to understand what the mere sight of American troops meant to the drooping spirits of the French people. Several hospital units were hastily organized within a few days after war was declared, rushed to England and then on to various parts of the British lines in France for no other reason than the psychological effect upon the British and French people. American destroyers were already in British waters to convoy them through the submarine zone. The Commander in Chief of the American Expeditionary Force, General John J. Pershing, followed shortly afterward, arriving in London June 9 and in Paris June 13. From that time on, detachments of troops from every department of the Army moved in ever-increasing numbers into the war zone. They were brigaded with the French and British troops all through the winter of 1917–1918. The United States was not prepared to equip them properly for modern warfare and relied heavily upon the British and French for artillery, machine guns, and particularly airplanes. Nor were we prepared to transport troops to France, Great Britain carrying no less than one half of our army across the Atlantic.

The reasons for haste in thus sending even small detachments to France was perfectly apparent. The Allied nations were close to exhaustion when the United States entered the war. Ambassador Page had notified President Wilson on March 5, 1917, that the British financial structure was threatened with collapse. German submarines had reduced the civilian population of the British Isles almost to the point of starvation. Shortly after our entry into the war, France and Great Britain were compelled to rush troops to Italy to prevent the complete collapse of the Italian armies. Russia, under the new Bolshevist regime, sued for peace with Germany and thus released Germany's eastern armies for operations on the Western Front. It was necessary for the United States to bolster the resources and ebbing morale of the Allies, and to do it quickly, or lose the war before it had fairly started. The result was that 1,750,000 troops were transported to France between March and October, 1918, and they constituted the decisive force in the final phases of the war.

The United States Shipping Board, created in September before war was declared, set up an Emergency Fleet Corporation with General George W. Goethals as its chairman. It started out with a fund of fifty million dollars to acquire ships by purchase, charter, and construction. Goethals and William Densman, Chairman of the Shipping Board, soon disagreed and were replaced by Charles M. Schwab and Edward M. Hurley. Shipyards were built and a huge construction program was initiated. Ships were purchased from other nations and the interned German ships were reconditioned. From all sources, the Shipping Board assembled ten million tons of shipping before the Armistice. Its efforts enabled the government to carry about half of its own troops and all supplies to France and to return them all to the United States in record time after the war.

Having made a feeble gesture at regimenting manpower in such a way as to place every individual in the position, civil and military, for which he was best equipped, the government next undertook to regiment the economic life of the nation under six regulatory agencies: the War Industries Board, the War Trade Board, the Food Administration, the Fuel Administration, the Railroad Administration, and the National War Labor Board. These agencies were created to increase production and reduce domestic consumption, to insure maximum efficiency in transportation, and to prevent disputes between capital and labor from interfering with the smooth functioning of the industrial process. The aggregate powers of these several boards and administrators constituted an economic dictatorship. Prices of many commodities, including steel, aluminum, copper, cement, lumber, wheat, and sugar, were fixed. Products were standardized. Submarginal mines were opened and submarginal land cultivated. No new industrial enterprise could be initiated without government consent. Processors were dependent upon the good will of bureaucrats for raw materials, for priorities in shipment, and for export permits. The housewife was no less irritated by the rationing of grocers and butchers and the assumed importance of the local dispensers of sugar. Meatless and wheatless days and fuelless Sundays were borne without protest or even with zealous show of patriotism, but in the hearts of millions was harbored a dull resentment against the attempt to put everyone in leading strings.

The War Industries Board originated as a committee of the Council of National Defense and was created a separate agency by executive order on July 8, 1917. Its chief members were Bernard M. Baruch, Daniel Willard of the B. & O. Railroad, Samuel Gompers of the A.F. of L., Julius Rosenwald of Sears, Roebuck and Company, and Judge Robert S. Brookings. It maintained strict control of all manufacturing and mining and approved all purchases by the United States and foreign governments. The War Trade Board, under the chairmanship of Vance C. McCormick, was empowered to regulate all exports and deny licenses to trade to any firm even remotely connected with German and Austrian commerce, to refuse permission for the export of certain commodities, and to allot shipping space to exporters. The Food Administration Board, supervised by Herbert Hoover, exercised the same powers over the production and consumption of foodstuffs as the War Industries Board over manufacturing. The task was infinitely more difficult because of the tremendous number of units of production and total lack of cooperative enterprises. Nevertheless, through the control of exports, purchases, and shipping, it did bring the production and distribution of agricultural products under control. Six months after wheat was selling for $3.45 a bushel in May, 1917, it set a price of $2.20 for the 1917 crop, increased wheat acreage from 45,000,000 in 1917 to nearly 76,000,000 in 1919, and set in motion an amazing voluntary conservation program in the use of foodstuffs, particularly of bread and meat. The Fuel Administration, headed by Harry A. Garfield, closed factories at will to conserve fuel, introduced daylight-saving time, and encouraged the expansion of the coal industry into what were previously regarded as submarginal deposits. The Railroad Administration was created in December, 1917, and placed under the supervision of Secretary of the Treasury William G. McAdoo. Inland water transportation and express companies were also brought under the same control. They were operated as a single unit with little thought for improvements, profits, or even replacements except as required by the single objective of quick and adequate transportation of the sinews of war.

The character of the war was such that most industries shared in the orders for war supplies. Others profited from the widespread prosperity created by the prodigious spending of our own and foreign governments between 1914 and 1919. Men became wealthy over night. Property values soared, especially those of agricultural lands. The cost of living rose steadily. Labor was in a strategic position during those years. Immigration from Europe virtually ceased at the outbreak of the war. Production was speeded up to supply the demands of the warring nations. The labor supply was further reduced by our entry into the war and the operations of the draft. A friendly administration was in power at Washington. Organized labor took advantage of conditions to increase its membership from 2,000,000 in 1913 to nearly 3,000,000 at the end of the war. Huge profits from the manufacture of war supplies made possible an increase in wages even more rapid than the increase in living costs. But the gains of labor were not made easily. The friendliness of the Wilson Administration for organized labor provoked stubborn opposition from capital. Fresh labor supplies were tapped in the agricultural South and violence was resorted to in the West against the Industrial Workers of the World. Industrial warfare was general during 1916 and 1917.

The Wilson Administration was faced with the necessity of keeping production at a maximum, but it refused to use its war powers to labor's disadvantage. An advisory council was given to the Secretary of Labor and a War Labor Conference Board was established in the winter of 1917–1918. Finally a National War Labor Board was created by executive order on April 8, 1918. The formulation of labor policies was largely the work of Felix Frankfurter; the direction of the War Labor Board was assigned to former President William H. Taft and to Frank P. Walsh. The purpose of this machinery was to settle by mediation and conciliation every controversy which might arise between employers and employees in essential war industries and related fields. This was to be done through mediation committees in local communities which were given power to summon all parties for a hearing and refer questions it failed to settle to the National Board. This Board, in such instances, was to choose an arbiter by unanimous vote or by lot from ten disinterested persons nominated by the President of the United States. The machinery of the Department of Labor was placed at the disposal of the Board, and the Secretary of that Department or either party to a controversy might bring a case to the attention of the Board. All committees appointed by the Board were to have equal representation from capital and labor. The principles laid down by law were as follows: (1) strikes and lockouts were banned for the duration of the war; (2) the right of collective bargaining was affirmed and could not be denied; (3) employees could not be discharged for union activities; (4) unions were forbidden to coerce non-union workers or employers; (5) standards of work and wages established by unions must be maintained where already existing; (6) equal pay for men and women in the same work was required; (7) existing eight-hour day agreements were to be continued and all other cases determined on the basis of governmental requirements and the best interests of the employees; (8) a national card index of available skilled labor was to be prepared by the Department of Labor; and (9) wages were to be maintained on a level insuring "health and reasonable comfort" to the worker's family.

The cost of the war amounted to $32,000,000,000. Nearly $1,000,-000,000 was loaned to the Allied nations within six months after our declaration of war, and a total of $10,338,000,000 went for war and rehabilitation purposes to the Allies and to the newly created states of Eastern Europe after the war. Great Britain borrowed $4,277,-000,000; France, $3,404,000,000; Italy, $1,648,000,000; Belgium, $379,000,000; and Russia, $192,000,000. Of the other nations, Poland received $159,000,000; Czechoslovakia, $92,000,000; Jugoslavia, $52,000,000; Austria, $24,000,000; Esthonia, $14,000,000;

Armenia, $12,000,000; Latvia and Lithuania each $5,000,000; and Hungary, $1,685,000. Practically all of this money was advanced in the form of credit for the purchase of foodstuffs and supplies in the United States. The government secured approximately the amount loaned to these nations, or one third the total expenditures of the war period, from taxes, largely income taxes on individuals and corporations, excess profits taxes, and excise taxes on telegraph and telephone messages, railroad and theater tickets, etc. The larger part, of course, came from income taxes which amounted to three billion dollars in the fiscal year 1917–1918. The normal rate on incomes was raised to 6 percent and surtaxes to a maximum of 65 percent. Twenty and one half billion dollars, about the cost of our own war establishment, was secured by the sale of Liberty Loan Bonds, Victory Loan Bonds, and War Savings Certificates. The amounts, dates and interest rates of these bond issues were as follows:

First Liberty Loan—June, 1917—3½%—$2,000,000,000
Second Liberty Loan—November, 1917—4%—$3,800,000,000
Third Liberty Loan—May, 1918—4¼%—$4,200,000,000
Fourth Liberty Loan—October, 1918—4¼%—$6,000,000,000
Victory Loan—April, 1919—4¾%—$4,500,000,000

The public had no more choice about buying bonds than the soldiers had about buying government insurance. The government did not directly coerce the purchase of its securities, but it worked the people into such a frenzy of patriotic hysteria that few people dared risk the disfavor of their neighbors by not purchasing irrespective of their ability to do so. Not only did the people respond to the government's appeal for funds, they supported most magnanimously such agencies of relief as the American Red Cross, the Young Men's Christian Association, and the Salvation Army as well as the several religious organizations for soldiers' aid.

PUBLIC OPINION

More important than all of these activities, over the long view, was the government's zealous effort to regiment public opinion. On

April 14, 1917, George Creel was placed in charge of a Committee on Public Information. The work of this agency was little short of sensational. Millions of pamphlets were distributed. Seventy-five thousand speakers were engaged to promote the sale of bonds and stimulate patriotism. The foreign-language press was censored and other newspapers persuaded to establish their own censorship. Every conceivable channel for the dissemination of propaganda in the country was utilized from motion pictures to stereopticon slides and foreign missions were sent out to convert the world to America's war-for-peace program. When Creel's work was finished every one confidently expected that a new world order was in the making and the repercussions which followed their disillusionment continued to reverberate throughout the world for many years. In the United States, the result was equally tragic. Carried away by the war hysteria, Congress passed the Espionage Act of June 15, 1917, and amended it with the Sedition Act of May 6, 1918, sweeping away at one stroke the most cherished principles of the American people: freedom of speech and of the press under all circumstances.

When Woodrow Wilson delivered his war message to Congress, he said: "We act without animus, not in enmity toward a people . . . but only in armed opposition to an irresponsible government which has thrown aside all considerations of humanity and of right and is running amuck." Wilson continued to differentiate between the German government and the German people; but the people of this country made no such distinction. They came to hate the German people as well as their government; they permitted suspicion to supplant facts in judging disloyalty, hurling bitter terms of denunciation at citizens of foreign birth and aliens; they discharged such persons from positions of honorable employment which they had long filled; they sought to ban the study of the German language and German literature from the schools by legislation, all but destroying it through force of public opinion; they inaugurated a widespread witch-hunt in the public schools, colleges, and universities in an effort to crush every one who was pacifically inclined or internationally minded; they found it impossible to go to war and remain true to their traditions of justice and tolerance.

The Committee on Public Information was designed to perform the twofold function of promoting publicity and invoking censorship. It established precedents in disseminating propaganda which were followed up with equal fervor and small regard for the truth by a host of self-anointed patriots and patriotic societies. Some stories, such as the mutilation of Belgian babies and soap-making from the cadavers of their soldiers fallen in battle by the Germans, emanated from foreign propaganda machines. A thousand others, manufactured out of whole cloth by suspicious individuals alarmed at unusual but harmless incidents, set the people everlastingly to suspecting every one of subversive activities. The number of actual spies thus apprehended was relatively so small that failure to discover them probably would not have resulted in any serious consequences. The historical importance of the whole phenomenon does not lie in the number of guilty individuals caught, nor in the inconvenience, injustices, and injuries inflicted upon unfortunate innocents, deplorable as such incidents were. It lies in the self-imposed restraints of free discussion and rational criticism through fear by every one. It lies, too, in the fact that intolerance, which is a vicious disease, carried over into the postwar period to follow the psychopathic trail into many phases of social and economic life. If there is one fact clearly revealed by the history of the abolition movement, the Civil War, and the reform movement, it is that the right of free discussion was an unquestioned principle of American life. We emerged from the war with the right of the individual to advocate publicly and freely whatever ideas he might have little more than a hollow pretense.

It is important to remember that war legislation set up a vast centralized control of nearly every phase of activity, and especially that the Selective Service Acts made every man between the ages of eighteen and forty-five a potential member of the armed forces. An individual, therefore, could scarcely speak, write, or print anything, however select his audiences, without influencing the armed forces. Whether the memory of Civil War dissent, the difficulties already experienced by the Allied governments, or Wilson's personal fear of criticism was responsible for federal legislation is a matter of conjecture. There are strong reasons for believing that it was the latter. A wartime President usually gets the type of legislation he desires from Congress. The original Espionage Act was an administration measure and was modified only after a bitter attack upon it by the press and a small group of Senators led by William E. Borah. Moreover, Wilson said: "If there should be disloyalty, it will be dealt with with a firm hand of stern repression." The Espionage Act was introduced shortly after the declaration of war and, certainly, was not a response to popular demand. It was followed, in point of time, by the activities of the Committee on Public Information. Then came the many repressive state statutes from one of which, that of Montana, the language was taken for the amendment to the Espionage Act, popularly known as the Sedition Act of May 16, 1918. It was under the original Espionage Act, however, that most of the government prosecutions were conducted. Wilson had risen to such heights of leadership, not of power alone, that he could have done much to modify the popular attitude had he chosen to do so.

The Espionage Act of June 15, 1917, imposed a maximum penalty of $10,000 fine and twenty years imprisonment upon any one who interfered with the operations of the draft, made false statements with intent to retard the success of the armed forces, or attempted to incite disloyalty. It was amended drastically, May 16, 1918, to include any one who discouraged the sale of government bonds; obstructed the making of loans by or to the United States; incited insubordination, disloyalty, or mutiny; uttered, printed, wrote, or published any "disloyal, profane, scurrilous or abusive language about the form of government of the United States," constitution, armed forces, or uniform; issued language intended to bring them into "contempt, scorn, contumely or disrepute"; discouraged production of war necessities; or taught, defended, or suggested the doing of any of these things—and certainly these "things" were open to broad interpretation.

These acts gave the Postmaster-General power to exclude from the mails not only anything which in his sole judgment violated the prohibitions but to deny the offender all use of the postal service for any purpose whatsoever. Postmaster-General A. S. Burleson did exercise the power thus conferred upon him to the extreme limit, excluding from the mails *The Masses* edited by Max Eastman, the *Milwaukee Leader* edited by Victor L. Berger, an issue of *The Nation* and many books and pamphlets, including Thorstein Veblen's *Imperial Germany and the Industrial Revolution*. The Department of Justice, under the control of A. Mitchell Palmer, ably assisted by courts and juries, sent nearly two thousand men and women to prison for terms ranging up to twenty years, including Eugene V. Debs, Victor L. Berger, and William D. Haywood. Several aspects of the trials and convictions under these wartime statutes are significant. The courts gave a broad construction to the law, holding all utterances to be in violation which had a tendency to do the things prohibited. Jury trial failed to safeguard the traditional principle of freedom of speech because of the widespread determination to suppress dissent. The Department of Justice and the Post Office, rather than Congress and President Wilson, were responsible for converting the law into an instrument for the persecution of pacifists and economic dissenters. It was the first establishment of political crimes in over a century of national development. The defense that government severity was necessary to forestall mob actions and the expressed fear of radical influence upon the Negro were undeniably pregnant with meaning for the future.

The extreme penalties provided in the law and the militant activities of the enforcement agencies thwarted all rational consideration of public questions. There could be no free discussion of fiscal policies with respect to taxation, bond issues, or war loans to the Allies; of the relative merits of conscription and volunteer enlistments; of mistaken administration policies touching upon neutrality; of the economic and imperialistic basis of Allied war aims; of profiteering and official corruption; or of the many other issues about which there are always honest differences of opinion and which can be approached intelligently only after free interchange of opinions. Many of these issues which carried over to test the wisdom of the postwar generation were far more perplexing than they necessarily would have been had the government been satisfied with an almost unanimous support of the people and not attempted to create an artificial unanimity of opinion.

The period presents the unique spectacle of a nation, whose President was the recognized champion of human rights everywhere, sending men to prison for twenty years whose humanitarianism was no less sincere, but whose formula for reaching the millennium differed from the prevailing one.

THE WAR IN EUROPE

The American Army was assigned the southern sector of the war zone with General Pershing's headquarters at Chaumont, supply headquarters at Tours and the principal seaports at Brest, Saint-Nazaire and Bordeaux. Railway lines, motor transport roads, telegraph and telephone lines were constructed from the ports of debarkation to the front lines and connecting the dozens of training camps, storage depots, and hospitals within the triangle from Le Havre to Chaumont to Bordeaux. The construction of docks, barracks, warehouses, recreation centers, etc., went on unceasingly until the Armistice. Millions of tons of equipment, food, munitions, and other supplies including railway rolling stock and motor trucks had to be transported through the submarine zone. So efficiently did the navy perform its services that the loss was almost negligible. The navy was not called upon to participate in any major engagements but effectively protected American convoys, and engaged in planting mines and destroying submarines. Its presence may have been the deciding factor in the decision of the German government not to risk a decisive naval engagement. It was almost a year before American troops in any numbers participated in actual fighting and not until August, 1918, that a separate American Army was created. Until that time, detachments were brigaded with British and French troops. Beginning in October, 1917, however, one division after another entered the lines on the more quiet southern sector.

The German high command had no choice in the spring of 1918 but to open a vast offensive on the Western Front. They had gambled everything on unrestricted submarine warfare in 1917 and had lost. Allied shipping losses had been appalling: 532,000 tons in February, 599,000 in March, and 869,000 in April. Then

Britain had met the crisis with one of the great innovations of the war—the system of convoys—and by mid-summer, with the American navy participating, the submarine was beaten. Thereafter, losses were negligible. In the second place, the United States had performed miracles in building an army and putting it into combat—3000 miles from the home base of supplies. There were 250,-000 troops in France by March, 1918, with new arrivals averaging 10,000 per day. It was a real achievement, unprecedented in American history, wholly unexpected by the Germans. Every week that passed increased the strength of Germany's opponents and lessened the advantage she had gained by the humiliation of Russia at Brest-Litovsk. There was peace talk in the Reichstag, mutiny in the navy, widespread rumblings of revolt among the subject peoples of Austria-Hungary.

The final German offensive began on March 21, 1918, and finally ended on July 18. These four months were critical. Germany had transferred her finest troops to the Western Front, marshaled all her resources, and was making a desperate bid for victory before the American Army could be assembled. The stimulating effect of our entry into the war was wearing off and the morale of the French and British troops had reached a new low point as the weary months of the winter dragged on without hope of immediate victory. The German attack was launched viciously and at the proper psychological moment to break the British lines. It almost succeeded in doing so, giving the Allied command some anxious hours until fresh support could be rushed into the breach. Three offensives in all were hurled at the war-weary Allied Armies: on March 21, from Arras to La Fere; on April 9, from Ypres to Armentières; and on May 26, between Noyon and Rheims. The attack of March 21 was unprecedented in fury, embracing 62 divisions, 1700 batteries, and 1000 planes. The stalemate had ended; this was a war of movement; victory or humiliating defeat. In desperation, American troops were rushed to critical points all along the line to the north, and plans for the immediate formation of an American Army appeared to be doomed. But the Allied governments agreed to surrender all differences among themselves and place their armies under the absolute authority of a supreme command. The French General Foch was chosen for the post and Foch consented to the American demands for united forces in their own section of the line. While this was being accomplished and during the German offensive, American troops engaged in strenuous fighting in the battles of the Aisne, Noyon-Montdidier, and Champagne-Marne.

The German offensive inflicted heavy casualties upon the British and French forces, and gained hundreds of square miles of territory; but the lines held, and on July 18 the Allied counter-offensive began. The Second Battle of the Marne which began that day was an unpleasant surprise to the Germans. They had not credited the French with strength to mount an offensive; nor had they expected to meet infantry supported by a wave of tanks. They had no defense against these new offensive weapons though the British had first used them at Cambrai in November, 1917. Between July 18 and August 6, an American force of about 250,000 men, co-operating with the French Army, regained the ground previously lost between Rheims and Soissons and straightened out the salient which, at its farthest point, included Château-Thierry. Two days later, the British began an attack which did not cease until November 11 on the Somme east of Amiens. This assault of Canadian and Anzac divisions, again supported by tanks, on August 8, completely overwhelmed the German positions. "August 8 confirmed the decline of our fighting powers" said Ludendorff of the German High Command. "The war," he said, "must be ended."

Ten days later (August 18), the French and American armies resumed their attack on the Oise-Aisne line between Rheims and Soissons and, the following day, the British and Belgians drove south and east from Ypres on a line toward Brussels. These concerted and continuous attacks made the shifting of troops by the German command precarious business and set the stage for the final drive of the full American Army through the almost impenetrable Argonne Forest to Sedan. The St. Mihiel salient was straightened out between September 12 and 16 and, on September 20, the drive began north of Verdun. The Germans sent their finest troops to stay the American advance but without success. It was the beginning of the end for Germany because that sector of the line protected the iron mines of Lorraine and the central transportation center at Sedan. The British Army broke through into Belgium and the American Army pushed forward to cut the German line of communications at Sedan.

13

Making the Peace

WILSON'S PEACE PROGRAM

WHEN the radical socialists of Russia, soon to be known as the Bolsheviks or Communists, engineered a coup d'état in November, 1917, established a dictatorship of the proletariat, and opened peace negotiations with Germany, Wilson was forced once more to take up the question of Allied war aims which he had allowed to lie dormant during the early months of America's war effort. So insistent did the demands of liberal, and particularly labor, groups in Great Britain, France, and the United States become, and so reluctant, or incapable, were the Allied governments to state a specific program, that Wilson once more assumed leadership in this respect. On January 8, 1918, he delivered a memorable address to Congress enumerating fourteen points as a basis for a peace settlement.

Six of these were general restatements of objectives previously mentioned in his public pronouncements: abandonment of secret diplomacy, freedom of the seas in peace and in war, removal of all trade barriers, reduction of armaments, readjustment of colonial claims in the interest of the native populations, and a League of Nations. Eight points dealt with specific territorial problems: evacuation of Russia and complete freedom for her to determine the nature of her own political institutions and public policies; evacuation and restoration of Belgium; evacuation of France and the return to her of Alsace-Lorraine; self-determination for the subject groups in Austria-Hungary; readjustment of boundary lines in the Balkans; self-determination for minorities in Turkey and internationalization of the Dardanelles; a free Poland with an outlet to the seas; and restoration to Italy of Italian provinces in Austria-Hungary. The ultimate importance of the speech lay (1) in the fact that it committed the United States, for the first time, to participation in the settlement of specific European problems as a prerequisite to world peace; and (2) in the fact that Germany appealed to Wilson for peace negotiations on the basis of these points when defeat stared her in the face. Wilson had also elaborated upon the theme of his original war message in an address at Washington, June 14, 1917, and in his message to Congress, December 4, 1917. Great emphasis had been placed upon certain general principles. Belgium was to be evacuated and restored as a "healing act" without which "the whole structure and validity of international law is forever impaired." Russia was to be evacuated and all questions touching that nation settled in such manner as would obtain for her "an unhampered and unembarrassed opportunity for the independent determination of her own political development" under institutions of her own choosing. There were to be no annexations and all territorial settlements were to be made on the basis of the best interests of the people involved rather than for the benefit of rival nations. All such settlements were to be consistent with permanent peace and without discrimination arising from war hatreds. Finally, there was to be a League or General Association of Nations, which was to replace all alliances between nations or groups of nations and have sole control of economic discriminations for the purpose of enforcing its mandates.

The disintegration of the German Empire began with the failure of the last German offensive. The German government, perfectly aware that the Allies would refuse any terms except a complete surrender, and under pressure from their own military leaders to open peace negotiations before the invading armies should reach German soil, turned to President Wilson in hope of salvaging something from defeat in the field. Had they not taken advantage of the Wilson peace program and sued for peace, the Allied and American Armies would have driven straight to Berlin.

Unwilling to risk the havoc of an invasion, they hastened to capitulate.

An exchange of notes between the United States and Germany and between the United States and the Allies took place during the month of October. The Allies were reluctant to accept peace on the basis of the Fourteen Points, partly because of previous secret treaties of their own as to the disposition of the territories of the Central Powers. Great Britain flatly refused to agree to the freedom of the seas in war which would have deprived her of the blockade as a weapon. The French insisted, and it was understood by all, that "evacuation and restoration of territory" would include compensation for damages to civilians and their property "by the aggression of Germany by land, by sea, and from the air." This reservation left the way open for the imposition of heavy reparations, and it was particularly emphasized by Wilson in his last note to Germany on November 5.

The German government, fearing that any effort to secure clarification of the Fourteen Points in her interest would lead to cessation of negotiations and complete rout of her armies, preferred to risk her chances at the peace table, knowing that she would probably lose Alsace-Lorraine, the Polish Corridor, and her colonies. Sentiment in the United States, also, was strongly against anything but a dictated peace. Wilson, having refused to discuss terms with the old German government, a parliamentary government was set up under the chancellorship of Prince Max of Baden. The old regime then began to crumble under the impact of strikes, communist outbreaks in the cities, and mutinies in the fleet and army. Kaiser Wilhelm fled to Holland and a new German Republic was established. Then, on November 11, an armistice was signed on terms dictated by the Allied high command.

President Wilson had informed Germany, October 23, that the terms of an armistice must be such as to make renewal of hostilities by Germany impossible. It was on those conditions that the German Armistice Commission proceeded to Foch's special train in the Forest of Compiègne and signed the terms of surrender on November 11, 1918. The terms were not easy; they could not have been in view of the tremendous power of the German military and economic system. German military forces were to withdraw from all occupied territory, and in the West, to a line 10 kilometers east of the Rhine. The German army was to surrender armament to the amount of 5000 guns, 25,000 machine guns, and 1700 airplanes; in transport equipment, 5000 motor trucks, 5000 locomotives, and 150,000 wagons; and in naval armament, 10 battleships, 6 battle cruisers, 8 light cruisers, 50 destroyers, and all her submarines. Germany was to return all gold and all inhabitants carried out of occupied countries, and all prisoners of war. The blockade was to continue. The treaties of Brest Litovsk and Bucharest were to be annulled. Thus ended a war which had cost the lives of 13,000,000 men in arms and an equal number of non-combatants.

TRAGEDY OF ERRORS

Looking back after nearly three decades one may well ask the question, What price victory? Millions of men must have pondered the thought, Woodrow Wilson among them. Wilson was now at the zenith of his power. He was, to all outward appearances, the leader of a united nation, commander in chief of the strongest military and naval power on earth. He was the acknowledged spokesman for suffering and oppressed humanity throughout the world. He had rallied the peoples of all nations in a great crusade to bring freedom, justice, and peace to everyone, everywhere. He had won a great diplomatic victory by bringing the war to a close on the basis of his reconstruction program. He was the leader of the moral forces of the world. He was looked upon with an adoration closely akin to worship by the masses of Europe. Never before did a man hold such tremendous power, so glorious an opportunity, so grave a responsibility; yet, in the end, Wilson's power was broken; his handiwork, the League of Nations, was repudiated by his own people; and he was driven to his grave by the loss of his cause. The United States remained out of the League and the World Court, insisting upon acting always according to its own judgment in any situation which might arise. Germany and Japan ultimately did likewise. Economic warfare followed. Irresponsible governments rose to power. National hatreds accumulated. National bigotry passed for patriotism. The eternal peace for which men fought turned out to be a sadly elusive goal as human life turned back many decades to isolation, violence, and despotism. The price of failure was the damaged morale of a generation of young people who grew up to know only idleness, starvation, turmoil, and oppression. The theory of safety in armaments, shattered and discredited by the events of the World War, was repeated and believed. Armaments piled upon armaments, adding their billions of dollars to the burden of taxpayers and kindling distrust in the hearts of men.

Reaction had already set in before firing ceased on the western front; and, in consequence, making the peace proved to be incomparably more difficult than winning the war. Its first fruit was a sordid sacrifice of lofty idealism to political expediency which weakened Wilson's position at the Peace Conference and then prevented our entry into the League of Nations. Wilson began it when, in October, 1918, he placed the question of supporting his policies on a partisan basis, implying, in an appeal to the electorate, that to be a righteous patriot one must first be a Democrat. Warren G. Harding followed with an open bid for the presidency by repudiating the idea that nations can be anything but potential enemies or that mankind can recognize higher motives for human conduct than mere selfishness. The spirit of the irreconcilable isolationists was permitted to prevail as the mass of people, deprived of inspired leadership, turned indifferently to more material things.

On October 24 before the Congressional elections of 1918, Woodrow Wilson made the following appeal to the people of the United States: "If you have approved of my leadership and wish me to continue to be your unembarrassed spokesman in affairs at home and abroad, I earnestly beg that you will express yourself unmistakably to that effect by returning a Democratic majority to both Senate and House of Representatives." A few days later the people went to the polls and gave the Republicans a majority of two in the Senate and forty-five in the House of Representatives. Wilson's appeal was in no way responsible for the results of the election. Its significance lies much deeper than that. For eighteen months the government had been attempting to destroy all diversity of thought by compulsion and regimentation. Congress was the tool of the President. He had demanded explicit faith and un-questioning support of his policies. What he asked of the electorate was the right to continue to dictate to Congress, to determine the national policies, and to draft men for their support. Only a few Republicans had been courageous enough to resist his dictator-ship from the first. George W. Norris and Robert M. La Follette were two, and he had denounced them and their associates as the "wilful twelve." But now that the war was virtually over and the necessity of formulating a reconstruction program approached, this question of executive power vs. Congressional prerogatives assumed new importance. Wilson's base appeal to partisan politics swept away the shroud of idealism which had given him the support of most Republicans and loosed the torrent of pent-up discussion and hostile criticism. It was then that Wilson's intolerance of others' desires, his dictatorial attitude with respect to policy, and his lack of followers genuinely devoted to him personally, counted so heavily against him.

There was another aspect of the situation which is too often ignored. For months, a mob spirit had been abroad in the land masquerading under the cloak of patriotism. Tarring and feather-ing, deporting, beating, and downright killing had finally impelled Wilson to say in July, 1918: "How shall we commend democracy to the acceptance of other peoples if we disgrace our own by proving that it is, after all, no protection to the weak?" But he did nothing about it. His great error had been in permitting the Espionage and Sedition Acts to be placed upon the statute books. Government agencies went on making America unsafe for liberal-ism with their bureaucratic autocracy while the President insisted the world must be made safe for democracy. The Department of Justice and the Post Office Department were particularly active during September, 1918, and the protest, however strong it may have been, was silently registered on election day.

Finally, making the peace and demobilizing the vast war machine were both in men's minds in the summer of 1918, the latter more than the former. Men were thinking in terms of whether the government should continue its control of industry; whether the nation should move farther away from or back to individualism in economic life; and what should be done about the national debt, the railroads, the merchant marine, the tariff, submarginal land and mines, and world markets. Wilson's display of partisanship was the occasion for a revival of party politics, with a presidential campaign not far distant, and a determination to have no extension of the domestic legislation of his first administration. There were four points, moreover, on which Wilson lacked the united support of either party, all vital to the peace program he had enunciated. They were (1) moderation in dealing with the vanquished nations; (2) reduction of economic barriers; (3) an association of nations; and (4) reduction of armaments. For the first time, Wilson needed the support of all the liberal forces in the country and they were completely disorganized. There had been so little discussion of the peace program developed by Wilson that no strong public opinion was created to strengthen his position at the Peace Conference. The strategic control of world diplomacy which passed into Wilson's hands with our entry into the war, and which even the publication of the secret treaties in the summer of 1918 did not damage, was lost by the election. He went to Europe the repudiated leader of the American people. He came back the discredited leader of liberalism throughout the world. All of this should not obscure the fact that men like Henry Cabot Lodge, Theodore Roosevelt, and William Howard Taft had endorsed a militaristic approach to the problem of peace and were demanding the prosecution of the war to the point of unconditional surrender, a dictated peace in Berlin; that the opposition was already demanding a return to high protective tariffs and government aid in the anticipated mad scramble for world markets; that fear of Bolshevism was rapidly replacing fear of Prussianism and not only reviving the spirit of isolation, but threatening the proposal that Russia be left free to adopt institutions of her own choosing; and that the farmers of the Middle West were hostile to Wilson because they regarded their war profits so very small compared to those of the industrialists.

Foreign governments promptly judged the election as a repudia-tion of Wilson's leadership. The Senate Foreign Relations Com-mittee was now in the control of his political opponents. Wilson then chose a peace commission of Colonel Edward M. House, Secretary Robert Lansing, General Tasker Bliss, and former Ambas-sador Henry White, completely ignoring the Senate, the Republi-cans, and the practical politicians of his own party. Finally, he an-nounced that he, himself, would go to the Peace Conference. Opponents of the administration criticized him severely for leav-ing the country, insisting that he was needed at home to deal with problems of reconstruction. Theodore Roosevelt insisted that Wil-son no longer had "any authority whatever to speak for the Ameri-can people," and others spoke disparagingly of his Messiah com-plex. Wilson, of course, was not free of human frailties, despite great intellectual endowments and an exalted humanitarian phi-losophy. He believed so firmly in his cause that he became arrogant, obstinate, and suspicious of all who opposed his ideas. He went to Paris contrary to the advice of his closest advisers in foreign affairs. He had to deal with men like Clemenceau of France who knew he did not have the united support of his nation and probably could not secure ratification by the Senate of his treaty.

Finally, there is the curious fact that Wilson ceased to champion the ideals of his original peace program with the same fervor as formerly. He had brushed aside as unimportant the secret treaties by which the principal Allies had agreed to dismember the Central Powers and divest them of all their outlying possessions, and never confronted their governments with these treaties during the nego-tiations leading up to the Armistice. He knew the announced in-tention of the British and the French to destroy Germany as a great power by depriving her of her economic resources and im-posing punitive reparations. This question of dealing with Germany is so important that it is best to consider again Wilson's previous pronouncements:

[January 22, 1917]—Victory would mean peace forced upon the loser, a victor's terms imposed upon the vanquished. It would be accepted in humiliation, under duress, at an intolerable sacrifice, and would leave a sting, a resentment, a bitter memory upon which terms of peace would rest, not permanently, but only as upon quick-sand.

[April 2, 1917]—We have no quarrel with the German people. . . . We are, let me say again, the sincere friends of the German people, and shall desire nothing so much as the early reestablishment of intimate relations of mutual advantage between us—however hard it may be for them, for the time being, to believe that this is spoken from our hearts.

[August 27, 1917]—Punitive damages, the dismemberment of empires, the establishment of selfish and exclusive economic leagues, we deem inexpedient and in the end worse than futile, no proper basis for a peace of any kind, least of all for an enduring peace.

[December 4, 1917]—You catch, with me, the voices of humanity that are in the air. They grow daily more audible, more articulate, more persuasive, and they come from the hearts of men everywhere. They insist that the war shall not end in vindictive action of any kind; that no nation or people shall be robbed or punished because the irresponsible rulers of a single country have themselves done deep and abominable wrongs.

[January 26, 1918]—The people won this war, not the governments, and the people must reap the benefits of the war. At every turn we must see to it that it is not an adjustment between Governments merely, but an arrangement for the peace and security of men and women everywhere.

[September 27, 1918]—The impartial justice meted out must involve no discrimination between those to whom we wish to be just and those to whom we do not wish to be just. It must be a justice that plays no favorites, and knows no standards but the equal rights of the several peoples concerned.

[February 24, 1919]—The men who are in Conference in Paris realize as keenly as any American can realize . . . that no man dare go home from that Conference and report anything less noble than was expected of it.

Conscious of the fact, as the war progressed, that a perfect world order could not be achieved by the fiat of a peace conference, Wilson sacrificed much to gain acceptance for his League of Nations. He did so because in the League was the machinery for ironing out whatever injustices there were in the peace settlement, and for providing not only permanent peace but that atmosphere of security so necessary to social and economic progress.

THE VERSAILLES TREATY

⌈The Treaty drawn up at Versailles between January 18 and May 7, 1919, was dictated in all essential features by Wilson, Lloyd George, and Clemenceau.⌉Wilson strove to maintain the principles of his previous pronouncements. The French insisted upon security by reducing Germany to economic impotence. Russia, in the throes of counterrevolution, was not represented. China, angry that Japan should be allowed to keep Shantung, refused to sign the Treaty. Italy, determined to have the Adriatic port of Fiume, withdrew from the conference. Wilson threatened to leave until France surrendered her demand for a Rhine frontier. Every nation, it seemed, paid lip service to Wilsonian idealism unless it touched its own territorial ambitions and sphere of influence.

The Treaty, in consequence of the prevailing tension of war-born hatreds, the growing fear of Bolshevism, and surviving imperialistic rivalries, represented a partial departure from the original Wilson program. It did, however, invoke the principle of self-determination in fixing boundary lines, with plebiscites, or popular votes, in doubtful areas; mandates, or trusteeships under the League of Nations, for former German colonies; and a League of Nations through which any injustices in the treaty and future matters of discord arising between nations could be eliminated. It was the repudiation of all the generous promises with respect to Germany which angered liberals. The socialists of France denounced it as a settlement which violated justice "in nearly every phrase." The *London Herald* could say: "There is no honor left for any of us." The Women's International Conference for Permanent Peace saw in it "discords and animosities which can only lead to future wars." General Jan Christiaan Smuts confessed the "promise of the new life, the victory of the great human ideals are not written in this treaty."

Germany was forced to sign a confession of guilt for the outbreak of the war and all damages to the Allied governments and their people. The Kaiser and other high officials were to be tried by the Allies for crimes against international morality and viola-

tions of the rules of war. She was stripped of all her overseas possessions, together with commercial rights in Morocco, Egypt, and
China. She lost Alsace-Lorraine, Schleswig, German Poland, Danzig, and the Polish Corridor. The Saar Basin was placed under the
control of the League of Nations and its coal mines given to
France for a period of fifteen years in payment for the destruction
of coal mines in northern France. The University of Louvain was
to be supplied with books equal in number and value to those destroyed when its library was burned in 1914. The German army was
reduced to 100,000. Compulsory military service was abolished,
all enlistments being voluntary and for a twelve-year period. The
General Staff was abolished. She was forbidden to manufacture
or import arms, munitions, or war materials, including heavy
artillery, tanks, and poison gas; to own any submarines, or more
than six battleships of 10,000 tons, six light cruisers, and twelve
destroyers; to manufacture or import any airplanes or engines for
airplanes.

In line of reparations, Germany accepted responsibility for restoring all losses incurred by the Allied and associated nations and
their people, including pensions to naval and military victims and
their families. She was required to pay $5,000,000,000 in gold before
May 1, 1921, for rehabilitation purposes and ultimately a sum, to
be fixed by a commission, sufficiently large completely to restore
the Belgian and French war zones. Meanwhile, she was to deliver
to the commission livestock, coal, and manufactured products, all
merchant ships above 1600 tons, one half of those between 1000
and 1600 tons, and build for the Allies 200,000 tons of shipping annually for five years. By these terms, Germany lost control of her
transportation system, taxation, exports and imports, navy, air
service, and merchant marine. She was reduced to economic impotence.

The important omissions of the Treaty provisions were as significant as the punitive sections. An economic basis for this supposedly
permanent peace was completely lacking. There were no provisions
for the disarmament of nations other than the vanquished. Germany and Russia were excluded from the League of Nations.
Finally, the manner in which the representatives of the three great

powers drew up the terms of the Treaty—sitting in secret and dictating to all the world, without counsel and advice from the leading neutral powers or opportunity of protest from the Germans, without representation from the important social and economic groups in the leading nations—all of this was looked upon as autocratic rule by the three powers, a repudiation of self-determination, and a return to the oft-condemned practices of secret diplomacy. These were the things which caused liberals in the United States, Great Britain, and France to reject the treaty, and, many of them, to consider Wilson's previous confessions of faith as mere camouflage.

The other provision of the Treaty which aroused strenuous opposition in the United States was the provision for a League of Nations. The governing agencies of the League were to consist (1) of an Assembly in which all member nations were to have equal representation and voting power; (2) a Council of nine members, consisting of one each from the United States, Great Britain, France, Japan, and Italy; and four to be chosen by the Assembly; (3) a Secretariat at Geneva; and (4) a World Court. The function of the League was to preserve peace by eliminating and curbing the development of all conditions leading to war. It was to guarantee the "territorial integrity and existing political independence" of its members; arbitrate international disputes; impose economic sanctions and, perhaps, military pressure, against violators of the Covenant's provisions; supervise the mandates over the territories of the former Central Powers; control slavery and traffic in women, drugs, and implements of war.

This provision for a League of Nations was the one point on which Wilson refused to yield either to the other nations or to the Senate of the United States. Other mistakes in the settlement could be rectified peacefully and by agreement only if the whole process of international relations was changed. Cooperative action to preserve peace and work toward a better world order required a permanent agency for the purpose. That agency, however much it might require future modification, was the League of Nations. In it lay the hopes of mankind for relief from the burden of armaments, freedom from the threat of force by aggressor nations, and protection of minority populations. It was the parent organization of a Committee on Intellectual Cooperation, an International Labor Organization, and a Permanent Court of International Justice. Small wonder Wilson staked everything on its success.

CONTEST FOR RATIFICATION

Wilson returned to the United States in February, 1919, for the purpose of consulting with the Foreign Relations Committee of Congress and afterward succeeded in having some alterations made in the final draft of the Treaty to insure its ratification by the Senate; but thirty-nine Senators of the new Congress agreed to reject any Treaty of Peace which included the Covenant of the League of Nations. The principal objections to the first draft of the Treaty which were rectified on Wilson's return to Paris were (1) that it did not recognize the Monroe Doctrine; (2) that it failed specifically to exclude the authority of the League over domestic questions such as immigration and tariffs; (3) that the right of a nation to withdraw was not recognized; and (4) that no cognizance was taken of the powers of Congress to make war and peace.

The text of the Treaty was withheld from the Senate until July 10, but copies were secured unofficially and a bitter attack was launched against it. It was opposed by the liberals, both because of its harsh treatment of Germany and its guarantees of the territorial integrity of nations which had appropriated to themselves the former possessions of the Central Powers. It was opposed by the western Progressives who represented the deep-seated tradition of isolation and abstention from foreign entanglements. It was opposed by the group of American imperialists who shuddered for the safety of the Monroe Doctrine and protective tariffs. It was opposed by German-Americans because of its punitive provisions, by Italian-Americans because Italy was not given Fiume, and by Irish-Americans because Wilson had not championed the cause of Irish independence. It was opposed by all who hated Wilson's domestic reforms and were willing to sacrifice civilization if need be to break his power. It was opposed for the sordid sake of party advantage. These forces brought together in opposition to its ratification such powerful men as Elihu Root, Charles Evans Hughes, William Howard Taft, and Senators Frank B. Brandegee, William E. Borah, Hiram Johnson, Philander C. Knox, Robert M. La Follette, Henry Cabot Lodge, Medill McCormick, George H. Moses, and Miles Poindexter. The Senate Foreign Relations Committee under the chairmanship of Lodge insisted upon amendments and engaged in interminable delay.

Wilson finally decided to carry his cause to the people, and left Washington on September 3, 1919, against the advice of his physicians and friends. He traveled more than 8000 miles, delivering 37 speeches over a period of twenty-two days. His opponents sent Borah and Johnson to follow over the same ground and speak against both Wilson and the League. Wilson's strength was not equal to the superhuman effort. He suffered a paralytic stroke at Pueblo, Colorado, was returned to Washington, and lay almost helpless for more than seven months.

The Senate Foreign Relations Committee made its report to the Senate on September 10, the week after Wilson left Washington on his fateful tour. The Committee reported forty-five amendments and four reservations. The Senate rejected the amendments, which would have required a reassembling of the Peace Conference for revision of the Treaty, and accepted a total of fourteen reservations, submitted by Lodge, for debate. The most important of these rejected completely Article X which pledged the members of the League "to respect and preserve as against external aggression the territorial integrity and existing political independence of all members of the League." This Article was particularly obnoxious to Irish-Americans, who insisted it would bind Ireland in perpetual slavery to Great Britain. Wilson regarded this Article as the "heart of the Covenant" and steadfastly refused to make concessions for its amendment or excision.

The reservations also rejected Article XVI, and reserved the right of Congress to authorize the use of armed force. They demanded voting power for the United States equal to that of Great Britain and her dominions. They reserved the right of Congress to decide the question of accepting a mandate under the League, to withdraw from League membership without obligations or penalties, and to exercise complete freedom of action in regard to the Shantung settlement which had so mortally offended China.

The Democrats in the Senate, with complete approval of Wilson, voted against the Treaty with reservations, in order to force a vote on the direct question of ratification. The Senate then refused to ratify the Treaty with reservations (41–51) and without reservations (38–53). Elihu Root and William Howard Taft now tried to obtain a compromise from Lodge and Wilson. Herbert Hoover, who feared the spread of Bolshevism in Europe, warned: "If the League is to break down we must at once prepare to fight: Few people seem to realize the desperation to which Europe has been reduced." But William E. Borah spoke of the rejection as "the greatest victory since Appomattox."

Wilson and Lodge both refused to yield. Representatives of national organizations with a combined membership of 20 million people demanded of Lodge that the Treaty be ratified. Colleges and universities joined in the plea. There can be little doubt that a majority of the people of the country, practically all of the intellectual leaders, and three fourths of the Senate membership favored ratification in some form or other. The discussion was resumed in the next session of Congress, with Lodge showing signs of weakening in his opposition. Borah threatened to disrupt the party if any concessions were made and Lodge's attitude stiffened once more. Wilson likewise was adamant, preferring to have a solemn referendum of the people in the presidential election. The vote of March 19, 1920, therefore, resulted in final rejection of the Treaty, 49 to 35. Wilson vetoed a joint resolution declaring the war with Germany at an end, and it was not until July, 1921 that President Harding signed another resolution bringing the war officially to a close.

THE END OF AN ERA

The presidential campaign of 1920 followed closely upon the final rejection of the Treaty by the Senate. All of the policies which liberals had sponsored and fought for in the first two decades of the country were at stake in the contest. It should have been a classic debate not alone on the question of continued world leadership for the United States, but also on the continuation of the philosophy of the Square Deal and the New Freedom in domestic policies. It was not, because the forces of liberalism were confused and without leadership; but the verdict of the people, tragically, took the country back to the isolation and governmental inaction of the seventies and eighties, and the two great leaders of the forces of liberalism—Theodore Roosevelt and Woodrow Wilson—passed away as their idealism receded into oblivion.

The Republican convention met in Chicago on June 11, 1920, with three strong contenders for the nomination: Major General Leonard E. Wood, Governor Frank O. Lowden of Illinois and Senator Hiram Johnson of California. Wood, who had not been permitted to go overseas during the war, had some following among the war veterans; but his availability received a severe blow when it was revealed by a Senate committee that his campaign fund amounted to $1,252,000, about half of which had been contributed by W. C. Procter, an Ohio soap manufacturer. He was, moreover, reported to be in sympathy with Attorney-General Palmer's anti-radical activities and was totally ignorant of social and economic questions. His campaign faded rapidly after he failed to secure more than 96,000 votes of 335,000 cast in the Michigan primary early in April. Lowden, a very capable governor, was the most prominent representative of midwestern agricultural interests during the decade of the 1920s. When the Senate committee discovered that he had spent $379,000 of his own money in a campaign fund of $414,000, his position was little better than that of Wood. Senator Borah of Idaho carried the fight against both men on the grounds of excessive campaign expenditures and threatened to bolt the party if either was nominated. Hiram Johnson was the most liberal of the three, but his campaign was poorly managed in the face of strong eastern opposition. Political expediency demanded the nomination of an inconspicuous candidate on a platform of negation. The Old Guard had been in favor of Warren G. Harding for several months before the convention. When neither Lowden nor Johnson showed winning strength in the balloting, Senators Frank B. Brandegee, Reed Smoot, and Henry

Cabot Lodge and Harry M. Daugherty, national committeeman from Ohio, engineered his nomination. Calvin Coolidge, an equally unknown machine politician, was chosen for the vice-presidency. Harding's nomination was received in the convention without enthusiasm, that of Coolidge with facetious observations about his luck.

Harding was owner of the *Marion Star*, a good small town newspaper. He had served in the state Senate, as Attorney-General of Ohio, and as United States Senator. His record was negligible except as the servant of the steel interests. He was a reactionary, narrowly partisan, in favor of high tariffs and universal military training. Calvin Coolidge also had served in his state legislature, as mayor of Northampton, as lieutenant governor of Massachusetts, and finally as governor. Nine months before the Republican convention met, he suddenly attained notoriety by virtue of the Boston police strike. Refraining from intervention until Mayor Andrew J. Peters had the situation well in hand, he wired to Samuel Gompers, President of the American Federation of Labor: "There is no right to strike against the public safety by anybody, anywhere, anytime." In normal times, the incident would scarcely have made the front page of the newspapers; but coming, as it did, during the worst period of industrial unrest in two decades, while the red hunt and deportation delirium were rampant, it gave him an availability not possessed by a half-dozen statesmen in the party. Another possible candidate was Herbert Hoover who, though looked upon with mistrust by the farmers and organized labor, was believed to be a good economist, and to possess great administrative ability and an acquaintance with the European situation. A vigorous campaign early in the year probably would have placed him at the head of the liberal forces in the country, but he refused to state in February whether he was a Democrat or a Republican until the parties had announced their principles. On March 11, he classed himself as an independent Progressive and by April 3 he was definitely identified as a Republican. By then, there was no time to organize an effective campaign for his nomination.

The Democratic convention met in San Francisco on June 28. The party had no recognized leadership and precious little talent.

Like the Republican convention, it met in an atmosphere of uncertainty and confusion with a membership made up largely of officeholders. John W. Davis, Ambassador to the Court of St. James and former Solicitor-General, was the most able candidate but little known. William G. McAdoo's weakness was his relationship, as a son-in-law, to President Wilson. James M. Cox, the mildly progressive Governor of Ohio, was opposed by William Jennings Bryan. A. Mitchell Palmer of Pennsylvania had shown almost no strength at all in the primaries and was wholly discredited as a result of his anti-radical activities. Alfred E. Smith, Governor of New York, was honest, capable, liberal and had a large personal following. In his message to the state legislature in January, 1920, he had recommended a minimum wage law; an eight-hour day for women in industry; maternity insurance; state medical service; state ownership and operation of water power; state-operated grain elevators; municipal ownership of public utilities; and classification of the production and distribution of milk as a public utility service. No other man in either party was as well qualified to take up the leadership of the progressive movement where Wilson had dropped it; but he was an anti-prohibitionist, a member of Tammany Hall, and a Catholic. The ascendancy of the Ku Klux Klan at the time ruled Smith out as an available candidate. Franklin D. Roosevelt, Assistant Secretary of the Navy under Josephus Daniels, a foe of Tammany, an old-school liberal, more independent than Theodore Roosevelt but with the same leanings toward imperialism, was only thirty-eight years of age. Cox was chosen for the Presidency on the forty-fourth ballot and Roosevelt was nominated for the vice-presidency. The country was presented with a choice between two mediocre newspaper editors from Ohio. Eugene V. Debs, a prisoner in Atlanta penitentiary, was nominated by the Socialists at New York on May 8. Another mildly socialist group, known as the Farmer-Labor party and made up of intellectuals, farmers and trade-unionists, nominated Parlay P. Christensen of Utah for the presidency.

The platforms of the two major parties offered the voters little inspiration, the speeches of the two contestants even less. Both platforms endorsed a federal child labor law and the right of collective bargaining for labor. The Republicans denounced the Treaty of Versailles without repudiating the idea of international co-operation. They favored an "Association of Nations." The Democrats endorsed the League Covenant and Cox, at the insistence of Wilson, tried to make of the election a solemn referendum on the question. They also endorsed the anti-sedition activities of Attorney-General Palmer, independence for the Philippines and territorial status for Puerto Rico, tariff for revenue only, and Wilson's Mexican policy. The Republicans favored privately owned and operated railroads and merchant marine, restriction of immigration, and a protective tariff. The Farmer-Labor platform endorsed a broad program of social legislation, government ownership of transportation and natural resources, and opposed the League of Nations. Cox made an extended tour of the country in support of our entry into the League. Harding was kept at home by his campaign managers and spoke to visiting delegations from his front porch in Marion, Ohio. The real issue in the campaign was Woodrow Wilson, not the League of Nations. Social and economic questions were scarcely touched. The League was a dead issue. Living costs, relations between capital and labor, civil rights, and transportation, each worthy of vigorous discussion, were evaded. Wilson had progressively ignored his Cabinet with the result that his administration had been distinguished by a lack of coordination between its several units. This emerged as a glaring weakness after his return from Paris and during his incapacity. He had taken the United States into the war almost immediately after being re-elected on the platform "He kept us Out of War." He insisted upon our ratification of the League Covenant without reservations, when millions of people believed that he had bartered away the aspirations of struggling humanity at Paris and that the League would be an agency for war rather than for peace. Some people were bitter because he had done nothing to stop the crusade of intolerance so utterly foreign to traditional American principles. Living costs were steadily mounting, but no action had been taken against the profiteers. Economic unrest was acute. All of these things created currents and crosscurrents of hostility to Wilsonism, which came to mean in the minds of many people, insincerity, inefficiency, needless entry into the war, dishonored Americanism. Men did not vote for Harding's cause. There was no enthusiasm for it or for him. His campaign was negative. They did not vote for reaction and a return of government to the control of the invisible forces Wilson had denounced in his New Freedom. They voted for a change without thought of where it would lead. Harding received 404 electoral votes to 127 for Cox. The popular vote gave the Republicans 16,152,200, the Democrats 9,147,353, the Socialists 919,799, and the Farmer-Labor Coalition 265,411. The Republicans were given majorities in the Sixty-seventh Congress of 22 Senators and 167 Representatives.

Wilson had hoped for the impossible, and when the people had rendered their verdict at the polls he sadly remarked: "The people of America have repudiated a fruitful leadership for a barren independence . . . soon we will be witnessing the tragedy of it all." But even Wilson could scarcely have suspected what lay ahead. The same may be said of Herbert Hoover, who had warned against "European chaos" if the Treaty were tampered with and prophesied "Even if we managed to keep our soldiers out of it we shall not escape fearful economic losses."

14

Postwar Accounts

DEMOBILIZATION

THE United States was no more prepared for peace than it had been for war. Neither the government nor private industry had a plan for reconversion. Congress had not even entered into a serious discussion of the question, though many suggestions of a specific nature had been made by responsible economists. Failure of the government to do any concrete planning in advance was due (1) to a prevailing notion that all energies must be devoted to winning the war; (2) to a complete lack of precedents, and (3) to a very widely held belief that there was no need for planning. The main problem was thought to be that of the returning veteran. There had been some discussion of the need for an efficient employment service, the wisdom of a comprehensive educational program, and the desirability of emergency public works, but nothing had been done.

The war had been expected to last into the summer of 1919, with as many as 5,000,000 men in the American Expeditionary Forces, and the entire nation was on a wartime basis when it ended. War contracts amounting to several billion dollars had to be cancelled. A ship-building industry which had produced more than three billion tons of shipping in 1918 had to be liquidated. All of the wartime controls had to be lifted and administrative agencies dissolved. Men in the armed services had to be returned from Europe, discharged, and assimilated into a peacetime economy. Arrangements had to be made for the collection of Allied debts. Tariffs and wartime taxes had to be reconsidered in relation to reduced government expenses. The war had drawn new workers into industry and new land into production. It had greatly expanded credit facilities, had dislocated foreign trade, and had created a rising spiral of inflation.

Many of these problems seemed to be relatively simple, yet some aspects of all of them were perplexing, costly, and controversial. There was, first of all, a tremendous conflict of interests. Labor, for example, feared the effect of a rapid demobilization of the army upon the labor market, yet service men, their families, and their friends were irked by every sign of delay. Everyone, apparently, realized the need for planned, effective, re-employment of veterans into peacetime industries, but large numbers of industrialists feared the United States Employment Service, in the Department of Labor, would foster unionism; and some were angered by its refusal to supply strike breakers. Living costs had to come down before the masses could better their standard of living, but labor fought to maintain high wages and industry to maintain its wartime margin of profits. These many conflicts militated against a meeting of minds on the most simple questions.

More important than conflicting interests was the trend toward complete freedom of enterprise. Lifting of wartime controls did not mean abandonment of the legal machinery created so laboriously over a thirty-year period for regulation of finance, industry, and commerce. Yet many thought it meant that, and a great many more were determined that it should. In a situation which called for an intelligent extension of the New Freedom, the trend was for a reversion to government inaction. On December 2, 1918, Wilson said: "Our people . . . know their own business, are quick and resourceful at every readjustment, definite in purpose and self-reliant in action. Any leading strings we might seek to put them in would speedily become hopelessly tangled because they would pay no attention to them and go their own way." This was, indeed, a radical departure from the philosophy of the New Freedom that *industrialists and financiers must no longer control the economic and social life of the nation*; and it was lamented by the liberal press of the country. Later, when the need for action became apparent, Wilson and Congress were too absorbed in the contest over the League of Nations to give the problem rational consideration, and during Wilson's long illness the country drifted without leadership.

Military personnel and civilian employees in war work were discharged rapidly, with 50 percent of the enlisted men in the United States back in civilian life within six months after the Armistice. Soldiers in Europe were returned home as rapidly as transportation could be provided. Eighty percent of the army was demobilized by August of 1919; and practically all of the American Expeditionary Forces, with the exception of the 17,000 men in the Army of Occupation, were back in the United States by Christmas of 1919.

All government contracts on which work had begun were adjusted by a Board of War Claims. Others were canceled for a saving of some seven billion dollars. All permanent structures in France, including warehouses, docks, railroads, telephone lines, and bridges, were sold to France for $400,000,000. Goods in Europe, worth slightly less than two billion dollars, were sold at half price. Liquidation of wartime control agencies was very rapid. Practically all of them had ceased operations by January 1, 1919, less than two months after the Armistice. War controls had all been removed and war production had entirely ceased by June 30, 1919.

Congress refused to provide adequately for the United States Employment Service, which was so essential to proper placement of returning veterans. The Service continued to function for a time, but only because key personnel were willing to work without salary and both religious organizations and private benefactors gave it financial support. It finally ceased operations on October 3, 1919, and veterans joined the ranks of other unemployed job-seekers. All together, the government found jobs for about one fourth of the veterans who wanted work, and it trained for new and useful work about one fourth of the partially disabled veterans. It was not an impressive record.

Inflation had raised food prices by 1920 to more than double those of 1913. People were being encouraged to "buy now" on the theory that prices would rise to new high levels. A wave of stock market speculation was sweeping the country, and everywhere there were signs of riotous extravagance. Worst of all was an enormous amount of profiteering. The wrath of the people was directed against profiteers, and every businessman from the corner grocer to the meat packer was considered a profiteer. Many of them were guilty of excessive profits, some of creating shortages by holding food in storage. Housewives finally organized buyers' strikes or boycotts in the summer of 1920. The people, or a considerable portion of them, blamed labor for the inflation of prices, and demanded both increased production and legislation against strikes.

President Wilson went before Congress, August 8, 1919, and recommended a broad program of legislation. It included the immediate sale of government surpluses, the seizure and sale of food hoards, government regulation of cold storage, compulsory price-marking by the producer, federal incorporation of business in interstate commerce, price control, and vigorous prosecution of violators of the anti-trust laws.

Congress failed to pass any new legislation, but did amend the Food Control Act to permit government seizure of hoarded food (Oct. 22, 1919). Subsequently, more than 2000 actions were brought against profiteers and much food was seized and released from storage. The Department of Justice began investigations of many large corporations, and secured some reductions in prices, but accomplished very little toward reducing the cost of living.

Finally, in May, 1920, prices began to decline. A depression had begun which continued for nearly two years. Foreign markets were uncertain. Renewal of war in Europe was considered possible. Agriculture in the United States began a ten-year decline. Business failures occurred involving losses of more than a billion dollars. Unemployment was general throughout the country, and a high percentage of the unemployed were veterans who had not found permanent jobs after their discharge. One of the most controversial problems, therefore, was that of veterans' compensation.

VETERANS' BENEFITS

The history of veterans' legislation, of course, does not begin with World War I, nor does it concern only veterans of that war.

No other governmental policy is as consistent and firmly established as that of placing ex-service men in a special class with respect to government gratuities. The principle that the government is responsible for relieving all distress growing out of war service by pensions to disabled veterans and to the widows and children of those killed had never been seriously disputed at any time. The facts that any period of service makes it difficult for the individual to readjust himself to normal civilian life, and also that wars are invariably followed by disturbed economic conditions, have ever made the government cognizant of the need for some special arrangements for easing the strain of the transition period after a war. During the nineteenth century the great resources of public lands were used for this purpose, veterans being granted special consideration in their disposal since the Revolutionary War. Beyond that, however, the considerable body of veterans in any constituency offered a temptation to men seeking public office to court their favor by supporting the principle of pensions to all veterans, to their widows and minor children. Thus a considerable number of widows remained upon the pension rolls long after the last veteran of a war had answered the final roll call. The last veteran of the War of 1812 died in 1905, but five widows still received pensions at an annual cost to the government of about four thousand dollars. The last veteran of the Mexican War died in 1929, with 351 widows still on the pension rolls at an annual cost of nearly $300,000. At the close of Hoover's Administration in 1933, there were still about 23,000 Civil War veterans and 125,000 widows of Civil War veterans on the rolls at an annual cost to the government of nearly $100,000,000. More than 200,000 Spanish War pensions were costing $110,000,000 annually. By the end of the fiscal year 1933, the country had paid out pension benefits to the following amounts: Revolutionary War, $70,000,000; War of 1812, $46,000,000; Mexican War, $60,000,000; Civil War, $7,500,000,000; Spanish-American War, $800,000,000; Indian Wars, $58,000,000. The principle involved is best shown by the fact that only 392,000 men were brought into the service in the Spanish-American War and there were not more than 10,000 casualties; but payments to veterans—businessmen, professional men, laborers, rich and poor alike—still amounted to more than $100,000,000 annually after thirty years.

The adoption of the selective draft system, bringing, as it did, several million men into the armed forces at the beginning of World War I, forced the government to consider a substitute for the pension system. A program designed by a commission under the chairmanship of Judge Julian W. Mack drew up a program which was endorsed by President Wilson, Secretary of the Treasury William G. McAdoo, and others and adopted by Congress as the War Risk Insurance Act on October 6, 1917. This act provided (1) for the support of servicemen's families by a fifteen dollar per month allotment from their pay plus an additional allowance from the government up to fifty dollars; (2) compensation to the amount of $30.00 per month for disabilities arising out of war service; (3) free hospitalization and rehabilitation through vocational training; (4) government war risk insurance. All payments under these provisions were protected against assessments for taxes and debts. Every man in the service was required, not by law but in effect, to buy this insurance up to $10,000. The premiums, based on the usual mortality tables, averaged $6.60 per month on that amount and were deducted from the service man's pay. The face value of the policy was to be paid upon death in monthly installments of $57.50. The cost of administration plus war losses in excess of normal expectancy was borne by the government.

The war brought about four million men into the armed forces in addition to their normal prewar strength. The Army of 4,057,-000 men was composed of 1,274,000 volunteers and the remainder of conscripts. The Navy forces numbering 596,000 and the Marine Corps of 104,000 were all volunteers. About half of the Army reached France during the war, but less than 1,000,000 men participated in major engagements. Following the Armistice, these 2,000,-000 men were returned to the United States as rapidly as possible and given their discharge with two months' pay or $60. The real history of veterans' legislation begins at this point and, to be honestly understood, must be divided into adjusted compensation for war service and rehabilitation and disability benefits.

Men who gave up their jobs and volunteered or who were

selected for military service from the more than 12,000,000 men
of military age, were assured on every hand that when they returned they would receive fair treatment economically. The general
understanding was that the serviceman would not have to suffer
economically by reason of his service. This financial obligation of
the country to the men in the service was constantly stressed by
public speakers during the war. At the close of the war, they came
back to find the country tremendously prosperous, with 1700 new
millionaires created by war profits and with thousands of others
exceedingly well-to-do. Their own former jobs were in most instances occupied by someone else. Dull resentment was the inevitable consequence, and bills were constantly pressed in Congress
for adjusted compensation. Meanwhile, seventeen states provided
bonuses of from $10 to $30 for each month of service rendered.
The first federal proposal, calling for a fifty-dollar bond for each
month of service, was bitterly opposed by President Warren G.
Harding who appeared before Congress in person to urge its rejection. Senator Tom Watson of Georgia countered with a proposal
to make the payments with greenbacks, and a new factor was injected into the controversy. President Harding's objections, as expressed in his veto message of September 19, 1922, were based
upon paying a bonus to men who themselves did not expect it at
the time of service, or to men who were physically fit and not in
distress. He insisted that such a bill must carry additional taxes to
provide for the payments, suggesting a sales tax; and he added:

Pledge to the able-bodied ex-service men now will not diminish
the later obligation which will have to be met when the younger
veterans of today shall contribute to the rolls of the aged, indigent,
and dependent. It is as inevitable as that the years will pass that
pension provision for World War veterans will be made, as it has
been made for those who served in previous wars. It will cost more
billions than I venture to suggest.

The fight continued in Congress, however, with the issue clearly
drawn on the manner of payment and the possibility of future
pensions. This question of whether payment should be made by
virtue of a sales tax, income and inheritance taxes, or by inflation
continued to be troublesome until the matter was finally disposed

of in 1936. The other question, that of pensions, was probably not settled even then.

The World War Adjusted Compensation Act was finally passed over President Calvin Coolidge's veto on May 5, 1924. Each veteran was given a twenty-year endowment insurance policy. These policies matured at death or at the end of twenty years, were nonnegotiable, and had a fixed scale of loan values. Their face value was determined by allowing $1.25 per day for foreign service, $1.00 per day for home service, with $625 maximum for overseas service and $500 maximum for service at home. To this amount was added 4 percent compound interest and the whole was regarded as a single premium for the purchase of a paid-up insurance policy. The largest single policies were somewhat less than $1600 and the average about $1000. About 3,500,000 veterans received the adjusted compensation certificates for a total amount of $3,500,000,000. President Coolidge's veto repeated the fear that pensions would follow and emphasized the effect of the law upon an already overtaxed treasury. The House passed it over his veto by a vote of 331 to 87 and the Senate by a vote of 61 to 27. Thus Congress evaded the necessity of enacting an unpopular sales tax while leaving the way clear to reduce income taxes, which it did five times between 1921 and 1929. It also minimized the probability of an immediate demand for pensions by giving the veterans a payment collectible twenty-six years after the war ended. The matter did not become an important political issue again for six years.

Meanwhile, the costs of payment for disabilities sustained in the service, for disabilities presumed to be of service origin, for vocational rehabilitation, for hospitalization and other benefits had risen to nearly $1,000,000,000 annually by 1933. Congress had established the Veterans Bureau by act of August 9, 1921, bringing together the work formerly handled by the Bureau of War Risk Insurance, the Federal Board for Vocational Education, and the Public Health Service. The Bureau was also given charge, by act of July 3, 1930, of the National Soldiers Home and the Bureau of Pensions, and was renamed the Veterans Administration. It included the central office at Washington under the Administrator of Veterans Affairs, thirty-eight regional offices, forty-four hospitals, and twelve soldiers' homes. The original War Risk Insurance Act of 1917 was amended on June 25, 1918, to provide that all men enrolled in the service were presumed to have been in sound condition at the time. The change was deliberately made to bring under the provisions of the act men who might become mentally deranged as a consequence of having been inducted into the service even though their active term of enlistment did not result in visible injury. An effort had been made, with little success, to weed out mentally infirm before enrolling them into the service, by setting up a special neuropsychiatric bureau, and by use of the army intelligence tests. How complete the failure was is shown by the fact that eventually almost half the ex-service men receiving hospitalization were neuropsychiatric cases. Congress also provided for vocational training at any school or college, with monthly allowances of $80 for single men and $100 for married men, for all veterans unable to pursue their original vocation.

The second fundamental change in the law came in 1924. This amendment declared that neuropsychiatric disorders, amoebic dysentery, and tuberculosis appearing before January 1, 1925, were to be classed as of service origin and the patient entitled to full compensation. Henceforth, these were known as presumptive cases. Compensation was increased to $80 per month with $10 for each child. The act also set up complicated tables by which degrees of disability were to be determined. Meanwhile, special pension acts, granting compensation to individual servicemen, were continually passed by Congress, nearly 8000 such laws being enacted during the Coolidge Administration, and nearly 15,000 before 1933. Meanwhile, too, the Spanish-American War pension list increased from 23,000 in 1919 to 193,921 on June 30, 1933. The first step toward civil disability allowances was taken in 1930. In that year, Congress provided that certain physical and mental disabilities appearing before January 1, 1930, were to be held as being of service origin and the veteran entitled to from $12 per month for 25 percent disability to $40 for 75 percent disability.

These liberal provisions had placed upon the pension rolls by the end of 1932, 853,827 World War I veterans and dependents at an annual cost of more than $315,000,000. By that time the total cost to the country of veterans' benefits had reached more than $14,000,000,000, including $2,205,000,000 for disabilities presumed to have been of service origin, and $644,943,000 for vocational training.

In the winter of 1930, agitation began for immediate payment of the face value of adjusted compensation certificates. Veterans, like millions of others, were in dire need as a result of the depression and the drouth. The claim was made that the addition of such a sum of money to the nation's purchasing power would break the back of the depression. Congress refused to pay the face value of the certificates but did pass over President Hoover's veto, February 27, 1931, an act enabling the holder of a certificate to borrow from the Treasury one half of its face value at 4½ percent interest. Hoover said in his veto message: "We cannot further the restoration of prosperity by borrowing from some of our people, pledging the credit of all of the people, to loan to some of our people who are not in need of the money. . . . If this argument of proponents is correct, we should make government loans to the whole people." How nearly the government came to doing that very thing will be seen later. This act made full payment at an early date an absolute certainty because the interest, if unpaid—and none expected it would be—would cancel the remaining 50 percent of the value of the policy before 1945.

In September, 1931, President Hoover appeared in person before the American Legion Convention in Detroit with a plea that further agitation for the payment of the adjusted service certificates be abandoned. The following June 20,000 veterans, many of them with their families, made their way to Washington, D. C., encamped on the "flats" and sought by their presence to bring pressure upon the government to meet their demands.

From that point payment of the certificates and demands for inflation were closely connected. Representative Wright Patman of Texas was the leading advocate of payment by a $2,300,000,000 inflation of the currency. A bill bearing his name, and backed by both the inflation lobby and the veterans' lobby passed the House of Representatives on June 15, 1932, by a vote of 211 to 176 and again on March 12, 1934, by a vote of 295 to 125. It was defeated each time in the Senate by votes of 62 to 18 and 51 to 31. There then occurred a break between the veterans and the inflationists, the former supporting a bill bearing the name of Representative Vinson of Georgia and providing no method of payment. Frank Belgrano, Commander of the American Legion, strongly supported the payment of the certificates by a bond issue. In May, 1935, the Patman Bill was passed by Congress but vetoed by President Roosevelt in a strongly worded message. He denounced it as a "complete abandonment" of the 1924 settlement and an opening wedge for the payment of service pensions to "all veterans, regardless of need or age." He added: "I hold that the able-bodied citizen, because he wore a uniform and for no other reason should be accorded no treatment different from that accorded to other citizens who did not wear a uniform." It was perfectly clear that the bill failed to pass over the President's veto because of its inflationary provisions and that, if a way could be found to eliminate those features, it would pass at the opening session of Congress in January, 1936. In fact, there was strong support from all quarters for the elimination of the question as an issue in the next presidential election and a feeling that in no other way could inflation of the currency be prevented. The inflation bloc in Congress was dangerous largely because it was constantly bidding for the support of the veterans' bloc. Bonus legislation, therefore, was made the special order of business when Congress convened and a bill for immediate payment was drawn up by the Ways and Means Committee of the House with the endorsement of the administration spokesman, Senator Pat Harrison of Mississippi. This bill was promptly passed by Congress with only sixteen Senators and fifty-nine Representatives voting against it. It was vetoed by President Roosevelt but immediately passed over his veto (January 27, 1936) with the support of Congressmen from both parties, even those who had been most insistent upon a balanced budget. The Act provided for the exchange of the Adjusted Compensation Certificates for Government Baby Bonds in denominations of $50 each, such bonds to be non-negotiable but to bear 3 percent interest and to be redeemable at any post office after June 15, 1936. The problem of finding the necessary funds to redeem whatever portion of the bonds should be presented was left to the Treasury Department. Thus was the final chapter written to a fourteen-year controversy. Every President during those years had opposed payment of adjusted compensation, vetoing bills of one kind or another. Not one of the measures passed by Congress, even the final act of 1936, had contained any provision for collecting the necessary funds by taxation, a fact which emphasizes the cumulative effect of pressure politics.

On March 15, 1933, Congress passed An Act to Maintain the Credit of the United States Government, popularly known as the National Economy Act, sponsored by President Roosevelt. It superseded all existing pension legislation having to do with the Philippine Insurrection, the Boxer Rebellion, the Spanish-American War, and the World War. Opposition to it was based upon the provision delegating to the President the power to make retrenchments in government expenditures. The debate brought from many members of Congress what Senator Simeon D. Fess of Ohio designated a "humiliating confession" that that body was powerless to make economies because of the pressure of organized minorities. Senator William E. Borah led the fight against the act, not because he opposed economies but because, as he said, "I am unwilling myself, in the midst of this awful calamity . . . to single out the Congress of the United States and say that that body, of all who were concerned in the matter, has been the signal failure and therefore we are called upon to abandon our function of seriously considering and passing such measures as we in our judgment feel are necessary for the situation." Under the provisions of the act, President Roosevelt removed 436,000 men from the pension rolls for an annual saving of $460,000,000. He then journeyed to the American Legion convention at Chicago to explain that the principle involved in his action was simply one of drawing the line between pensions for disabilities incurred in war service and those not incurred in service. The Economy Act was designed to give the President wide discretionary powers in fixing disability rules on the assumption that the executive department is not under as great pressure from the veterans' lobby as is Congress. Within a few weeks after President Roosevelt's action, Senator Connally introduced a bill designed to restore $170,000,000 of the veterans' cuts. The Administration forces compromised on $100,000,000, restoring to the pension rolls 29,500 totally disabled veterans whose disabilities were not incurred in the service and submitting the presumptive cases to special review boards. The review boards, 128 in number, were composed of five members, including a physician, a veteran and three citizens. These boards rejected 43 percent of all cases reviewed, some of men who were discharged a few days after being called in the draft but had drawn stipends of $100 per month.

In March, 1934, Congress passed over President Roosevelt's veto the Independent Office bill, restoring to the pension rolls the 29,000 veterans whose cases were rejected by the review boards, and several thousand Spanish War veterans whose disabilities were not of service origin. It also limited to ten percent all Spanish War pension reductions. In his veto message, Roosevelt said: "The Spanish-American War veterans' amendment to this act provides for service pensions. . . . I am wholly and irrevocably opposed to the principle of the general service pensions, but I do seek to provide with liberality for all those who suffered because of their service in that war." In August, 1935, Congress passed the Spanish War Veterans Act restoring to veterans of that war, the Boxer Rebellion and the Philippine Insurrection the full allowances taken away by the Economy Act of 1933—a total of about 50,000 at an annual cost of $45,581,000. Only one Senator, Hastings of Delaware, voted against it. President Roosevelt signed the bill with a statement, directly contrary to his former position, that Spanish War veterans and World War veterans were in a different class.

MERCHANT MARINE AND AVIATION

Another government policy as venerable as pensions for veterans was subsidies for the merchant marine. Prevailing economic philosophy at the close of the war decreed that the government-owned merchant fleet be disposed of as quickly as possible to private owners and operators. It was only natural, therefore, that Congress should turn to subsidies for merchant shipping and aviation as an integral part of the program of national defense.

The first subsidy in American history for merchant vessels was passed on July 4, 1789, and was in the nature of an average 10 percent reduction of custom duties on all goods imported in American-built and -operated vessels. Hyson tea, for example, was taxed 20 cents per pound if imported from the Far East in American vessels, 26 cents per pound if imported from Europe in American vessels and 45 cents per pound if otherwise imported. In 1845, Congress inaugurated indirect subsidies through the postal service. Two years later it permitted shipowners to borrow money from the government to construct vessels for mail service. Some $21,000,-000 were expended in indirect subsidies before 1877. These subsidies aided materially in the development of the American fleet of clipper ships to the point where only Great Britain was superior in total tonnage owned and operated; but the outmoding of wooden vessels, coupled with the destruction of vessels flying the American flag by Confederate cruisers, virtually destroyed the American merchant marine during the Civil War.

The government made no effort to revive the merchant marine, withdrawing subsidies in 1877. These were revived in 1891, however, when an act was passed allowing liberal sums, beyond the rates for actual poundage carried, to shipowners holding mail contracts. This law, which remained in force until 1928, cost the government an estimated $30,000,000. It did not, however, revive the merchant marine. By 1900, American-owned vessels were carrying only 9.3 percent of the goods entering into our foreign trade. When President Theodore Roosevelt sent the fleet around the world in 1907, it was necessary to rely upon foreign merchant vessels to provision it; and the entry of the United States into World War I found us still without the necessary troops and supply ships. Congress promptly created the Emergency Fleet Corporation with a capitalization of $50,000,000 and authority to "purchase, construct, equip, lease, charter, maintain, and operate merchant ships in the commerce of the United States." It was under the direction of George W. Goethals and, later, of Charles M. Schwab. Four large shipyards were constructed, some vessels were built, others were purchased, and the interned German ships were repaired and placed in service. A total of $3,000,000,000 was spent in one form or another to acquire a merchant fleet during the war. The money thus spent was borrowed as a part of the Liberty Loans and cost in interest alone a minimum of $100,000,000 annually after the war. Much of it was wasted in poorly constructed and unserviceable vessels. Nevertheless, the United States Shipping Board had under its jurisdiction 10,000,000 tons of shipping at the close of the war and these vessels were carrying 42.7 percent of the country's foreign trade when Congress took up the question of their disposal in 1920.

The Jones Act, sometimes called the Merchant Marine Act of 1920, was passed after long and bitter debate. The one fundamental principle on which everyone agreed was the desirability of maintaining permanently an American merchant fleet, either privately or publicly owned, as an auxiliary to the Navy in time of war. National pride was a most important motive in the congressional decision. The Shipping Board was authorized to sell the vessels under its control to private owners. It was the purpose of Congress, and was clearly understood at the time, that the Board was to sell only when convinced that by so doing the development and maintenance of a permanent merchant marine would be promoted. Purchase of ships was restricted to corporations in which the majority of the stock was held by citizens of the United States, 75 percent if the vessels were to be operated in coastwise trade. Ships not sold were to be operated by the Shipping Board, which had the authority to map out new trade routes and loan money to companies operating over them. The principle of the act of 1789 was re-established and preferential tariff rates were authorized for goods imported in American-owned vessels. Presidents Harding and Coolidge both refused to act under this provision because it violated existing treaties with other nations and succeeding Congresses did not press the point. The Act also permitted indirect subsidies in the form of mail contracts. This provision was also ignored for several years, a total of only $5,000,000 being spent in that manner before 1928. The Act contained three fatal defects. It made no provision for building new ships. It did not provide specifically for reconditioning old vessels. It left wide discretionary powers in the administration board. The board did establish thirty-five new trade routes between 1920 and 1928. It sold 1141 ships and nine shipping lines and guaranteed the losses of companies willing to operate over the new routes. Many of the vessels, however, which had cost an estimated $200 per ton to build, were sold for as low as five dollars per ton and were scrapped by the purchasers. The fleet was operating 392 vessels with a tonnage of 3,378,342 in 1923 and 286 vessels with a tonnage of 2,548,648 in 1928. During that period its operating deficits were regularly supplied by Congressional appropriations as follows: 1922, $48,500,000; 1923, $12,000,000; 1924, $50,000,000; 1925, $30,000,000; 1926, $24,000,000; 1927, $13,000,000; 1928, $17,000,000. Many of the vessels, built hastily and for war purposes, were slow-moving and ill-adapted to competitive commerce. Meanwhile, about half of the world's tonnage had been dieselized while the Shipping Board had no funds for that purpose. By 1928, the percentage of foreign commerce carried in American vessels had shrunk from 42.7 as of 1920 to 32.2. It was a sorry return for the interest on money, spent to accumulate the fleet and the operating deficits combined, amounting to more than $150,000,000 annually.

When Congress again took up the question in 1928, the Shipping Board had a total of 485 vessels permanently inactive. Of this number, 129 were fit only to be scrapped. The remainder were in need of extensive repairs before being put into service. Congress approached the problem vigorously with strong support for a publicly owned merchant marine. In the end, however, it was decided to fall back upon the same principle followed in railroad construction: liberal subsidies to private builders and operators. The Jones-White Act appropriated $250,000,000 for construction loans. Long-term, liberal mail-carrying contracts were authorized. Vessels remaining in the hands of the Shipping Board were to be disposed of at whatever price operators were willing to pay. Between 1928 and 1931, seventeen shipping lines were awarded mail contracts costing $5,588,000 annually. The difference between that sum and an estimated actual cost of carrying the mail of $92,000 annually constituted an indirect subsidy.

The construction of 68 new vessels to operate over 39 new routes at a cost of $281,000,000 was also provided for in mail contracts.

Mail subsidies under these contracts brought the total to $23,000,-
000 annually in 1933. Meanwhile, the Shipping Board sold, for
$23,000,000, 104 vessels which had cost the government $258,000,-
000. That the government had failed to accomplish the purpose
back of its entire merchant marine policy after the war was clearly
evident by 1933. The La Follette Seaman's Act, together with the
higher standard of living maintained in the United States, placed
shipping interests at a tremendous disadvantage in competition
with foreign operators. Even more important was the devastating
effect of tariff barriers, particularly the Hawley-Smoot tariff, which
contributed to the decline of foreign trade, drove American manufacturers to establish branch factories in foreign lands, and thoroughly counteracted all efforts to develop shipping by liberal subsidies. The policy of merchant marine subsidies, in the words of
the Black Committee of the Senate, had turned out to be "a sad,
miserable and corrupting failure."

Equally important as a part of the national defense program
was the policy of encouraging the development of aviation by
mail subsidies to a total of $20,000,000 annually. Congress under-
took to encourage aviation because of its increasing military importance and the government's failure to complete adequate aircraft
construction during World War I. There had been much loose
talk at the beginning of the war about throwing a fleet of 100,000
planes into the contest, and Congress made ample appropriations
for building the planes. Few planes were built, however, in time to
be of any service to the fighting forces. The Army in France was
compelled to rely heavily upon the Allies for planes. An investigation disclosed that there had been some administrative inefficiency
and mismanagement, but that the chief difficulty was almost a
complete lack of construction facilities and personnel. Congress
decided to subsidize commercial aviation as an integral part of the
national defense program.

A Senatorial investigating committee, under the chairmanship
of Hugo Black of Alabama, revealed in January, 1934, that these
subsidies had been diverted from their original purpose of fostering
aviation and prostituted to party politics, private graft, and stock
promotion schemes. Air mail routes had been divided by the large

company operators themselves in May, 1930, without competitive bidding. Postmaster-General Brown had brought pressure upon small companies to merge with larger companies. The testimony revealed that one official had started with forty dollars and manipulated his stock to a market value of $5,000,000. Stock-watering, salary bonuses, etc., had ended with more than 18,000,000 shares of outstanding stock on which only a few thousand dollars of dividends had been paid.

The subsidies themselves had amounted in 1933 to the difference between fifty-four cents per mile paid and the fifteen cents per mile estimated cost of operation. Total subsidies between 1926 and 1933 were estimated at more than $60,000,000. Following the disclosures, all air mail contracts were cancelled and the duty of carrying the mails thrust upon the Army Air Corps. There followed a series of disasters in which twelve pilots were killed. Extraordinary flying conditions, poor equipment, unskilled pilots, and the fact that many pilots had been called back hurriedly from CCC camps all contributed to the debacle. Not the least important result of the disasters was the fact that it drew the attention of the country from the disgraceful situation revealed by the Senatorial investigating committee. The service was again returned to private companies and a special committee was appointed to investigate conditions in the Army Air Corps. Newton D. Baker, former Secretary of War, was chairman of the Committee composed in part of expert aviators. The Committee went beyond the question of Air Corps efficiency and discussed the relative strength of aviation in different countries. It recommended: (1) an increase in the Army Air Corps to 2320 planes; (2) purchase through negotiated contracts; (3) continuation of air defense as a supporting branch of both the Army and Navy Departments; (4) increased attention by Congress to army aviation; (5) the retirement of aviators at forty-five years of age; and (6) aviation training for all West Point cadets.

RAILROADS AND ELECTRIC POWER

At the close of World War I, Congress was faced with the task of formulating a new transportation policy before returning the railroads to private control. There was strong agitation for government ownership and operation. The Director-General wanted continued government operation for five years. The owners wanted the roads back and a law for compulsory arbitration of labor disputes. Stockholders wanted a government guarantee of 6 percent. The employees wanted public ownership, with one half of all profits over 5 percent going to the workers.

Congress was determined to return the roads to private control. The Transportation Act of 1920 or the Esch-Cummins Act was passed and approved on February 28, one day previous to the termination of government operation. This Act increased the size of the Interstate Commerce Commission to eleven members and their term of service to seven years. It also created a Railroad Labor Board of nine members. Employees of the roads and the management were each to nominate six men for membership on the Board. The President and Senate were to appoint three from each of these groups and an additional three representing the public. This Board was to hear and settle all disputes with respect to wages, taking into consideration "the scale of wages paid for similar kinds of work in other industries; the relation between wages and the cost of living; the hazards of the employment; the training; the skill required; the degree of responsibility; the character and regularity of employment; and inequalities of increases in wages or of treatment, the result of previous wage orders or adjustments." The Board was not given authority to enforce its decisions and was replaced by a Federal Board of Mediation in 1926, with authority only to serve upon the voluntary request of the management or employees.

The second important feature of the Act was the Recapture Clause. The Commission was given the power to establish rates, including the prescription of minimum rates on the basis of "a fair return upon the aggregate value" of the railway property of the country, which the Supreme Court later defined to mean re-production cost new. The Act said, however, that since it was impossible to establish uniform rates on that basis without allowing some roads more than a fair return on the value of their property, all roads receiving more than a 6 percent return should place one half of the excess in a reserve fund and the other half in a contingent fund to be used by the Commission in making loans for capital expenditures to less prosperous roads. The third important departure from precedent gave the Commission the power to consolidate the four express companies into one and to consolidate the railway lines into a few systems on an economic rather than geographical basis. These combinations were to be exempt from the force of the anti-trust laws. The pooling of traffic for economy in operation was permitted. Interlocking directorates were prohibited. The sale of securities and expenditures of funds received therefrom were placed under control of the Commission. Finally, the control of the Commission was extended sufficiently to eliminate discriminations between intrastate carriers and interstate carriers.

In 1926, the Interstate Commerce Commission published a plan to consolidate all railroads into nineteen systems. It was abandoned as a result of the opposition of the roads and management itself was requested to offer a substitute plan. In 1930, in accordance with their own request, all of the roads in the North Central States and west of the Hudson were consolidated into the Baltimore and Ohio, the Chesapeake and Ohio, the New York Central, and the Pennsylvania.

The year 1920 marked the end of an era in railroad history. For a quarter of a century, the railroads had enjoyed a monopoly of transportation. They had bitterly opposed, and for the most part successfully resisted, regulation. Whether the Esch-Cummins Act represented the final triumph of government over the unsocial practices of a great monopoly or the first acknowledgment by railway management that there was nothing more to gain by further opposition is difficult to say. In any case, the railroad barons were reduced to humble petitioners of the government they had so long defied, not by the majesty of the law and the Courts but by competition. The railroads were the leading American industry before World War I with a capitalization of approximately $20,000,000,-000. Then, in slightly more than a decade, the government and technology created a great competitive transportation system of inland waterways, the Panama Canal, pipe lines, air transport and 900,000 miles of paved highways. Passenger automobiles, buses, and trucks robbed the railroads of more than 50 percent of their business. There were 24,000,000 automobiles on the highways in 1930, and local freight and passenger traffic on the railroads had ceased to exist. Nearly six times as much traffic passed through the Panama Canal in 1930 as in 1920, and the Inland Waterways Corporation, established by the government in 1924, was doing a business of $6,000,000,000 annually with its barge lines. Beginning in 1926, commercial aviation forged to the front, increasing its passengers carried from less than 6000 in that year to 165,000 in 1929 and to 450,000 in 1933. All-daylight flying schedules were introduced from New York to San Francisco, trans-Pacific service was inaugurated, and service across the North Atlantic was being planned.

Air and motor transport were to the railroads what railroads had been to the earlier prairie schooners and stagecoaches. Flexible, fast, and relatively inexpensive, they rapidly became indispensable to modern society; and their growth created problems for the railroads and the government alike. The railroads were caught in the worst possible condition to meet the new competition. They had been plundered by speculative promotion and banker control, and overcapitalized to the point where rate reduction, though absolutely essential, was difficult. Notoriously lax in creating capital reserve funds, they were in no position to replace outmoded equipment with lighter and faster rolling stock or to eliminate the grade crossings which were a prerequisite to faster service. They were prohibited by law from reducing their labor costs and from abating their services to the public. Their capital structures were so integrated with the savings of the people as to eliminate almost automatically the hope of wringing out the water. Of the $11,000,000,000 of outstanding bonds in 1933, $5,000,-000,000 were owned by insurance companies and savings banks and

$2,000,000,000 by endowed churches, colleges, and hospitals. Railroad stocks were owned by thousands of individual investors, privately or in trust funds. Finally, the strict regulation exercised by the Interstate Commerce Commission had not been extended to their competitors.

About the time railroading had ceased to be a profitable field of adventure for private capital and adequate regulation in the public interest became a possibility, a new industry emerged, second only to railroads from point of investment: the electric utility industry. It, too, was a natural monopoly, and, for the most part, free from state regulation because it moved in interstate commerce. It developed as rapidly as had the railroads, under the same driving force of reckless search for private gain. Its management fought as bitterly as had railroad management against federal regulation. New techniques in propaganda and in finance greatly complicated the problem. There were, however, two aspects of the problem of regulation which did not enter into the long controversy over railroad regulation. The first was the existence of the holding company. Like holding companies in every field of industrial and commercial enterprise, many served a useful function in economical financing, engineering, management, and mass production; but many, too, when pyramided one above another, were prostituted to the purpose of defrauding investors, increasing rates unnecessarily to consumers, making capital structures so complex as to defy reasonable accuracy in rate regulation. Above all else, the system served as a device by which economic power was concentrated in a few hands, giving to a few men control over the honest savings of thousands of small investors in operating companies. The second new element was the possibility of public competition, which was far more effective in eliminating abuses than any amount of regulation could possibly be, and which the utility magnates feared far more than they feared regulatory agencies. The history of the struggle for power control extending over two decades centers about the holding company and public ownership. The fight for federal regulation was led by Senators Thomas J. Walsh, Burton K. Wheeler, and Frank Couzens and its history includes the Federal Water Power Act of 1920, an extended investigation by the Federal Trade Commission during the late twenties, and the Wheeler-Rayburn Act. The fight for public ownership and operation, so far as the federal government was concerned, began with the building of nitrate plants at Muscle Shoals during the World War, and included the Norris Resolutions vetoed by Presidents Coolidge and Hoover and the creation of the Tennessee Valley Authority.

The Federal Water Power Act of 1920 created a makeshift Federal Power Commission consisting of the Secretaries of War, Interior, and Agriculture. This Commission was authorized to issue licenses for power projects on the navigable waters, public lands, and Indian reservations of the United States. These licenses were to run for a period of fifty years, at which time they might be revoked by payment of the amount invested. The Commission could regulate rates on all power moved across state lines by the licensed companies or their subsidiaries, and was given full access to books and records of such companies with authority to regulate accounting practices. Public ownership for sale of electricity without profit was encouraged by exempting state and municipally owned projects from license fees. This system of control proved to be wholly insufficient to cope with an increasingly complex problem. Not more than one fourth of the power being generated was from hydro plants, and of those, not more than one fourth were under federal license. Moreover, the complex structure of holding companies was free from any regulation whatsoever.

In 1928, Senator Thomas Walsh of Montana introduced a resolution into the Senate providing for a committee investigation of the power and light industries' financial and propaganda practices. One of the most powerful lobbies ever assembled in Washington succeeded in assigning the task to the Federal Trade Commission in order to keep it out of the hands of Walsh whose relentless investigations had ferreted out the oil scandals. The Federal Trade Commission's report of 7,000,000 words was the most sensational since that of the Pujo committee. It revealed, by the admissions of the industry's own propaganda agents (1) that the National Electric Light Association was spending millions of dollars annually for propaganda; (2) that unlimited quantities of printed

material were placed in the hands of newspaper editors, businessmen, professional men, and labor leaders; (3) that the tentacles
of this vast propaganda machine had reached into every department of the educational system, including the kindergartens;
(4) that professors in universities and the President of the General Federation of Women's Clubs were on its payroll; and
(5) that pressure of advertising was brought to bear upon the
press for friendly publicity.

The revelations of the committee's report furnished material
for wide discussion in news articles, editorials, and monographs,
among the latter being Ernest Gruening's *The Public Pays*, Stephen Raushenbush's *The Power Fight*, and Ernest M. Patterson's
Power and the Public. A wave of popular indignation swept over
the country, culminating in a demand for lower utility rates,
strengthening the Senate group's demands for strict regulation of
the power companies, and discrediting the negative attitude of
Presidents Coolidge and Hoover. The collapse of the Insull utility
empire came as a dramatic climax to ten years of bitter controversy and paved the way for a sweeping reform.

Meanwhile, Senator Norris carried on a persistent crusade for
government operation of the Muscle Shoals power and nitrate
plant. The two nitrate plants, with an estimated annual output
of approximtaely 50,000 tons of fixed nitrogen, were constructed
by the government during the war. The cost of these plants and
of the Wilson Dam, which was to supply the electric power, was
about $150,000,000. The nitrate plants were not used after the
war and the power generated at Wilson Dam was sold to the
Alabama Power Company. Senator Norris, marshaling an array
of facts and figures to prove that public owned hydro plants in
Canada were furnishing power to consumers at less than half
the average American price, succeeded in getting, in 1928, Congressional approval to his resolution providing for the completion
and operation of the Muscle Shoals properties; but it was pocket-
vetoed by President Coolidge. Numerous studies were published
supporting the demand for reduction of rates, one in particular,
by Morris Llewellyn Cooke of the New York Power Authority,
estimating excess rates to the American domestic consumer at

more than $300,000,000 annually. It was from the standpoint of the small consumer, principally, that the production of electric power was a monopoly. Large consumers, who might produce their own power, enjoyed drastically reduced rates in comparison to the average householder.

Senator Norris's resolution again passed Congress in 1930. This revised program provided for the building of another dam on the Tennessee River, the construction of transmission lines, and government manufacture and sale of both power and fertilizers. Coolidge had vetoed the original act in silence. Hoover, on the other hand, condemned it with visible emotion, (1) because private interests were now able to furnish all requirements of nitrogen for war purposes; and (2) because he was opposed to government competition with private enterprise. Nothing reveals more clearly than his veto message how much the operation of the government plant was regarded as an effectual corrective of public utility abuses. On that point, he said:

Involved in this question is the agitation against the conduct of the power industry. . . . The remedy for abuses in the conduct of that industry lies in regulation and not by the Federal Government entering upon the business itself. . . . I hesitate to contemplate the future of our institutions, of our country if the preoccupation of its officials is to be no longer the promotion of justice and equal opportunity but is to be devoted to barter in the markets. . . . Muscle Shoals can only be administered by the people upon the ground, responsible to their own communities and not for purposes of pursuit of social theories or national politics.

It was this avowed purpose of the sponsors of government operation to make the Muscle Shoals plant a laboratory to determine the actual cost of the manufacture and distribution of electricity which the power interests fought so bitterly. For ten years, it stood idle as the cost of a universal public service soared and the architects of utility holding companies peddled their worthless stocks. Concerning these companies, Chairman Frank R. McNinch of the new Federal Power Commission created in 1930, said: "The holding company dynasty, with its absentee ownership and management, its sovereignty over far-flung dominions in many states, but subject to the direct jurisdiction of none, its fees being taxation without representation of the operating companies, is a grave economic and social peril."

Governor Franklin D. Roosevelt of New York had said, meanwhile, that control of holding companies and super-utilities had proved so difficult as to be impracticable and had urged federal control. Later his candidacy was opposed by the power interest, which went so far as to deluge the Chicago Convention with telegrams in an effort to secure Newton D. Baker or Albert Ritchie as the candidate of the Democratic party. In his campaign speeches, he advocated government development of water-power sites with control of distribution costs and services through contracts with private companies, control of security issues, and the regulation of holding companies. He was known to be favorable to the Norris resolution, to regulation of all power entering into interstate commerce, and to rigid enforcement of the Federal Water Power Act. Few people, however, expected the devastating attack about to be made upon the power utility monopoly from at least five directions. They were (1) the Tennessee Valley Authority Act (May 18, 1933), (2) the Public Works Program, (3) the creation of the Electric Home and Farm Authority, (4) the Electric Rate Investigation Resolution and (5) the Wheeler-Rayburn Act.

INTERALLIED DEBTS

If one may regard the American people as reasonably entitled to expect repayment of loans made to European nations, then the cost of the war to American taxpayers had scarcely begun when the Armistice was signed. The total loans of the United States government to foreign nations amounted to $10,350,490,000. The loans of $4,277,000,000 to Great Britain, $3,404,818,000 to France, $1,648,034,000 to Italy, $379,087,000 to Belgium, and $192,601,000 to Russia were in the nature of financial assistance to Allied nations engaged in a common undertaking and for rehabilitation work; but, of the $3,000,000,000 post-Armistice loans, much went to the new nations created by the Versailles settlement, some to the recent enemy nations. Austria received $24,055,-

000; Czechoslovakia, $91,879,000; Jugoslavia, $51,759,000; Poland, $159,668,000; Latvia, $5,132,000; Lithuania, $4,981,000; Esthonia, $13,999,000; and other nations smaller amounts.

The Versailles Conference of 1918–1919 did not attempt to decide upon the total amount of indemnity to be imposed upon Germany but amounts as high as $125,000,000,000 were mentioned. By June, 1920, the Allied nations had considered the matter more calmly and talked about $64,000,000,000. In April of the following year, the Reparations Commission set up by the Versailles Treaty notified Germany that her bill for the war was $31,680,-000,000. This action was based upon the theory that Germany was solely responsible for the war. The major portion of this amount, approximately nine tenths, was to go to the four largest debtors to the United States, and in about the same relative proportions as their debts.

On February 9, 1922, Congress created a World War Foreign Debt Commission to arrange terms of settlement between the United States and its debtors without reference to the question of German reparations. This Act of Congress laid down certain rules which must be followed in the negotiations. All debts were to be paid before June 15, 1947, interest was not to be less than 4¼ percent per year, and there was to be no reduction in the principal amounts due. France refused to discuss such terms, and the Commission was forced to make important modifications in the arrangements with Great Britain which were ratified by Congress. Payment was extended over a period of sixty-two years and the interest rate was modified sufficiently to reduce the total amount, principal and interest combined, to slightly less than $10,000,000,000. The negotiations with other nations continued over a period of years; and, by 1930, all of the principal debtor nations except Russia had agreed to terms. Their payments were all extended, as in the case of Great Britain, over a period of sixty-two years. Belgium was granted an interest rate of 1.8 percent; France, 1.6 percent; and Italy, .4 percent. The other nations were charged an average of 3.3 percent. These interest reductions lowered the total indebtedness of Great Britain 20 percent, France 50 percent and Italy 75 percent, but still left the total to be paid more than twice the amount originally borrowed and about equal to the amount of the United States government bonds outstanding as a result of war financing.

Each year that passed saw a more complicated situation developing. The fighting had scarcely ceased in Europe when a reversion to intense nationalism set in. An economic warfare was inaugurated and carried to the point where tariff barriers lessened international trade by half. The rising generation, pushed to the limit to human toleration by starvation, turmoil, and oppression, revolted against paying for the devastation of the war. Germany defaulted from the first on her reparation payments. The Allies indicated that their payments to the United States must depend upon German payments to them. The United States government refused to admit officially that there was any relation between reparations and debts. The combined intelligence of the world was never able to state how the transfer of the huge sums involved could be made from one nation to another in the absence of foreign trade.

An International Debt Commission, under the chairmanship of Charles G. Dawes, drew up a new reparations arrangement which went into effect in 1924. This plan advanced a loan of 800,000,000 marks to Germany, allowed her a moratorium for one year, and cut her initial annuities to 20 percent of the original payments. The total amount of reparations was not reduced, but the mystifying problem of finding a method of transfer was shifted to the Allies. Faced with the problem of finding a means of transfer from Germany to themselves and of transferring their own payments to the United States, it was inevitable that they should link the two together officially, if possible. The inability of Germany to meet her obligations under the Dawes Plan resulted in a new Reparations Commission headed by Owen D. Young. In the Young Plan, announced in June, 1929, Germany's reparations were cut, for the first time, to $26,000,000,000, a sum still substantially larger than the total amounts due the United States. The most important item in the new arrangement, however, was that which finally fixed the amount due from Germany at $26,800,000,000 to be paid over a period of fifty-nine years. These payments were separated into two divisions. One hundred and sixty-five million dollars annually for thirty-seven years was specifically required. The remainder, amounting to more than $350,000,000 annually over a period of fifty-nine years, was to be reduced in proportion to whatever reductions the Allies were able to secure in their debts to the United States.

By 1931, the economic structure of the whole world was in such a state of collapse that President Hoover announced a moratorium for one year on all international debt payments. This was the first official recognition by the United States government of any connection between debts and reparations. It altered the entire nature of the problem. Premier Laval of France visited Washington in October of that year and issued in conjunction with President Hoover a statement to the effect that further arrangements concerning intergovernmental debts must be made before the expiration of the one-year moratorium, the first steps to be taken by European nations relative to German reparations.

The Allied nations—Great Britain, France, Italy, Belgium, and Japan—met with Germany at Lausanne and entered into an agreement, July 8, 1932, reducing reparations to 2 percent of the original amount, approximately $714,000,000. This amount was to be paid in the form of 5 percent German bonds to be delivered to the Bank for International Settlements created by the Young plan. These bonds were to bear no interest until placed upon the market at the end of three years and might be redeemed by Germany at any time. By this action, France completely reversed her postwar attitude, agreeing to virtual cancellation of all further reparations although continuing the fiction of collection. This altered the entire nature of the problem of debts to the United States. The question no longer was how to make the transfer of payments from one nation to another nor how large the payments should be. It was now a choice of fulfilling the spirit of the Hoover-Laval pronouncement by drastic reduction or cancellation or refusing to act and thus forcing our debtors into repudiation. Shortly before the Lausanne settlement was announced, the Democratic convention adopted as a plank in its platform a pledge against war-debt cancellation. That party was victorious in November, and Congress refused to act. France, therefore, repudiated her debt in December. President Roosevelt announced that nations making partial payments of their annuities would not be considered in default and Great Britain continued to make token payments until December, 1933. At that time France, Poland, Hungary, Belgium, and Esthonia paid nothing. The other nations, following the lead of Great Britain, made only small token payments amounting to about nine million dollars in all, slightly more than 5 percent of the total amount due. Meanwhile, Germany sold bonds to private investors in the United States to the amount of $2,500,000,000. The debtor nations paid about $2,600,000,000 to the United States. Germany, in 1933, repudiated her foreign bonds, so that private citizens in the United States lost about what the government received.

Congress passed the Johnson Act in 1934, prohibiting any defaulting nation to float loans in the American market. Thereafter, only Finland continued to meet her payments. The question of willingness to pay was never a fundamental part of the war debt question. It was, from the first, a question of how the payments could be made. The United States refused to buy Europe's goods, raising its tariffs three times after the war, in 1922, 1930, and 1932. The collapse of the American market in 1929 reduced the flotation of foreign bonds to zero before Congress passed the Johnson Act. We virtually stopped immigration in 1924, and we subsidized our merchant marine. There was no other way by which the debtor nations could recover for purposes of continuing payments the gold they originally sent to this country. It is true there was some sentiment in European countries against payment in any case. In fact, at times there were vigorous campaigns in those countries against payment. Taxes were far heavier there than in the United States; war losses had been greater; distress was more general; but, from the first, payments had been possible only through sale of securities in this country. It amounted to a lowering of their debt to the United States government by increasing their debt to the private investors of the United States. When the market for their securities in this country collapsed, payment became impossible. The Johnson Act merely closed the door to a resumption of payments and unjustly attached the stigma of defaulters to nations like Great Britain which were willing to raise the money by taxation but could find no way to transfer it to this country. When President Hoover agreed to payment in pounds sterling to be earmarked and deposited in London, he merely resorted to fictitious payment for the sake of political expediency. Until some way of transferring the sums could be found, there was no payment in fact.

The problem was loaded with political dynamite in this country. Politicians evaded it when possible, or encouraged continued unsound thinking by asserting that the debts must be paid when most of them were too good economists to believe that it was possible. The people of the United States were in personal difficulties financially and were confronted with increasing tax burdens. They were even less disposed to think in terms of cancellation than they would have been had Europe used some discretion in expenditures for armaments. They failed to realize that government expenditures within a nation's own domestic economy and payments to another nation were two different things. Congress merely reflected the attitude of the people. The problem which faced the Hoover Administration and the Roosevelt Administration was to find some means of cancelling the debts which would be acceptable to the people; in short to cancel without admitting it. Several possibilities existed: (1) to collect the principal of the loans without interest; (2) to regard all moneys lent before the Armistice as a part of this country's contribution to the war, and collect only the post-Armistice loans; (3) to reduce amounts due in proportion to the reduction which had taken place in world price levels, international trade, or on some other fair ratio; (4) to accept the Allied nations' point of view and balance debts to us against German reparations. The unwillingness of the United States to agree upon one or another of these formulae before the debtor nations were forced into repudiation reduced their chances of ever receiving anything either in the way of financial return or concessions toward the stabilization of

world trade. The debts gave to the United States strong bargain
ing power in the field of diplomacy. They could have been sacrificed in the interest of foreign trade through lowering of tariff
barriers. They could, as an absolute minimum, have been used to
purchase international friendship and good will.

15

Labor in Postwar America

LABOR'S EXTREMES

THE most conservative and the most powerful labor organization in the world in 1918 was the American Federation of Labor. Yet, there were some indications that the A. F. of L. might be going the way of the Knights of Labor which had ceased to be of practical importance after 1890.

The A. F. of L. was organized on a craft basis, and craft organization had become more antiquated with each passing year. Machinery freed the employer from dependence upon workmen skilled in the handicrafts. It struck a body blow at apprenticeship and opened wide the doors of the factories to labor fresh from the fields of agriculture. It brought into a single factory the members of a dozen crafts, who dissipated their strength in petty quarrels among themselves and confounded the wisdom of the best intentioned employers to devise a program of operation suitable to the demands of so many minds.

The fundamental principle of industrial relations, recognized by government, capital, and labor alike, was the pitting of the economic strength of employers against the economic strength of labor; but employers were organized on an industrial basis while organized laborers remained wedded to the decentralized craft unions. The reason for this was the secure status of the craftsmen relative to that of the great mass of wage earners. They were an aristocracy within their economic group. Their gains in the form of wage increases frequently were at the expense of the unorganized and unskilled workmen. Actually, therefore, the skilled workmen of the A. F. of L. had little to gain by interesting themselves in the broader problems of labor as a whole. They fought valiantly for the principles that labor was not a commodity; that employers must recognize the right of collective bargaining; and that the government must throw no legal obstacles in the way of labor's use of its only effective weapon, the strike. They maintained high membership fees, large strike funds, and benefit payments to make their strikes effective. They refrained from too frequent use of their strike and boycott weapons. They repudiated the sympathetic strike.

The above policies of the A. F. of L. served its membership well for many years; but the failure to organize unskilled workmen eventually proved to have been a shortsighted policy. It left unorganized such basic industries as steel, rubber, and oil, and new mass-production industries such as automobiles. Capital insisted upon the right to purchase labor in a competitive market and to maintain the open shop. It was able to do so after the war because organized labor had steadfastly refused to interest itself in women and children, Negroes, and agricultural laborers.

Every factory had in it a dozen or more craft organizations although the mass of workmen were unorganized. Employers, to counteract the strength of these craft organizations, began to organize company unions. The company union takes second place only to craft unions as an archaic institution. Every company union was an entity unto itself. The employees in a factory lacked cohesion in dealing with their employers under the craft system, but they did have some contact with similar craftsmen in other factories and other industries and the advice, leadership, and financial support of men whose sustenance emanated from some other source than their own. Company unions made for cohesion within the factory unit but severed all connection between its members in other factories of the same industry and from those in other industries. One of the great weaknesses of the labor movement during the twenties, particularly in the South, was the constant draining away from labor into managerial positions of its natural leaders. Company unions accentuated this process. It enabled the employer to dictate the appointment of its employees' representatives. Labor's representatives, however free from employer influence their choice might be, were still employees of the men with whom they were supposed to bargain. All manner of subtle coercion was employed to destroy labor's bargaining power under the company union.

Among the great mass of unorganized workers were certain lowly groups of the South. These were the textile workers, the coal miners, and the agricultural workers. The company town of the textile mills and the coal mines presented a mode of life little removed from feudalism. Families lived in company houses, bought at company stores, worshipped in company churches, and sent their children to company schools. If the companies did not own and operate these agencies outright, they controlled them. They ruled the sheriffs, the deputies and, too often, the courts. Workers were ofttimes in arrears on house rent or for food supplies just as were the crop renters of the Cotton Belt. The vast majority of agricultural laborers, including crop renters, of coal miners, and of textile workers never really had been on a money economy. They labored, year in and year out, for a meager subsistence wage which came to them through the crop *lien* and credit system, company stores, and welfare projects of the company towns. In agriculture and in the textile industry, the system approached serfdom, because the labor of women and children was a requisite to employment. One would have to be naïve indeed to suppose that workers possessed freedom of action under such a system of economic subserviency. The companies could shut down their plants or discharge recalcitrant employees to force their will upon the workers. Elaborate spy systems in many plants kept employers fully informed of any contacts between employees and outlanders, and strict rules against fraternizing, even in private life, between supervisors and workers completed the isolation. Nowhere was this more true than in the textile districts and coal fields of the South where to get within the zone of possible communication entailed trespass upon company property; where the workers' distrust of outside leadership and public resentment of northern interference robbed labor of all outside support.

MILITANT LABOR

Opposed to the structure, aims, and methods of craft and company unions was an entirely different type of labor movement which had been slowly growing in strength through the years. The workers in this movement, regardless of the particular organization to which they belonged, lacked the stabilizing, conservative influences of home ownership, permanent employment, and relative security so characteristic of the craft union membership. They organized along industrial lines. They rejected the basic principles of capitalism. They did not believe in the A. F. of L. philosophy that there was an essential harmony between the interests of capital and labor. They inclined rather to the Marxian theory of class conflict. They belonged to the most oppressed and underprivileged working groups, such as the Negroes, the women in the textile mills and garment factories, and the longshoremen and lumber workers.

The first of these militant labor groups was organized by the socialists. Samuel Gompers, President of the American Federation of Labor until 1924, was opposed to bringing the labor unions into politics, preferring to have them act as a pressure group upon both political parties. It was this attitude which resulted in the withdrawal of the socialists from any connection with the American Federation of Labor in 1895 and their formation of the Socialist Trade and Labor Alliance under the leadership of Daniel De Leon. Thenceforth, Gompers regarded the socialists as the most dangerous enemies of the laboring class. This was essentially the attitude of other Federation leaders, including Peter McGuire, James Duncan, James O'Connell, John Mitchell, and Frank Morrison. They were practical men who, as time passed, became more and more conservative, interested in promoting harmony between capital and labor, and in defeating the aims of "radicals" who believed in class conflict.

The Socialist Trade and Labor Alliance never took root among the organized workmen, but its principle of dual unionism became an important issue in the labor movement. Sceptical of any possibility of changing the philosophy of the American Federation of Labor, it sought to withdraw the radical elements and establish industrial unions dedicated to the task of overthrowing the capitalistic system. Its technique included the general strike, and its objectives those of syndicalism. Its political support was given to the Socialist Labor party. De Leon has been called the "intellectual father of American syndicalism," though probably without justification. Nevertheless, Lenin spoke of him in 1917 as the only socialist who had added anything to the Marxian thought and as the progenitor of the Soviet idea. His contributions to the American labor movement were those of dual unionism and revolutionary industrial unionism, but his organization failed because it was dogmatic, sectarian, and produced no immediate benefits to its members.

The failure of the Socialist Trade and Labor Alliance was followed by the formation of the Socialist party in 1901, and the Industrial Workers of the World in June, 1905. The latter organization was formed at Chicago by Eugene V. Debs, De Leon, and William D. Haywood, all supporters of industrial, revolutionary, class-conscious unionism. Delegates were said to represent 27,000 members of the Western Federation of Miners, 16,750 members of the American Labor Union, 3000 United Metal Workers, 2000 United Brotherhood of Railway Employees, and 1450 members of the Socialist Trade and Labor Alliance. Among the delegates were William E. Trautmann, editor of the *Brauer Zeitung*, the official organ of the United Brewery workmen; Charles O. Sherman, General Secretary of the United Metal Workers International Union; A. M. Simons, editor of the *International Socialist Review*; and Thomas J. Hagerty, a Catholic priest and editor of the *Voice of Labor*. The preamble of the constitution drawn up by the convention was as follows:

The working class and the employing class have nothing in common. There can be no peace so long as hunger and want are found among millions of working people and the few, who make up the employing class, have all the good things of life.

Between these two classes a struggle must go on until all the toilers come together on the political, as well as on the industrial field, and take and hold that which they produce by their labor through an economic organization of the working class, without affiliation with any political party.

The rapid gathering of wealth and the centering of the management of industries into fewer and fewer hands make the trade unions unable to compete with the ever-growing power of the employing class, because the trade unions foster a state of things which allows one set of workers to be pitted against another set of workers in the same industry, thereby helping defeat one another in wage wars. The trade unions aid the employing class to mislead the workers into the belief that the working class have interests in common with their employers.

These sad conditions can be changed and the interests of the working class upheld only by an organization formed in such a way that all its members in any one industry, or in all industries, if necessary, cease work whenever a strike or lockout is on in any department thereof, thus making an injury to one an injury to all.

Following the organization of the I.W.W., the American Federation of Labor launched a bitter attack upon both it and the Socialist party and in May, 1906, a factional fight led to the secession of the Western Federation of Miners. All three groups, however, rallied to the defense of the leaders of the W. F. of M., Charles H. Moyer, William D. Haywood, and George A. Pettibone, who were accused of the murder of former Governor Steunenberg of Idaho in February, 1907. Defense funds poured in from all classes of labor throughout the country and Eugene V. Debs wrote his famous "Call to Arms" editorial asking for a million armed revolutionists to free the accused men if they were convicted. They were acquitted in July, 1907, leaving the Western Federation of Miners a strong organization and the Industrial Workers of the World financially bankrupt. The following year, the latter organization was purged of the Social Laborites under De Leon, and control passed into the hands of the "industrial actionists," Vincent St. John and William Trautmann. The followers of De Leon set up their own headquarters in Detroit and posed as the true I.W.W., but in 1915 changed the name of their organization to Workers International Industrial Union. They carried on a series of textile strikes in 1911–1912 with little permanent gain and officially dissolved their organization in 1924.

The Industrial Workers of the World, after purging their organization of the De Leon group, added the two following paragraphs to their declaration of principles:

Instead of the conservative motto, "A fair day's wages for a fair day's work," we must inscribe on our banner the revolutionary watchword, "Abolition of the wage system!"

It is the historical mission of the working class to do away with capitalism. The army of production must be organized, not only for the every-day struggle with capitalists, but also to carry on production when capitalism shall have been overthrown. By organizing industrially we are forming the structure of the new society within the shell of the old.

Thereafter, it remained bitterly opposed to participation in politics. The majority of its members were migratory workers from the West who could seldom vote because of residence requirements—men who were, from the nature of their existence, distrustful of small-town politicians and law enforcement agencies. Their philosophy of life was that of the anarchist rather than of the socialist. Alien members, likewise, were not interested in politics. Eternal warfare against capitalism and ultimate control of industry by the working class was their motto. Having nothing to lose and being migratory workers, they struck hard and fast, winning quickly or not at all. If they lost, they moved on to another job. There were no strike funds, no strike benefits, no long strikes, and no binding agreements with the employer. When the strike failed, they resorted to sabotage. Industrial peace under the wage system was, to them, impossible. Year by year, they increased their strength among the migratory harvest hands, the foreign-born steel workers, the lumber-camp workers, the textile workers—all groups which were unskilled, poorly paid, and ignored by the American Federation of Labor.

Meanwhile, the Socialist party spread its gospel of "striking at the ballot box" among all classes of workers. Maintaining a neutral position on the question of craft versus industrial unionism, though sympathetic to the latter, it adopted the following rule in 1912:

Any member of the party who opposes political action or advocates crime, sabotage, or other methods of violence as a weapon of the working class to aid in its emancipation shall be expelled from membership in the party. Political action shall be construed to mean participation in elections for public office and practical legislative work along the lines of the Socialist Party platform.

THE WAR YEARS

Of the three organizations—Industrial Workers of the World, Socialists, and American Federation of Labor—only the latter came through the war period unscathed. Peace sentiment, or isolationism, was strong in the middle western and Pacific Coast states as the war approached. This sentiment led to the organization of Labor's National Peace Council by trade unionists in these areas, with strong support from the American Neutrality League and the American League to Limit Armaments. The charge was made, with strong justification, that this peace movement was inspired by German agents.

Samuel Gompers, President of the A. F. of L., on the contrary, dropped all pretense of pacifism as early as 1915. He led the attack upon the new peace movement in the West, and succeeded in weakening it to the point where its maximum demands were for continued neutrality without an embargo on the sale of munitions. Gompers also joined in the preparedness for national defense campaign being waged in 1914 and 1915, became a member of the Advisory Commission of the Council of National Defense in 1916, and supported the ruthless suppression of the International Workers of the World which followed. Membership in the American Federation of Labor increased steadily as a result, with applicants for membership almost having to beg admittance. It went so far as to refuse to recognize the Amalgamated Clothing Workers of America following a split in the ranks of the United Garment Workers, and the new organization went on as an independent, industrial union to gain a membership of 200,000 by 1920. The American Federation of Labor, however, increased its membership from 2,000,000 in 1914 to 4,078,000 in 1920.

On August 12, 1914, the Socialist party took a position directly contrary to that of the A. F. of L. It condemned the war in strong terms as a war of imperialism and called upon labor to recognize it as such. Within a year, it amended its constitution to provide for the expulsion of any member lending support to military or naval credits. Its presidential campaign in 1916 was little more than an appeal for labor to unite in opposition to war. On April 7, 1917, members of the party met at St. Louis, denounced our entry into the war, and pledged themselves to oppose it by every means within their power. Only a few, however, had courage to go through the ordeal, Victor L. Berger, Eugene V. Debs, and Max Eastman among them.

The two most interesting cases were those of Debs and Berger. The first, four-times candidate of the Socialist party for President and one of the most beloved citizens of Terre Haute, bitterly assailed the Wilson Administration for its persecutions under the Espionage and Sedition Acts. Following a particularly strong speech at Canton, June 16, 1918, he was indicted, tried, and sentenced to ten years' imprisonment. Victor L. Berger, Conservative Socialist editor of the *Milwaukee Leader* and former Congressman, had his paper barred from the mails by Postmaster-General Burleson and was indicted under the Espionage Act. Specifically, he was charged with having said that we entered the war to save our financial interests in Allied success and to maintain munition profits; that war would enable the capitalists to suppress labor disturbances as treason; that insanity was a common consequence of active service; that conscription had a taint of dishonor; and that the Bible was a pacifist document. He was elected to Congress while under indictment, but was refused his seat. In November, 1917, he was sentenced by Judge Kenesaw Mountain Landis to twenty years' imprisonment. An appeal was filed, and Berger was meanwhile returned to Congress by an increased vote of 8000 over that he formerly received; but Congress again rejected him. The peak of Socialist proscription came in January, 1920, when five members of the New York Legislature were expelled for no other reason than that of belonging to the Socialist party. The conservative and liberal press alike protested most vigorously, as did the New York Bar Association under the leadership of Charles Evans Hughes. The protests did not alter the action of the Legislature, but the episode marked the beginning of a sharp decline in wartime hysteria and a restoration in part at least of the principle of free political discussion.

The conviction of Debs had aroused a great deal of protest. He was nominated for the presidency a fifth time, in 1920, and received nearly a million votes while a prisoner in Atlanta penitentiary. From his prison cell he wrote in acceptance of the nomination:

I am thinking this morning of the men in the mills and the factories. I am thinking of the women who, for a paltry wage, are compelled to work out their lives; of the little children who, in this system, are robbed of their childhood and in their early, tender years are seized in the remorseless grasp of Mammon and forced into industrial dungeons to feed the machines, while they themselves are being starved in body and soul. I can see them dwarfed, diseased, stunted, their little lives broken and their hopes blasted, because in this high noon of our twentieth-century civilization money is still so much more important than human life.

The following year President Harding released him from prison without the restoration of citizenship. The long period of official persecution, however, together with the recusancy of most of its leaders destroyed the Socialist party as an effective agency in the labor movement.

It was the Industrial Workers of the World who bore the brunt of the war hysteria. Three acts of violence marked the year 1916. On July 22, a bomb killed many people participating in a preparedness day parade in San Francisco. Thomas Mooney and Warren K. Billings were indicted, tried, and sentenced to death. The death sentence was later commuted to imprisonment for life. Substantial proof, though not wholly convincing proof, was later presented to show that they had been convicted on perjured testimony, but all efforts to secure a new trial or release for the convicted men proved unavailing. The second event was the death of several persons during a "free speech" fight between Industrial Workers of the World and a "citizens' committee" at Everett, Washington, on November 6. The third was a violent contest between 15,000 striking iron miners led by Industrial Workers of the World in the Mesabi Range and imported gunmen. The entry of the United States into the war inaugurated a terrific official drive against the organization. More than 1000 members were imprisoned in the course of two years, many being given long-term sentences, and others being deported. The nature of the suppression may be judged from the fact that indictments were drawn up against men who had been dead for years, but who had been active at one time in the organization. Fifty thousand lumber-camp workers in the Northwest struck for and won the eight-hour day on June 1, 1917. This was the signal for an outburst of terrorism. Frank Little, a member of the general executive board of the organization, was kidnapped and hanged to a railroad trestle outside Butte, Montana, on the night of August 1. Twelve hundred strikers at Bisbee, Arizona, were shipped to Columbus, New Mexico, and detained in military prison camps for three months. The result was increased rather than decreased labor unrest—4233 strikes occurring during the year—and the setting up of the President's Mediation Commission and the War Labor Board on May 7, 1918. These Boards were largely ineffective and were dispersed shortly after the signing of the Armistice.

Under pressure from Criminal Syndicalism laws and government prosecution, the I.W.W. declared in 1920 that their organization "does not now, and never has, believed in or advocated either destruction or violence as a means of accomplishing industrial reform." Within two years, factional disputes, imprisonment of its leaders, conflict with the communists, and the decline of the importance of migratory workers completely disrupted the organization. Remnants of the group lingered on, and, in October, 1927, led a strike of 6000 Colorado miners. Failure of the strike practically eliminated the I.W.W. from the labor movement.

POSTWAR REVERSES

The War Labor Board had formulated a set of principles during the war, the most important being the right of workers to organize and bargain collectively, and the protection of workers against discharge for union activities. This was considered a great gain by labor, but it proved to be a temporary one. The war ended with revolutions sweeping Europe, with labor restless throughout the entire world, and with American workers anxious to extend the systematic labor policy of the war period. They counted heavily upon the Clayton Act to protect them against injunctions, and upon their ability to maintain the principle of collective bargaining. In spite of their steadily increasing membership, however, the unions were faced with severe handicaps. The war had stimulated the flow of manpower from the farms to industry, and particularly from the rural South to northern industrial centers; it had drawn an increasing number of women into the factories; and it had hastened the use of new labor-saving devices in all types of work. The end of the war threw many men out of employment where industries had expanded into submarginal areas. More important still, it had unloosed a terrific offensive against the socialists and the Industrial Workers of the World. Once government control agencies were dissolved, industry began a devastating open-shop drive. The issues involved in the contest which followed were confused by the rise of communism and the anti-Red agitation which swept the country. Finally the Supreme Court had seriously crippled labor's hopes for a new era by upholding the legality of yellow-dog contracts which bound employees not to join labor unions under penalty of losing their jobs (*Hitchman Coal Company v. Mitchell*, 1917). It followed this action, in 1921, by narrowly interpreting the prohibitions of the Clayton Act against the use of injunctions (*Duplex Printing Press Co. v. Deering*).

Early in 1919, several large industries began a movement for the open shop and reduction of wages. Unions affiliated with the American Federation of Labor resisted in a series of strikes. Thirty-two thousand members of the United Textile Workers Union of Lawrence, Massachusetts, struck against a reduction of wages and for a 48-hour week on February 3. Ten thousand Irish-American and French-Canadian workers deserted and went back to work but the remainder, made up of Italians, Lithuanians, Russians, Ukrainians, Syrians, Germans, and Jews, continued the strike. After sixteen weeks of terror and police brutality they won their demands on May 20. One hundred and ten American Federation of Labor unions struck in Seattle on February 6 in support of 32,000 shipyard workers. It was, in reality, a test of workers' solidarity, and the strike was abandoned on February 11 after every important function in the life of the city, including the police service, had been in the control of the strikers' committee for seven days. There was no violence during the strike, but the demonstration served to solidify the ranks of both capital and labor for a major test of strength. It came in the steel industry. The American Federation of Labor authorized an attempt to unionize that industry at its 1918 convention. William Z. Foster directed the project, presenting labor's demands to the United States Steel Corporation on July 20, 1919. The corporation, as was expected, refused to negotiate and a strike was called for September 22. This was the third attempt in twenty years to organize the steel workers, the others having been in 1901 and 1909. It was, without question, the most terrific battle between capital and labor and the most disastrous defeat for organized labor in the twentieth century. The Amalgamated Clothing Workers alone contributed $100,000 to the strike fund. Three hundred and sixty-five thousand workers were out by October 9, but the Amalgamated Association of Iron and Steel Workers indicated a willingness to negotiate separately, the American Federation of Labor withheld its full support, 40,000 Negro strikebreakers were imported, charges of communism were injected into the controversy, and the strike was broken on January 8, 1920.

Meanwhile the United Mine Workers called a strike on October 31, 1919, asking for a 60 percent wage increase and a thirty-hour week. Four hundred and twenty-five thousand miners left the mines. On October 24, President Wilson declared the strike to be illegal on the ground that the country was still at war, although war regulations had ceased to function as far as the operators were concerned. Attorney-General A. Mitchell Palmer secured injunctions against the Union; and, on November 10, John L. Lewis called off the strike with the words, "we cannot fight our government." Many miners refused to work, however, until the Fuel Administration negotiated a 14 percent wage increase on December 9, 1919.

A general wage reduction began in industry early in 1920. The American Federation of Labor lost 700,000 members in a single year, and declined to 3,000,000 by 1932. The tide against the unions was stemmed by a two-year strike of the International Typographical Union which began on May 1, 1921, and cost the Union $15,000,000. Six hundred thousand United Mine Workers struck against a 35 percent wage reduction and for a single agreement covering the anthracite and bituminous fields on April 1, 1922. Violence was prevalent, reaching the point of pitched battles in southern Illinois. An agreement was signed with the bituminous operators on August 15 and the anthracite operators on September 3. There was no change in the wage scale, but contracts of the two classes were to expire at different times and the miners of West Virginia and western Pennsylvania were left out of the settlement entirely. Six crafts of the railway shopmen, representing 400,000 men, struck on July 1, 1922, against wage cuts and the abrogation of agreements made under the jurisdiction of the United States Railway Labor Board. Attorney-General Daugherty, at the instance of President Harding, secured an injunction against the unions under the Sherman Act and the Transportation Act of 1920. The strike was broken and the men returned to work on September 15.

The entire decade of the twenties, thereafter, was a period of union stagnation. Industry sought to make its freedom from labor disturbances permanent by promoting pension plans, company unions, and profit-sharing programs. Many industries moved to the open-shop country of the South, and mass-production industries, in which the A. F. of L. had little strength, absorbed an ever larger proportion of the employees in industry.

THE RISE OF COMMUNISM

Beginning with 1918, the left wing of the Socialist party became powerful and well organized. In 1919, two radical groups seceded or were expelled from the party which then became almost as conservative as the A. F. of L. Its membership declined from

104,000 in 1919 to 11,000 in 1922, and it ceased to be a factor in labor history.

The first of the radical groups formed the Communist Labor party and the second formed the Communist party, at the end of August, 1919. Both groups were hostile to the political program of the socialists and in favor of a militant struggle against capitalism. These communist organizations had the backing of the majority of the revolutionary working class in the country, and they took orders from the Communist International of Moscow. The anti-radical campaign of Attorney-General Palmer, however, struck a severe blow to the communist movement in 1919. Only the strongest believers, the convinced communists, dared to remain active in the two parties and less than 12,000 members were represented at a joint or unity convention in May, 1921.

Seeing that the attempt to maintain independent organizations had ended so disastrously both for the I.W.W. and themselves, the communists decided to function as a revolutionary group within the ranks of the American Federation of Labor. This was the beginning of the "boring within" tactics of the communists which have been so irritating to most Americans. Under the leadership of William Z. Foster all of the communists in the various unions of the A. F. of L. were united in an organization called the Trade Union Educational League. This organization announced in 1922, that it was "an informal grouping of the progressive and revolutionary elements throughout the entire trade union movement . . . to develop the trade unions from their present antiquated and stagnant condition into modern, powerful labor organizations."

Then began the modern contest between the American Federation of Labor and the Trade Union Educational League. The radical or communist members of the various unions affiliated in the A. F. of L. were pushing their program of transforming these craft unions into industrial or so-called "vertical" unions and the officials of the American Federation of Labor were resisting the trend with every means at their disposal. The A. F. of L. also had tried in 1919 and 1920 to get the Railroad Brotherhoods to affiliate with it, without success; and it continued to oppose political action.

After losing the shopmen's strike, the railway unions undertook to organize a Conference for Progressive Political Action with the support of many state and city federations of labor, international unions, the Socialist and Farm Labor parties, farm organizations, and church groups. They took an active interest in the congressional campaign of 1922, and then undertook to crystallize the movement through the organization of an independent labor party. All interested groups were invited to a conference in 1923; but the leaders of the movement made the mistake of inviting the Communist party to send representatives. Other organizations thereupon refused to participate further in the undertaking, and it collapsed. A. J. Muste of Brookwood Labor College revived the movement in 1935 and succeeded in organizing an American workers party, but it was absorbed by the Socialist party to the disappointment of those who had hoped for a militant labor party based on communist principles.

The loss of an additional 269,000 members in 1923 by the American Federation of Labor forced it to undertake a more aggressive program at its Portland convention. Delegates suspected of communist leanings were expelled, a news service and a legal information bureau were authorized, and a union lobbying agency was planned. The entire support of the Federation was thrown behind La Follette and Wheeler in the 1924 presidential campaign. Injection of radicalism into the campaign, followed by the failure of La Follette to secure any electoral votes except those of Wisconsin, caused the Federation to return to its old non-partisan policy and to inaugurate a rigorous drive against the Trade Union Educational League members of the garment workers' unions. Sixty thousand more members were lost during the year, and President Samuel Gompers died on December 13, 1924, on his return trip from the San Antonio convention.

While the American Federation of Labor was attempting to formulate a new policy under the leadership of its new President, William Green, the communists, having organized in 1921 under the name of Workers (Communist) party which openly proclaimed itself the American section of the Communist International, renewed their activity among factory workers. Thus the strike in the Botany textile mills of Passaic, New Jersey, on January 25, 1926, was the first in the history of the country under communist leadership. The workers were quickly organized into a union, and affiliation with the American Federation of Labor was requested. This request was granted only after Albert Weisbord, communist leader of the strike, agreed to withdraw. The workers were admitted to the United Textile Workers Union and the American Federation of Labor backed their demands for a 10 percent wage increase, a 40-hour week, and recognition of the union. A compromise was reached on December 13 and the strike came to an end. The interesting feature of the strike was that a group of workers, formerly ignored by organized labor and revolting against intolerable conditions, were organized on an industrial basis by communist leaders and then admitted into an affiliate of the American Federation of Labor after those leaders voluntarily withdrew. It was the beginning of a new chapter in labor union history. The Trade Union Educational League, discouraged by consistent action against it by trade union leaders, and encouraged by a partial sanctioning of "revolutionary unions" by the Communist International, began to look favorably upon the idea of dual unionism. They began with the organization of the National Miners Union, the Needle Trades Workers Industrial Union, and the National Textile Workers Union. They insisted that none of these were dual unions; that they were simply organizing workers not acceptable to the American Federation of Labor. Actually, they were withdrawing the militants from the conservative trade unions and were rightfully called disrupters by the union officials. They reorganized the Trade Union Educational League into the Trade Union Unity League on September 1, 1925, and it became, in spite of consistent denials, a dual union center. By 1932, the communists had eleven independent unions.

BASIS FOR POLITICAL ACTION

The strength of the communist movement in the twenties was evidence of how completely the American Federation of Labor had failed to develop a broad program of improvement for the whole of the wage-earning group in the country. Federation leaders had refused to organize labor outside the ranks of the skilled craftsmen; to develop a program of political action; or to acknowledge the wisdom of public social security measures. The weakness of this position over the long view became apparent after World War I because of (1) the increased employment of women; (2) the migration from agriculture to manufacturing; (3) the entrance of the Negro into manufacturing; (4) the greater productivity of labor as a result of mechanization; (5) the slackening rate of population increase; and (6) the decline in immigration. It would be difficult to determine the total net influence of these things upon wages, unemployment, standards of living, and general cultural advantages after each had been balanced against the other; but they did promote sweeping changes in human relationships. They laid the basis for a definite labor vote, for a new type of powerful labor union, and for an increasing interest by the government in labor problems.

Negro migration away from the Black Belt set in strongly in 1918. The depression of 1929 virtually halted its northward movement; but there were three million Negroes outside the South by that time, including a million in the North Central States, nearly two hundred thousand in the Mountain and Pacific Coast States, and more than two hundred thousand each in New York, Philadelphia, and Chicago. Negro men took over the disagreeable types of labor formerly monopolized by the most recent arrivals among the immigrants. They worked in the fertilizer factories and the stockyards, as longshoremen and hod carriers, in the furnace rooms of the steel mills. Negro men and women alike became marginal laborers in the North. A million Mexicans moved in to take their places in the South, some 300,000 going to the sugar-beet fields in the Platte counties of Colorado and to the cantaloupe plantations of the Imperial Valley in California. Native whites entered the services long monopolized by Negroes in the southern states. Negro women and children who migrated to the North dropped out of the class of agricultural laborers. The children went into the schools and some of the women into domestic service. The race developed its own economy in the northern cities, with its many services and skills. There always had been many aliens in the North who did not enjoy the franchise. Negroes were disfranchised at the South; but they voted in the North. Thus the lowliest of the low among laboring men became a force to be reckoned with in politics. Because organized labor at first excluded them from its ranks and did nothing to alleviate their sordid condition either in northern industries or southern agriculture, they constituted a fertile soil for the seeds of communism; and among the devotees of capitalism, fear of violence from alien workers was supplanted by fear of radical labor ballots. The Communist party platform of 1932 demanded for the Negro: political and social equality; abolition of Jim Crow laws, disfranchising laws, segregation ordinances, and the convict lease and chain gang systems in penal institutions; abandonment of separate educational institutions; freedom for interracial marriages; Negro jury service; a federal anti-lynching law; admission to labor unions; and equal pay for equal service.

The number of women classed as wage earners increased more than 2,000,000 between 1914 and 1930, reaching a total variously estimated between 10,000,000 and 11,500,000. This was nearly one fifth of all persons gainfully employed. About 100,000 moved into managerial positions and cannot be classed as laborers. Another 1,500,000 entered the professions. Domestic and personal service, including the restaurants, hotels, and laundries, required the services of 3,000,000, an increase of one third in twenty years. The number in agriculture decreased, standing at about 1,000,000 in 1930. There were about 1,000,000 in the trades, and 2,000,000 each in clerical positions and factories. In manufacturing, they furnished about one half of all workers in the rayon mills, 50,000 each in automobile factories and rubber factories, and about 100,000 each in production of electrical supplies and chemicals. Of all the women wage earners at the close of the period, 2,000,000 were Negro. Forty percent of all women wage earners were under twenty-five years of age, including more than 200,000 under sixteen and 1,000,-000 between the ages of sixteen and twenty. The nation was putting its young women to work even in the teaching profession. The National Educational Association reported in 1931 that more than three fourths of all cities in the country were refusing to employ married women. The result was a more rapid turnover in the teaching profession. It was a retarding influence against the early marriage of young women teachers, and it deprived children of guidance by those best qualified to understand their emotions. Only about 3 percent of women wage earners were organized. Their competition kept the wages of men low; but minimum wage laws too often served to level off all wages in an industry and make a maximum wage of the minimum fixed by statute.

Finally, after World War I, there was a steady migration of farmers to the more prosperous industrial centers. Some of this migration came from all parts of the country, but the bulk of it was from the Southern Appalachian Highland, the Cotton Belt, the cut-over timberlands of the Great Lakes area, and the Great Plains of the West. These areas were submarginal from the standpoint of agricultural production. The farms were incapable of supporting the population. Standards of living were low. There were few such modern conveniences as automobiles, telephones, and electric lights. Medical service was inadequate. The common diet of the people was sadly deficient in calcium and vitamins. But the people who migrated were hardy, deeply religious people, who had been reared in the best American traditions. They went to the industrial centers like Pittsburgh, Cincinnati, Detroit, and Chicago. They went into mass production industries like iron and steel, food packing, automobiles, and rubber products.

These new industrial workers knew nothing about labor unions. The industries which they entered were free from unionization, 70 percent of the union membership of the country being concentrated in transportation, building, printing, public service, and theaters. They had no leadership, therefore engaged in few strikes although their dissatisfaction increased from year to year. Their strongest potential weapon was the franchise, and eventually their members increased to the point where they held the balance of political power in the country. Then politicians undertook to do for them what labor leaders had failed to do.

BASIS FOR SOCIAL SECURITY

Of the 17,000,000 increase in population between 1920 and 1930, less than 2,500,000 was in rural areas. Agricultural production, however, increased nearly 50 percent between 1900 and 1930: cotton from 10,000,000 bales to 14,000,000 bales; wheat from 602,000,000 bushels to 850,000,000 bushels. Approximately 150,-000,000 acres were added to the total farm acreage of the country, although the average size of farms continued to fluctuate slightly around 150 acres. This increased production with less manpower was due to the development of labor-saving machinery. To some degree, the shifting population was re-absorbed into other fields of production, particularly manufacturing, transportation and mining, although much of it went into new types of service created by an expanding urban population. The latter group remained an unknown quantity and greatly complicated the formulation of a recovery program after the collapse of 1929–1930. Mining, manufacturing, and transportation industries each increased more than 300 percent during these thirty years; but the number of workers employed in these industries did not increase in any such proportion. Science and technology entered into the picture to slow up the re-adjustment and in some cases actually displaced men already employed. Labor-saving machinery and power outdistanced the increased consumption of minerals and manufactured goods. The increased cost of mining, for instance, after the more accessible deposits were exhausted, was met by replacing hand labor with machines. By 1930, the average coal miner was producing twice as much coal as he had thirty years earlier. There were only 125 loading machines in the coal fields in 1923. That number had increased to 3089 by 1934. In that year machines were loading 12 percent of the bituminous coal and 20 percent of the anthracite. The efficiency of steel workers increased 50 percent after World

War I; that of the automobile worker 300 percent. There was perfected a steam shovel which would do the work of 200 men; a bread-wrapping machine which would do the work of 20 men; a clothes-making machine which would do the work of 25 men.

This increased output per man hour in industry was greater than the increased demand for their products. The power generated in the oat and hay fields was replaced by that which came from the oil fields as the tractor, truck, and passenger automobile came into general use. The coal-mining industry suffered from increased production of water power, oil, and natural gas. The rate of increased production in iron mining slowed down as more and more scrap from accumulated stocks went back into the manufacturing process. New, rich fields of exploitation were discovered and older fields were abandoned. In some cases it amounted to a migration within the nation's own domestic economy, in others to importation of minerals from Central and South America. The first process always left behind a destroyed local economy as in the copper districts of Upper Michigan, the gold fields of the Cripple Creek area, the oil fields of Pennsylvania and Ohio. In the second process there was competition from richer deposits outside the domestic economy: of anthracite coal from Russia, of copper and oil from Latin America. By 1930, agricultural imports were larger than agricultural exports by more than $300,000,000. Imports of copper were almost negligible in 1900; but thirty years later they were only 2 percent less than exports. Imports of crude oil were only 30 percent less than exports. In every case, three factors operated to create unstable conditions in the extractive industries: (1) overproduction resulting from unrestricted competition and production for profit; (2) the development of substitute products; and (3) the development of new fields of operation at home or abroad. These unstable conditions in our national economy affected both man and material. Between World War I and 1930 250,000 coal miners and 535,000 railroad men lost their jobs. One hundred and fifty million tons of coal were forever lost each year by destructive processes of extraction. The situation in the oil and gas industries was even worse, with enough gas being wasted in the Texas field to supply large industrial cities of the North and East.

It was customary in the days when the American economic system was regarded as 100 percent perfect to dismiss the subject of technological unemployment with the traditional fiction that other enterprises made possible by invention took up the displaced workmen. This of course did not benefit the individual worker who lost his means of livelihood. How many blacksmiths became garage mechanics when automobiles replaced horses? How many piano tuners went into the radio business? How many operatives in the New England textile mills moved south into the Piedmont Crescent when the manufacturers shifted their field of operations? How many employees of the shoe factories of New England moved to St. Louis? How many mountaineer farmers in the South went into the textile mills with their wives and children? The answer in any case is: precious few. How many cotton fields went untended when 135,000 Negroes moved out of Georgia? What became of the millions invested in houses, schools, and streets when a town shrank from several thousand to a few hundred population? Who provided for the aged and infirm when young men and young women left the farms for distant manufacturing centers? The answers to these and other questions provide the dark shadows in an economy of reputed superabundance. One does not have to dig very deep into the life of any community in the 1920s to find men whose experience and skill in a particular trade became useless to them when they were past the age of adaptation; men who lost their jobs in periods of seasonal or cyclical unemployment and walked the streets for months before they found someone who would risk employing persons above the age of forty-five; men whose factory or mine or oil field was moved away from them over night and were unable to follow because of age, or homes, or other local attachments. No one can say how many there were at any time because those who suffered these reverses usually found temporary or less desirable employment after using up their savings and passing through a period of despondency, perhaps undernourishment and despair. Statistics of unemployed are useless in measuring these things; but even so there was not a single year after World War I when ordinary measurements showed less than 2,000,000 unemployed. It was more than 4,000,000 in 1921 and probably close to that figure in the peak year of prosperity, 1928. By 1932, it had increased to an estimated minimum of 15,000,000. Unemployment among laboring men resulting from technological advance, shifting fields of operation, and cyclical depressions, was matched by equal casualties among those business and manufacturing enterprises unable to keep up with the rate of increased output per man hour. The increased wealth represented by new factories, homes and civic improvements in the textile districts of the South little more than offset the depreciation represented by idle factories and falling real estate values in New England. So with every phase of the economic system. One man's gain was another man's loss. People began to buy automobiles, radios, electrical appliances, and all the other numerous modern conveniences; but unless their incomes increased proportionately, they purchased less of food, clothing, and other commodities. When they turned to fabricated homes, they bought less lumber. The automobile drove down the value of horses. Silk and rayon replaced cotton. The effects of changing standards of living were especially severe upon agriculture. The increased consumption of many of these new artifacts led to the general assumption that standards of living were rising. It was more apparent than real. When the total volume of consumption made possible by mortgages on agricultural lands and on the future earnings of urban residents through installment buying is deducted, the result is startling.

By the end of the twenties the country had accumulated such a staggering load of personal and public indebtedness, so many unemployed and unemployables, that a broad program of public welfare could no longer be avoided.

16

Postwar Reaction

DEPORTATION OF ALIENS

THE immediate postwar period was one in which society felt in grave danger of losing its ideals and customs and struck out in blind intolerance against all who dissented from the established order. In Europe, it was said, the capitalistic system was rapidly passing and with it the Protestant faith; that the middle class economic system of exploitation and production for profit, re-enforced by the Protestant virtues of thrift, industry and self-reliance, were on the decline. A new social order was being constructed, painfully and often violently, in many spots on the Continent, particularly in Russia. Lloyd George and President Wilson both offered the menacing unrest in Europe as an excuse for the haste with which the Versailles Treaty was thrown together. There is no space here to enumerate all the interesting aspects of the revolution in human institutions. Suffice it to say that men and women everywhere were facing the facts of their environment in a new and more realistic manner, and were undertaking to re-model that environment along new lines. That phase of the change which had to do with human relationships proved most confusing, and, therefore, most disconcerting. That is why men said our social institutions had not kept pace with our scientific advance. It was the secret of the amazing appeal of Wilson's promise of a new world order to bewildered humanity everywhere. That was why men turned from him in despair after the Treaty of Versailles and took into their own hands the reconstruction of a new world. It was a vindication of the socialist claim that hope for world peace based on justice was utterly out of the question until the social and economic order at home was reconstructed on the same principle. This attitude explains why the socialists who believed in political action came to be tolerated and those who advocated direct action were suppressed.

It should be remembered (1) that the socialist program called for a fundamental reorganization of production under social ownership and control; (2) that the South, still in the growing pains of industrial development, had millions of Negroes in its midst whose status in society was such as to make them peculiarly susceptible to violent reform ideas; (3) that the American Federation of Labor was a conservative organization, representing the aristocracy of labor and in no sense representative of the great groups of unskilled workers: the domestic servants, the agricultural laborers, the western transients, and the Negro; (4) that economic rivalry as the fundamental cause of World War I, President Wilson's grand theme of Democracy versus Aristocracy, and other equally thought-provoking theses had evoked an intellectual ferment nonacademic in character and all-inclusive in its evaluation of human institutions; (5) that the rule of the proletariat became an accomplished fact by violent revolution in Russia in 1918; and (6) that there were millions of recent immigrants in the United States, not yet thoroughly assimilated, many of whom had fled to this country to escape the militarism and oppressions of the Old World autocracies.

Not the least important aspect of the shifting American scene was political. The Democratic and Republican parties had remained definitely middle class in their economic philosophy with some modifications due to the increasing number of extremely wealthy men; but opposed to them were the Socialist party, the Industrial Workers of the World, and the Non-Partisan League. Each of these parties had a definite program that touched the fundamental principles of economic life. The purpose of the I.W.W. was to overthrow capitalism by direct action. Its members were outspoken in denouncing the war as a capitalistic enterprise, and were actively engaged in sabotage during the war. The arrest

338

and conviction of 93 members of the party in Chicago in 1918, including the head of the organization, William D. Haywood, virtually destroyed it. The mopping up process was continued after the Armistice under state syndicalist laws and the federal Alien Act; but its place at the extreme left was taken immediately by the Communist party or American branch of the Third International. The Socialist party had always advocated public ownership of publicly used property but had sought to accomplish it by orderly governmental processes. As we have seen, the Socialists expelled the radicals in 1919, became conservative, and ceased to be a factor in public affairs. Remnants of the I.W.W. and the former radical Socialists organized the Communist party and frankly admitted their support of the Russian revolutionary program. Though few in number, the mere fact of their existence has vitally affected the course of American history.

The Russian revolutionists had created the Union of Soviet Socialist Republics. The Communist party, comprising a small minority of the people, had established a dictatorship by ruthlessly suppressing all who opposed their ambitious program. The central committee of the party was the government of Russia. Its power was established by force, and it was maintained by rigid censorship, the suppression of free inquiry and discussion, and state ownership of all the instruments of production and distribution. In 1919, the Third Communist International, or Comintern, was organized at Moscow. The Communist parties of all nations were brought together in this union for the purpose of precipitating world-wide revolution; and from that day till its dissolution in 1943, the Comintern advocated the overthrow of the economic and political system of the United States.

Communism throve on misery and poverty. Communists sought, therefore, by every means in their power, to create unrest, confusion, and divided counsels in the solution of domestic problems. They bored into the labor unions, and proselyted among the foreign-born of the urban centers and the Negroes of the South. Their activities and their methods were a hindrance to democratic processes. Americans opposed communism because its objective was to destroy free enterprise; but more than all else, because its methods of violence, disruption, and subversion were contrary even to common decency in human relationships.

On October 16, 1918, Congress passed an act authorizing the Secretary of Labor to take into custody and expel from the United States any alien who advocated or who belonged to any organization which advocated the overthrow of government by force, assassination of public officials, no human government, or the unlawful destruction of property. The act was amended, May 10, 1920, to give the Secretary of Labor authority to take into custody and to deport if, after a hearing, he found them "undesirable residents of the United States," all aliens convicted of violation or conspiracy to violate any of the wartime statutes, such as the Espionage Act, the Trading with the Enemy Act, etc. There were two distinctive features of these Alien Acts: (1) they gave into the hands of an administrative officer, the Secretary of Labor, plenary power, without appeal even to the President of the United States or the safeguards of court procedure, to impose upon aliens, irrespective of their length of residence in this country, the most drastic punishment conceivable, namely, that of being summarily torn from family, friends, and property and transported beyond the sea; and (2) they subjected to the possibility of such punishment individuals who had committed no overt act, who might even not endorse such principles as those designated, but who from some circumstance or other had become affiliated with men who did.

The feeling of animosity toward radical aliens was nation-wide. Communism and anarchy came to mean violence, intrigue, terror, murder, and assassination to most people, and public disquietude reached the point of hysteria in 1919. Newspapers carried stories almost daily of plots to overthrow the government. Beginning in May of that year, bombs were sent through the mail to many public officials, including Mayor Ole Hanson of Seattle, Attorney-General A. Mitchell Palmer, Postmaster-General A. S. Burleson, Justice Oliver Wendell Holmes, and to J. P. Morgan and John D. Rockefeller. Sixteen of these bombs were intercepted in the New York post office, but one reached its destination, seriously injuring the wife and maid of former Senator Thomas W. Hardwick of Georgia. The house of Attorney-General A. Mitchell Palmer was damaged by a bomb. An explosion in Wall Street killed thirty people, injured several hundred, and damaged the office of J. P. Morgan and Co. Other bombs damaged the rectory of a Roman Catholic Church in Philadelphia, and the homes of a silk manufacturer in Patterson, a judge and a Congressman in Boston, a federal judge in Pittsburgh, and the Mayor of Cleveland. Finally, an Armistice Day parade in Centralia, Washington, was fired upon and four men were killed. The strikes of 1919 numbering 3374 and involving 4,000,000 workers added to the general feeling of unrest. Labor had real grievances in most of these strikes, and probably would have had the support of public opinion under normal circumstances, but communists were involved in most of them, emphasizing their objective of gaining worker control of industry.

The first action under the Alien Acts was taken in December 21, 1919, when 249 Russians were deported on the transport *Buford*. The next month over four thousand persons were taken into custody in a carefully planned raid throughout the country, but many were later released for insufficient evidence.

These activities against aliens were vigorously pressed by Attorney-General Palmer. The enforcement of the law was under the jurisdiction of the Secretary of Labor, William B. Wilson; but the government agencies were disorganized in the winter of 1919–1920. President Wilson was dangerously ill, the country was drifting, and reactionary elements were in control. The orders for the January raids, for instance, were signed by J. W. Abercrombie, acting solicitor for the Department of Labor but a member of the Department of Justice, and A. Carminette, Commissioner-General of Immigration. Secretary Wilson was ill at the time and, in his absence, important changes were made in the rules of procedure, one such denying the person in custody the benefit of counsel. Everywhere throughout the country, the industrial unrest became much more of a class warfare than it would have been had not the Justice Department taken the lead in pursuing labor agitators suspected of communist leanings.

Moreover, Palmer's zeal to rid the country of all vestiges of radical thought caused him to disregard many of the constitutional guarantees of individual freedom. Arrests were made without warrants, and both aliens and citizens were arrested en masse for mere presence in or about radical meetings. Persons were detained for long periods without benefit of counsel. Private property was wantonly destroyed. Agents-provocateurs were employed. Finally, the Department of Justice was perverted into a propaganda bureau to prejudice the people against aliens and citizens of radical beliefs.

It is perfectly clear that the Alien Acts and the deportations were popular throughout the country. In the South, much was said and believed about the danger of communist agitation among the Negroes. The American Federation of Labor was not sympathetic to radical labor groups which sought to penetrate their organization and discredit their policies. Industrialists were satisfied to see their adversaries clapped into jail for long terms under the state syndicalist laws or deported to foreign lands. Returned soldiers were unfriendly to a radical labor group which had been so actively identified with opposition to the war. The exhilaration of silencing economic dissenters by suppression was as pleasurable as silencing pacifists and German sympathizers had been, especially when the victims were foreigners against whom there was a prevailing though perhaps subconscious dislike. Many people agreed with Attorney-General Thomas W. Gregory and his successors that free expression of opinion was dangerous to American institutions, and a great many more preferred not to have to think about the social and economic injustices which agitators were constantly bringing to their attention. Many thought, and continue to think, that safety lay in splendid isolation with the minds of mature men and women safeguarded against strange new ideas. These conditions combined to give to the postwar decade an atmosphere of dull resentment and surprising indifference to internal disorders. It was a decade of racial and class hatreds, of open and defiant lawlessness, of religious bigotry, of widespread intolerance, and of intellectual dishonesty.

KU KLUX KLAN

During the early days of the war, a moving picture made its appearance, called *The Birth of a Nation*. The picture, supposedly historical but a grossly inaccurate and distorted portrayal of the Reconstruction Period, made a sensational appeal to race prejudice. It was shown to packed houses throughout the nation at a time when other disturbing factors in race relations were threatening open warfare. The feeling of hostility between the Negroes and whites had been slowly dying out in the South after the turn of the century. Confidence, born of understanding and cooperation, was taking its place. Booker T. Washington, the great Negro leader and educator, had pioneered in the field. His work at Tuskegee had stimulated racial pride among the Negroes, contributed to improvement in every field of human endeavor, and established the principle that the only solid foundation for sectional advancement was equal justice to all. His thesis that the two races had talked "too much about each other and not enough to each other" was acted upon by several agencies. The National Urban League set up interracial boards to assist migrating Negroes to adjust themselves to urban conditions. The Southern Publicity Committee, financed by the Phelps-Stokes Fund, made press releases of notable Negro achievements. Dr. Willis D. Weatherford, President of Southern College, working through the college Y.M.C.A., promoted special studies along scientific lines of the race problem. The organization created interracial boards and established a summer school at Blue Ridge, North Carolina, for a study of the question. In 1912, the Southern Sociological Congress, composed of representative southern men from all walks of life, held its first meeting at Nashville. A special committee on race relations, under the chairmanship of James H. Dillard, was created. Its meetings and reports were a real stimulus to continued activity. Dillard, Director of the Anna T. Jeanes Foundation, organized the University Commission on the Southern Race Problem. The Commission, representing all southern state universities, studied the conditions of Negro life, and issued many open letters summarizing at length such problems as lynching, education, and migration.

Then came the World War, the most trying period in race relationship since Reconstruction, and a return of all the old passions and misunderstanding. *The Birth of a Nation* with its scenes of Negro terrorism revived the Ku Klux Klan. There probably would have been a proscriptive organization of some sort in any case, but the mere use of the name was an incentive to all the old oppressions fifty years after the event and under strangely different circumstances. The name struck terror into the hearts of the Negroes with their inherited traditions of unlawful persecutions; it revived dormant prejudices in the hearts of competing groups of whites; it gave some degree of legitimacy to the use of robes and masks. The Selective Service Act took nearly 400,000 Negroes into the armed forces, about half of them to Europe. That there was intentional discrimination against them would be difficult to prove; but it was apparent that they had grievances, real or imaginary. It was said and believed that proportionately more Negroes were drafted into the service than whites; that Negro officers were discriminated against in travel; that Negro soldiers were discriminated against by the Y.M.C.A. More important, however, were the lynchings of 34 Negroes in 1917 and 60 in 1918, including five Negro women; and race riots in East St. Louis, Chester, Pa., Philadelphia, Houston, Omaha, Chicago, Washington, D. C., and Elaine, Arkansas. The feelings of Negro soldiers carried off to France to battle against German atrocities, about the situation at home, were not conducive to racial harmony. In addition, there was the fear among the whites that Negro freedom in army life in France would disrupt the normal relationship between the races at the South. This fear led to repressive measures to stop the migratory movement which, in turn, succeeded only in providing further excuse for the migration. More than 600,000 migrated to the North between our entry into the war and 1924. Hundreds of Negroes, waiting at railway stations, were arrested and thrown into jails. Northern labor agents were heavily fined. All these conditions contributed to a sense of impending peril.

Early in 1919, there met in Atlanta five men who had been

active in promoting interracial cooperation: John J. Eagan, a steel manufacturer of Atlanta; M. Ashby Jones, an Atlanta clergyman; R. H. King, Executive Secretary of the National War Work Council for the Southeast; W. W. Alexander, prominent clergyman and army Y.M.C.A. executive; and J. H. Dillard. These men planned and inaugurated the Atlanta Conference of representative Negroes and whites from all parts of the South. Out of that Conference, where there was more honest and frank interchange of opinion than ever before, came a proclamation and the permanent organization of a Commission on Interracial Cooperation. The proclamation clearly reveals the gravity of the crisis:

We a group of Christians, deeply interested in the welfare of our entire community, irrespective of race or color distinction, and frankly facing the many evidences of racial unrest, which in some places have already culminated in terrible tragedies, would call the people of our own beloved community to a calm consideration of our situation before extremists are allowed to create a condition where reason is impossible.

The Commission on Interracial Cooperation, financed by the Y.M.C.A., established headquarters at Atlanta. Under its guidance, executive boards were established in each southern state, interracial committees in more than eight hundred counties, and a network of committees in local communities. The organization was flexible but permanent, devoting its efforts toward insuring justice in the courts, the repression of mob violence, adequate school and recreational facilities for Negroes, etc. It worked in close cooperation with local institutions such as boards of education, chambers of commerce, and churches. The presidents of leading Negro schools, Robert R. Moton of Tuskegee Institute, James E. Gregg of Hampton Institute, Isaac Fisher of Fiske University, and John Hope of Morehouse College were active in the organization from its inception. The two fundamental objectives were (1) to correct injustices and inequalities of conditions affecting the Negro; and (2) to improve those interracial attitudes out of which intolerable conditions arise. The attainment of the first objective was specifically the task of local committees; that of the second the function of a press service reaching 2000 publications with a combined circulation of

20,000,000. The Commission was responsible for the establishment of college courses for the study of race relations in more than sixty institutions, and for the appointment of a committee on race relationship by the Federal Council of Churches of Christ in 1921, and is generally given credit for the sharp reduction in the number of lynchings after that year, in addition to effecting marked improvement in conditions touching household servants, the founding of day nurseries, kindergartens, and child clinics.

Meanwhile, the Ku Klux Klan, with its organized defiance of the law and its attempt to direct the affairs of men through an invisible empire, was working in the opposite direction. The Klan was conceived by William J. Simmons of Atlanta, organized under a Georgia charter in 1916, and promoted along lines of high-pressure salesmanship by Edward Young Clarke. By 1925, its membership had reached a total of over 5,000,000 with half the total members in New York, Ohio, Indiana, Texas, and California. Its fundamental creed was religious and racial intolerance combined in hostility to Negro, Jew, and Catholic. Its practices were utterly foreign to the fundamental tenets of Americanism of which it claimed to possess a 100 percent monopoly: the boycott and proscription of Catholics, foreigners, and Jews; secret trial and punishment of Negroes in particular but of all without distinction who incurred its displeasure; the utter disregard of law and Constitutional guarantees of individual liberty. The reasons for its phenomenal growth, estimated at 100,000 per week for a time, are perfectly clear. The deep concern about the large number of foreigners unrestricted immigration was bringing into the country was crystallized by Wilson's denunciation of hyphenated Americanism. In the minds of many people there was an association of aliens and Jews with radical economic theories, and a fear that postwar Europe was about to deluge the country with a new flood of immigrants. The moral reform movement, which reached its dramatic climax in emphasis upon the prohibition of alcoholic beverages, was beginning to encounter serious resistance. The effects of the war were draining the South of its agricultural laborers and creating unrest among the Negro population. More than half of the nation's population was living within fifty miles of its boundary

346

lines. Here were concentrated the wealth, the foreign born, the freedom from religious restraints, the opposition to prohibition, the intellectual heresies, the Catholics. The interior region, predominantly agricultural, native-born American and Protestant, was precisely the region which nourished the prohibition movement and fundamentalism, raised its voice against the encroachments of industrialism, viewed with alarm the changing status of Negroes, and harbored a genuine fear of Popery.

The Klan capitalized on all of these things. It was more than a mere organization; it was an attitude of mind—a body of thought —which was the direct antithesis of justice, liberty, and equality. Professional organizers and propagandists were drawn into the movement by the high percentage of initiation fees they were allowed to retain. The result was that the lunatic fringe of society furnished more than its quota of members. The Protestant ministers took up the banner and added a degree of respectability to it. Professional and business men were forced to join as a means of self-preservation. The press was silenced in many places, and politicians feared to lift their voices in protest. Anonymous telephone calls and fiery crosses came to direct the conduct of men. The organization became so strong that neither the Democratic nor the Republican party had the courage to do more than evade the issue. Even after it had ceased to be a force to be reckoned with in politics, its lingering spirit cast a blight over the land. It is doubtful if such organizations ever die out completely. Fiery crosses may still be seen on occasion in the Black Belt. The campaign against the Democratic presidential candidate, Alfred E. Smith, in 1928, was based upon the Ku Klux Klan vendetta. Religious and social hatreds are peculiarly sensitive to sly propaganda, and propaganda has developed into an esoteric art.

FUNDAMENTALISM

A second aspect of the postwar reaction was the fundamentalist movement. Economic and religious fundamentalism are inseparable in history. Each represents eighteenth-century dogma in its respective field, and they were brought into concert by the increasing emphasis upon social welfare in the Protestant churches. Rural Southerner and wealthy Northerner found common ground in opposition to this sociological trend which threatened to interfere with the exploitation of Negro and white workers. The religious fundamentalist remained faithful to the literal interpretation of the Bible; the economic fundamentalist clung to the sacred formulae of parental authority, individual liberty, and property rights. The former opposed every effort to reconcile the teachings of Christian religion with modern scientific thought; the latter denied the need for new relationships between the individual and the changing social order. The prestige of the pioneering modernists in the Church—Harry Emerson Fosdick, A. C. McGiffert, Preserved Smith and others—finally reached such heights that the fundamentalists sought to throw up legislative barriers against their heresies. Their efforts were followed by an equally determined minority who hoped to accomplish the same thing with respect to social and economic theories. The public schools have become the clearing house for the accumulated mental pabulum of the human race. Some groups doubted the ability of young people to choose correctly between conflicting theories. Others questioned the impartiality of instructors in their presentation. Others, more certain that their own philosophy constituted the correct way of life, insisted that it be emphasized to the exclusion of everything else. Still others sought to prostitute the educational system to their own selfish ends. The aim of the school personnel, then, to teach children to think and to take what they read and what they hear, not as facts, but as data for their consideration, became increasingly difficult. The campaign of the Ku Klux Klan to require the reading of the Bible in the public schools and to eradicate parochial schools, was followed by the religious fundamentalists drive against the teaching of evolution; and that, in turn, by the economic fundamentalists drive for teachers' oaths to uphold the Constitution. Interwoven with the whole movement was the effort to use the schools as an agency for propaganda by the prohibition forces, certain elements of the privately owned utilities, and other special pleaders.

The anti-evolution agitation coursed through the entire nation for a decade after the war. Its great protagonist was William Jennings Bryan who had contributed more than any other individual to the cause of prohibition. His plea for a return to the old-time religion was as eloquent as that of Billy Sunday, but he made it directly to legislative bodies for statutes to stamp out modern heresies. Interest was largely localized with little notice by the press until the Scopes trial at Dayton, Tennessee, in the summer of 1925. The man who introduced the bill in the Tennessee legislature was John W. Butler, a primitive Baptist farmer of Fayetteville. The bill as passed forbade the teaching in state-supported schools of "any theory that denies the story of the Divine Creation of man as taught in the Bible." There were immediate demands for its enforcement. John T. Scopes, a high school teacher of Dayton, acting on the suggestion of a group of friends, made a test case of the law. There followed one of the famous trials in the history of the country. William Jennings Bryan assisted in the prosecution and the Civil Liberties Union employed Clarence Darrow, Dudley Field Malone and Arthur Garfield Hayes for the defense. Scopes was convicted and the state Supreme Court, on an appeal, upheld the constitutionality of the law. Little was said in the trial about the relationship between state and church, or about academic freedom in the broad sense of the term. Bryan summed up the theory of the fundamentalists when he said: "Power in this country comes from the people; and if the majority of the people believe that evolution breaks down a religious faith and threatens Christianity, they have a right to demand that it be suppressed or at least confined to the little group of research men who may study it as a theory not yet proven." The defense made no great effort to prove the law unconstitutional. Instead, it sought to show that the theory of evolution was not contradictory to the Bible. The nature of the controversy accompanying the trial gave further convincing proof of the rural South's conservatism and of its sensitiveness to outside criticism, of the ignorance of many of its religious leaders, and of its lag in general cultural progress. The trial contributed to a general nationwide introspection which turned the tide against religious fundamentalism, against the Klan, and against lynchings.

The reaction was generally favorable to educational processes and more courageous leadership.

The success of the anti-evolutionists in Tennessee encouraged them to greater efforts elsewhere; but their great leader was gone. Bryan had died during the Scopes trial, a crusading reformer to the last. Two organizations were founded about this time to aid in the movement: The Supreme Kingdom and the Bible Crusaders of America. The former was founded by Edward Young Clarke, former Imperial Wizard of the Ku Klux Klan. The latter was said to have been financed by the millionaire George F. Washburne, who published a list of fifty-four institutions of higher learning where young people could receive an education without their faith in the book of Genesis being disturbed. He was also chairman of a committee for founding a memorial university to Bryan at Dayton. T. T. Martin of the Bible Crusaders of America and author of *Hell and the High Schools,* carried the fight into Mississippi, most rural of all the states, where an anti-evolution act was placed upon the statute books in 1926. A similar measure was defeated in Louisiana only by partliamentary maneuver and in Kentucky by a vote of 42 to 41. Martin then transferred his lobbying headquarters to Charlotte, North Carolina. Heroic work by President Harry W. Chase of the state's great university defeated his efforts, the fight ending finally in 1927. The same year an anti-evolution act was passed by popular referendum in Arkansas by a majority of 45,000.

The anti-evolutionists next turned their attention to textbooks and teachers, fomenting strife at many schools including the University of Tennessee, the University of Texas, and Southern Methodist University at Dallas. The Southern Baptist convention, in 1926, adopted a resolution stating: "This convention accepts Genesis as teaching man was a special creation of God and rejects every theory, evolutionary or otherwise, which teaches that man originated or came by way of lower animal ancestry." The Southern Presbyterian General Assembly, in 1931, broke away from the Federal Council of Churches of Christ in America because it endorsed the practice of birth control. The burden of the fight against these phases of reaction was carried by a group of independent southern newspapers: the Norfolk *Virginia Pilot*, edited by Louis I. Jaffe; the Raleigh *News and Observer*, owned and edited by Josephus Daniels; the Chattanooga *Times*, edited by L. G. Walker; the Columbus (Ga.) *Enquirer Sun*, edited by Julian Harris; and the Montgomery *Advertiser*, edited by Grover C. Hall. Pulitzer prizes were awarded to the *Virginia Pilot* for its campaign against lynching and might with equal justice have been given for its bold denunciation of A. Mitchell Palmer's Red hunts; to the *Enquirer Sun* for its relentless crusade against the anti-evolutionists; and to the *Advertiser* for its fight against the Klan. Just as the Klan, anti-evolution, lynchings, and anti-communism were inseparable, so too was the fight against them. The combined efforts of this group of newspapers, and others to a lesser degree, constitute a brilliant epoch in American journalism, the more so because they were located in the heart of the reactionary region and were a hundred times more effective than northern newspapers would have been.

The same cannot be said for men in public life. Most politicians fought shy of the Klan issue, insisting that it was of minor importance and would soon disappear. They refused to admit that the Klan was seeking to put its doctrines into practice by seizing control of the government. In fact, politicians turned the situation to their own account, basing their appeals for support upon the prevailing spirit of intolerance. Robert M. La Follette, in the presidential campaign of 1924, was denounced as a dangerous radical, whose election would sound the death knell of American institutions. Charles G. Dawes and Calvin Coolidge, the Republican candidates, spoke passionately of the menace of Bolshevism and with deep affection for the Constitution. The campaign slogan of the Republican party was *Coolidge or Chaos*. Thus was the attention of the country skillfully turned from the corruption of the previous administration by an appeal to irrational thought. A straw man was set up and every one was invited to the kill. The idea worked so well that it was repeated with each presidential campaign. When succeeding generations are able to view the period with a better perspective than the present permits, it may well appear to have been the most damaging blow ever dealt to the country.

The worst depression in the nation's history brought financial ruin to millions and forced one man in five into the breadlines. The Roosevelt Administration in 1933 commanded the largest working majorities in history and faced tremendous problems. It was a situation which called for the most vigorous and intelligent minority leadership that could be mustered; but the minority had talked about communism for so long it could not think in any other terms. After a while it began to denounce the administration program as all wrong, un-American, radical, destructive of individual liberty, inspired by Moscow. There was no difference between the appeal of the southern politicians to race prejudice and of northern politicians to the fears of Bolshevism. Both made grand themes for the hustings: dramatic, emotional, and non-controversial. Both created an atmosphere in which self-appointed guardians of the nation's security insisted upon banding themselves together into organizations for the purpose of non-legal control. They were variously opposed to Catholics, Negroes, Jews, aliens, communists, labor leaders, liberals of all kinds and, particularly, pacifists. The Silver Shirts, known to have had organizations in forty-six states, charged the Jews with responsibility for all the ills from which humanity has ever suffered. The Crusaders for Economic Liberty in Tennessee and the White Legion of Alabama were particularly hostile to agitation among the Negro and white share-croppers. There were, also, the Pioneer American Protective Association of New England; the Union of Fascists of New Jersey; the Order of '76 of New York; the Black Legion of Michigan; and the Vigilantes of San Francisco and Tampa.

The attack of the economic fundamentalists upon the educational system met with greater success than that of the anti-evolutionists because of the subtle fashion in which the meaning of patriotism was broadened to include not only devotion to our democratic political system, but to the existing social order and willingness to defend the latter even to the point of denying the right to discuss freely social and economic questions. Academic freedom was seriously imperilled all over the country by Red hunts and legislative investigations. A group of students was expelled from one university for inviting Harry Elmer Barnes to speak on the Mooney-Billings case; students from another university were chastised for vigorous opposition to compulsory military training; students from still another were punished for various offenses ranging from peace parades to inviting John Strachey to speak on the campus. Some leading educators of the country endorsed the idea of teachers attending summer school at the University of Moscow, there to learn at first hand the principles of the social and political system of the Soviet Union. We maintain great universities to teach young people about social practices from the Court of St. James to the cannibalism and eroticism of the heathens; about political theories from Aristotle to Calhoun; and about every conceivable kind of economic institution; but, because some intelligent people proposed to find out what the Russian people were thinking and doing, a great chain of newspapers was ready to drive them into exile. That the movement did not go farther was due to a vigorous counteroffensive. The Board of Regents of the University of Wisconsin went on record as believing that "students should have and do have the right to study social problems and should not be suppressed from expressing or advocating doctrines in which they sincerely believe, provided always the bounds of law or of decency are not exceeded." Secretary of the Interior, Harold Ickes, said before the Teachers Welfare Organization of Chicago: "To justify its existence, a school system in America, from kindergarten to university graduate school, must be staffed by intellectually honest men and women who are undaunted in their search for truth, fearless in its dissemination and unshackled by ancient superstitions or bugaboos, free to think and think aloud." President Robert M. Hutchins of the University of Chicago, Thomas W. Lamont of J. P. Morgan and Company, the *St. Louis Post Dispatch*, the *Baltimore Sun*, the *Christian Science Monitor*, and others added their protests so vigorously that the movement was checked before great damage was done. That was not true, however, of the public schools.

Twenty-two states had adopted teachers oath laws before January 1, 1936. The first of these laws since the period of the Civil War was enacted in Rhode Island in 1917. This oath, which every teacher in the public schools was required to take, was the only one of its kind until 1935 and, in some respects, still remains in a class by itself. It reads:

Rhode Island—1917

I, as a teacher and citizen pledge allegiance to the United States of America, to the state of Rhode Island and to the American public school system.

I solemnly promise to support the constitution and laws of Nation and State, to acquaint myself with the laws of the State relating to public education, and also the regulation and instruction of my official superiors, and faithfully carry them out.

I further promise to protect the school rights of my pupils, to conserve the democracy of school citizenship, to honor public education as a principle of free government, to respect the profession of education as a public service, and to observe its ethical principles and rules of professional conduct.

I pledge myself to neglect no opportunity to teach the children committed to my care loyalty to Nation and State, honor to the Flag, obedience to law and government, respect for public servants entrusted for the time being with the functions of government, faith in government by the people, fealty to the civic principles of freedom, equal rights and human brotherhood, and the duty of every citizen to render service for the common welfare.

I shall endeavor to exemplify in my own life and conduct in and out of school the social virtues of fairness, kindliness and service as ideals of good citizenship.

I affirm in recognition of my official obligation, that, though as a citizen I have the right of personal opinion, as a teacher of the public's children I have no right, either in school hours or in the presence of my pupils out of school hours, to express opinions that conflict with honor to country, loyalty to American ideals, and obedience to and respect for the laws of the Nation and State.

In all this I pledge my sacred honor and subscribe to a solemn oath that I will faithfully perform to the best of my ability all the duties of the office of teacher in the public schools.

Ohio adopted a teachers oath law in 1919, and Colorado, Oklahoma, Oregon, and South Dakota in 1921. Florida required the signing of a pledge after 1925. West Virginia enacted an oath law in 1928 and Indiana in 1929, the latter serving as a model for those adopted in 1931 in California, Montana, North Dakota, and Washington. An oath law was enacted in New York in 1934 and the following year in Arizona, Georgia, Massachusetts, Michigan, New Jersey, Texas, and Vermont. Moreover, such bills were introduced in the legislatures of sixteen states in 1935 but were defeated in seven and vetoed by the Governors of Delaware and Maryland. Propaganda behind such laws was thoroughly organized in that year as a part of a broad program including stringent sedition bills and bills barring radical parties from the ballot. All of these laws were similar either to that of Oklahoma or Oregon or Indiana, except those of Georgia, Florida and Vermont which belong in a class with that of Rhode Island. The substance of these laws reveals in a better way than can otherwise be shown, the progression of the movement.

Oklahoma—1921
I . . . do solemnly swear (or affirm) that I will support, obey, and defend the constitution of the United States and the constitution of the State of Oklahoma.

Oregon—1921
I solemnly swear, or affirm, that I will support the constitution of the state of Oregon . . . and the laws enacted thereunder, and that I will teach, by precept and example, respect for the flags of the United States and of the state of Oregon; . . . reverence for law and order and undivided allegiance to the government of our country, the United States of America.

Indiana—1929
I solemnly swear (or affirm) that I will support the constitution of the United States of America, the constitution of the State of Indiana and the laws of the United States and the State of Indiana, and will, by precept and example, promote respect for the flag and the institutions of the United States and of the State of Indiana, reverence for law and order and undivided allegiance to the government of the United States of America.

Georgia—1935
Uphold, support and defend the Constitution and laws of this State and of the United States, and will refrain from directly or indirectly subscribing to or teaching any theory of government of economics or of social relations which is inconsistent with the fundamental principles of patriotism and high ideals of Americanism.

355

Vermont—1935

I, . . . , do solemnly swear (or affirm) that I will support and defend the Constitution of the United States against all enemies, foreign and domestic; that I will bear true faith and allegiance to the same; that I take this obligation freely, without any mental reservation or purpose of evasion; and that I will well and faithfully discharge the duties of the office on which I am about to enter. So HELP ME GOD.

Florida—1925

I believe in the United States of America as a government of the people, by the people, for the people, whose just powers are derived from the consent of the governed; a democracy in a republic; a sovereign nation of many sovereign States, a perfect Union, one and inseparable, established upon those principles of freedom, equality, justice, and humanity for which American patriots sacrificed their lives and fortunes.

I therefore believe it is my duty to my country to love it; to support its Constitution; to obey its laws; to respect its flag; and to defend it against all enemies.

This amazing legislative concern with the patriotism of teachers has but one explanation. It is that during World War I and the two periods of economic unrest after the war any one was an object of suspicion by certain vested interests who suggested changes in the economic and social order or who even desired to discuss the merits of suggested changes. Middle-class philosophy and intense nationalism were masquerading as patriotism. The prevailing philosophy was the direct antithesis of that expressed by Justice Holmes in the Rosika Schwimmer case when he said: "If there is any principle of the Constitution that more imperatively calls for attachment than any other it is the principle of free thought —not free thought for those who agree with us but freedom for the thought that we hate." The purpose back of every teachers oath was to induce those who took it so to present the facts in classroom discussion as to make the *status quo* appear to be the wisest and best of all human endeavor. How could any teacher have sworn in 1850 to promote, by precept and example, the institutions of the United States without being a slaveholder? If ever there was a distinctly American institution, it was slavery in 1850. How could any teacher have taken such an oath in 1920 without being a staunch prohibitionist? The prohibition was a part of the Constitution. How could any teacher have taught pupils respect for some of the public servants at Washington during the Harding Administration? The amazing thing about the whole procedure was that, in setting up the Constitution as a symbol to which teachers must swear allegiance, no thought was given to the fact that the Constitution itself provides a form of amendment by which every feature of the government may be altered or abolished if the people so desire.

Every teacher who ever took such an oath in the United States knew that the purpose of those who sponsored its requirement was that, so frankly stated in the Georgia oath, of preventing a full and frank discussion of social, economic, and political questions. The damage done to the school system cannot be measured in terms of those rare cases where teachers refused to take the required oaths or were dismissed from the service. The damage, and no one can adequately measure it, resulted from the fact that teachers, already suffering the effect of drastic salary cuts, concealed whatever spark of liberalism and disposition they might have to acquaint their pupils with a broad knowledge of human thought, rather than antagonize conservative interests in the community. One could find school districts in every state where teachers voluntarily refrained from a discussion of one or another of the questions of banking, dishonest advertising, industrial labor policies, child labor, old-age pensions, unemployment insurance, the tariff, crop renters, lynching, or pacifism.

Back of the movement for teachers'-oath laws was a continuous agitation by a number of newspapers and patriotic organizations over the menace of Bolshevism, communism, and regimentation. There can be no question but that the widespread denunciation of the Roosevelt Administration on these counts had some connection with the drive for teachers'-oath laws in 1935. That the movement was definitely checked by the following year was due to the courageous efforts of many men and women in the leading eastern universities including George Counts, Carl Becker, Alice Snyder, Mary Woolley, Christian Gauss, Kirtley Mather, Howard K. Beale,

Charles A. Beard, Merle Curti, John Dewey, and Harold U. Faulkner.

Meanwhile, the Customs Bureau of the Treasury Department and organizations such as the Boston Watch and Ward Society and the New York and Philadelphia Societies for Suppression of Vice were busy protecting individuals against their own indiscretions by the censorship of books, theater productions, moving pictures, and art exhibits. The Tariff Act of 1894 prohibited any person from importing into the United States from any foreign country, "any obscene book, pamphlet, paper, writing, advertisement, circular, print, picture, drawing, or other representations, figures, images, etc." Beginning in 1909, when the Bureau sought to prevent the Field Museum from importing Chinese pictures and manuscripts claimed to be obscene, a black list of hundreds of book titles has been compiled. Among those books which have been excluded at one time or another since then are Rousseau's *Confessions*, Voltaire's *Candide*, Boccaccio's *Decameron*, Joyce's *Ulysses*, and Lawrence's *Lady Chatterley's Lover*. Police censorship in large municipalities of books, plays, and movies barred from the bookstores and from the stage such eminent productions as Eugene O'Neill's *Desire Under the Elms* and *Strange Interlude*, Sinclair Lewis' *Elmer Gantry*, Upton Sinclair's *Oil* and *Boston*, Theodore Dreiser's *American Tragedy*, Lee Shubert's *Bunk of 1926*, Maxwell Anderson's *Gods of the Lightning* and *Winterset*, Ernest Hemingway's *Farewell to Arms*, Lion Feuchtwanger's *Power*, Carl Van Vechten's *Nigger Heaven*, Sherwood Anderson's *Dark Laughter*, Samuel Raphaelson's *Young Love*, Clifford Odets' *Waiting for Lefty*, and Jack Kirkland's *Tobacco Road*. Margaret Sanger was refused permission to speak in Boston on the subject of birth control. Mary W. Dennett was arrested and brought to trial for circulating a treatise originally written for her adolescent sons explaining the physiological basis of sex life. Rosika Schwimmer, one of the really fine characters of the age and an internationally known pacifist fifty years of age, was denied citizenship because she refused to agree to bear arms in defense of the country. Charlotte Whitney was convicted for membership in the Communist Labor party which was a criminal offense under the laws of Cali-

fornia. Editors of student publications in
universities were forbidden to discuss compulsᴇ
Large radio stations "cut out" of network proᵧ
munist, socialist, and pacifist speakers went on the
Criminal Syndicalist laws were enacted in thirty-twᴇ
punishing the display of the red flag as a political emblem .
eight states; laws requiring the reading of the Protestant ɪ
the schools in seventeen states; laws prohibiting atheists   .ɴ
testifying in court or holding public office in six states; laws segregat-
ing Negroes in public conveyances, schools, and recreation centers
in seventeen states; and laws establishing censorship of the movies
in six states. Laws dating from reconstruction days were revived
in some southern states and used against labor organizers. In the
cities, ordinances were written against disorderly conduct, disturbing the peace, parades or street meetings without permits, distribution of literature in public places—all of which gave discretionary
power into the hands of police officials which was used to deny
freedom of speech, press and assemblage to dissentient groups.
Bills were introduced into Congress and received substantial support to deport all alien radicals, register all aliens, and suppress
sedition and syndicalism.

GROWTH OF THE UNDERWORLD

The most spectacular attempt and failure to achieve uniformity
in American life during the twenties was the prohibition debacle.
It was expected by those who sponsored the Eighteenth Amendment that crime and poverty would disappear from the land. Instead, all the previous gains for temperance were lost; and disrespect for the law, the criminal underworld, and official corruption
increased at an alarming rate.

The most disturbing feature of the experiment was the financing
of criminals. The manufacture of illegal alcoholic beverages became
as common in the cities as it had formerly been in the mountains.
Whole fleets of rumrunners poured a steady stream of illegal
beverages into the country from abroad. Bootlegging became a
major industry, highly profitable, and under the control of the most

depraved elements in society. Yet, however vicious personnel of the liquor business, and in spite of the illegality of the trade, respectable people in such numbers purchased such goods that the flow of drink underground became as great as it had ever been in legitimate channels. Enormous profits led to the organization of gangs in every city, all armed and thoroughly ruthless in their dealings with competitors and law enforcement agents. The Al Capone gang of Chicago, for example, numbered 700 thugs, and collected annual revenues of $60,000,000. Five hundred murders in ten years in that city alone were directly traceable to the liquor business.

It was inevitable that an illegal business which so handsomely enriched its agents, should branch out into other fields. Kidnaping and bank robbery increased at an alarming rate; and a new type of crime, known as racketeering, spread like a deadly virus through the economic life of the nation. There were nearly one hundred different kinds of rackets, all based upon the single principle of levying weekly or monthly tribute upon honest businessmen. Men paid to escape being shot, or having their business establishments destroyed, or having their children kidnaped. They paid because law enforcement agencies had become so corrupt and inefficient that no man's life or property was safe.

17

The Harding Administration

THE PHILOSOPHY OF INACTION

THE Harding-Coolidge-Hoover administrations constitute an epoch in American history. It began with the precipitate collapse of the great reform movement. It ended in disillusionment and despair. In one short decade the moral tone of public life sank to the lowest depths possible without losing every semblance of responsibility for the public welfare. Warren G. Harding's election was heralded as a return to "normalcy," meaning an abandonment of Wilsonian idealism in international relations, and of the honest effort to regulate business practices in the common interest at home. Long the servant of special interests, President Harding inaugurated a philosophy of government which his successor, President Coolidge, cryptically defined with the words: "The business of the United States is business." The deep concern of the three preceding Presidents—Roosevelt, Taft, and Wilson—about the rapid development of an industrial and financial feudalism in the country was scorned. The system of controls, which had been so painfully constructed, was allowed to fall into disuse. Financiers and industrialists were given free reign and the government adjusted its policies to theirs.

Harding's administration pointed the way to the policies which the Republican party steadfastly maintained for 12 years. They were to take government not only out of business but out of regulating business, to give the captains of industry and finance free reign in the economic field, and to bring them into the government to formulate its policies. Unprecedented prosperity was to be achieved (1) by maintaining a high protective tariff; (2) by reducing high income and corporation taxes; (3) by delivering the regulatory commissions into the hands of the corporations, suspending the anti-trust laws, and encouraging large-scale combinations. The principle of enforced competition was abandoned in favor of cooperation in the business world and between government and business. The party had no program for agriculture except the tariff; none for labor except the indirect benefits of industrial prosperity. It was interested in production, not in consumption. The consequence was a period of great corporate prosperity in which neither labor nor agriculture shared, which produced an increasingly unequal distribution of wealth, an orgy of inflation and speculation, and a perfect network of trade cartels, holding companies, and industrial monopolies.

The Federal Reserve System was so loosely controlled as to contribute heavily to wild speculation on the stock market, but President Coolidge refused to interfere, with the statement: "Everything is fundamentally sound." Millions in foreign government bonds were peddled to private investors by men who knew they were worthless, but the Department of State, which also knew it, was restrained from making the information public. Millions in income taxes were evaded because the law was poorly written, but Andrew Mellon, Secretary of the Treasury for 11 years, failed to inform Congress of what was taking place. Of the four Attorney-Generals—Harry M. Daugherty, Harlan F. Stone, John G. Sargent, and William D. Mitchell—only Stone was distinguished enough to justify the conclusion that he measured up to the important functions of his office. Daugherty was driven from office by outraged public sentiment following disclosures by the Brookhart investigating committee, but his resignation was accepted by President Coolidge with a statement of confidence and regret. The Director of the Veterans Bureau, Charles R. Forbes, was found by a Senate committee to have been guilty of such flagrant corruption that he was brought to trial in the courts and convicted of conspiracy to defraud. Great naval oil reserves were bartered away by the Secretary of the Interior, Albert B. Fall, without a protest from the other members of the Cabinet. The Secretary of the Navy, Edwin Denby, agreed to the transfer of the reserves to the Department of the Interior. His assistant secretary carried the orders for the transfer to President Harding for his signature. Calvin Coolidge, Vice-President when the leases were granted and President when the transaction was bared, did not lift his voice in protest nor offer the slightest assistance to the Senate investigating committee. The anti-trust laws went unenforced. The Federal Trade Commission became moribund. The Tariff Commission ceased to function except to justify increased rates on the products of special industries. The growth of monopolies was smiled upon. Tariff rates were increased until they assumed the proportions of an embargo. Income and corporation taxes were reduced again and again under the prodding of the Secretary of the Treasury. All these facts, and more, reveal the complete reversal of those policies which men in public life sponsored and fought for in the first two decades of the century. They leave no escape from the conclusion that the prevailing philosophy of government in this period had no precedents in 150 years of national development.

Harding's Cabinet was the dismay of every intellectual liberal in the country, the most competent appointments being those of Charles Evans Hughes as Secretary of the State and Herbert Hoover as Secretary of Commerce. Even in the case of Hughes, however, Harding was saved from a blunder only by the fact that his first choice, George Harvey, declined the office. Andrew Mellon, wealthy Pittsburgh banker and reputed head of the aluminum trust, was Secretary of the Treasury. These three appointments received general approval throughout the country. These men carried the burden of the Administration's policies; and, since Mellon remained in the Treasury Department until 1932 and Hoover in the Commerce Department until the campaign of 1928, in which he was elected to the presidency, there was a definite continuity of policy with respect to industry and finance from the beginning of Harding's administration in 1921 until the depression of 1929. Charles Evans

Hughes retired from the State Department to become a corporation attorney in 1925 and was replaced by the lame-duck politician, Frank B. Kellogg.

Harding's other original appointments were political in character, and revealed his poor judgment of men. Many of them were personal friends who betrayed him, lowered the moral tone of his Administration, and drove him to his grave amidst revelations of widespread corruption and dishonor. Will H. Hays of Indiana, an exceedingly adroit politician who somehow had discovered ways and means to fill the party's campaign chest, was Postmaster-General. Albert B. Fall, objectionable from the standpoint both of character and previous record, who made his position an easy road from cattle ranch to federal penitentiary, was Secretary of the Interior. Harry M. Daugherty, archlobbyist and political patron of Harding's, who later barely escaped going to the penitentiary, was Attorney-General. Edwin Denby, wholly ignorant of naval organization and naval strategy, was Secretary of the Navy.

Harding lacked the qualities of firm leadership and vigilance for the public welfare. He believed a President should carry out the policies determined by his Cabinet members in their respective fields. It was this which made his weak judgment of character so fatal to good government. He believed in cooperating with Congress, but he chose as confidants from senatorial ranks the lesser intellectual lights. He preferred to abandon his own ideas, such as the establishment of a department of public welfare and adherence to the World Court, rather than oppose his party's policies. He called Congress into special session, April 11, 1921, and recommended an emergency tariff act, the restriction of immigration, the readjustment of war taxes, the creation of a federal budget system, assistance to the farmers, and retrenchment in government expenditures; yet, in spite of this favorable beginning, not a single constructive measure, comparable to those of Wilson's Administration, was enacted during a period of two years.

The first act of Congress was to pass an emergency tariff act (May 27, 1921) which Wilson had vetoed, and which raised rates on wheat, meat, wool, and sugar, and prohibited the importation of dyestuffs from Germany. Congress then passed the Budget Act

(June 10, 1921) which Wilson also had vetoed. The Act marked the culmination of a movement, dating back to the administration of President Taft, to provide a Budget Director and Comptroller who would be responsible, respectively, for submitting an annual budget and for auditing all expenditures. Wilson had objected to a 15-year term of office for the Comptroller without power of removal by the President. President Harding signed both acts, and then appointed Charles G. Dawes, a Chicago banker, as Director of the Budget.

MELLON'S FISCAL POLICIES

Politically, the history of federal taxation during the Harding-Coolidge Administration was a contest between those who favored excise taxes and those who favored high income and inheritance taxes. Income taxes not only followed the principle of ability to pay, but they furnished services for the population which it could have afforded as individuals only through a more equitable distribution of the returns from industry and services. Because all income taxes have back of them this intentional levelling process, organized wealth always has opposed them bitterly. On the other hand, neither sales taxes nor nuisance taxes have any relation to ability to pay. They bear heavily upon the poor, reduce consumption, and arouse little counteropposition to government spending because they are invisible. Income taxes, with even small assessments on a broad base, have a tendency to make the people tax conscious and critical of government spending. The remnants of the Progressive bloc in Congress insisted that the government could not reasonably expect to pay its domestic debt of $34,000,000,000 from World War I debt settlements, and that wartime rates on private and corporation incomes should be retained. Secretary Mellon, with the support of Presidents Harding and Coolidge, insisted that these taxes were retarding the expansion of business enterprise and should be repealed. Mellon's arguments were in accord with the principle that general welfare could be promoted best by lending every encouragement to the expansion of production with little thought to the problems of distribution or consumption. He asserted that the development of industrial enterprise was seriously restricted by high income taxes—the same argument later advanced against the Securities Act of 1933. President Coolidge lent his support with the argument that surtaxes were passed on to the consumer which, of course, they were not or the whole power of wealth would not have been thrown back of the movement for their reduction without disturbing consumption taxes such as the tariff duties. Until 1926, Congress refused to accept their program in its entirety. The Progressives predicted that the whole structure of international reparations and debt settlements was unsound; that the United States could not safely rely upon foreign debt settlements to retire its own domestic debt; and that wartime rates on incomes should be retained to reduce the debt as rapidly as possible. They were overruled, and the result was disastrous speculation instead of healthy industrial expansion, with ultimate collapse of foreign debt settlements as they had predicted.

Taxation during the World War had brought into the federal treasury only slightly more than the $10,500,000,000 loaned to European governments. Our own expenditures had approximated the $21,000,000,000 secured in five loans. The income tax of 1913 had imposed 1 percent on incomes over $3000 for single men and $4000 for married men, and a surtax ranging up to 6 percent on all incomes in excess of $500,000. The basic income tax had been raised from 1 to 2 percent in 1916, to 4 percent in 1917, and to 12 percent in 1918. Surtaxes had been raised from a maximum of 6 percent to 50 percent in 1917 and to 65 percent in 1918. Exemptions had been reduced to $1000 and $2000. Secretary Mellon wanted surtaxes reduced from the wartime rate of 65 percent to 40 percent. Congress finally agreed to reduce the maximum rate to 50 percent in 1921, then to 40 percent in 1924, and finally to 20 percent in 1926. The basic tax on incomes was not changed, nor were the basic exemptions of $1000 for single persons and $2000 for married persons in 1921. Beginning in that year, however, there was a further exemption of $400 for each dependent child under 18 years of age. Then, in 1926, basic exemptions were raised to $1500 for single persons and to $3500 for heads of families.

The law of 1913 also had imposed a tax of 1 percent on corporation profits in excess of $5000. This had been raised to 6 percent in 1917 and to 10 percent in 1918. In addition, there had been imposed an excess profits tax of 25 percent of all profits between 15 and 20 percent of capital stock, 35 percent between 20 and 25 percent of capital, and 45 percent between 25 and 35 percent of capital. The excess profits tax had brought into the Treasury $1,638,748,000 in 1917, $2,505,566,000 in 1918, and somewhat lesser amounts thereafter. This was repealed in 1921 and was not restored until during the depression. The normal tax on corporations, however, was raised from 10 percent to 12½ per cent.

On the matter of estate taxes, Congress refused to yield. The estate tax of 1916 had been fixed at a maximum of 10 percent with a basic exemption of $50,000. The rate had been raised to a maximum of 25 percent in 1917. Congress left it alone in 1921, but raised it to 40 percent in 1924. In 1926, the basic exemption was increased to $100,000.

As a result of these tax revisions, receipts from income taxes dropped to $3,228,000,000 in 1921, to $2,000,000,000 in 1922, and to $1,698,000,000 in 1923. This was, in part, due to the decision of the Supreme Court in *Towne v. Eisner* (1918) that stock dividends were not taxable income. There followed a veritable avalanche of stock dividends, many corporations splitting their stock as much as five to one. Overcapitalization and wild speculation were the two most noticeable results, but lessened revenues from income taxes were equally important. There was a strong suspicion, however, that evasion of income taxes was prevalent. Congress, therefore, insisted on writing a publicity clause into the tax law of 1924. What was intended to be a corrective measure for suspected dishonesty in making income tax returns, was seized upon by the yellow press, unscrupulous politicians, and gold-diggers and wretchedly abused. Whether abuse of publicity was as great as abuse of secrecy, would be difficult to determine; but in one case the Treasury suffered, and in the other wealthy private citizens. Congress, therefore, repealed the publicity clause in 1926. The Progressives returned to the attack and, in 1934, Congress authorized the Senate Finance Committee and House Ways and Means Committee to investigate all income tax returns at their discretion. It also provided for what was known as the "pink slip" return—a separate statement to be made out by the taxpayer and open to public inspection for three years. A storm of protest resulted in the repeal of the latter provision one year later; but publicity was required on all incomes over $15,000 received by individuals from corporations.

TRIUMPH OF PROTECTION

A reversal of Wilsonian tariff policies was as inevitable as the reduction of corporation taxes. The Hamiltonians were in power. The Underwood Tariff of 1913 had been the only serious interruption of the upward trend in tariff duties since the Civil War; and it had never operated under normal conditions because of the abnormal war trade. A return to "normalcy," so far as the special interests were concerned, meant a restoration of high protection. The policy was established in the Emergency Tariff Act of 1921, and continued in the Fordney-McCumber Act of 1922 and Hawley-Smoot Act of 1930. Here again there was a sharp division of opinions on the matter of policy.

The war had in no way lessened the growth of business combinations and monopolistic practices. The argument that a protective tariff was the mother of monopolies was as valid in 1921 as it had been in 1913. The war had, however, greatly altered the position of the United States in world economy, and the resultant changes strengthened the arguments for tariff reduction. Protection had triumphed in the early years of industrial development, when the United States was a debtor nation. We had emerged from the war a creditor nation, and it was argued correctly that true national interest required our leadership in the restoration of international trade and a stable world economy. Public policy, however, was not determined by national interest but by very powerful economic minorities, and the tariff was twice raised at the behest of interests already rich beyond all precedent.

National economy had grown to such proportions, and tariff schedules had become so long and complex by 1916, that a mere legislative body could not possibly construct an intelligent rate structure. However honest the inclination of Congress, special interests had a great degree of freedom to write their own tariff rates, with Congress doing little more than maintaining the fiction of defining public policy. Congress, in consequence, had created a United States Tariff Commission in 1916, as a fact-finding agency. It was the duty of this non-partisan board of six members to provide data for scientific tariff rates, meaning rates which equalized the cost of production at home and abroad.

The Fordney-McCumber Tariff Act (September 21, 1922) raised tariff rates about 25 percent above the levels of the much condemned Payne-Aldrich Act of President Taft's Administration. It was the highest tariff schedule in the history of the country up to this time, and was condemned even by conservative Republicans as extreme and highly injurious. The *Wall Street Journal* called it a "selfish, short-sighted and extravagant" law. It retained the Tariff Commission for the purpose of investigating the costs of production of commodities offered for import, such investigations to be followed by recommendations to the President of changes in rates to equalize the costs of production abroad and in the United States. The President was given the discretionary power to raise or lower rates on specific commodities by as much as 50 percent in line with these recommendations.

The whole purpose of those who originally devised the Tariff Commission had been to take the tariff out of politics. That purpose was lost sight of in these days of corruption and political intrigue. Politics was introduced into the Tariff Commission, as indeed into all of the administrative boards, by the appointment of prominent tariff lobbyists to the Commission. The Commission, in consequence, recommended only 37 changes in existing rates during the Administrations of Presidents Harding and Coolidge, and only five of these were for downward revisions. Rates were reduced during the period on mill feed, bobwhite quail, paintbrush handles, phenol, and cresylic acid. They were raised the maximum amount on 18 items, including iron ore. The conclusion is inescapable that the Commission was perverted from its original purpose by the high protectionists into a device to accomplish their purpose without suffering the resentment of public opinion which would arise from congressional action. Nevertheless, protection was adhered to so strongly as a Republican party policy that the Hoover Administration undertook still higher revision on the eve of the disastrous panic of 1929.

QUOTAS FOR IMMIGRANTS

In 1917, Congress had passed over President Wilson's veto an act embracing the principle of the literacy test in the selection of immigrants. Those who could not read were now excluded in addition to anarchists, idiots, lunatics, convicts, beggars, polygamists, tubercular patients, vagrants, and contract laborers. Contract laborers had been added to the list of undesirables at the behest of labor unions, but all other categories embraced persons thought to be undesirable citizens. The literacy test was not adopted to keep out undesirables, but to exclude large numbers of immigrants, and therefore represented the principle of restriction rather than of selectivity. Congress did not adopt it hastily. In 1907, Congress had created an Immigration Commission to study the whole problem. Its report, published in 1911, represented four years of labor and an expenditure of several hundred thousand dollars. It placed emphasis upon three features of a proposed program: (1) selection on the basis of easy assimilation, preferably by the literacy test; (2) government action to encourage naturalization and proper geographic distribution; and (3) consideration of economic aspects to prevent exploitation by industry and injury to American standards of living. On the other hand, the act of 1917 had been passed largely by a combination of those elements from the South and West which were soon to enter upon the crusade for 100 percent Americanism.

The pressure for exclusion of foreign people in 1921 was even greater than for exclusion of foreign goods. Everyone knew that immigration had declined after 1917 because of the war and not because of the literacy test. Everyone knew, too, that peace in Europe would bring a flood of people to the United States, some predictions being as high as ten million. The fear of communism, the deportation delirium, and the Ku Klux Klan vendetta were evidences of widespread fear for the safety of American institu-

370

tions. President Coolidge paid tribute to this fear in 1923 in his first annual message to Congress when he said: "American institutions rest solely on good citizenship. They were created by people who had a background of self-government. New arrivals should be limited to our capacity to absorb them into the ranks of good citizenship. America must be kept American. For this purpose, it is necessary to continue a policy of restricted immigration."

Congress, in 1921 and 1924, passed quota laws limiting the number of people who might come in any one year from each country, without abandoning the previous restrictions on undesirable individuals. Immigrants to be admitted were not to exceed 3 percent of the total number of their nationality in this country in 1910. The law did not apply to nations in this hemisphere nor to other aliens resident in those countries for one year. One year later this period of residence was raised to five years.

In 1924, the number of immigrants was reduced to 2 percent of the nationality resident in the United States in 1890. This was to apply until 1927, when the total number of immigrants in any one year was fixed at 150,000. Each nation was to be allowed the same proportion of that number as it had nationals in the population of the United States in 1920. Members of the immediate families of American citizens and skilled agriculturalists were to be given preference up to 50 percent of a nation's quota. Wives of citizens could come without being counted in the quotas, a provision which admitted at once the wives of servicemen serving overseas in World War II. The change was not made in 1927 because the Secretaries of State, Commerce, and Labor were unable to determine the quotas. Congress refused to grant President Hoover's request for a repeal of the provision and it went into effect in 1929. In 1931, the executive department of the government decided that anyone was likely to become a public charge who possessed less than $1000 and permitted only 48,500 to enter under the law. Mexican labor was also cut down under this provision of the law. Nearly 500,000 came in during the twenties, but only 3000 in 1931.

Both the quota and the national origins principles were adopted because of the heavy immigration to this country from the southern and eastern regions of Europe which had begun in the 1890s. There were in the United States in 1890, for example, only 182,000 Russians, but there were 1,343,000 in 1910. The number of residents who had been born in northern European countries, however, had not changed very much during the period, England having 909,000 and 877,000 for the two dates, Norway 322,000 and 403,000, and Germany 2,784,000 and 2,311,000. The quota system as established gave advantage to northern Europeans who were thought to be better educated, more accustomed to institutions like our own, and more likely to become citizens and permanent residents. The new law gave the following quotas to the principal European countries: Great Britain and Northern Ireland, 65,721; Germany, 25,957; Irish Free State, 17,853; Poland, 6524; Italy, 5802; Sweden, 3314; France, 3086; Netherlands, 3153; Czechoslovakia, 2874; Russia, 2712; and Norway, 2377.

No nation was to have a quota of less than one hundred; but the Chinese had been excluded entirely in 1882, and this was not changed. Japan had entered into an agreement in 1907 to refuse passports to Japanese laborers, and less than 14,000 Japanese had come into the United States after that date. The new law excluded Japanese entirely, denying them even the minimum one hundred granted to other nations. This was the result of a serious indiscretion on the part of the Japanese Ambassador at the time the bill was under discussion in Congress. An amendment to the bill, providing equal treatment for Japan with other nations was under consideration, when the Ambassador wrote Secretary of State Hughes of "grave consequences" which unequal treatment of Japan would "inevitably bring upon the otherwise happy and mutually advantageous condition between our two countries." Congress reacted violently, Senator Henry Cabot Lodge saying, "I will never consent to establish any precedent, which will give any nation the right to think that they can stop by threats or compliments the action of the United States when it determines who shall come within its gates and become part of its citizenship."

The United States had regarded itself always as the haven of refuge for the oppressed of other lands, as the temple of responsible, individual freedom, and as a land of opportunity for suffering humanity. It had, for so many decades, invited other people to come and share its blessings and bounty, that the immigration laws of the 1920s constitute one of the major reversals of national policy in all history. There was, moreover, another factor to be considered over the long view. The steady migration of people from Europe and from the rural sections of the United States to the cities before the mid-1920s had furnished expanding industry with a ready supply of mature labor. One may fix the cost of rearing a child at any figure within reasonable limits and it represents a substantial sum if paid out in wages. Industry had never paid for rearing its labor supply. It had come as a gift from Europe and rural America. Industry had never cared for all of its unemployables. The children and aged were left behind when mature young men and women migrated to the industrial centers. Industry was faced with the necessity of doing both if the restrictions on immigration were maintained: of curtailing its previous rate of expansion if the population ceased to grow, the birth rate in the cities being consistently lower than in rural sections; of absorbing within its own economy the loss of sales due to a declining agricultural market.

ISOLATION

Wilson's theory that the United States could not long remain neutral in event of another war, and that our only hope lay in active cooperation with other nations to prevent war had been repudiated by the election of 1920. For fifteen years the isolationist theory prevailed: that any cooperative action with other nations was certain to thrust us into war. Harding had made vague references during his campaign to the desirability of an "Association of Nations" without specifying in what respects it should differ from the League of Nations. He did not enlarge upon the idea after the election, although insisting that the United States would have nothing to do with the League. His statement that the League was "as dead as slavery," may have been wishful thinking. In any case, Secretary Hughes behaved as if it were non-existent, refusing to answer any of its communications until six months after the inauguration of President Harding. He then answered the accumulation of documents in a non-committal fashion, and sent unofficial observers to Geneva to cooperate on a limited scale in conferences dealing with the international traffic in white slaves, opium, poison gas, and munitions. This official unconcern toward the problems of Europe continued throughout the twenties.

President Wilson had already established a policy of non-recognition of the Soviet regime in Russia, which the Harding Administration continued. Russia repudiated her foreign debts, including nearly $200,000,000 officially owing to the United States government and nearly $400,000,000 in private claims of American citizens and corporations for property destroyed or confiscated during the revolution. This repudiation of debts was ofttimes advanced as the cause of continued unfriendly relations between the two nations, but the basis for non-recognition had been determined on other facts. Refusal of the Wilson Administration to recognize the Soviet regime was based on the principles laid down in its Mexican policy: the Soviet government did not give substantial evidence of permanence; it did not represent the will of the people freely expressed; it did not observe the principles of good faith in its dealings with other nations; and it was responsible for world-wide subversive activities being carried on by the Third International or Comintern.

The Harding Administration continued the policy of indirect relations with Russia as with the League of Nations. The Secretary of Commerce, Herbert Hoover, insisted that Russia's economic system did not lend itself either to exports or imports, but he directed a broad program of relief for famine-stricken Russian peasants in 1921–1922. President Harding was sharply denunciatory of Soviet domestic policies. Secretary Hughes and his successor, Frank B. Kellogg, refused to countenance diplomatic relations. Senator William E. Borah, Chairman of the Senate Foreign Relations Committee, was the only one connected with the conduct of foreign affairs who argued for recognition as an aid to the maintenance of world peace.

Although the Republican isolationists had prevented the United States from joining the League of Nations, they dared not ignore the dangerous situation which was developing in the Far East.

Relations with Japan, long strained over the land and immigration policies of this country, and over our efforts to force respect for the Open Door policy, became steadily worse after Wilson threw his support back of the British to prevent a declaration of racial equality from being inserted in the League Covenant. There were strong indications that the United States, Great Britain, and Japan were embarking upon a naval building race, with the two latter nations bound by an alliance which many believed might involve the United States in a war with Great Britain in event of trouble with Japan.

Few informed people questioned the potential danger of war, in view of the active penetration of Japan into Manchuria and her persistent thrust toward the Southwest Pacific. Her refusal to surrender control over Shantung had been advanced as one argument against ratification of the League Covenant. Her mandate over former German possessions lay directly across the line of communications between the United States and the Philippines. The Canadians especially were anxious to have a termination of the Anglo-Japanese Alliance. The Australians were becoming increasingly restless over the Japanese menace to their security. The United States, therefore, could not do otherwise than insist upon maintenance of the status quo in the Pacific and offer firm resistance to the pretensions of Japanese imperialism.

Senator Borah succeeded in adding an amendment to the naval appropriation bill of May 21, 1921, authorizing the President to call a conference for naval limitation. The President was not enthusiastic, but acquiesced probably because limitation of armaments was one way to promote economy in government expenditures. Secretary Charles Evans Hughes issued the invitations on August 11, 1921, to Great Britain, France, Italy, Japan, Belgium, China, the Netherlands, and Portugal.

The first session of the Washington Conference met on November 12, 1921, and listened to an amazing proposal by Secretary Hughes that no more capital ships be constructed for 10 years, and that enough ships in service or under construction be scrapped to give the United States, Great Britain, and Japan a ratio of 5-5-3. This proposal involved the destruction of 1,878,000 tons, nearly half of it by the United States. There was a great deal of opposition from Japan, which resented the position of inferiority assigned to her, and from the French, who wanted to increase their existing ratio of 1.75 to twice that amount. The French, of course, had insisted from the close of the war that they could not disarm until promised security against further German aggression, not only by the collective security of the League of Nations, but by a treaty of alliance with the United States and Great Britain. The Japanese finally agreed to the proposed ratio on the basis that the United States would not increase her fortifications in the Philippines, Guam, Samoa, and the Aleutian Islands. France agreed after a personal appeal from Secretary Hughes to Premier Briand, but she would not consent to a limitation on cruisers, destroyers, or submarines.

The limitation on capital ships was followed by the Four Power Treaty. This Treaty abrogated the Anglo-Japanese Alliance, and bound Great Britain, France, Japan, and the United States to respect the rights of each other in the Pacific and to consult in joint conference about any disputes which might arise. It also provided for full consultation and joint action by the four powers in case of encroachment upon the rights of anyone by another power not a party to the Treaty. The Conference then entered into a Nine Power Treaty (February 6, 1922) by which all of the powers represented agreed to uphold the principle of the Open Door and to respect the sovereignty, independence, and territorial integrity of China. Japan signed this treaty only after strong pressure was exerted by the United States and Great Britain. The Senate approved these treaties with the reservation that they in no way committed the United States to an alliance or to the use of armed force. The most beneficent result of the conference from the standpoint of the United States was the abrogation of the Anglo-Japanese Alliance, for which we paid the price of potential naval superiority and the right further to strengthen the fortifications of our possessions in the Pacific.

CONFUSION AND CORRUPTION

By the spring of 1923, the Harding Administration had fallen into utter confusion. The first signs of revolt were appearing in the farm belt of the Middle West. The decline of agriculture had begun. Farm ownership and operation had become capitalistic ventures, and the average price of farm lands in the North Central States had risen to $125 per acre. An additional acreage of 37,000,-000 had been put into production to supply the needs of Europe during the war. Prices had increased until the farmers' portion of the total national income reached 15 percent. Beginning in 1921, however, the relative position of the farmer began to change. Cheaper lands in other countries came into production. The new tariff act, coupled with war debt payments to this country, brought a sharp decline in exports. Mortgage foreclosures, bank failures, and bankruptcies were beginning, and farmers were becoming increasingly apprehensive.

The economic plight of the farmers, the special-interest character of the tariff and tax laws, and the confusion in industrial relations produced a sharp reaction in the Congressional elections from the landslide of 1920. The Republicans lost six Senators, their number in the House of Representatives was reduced from 299 to 222, and Republican majorities in the two Houses were reduced to eight in the Senate and five in the House. The farm bloc in the new Congress would hold the balance of power. The elections were scarcely over when rumors began to be heard of widespread corruption in government circles. The Navy Department, the Department of Interior, and the Justice Department were all involved in investigations sponsored by Senators Thomas J. Walsh of Montana, Smith Brookhart of Iowa, and Burton K. Wheeler of Montana. The complete corruption of the Attorney-General's department necessitated the prosecution of the investigations by outside legal talent. Over $250,000,000 of veterans' appropriations had been diverted from proper channels and Charles R. Forbes was driven from office. Attorney-General Harry M. Daugherty's friends were enriched by illegally withdrawing alcohol from government warehouses. One of them, Thomas W. Miller, was involved in theft from the proceeds of sales in his department, was fined $5000, and was imprisoned for 18 months. Secretary Edwin Denby transferred to the Department of Interior three naval oil reserves in California and Wyoming. The transfer was carried out by executive order of President Harding. Harding had been an intimate friend of Albert B. Fall when both were in the Senate. It was impossible for him or any one else who knew of the transfer to have been unaware of what was behind the transaction because Fall's hostility to conservation was an open record. That alone should have disbarred him from his office. After the transfer, Fall secretly leased the Teapot Dome Reserve to Harry F. Sinclair and the Elk Hills Reserve to Edwin M. Doheny. These men stood to make a profit of $100,000,000 from the transaction. In return, the government was to receive the use of a few storage tanks at Pearl Harbor, Hawaii. Fall had already received $100,000 from Doheny and the Republican campaign fund had likewise received large contributions from Sinclair. In the end, Fall was fined $100,000 and sent to prison for one year, and the oil reserves were recaptured for the nation. Sinclair served short jail sentences for contempt of the Senate and for shadowing jurors.

The full extent of the corruption was not known in the spring of 1923, perhaps not even by President Harding himself; but he knew that he had been betrayed by trusted friends and official advisers. He was stunned by the enormity of the offenses, perplexed as to what course to pursue. On June 20, 1923, the President and Mrs. Harding, with a large party, began a transcontinental tour. He was worried, anxious, and obviously ill. He went on to Alaska, returned to Seattle on July 27, and died of bronchopneumonia at San Francisco on August 2, 1923. There can be no doubt that his collapse was hastened, if indeed it was not caused, by the betrayal of men he had trusted. Harding's death brought into the Presidency a man whose virtues were as marked as were his predecessor's weaknesses, and probably saved the Republican party from defeat in the election of 1924. It was good politics for the surviving politicians to blame everything on the departed President. They did so, repeatedly, and few could be found to defend his name or official record. He had failed because his vision embraced his party, not the nation, and because he served his party, not the people. He was a local politician and of all the people he gathered together in public office, few could be classed as capable public servants.

18

The Administration of Calvin Coolidge, 1923-1929

THE ELECTION OF 1924

CALVIN COOLIDGE, President of the United States by virtue of Harding's untimely death, was a cautious, discreet party servant. He was frugal, taciturn, and conservative. He was honest, industrious, and self-reliant. His personal qualities reflected his early environment and training in rural Vermont. They were qualities which were in general eclipse in the rampaging, corrupt society of the golden 1920s. Coolidge completely lacked the warmth and generosity that cement personal friendships. He had no personal following. He lacked breadth of interests, particularly in people, and had no appreciation of the problems of labor and agriculture. He lacked imagination and intellectual interests. He paid so little attention to foreign affairs that he failed even to mention them in his autobiography. He saved his pennies and paid extraordinary deference to the masters of business and finance. He created no legislative policies. His public utterances were a curious combination of dry humor, platitudes, and generalities. The country, however, was in a mood to mark time. The masses liked his simplicity. Special interests wanted anything but vigorous leadership in the White House. They applauded his willingness to give them free reign and to that policy the country generally credited the prevailing prosperity.

The death of President Harding nearly a year before the presidential campaign of 1924 gave renewed hope to the party managers who had begun to despair of a victory. The energies of everyone in the party, except the Progressives, were bent to the task of minimizing the enormity of the corruption. By studiously avoiding any defense of the late President, they created the impression that he alone had been to blame. For the next six years, the party capitalized on prosperity and talked about the dangers of radicalism. It was not necessary to meet the opposition on a discussion of issues, for the Democrats were too busy quarreling among themselves to furnish much in the way of real opposition to the party in power. The nomination in 1924 went to President Coolidge without a contest. His virtues were too apparent, and in too sharp contrast to the weaknesses of his predecessor for the party to think of nominating any one else. Governor Frank Lowden of Illinois refused to accept the second place on the ticket, and it was given to Charles G. Dawes. The party platforms emphasized economy, tax reduction, a protective tariff, limited aid to agriculture, and membership in the World Court.

The Democratic convention at Madison Square Garden lasted from June 24 to July 10 and balloted more than 100 times before nominating a candidate. There were deep cleavages in the party. The South, solidly Democratic, had a rapidly growing industrial area and primitive exploitation of labor in the Piedmont Crescent, a submerged population of agricultural laborers and tenant farmers, and a restless Negro population. It wanted no part in a broad social and economic reform program such as had been initiated in the Wilson Administration, and such as the Democrats of the northern industrial areas were determined to revive. There was a strong Catholic element and almost unanimous opposition to prohibition among northern Democrats, while Southerners were Protestants, opposed to repeal of the Eighteenth Amendment, and heavily involved in the Ku Klux Klan vendetta. The movement of industry to the South had caused a decline of interest in free trade in that section. The party was, in reality, a coalition, without principles and leaders strong enough to hold it together, and only the existence of the Solid South had kept it from going the way of the Whig party of a century before. William G. McAdoo had the support of the southern wing of the party. His services to the oil interests as charged in testimony before the Lenroot Senate Committee injured his chances for the nomination; yet McAdoo, the choice of the Ku Klux Klan and the political lawyer of Doheny, appeared in the convention as the leader of reform against big business and the liquor interests. Alfred E. Smith had the support of the northern wing of the party. Smith was the most progressive man in the list of possible candidates but the Klan and prohibition were still too strong to permit his nomination. Nevertheless, the Democratic convention presented the first and only open debate of the Klan issue by a political party. It was in this convention that Smith initiated his long and successful offensive against the Klan and prohibition. The convention finally faltered on the question of denouncing the Klan by name, refusing to do so by a vote of 541 to 546; but no one could have listened to the proceedings without realizing that men in public life had finally found courage to fight it even at the risk of political oblivion or worse. The rapid decline of its power dates from those July days of 1924. John W. Davis of West Virginia was nominated after a bitter contest between the Smith and McAdoo forces and Governor Charles W. Bryan of Nebraska, brother of William Jennings Bryan, was named for the vice-presidency.

The Democratic platform favored a government-owned merchant marine, independence for the Philippines, and submission to popular referendum of the question of joining the League of Nations.

The western Progressives, representing for the most part the agricultural states of the North Central section, and led by Senators George W. Norris, Robert M. La Follette, and William E. Borah, remained in the Republican party during the twenties. They consistently opposed the administration policies of Harding, Coolidge, and Hoover, but their constituents were Republican by tradition and would not vote for Democratic candidates for President. In the campaign of 1924, however, La Follette led a movement out of the party. This third party was organized originally in February, 1922, as the Conference for Progressive Political Action. It had participated in the Congressional election of 1922, and had succeeded in sending to Congress such men as La Follette of Wisconsin, Henrik Shipstead of Minnesota, Lynn Frazier of North Dakota, Smith W. Brookhart of Iowa, and Burton K. Wheeler of Montana. Meeting in convention, July 4, 1924, it nominated as its candidates La Follette and Wheeler. It was the only party which offered a frank statement of principles in its platform: high inheritance taxes, excess profits taxes, government ownership of the railroads, reduction of tariff rates, abolition of child labor and of the injunction in labor disputes, the direct election of Presidents, a federal initiative and referendum, and the power of Congress to override Supreme Court decisions by a two thirds vote of each House.

The nomination of Davis by the Democrats cast the dark shadow of the League of Nations over the party again. Moreover, he was properly looked upon as a conservative. He had been Solicitor-General in Wilson's first term and was known to be a brilliant lawyer. He had been Ambassador to Great Britain from 1918 to 1921. Upon his return, he entered the private practice of law, representing the house of Morgan, the Erie Railroad, the Guaranty Trust Company, and Standard Oil. His own private fortune, his close association with large corporations, and his hostility to the release of dissenting opinions by the Supreme Court, all raised grave doubts as to his liberalism on social and economic questions. Many Democrats deserted the party because it did not denounce the Klan by name, many because Smith had been defeated for the nomination. La Follette was supported by the railway brotherhoods and the American Federation of Labor, both representative of the most conservative labor groups in the world; by the northwestern wheat farmers; and by the Debs Socialists. La Follette's strong denunciation of the Klan, and Wheeler's long record of service to the underprivileged, plus his indefatigable labors in uncovering corruption in the Attorney-General's department, won them many votes.

Coolidge received 15,725,000 popular votes; Davis 8,386,500; and La Follette, 4,822,000. In the electoral college, Coolidge had 382 votes, Davis 136, and La Follette 13. The popular vote in this election, however, is an unsatisfactory criterion by which to judge the strength of the party candidates. Only 52 percent of the qualified voters of the country went to the polls, as compared to 49 percent in 1920; 62 percent in 1912; 73 percent in 1900; and 80 percent in 1896. Figures compiled by the National Association of Manufacturers showed that only 8 percent of the qualified voters cast their ballots in South Carolina, 10 percent in Georgia and Mississippi, and less than 20 percent in Alabama, Arkansas, Florida, Louisiana, Tennessee, and Virginia—all solidly Democratic states. La Follette received the 13 electoral votes of Wisconsin, not more than 100,000 votes in the entire South, but four times as many as Davis in California and twice as many in seventeen states west of the Mississippi. In only nine small states did Coolidge's vote fail to exceed the combined support of his two opponents. Republican majorities in Congress were 12 in the Senate and 60 in the House of Representatives.

The next four years were a period of as complete government inaction as any in American history. President Coolidge offered few recommendations to Congress, exerted almost no influence over its deliberations. Public opinion was apathetic, being more interested in prices on the stock market than debates in Congress. Labor was quiescent. Only the farmers demanded change from the status quo, and debates on the measures they proposed occupied the major portion of congressional activity.

THE AGRICULTURAL PROBLEM

Agriculture always has been the foremost industry in the United States. It nourished the institution of slavery and has sustained the major portion of the Negro race since emancipation. It lured millions of immigrants to American shores and on into the wilderness where the greatest timber resources any one nation ever possessed were sacrificed in men's haste to till the soil. For nearly a century, it furnished the men who assumed leading positions in every walk of life and controlled the thought and governmental policies of the nation. It still dominates the policies of most state governments. It furnished much of the labor supply for expanding industry, re-absorbing industry's unemployed from time to time. It provided the exports which were exchanged in the intricate processes of world economy for the capital resources needed to build the nation's industries. It embraced, at the close of World War I, an area of 350,000,000 acres cultivated by 6,500,000 farmers and sustaining directly five times that many people or about one fourth of the total population of the country. Above all else, it served as the great shock absorber for a mismanaged national economy, supporting its own workers and those who failed to find sustenance elsewhere, operating with profit or without, providing an ever-increasing consumers market for the artifacts of manufacturing enterprise, and supplying one half the freight traffic for the $20,000,000,000 railway system.

The agricultural population of the country was never wholly self-sufficing, though it came close to being so before the Civil War. Within the rural areas of the North and West were hundreds of small towns whose populations were engaged in supplying the various types of services needed to supplement labor on the soil. It was, in the beginning, a simple agrarian economy, embracing 90 percent of the population of the country. That does not imply uniformity, identity of interest, nor singleness of purpose on the part of the several types of producers. Cotton, tobacco, sugar, cereals, dairy products, meat, fruit, and vegetables indicate the infinite variety of products which come from the soil. Each requires its own peculiar soil, proximity to markets, and degree of labor. They are not equally sensitive to world market conditions, nor equally adaptable to large-scale production. They require various amounts of capital investments, of processing before consumption, of systematic marketing arrangements. Yet agriculture constituted a singular unity during the twenties from the points of world trade, governmental policies, soil depletion, flood control, and its complete prostration.

Agriculture always has lacked stability, to an even greater degree than the manufacturing and extractive industries. If the exploiters of copper, coal, and oil and the employers of human labor have roamed about over the country in search of virgin regions, so too have the farmers. The steady march of grazing herds, of cotton fields, and waving cereals across the continent is as familiar as the westward movement itself. Virgin lands were so plentiful until recent years and so easily obtained by pre-emption or purchase that men did not hesitate even to abandon exhausted land and seek their fortunes elsewhere. So many riches were made from unearned increment that land speculation frequently became as general as the speculation in corporate stocks of the twenties. Land owner-ship lacked permanence. Every migration to the West and to the cities meant that countless farms passed to new owners. At any given time, therefore, land ownership represented either an actual capital investment of considerable proportions or of a small equity supported by a land mortgage. In either case, the maximum pro-duction was desired, with a minimum of cash returns expended for replacement of soil fertility. The result is that the United States today has no less than 300,000,000 acres of marginal and sub-marginal land under cultivation. One third of that amount has been totally destroyed by erosion.

Equally important was absentee ownership. The large landed estates in the South were broken up by the emancipation of the slaves. Thereafter, landholdings were equally large but they were not operated as a unit. The owners, for the most part, resided in the urban centers and depended upon crop renters, both Negro and white, for their farming operations. In the North, thousands of farmers moved to the small urban centers where modern con-veniences rendered life more attractive, and rented their farms on a cash or crop-sharing basis. Thirty-five percent of those who tilled the soil were renters at the close of World War I, more than 50 percent in 1933. A large proportion of the absentee landlords at the beginning of the period were farmers in their own right and absent by choice. The increase after the war was the tragic conse-quence of falling prices, credit stringency, and lower profits which wiped out the owner-operator's equity and transferred title to his creditors. This increase was largely in the North Central states, where diversified farming and relatively small landholdings had provided a normally prosperous and sturdy yeomanry.

A third group in the farming industry was that of agricultural laborers. They neither owned nor rented land, but supplied the seasonal labor required in harvesting certain crops. The region of diversified agriculture, embracing the New England, Middle

Atlantic, and North Central states had fewer of them than the South and West. There were exceptions, such as in the cranberry marshes, the truck farms, the onion and beet fields, and the orchards; but the extra help required for a short period was usually supplied in these regions by the female members of the farmers' families or by pooling neighborhood resources. In the West, transient laborers worked in the wheat fields, moving from the Texas Panhandle to the Canadian prairies as the harvesting season progressed and seeking refuge from winter's blasts in Chicago and other western cities. In the South, there were between 2,000,000 and 3,000,000 men, women, and children, who lived on the extreme margin of civilization and eked out an existence from a short period of labor in the fields during the cotton-picking season or on the wharves and docks as the crop moved to market. Their ranks were augmented by several hundred thousand transient Mexicans who worked from Texas to California and occasionally found their way as far north as the cherry orchards of western Michigan. Agricultural laborers worked for a cash wage, something less than $500 annually on the average. Crop renters received their share of marketable produce, if any, at the end of the harvesting season. Northern renters seldom failed to produce their food as a bare minimum and normally derived some additional supplies from the barter or sale of by-products such as eggs, milk, and vegetables. Southern renters, however, caught in the vicious cotton complex, relied upon the country merchant for the simplest items of their diet and surrendered the advantages of a cash economy for the convenience of a credit and crop lien system.

In every section—North, South, East, and West—the most striking characteristic of the American farmer ever has been his unwillingness to join in cooperative regimentation. Increasing production, trusting in a beneficent Providence for the return of a better day, and relying ultimately upon the assistance of an ever-generous government, he remained the victim of his own intransigence. The manufacturer, following closely the trends of business cycles, bent every effort to adjust production to fluctuating purchasing power. He established stable prices by creating monopolies or by agreement. Circumstances favored the manufacturer in this respect. The farmer could not take land out of production for less than one year. Six million farmers could not be brought into agreement so easily as a half dozen manufacturers of a particular commodity. Land ownership fluctuated more rapidly than the directorship of corporations. The farmer did not have a closed market behind tariff walls in which to operate. He could not build up capital surpluses to tide over periods of non-production. Nevertheless, the American farmer did not join in cooperative movements to eliminate the middlemen as has been proved a possibility by the farmers in Scandinavian countries.

Much of the farmers' difficulty arose from the expectation of exorbitant returns from his labor. Farm ownership and operation had become capitalistic ventures by the second decade of the twentieth century. The average sale price of farm lands in the North Central states rose to about $125 per acre by 1920. Much of the better land was selling for $300 or more. Men who purchased at this price had a capital investment ranging from $10,000 upward on a hundred-acre farm. If part of the purchase price was represented by a first mortgage, the annual interest payment alone was a heavy fixed charge. Many farms carried additional second mortgages on which the interest plus service charges amounted to usurious sums. Periods of decreasing land values would wipe out the owner's equity faster than it accumulated. Declining prices not only reduced the margin between total income and fixed charges, representing consumer's purchasing power, but increased the initial debt in terms of what the farmer had to sell. Expensive machinery—binders, mowers, hay loaders, tractors, automobiles, and myriads of other items of the machine age—was introduced. They could not be manufactured within the rural economy, but were produced by monopolies and represented an additional capital investment. Moreover, the standard of living of farm families advanced in line with that of urban folk. New and expensive furniture, electrical appliances, education, and commercial amusements added to the cost of living. The farmer did not sell his labor, nor was he ever without employment; but the products of his labor and his soil were sold and the difference between his cash returns on the one hand and fixed charges and replacements on the other represented his wages. As it grew less his ability to purchase goods declined or was maintained by abandoning the use of fertilizers, then postponing repairs on buildings, fences, drainage, and the like, then by allowing taxes to accumulate, finally by increasing the mortgage if possible, otherwise defaulting on interest payments and reverting to the status of tenantry. Little of this is revealed in statistics of total farm mortgages. There is no completely accurate way of measuring the actual losses incurred or the resulting derangement in the economic life of the nation, but they assumed damaging proportions in the midst of fancied national prosperity. There was very little difference between the amount of farm produce required to purchase a given amount of consumers goods in 1914 and in 1920. Thereafter, the prices of farm products declined much more rapidly than that of the things the farmer purchased until, by 1933, his purchasing power in terms of what he produced was little more than 60 percent of what it had been in 1920. The farmer's portion of the total national income dropped from 15 percent in 1920 to 9 percent in 1929 and to 7 percent in 1933. Taxes likewise increased until tax delinquency on 40,000,000 acres of farm property forced many states to resort to general sales taxes to meet ordinary revenues of the government.

The farm mortgage problem after the World War centered in the twelve North Central states. The value of farm lands in these states decreased 40 percent in ten years. The total amount of farm mortgages in these states increased from $4,791,000,000 to $5,496,-000,000. Sixty percent of the national total was in these states, with one half of it in Illinois, Iowa, and Nebraska. By contrast, the farm debt of the New England and Middle Atlantic states increased from $508,000,000 in 1920 to $624,000,000 in 1930, about 5 percent of the national total; and that of the Mountain and Pacific Coast states from $1,178,000,000 to $1,343,000,000.

There were powerful forces beyond the control of the farmer which precipitated this revolution in agricultural economy. One was the tremendous increase in world acreage under cultivation; another, increased mechanization and the use of power. Fifty million acres of land were taken out of production in Europe during the war and, because the United States was extending loans and credits to the Allied nations, 37,000,000 additional acres were put into production in this country to supply the deficiency. Sales from this country continued through 1919–1921 because of the further extension of postwar loans for rehabilitation purposes. Then cheaper land in other countries immediately came into cultivation. Approximately 42,000,000 acres of wheat in excess of 1914 were being grown in Canada, Australia, and Russia in 1930. The combined world acreage of all crops increased by more than 100,000,000 during the same period. Immediately after the war, also, tractors began to replace horses and mules in the United States until there were 800,000 more tractors and 9,000,000 less draught animals in the country, and 30,000,000 acres of land formerly used to produce food for animals had been converted to other crops. Changing habits of food and dress further complicated the problem of surpluses. People ate less cereals, meat, and potatoes, more sugar, milk, and fruits. They wore less wool and cotton, more silk and rayon. Domestic consumption declined, production increased, and the government made no effort to revive exports. Nothing short of a restoration of world trade could have accomplished much. So long as the United States expected annual payments on the war debts and raised its tariff barriers against foreign imports, European nations had nothing to send us in exchange for agricultural commodities. Every nation entered upon a program of economic self-sufficiency which reduced our agricultural exports, caused surpluses to accumulate and rendered ineffective tariff duties on any such products in so far as the domestic price was concerned. Wheat exports to Europe declined from 120,000,000 bushels to 20,000,000 bushels and the domestic price from $1.26 to 47 cents. Cotton prices fell from 18 cents per pound to 5 cents; hogs from 11 cents to 2 cents. Tariff duties benefit but a small portion of the farmers—those who produce sugar, wool, flax, and perhaps a few other minor products. They have no value to the producers of those crops in which there are exportable surpluses, estimated at no less than 85 percent of the total production. More than one half of the cotton produced in the United States, nearly one half of the tobacco and one fourth of the wheat were normally exported. It was in the 1920s that the farmer, after more than a half century, finally realized how detrimental the ordinary tariff system was to his interests, and devised certain modified tariff subsidy schemes.

GOVERNMENT ASSISTANCE

Farmers had fared well at the hands of the government during Wilson's Administration. On August 11, 1916, Wilson wrote to A. F. Lever, Chairman of the Committee on Agriculture, that the legislative record of Congress for the betterment of rural life was "a remarkable one." It included the Federal Reserve Act (1913), the Federal Farm Loan Act (1914), the Grain Standards Act (1916), the Bonded Warehouse Act (1916), the Federal Road Act (1916) and the Agricultural Extension Act. The Federal Reserve Act, designed to keep reserve funds available for local needs, allowed National Banks to loan on farm mortgages and Federal Reserve Banks to re-discount agricultural paper. The Federal Farm Loan Act was designed, in the words of Wilson, to "introduce business methods into farm finance . . . reduce the cost of handling farm loans, place upon the market mortgages which would be a safe investment for private funds, attract into agricultural operations a fair share of the capital of the nation and lead to a reduction of interest." It established the Federal Farm Loan Board and twelve Federal Farm Loan Banks. It authorized farmers seeking loans to form farm loan associations and interested parties to establish Joint Stock Land Banks. The Cotton Futures Act and the Grain Standards Act were designed to improve the quality of production by establishing uniformity in grading and regulation of the Cotton Futures Exchange. The Bonded Warehouse Act was designed to promote better storage facilities and make available negotiable warehouse receipts to farmers for grain in storage. The Federal Aid Road Act made available $240,000,000 for road building, as an incentive to increased state and local appropriations for that purpose, to "stimulate larger production and better marketing, promote a fuller and more attractive rural life, add greatly to the convenience and economic welfare of all the people, and strengthen the national foundations." The Agricultural Extension Act provided for farm demonstration work by two agents in each of the 2850 rural counties through joint federal and state appropriations.

Admirable as the Wilson program had been, it did not meet the needs of the farmers after World War I. As has been seen, two of their major difficulties were overproduction in terms of what the domestic economy could absorb, and a heavy mortgaged debt which could not be liquidated at prevailing prices of farm products. They inevitably turned to the government for assistance, and they controlled a considerable *bloc* of votes in both the Senate and House of Representatives. In fact, the *farm bloc* held the balance of power in Congress after the congressional elections of 1922. The Farm Bureau Federation, embracing farm bureaus in nearly every county in the country, wielded tremendous political power.

Congress, in consequence, passed the Federal Intermediate Credit Act in 1923, making available an initial sum of $60,000,000 for short-term loans as a supplement to those available through National Banks, Farm Land Banks, and Joint Stock Land Banks. The Intermediate Credit Banks were to be adjuncts of the twelve Federal Land Banks and were to rediscount agricultural paper held by banks, trust companies, and credit corporations and make loans on warehouse receipts. The Federal Land Banks could lend only on real estate, whereas the new Intermediate Credit Banks could lend on livestock, growing crops, and farm implements. The Act authorized the establishment of agricultural credit corporations, and extended the facilities of the Federal Farm Loan Bank and Federal Reserve Banks by increasing the maximum loans permitted and the period of loans. By 1932, farmers had availed themselves of nearly $4,000,000,000 in loans from the three sources.

What the farmer needed, however, was increased prices for his products. The basic problem, therefore, centered around the question of foreign and domestic markets. The Fordney-McCumber Tariff Act of 1922 and the Hawley-Smoot Act of 1930 both raised tariff duties on agricultural products to the highest point in history. In addition special tariff acts in 1924 and 1926 raised the tariff on wheat to 42 cents per bushel and on butter to 12 cents per pound. Farmers, however, came to realize the futility of tariffs on any crop of which there continued to be an exportable surplus, because the price of that consumed in the domestic market as well as that which went for export was determined by world price conditions. They designed, therefore, two subsidy schemes to make the tariff as effective for agriculture as it was for manufacturing where exportable surpluses were non-existent. The first, known as the equalization fee program, was incorporated in the McNary-Haugen bill twice passed by Congress and twice vetoed by President Coolidge.

The McNary-Haugen bill was first introduced in Congress in 1924, endorsed by such men as Henry A. Wallace, Sr., Frank O. Lowden and Charles G. Dawes. It provided for the creation of a Federal Farm Marketing Board of twelve members whose function was to get rid of agricultural surpluses over and above the demands of the domestic market in order that prices of farm products at home might be raised by the amount of the tariff duties. The Board was to accomplish this increase in price by contracting with exporters for the sale abroad of a sufficient quantity of each product and to reimburse them for losses incurred to the amount of the tariff duties. Assuming that the export of 200,000,000 bushels of wheat would be necessary to accomplish this objective and the full payment of 42 cents per bushel required, the scheme would call for an expenditure of $84,000,000 which was to be raised by a tax on the total wheat crop of about 800,000,000 bushels. The net profit to the wheat grower in higher prices would then amount to $252,000,000. The plan was vigorously opposed as a burden, in the form of higher prices for bread, upon the American workingman to the benefit of foreign labor. It was predicted that the scheme would fail because it would further stimulate production, decrease consumption, and lead to foreign retaliation. Farmers, however, were confident that it would work, and would stabilize the prices of commodities involved, such as cotton, wheat, corn, rice, hogs, and tobacco. In short, a government agency, by buying in the domestic market and selling abroad, would fix prices and distribute the cost of its losses among the producers of each particular commodity.

President Coolidge had worked on a Vermont farm in his youth, though there is no evidence that he ever had any real interest in farming. The extent of his personal ideas for solving the farmers' problem was reduced taxes, better transportation, and cheaper fertilizers. He maintained an inflexible opposition to the fixing of prices or the buying and selling of farm products by the government. He insisted, also, that the tariff on farm products benefited the farmer, which of course it did not do where there were exportable surpluses. He appointed a presidential commission to study the farm problem and submitted its recommendations to Congress on January 28, 1925. They were, in the main, for cooperative control of production and selling by farm organizations under the guidance of a Federal Cooperative Marketing Board. Lacking subsidies for taking land out of production, the plan made no appeal to the farmers. President Coolidge vetoed the McNary-Haugen bill in February, 1927 and again in May, 1928.

The sentiment of the country, aside from the farming population, was undoubtedly sympathetic to President Coolidge's veto. The plan disappeared from congressional debate in 1928 after four years of bitter controversy, and the export debenture proposal was substituted. This plan provided for a slightly different system of financing and a reduction of the amount of subsidy by 50 percent. Exporters were to receive export debentures for all exports of farm products equivalent in amount to one half the existing tariff on each unit. These debentures were negotiable and could be used in the payment of import duties. The total subsidy to the farmer, therefore, would be lower than under the McNary-Haugen proposal, and the cost of the export subsidy would come from the Treasury in the form of a reduction in tariff receipts. In the end, the consumer would pay an increased price for commodities and additional taxes would be imposed to replace the Treasury deficits. The debates on this proposal carried over into the Hoover Administration. President Hoover staunchly opposed the debenture scheme, insisting that "no Government Agency should engage in buying and selling and price-fixing of products."

THE COMMERCE DEPARTMENT

Faith in competition had long been the dominant note in American economic philosophy. It was to preserve competition that the Sherman Anti-Trust Act of 1890 was written, the trust-busting activities of Roosevelt and Taft were conducted, and the Federal Trade Commission was established in 1913. These acts failed, however, as did the Clayton Act, to preserve competition. Integration of industrial and financial control continued until, at the time of our entry into World War I, modern economic feudalism was well on its way to becoming an accomplished fact. The first stage of economic development, distinguished by free competition, came to an end. The individualism of businessmen and Supreme Court decisions had prevented more than the loosest sort of associations among independent producers and traders previous to this time. During the war, however, the War Industries Board and the several Commodity Administrators, particularly Hoover and Garfield, went far toward setting up temporary associations with the worse evils of such organizations, control of production, and open price fixing as the primary objectives. At the end of the war, the government agencies were liquidated, and presumably the anti-trust laws were to be enforced again by the Federal Trade Commission and the Department of Justice. The wartime machinery disbanded in the trying postwar period when industry was shifting back to peacetime production, and many independent producers were finding it difficult to survive with tumbling prices, cut-throat competition, and high labor costs. It was in this situation that Herbert Hoover, former Belgian Relief Administrator, Food Administrator, and organizer *par excellence*, was appointed Secretary of Commerce.

Secretary Hoover believed that industrial waste should be eliminated by cooperative action. He believed it possible to obtain the benefits of cooperation between producers in a given industry without destroying equality of opportunity and individual initiative. In his first *Annual Report*, he said: "No one would contend that there be a relaxation in the restraints against undue capital combinations, monopoly, price fixing, domination, unfair practices, and the whole category of collective action damaging to the public interest." But he believed the public interest suffered a greater loss through the restraints of the Sherman Act than it would suffer from the use of associations as a cloak for the above named activities. He requested that the Sherman Act be amended to permit cooperative organizations "to file with some appropriate governmental agency the plan of their operations, the functions they proposed to carry on, and the objectives that they proposed to reach; that upon approval, such of their functions as did not apparently contravene public interest might be proceeded with." What he proposed was that associations be formed for the following purposes: (1) the preparation of statistical abstracts from information supplied by the members as a guide to future production; (2) standardization of products along the lines of variety, grade and quality; (3) uniform credit policies; (4) settlement of trade disputes by arbitration instead of litigation; (5) elimination of unfair practices and misrepresentation of goods; (6) promoting uniform improvement of laboring conditions; (7) cooperation for economy in insurance; (8) establishment of common agencies to handle all problems of transportation; (9) cooperative research.

Early in 1923, Secretary Hoover appointed a Committee on Business Cycles and Unemployment to study the feasibility of his proposed program. This Committee reported that if industrialists were provided with "more adequate information as to the tendencies in production, stocks, consumption of commodities and unemployment," cyclical unemployment and business depressions could be eliminated. Secretary Hoover followed this by insisting that the standardization of products then being sought by legislation could be accomplished better by voluntary agreements within trade associations. More than two hundred trade and industrial conferences were held during the first four years of his incumbency in the Commerce Department. They were attended, presumably, by producers, distributors, and consumers, though the ultimate consumer was seldom represented at all. Standardization of products was but a small item on the agenda of these conferences. What was sought and ultimately accomplished was the exchange among competitors of information relative to prices, sales, stocks, and shipments sufficient to achieve open, intelligent, uniform price fixing. In 1923, the Department of Commerce published a handbook entitled *Trade Association Activities* designed to spread the gospel of cooperative action. In four years, 1921–1925, American industry was regimented within the framework of a vast trade and industrial association structure.

This development, nourished by the Commerce Department, was directly contrary to the spirit of the Sherman Act as interpreted by the Department of Justice and the Supreme Court. Attorney-General Harry M. Daugherty insisted that the gathering and distribution of information and statistics among the members of a trade association was in violation of the law. The Supreme Court in the case of *American Column and Lumber Co. v. United States* (1921) held that the pooling of information, known as the Open Competitive Plan, by the American Hardwood Manufacturers' Association was in restraint of trade. Justice John H. Clarke, rendering the majority opinion, said:

Genuine competitors do not make daily, weekly and monthly reports of minutes and details of their business to their rivals, as the defendants did; they do not contract to submit their books to the discretionary audit and their stocks to the discretionary inspection of their rivals for the purpose of successfully competing with them; and they do not submit the details of their business to the analysis of an expert, jointly employed, and obtain from him a harmonizing estimate of the market as it is; and . . . promises to be . . . if it did not stand confessed a combination to restrict production and increase prices in interstate commerce . . . the conclusion must inevitably have been inferred from the facts which were proved.

Justice Louis D. Brandeis, in a dissenting opinion concurred in by Justices Oliver Wendell Holmes and Joseph McKenna, denied it was in violation of the law, largely because membership was voluntary and "no information gathered under the Plan was kept secret from any producer, any buyer, or the public." But the opinion of the majority prevailed that it was "an old evil in a new dress and with a new name. . . . the gentlemen's agreements of former days, skillfully devised to evade the law."

The members of the American Hardwood Manufacturers' Association produced but 30 percent of the hardwood in the United States. Two years after the adverse opinion against them, an Association of Linseed Oil producers, twelve in number and controlling 70 percent of the production in the industry, was held to be a combination in restraint of trade by the Supreme Court (*United States v. Linseed Oil Co.*). Chief Justice Taft, in rendering the majority opinion of the Court, said:

> With intimate knowledge of the affairs of other producers and obligated as stated, but proclaiming themselves competitors, the subscribers went forth to deal with widely separated and unorganized customers necessarily ignorant of true conditions. Obviously they were not *bona fide* competitors. . . . Their manifest purpose was to defeat the Sherman Act without subjecting themselves to its penalties.

Secretary Hoover then took the final step in using the machinery of his department to circumvent the restraints of the Supreme Court and the Department of Justice. Voluntary committees within the industrial and trade groups sent statistical data to the department. This was combined with data furnished by the Bureau of Census and the Bureau of Foreign and Domestic Commerce, analyzed, and returned to the associations to be distributed among their members. The Federal Trade Commission denounced the practice as open price fixing through the agency of the Department of Commerce. This was followed by two Supreme Court decisions (*Maple Flooring Manufacturers' Association v. United States*, and *Cement Manufacturers' Protective Association v. United States*) in which the Court held that associations were not combinations in restraint of trade providing they gathered and published without comment information respecting "the cost of their product, the volume of production, the actual price which the product had brought in past transactions, stocks of merchandise on hand, shipping costs," and held meetings where this information was discussed "without reaching or attempting to reach an agreement." Justice James C. McReynolds, however, in a vigorous dissenting opinion in the latter case held that "pious protestations and smug preambles but intensify distrust when men are found busy with schemes to enrich themselves through circumvention."

These decisions opened the way to further progress in price fixing. The associations had proved profitable for purposes of combined research, advertising, insurance, regulation of traffic, and lobbying. They had approached the borderline of illegal activity by gathering and disseminating statistics and by the standardization of products. They now turned to uniform accounting methods, exchange of credit information, and joint purchases. But beyond all else, they introduced codes of ethics or trade practice agreements. These agreements were more in line with what the Federal Trade Commission had been trying to achieve. They outlawed bribery, misbranding, misrepresentation of products, refunds, rebates, discounts, freight allowances, etc. Two hundred forty-three such trade agreements were devised through the good auspices of the Department of Commerce before 1927. Secretly, there were added to the list of unfair practices such items as sales below cost and price cutting. In business ethics, thereafter, lowering prices from those fixed by agreement was a crime. Standard prices became an accepted feature of the competitive system.

The final step in the movement was the formation of institutes or incorporated trade associations. The Cotton-Textile Institute was the first to be formed. It was followed by the formation of institutes in carpet manufacturing, copper, sugar, woolen goods, industrial alcohol, and rubber. The Cotton-Textile Institute cut production and raised the price level, both by 25 percent, showing profits in 1926 for the first time in years. Carpet prices failed to fluctuate in 1928 for the first time in twenty years. Copper prices were raised from 15.4 cents per pound to 18 cents per pound and profits increased 300 percent. The price of sugar was set at intervals by the Institute and announced over the telephone and that of alcohol at monthly meetings. The Rubber Institute failed to maintain fixed prices because the Firestone Company refused to participate in the monthly meetings. The institute of particular concern to the Secretary of Commerce was that of petroleum. Oil and coal were the two industries suffering most severely from overproduction and cut-throat competition. In oil, about one half of the crude oil production was controlled by two interests: the Standard and the Royal Dutch Shell. Twelve thousand smaller producers accounted for the remainder. Few of the 12,000 were ever far removed from bankruptcy. Secretary Hoover first suggested voluntary curtailment of production in 1922. The task of persuading the 12,000 independents to join in a cooperative movement for curtailing production was undertaken by the Petroleum Institute. A plan was drawn up and agreed to in March, 1929. The agreement was recognized, even by some of its proponents, as an open violation of the Sherman Act, and when Attorney-General William D. Mitchell declared it illegal the plan was abandoned without being put into operation.

The formation of trade and industrial cartels revolutionized competition. Competition by price cutting between producers within an industry largely disappeared and in its place appeared competition between industries and commodities. In recognition of this new condition, the Department of Commerce reported: "Competition has changed from the contest of merchant with merchant to a gigantic struggle of industry with industry, for outlets, for space on the dealers' shelves, and for a place in the consumer's budget." It was no longer a contest between lumber dealers but between the lumber, brick, cement, and steel men in the sale of building materials. Hoover could say: "I believe that we are, almost unnoticed, in the midst of a great revolution, or perhaps a better word, transformation of the whole superorganization of our economic life. We are passing from a period of extremely individualistic action into a period of associated activities." Thus spoke the great champion, in later days, of "rugged individualism" in economic life.

The public was indifferent to the new development and business was exceedingly sympathetic. Few public officials had the courage to oppose what all knew to be illegal and contrary to national policy as defined in the anti-trust laws. The general attitude was one of waiting for Congress to decide whether to repeal the Sherman Act or silently acknowledge its demise. John Lord O'Brian, Assistant Attorney-General, said, in 1931, that more than fifty associations had been investigated and most of them found to be in violation of the law. The Federal Trade Commission discovered among the methods designed to control prices and increase profits "at the expense of the public generally," such things as "exchange of price information, prohibitions of selling below cost, weekly reports by committees as to what was considered a fair price, discussions at meetings to deter price cutting, publication of bulletins designed to prevent price cutting, exchange of price lists, and agreements to operate on a part time basis." Suit was filed by the Department of Justice against the Sugar Institute in March, 1931, but was not pressed. Attorney-General Mitchell asked for an injunction against the Wool Institute in 1930 and forced its dissolution. But these were isolated incidents in the general program of sympathetic aid to the movement which was the handiwork of Herbert Hoover as Secretary of Commerce and as President.

FOREIGN RELATIONS

President Coolidge left the conduct of foreign affairs almost entirely to Secretaries Hughes and his successor, Frank B. Kellogg. Like President Harding, he was aware of general indifference toward the League of Nations and of active hostility toward it by the isolationists. President Harding, however, had expressed a willingness to have the United States join the Permanent Court of International Justice (World Court) but had failed to press the matter against violent objections in Congress. Coolidge revived the World Court issue when sentiment in the country appeared to be favorable. The American Bar Association, the American Federation of Labor, and the American Council of Churches of Christ in America continued to agitate for adherence and both party platforms declared for it in the election of 1924.

The House of Representatives passed a resolution favoring adherence by a vote of 303 to 28 on March 3, 1925. Senator Henry Cabot Lodge had died, but Senator William E. Borah had taken his place as spokesman for the isolationists. The Senate, under the leadership of Borah, added five reservations to the House resolution. These were designed to safeguard the United States against commitments to the League, give it a share in filling vacancies on the Court, recognize its obligation of financial support to the

Court, and permit it to withdraw from the Court at any time. A fifth reservation, designed to safeguard the Monroe Doctrine and American immigration policies, forbade the Court to render advisory opinions on any subject of interest to the United States. The Senate voted to join with the reservations, 76 to 17. The League expressed a willingness to accept all of the reservations except the one dealing with advisory opinions. President Coolidge interpreted the League action as a rejection of Senate demands and the entire matter was dropped. Elihu Root later attempted to work out an acceptable formula without success. Secretaries Hughes and Kellogg both served as judges on the Court at later dates, but the United States officially remained aloof. The practice of sending unofficial observers to Geneva, however, was changed. Official delegates were sent in 1924 to participate in the Second Opium Conference of the League, and to many such conferences thereafter. Five permanent officials of the United States were stationed at Geneva by the end of Coolidge's Administration.

In April, 1927, Foreign Minister Briand of France announced that France was prepared to enter into a treaty with the United States outlawing war. Urged on by Senator Borah, Secretary Kellogg, in December, 1927, suggested that other nations be asked to join in such a pact. The result was the Pact of Paris, or Kellogg-Briand Pact, August 27, 1928, in which fifteen nations (including Great Britain, France, Germany, Italy, and Japan) agreed not to engage in offensive war, and to submit disputes to a court of arbitration:

Article 1. The high contracting parties solemnly declare . . . that they condemn recourse to war for the solution of international controversies, and renounce it as an instrument of national policy in their relations with one another.

Article 2. The high contracting parties agree that the settlement or solution of all disputes or conflicts of whatever nature or of whatever origin they may be, which may arise among them, shall never be sought except by pacific means.

The agreement had no force back of it except the good faith of the signatory nations. It represented complete reliance on moral forces in international relationships.

Wilson's refusal to violate the rights of the Mexican people to control their own domestic affairs, and his championship of democratic government had laid the basis for a solution of the Mexican problem in President Coolidge's Administration. It constituted, also, the beginning of the end of imperialism and the formulation of a new national policy in Latin American affairs. Secretary of State Hughes and his successor, Frank B. Kellogg, sought to follow the old dictatorial policy between 1921 and 1927 without success. The chief difficulty with Mexico centered about the Mexican constitution of 1917 which nationalized all mineral and oil resources. President Obregon agreed in 1923 not to make the provisions retroactive and thus recognized all American rights acquired before 1917. He also agreed to settle the claims of American citizens growing out of the revolutionary period before 1920. President Calles, however, who came into office in 1924 with the support of the agrarian, anticlerical elements in Mexico, showed a disposition to make the provisions of the constitution retroactive. Petroleum and Alien Land Laws were enacted substituting fifty-year concessions for existing titles. Some American interests agreed to this; others did not, and renewed their agitation for intervention. Catholics joined in the pressure upon the government because of harsh antichurch activities of the Calles government. A charge by the State Department that communists were using Mexico as headquarters for propaganda against the United States in Central America added to the confusion.

Secretary Kellogg adopted a belligerent attitude, saying that the government of Mexico was on trial before the world, and that the United States expected payment for any violation of the property rights of her citizens. "We have been patient," he said, "and realize, of course, that it takes time to bring about a stable government, but we cannot countenance violation of her obligations and failure to protect American citizens." President Coolidge was determined to avoid war, and was sensitive to the storm of criticism over his policies in Nicaragua, where more than 5000 United States marines were carrying on a miniature war in defense of American lives and property. In the crisis, he called upon an old Amherst classmate, Dwight Morrow of J. P. Morgan and Co. to go as

Ambassador to Mexico, and upon Henry L. Stimson to go as special agent to Nicaragua. Morrow's instructions were to solve the Mexican tangle, and Stimson's to restore order in Nicaragua without impairing the country's independence.

Morrow's skill as a diplomatist and, more particularly, his appreciation of the domestic problems of the Mexican government, secured a modification of the Petroleum Law, an adjustment of the controversy between the government and the Church, and a spirit of mutual sympathy and cooperation between the two neighboring peoples which had never existed before.

The situation in Nicaragua was confusing to everyone. The United States was compelled to safeguard the Canal Zone and also its rights to build another canal in Nicaragua. American interests, however, had investments totaling $12,000,000 in the country, and anti-imperialists insisted our intervention was for the purpose of protecting these special interests. President Diaz was an ultraconservative, if not a dictator. The United States was supporting him against various revolutionary groups, some of whom were receiving aid from Mexico. Stimson arrived in Nicaragua in April, 1927, and worked out an agreement by which both sides in the civil war surrendered their arms and the United States supervised an election. The liberals gained control as a result of the free election, but one recalcitrant rebel leader, Sandino, carried on a private war against the presence of American troops for many months.

Meanwhile, military occupation of Santo Domingo was terminated in 1924. President Hoover announced in 1930 that marines would be withdrawn from Haiti after the expiration of the tenyear treaty in 1936. In 1931, he announced that military occupation of Nicaragua would be terminated after the election in that country in 1932. President Franklin D. Roosevelt and Secretary of State Cordell Hull speeded the movement already begun. Troops were withdrawn from Haiti without waiting for the termination of the treaty. The Platt Amendment was speedily abrogated by the Senate. Meanwhile, Secretary of State Stimson, in 1930, completely repudiated the interpretation placed upon the Monroe Doctrine by President Theodore Roosevelt, and justified whatever action had been taken in the Caribbean on the needs of national defense as related to the Isthmian Canal.

The independence promised to the Philippines by the Jones Act of 1916 was indefinitely postponed with the return of the Republican party to power in 1921. President Harding sent Major General Leonard Wood and W. Cameron Forbes to investigate conditions in the Islands. Wood was a Republican, seeking to restore his political fortunes, and violently opposed to Philippine independence. His report, so far as recommendations were concerned, might well have been written before his departure from the United States. It was so clearly biased that the legislature promptly sent a committee to the United States to refute its charges that the people had misused their powers of self-government. The spirit of independence was so general that even Wood could find no opposition to it except among the 400,000 Mohammedan Moros and the American colony. In spite of popular resentment in the Islands over Wood's report, Presidents Harding and Coolidge kept him in the Islands as Governor General until 1927. It was a period of strife and misunderstanding, during which most of the progress made under Governor General Harrison was undone. Government enterprises were turned over to private capital, and the Council of State was abolished. At one time, the entire Cabinet resigned. Hostility to the Wood regime became so open in the Islands and criticism so severe in the United States that President Coolidge sent Carmi A. Thompson out to investigate in 1926. Governor Wood died while in the United States fighting to retain his position.

Thompson's report was a masterful politician's compromise between the demands for immediate independence by the Filipinos, for more autocratic power by Wood, and for relief from a trying situation by President Coolidge. He advised that "independence be postponed for some time to come" (1) because of the Islands' lack of financial resources, a common language, and controlling public opinion; (2) because they were necessary to the United States as a commercial base and free trade with the United States was essential to their economic security; and (3) because granting their independence "might complicate international relations in the Orient." He just as definitely, however, condemned the proposed repeal of the Jones Act and of the land laws which stood in the way of large-scale exploitation by the rubber interests of the United States. He recommended immediate restoration of cooperation between the Governor General and Philippine Legislature, presumably by the appointment of a new Governor General from other than Army ranks, extension of the Federal Reserve System to the Islands, and sale of Philippine national properties to private capital. Finally, he recommended a new department of Colonial Administration of Alaska, Hawaii, Puerto Rico, and the Philippines. President Coolidge was himself opposed to independence for the Islands, offering as his reason the additional economic burden which would be thrown upon them in providing for their own defense and in becoming subject to the tariff duties on foreign commerce with the United States. Governor General Wood was succeeded by Henry L. Stimson, who restored the Council of State, subjected department heads to legislative control and, in other ways, adopted a policy of conciliation.

The refusal of Congress to tamper with the Jones Act, coupled with the return to the Harrison policies by Governor General Stimson, ended whatever hopes had existed on the part of industrial interests that the Philippines would be turned over to economic exploitation. There were no large investments of American capital in the Islands to influence their retention. They had proved valueless as a base for developing commerce in the Orient. Naval experts regarded them a liability rather than an asset in event of war. Importations of sugar, coconut oil, and tobacco on a free-trade basis after 1913 added to the advocates of Philippine independence all those domestic producers who suffered from this competition. Finally, there was a growing consciousness that the task undertaken at the conclusion of the war with Spain was completed. It had cost several hundred million dollars; but it stood as a magnificent monument to the benevolence of the American people. The Philippine people longed for independence. Neither they nor the United States had anything further to gain by longer delay, and the question of independence was renewed in Congress during the Administration of President Herbert Hoover.

19

Economic Trends in the Coolidge Era

A COMPLETE ECONOMY

THERE was a time, when the nation was predominantly agricultural, that the desire for a home, a few acres of land from which to draw sustenance, and a fair start in life for their children was the principal objective of enterprising people. The same was true of those engaged in manufacturing enterprise during the first stages of industrial development. These people were drawn rapidly into the cities, where they lived in a money economy. They went to work in the factories, in business establishments, and in the several types of services for a money wage. The factory—the unit of production—was not theirs. They had no voice in determining when it should operate. They were paid only when it did operate—not an annual wage, but a monthly, weekly, or hourly wage. If they saved money, it was invested sometimes in a home, but more often in real estate mortgages or industrial stocks and bonds, either directly or through the medium of savings banks, trust companies, or insurance companies. The value of these investments, like their wages, depended upon the operation of the factories in which they worked. There was a particular exception in the case of government bonds, foreign, United States, or municipal. The manufacturing process could function only so long as there was a market for the artifacts produced. The market was foreign and domestic. The domestic market was urban and agricultural. The agricultural market in turn depended upon the ability of farmers to sell their products at home or abroad. The system was highly dependent upon the proper functioning of each of its parts. It also was vulnerable at many points. Anything which affected the farmers' ability to purchase, destroyed a most important part of the industrial market. Tariffs were one. A currency with a fluctuating purchasing power was another. The urban market was a third. Anything which affected the value of investments likewise destroyed purchasing power. It was one thing to buy securities with the idea of receiving a fairly constant return on the investment, but quite another to purchase them with the idea of selling the next day to some one else for a profit. It was one thing to use that profit to purchase consumers goods and another to re-invest it until one's income passed beyond one's ability to consume. The sale of securities on the stock market, then, was a second important factor. Its relative importance depended upon the disposition of the people to speculate rather than to invest and upon their ability to determine the true investment value of securities. The third important factor was the relative proportion of industrial profits which went to invested capital in the form of dividends, to management in salaries and bonuses, to labor in wages, and to reserve for replacements and expansion. The portion which went to labor for the most part, and to investors in some degree, was used to purchase consumers' goods and keep the factories in operation. These fundamental facts, simple as they may seem, are essential to an understanding of the history of the Golden Twenties.

It must be remembered, of course, that the economic problem was greatly complicated by the effects of World War I and the tariff policies of the Harding-Coolidge-Hoover era. These effects were far reaching. Production was expanded to meet the war needs of the nation and its allies. It began with the outbreak of the war in Europe and continued until nearly two years after the Armistice because of the need for private and public rehabilitation work. Fifty million acres of land were taken out of production in the warring nations of Europe. Thirty-five million Europeans lost their lives in combat or as a result of disease over and above the normal death rate. The efficiency of more millions was lessened by injuries. Every nation emerged from the war with a tremendous internal debt, impoverished beyond belief, and owing the United States government a combined total of more than $10,000,000,000. They eliminated their internal debts in whole or in part by confiscating the savings of their people with depreciated currencies. They delayed debt-funding negotiations with the United States, made some slight payments, and then defaulted. They entered upon intensive industrialization programs and purchased machinery from the United States with short-term and then long-term credits. When necessary, they purchased foodstuffs from those nations possessing an abundance of cheap land: Australia, Canada, and South America. They also initiated extensive trade wars with tariffs and fluctuating currencies as their weapons. The United States could not escape the effects of this abnormal situation. The farmers, unable to take high-priced land out of production without government subsidies, and forced to depend upon the domestic market, accumulated crop surpluses and mortgage debts.

Industry cut across tariff barriers by building factories in foreign lands. Private investments and loans in foreign countries were increased to a total of $12,000,000,000. The point is that we exported both commodities and capital, but nothing came back to the United States in return. The money went into manufacturing plants, mines, public utilities, oil lands, and agricultural lands. By the end of the 1920s the automobile industry had 76 subsidiary plants abroad, radio 31, telephone 32, petroleum refining 61, and rubber 41. American plants in foreign countries employed 250,000 workers. Moreover, industry imported absolute essentials to the manufacturing process, including manganese, nickel, tin, antimony, pyrites, asbestos, asphalt, bauxite, graphite, silk, wools, wood pulp, palm oil, crude rubber, furs, and copra. When we add to all of this the fact that the United States normally exported substantial amounts of many commodities, including 33 percent of its tobacco, 56 percent of its cotton, and 32 percent of its copper, it is apparent that the national economy was bound up with world economy despite all the talk of economic isolation and national self-sufficiency of those who controlled the national policies.

DISTRIBUTION OF INCOME

The total wealth of the United States rose from an estimated $192,000,000,000 at the outbreak of World War I to $362,000,-000,000 in 1929; the total national income from $34,000,000,000 to $83,000,000,000. This evident increase in material prosperity was credited to scientific production and management which enabled men to produce vastly more per hour of labor than ever before. The productivity of labor actually increased 50 percent in ten years. There were, however, more things involved in the general process than merely total production and wealth. The ever-increasing supplies of marketable goods had to be distributed at home and abroad. The degree of equitable distribution both of the finished product and of the returns from the industrial process is the only criterion by which to judge the general welfare of the people. In view of the fact that the output of factories operating under the modern system of mass production cannot be sold to a small percent of the population, unless there are extensive foreign markets, it is the only criterion by which to judge the general stability of the industrial system. The shift in population from rural to urban centers made the purchasing power of the urban masses a vital element in the industrial market. At the turn of the century, labor was receiving in wages 17½ percent of the total value of the goods it produced. In 1929, it was receiving 16½ percent. Industry increased its output about 50 percent during the 1920s, but the wages received by the workers, translated into real income, amounted to less than a 30 percent increase. The volume of consumers' goods increased about 30 percent during the same period, while that of capital goods, including machinery and construction other than residential, increased much more rapidly. The volume of unemployment was not due to lack of plant equipment, which had never operated to full capacity, but to lack of consumption. It is estimated that the average man purchased one suit of clothes per year during this period; that nearly one half the dwellings in many cities were without electric lights and furnace heat; that nine tenths of the urban homes had no electric refrigera-

tion. This was true, in spite of the fact that an ever larger proportion of family incomes was going into these so-called durable goods.
Consumption of food and clothing increased less than 20 percent,
while that of durable goods increased more than 70 percent. The
reward of greater productivity went to capital and not to labor.
Prices did not rise; but they should have fallen and did not do so.
Limitations on competition, imposed by the trade and industrial
associations, enabled business firms to maintain prices with lower
unit costs of production.

These things were, true because not only the real income, but
the money income of the wage earner was pitiably small. There
were more than 7,000,000 families living in cities whose income
was less than $1500 per year; and 15,000,000 whose income was
less than $2500. Not a single study by government or private re-
search investigators has ever been published which would indicate
that these families enjoyed more than the barest subsistence. Evidence is conclusive that the capacity of American farms and factories to produce would have been taxed, had every American
family enjoyed a liberal allowance of life's simple necessities.
Further evidence of a hopelessly inadequate system of distribution
was furnished when, in the depression, millions were on the verge
of starvation in the midst of an abundance of food. Norman
Thomas described it as "bread-lines knee-deep in wheat." Secretary
Wallace called it "the tragic nonsense of misery and want in the
midst of tremendous world stocks of essential goods."

By 1929, three fifths of the nation's wealth was owned by 2
percent of the people. Those with family incomes over $5000
received 42 percent of the national income. The amount received
by the 503 persons with the largest incomes equalled the annual
wages of 615,000 automobile workers. More than half of the corporate wealth was in the possession of 200 corporations, which
were under the control of a few hundred men. There had developed, for the most part since 1900, a modern industrial feudalism
in which the instruments of production were owned by a relatively
few stockholders and controlled by a much smaller number of
directors. Almost one fourth of the total income of the nation
flowed from the industrial process. The simple necessities of food,

clothing, and shelter for millions of people depended upon its uninterrupted operation. It is agreed that nine tenths of the income of families receiving less than $2500 per year went for goods and services; that those receiving $100,000 per year spent about one half for goods and services; and that families receiving $500,000 or more probably spent little more than one tenth for goods and services. People with large incomes put their money into investments and speculation. The income tax returns showed that 513 people had incomes above $1,000,000 in 1929. There were only 20 such in 1932, but the increase began again thereafter and rose to 46 in 1933. There were 14,816 families with incomes above $100,000 in 1929; and it was estimated that there was about an equal amount received by 11,000,000 low-income families and 36,000 high-income families. There was, moreover, a steady growth in the unequal distribution of income

INVESTMENT AND SPECULATION

The decade following World War I was an era of rackets. One man shrank from denouncing another man's racket for fear of having his own exposed. Children were brought up to feel that anything one did was all right providing one could get away with it. They did not need to be told. It was in the very air they breathed. Scarcely a ripple of excitement followed the exposure of corruption in high government circles during Harding's Administration. Few realized the extent to which this philosophy of life was undermining the economic structure of the nation, for it was a matter of economics as much as a matter of morality and ethics. The idea that a nation of people could become wealthy by gambling was an economic fallacy of the first order; yet everyone was trying to get something for nothing.

Farm mortgages rose from $3,500,000,000 in 1910 to $9,500,-000,000 in 1925. The number of renters increased proportionately. There were several reasons for it, but not the least was the constant appreciation of land values which went on before and during World War I. This appreciation was fictitious. It was not the result of increased productivity of the soil, because the soil was being depleted by erosion and lack of fertilization. It was not due to increasing profits, for most farms were being operated at a loss. Nevertheless, landowners, seeing the value of their land increase, thought they were rich and moved to the hundreds of small towns throughout the Mississippi Valley. The same land that had previously provided sustenance for one family as the result of that family's labor now was expected to provide sustenance for two families from the labor of one, the other joining the leisure class. What farm mortgages made possible in agriculture, was equally true in city real estate. Every city had its horde of real estate speculators who reaped their harvest from the unearned increment produced by concentrating populations. Millions of people bought homes, paying for them in part with accumulated savings and from their monthly earnings, only to find themselves unable to continue payments as a result of unemployment or to find their equities wiped out when serious depressions arrived. The social inventions of the people did not include a plan for equal sharing of depreciation and remaining values. The railroads had been burdened down year after year by additions of watered stock to their capital structure until the volume of earnings required to meet interest and dividend payments on bonds and stocks outstanding made reductions of rates to compete with automotive carriers an impossibility.

The last and most important addition to the process, however, was that of corporate stocks. No-par-value stocks lent themselves as readily to the gambling fraternity who played the "big board" as blue chips to those who sat by the poker table. The objective was identical in each case: to get something for nothing. When many industrial enterprises were brought together into one corporation, the amount of the capitalization of the new corporation was always greatly in excess of the actual value of the constituent properties. Whatever else was done in the process of financial organization, a considerable block of common stock went to the men who engineered the transaction. This stock had no equivalent value in property belonging to the company. The actual assets of the company were represented by bonds and preferred stock outstanding. The common stock was valuable to the promoters only because they could find some one willing to buy it. It was valuable to the purchaser only if the profits of the company were large enough to permit dividend payments. The same thing was done in the organization of virtually every large corporation, and invariably the promoters unloaded this stock upon the investing public through the medium of the stock exchange. The whole business would have been impossible had the people who purchased stocks done so for investment purposes rather than for speculation. It is agreed that no less than one million people from all walks of life went into gambling in stocks on margin. They were told that any man could become wealthy by saving a few dollars a week and investing in common stocks.

The result was the wildest orgy of speculation in the history of the nation. Hundreds of thousands of investors were drawn into the net by the promoters of colossal swindles. Foreign bonds were floated without the truth being told about the economic conditions of the debtor nations. Holding companies were pyramided one above another until, when the crash came, neither the promoters nor the courts could untangle the complicated structures. Pools were organized to drive up the price of selected stocks so that those on the inside might profit handsomely from the transaction. The partners of Dillon, Read and Company's investment trust, the United States and International Securities Co., thus disposed of stock which cost them twenty cents a share for $52 per share. Investment trusts and commercial banks were drawn into the operations. Prominent men in all walks of life, including public officials, were placed on preferred lists and sold stock, about to be fed to the public, at tremendous discounts from the market price. Insull Investments was thus sold for $7.48 to insiders before being placed on the Chicago Exchange at $30. President Coolidge was deeply embarrassed after his retirement when Standard Brands stock, of which he had bought 3000 shares on the inside at $32, was put on the market at $40. Worthless securities were unloaded into trust funds established for the protection of widows and orphans. Thus unscrupulous financiers, occupying positions of public trust, not only speculated with their own money but gambled with the savings of the others. Hundreds of millions of dollars were drawn into the market from foreign countries, complicating an already precarious economic situation in foreign nations. It is estimated that 90 percent of the stock market transactions during the 1920s were speculative rather than for investment purposes. The extent of the economic misery throughout the nation following the collapse of the market in 1929 is a measure of how far money was drawn from normal channels of trade for speculative purposes.

The effect of this abnormal condition upon consumption of goods is immediately evident. Money which would otherwise have been used to purchase life's necessities went into the market and was transferred eventually to the bank accounts of men whose incomes were far beyond their capacity to consume. The people probably lost close to $25,000,000,000 through speculation in one short decade. Men who purchased 100 shares of stock for ten dollars a share and saw it rise to twenty dollars a few days later, figured they had one thousand dollars to spend. Retaining the stock for future profits, they bought the new automobile, washing machine, or furniture on time payments. How many more who had no money to gamble on the market, thus mortgaged their future earnings through credit accounts is difficult to say. The important points are (1) that a large part of the consumers' goods which was sold in the twenties was sold because men were mortgaging their farms or their future wages—living from past savings and prospective earnings; (2) that much of the wealth of millions of people was in stocks which had no real value and was certain to be erased by a sudden slackening in business; (3) that, because of the necessity to pay dividends on large volumes of watered stocks, the directors of industries were forced either to sell their products at a higher price than would have been necessary otherwise or pay labor less, or both.

The actual ownership of agricultural lands, mines, transportation companies, and corporations was widely distributed. Farm lands were worth about $78,000,000,000 at the close of the war, $57,000,-000,000 in 1930. In addition to the large portion of the returns from agriculture which went to non-producing owners, there was the portion which went to the holders of farm mortgages. The mortgage debt of farm owners was a little less than $10,000,000,000 in 1930, of all farmers about $4,000,000,000 more. The interest payments on this indebtedness was nearly $1,000,000,000 per year. Insurance companies owned 23 percent of the total, Federal Land Banks and Joint Stock Land Banks 20 percent, private lenders in agricultural communities 25 percent, and commercial banks 10 percent. The increased take of absentee landlords and money lenders through the years placed a steadily increasing burden upon the soil and reduced the volume of goods farm operators were able to purchase. The railroads were capitalized at $25,000,000,000, representing an actual investment of about half that amount. The stockholders numbered 850,000. The holders of $11,000,000,000 bonds, having first claim upon the assets of the companies, were largely savings banks, insurance companies, and numerous kinds of trusts, representing no less than 60,000,000 policy holders and depositors. At least $2,000,000,000 of that amount was owned by educational, religious, and charitable institutions. There were about 4,000,000 holders of corporate stocks in 1900, 20,000,000 in 1930. Making allowance for those who held stock in more than one company, there still was an amazing distribution of ownership. The stimulating effects of inflation and the devastating effects of deflation upon consumer purchasing power are readily discernible.

GOVERNMENT SPENDING

A historical treatment of public finance during the period under consideration involves more than statistics of expenditures and tax collections. The bitter controversy that raged over every incidental aspect of fiscal policies bears witness to the complexity of the problem. Taxation long ago ceased to be a matter of meeting ordinary governmental expenditures in the most painless manner possible. Tax laws became weapons for controlling the social and economic life of the nation. At times, they came dangerously close to political regimentation as well. Taxation ceased to be a measure of public expenditures, credit and tax exempt securities easing the way for extraordinary services required by the exigencies of the times. The burden was simply passed along to future generations.

Almost one third of public expenditures during the period of 1916–1936, not including World War I and the depression, were from borrowed money. Taxation came to serve as a corrective for inequitable distribution of wealth made possible by technological progress. It drove deep cleavages between various classes in society as the real estate owner sought to shift the burden to the consumer by sales taxes, and the poor man, in turn, sought to shift it to incomes, inheritances, and estates. Fiscal policies also involved the nature of the currency, with a revival of two ancient problems: bimetallism and inflation. They aroused a critical analysis of obsolete units of government, and a violent discussion of the question of judicial review as the Supreme Court indicated probable limits to the legislative prerogatives of taxation and spending. In short, aside from the direct questions of revenues and expenditures, fiscal policies touched almost every phase of American life.

During the period of the 1920s the federal and state governments were forced to assume no less than a half dozen extraordinary financial burdens, every one a permanent annual charge against society. They inclued: (1) greatly increased army and navy budgets; (2) retirement of the World War I debt; (3) veterans' benefits; (4) education; (5) highway construction; (6) unemployment relief. In spite of the fact that the revenues of federal and state governments had reached a combined total of $11,500,000,-000 annually at the end of the period, every unit of government except the state of Nebraska had greatly increased its bonded indebtedness. The public debt of the federal government had been $1,023,479,000 or $13.47 per person in 1900. In 1914, it was $967,-953,000 or $9.88 per person. At the close of World War I expenditures, August, 1920, it stood at $24,061,000,000 or $228 per person. On June 30, 1930, it was $16,185,000,000 or $134 per person. The federal government, therefore, in spite of the repeal of high wartime taxes and the failure of European countries to pay their debts steadily improved its financial position. On the other hand, the expenses of state, municipal, and other local units of government increased largely as a result of expanding educational systems and highway construction. Education, which was costing all units of government less than $1,000,000,000 in 1916, required about

$3,000,000,000 in 1930, only an insignificant amount being contributed by the federal government. Highways cost less than $500,-000 in 1916, but about $2,000,000,000 in 1930. If we add together the national defense budget and cost of veterans' benefits, the state and local school and highway budgets, and the $2,500,000,000 interest and amortization costs of all public indebtedness in 1930, it amounts to about 75 percent of the total public expenditures for that year.

TAXATION

The extraordinary items included in the complicated tax structure of today should not confuse us with respect to certain general principles involved in the history of taxation during this period. Many taxes were levied on the principle of making government undertakings self-liquidating. Automobile owners for example demanded paved highways and so special weight taxes and sales taxes on gasoline were levied in most states to provide road funds. This sort of tax continued to be popular when the government was hard pressed for funds after the depression. The purpose of the Agricultural Adjustment Act was to restore a normal balance between agriculture and manufacturing within a self-contained national economy by diverting some of the benefits of the tariff to the farmers; and so the funds for benefit payments were sought from processing taxes. The fact that they were passed on to the consumer does not alter the principle on which they were first applied. When the unemployment insurance scheme was drawn up, funds were provided for by a tax on payrolls.

In addition to taxes for particular purposes, there were taxes for social reform. Excise taxes on cigarettes, liquors, and playing cards are favored because they are taxes on non-seasonal and non-depression commodities: but they are also taxes which, when first levied, were on commodities the use of which a considerable portion of the population thought should be discouraged. During the depression many governors and mayors advocated the legalizing of institutions previously outlawed, such as dog and horse racing and lotteries. Not the least argument for the repeal of the Eighteenth Amendment was the expectation of much needed revenue from taxes on liquors and beer. Inheritance and real estate taxes have a strong appeal aside from derivative revenues because they serve the popular fancy of promoting equality of economic opportunity for the youngsters of each succeeding generation.

Finally, agricultural prostration, real estate speculations, and increasing governmental budgets combined to force the exploration of new fields of taxation for the relief of real property. Not only did sales taxes lift some of the burden from farm lands, but they fell very lightly upon those who derived their living from the soil. Farmers who could, in an emergency, produce most of what they consumed and who figured income from the point of putting cash in the bank, did not hesitate to throw their support to sales and income taxes. Retail grocers demanded special chain store levies to force up the price of consumers goods to a level permitting continued competition. The urban consumer, who, of all groups, had no organization, paid real estate taxes in rents, processing taxes and chain store taxes in food prices, insurance taxes from nearly every type of recreation and amusement, and regarded the income tax with a substantial exemption for the low-income groups as most virtuous of all.

At least eight major trends in fiscal history are discernible during the period: (1) The adoption of the Eighteenth Amendment and the Volstead Act reduced annual receipts from liquor excises by approximately $300,000,000. The stagnation in foreign trade resulting from world-wide resort to national self-containment, international debts, and tariff walls reduced the percentage of customs receipts in the total federal revenues by more than one half, although actual receipts increased. The collapse of war debt payments from European nations in 1931, with the probability that they never would be renewed, necessitated further heavy additions to the tax burden. (2) Income, estate and inheritance taxes furnished a fair proportion of the extraordinary expenditures of the war period, provided an annual surplus for debt retirement in the postwar period, but failed completely in the crisis of the depression. (3) Congress abandoned most of the nuisance taxes after the war, but hastened to resume them and liquor taxes when the income tax receipts dropped off sharply after 1929. (4) The general property tax remained the principal source of revenue for the state and local governments, furnishing more than half of all public revenues even at the end of the period, but reached the point of diminishing returns in 1930 as real estate values fell and tax delinquencies mounted. Meanwhile North Carolina, Oklahoma, Virginia, and Wisconsin, which had income tax laws before the federal law of 1913, were joined by sixteen other states during the twenties, and by seven more during the depression with total returns from such state levies rising to about $250,000,000. All states adopted some form of inheritance and estate taxes. Sales taxes were introduced by West Virginia and tobacco taxes by Iowa in 1921. They were followed by numerous chain store taxes after 1925. (5) The desperate rush for revenues by state legislatures and Congress at the beginning of the depression resulted in general resort to sales and nuisance taxes. (6) Unable to finance the extraordinary burden of relief after 1929, all units of government fell back upon the inexhaustible resources of federal credit, which was extended to tottering business enterprises, subordinate units of government, and private individuals. (7) The burden was finally assumed wholly by the federal government through expenditures for direct relief and public works. (8) An entirely new innovation appeared in the process: the delegation to administrative units of discretionary power to spend large sums made available by legislative action.

TAX EVASION

That there had been widespread evasion of the income tax laws during the twenties was revealed by the Senate Banking Committee's investigation of 1933–1934. It revealed, moreover, that tax evasion had come to be a respectable avocation, and had furnished the legal profession with substantial revenues. Tax laws were complicated and often unintelligible to the average layman. It was necessary, in the interest of reasonable accuracy, to consult legal advice in making out tax returns; but too often the spirit of evasion, of circumventing the clear intent of the framers of the law, prevailed. The responsibility of keeping Congress informed on how its tax policies were actually working out in practice belonged to the Treasury Department. That there were loopholes in the income tax laws, both private and corporate, there can no longer be any doubt. The amazing sums of Treasury refunds finally aroused Congress to a realization that something was wrong. Whether the practice of refunds was being prostituted, as both Senator Couzens and Congressman John N. Garner charged, to the encouragement of political campaign contributions, is a moot question. Secretary Mellon certainly did not take the initiative in seeking to have necessary corrections made in the structure of the laws which permitted evasions. Instead, he took advantage of the law's infirmities in making his own personal returns. When the government finally brought proceedings before the Board of Tax Appeals for an additional $3,089,000 for the year 1931, it was revealed that he had transferred large blocks of stocks to holding companies controlled by members of his family to establish losses in that year. The tax of $647,559, which he paid, was frankly admitted to have been voluntary because he felt that, having a substantial income, he should pay something.

Not only were surtaxes in the higher brackets evaded by splitting incomes among the members of one's family, but so-called wash sales of stock were made to establish losses. The most famous case was that of Charles E. Mitchell, President of the National City Bank, who sold 10,000 shares of stock to his wife at a loss of $2,800,000, thus depriving the Treasury of $657,112 in income tax. President Albert Wiggin of the Chase National Bank devised the technique of organizing a small corporation in Canada, to which he sold stock at its original purchase price but which he entered on the books of that corporation at the market price as allowed by Canadian law. J. P. Morgan and his partners cancelled the profits of certain subsidiaries and affiliates against the losses and depreciation of others by making joint returns as permitted by law. The government lost further large sums because an estimated 20 percent of those subject to income taxes did not make returns. How general this form of evasion became is shown by the fact that between 1927 and 1933 a total of $182,000,000 was discovered by the Intelligence Unit of the Bureau of Internal Revenue. More than $100,-

ooo,ooo annually was lost because, under the act of 1928, the government was allowed a maximum of two years to make its investigations. How much more was lost through evasion by gifts is difficult to determine. The law of 1924 placed gifts in the same category as inheritances for taxation purposes and made gifts within two years of death *prima facie* evidence of attempt to evade. The Supreme Court invalidated this provision, and in 1926 Congress restored all taxes collected under the law by repealing the gift tax retroactively. Gift taxes were again placed on all sums over $10,000 in 1932. Corporations evaded taxes by establishing dummy corporations which leased factories and subleased them to the parent corporations at exorbitant rentals or which acted in the same capacity for the purchase of materials. Four hundred and ninety eight thousand, one hundred and ten corporations filed income tax returns in 1930, but less than 40 percent of that number paid any tax.

Evasions under the general property taxes of subordinate units of government also became so general as to evoke concern. The exemption of property held by churches, schools, and benevolent societies induced many such institutions to invest their funds in valuable real estate in anticipation of unearned increments. Large gifts of otherwise taxable city property were made to such institutions in return for guaranteed annuities over a period of years. Such property could be rented for less than other property to which an additional tax burden was shifted, the donor was assured a fixed income for himself or his heirs and the endowed institution an eventual enlargement of revenue-producing endowment. Nearly one fourth of all real estate in New York City in 1930 was tax exempt. More than $3,000,000,000 of that amount was government-owned property, but real estate worth $419,000,000 was owned by religious institutions and $37,000,000 by fraternal and benevolent organizations. Under the federal income tax laws, the income of labor organizations, agricultural cooperatives, religious, charitable, scientific, literary, and educational institutions was exempt from taxation. Many states met the issue by placing limits on the amounts of tax-exempt property such institutions might hold.

The most notorious method of tax evasion, however, was

through investment in tax-exempt securities. Amendments giving Congress power to tax such property were introduced into Congress numerous times but never received much support. Cordell Hull said, in support of such an amendment: "We have some 36 billion dollars of Federal, state, and local securities, largely exempt from all taxation. . . . It is unwise to create a class in the country which cannot be reached for tax purposes. Such policy is utterly inconsistent with any system of graduated income taxes, and it would ultimately destroy the latter. In event of war, it would be an unspeakable tragedy to have locked up in tax-exempt securities 40 to 70 billions of dollars, owned by a privileged class which could not be reached, even for the most urgent emergency war tax." Presidents Harding and Coolidge both recommended that tax exemption be abolished. Herbert Hoover took the same position both as Secretary of Commerce and as President. Secretaries of the Treasury Andrew Mellon and Ogden L. Mills both supported the reform. Mills said in the House of Representatives in 1923 that the government lost $240,000,000 annually because of the exemptions. He added: "A progressive income tax at high rates and tax-exempt securities can not exist side by side." As Secretary of the Treasury, he said in his report of June 30, 1932, that there were $22,536,000,000 such securities exempt from income and surtaxes. Professor E. R. A. Seligman of Columbia University placed the annual loss to the government at $300,000,000. Secretary Mellon argued that high income taxes and surtaxes drove capital out of productive enterprise into tax-exempt securities. It was never quite clear whether he was most concerned about having taxes lowered or tax exemption abolished. Finally, tax-exempt securities were looked upon as the strongest influence to government extravagance, making it easy for the several units to borrow money instead of holding expenditures within general revenues.

Opposition to any action in the way of abolishing such securities was based on the theory of reciprocal balance between exemption from taxation and lower rates of interest. The government, it was contended, neither lost nor gained by the practice. Mellon, however, was always accused in Congress of keeping interest rates on government bonds too high, and there was an equally pronounced agitation for refunding the national debt at lower rates. Nothing was accomplished, however, until Franklin D. Roosevelt's Administration. It was maintained also that ability to tax such securities would give the federal government a powerful weapon for taxing states out of existence at some future time should it decide to do so. Finally, the argument of those who sponsored a change in order to reach wealthy slackers was weakened by the assertion that less than 15 percent of tax-exempt securities were owned by persons whose taxable incomes exceeded $10,000; that large amounts of them were owned by educational and charitable institutions whose need was for safe investments rather than large incomes; and that further large amounts were held by people of small means who did not fall within the group of 60,000 persons who paid 80 percent of the income taxes. On the other hand, the Treasurer's report for 1932 maintained that $3,609,053,815 worth of tax-exempt securities were owned by those whose incomes exceeded $5000; and that their interest return, not subject to taxation, amounted annually to $202,684,000; and that two persons whose annual incomes exceeded $4,000,000 received $4,344,491 in non-taxable income from such securities. Those who considered the matter from the point of social reform contended that non-exemption and higher interest rates would place more of such securities in the hands of the small investors who needed security but were not subject to income taxes.

ATTITUDE OF THE GOVERNMENT

The attitude of the government toward the more fundamental problem was one of inaction. The nationalist, or isolationist, point of view prevailed that the political and economic fate of European countries was none of our concern, that they should pay their debts and keep both their goods and their people at home. The opposing view, and it was a minority view in the twenties, was that world peace and economic stability were essential to American security, that we should encourage world trade, if necessary by cancellation of the war debts.

With regard to domestic problems, the same attitude prevailed. In 1921, at the instigation of President Harding, there was held the

President's Conference on Unemployment under the chairmanship of Secretary Hoover. Its report, *Business Cycles and Unemployment*, expertly prepared, recommended rigid control of the expansion of construction, industry, and credit, and safeguards against recurring unemployment. The report was filed away and forgotten. For twelve years nothing had been done about the vast concentration of economic power into a few hands which had so greatly disturbed Theodore Roosevelt, Taft, and Wilson and had been so ably demonstrated by Brandeis and the Pujo Committee. Taft's pleas for a curb on overcapitalization, for publicity of corporate affairs, and for federal incorporation had gone unheeded. The consequence was nefarious holding companies, gambling on the stock market by the directors of corporate management, an alliance between investment and commercial banking, and a tremendous distribution of stocks to the investing public at fictitious values. Nothing had been done about reducing foreign debts on the principle of capacity to pay. Nothing had been done about the tariff except to increase it to the point where foreign nations were forced to repudiate their debts and enact retaliatory tariffs, and American manufacturers, in turn, were forced to establish their branch factories in foreign lands. Nothing had been done to relieve the unequal tax burden either by drastically reducing the debt through high income and inheritance taxes or abolishing tax exempt securities. Nothing had been done to counteract technological unemployment. Nothing had been done to maintain an even economic balance between industry and agriculture. Nothing had been done to relieve the railroads from the burden of destructive competition, to promote flood control, or soil conservation. The government refused to assume any responsibility for the poverty and distress of share croppers, textile workers, and miners; or to admit the need for increased public welfare. These were the "big problems" which President Coolidge confessed he had avoided. The Sherman and Clayton Anti-Trust Acts remained on the statute books but the traditional method of enforcement so characteristic of the Roosevelt-Taft period—criminal prosecution by the Department of Justice—was abandoned. The Federal Trade Commission remained in existence but its cease and desist orders dealt with trivialities and its investigations were ignored. Trade associations, whose ultimate objective was the elimination of competition, were encouraged and carefully fostered by the Commerce Department. Towering high in the economic system were a few absolute monopolies, secure behind the tariff walls and more powerful than the government itself.

20

The End of an Era

THE ELECTION OF 1928

MILLIONS of people in the United States believed that business had found the secret of a modern utopia, that prosperity would go on and on if the policies of the Coolidge Administration were continued. Herbert Hoover had done more than any other man to popularize that idea, and his nomination by the party to succeed Coolidge was inevitable. The Republicans had a number of candidates for the nomination. Frank O. Lowden of Illinois, a wealthy businessman and gentleman farmer with farms in Illinois and plantations in Arkansas and Texas, could not be disregarded. He had proved to be a capable governor, had favored the McNary-Haugen farm bill, and was in sympathy with high income taxes. He had three weaknesses: unusual intolerance during the war, the unethical use of money by his supporters in the pre-convention campaign of 1920, and his age of sixty-eight years. Vice-President Charles G. Dawes, many things to different people, was known to be vindictive toward opposition, bitterly opposed to labor unions, fascist in his tendencies, and demagogic in his attacks upon liberals. William E. Borah of Idaho was a unique personality in public life. He was a resourceful debater, an authority on constitutional law, and a master of detailed facts. He was an opponent of monopoly with a curious idea that economic competition could be restored, of imperialism in Central America, and of the Lily White movement in the Republican Party South. He was the great champion of civil rights and of Russian recognition, but was never concerned about the question of the tariff.

427

Herbert Hoover was the most sensitive to criticism of any man in public life. He probably would have heartily endorsed the peculiar idea then prevalent in the land that it was unpatriotic to criticize the President. In those two respects, and in his rapid assumption of an air of self-importance, he was remarkably like Woodrow Wilson. He held to the theory of self-government in industry, professing to believe that voluntary cooperation within the several units of industrial life could more effectively eliminate abuses than any degree of government compulsion. When he announced his entry into the Ohio primaries, he said, "If the greatest trust which can be given by our people should come to me, I should consider it my duty to carry forward the principles of the Republican party and the great objective of President Coolidge's policies—all of which have brought to our country such a high degree of happiness, progress and security." It is true that pronouncements of this nature and his approval of Coolidge's McNary-Haugen veto were calculated to win him the support of the President in the contest for nomination. It is, however, doubtful if that had very much to do with the nomination. It was the sequel to years of planning and skillful publicity. The Hoover myth is one of the most firmly established in American history. Whatever may be final judgment as to his work in the Department of Commerce, it is certain that it gave him more intimate contact with more people in the country than was true of any other man in public life. Time after time he wrested the front page from President Coolidge. That and his career as Director of Belgian Relief and as Food Administrator were sufficient in themselves to have made him President. He early had the support of such newspapers as the *Chicago Tribune*, and when the Scripps-Howard papers declared for him in January, 1928, in preference to Dawes and Lowden, there was no question about his nomination. The Republican convention at Kansas City nominated him on the first ballot and named Senator Charles Curtis of Kansas, the majority leader who spoke in monosyllables, for the vice-presidency.

The Democrats also had several possible candidates. Governor Albert C. Ritchie of Maryland was probably the most available. He had proved equal to the task of reorganizing a state government in much the same fashion of Alfred E. Smith of New York and Frank O. Lowden of Illinois, introducing a state budget system, a civil service, a reformed prison system, and modern educational facilities. He was an old-line champion of state rights who had earned the right to be so by making his state government function. He stood by his state rights principles to the point of opposing the federal child labor amendment, federal inheritance taxes, and prohibition, and favoring a popular referendum in the states on federal constitutional amendments. He steadfastly refused to use troops to suppress strikes; and he flatly refused to participate in the preparedness day mobilization Coolidge had sponsored. Economically he was opposed to government interference with business other than public utilities or to its entering into competition with private enterprise. Thomas Walsh of Montana was the most liberal man in the party with a splendid record; but he was a Catholic and from the state of Montana which was not a pivotal state. He had uncovered the oil scandals by relentless digging against tremendous opposition; had led the fight against seating Truman H. Newberry of Michigan as well as for the seating of Louis D. Brandeis on the Supreme Bench and for an investigation of the propaganda activities of public utilities; and favored the child labor amendment and woman's suffrage. He had helped draft the Federal Reserve Act. He was opposed to the use of the anti-trust laws against labor. Finally, he was a dry. Governor Vic Donahey of Ohio was much the same type as Smith as to origins and human interests. He was, moreover, from a pivotal state of which he was the only governor who had ever served three terms. He was for economy in government, a Methodist, an ardent prohibitionist, an opponent of the Klan, and sympathetic to labor. There was less contest in the preconvention stages of the campaign than in any other in three decades. Smith's nomination became a certainty at an early date as a result of his splendid showing in the primaries, and he was nominated on the first ballot at Houston with Senator Joseph T. Robinson of Arkansas as his running mate. Thus was the attempt made to bridge the deep chasm between the several divergent elements in the party.

The campaign which followed is indescribable. The one in 1924

had missed being a complete sacrifice to intellectual sterility because of the ferment injected into it by the La Follette-Wheeler
campaign. The campaign of 1928 lacked even that saving quality,
and degenerated into the most shameful political depravity since
the days of Know-Nothingism. The nation was in the grip of a
fictitious stock-market prosperity; but there were not less than four
million unemployed, and hunger and privation were already abroad
in the land. The coal industry was in a state of chaos. The oil
industry was engaged in a destructive and wasteful competitive
warfare. Agriculture was bordering on a state of collapse. The railroads were facing the inevitable consequences of speculative banker
control. Economic experts were privately warning their friends to
get out of the market before the crash came. There were great
problems like prohibition, the increasing crime wave, the disposition of Muscle Shoals, flood control, veterans' benefits, and international debts crying for solution. It was a situation which called
for vigorous discussion of governmental policies touching social
and economic questions; yet the most important topics in the
world seemed to be Smith's grammatical errors, the exact degree
of culture possessed by his family, and the depravity of the Catholic
Church.

Hoover and Curtis did not say very much about anything. It
was not necessary. They simply remained silent and rode into office
on the most powerful whispering campaign ever set in motion. It
was the final flareback of a dying postwar intolerance which gathered race, religious, and moral prejudices into a torrent of opposition to Alfred E. Smith, the Catholic, anti-prohibition representative of Tammany Hall. Hoover carried forty states, five in the tra-
ditionally Democratic South: Virginia, North Carolina, Florida,
Tennessee, and Texas. His popular vote was twenty-one million to
fifteen million for Smith. Their electoral votes were 444 to 87 respectively. It had the appearance of a great victory for the candidates
of the Republican party; but never were statistics more deceiving.
Smith received six million more votes than any candidate of the
Democratic party had ever received previously. He received 40
percent of the total vote cast, whereas Cox had received but 34
percent in 1920 and Davis 30 percent in 1924. Moreover, the results

EXPECTANCY

of the elections in Minnesota, Wisconsin, Nebraska, North Dakota, Washington, and Arizona were pregnant with meaning because in all of those states independent progressives who openly opposed the Republican candidates and policies were elected by tremendous majorities while Smith was being repudiated. Smith lost Minnesota by only 100,000 votes and Shipstead, Farmer-Laborite, carried the state against the Republican candidate by 400,000. It is certain that, despite the association of Republicanism and prosperity as synonymous terms in the minds of many people, Smith would have come close to winning had he not been a Catholic and Tammanyite. Republican majorities in Congress were increased to 15 in the Senate and 101 in the House of Representatives.

EXPECTANCY

Hoover had been elected as the representative of industrial efficiency—as one whose peculiar equipment, by his own admission, would guide the nation to yet undreamed of abundance. In his acceptance speech, August 11, 1928, he said:

One of the oldest and perhaps the noblest of human aspirations has been abolition of poverty. By poverty I mean the grinding by undernourishment, cold and ignorance, and fear of old age of those who have the will to work. We in America today are nearer to the final triumph over poverty than ever before in the history of any land. The poorhouse is vanishing from among us. We have not yet reached the goal, but given a chance to go forward with the policies of the last eight years, and we shall soon with the help of God be within sight of the day when poverty will be banished from this nation.

At a later date, he expressed more fully his hopes and ideals:

In the field which is more largely social our first obligation should be the protection of the health, the assurance of the education and training of every child in our land. In the field which is more largely economic our first objective must be to provide security from poverty and want. We want security in living for every home. We want to see a nation built of home owners and farm owners. We want to see their savings protected. We want to see them in steady jobs. We want to see more and more of them insured against death and accident, unemployment and old age. We want them all secure.

431

Here was an expression of hope for a better America from the heart of a great humanitarian.

What Hoover might have accomplished along these lines under different circumstances, the world will never know. He believed society should care for its children, its aged, its sick, disabled, and unemployed, but that it should be done by voluntary association of the people and through local government agencies. It was the duty of the federal government to guide and direct, but not to regiment progress under a vast bureaucracy. Moreover, it was his firm belief that any interference with economic freedom would inevitably destroy spiritual freedom. His economic policies embraced absolute faith in individual initiative, enterprise, and opportunity, without governmental interference. "You cannot," he said, "extend the mastery of government over the daily working life of the people without at the same time making it the master of the people's souls and thought."

It was typical of the man that scientific investigation should precede action; and so he established many able research committees on social and economic problems. The most important of these, in view of the later prominence of social security in the New Deal program were the Committee on Recent Social Trends, and the White House Conference on Child Health and Protection. The first of these, appointed in September, 1929, was a committee of distinguished economists and sociologists who undertook a complete survey of social problems, with a view to providing "the basis for the formulation of large national policies looking to the next phase of national development." The report of the Committee was the most elaborate of its kind ever published, but we have no way of knowing what recommendations the President would have made on the basis of its findings because it was not completed until January, 1933, after his defeat for re-election.

Hoover had long been interested in child welfare. He had organized the American Child Health Association in 1921, and served as its chairman for twelve years. He had worked diligently for a constitutional amendment to permit the abolition of child labor. As President, he urged the Director of the Budget to deal liberally with the Children's Bureau. On July 2, 1929, he called a White

House Conference on the Health and Protection of Children, the first of its kind since that of Theodore Roosevelt in 1909. The Committee, after exhaustive research, formulated and published "The Children's Charter" in November, 1930, stating the minimum requirements of health and welfare, and recommending district, county, or community organization with full-time officials, nurses, and laboratories "for the relief, aid and guidance of children, in special need due to poverty, misfortune or behavior difficulties, and for the protection of children from abuse, neglect, exploitation or moral hazard." President Hoover repeatedly urged Congress to provide federal subsidies for these purposes without response. He appointed a committee of educators to consider the question of establishing a federal Department of Education; a committee to study the problem of adult education; and held a White House Conference on Home Building and Housing.

These things, taken in connection with the encouragement of trade and industrial associations during the early twenties, constitute a broad program of social and economic planning far removed from the sterility of ideas and inaction of Presidents Harding and Coolidge. It was a program based entirely upon voluntary and co-operative action, but it laid much of the foundation for legislation in the next administration.

THE TARIFF AND AGRICULTURE

The Hoover Administration opened with great promise. In the field of foreign relations, the Kellogg-Briand Pact, pledging all of the leading nations to preserve the peace, had been ratified. Germany was meeting her reparations payments, the European countries were paying their regular installments on the war debts, and the Young Commission had concluded a settlement which embraced complete freedom for Germany from Allied control at an early date. Conversations with Great Britain were initiated for further naval disarmament. The country's industrial plant was in full operation, there were no strikes or impending strikes, and prices were rising rapidly on the stock market.

Trouble began when President Hoover called Congress into

special session on April 15, 1929, for the purpose of altering the tariff rates in the interest of agriculture. Congress first passed the Agricultural Marketing Act of June 15, 1929. This Act created a Federal Farm Board of eight members, which was to encourage the organization of farm cooperatives, establish stabilization corporations for buying and selling in the open market, and guarantee both against financial loss. The Board established several national cooperatives such as the Farmers National Grain Corporation, the American Cotton Cooperative Association, and the National Livestock Marketing Association. It loaned them $165,000,000 for marketing purposes. It created the Grain and Cotton Stabilization Corporation, which lost $239,000,000 buying and selling on the wheat and cotton markets. It carried on an extensive campaign to encourage voluntary reduction of acreage. In short, it did exactly what President Hoover said no government agency should do: "engage in buying and selling and price-fixing of products." Its losses were a heavy burden upon the taxpayer without the slightest gain toward checking overproduction or stabilizing prices. The export debenture and equalization fee proposals were no less sound economically and neither could have failed more completely.

In February, 1931, Congress again came to the relief of drought-stricken farm areas with appropriations of $67,000,000 for direct loans to be used for seed, feed, fertilizer, food, medical supplies, and voluntary crop reduction. One year later, in setting up the Reconstruction Finance Corporation, it provided for additional credit to Federal Farm Land Banks. Until 1933, therefore, the Department of Agriculture of the federal government and the several state departments continued to stimulate production by encouraging better farming methods. Otherwise, the government did nothing except provide machinery for easy credits to farmers and encourage cooperative associations to some extent. No effective action was taken to restore foreign markets, but they were further restricted by increases in the tariff and non-cancellation of the war debts. Having entered upon a narrow program of economic isolation, nothing was done to reduce crop production to the needs of the domestic market.

Congress worked much more slowly on the tariff and not until

434

after the turn of the year was the Hawley-Smoot bill ready for approval. Of the 3218 dutiable items in the tariff schedule, 887 were increased and 235 were reduced. The others remained unchanged. Large increases were made on such articles as cereals, meats, dairy products, cotton, sugar, and leather, and some decreases were made on important items such as plate glass, aluminum, and automobiles; but the Act increased protection, in general terms, about 7 percent, at a time when the greatest collapse in world economy of modern times was under way.

More than 1000 trained economists petitioned President Hoover to veto the bill on the grounds that it would increase prices, that it would restrict imports and lead to further retaliation in foreign countries, and that it would be of no benefit to farmers because there were exportable surpluses of nearly all farm products. Hoover ignored the protest; signed the bill; defended it in the ensuing campaign; and did nothing to protest the action of the National Republican Committee in denouncing the economists as radicals, socialists, and communists.

Foreign countries promptly retaliated with increased tariffs and thus increased the dangers of an impending economic collapse throughout the world. Canada, for example, promptly raised her rates on all imports from the United States. Between 1929 and 1933, exports to that country dropped from $949,446,000 to $210,-651,000 and imports from $503,496,000 to $185,408,000. In 1929 we exported to Canada $11,997,000 worth of structural steel, $13,808,000 worth of tractors, and $33,353,000 worth of automobiles. Four years later the value of these items exported amounted to $345,000, $119,000, and $574,000, respectively. Meanwhile the tariff had driven manufacturers to the expedient of establishing branch factories in foreign lands: 48 in Europe; 12 in Latin America; 28 in the Far East; and 71 in Canada.

PANIC OF 1929

Hoover's troubles really began in the late autumn of 1929. The nation had been in the grip of a fictitious stock-market prosperity; and economic experts had been warning their friends privately for many months to get out of the market before the crash came. Stocks had been forced up by speculative buyers to fabulous prices: A. T. and T., for example, to $304 a share and United States Steel to $241. New securities worth $15,000,000,000 had been issued in one year. Trading had increased on the market from 223,000,000 shares in 1920 to 1,124,000,000 shares in 1929. Finally, the stock market crashed on October 23, wiping out an average of more than a billion dollars' worth of paper values a day. The previous frenzy of speculation gave way to a mad scramble on the part of everyone to get liquid. Every transaction drove down the market value of what had been considered gilt-edged securities. Gold flowed out of the country and both gold and Federal Reserve notes into the safety deposit boxes of private citizens. Unemployment mounted to more than 7,000,000 within a year, ultimately to the staggering total of 15,000,000, and those who continued to work did so under greatly reduced wage scales. For three and one half years ruinous deflation continued and its paralyzing effects spread to all parts of the world. Millions of people lost savings invested in gilt-edged securities. Millions more were reduced to beggary. Private charity proved incapable of sustaining the destitute. Little by little the totality of the collapse dawned upon an incredulous people. Destitution, despair, and divided counsels prevailed. No man of vision came forward with a program of relief. It was the price a people paid for more than a decade of political stagnation. Economists are pretty generally agreed on the causes of the economic debacle though there is less agreement on the relative importance of each:

1. There was an unbalanced world economy, with European nations staggering under tremendous burdens of debts and taxes, with depleted gold stocks, and with adverse trade balances. World War I purchases, payments on war debts, the fever of speculation, and fear of another European crisis had drawn to the United States the gold which the rest of the world needed for normal business purposes, and tariff walls kept them from getting it back again through normal trade processes.

2. The abnormal business conditions of the war and immediate postwar period had merged, in the United States, into a spec-

ulation boom in the late twenties which carried prices, and particularly prices of corporate stocks, far above real values. Year after year larger amounts of bank loans went into the speculative markets instead of into legitimate business channels. Banks were weighted down with government bonds, real estate mortgages based on greatly appreciated valuations, and highly speculative securities.

3. The approach of business and of government to the economic processes had been from the viewpoint of production. The vaunted prosperity had been a corporation prosperity. The problem of consumption had been ignored. Agricultural surpluses piled up as prices of farm products declined until farmers could no longer purchase the products of the factories. The returns from machine production were unevenly distributed. Technological unemployment increased, and year after year, larger amounts of money flowed out of the channels of consumers' trade and into the savings deposits of the relatively well-to-do. In short, the take of capital was too large, and the country was suffering from underconsumption not from overproduction.

4. The government, and particularly the Federal Reserve Board, had not checked credit inflation or imposed any sort of other restraints to keep inflation from getting out of control. It had not taken a realistic attitude toward the problems of agriculture, world trade, or labor.

Business adopted the attitude that deflation would have to run its course before recovery could begin again; that there should be economy in all branches of the government; and that expenditures for relief should come from sales taxes. The basic industries continued to reduce their labor forces and to pay dividends out of accumulated surpluses. Eighty-three corporations increased dividends on common stock a total of 5.9 percent during the first year of the depression although their earnings decreased 19.8 percent during the same period. Many corporations continued to pay the usual dividend rates after their earnings dropped to zero; and, at the same time, they were making wage cuts, laying off men, and reducing others to part time. Wages dropped 60 percent in three years. President Hoover made repeated appeals to prevent wage-cutting and the discharge of employees by industry, but to no avail. He held a series of conferences at Washington where he insisted that the shock of the depression ought to fall upon profits instead of wages, and that there ought to be no wage cuts if they could possibly be avoided. Industry, however, refused to act upon the principle that recovery depended upon restoration of the purchasing power of the masses.

The Administration, also, probably in the belief that the depression would be of short duration, approached the problem of the unemployed from the viewpoint of relief rather than restoration of purchasing power. It, therefore, refused to countenance the use of federal funds for relief purposes. Only at the end of his administration did President Hoover agree to loans of federal funds to states whose resources had been exhausted by the burden of caring for the unemployed. His approach was the indirect one of revitalizing industry so people could go back to work, instead of increasing purchasing power so industry could resume production. More than $2,000,000,000 was appropriated for public works, including the Boulder Dam project on the Colorado River; but the two chief measures of the administration program were the creation of the Reconstruction Finance Corporation and the Home Owners Loan Banks.

The Reconstruction Finance Corporation Act passed Congress in January, 1932. It created a corporation under a board of seven directors, including the Secretary of the Treasury, the Governor of the Federal Reserve Board, and the Farm Loan Commissioner. It was capitalized at $500,000,000 and was authorized to sell a maximum of $1,500,000,000 worth of five-year notes or bonds to the public or to the Treasury of the United States. Regional offices were established for the purpose of making loans. These loans could be made directly to banks and railroads, to agriculture through the Department of Agriculture, and to industry by acceptance of bills of exchange. Loans were limited to five years and to a maximum of $100,000,000. Not even Congress was to be allowed information as to what loans were made, except the aggregate amount in each class and state. In July, 1932, the capital funds of the corporation were increased to $3,800,000,000; $500,000,-

ooo for initial capital, $1,500,000,000 for loans to corporations, the same amount for construction loans on self-liquidating projects, and $300,000,000 for relief loans to states.

The Home Loan Bank Act of July, 1932, established a system of Home Loan Banks to discount home mortgages held by building and loan associations, savings banks, and insurance companies. The primary purpose of the Act was to rescue the banks. The Reconstruction Finance Corporation, during the first year of its existence, loaned $1,000,000,000 to banks. Nothing, however, seemed able to stop the trend toward a bank panic. Withdrawals continued, bankers refused to borrow and lend, and confidence was not restored. It became increasingly evident that the banks must close and, in financial circles, that the gold standard would have to be abandoned. The banking crisis came at the close of Hoover's administration. Nearly 7000 had closed in the previous eight years, more than 2000 of them in 1931, and the entire structure was shaky. Banks were temporarily closed by governors' proclamations in Nevada in January, and in Louisiana in February, 1933. Governor Comstock of Michigan closed the banks of that state on February 14. By March 1, the holiday had been extended to more than half the states and, three days later, was decided upon in New York City. Almost the entire country was without banking facilities and without currency. On March 5, President Roosevelt by proclamation closed every bank in the country and ordered all movements of gold and silver stopped. That date marked the bottom of the depression.

LABOR UNREST

The Coolidge era had been relatively free from labor disturbances. The unions had seemed to be stagnant; in fact, A. F. of L. membership had dropped from 4,000,000 in 1922 to about 3,000,000 in 1929. Meanwhile, the communists had been gaining strength, and their gains caused the American Federation of Labor, for the first time, to turn its attention to the new industrial South. Here was a region with a rather primitive economic structure and an agricultural philosophy—a philosophy of individualism and a traditional paternalism. Craft unionism existed in the skilled trades of the urban centers, but the factory workers of the Piedmont Crescent and the miners of the mountains were unorganized, isolated, subject to fluctuating economic conditions, and under constant pressure from a tremendous surplus of labor. Besides these there were the Negro laborers, the agricultural laborers, the common laborers in untold numbers with only seasonal and intermittent employment. All of this vast conglomeration of wage earners constituted a wide open and fertile field for the collective philosophy of the communists. The autocratic control exercised by the mill owners, tempered at first by a fine sense of responsibility for the welfare of the dependent worker, had become, in the second generation, an intolerable despotism over every phase of human existence. The mill workers were ripe for revolt, not necessarily against prevailing wages and hours and working conditions, but for social and spiritual freedom—for the right to order their own lives, earn an honest wage, and spend it according to the dictates of their own consciences. Unionization had been delayed far beyond the normal period by the surplus of cheap labor, the lack of leadership, the prevailing distrust of outsiders, and the ever-present race prejudice.

The communists led the way. The National Textile Workers Union organized and called a strike in the mills of Gastonia, North Carolina, on April 2, 1929. The strike was primarily for union recognition, though the workers had plenty of other grievances, including the introduction of the stretch-out system, low wages, etc. Nothing but a deep sense of oppression and unrest could have inspired the zeal with which the workers followed the lead of a handful of avowed communist agitators. National guard, imported gunmen, injunctions, kidnaping, wholesale arrests on trumped-up charges—all the brutal methods associated with labor controversies were used to break the strike and force the union underground. Meanwhile, the American Federation of Labor organized the workers at Elizabethton, Tennessee, and called a strike in those mills on March 12. The same methods were used by the authorities there with the same results. The United Textile Workers of the A. F. of L. then turned their attention to the mills of Danville, Virginia, where a strike was called in September, 1930. It failed as miserably as the others.

Even though the movement to unionize the southern textile mills failed, the strikes were important in many ways. Employers became more cautious and began to modify their worst practices. The prestige of the American Federation of Labor received a damaging blow. The workers became group conscious and aware of the necessity of relying upon leaders from among themselves. They learned that outside leadership, in part at least, cost them the support of public opinion. The brutality used in suppressing the strikes aroused liberal sentiment all over the country in a way few other strikes had ever done. The southern people, and particularly the newspapers, became conscious of existing social and economic evils. Social legislation received renewed support in an effort to eliminate the causes of labor's unrest. When the depression set in, the communists began the organization of Unemployed Councils in every city of the country. Demonstrations, supported by the Communist party, the Trade Union Unity League, and the Unemployed Councils, were held on March 6, 1930, with more than 100,000 participating in New York and Detroit. Fifteen hundred delegates of the unemployed staged a National Hunger March to Washington in December, 1931. On March 12, 1932, 40,000 marched in the funeral procession of four men killed in the demonstration before the Ford plant at Dearborn on March 7. A second National Hunger March was sent to Washington. Finally, 20,000 unemployed veterans commandeered freight trains and went to Washington to demand payment of the Adjusted Service Certificates. Continuation of these conditions would certainly have led to tremendous gains by the communist group, but the creation of the National Recovery Administration on July 16, 1933, changed the entire situation.

Meanwhile, Congress passed the Norris-La Guardia Act, outlawing injunctions and yellow-dog contracts, on March 20, 1932. This Act placed government approval upon the principle of collective bargaining and declared illegal all infringements upon its exercise. Specifically, it named yellow-dog contracts and forbade the issuance of injunctions against laborers ceasing to work, joining a union, paying strike benefits, giving full publicity to any facts pertaining to a strike, assembling peaceably, or persuading others to do these things. No officer or member of a union could be held responsible for unlawful acts of other officers or members unless they had authorized or ratified such acts. Section 7 of the Act said that no federal court might issue even a temporary injunction "except after hearing the testimony of witnesses in open court (with opportunity for cross examination) in support of the allegations of a complaint made under oath, and testimony in opposition thereto, if offered, and except after findings of fact by court, to the effect" (1) that unlawful acts had been threatened or would be committed; (2) that substantial or irreparable injury to property would ensue without the restraining order; (3) that the complaining party would suffer greater injury by the denial of an injunction than the defendants by its issuance; (4) that the complaining party had no adequate remedy at law; and (5) that law enforcement agencies were unable or unwilling to protect the property of the complainant. Furthermore, contempt cases, unless involving contempt committed in the presence of the court, were to be conducted on the basis of "speedy and public trial by an impartial jury of the state and district wherein the contempt shall have been committed."

DIFFICULTIES ABROAD

The United States had refused from the beginning to recognize any relationship between German reparations and Allied debts to the United States, and had insisted that the debts be paid. Actually, the entire pattern of international financial arrangements was a highly integrated one. Great Britain had loaned large sums to France, Italy, Russia, and the smaller nations. France had loaned to Italy, Rumania, and other nations. The United States had loaned much greater amounts to all of them. Germany had paid her reparations to the European countries only because she had continued to borrow heavily from private American sources. Allied governments had paid the United States only because Germany paid her reparations. The Allied debt to the United States government was being reduced because Germany's debt to American private interests was being increased.

As American citizens became more and more involved in stock market speculations, Germany had greater difficulty borrowing in this country. After the crash of the stock market in October, 1929, she found it virtually impossible. Germany was facing bankruptcy which meant collapse to the entire international credit structure. The United States, of course, stood to lose everything. President Hoover, therefore, privately secured consent of congressional leaders and then announced, June 20, 1931: "The American Government proposes the postponement during one year of all payments on inter-governmental debts, reparations and relief debts, both principal and interest." Other nations agreed; and Congress approved, December 22, 1931, but refused to accept a recommendation by Hoover that the war debt commission be revived further to examine the whole question. Premier Laval of France came to the United States, in October, 1931, for a conference with President Hoover concerning war debts, reparations and the gold standard. No statement was made of what decisions were arrived at in the conference; but France, shortly afterward, reversed her position on reparations and agreed to the Lausanne settlement by which German reparations were reduced to $714,-000,000. The next year an epidemic of defaults began which finally left only little Finland meeting her installments as they came due.

Late in 1929, Russia and China began fighting over the Chinese Eastern Railway without a declaration of war. Russia was clearly in violation of the Kellogg-Briand Pact, which both nations had signed, but she resented the fact that we tried to interpose when we never had officially recognized the new Russian government. Two years later, September 18, 1931, Japan invaded South Manchuria in such a manner as to indicate long and careful preparation. Secretary Stimson called the attention of Japan to her violation of the Kellogg-Briand Pact, without results.

After unsuccessfully seeking some action from the League of Nations, Stimson informed Japan, January 7, 1932, that the United States would never recognize "any situation, treaty, or agreement" which might be achieved in violation of the terms of the Pact of

Paris. This was not only a statement of policy, to which the United States has adhered, but an invitation for public opinion in other nations to rally to the support of the non-aggression principle. Neither Great Britain nor France supported the position of the United States, and Japan, knowing the United States would not resort to force, ignored the protest. On January 28, 1932, Japan invaded China at Shanghai, and once more the United States protested; but President Hoover resisted the demands for an economic boycott on the ground it would lead to war. Secretary Stimson undertook to secure the cooperation of other nations in invoking the Nine-Power Treaty of 1922, but the British Foreign Secretary, Sir John Simon, refused to cooperate. Stimson then announced the doctrine of non-recognition of any new order established by force in the Far East. In fact, he went much farther than that in a public address, August 8, 1932, and stated that the Kellogg-Briand Pact had altered the entire concept of international law respecting war and neutrality. War no longer had any standing in international law.

It is no longer to be the principle around which the duties, the conduct, and the rights of nations revolve. It is an illegal thing. Hereafter, when two nations engage in armed conflict either one or both of them must be wrong-doers—violaters of this general treaty law. We no longer draw a circle about them and threaten them with the punctiliousness of the duellists' code. Instead we denounce them as law-breakers.

The United States thus embarked upon an independent course of action in dealing with Japanese aggression and steadfastly refused to recognize the Japanese puppet state of Manchukuo.

Shortly thereafter Congress reopened a discussion of the Philippine question, and passed the Hawes-Cutting Act on December 29, 1932. This Act provided for the adoption of a Philippine constitution acceptable both to the Filipinos and to the Congress of the United States which would serve as an instrument of government during a ten year period. During this period the Islands were to be a protectorate of the United States with a High Commissioner in the Philippines and a Philippine Commissioner in the United States. The United States was to retain naval coaling stations and military posts in the Islands. Philippine foreign relations were to be under the supervision of the United States and appeals permitted from the insular courts to the Supreme Court of the United States. Philippine immigration to the United States was limited to 50 annually and imports of sugar and coconut oil were placed on a quota basis. American exports to the Islands were to be duty free. President Hoover vetoed the bill on the grounds that it would project the Philippines into economic and social chaos with subsequent collapse of government and degeneration of free institutions; that it would lead to peaceful infiltration or forcible entry of neighboring peoples; and that it would weaken the authority of the United States to a dangerous point during the probationary period. Congress promptly passed the Act over the President's veto but the Philippine legislature objected strenuously to its economic and immigration features and permitted it to lapse by default, failing to call a constitutional convention within the prescribed twelve months' period.

President Roosevelt requested, March 2, 1934, that the Hawes-Cutting bill be revived and amended. It was revived and passed as the Tydings-McDuffe Act and signed by President Roosevelt on March 24, 1934. The only change from the original act was the surrender by the United States of its right to maintain military establishments in the Islands. The Filipinos accepted the Act, and all American officials were withdrawn except a High Commissioner who was to have only powers of investigation and advice. Ten years were allotted to the two governments to solve the problems of economic independence for the Islands, involving the necessity of finding new markets at a time of worldwide economic nationalism. Equally important was the necessity of providing international guarantees of the Islands' independence. Failure to do these two things would make independence a mockery and vindicate the dire prophecies of Presidents Coolidge and Hoover.

21

The Conflict of Ideas

THE wild orgy of war and postwar days having come to a tragic end on that Black Thursday in October, 1929, America turned sadly to the task of studying the three R's: Relief, Recovery, and Reform. The economic collapse was so complete that virtually every one wanted relief, as much and as quickly as possible. Every one, too, hoped for recovery; some for the recovery of their lost paradise; others for the recovery of the sanity and stability of prewar days. Few wanted reform, if reform interfered with their own particular interests. Men knew that there was a surplus of consumers' goods, both of agricultural and of manufactured products, in terms of what the people could buy. They knew that there was a surplus of capital in the control of a relatively few people who could use it only for investment purposes. They knew that the purchasing power of the farmers had been destroyed by low prices. They knew that purchasing power of consumers must be restored by increasing the price of agricultural products and by re-employment of idle wage earners before recovery could be accomplished; but they disagreed as to the cause of the condition and the remedial measures required. Did tariff barriers, foreign debts, and reparations payments destroy world trade? Did the cartels so assiduously promoted by Hoover and the monopolies three administrations had tolerated foster artificially high prices and result in an unbalanced economy? Was the collapse due to overspeculation and, if so, were the banking policies or the tax policies at fault? Had the increased

446

productivity of the machine age produced a permanent technological unemployment which could only be remedied by shorter working hours? Had the "take" of capital out of industrial profits been
too great as compared with that of labor? On these questions,
there was a sharp division of opinion which cut squarely across
party lines and called for courageous leadership. No one will ever
understand the events from 1929 to 1936 who thinks in terms of
politics. The problem must be approached from the viewpoint of
conflicting social and economic philosophies.

THE BOURBON PHILOSOPHY

The country was deep in the mire of depression, and unemployment mounted to staggering totals between 1929 and 1933 because
producers of goods could no longer sell their products at a price
which would permit continued operation. Recovery required not
only that consumers' purchasing power be restored by placing
money in their hands through government largess or re-employment, either private or public; but that prices be restored to such
levels that profits from production were once more a possibility.
Restoration of economic stability on the basis of low prices and
low wages was impossible because of the tremendous burden of
private and public debt which could only be reduced by wholesale bankruptcy or default and dangerous curtailment of essential
public services. Restoration on the basis of high prices and low
wages was impossible because it was the very thing which added
momentum to the deflation process at the outset.

The Hoover Administration proceeded from the first on the
theory that the economic structure of the country was fundamentally sound. It would require time to liquidate inflated values of
stocks, real estate, commodities, debts, and wages, but the period
of deflation must necessarily be short if confidence could be restored. It brought pressure to bear, without success, upon industrialists to check the discharge of employees and wage-cutting.
It urged business to embark upon a program of construction, with
some success; and expanded the federal building program to $410,-
420,000 in 1930, to $574,870,000 in 1931, to $655,260,000 in 1933.

It issued optimistic statements from time to time about the imminence of recovery, perhaps partly from a failure to realize the totality of the collapse and partly from a desire to maintain confidence and prevent a bank panic.

Hoover refused, however, at any time to resort to direct federal relief for the unemployed. On that point, he said:

This is not an issue as to whether people shall go hungry or cold in the United States. It is solely a question of the best method by which hunger and cold shall be prevented. It is a question as to whether the American people on the one hand will maintain the spirit of charity and mutual self help through voluntary giving and the responsibility of local government as distinguished on the other hand from appropriations out of the Federal Treasury for such purposes. My own conviction is strongly that if we break down this sense of responsibility of individual generosity to individual and mutual self help in the country in times of national difficulty and if we start appropriations of this character we have not only impaired something infinitely valuable in the life of the American people but have struck at the roots of self-government.

By April, 1930, there were 3,187,000 unemployed, by government figures. This increased to 4,000,000 by October, 1930; and then Hoover created a Presidents' Emergency Relief Organization, which in turn encouraged state and local governments to establish some 3000 relief committees. Unemployment reached 7,000,-000 in July, 1931, and 10,000,000 in February, 1932. At this point Hoover approved an authorization by Congress for the distribution through the local committees of Farm Board surpluses: 45,000,000 bushels of wheat and 250,000,000 pounds of cotton. Finally, in May, 1932, he agreed to permit the Reconstruction Finance Corporation to loan up to $300,000,000 to state governments for relief purposes.

The question of relief for the unemployed was the most serious one facing the country, and however deeply President Hoover may have felt about the issues involved, the inescapable fact is that he set himself inflexibly against federal expenditures to feed the starving. His recovery program consisted of passing out millions to save from bankruptcy corporations which had turned out millions of men to starve until they could be re-employed at a profit. In July, 1932, a great army of veterans went to Washington and encamped on government property. They were there because they were unemployed, not primarily because they were veterans. They were well-behaved and well-disciplined; but they were driven out with cavalry, infantry, tanks, and machine-gun troops. Two men were shot; 1000 men, women, and children were gassed. Whatever hope of re-election remained was effectively destroyed on this July 28 by one of the worst exhibitions of official blundering and cruel oppression the country had ever witnessed. The country has long since forgotten the dark forebodings of disaster everywhere; but people were almost driven to strike out blindly for relief and the danger was real.

Long after he had been relieved of responsibility and the nation was well along the way to recovery, Hoover kept insisting that it was lack of confidence, fear of what the Roosevelt monetary policies would be, which delayed rapid recovery in 1932–1933. There is, indeed, some evidence of recovery in 1932, and the impending election, as always, may have had some further depressing effects upon business. Wherever one touches the controversy in its early stages, one inevitably comes back to this question of monetary policies. The dark shadow of 1896 and the darker shadow of post-war Europe hung like a pall over the White House. Hoover insisted the gold standard must be maintained, government expenditures must be reduced, and the federal credit must be kept unimpaired.

The Constitution gives to Congress complete power to establish a monetary system and regulate the currency of the country. During the Civil War, it taxed the paper currency issued by state banks out of existence. In 1873, it demonetized silver. Great Britain had been on the gold standard since early in the nineteenth century. Every leading nation except China had followed the example of the United States and Great Britain before the turn of the century. Thereafter, the world price level of commodities rose or fell in terms of gold as the supply of gold and the demand for it fluctuated. Gold did not increase in amount between the action of 1873 and 1896, but business and trade did expand and prices declined sharply. The demand for remonetization of silver emerged, and the battle for the restoration of free coinage at a ratio of 16 to 1 was fought to a conclusion in the United States in 1896. The silver forces were defeated and from that time forward the position of the country remained substantially one of opposition to bimetallism except by international cooperation. The fundamental principle for which the free-silver forces were contending in 1896, however, was written into the monetary system of the country by the Federal Reserve Act of 1914. It was that of a greatly expanded and flexible currency system. That act made commercial and agricultural paper instead of government bonds the basis of the paper circulating medium. Any member bank could take such paper to the Reserve bank for rediscount or it could take government bonds as collateral for loans and receive Federal Reserve notes in exchange. The amount of paper notes in circulation, then, and the aggregate amount of deposits subject to check, depended upon the willingness of people to borrow and spend and upon the willingness of bankers to loan and rediscount or borrow from the Federal Reserve banks, subject only to the following limitations: a 40 percent gold coverage for Federal Reserve notes must be maintained, and banks must keep cash reserves for demand deposits of 15 and 12 percent, depending upon their location, and 5 percent for time deposits. These ratios were reduced in 1917 to 13, 10 and 7 for demand deposits and 3 for time deposits. The amount of gold, thereafter, operated only as a check upon the expansion of credit beyond certain limits. If business languished, credit stringency ensued, and the percentage of gold coverage and cash reserves rose, then gold ceased to be a vital force in the general price situation. Within the limits of the rates of cash reserves set by Congress, the Federal Reserve System could control the volume of credit available by raising or lowering rediscount rates and by the indirect method of the purchase and sale of securities.

World War I which followed laid the basis for a tremendous expansion of credit in the United States by transferring to this country an extraordinary proportion of the world's supply of gold, and by the issue of more than $25,000,000,000 worth of government bonds. At the same time, however, the gold stocks of other nations were depleted to the point where they did not have enough gold with which to do business. They continued to buy from us only so long as we were willing to extend public or private credit for what we sold abroad and then world trade collapsed. Economists saw what was coming and warned of the danger of too much gold being concentrated in France and the United States while other nations remained on the gold standard. European nations had staggering internal and foreign debts. We had a large domestic debt, but, with respect to the rest of the world, we were a creditor nation. They had depleted gold stocks. We had more than we needed. Foreign trade balances were running heavily against them and in our favor. Government deficits faced them year after year. We had government surpluses to be applied to our debt all through the twenties. Because of the intricate nature of world trade, it was impossible for the United States to prosper, in spite of its 40 percent of the world's gold supply, when other nations were impoverished. The abnormal business conditions of the war and immediate postwar period merged into the speculation boom in the late twenties which carried the country to the dizzy heights of an economic fool's paradise and served to compound the calamity of deflation when it came. Year after year, larger amounts of money flowed out of the channels of consumers' trade and into the savings deposits of the relatively well-to-do. This was estimated by Hoover in 1932 at $1,500,000,000. Ever larger amounts of bank loans went into the speculative markets instead of into legitimate business channels. It is estimated that there were $11,000,000,000 in loans against speculative stocks when the stock market crashed, which were reduced ultimately, with the aid of the Federal Reserve System, to $2,000,000,000. Banks were weighted down with government bonds, real estate mortgages based on greatly appreciated valuations, and speculative securities.

Meanwhile, European nations had bowed to the inevitable and inflated their currencies. France inflated her currency 80 percent, Great Britain 30 percent, Italy 66⅔ percent, Belgium 40 percent and Austria 44 percent. Germany and Russia went all the way to uncontrolled inflation and printed fiat money until their currencies were depreciated to utter worthlessness. The fear of such uncontrolled inflation with its destruction of all savings, and the feeling that such methods are little more than legalized robbery for the benefit of improvident debtors, restrained the United States from action of any kind for some time. At length, the pressure from large industries, banks and service companies became so great that Hoover resorted to relief from the credit stringency by recommending the establishment of the Reconstruction Finance Corporation. The purpose of the move was to make available to hard-pressed key organizations the credit which the crumbling banking structure was unable or unwilling to extend.

On February 27, 1932, Congress had passed an amendment to the Federal Reserve Act permitting the use of Government bonds instead of commercial paper as collateral for the issuance of Federal Reserve notes, the lending of money to member banks without collateral, and to individuals. The Reconstruction Finance Corporation was transferred from the status of a relief to a recovery agency by permitting construction loans for self-liquidating projects. Loans to subordinate units of government for relief work, to agricultural export agencies, and to farmers through agricultural credit corporations were also authorized. The secrecy provision was also dropped, and monthly reports to the President and to Congress, including the names of borrowers and amounts of loans, was required. This action was taken because the former Chairman of the Board of Directors, former Vice-President Charles G. Dawes, had secured a $90,000,000 loan from his Chicago bank shortly after resigning. The amendment prohibited such loans in the future and Dawes' bank filed court proceedings to keep from repaying $60,000,000 which had been authorized but not transferred until after the amendment was passed by Congress.

The Reconstruction Finance Corporation eventually became a banking institution for short-term loans to banks, railroads, agriculture, and local relief, loans to banks and railroads constituting a substantial majority of the total amount. As government revenues declined, business stagnated, and unemployment increased, it became perfectly apparent that neither income taxes nor sales taxes could go far toward balancing the budget, nor could continued spending with increasing deficits do much more than equalize poverty until production, consumption, and normal price levels were restored. It was inevitable that inflation of credit begun with the creation of the Reconstruction Finance Corporation should be followed by demands for inflation of the currency through devaluation of the dollar in terms of gold, restoration of silver to the status of money, or the issue of greenbacks.

The first thought of the Chamber of Commerce and other businessmen's organizations was for economy in government and retrenchment in education. No other nation in the world ever undertook to educate its masses to the same degree as the United States. No other nation ever built an economic and political system so dependent upon the literacy of its people. No other nation so large and with a population so diverse in its origins and social backgrounds ever relied upon its educational system so heavily to train its people in the art of living harmoniously together. If ever there was a time when huge expenditures for education by past generations justified themselves, it was in 1929–1933 when everyone was in trouble, everyone needed to be tolerant, everyone needed to be thoughtful yet critical that the nation's political and social solidarity might not perish. If there was one institution which measures of economy should have passed by, it was the educational system. Yet the United States Chamber of Commerce and businessmen's organizations inaugurated a nation-wide drive against the cost of education which, before it was stopped, all but ruined the school system.

These organizations followed it with a bitter and concerted drive, which never ceased, against expenditures of public funds for the relief of the unemployed and for sales taxes to balance government budgets. They were determined that wealth should not be made to bear the burden either of relief or recovery. In short, industrialists refused to admit, or at least to act, upon the basic principle, now recognized by all competent economists, that recovery depended upon restoration of the purchasing power of the masses. However much they might give lip service to the theory that economic stability in a highly mechanized civilization required widespread economic equality among the people, they denied that there was anything fundamentally wrong with a system which ultimately placed 60 percent of the nation's wealth in the hands of 2 percent of the people. They believed and acted upon the thesis that recovery could be accomplished without reform; and they opposed all recovery measures which involved or were likely to lead to changes in the economic structure of the nation.

Two plans for recovery, slightly different from that of the Reconstruction Finance Corporation, were proposed and widely discussed in business circles. In the spring of 1931, Albert L. Deane, former head of the General Motors Acceptance Corporation and later Deputy Administrator of the Federal Housing Administration, published his Mutual Security Plan. It included the three principles of work spreading, permanent public works, and a tax system to sustain purchasing power. Its object was to control purchasing power by 100 percent employment and stability in wages and consumers' demand. The plan itself called for a revolving reserve fund from which to supplement the wages of all workers whose hours of employment in a given month fell below a long-term average. The long-term average, to be computed over a ten-year period, and the average hours of employment for each preceding month were both to be derived by dividing the total man hours of employment by the total number of employees. If the monthly average fell below the all-time average, every man's pay was to be supplemented with a government check on the reserve fund to the amount of 1 percent per man-hour of deficiency. The fund was to be sustained by a tax on the payrolls of employers who worked their employees more hours in any given month than the long term average. The tax was to amount to 1¼ percent on the total pay for each excess hour. The government should also provide a permanent public works program for all eligible workers unable to find employment in private industry. The program was to be carried out by a National Employment Reserve Corporation with an initial capital of $500,000,000 and authority to borrow $5,000,000,000. It was offered as a substitute in Congress for the NRA in March, 1933, and was again presented by Representative Frank W. Baykin of Alabama in April, 1935.

A somewhat similar program, known as the Kent Plan, was

submitted to the Senate Committee on Manufacturing by Charles
A. Miller of the Reconstruction Finance Corporation. As a substitute for paying men on relief for doing nothing, he proposed
that the RFC conclude a survey to determine the extent of employment, amount and kinds of raw materials used, etc., in normal
times, and the amount of capital required by each unit of the industrial system immediately to restore normal operations. Banks
would then be authorized to lend this required capital with a guarantee against loss by the RFC and with 50 percent of any increased
profits accruing to an industry going to the government.

TECHNOCRACY AND SHARE THE WEALTH

Precisely at the time when unemployment had reached its peak
and when the banking crisis was approaching an acute stage, a
dire prophecy of impending disaster coupled with a most amazing
revolutionary scheme was thrust before the people. At exactly the
same time Senator Huey P. Long appeared in the Senate with his
idea for making every man a king. It is only necessary to recall,
at this point (1) that the traditional policy of the nation, as written into the anti-trust laws, was based upon faith in competition
to maintain economic stability; (2) that the Hoover philosophy envisioned not only stability but an economic utopia arising from
an era of self-government of industry through trade associations
or cartels; (3) that fundamentally opposed to these ideas were
the socialists' doctrines of public ownership and control of all
instruments of production in a democratic political system and
the soviet theories of the communists. In the winter of 1932–1933,
from September to February, the most widely discussed subject
in the United States was a new plan for remaking the state known
as Technocracy. The term was originally applied to an organization
for research, but later was used in the sense of applying science to
remaking the social order. It began in 1919 with the publication
of Thorstein Veblen's *The Engineers and the Price System*, in
which he condemned the restraints placed upon technical achievements by industrial management for the purpose of securing maximum profits. Veblen's suggestion was for industrial control by

technicians to the end of securing maximum production at minimum cost. Shortly afterward, a group of men including Howard Scott, Charles Steinmetz and Stuart Chase were associated in an endeavor to test Veblen's thesis. In September, 1920, Scott entered the services of the Industrial Workers of the World and published an article in their magazine, *One Big Union Monthly*, in which he said: "It is possible under a system of scientific administration to increase the present standard of living 800 percent. Given a plan or design of industrial administration, the movement of the mass can be directed into constructive channels, but without such the country shall be plunged into a maelstrom beside which the Russian Revolution is but a tempest in a teapot." Controversy between Scott and Ralph Chaplin caused the former to sever his connections with the I.W.W. and, until the depression, he receded from public notice. In 1931, he became acquainted with certain men in Physics and Industrial Engineering at Columbia University and was allowed to use office space in the University to carry on the old Technical Alliance's Energy Survey of North America, 1830–1930. This study included what he called 3000 basic industries. Unemployed architects and engineers were put to work and an announcement was made that the Department of Industrial Engineering and the Architect's Emergency Committee of New York City were jointly sponsoring the survey. A report of the Department of Public Information of Columbia University drew attention to the survey in September, 1932. The amazing audacity of the survey's conclusions riveted the attention of the world upon them for six months.

Technocracy rested upon the thesis that technological unemployment was permanent and destined to increase. Manpower had ceased to be of importance in production. Employment had reached its peak in the United States in 1918 and had steadily declined as production increased to its peak in 1929. Consumers' labor no longer being necessary to production, money no longer flowed into their hands to purchase the production output. Under the price and profit system debt increases faster than production. Debt must give way to machinery. The price system, private enterprise, money, banking, securities, the political system—all such institutions must be discarded and a new economic utopia known as Technocracy set up. In this Technocracy, which should embrace a self-contained American continent, each individual would be required to fulfill a period of service to the state known as an energy contract. This period need be only for four hours per day, 165 days per year, between the ages of twenty-five and forty-five. Relative costs of all consumers' goods were to be determined by the relative amount of energy required to produce and deliver them. Every individual in the state would receive periodically an energy certificate from which would be deducted the amount of each purchase. There would be no profits under this scheme of complete social ownership and every one would have an equal income through life. Scott predicted absolute chaos in eighteen months unless his plan were adopted, on the grounds that 45 percent of the unemployed could never be reabsorbed in industry. The plan was so unintelligible in parts as to appear profound to many people. It was completely rejected after a short period of hysteria arising from fear of the total collapse of the economic system; but not until it had been presented in all seriousness before the American Association for the Advancement of Science at Atlantic City, December 29, 1932, and Scott had presented it in a national broadcast on January 13, 1933. Devastating articles by Walter Lippmann, Norman Thomas, Paul Blanshard, Stuart Chase and the Vatican newspaper *Osservatore Romano* did much to bring the nation out of the hysteria. All connections between Scott and Columbia University were disavowed on January 23, 1933. Scott then organized Technocracy Incorporated, called the Technological Army of New America. A separate organization known as the Continental Committee claimed 250,000 members by May, 1933.

Senator Long's Share the Wealth program was not so easily laughed away as was that of the Technocrats. For one thing, Long was no fly-by-night adventurer in the realm of economic philosophy. He was a practical politician and the absolute dictator of the sovereign state of Louisiana. Moreover, he had demonstrated a capacity to translate his proposals into practical realities to the utter discomfiture of business interests. He had lifted himself out of a backwoods environment into the governorship of his state as the champion of the underprivileged. He had wrested control of the state government out of the hands of a Bourbon oligarchy and centralized it; shifted the burden of taxation onto the wealthy; built a magnificent system of state highways; remodeled the school system by providing an eight-month term, free textbooks, and an outstanding state university; stamped out illiteracy; and curbed the power of utility monopolies. He took his seat in the United States Senate in January, 1932, and immediately launched a campaign to save the country by redistributing its wealth. The favorite quotation by which he later justified his program was from Governor Roosevelt's speech at Atlanta, May 22, 1932: "Our basic trouble was not an insufficiency of capital, it was an insufficient distribution of buying power coupled with an over-sufficient speculation in production"; and his favorite admonition was "Ye rich men, weep and howl, for your miseries that shall come upon you." On April 1, 1932, he introduced Senate Resolution No. 204 instructing the Senate Finance Committee to reform the revenue act under consideration "so that no person shall have an annual income in excess of $1,000,000, so that no person during his or her life time shall receive by gifts, inheritance or other bequests more than $5,000,000." On April 21, 1932, he first explained in the Senate his philosophy of redistributing wealth by a capital levy. His plan was for a capital tax of 1 percent on fortunes between $1,000,000 and $2,000,000, 2 percent on fortunes between $2,000,000 and $3,000,000, 4 percent on fortunes between $3,000,000 and $4,000,000, etc., doubling the rate on each successive million with a tax of 99 percent on everything in excess of $8,000,000. His plan was further developed in two radio addresses: "Decentralization of Wealth" on March 17, 1933, and "Currency Inflation" on April 21, 1933. On January 4, 1934, he introduced Senate Resolution No. 65 providing for old-age pensions of $30 per month for all persons over sixty years of age with less than $10,000 worth of property or net incomes of less than $1000 per year. His complete program, which he called a "Plan to Carry Out the Command of the Lord," was presented in the Senate February 5, 1934. It was the program of his Share Our Wealth Society, the motto of which was "Every Man a King." The principles of his program, in addition to old age pensions, were:

1. To limit poverty by providing that every deserving family should . . . possess not less than $5000.
2. To limit the hours of work to such an extent as to prevent over-production and to give the workers of America some share in recreations, conveniences, and luxuries of life.
3. To balance agricultural production with what can be sold and consumed according to the laws of God, which have never failed.
4. To care for the veterans of our wars.
5. Taxation . . . by reducing big fortunes from the top . . . to provide employment in public works wherever agricultural surplus is such as to render unnecessary in whole or in part one particular crop.
6. There shall be guaranteed a homestead to every family in the United States of America . . . which said homestead shall not be less than one-third the wealth of the average family in the United States of America.
7. The income of every family of America shall not be less than from one-third to one-half the average family income of the particular year. The income of no one person shall be more than 100 times the income of the average family for that year.

The nearest Long ever came to explaining how the wealth of the country could be redistributed short of the complete nationalization of property was to say: "We are going to take into the ownership of the United States of America every dollar, every bit of property that anybody owns above a few million dollars, and we are going to distribute that property, either by selling it and distributing it or otherwise, to those who have less than a homestead, of around $5000. That is how we are going to get it." He continued to popularize his dream of a debt-free home, a motor car, an electric refrigerator, and a college education for everybody until his assassination in the late summer of 1935. It was his ambition to defeat the Administration Senate leaders Pat Harrison of Mississippi and Joseph Robinson of Arkansas and to prevent President Roosevelt's re-election by shifting five million votes to some other candidate. After his death, the burden of accomplishing this was carried by his lieutenant Gerald L. K. Smith of Shreveport who claimed the support of six million people by the summer of 1936.

INDUSTRIAL DEMOCRACY

Midway between the ideas or lack of ideas of the radical and conservative extremists was the basic principle on which "New Deal" legislation was to rest. It was that the consumers' market could be recovered and retained only by raising the real income of farmers to prewar levels and by giving wage-earners a larger share of what they produced; in short, by increasing the return from production going to consumers and decreasing the returns going to investors and speculators. It was an approach to, though not an open endorsement of, the idea that our industrial system had developed to the point where a smooth functioning could be achieved only by putting capital instead of labor on a wage basis.

Edward A. Filene, a Boston merchant and philanthropist, proposed in January, 1933, that business and industry as a whole immediately adopt a thirty-hour week without any reduction in weekly wages and that thereafter workers be regarded entirely in the light of consumers with minimum wages based on unit cost of production. A. B. Lambert, a practical businessman of St. Louis, suggested a 100 percent Profits Tax Plan similar to the excess profits tax of World War I days. His argument was that any industry which utilized machinery to the exclusion of man-power and made large profits was a parasite on other industries, selling its products to their workers and providing no market in turn for their products. He proposed placing a 100 percent profits tax on all profits above 6 percent of the actual working capital and the use of the money so derived for the support of the unemployed.

It is only when the theory behind these suggestions is set over against the prevailing attitude of businessmen and industrialists from 1929 to 1933 that one begins to realize the tremendous difficulty of trying to solve the problem with reason rather than rhetoric, with intelligence rather than passion. The theory was that the country was dealing with a social revolution rather than an economic depression; that, in the new industrial age, the buying power of the masses must be increased by raising wages and lowering prices. Businessmen who had always been accustomed to think in terms of stabilizing prices at the highest possible levels and bargaining for the cheapest possible labor in order to increase the margin of profits, naturally found it difficult to change their attitude or to believe that economic changes had made it necessary for them to do so. The fact that there was a distinct moral tone to the reform movement—and the recovery measures were predicated upon the thesis that industrial relations were matters of social justice, of ethics, of morality as much as they were matters of economic expediency—did not make their endorsement by hard-headed businessmen any easier. This idea that recovery required a larger share of returns to labor was stressed by President Roosevelt when he signed the National Industrial Recovery Act. We shall see how the refusal of businessmen to accept the thesis caused that experiment to fail. In a demagogic way it was back of Huey Long's Share the Wealth program and, later, of Father Charles E. Coughlin's Union for Social Justice. On the other hand, it was significantly absent from the programs of the industrialists. It was the point at which men separated into new political alignments.

The man who, more than any other, presented a plan by which both economic liberty and economic prosperity might be retained was Monsignor J. A. Ryan, Professor of Moral Theology and Industrial Ethics at the Catholic University. Ryan's program for an industrial democracy is important to the historian not only because he belongs among the really great leaders of social reform, but because his philosophy represents that of so many men whose business it is to analyze social forces and because of the tremendous influence it had on the Roosevelt Administration. Ryan's program was unique among the many because it was not suggestive of a quick cure-all for existing difficulties but consisted of proposed modifications in the economic system. Recovery depended upon increasing the purchasing power of those who buy consumption goods. The new demand for consumers' goods and services would be followed by a demand for capital goods. The real income of farmers and wage-earners should be increased, because they purchase consumers' goods; and increased at the expense of those who invest and speculate with their incomes.

This increase in real income can be accomplished first by raising money wages through the agency of strong labor unions and minimum wage laws. The increase in money wages could then be transformed into an increase in real wages by indirect action such as forcing down interest rates by offering low rates on government securities and bank deposits and by government competition with those private industries which insist upon maintaining high prices and low wages. It could be accomplished directly by establishing a thirty-hour week by law with no reduction in weekly wages. In so far as this would destroy marginal and inefficient producers artificially kept alive by the tariff, it would benefit society. Finally, purchasing power could be increased by large governmental expenditures for public works until the unemployed were re-absorbed into private business, the money to be derived from high income, inheritance, and excess profits taxes. Public works should be of those types unattractive to private capital, such as the elimination of grade crossings and construction of low cost housing. There should be a restriction on the production of those agricultural commodities which would not be absorbed by the market if consumers were fully able to purchase, but not otherwise. Recovery should envision an increase in small farms and subsistence homesteads with the cooperative use of farm machinery and community industries. Finally, there should be a distinct reform in the ethical standards which governed economic relations.

Rejecting collectivism of every sort, whether it be socialism, communism, or fascism, Ryan evinced a sublime faith in the democratic system by advocating its extension to the industrial order. The objective should be an industrial democracy embracing living wages, social insurance, and a division of surplus profits between labor and management with a guaranteed fixed wage to capital. Such a system would necessitate the abandonment of individualism and bring the managers, the owners and the employees of an industry into a single unit for the control of wages, dividends, prices and working conditions. These occupational groups might be federated in a national council for the industry and all of them brought under the restraining influence of the state. It would place in the hands of wage-earners some influence over their environment, curb the power of the unscrupulous individualists, and eliminate conflict between classes. It was, in reality, a compromise program between socialism and individualism, between capitalism and communism.

UNEMPLOYMENT RELIEF

The United States was as completely without a plan for the relief of the unemployed in January, 1933, as it had been at the beginning of the depression. One of the important aspects of our economic system had been that society must bear the burden of supporting, in times of depression, the surplus labor supply of industry. Labor was recruited in the open market when needed, discharged when no longer required. During the twenties this recruitment of labor had been in the agricultural region of the South. Thousands of families were moved long distances by industry and given employment for a time, then dismissed. The determining factor was the ability of industry to sell at a profit the artifacts it produced. When the demand for its products slackened, whether it be for a few days or, as in this case, for months without end, labor was turned out to shift for itself. Families lived, during these periods, from savings, if any, returned to the comparative security of their former homes to live by the generosity of relatives or friends, did odd jobs for a meager wage, or depended upon private and public relief agencies. The same was true when wage-earners were discharged because of physical disability, old age, or technological improvements. County poor farms, public hospitals, clinics, etc., bear witness to the efforts of society to care for the derelicts of the industrial system. Organizations of private charity were spending $100,000,000 a year before the depression, probably 20 percent of which was contributed by industrial and business institutions. There were no expenditures of federal funds for the purpose and little, if any, of state funds. The problem was regarded as a purely local responsibility, and for the most part as a service of charity. There is no escaping the fact that the United States had been dilatory about setting up safeguards against the hazards of unemployment. Few people thought in terms of the insecurity of labor.

No one knows how many wage-earners were unemployed at any time during the depression because no census was ever taken. It was variously estimated between 12,000,000 and 15,000,000 at the peak. The National Industrial Conference Board said it was 13,-203,000 and the American Federation of Labor said 13,689,000 in March, 1933. In May, 1934, the two agencies placed it at 7,899,000 and 9,807,000 respectively; but some authorities maintained it was no less than 10,500,000 as late as the spring of 1936. Two facts became increasingly clear as the years came and went after 1929. The first was that shrinkage in the relief rolls was not keeping pace with industrial recovery. President Roosevelt professed to believe it was due to the increased use of machinery during the depression. His political opponents said people were being retained on the relief rolls unnecessarily for political reasons. There was probably some truth in both observations. A less partisan approach to the problem would have revealed (1) that as some persons left the relief rolls because of finding work, others were added whose private savings had finally become exhausted; and (2) that several million young men and women had reached the status of wage-earners with no opportunity to work. The second fact was that restoration of complete normality in business and industry would leave 5,000,000 persons and their dependents a permanent liability against society. Most of them were unemployables; persons who because of advanced age or physical disabilities, or because of the loss of means of support at an advanced age, must depend on charity. Others were marginal laborers who could be reabsorbed into productive enterprises only by a restoration of world trade and the recovery of foreign markets.

Not only, then, was there no preconceived plan for relief but the problem constantly became more complicated as time went on. From the very first, there were two schools of thought as to how the relief problem should be handled. President Hoover was inflexibly opposed to the use of federal funds, insisting that the responsibility belonged to state and local governments and, for the purpose of maintaining public morale, to private charity. Needless to say, his position was untenable and received little support. Local and state funds were soon exhausted and appeals were made on every hand for aid from the inexhaustible resources of the federal treasury. Those who insisted that the federal government assume the burden were not without reason. The relief burden was heaviest at first in the industrial centers. Municipalities simply could not maintain essential public services with decreased revenues, and, at the same time, provide thousands of unemployed with relief adequate enough to maintain health and decency and counteract the appeals of radical revolutionary groups. The destitution wrought by the ensuing droughts throughout whole groups of agricultural states ably supported their contention. Unemployment was so general as to be a national problem and only the federal government could reach the resources of accumulated wealth concentrated in the industrial North and East. The southern states which had, for more than a decade, been wrestling with the problem of caring for the non-productive people left behind as young men and women migrated to the northern industrial centers, now suddenly found those same persons returning in a state of destitution. It was no simple affair when a state like South Carolina suddenly found its population increasing 16 percent during the depression and Georgia 15 percent. Some of the western states even resorted to border patrols to prevent destitute persons from entering the state. State and municipal funds, if forthcoming at all, must be derived from sales taxes which were an added burden upon the poor. On the other hand, those who opposed federal relief and continued to insist upon its abandonment at the earliest possible moment were equally sound in their position. Relief was, after all, a matter of individual adjustment. Local officials and existing welfare agencies were in a position to know how much assistance was necessary in a particular case and when it might properly be withdrawn. Local politicians were inclined to shirk their own responsibility for political reasons under a federal dole. They could be lenient in dispersing federal funds without offending local taxpayers and, on occasion, turn that leniency to good political purposes. Long-continued government support had a demoralizing effect upon the individual. It fostered pressure politics instead of self-reliance and had a demoralizing effect upon the recipient's family.

Men were equally torn between their real fears of excessive public expenditures and their human sympathy for those in distress. It was said, and was probably true, that continued deficits would lead to uncontrolled inflation; and that fear of inflation was retarding recovery. Generous relief for the unemployed, therefore, was simply preventing the reemployment of the recipients into private industry. This was the difficulty in making a decision between work relief and direct relief. Work relief was expensive and meant larger capital expenditures or aid for fewer people. Direct relief was cheaper, and could be extended to a larger number, but it carried a stigma that destroyed self-respect. Moreover, a minimum dole was of no assistance in restoring the consumers' market. Unless sufficient funds could be placed in the hands of the unemployed to stimulate buying, it was purely a relief and not a recovery measure.

The problem of working out a formula for the care of the unemployed was quickly complicated by the existence of such a large number of unemployables, particularly of the aged. It is a significant fact that Dr. Francis E. Townsend, promoter of the Old Age Pension Plan which bears his name, was nearly seventy years of age when he lost his savings and his position at the beginning of the depression; and he is said to have evolved his plan after seeing three old women searching garbage cans for food. The plan, originating in 1933 and printed in the form of a petition to Congress, provided that every worthy citizen over sixty years of age who was willing to cease work should receive $200 per month from the federal government. The money was to be raised by what actually amounted to a 10 percent sales tax and each pensioner was to be required to spend his $200 within thirty days. The economic aspects of the plan, first presented as a recovery measure, were obscured by the sentimental appeal of caring for the aged. It was reduced to a concrete formula by Robert Clements and finally introduced in Congress by Representative John S.

McGroarty of California on January 16, 1935. Meanwhile, an organization, known as the Old Age Revolving Pensions, Ltd., was formed and incorporated in California and a magazine, *The Official Townsend Weekly*, was established. By February, 1934, clubs were being organized at the rate of 100 per day. The membership fee was twenty-five cents and the charter fee for local clubs twenty-five dollars. By 1936, there were 6500 local clubs with 5,000,000 members and regional offices in Washington, New York, Chicago and Los Angeles. Every club meeting was opened with prayer and a religious fervor soon permeated the whole movement. Its strength was among the ne'er-do-well groups of the small towns and rural districts which were unfamiliar with or unaffected by the philosophy of the labor movements; but it was viewed with favor by an amazing number of people from all walks of life. The plan was supported as an immediate stimulus to business recovery and as a solution to the problem of caring for the aged. Its economic fallacies were painstakingly exposed by so many people so many times that it should have disappeared as quickly as Technocracy; but recovery and not reason soon appeared to be the only antidote. Speaking to the first national convention of the organization at Chicago, 1935, Townsend said:

For every hundred delegates assembled here today, a million prayers go up to the God of Justice that our efforts in this Convention may not fail. Our plan is the only hope of a confused and distracted nation. . . . We have become an avalanche of political power that no derision, no ridicule, no conspiracy of silence can stem.

Making allowances for over-enthusiasm, it is true, nevertheless, that pressure politics put many Congressmen in an uneasy state of mind. Memorials from local clubs and the legislatures of Arizona, California, Colorado, Idaho, and North Dakota in favor of it, finally forced Congress to appoint a special committee in the House of Representatives to investigate the financial transactions of the organization as violating the Corrupt Practices Act. Fear of the political strength of the organization prevented the committee from citing Townsend for contempt when he refused to complete his testimony after three days of questioning. No one was quite certain how much truth there was to his claim of controlling the votes of 30,000,000 people; nor will any one ever know because of the rapid progress of recovery before the presidential election.

22

The New Deal: Relief

THE Republican party had no choice but to renominate President Hoover. To have done otherwise would have been to acknowledge failure of his administration, and that is something politicians are very reluctant to risk in a presidential election. The Republican convention met at Chicago on June 14, 1932. President Hoover controlled the convention, dictated the party platform, and received all but 28 votes for renomination on the first ballot.

In the Democratic party, there was a real contest. Franklin D. Roosevelt had emerged from the election of 1928 as the most available man in the party. He had been Assistant Secretary of the Navy in Wilson's Administration and Vice-Presidential candidate on the ticket with James M. Cox in 1920. He had attracted a great deal of attention with his speech placing Alfred E. Smith in nomination in 1924, and in 1928 Smith had prevailed upon him to run for the governorship of New York. He did so, being elected by a substantial majority while Smith failed to carry the state. He was re-elected in 1930 by a very large majority. During these four years, he proved a capable governor and a very shrewd politician. He had met the depression in the state by increasing income taxes 100 percent and using the money for direct relief. There was much doubt, however, about his being classed as a liberal and, also, about his ability to formulate a definite program of action. His strongest opponent for the nomination was John N.

Garner of Texas, who had been sponsoring a sales tax to balance
the budget in the last Hoover Congress. He had been in Congress
since 1903 and no one questioned his ability, least of all Andrew
Mellon whose tax proposals had more than once been defeated
by Garner's opposition. The Hearst newspapers and William G.
McAdoo both favored his nomination. The third prominent candidate was Alfred E. Smith who had broken with Roosevelt and
had the support of the Scripps-Howard newspapers. Albert Ritchie
and Newton D. Baker were considered possible compromise candidates. Roosevelt's managers made a tactical blunder in seeking
to repeal the ancient two-thirds rule for nomination in the convention and failed. A deal was then consummated whereby the Garner
votes from Texas and California were thrown to Roosevelt and
Garner was given the Vice-Presidency. The resulting bitterness
of the Smith forces was to remain a source of annoyance even
in the next campaign.

Hoover's renomination drove the Progressives out of the party.
No one among them attempted to lead a third-party movement as
Theodore Roosevelt had done in 1912 and Robert M. La Follette
in 1924. Five million people had voted for La Follette and Wheeler
in 1924 because theirs was the only platform that an intellectually
honest man could support. There had been no La Follette party
in 1928 in fact, but in reality there was just that. How many votes
went to Hoover instead of Smith as the lesser of two evils but
at the same time were given to dissenters like Henrik Shipstead,
George W. Norris, Henry F. Ashurst, C. C. Dill, Peter Norbeck and
others, one may only guess; but it is safe to say more than 5,000,000.
In short, if the Democratic party or any other party had presented
a platform in 1928 like the La Follette platform of 1924 or the
Democratic platform of 1932, Hoover would have gone into
office, if at all, with far less than a 6,000,000 majority of the popular
vote. It was the Democratic platform of 1932 which made it possible for the Progressive Republican leaders to support Franklin D.
Roosevelt—in fact the platform made it impossible for them to do
otherwise and remain true to their political philosophy. Senator
George W. Norris of Nebraska took the lead and was followed by
Robert M. La Follette, Jr., of Wisconsin, Bronson Cutting of

New Mexico and Hiram Johnson of California. They were denounced by Hoover as dangerous radicals, but in public opinion they were spokesmen of great constituencies, and as a group they were the most consistently intellectually honest men in public life. They came from the great agricultural states. Their people had voted Republican since the days of Abraham Lincoln; but their economy had nothing in common with that of the industrial East; their philosophy could not be reconciled with that of the Republican hierarchy; they had been Republican in nothing but name; they did not become Democrats.

The Republican platform was conservative and conventionally non-committal. The Democratic platform was concise, understandable, and liberal. The Socialist platform was, by comparison, radical. The Republicans had successfully sounded the alarm of radicalism so often that it had become habitual and again found its way into the platform. They promised to balance the budget, but said nothing about the tax program for doing it. They endorsed pensions for veterans suffering both from service and non-service disabilities, the gold standard, restriction of immigration, and the removal of submarginal land from production. They promised to maintain and extend the tariff schedules, and to submit a modified prohibition amendment. The Democratic platform would reduce government expenses 25 percent; tax on the basis of ability to pay; pay pensions only to those disabled in service; divorce investment banking from commercial banking; extend public works and federal credit for unemployment relief; enact state unemployment and old-age pension laws; control crop surpluses; collect the war debts; repeal the Eighteenth Amendment; and seek tariff reduction by negotiation. The Socialists demanded social ownership of principal industries; increased income and inheritance taxes; abolition of tax-exempt securities; a national banking system; ten billion dollars for direct relief and public works; abolition of the R.O.T.C., of conscription, and of munition sales; the recognition of Russia; entrance into the League of Nations; cancellation of war debts; disarmament by example; minimum wage laws; social insurance; the direct election of the presidents, proportional representation and abolition of judicial review.

In the campaign, Hoover staunchly defended the Hawley-Smoot Tariff, and the National Committee denounced the economists who had protested against it as radicals, socialists, and communists. Ogden L. Mills defended the policies of the Administration as 100 percent perfect. Hoover assumed the role of savior of the country by hinting with an air of secrecy at grave dangers which the Administration had overcome. Ex-President Coolidge wrote in the Saturday Evening Post of the great wisdom of President Hoover in avoiding the dole, although millions were receiving local and state relief at the time. He and others repeatedly asserted that the standard of health in the country had been raised under Republican Administrations—even during the depression. The prohibition forces threw their support to the Republican party, which redounded to the benefit of their opponents. The efforts of the Republicans to disclaim responsibility for the economic catastrophe were futile. They had claimed the benefits of prosperity too long to evade the consequences of the depression. That and prohibition were the deciding factors. Prohibition had been a dismal failure. Moreover, it had been dragged into every campaign to the confusion of other and more important issues. It had to be settled before there could be any rational consideration of pressing economic questions. Millions voted for the party which promised outright submission of an amendment for repeal. The general accumulation of dissatisfaction with three Republican Administrations, the failure of the party in power to arrest the deflation, and its refusal to face squarely the failure of the prohibition experiment combined to deprive the party of all but regular votes. The independent vote went to Roosevelt instead of Norman Thomas. Roosevelt received 472 electoral votes to 59 for Hoover; the popular vote was 22,809,000 to 15,758,000. Hoover carried only six states: Maine, New Hampshire, Vermont, Connecticut, Delaware and Pennsylvania. It was more than an election. It was a veritable political revolution. Only eight Republican governors were elected and such stalwarts as Senators George H. Moses of New Hampshire and Hiram Bingham of Connecticut went down to defeat. The House of Representatives was Democratic by almost three to one.

The weeks between the election in November and the inauguration in March were the most depressing the nation had witnessed since the winter of 1860–1861. Deflation had been running for more than three years. Unemployment had reached an estimated peak of 15,000,000. More than 200 cities were facing imminent bankruptcy. There was no way under the law by which fixed charges on bonded indebtedness might be reduced. Retrenchments, therefore, were being made at the expense of essential public services: schools, fire and police protection, garbage disposal, maintenance of streets, public buildings, and playgrounds. Farm and city home owners were unable, under the law, to reduce debts in proportion to the decline in prices and wages. Property was forfeited and millions of people had lost their hard-earned equities. Home building had long since ceased; but there was actually a surplus of homes as families doubled up or returned to rural communities. Private and local relief could no longer bear the burden of these unprecedented conditions. Several hundred thousand boys, many scarcely out of their teens, were roaming the country without purpose and in hopeless despair. Millions had reached maturity without prospect of honest labor. The situation was not only acute; it was desperate. Prime Minister Ramsay MacDonald said at the London Economic Conference in 1933: "This can not go on. The world is being driven upon a state of things which may well bring it face to face again with a time in which life revolts against hardship and the gains of the past are swept away by the forces of despair." He was not indulging in mere rhetorical bombast. The danger was as real in the United States as in Europe and more ominous because it was more silent.

RELIEF TO THE NEEDY

The inauguration of Franklin D. Roosevelt on March 4, 1933, initiated the most sweeping social and economic revolution in the history of the United States. Congress convened in extra session on March 9, and in one hundred days enacted an unprecedented body of legislation. It is impossible to determine what measures were intended strictly as relief, or reform, or recovery acts for there was an element of each in every statute and executive proclamation. The new President insisted that the country was facing a crisis not unlike a foreign invasion; that the people demanded action; and that, if it should be found necessary to depart from precedent and delegate broad executive powers, that would be done. Broad powers were delegated to the President by Congress, and by him to administrative officers. Much of the Hoover program was continued and implemented by law to make it effective, particularly with respect to industry and agriculture. The Wilson program of creating federal regulatory agencies was revived and expanded. The federal government assumed the burden of relief. It embarked upon a program of social planning. It dealt vigorously with long standing problems like child labor, collective bargaining, and labor standards. It established a comprehensive social security program. It drastically altered the banking, currency, and credit systems. It modernized the tariff system. The country got action, and was bewildered by its suddenness, but within three months the morale of the people was restored and recovery began.

The most difficult problem with which the Roosevelt Administration had to deal was that of unemployment relief. The formulation of a program was largely the work of Secretary Frances Perkins and Senators Robert Wagner of New York, Edward P. Costigan of Colorado, and Robert M. La Follette, Jr., of Wisconsin. The purpose of the Administration was to relieve distress among the unemployables until the financially embarrassed local governments could resume the burden, and to avoid the dole by giving men work wherever possible on socially useful projects with sufficient pay to provide the necessities of life and to restore purchasing power until the increased demand for consumers' goods reabsorbed them into private industry. To accomplish these two things Congress created (1) the Civilian Conservation Corps on March 31, 1933; (2) the Federal Emergency Relief Administration, provided by act of May 12, 1933, and inaugurated by the appointment of Harry L. Hopkins as Administrator on May 22, 1933; and (3) the Public Works Administration, provided for in the National Industrial Recovery Act of July 16, 1933. The slowness with which the Public Works program got under way necessitated the setting

474

up of a temporary program of quick relief on made-work projects during the winter of 1933–1934. This was the short-lived Civil Works Administration. Contributions for the care of all not employed in public work were made jointly by the state and local governments and the Federal Emergency Relief Administration. This continued until the spring of 1935 when unemployables were turned back to the local governments, the Federal Emergency Relief Administration was abandoned, funds for the Public Works Administration were virtually stopped and all federal aid was brought together under a new agency, known as the Works Progress Administration.

It will be noticed that the very first agency established for public works was the Civilian Conservation Corps. The purpose of the project was to restore the nation's forests and salvage the young men of the country from the attitude of despair so widely prevalent. As has been said, one of the most discouraging aspects of the depression was the indiscriminate hordes of homeless youth wandering aimlessly about the country. Secretary Frances Perkins and Senator Robert Wagner devised the plan for emergency conservation work and the act was passed and approved on March 31, 1933, after bitter debate. President William Green of the American Federation of Labor objected strenuously to what he called regimentation of labor in peacetime, to the wages of $30 per month, to the forced allotment of a portion of the wage to dependents, and to the requirement for a physical examination. Chairman William P. Connery of the House Committee on Labor and Education demanded a wage of $80 per month for married men and $50 for unmarried men. Unable to agree on the details of the plan, Congress omitted all controversial features and left to the Administration the task of supplying them.

Robert Fechner, Vice-President of the International Association of Machinists, was appointed Director of Emergency Conservation Work, with an advisory Council representing the Departments of War, Interior, Agriculture and Labor. Members of the Conservation Corps consisted mostly of young men between the ages of seventeen and twenty-eight. They received $30 per month, of which $22 was sent to their dependent families. Five percent of each company were allowed $45 per month for meritorious work and an additional eight per cent $36 per month. The age requirement was waived in the case of veterans who were sent to separate camps. A representative of the Department of Labor in each state selected the men through local public welfare agencies. Enrollment was entirely voluntary and selection was made from the most needy families. As soon as men were selected, they were sent to Army stations for physical examinations and two weeks of conditioning exercises. There was neither military training nor military discipline, but the War Department was responsible in all camps for food, clothing, camp construction, sanitation, medical service, education and religious services. The educational program was essential because there were 10,000 illiterates among the 350,000 enrolled; 50 percent had not completed the eighth grade; 46 percent had gone to high school, but only one-third of those had graduated; and only one-fifth of one percent had graduated from college. Participation in the educational program was optional, with 60 percent participating in June, 1935, about 9000 of whom were learning to read and write. Courses in vocational training, dramatics, music, and debating were offered. Libraries and newspapers were provided. The Department of Interior supervised all works in national parks, Indian reservations, and reclamation projects. The Department of Agriculture was responsible for reforestation and erosion control. Among the types of work undertaken were the building of telephone lines, fire breaks, truck trails, erosion control dams, reservoirs for wild-life, diversion dams; planting of trees; fighting forest fires; controlling insect pests and rodents. During the first eighteen months, 5,000,000 acres of forest lands were added to the national forests and 67,000 acres to national parks; 15,000,000 trees were planted; 34,570 miles of truck trails, 23,000 miles of fire breaks and 609,000 soil erosion dams were constructed.

The service cost $851,009,459 before the end of the fiscal year 1934–1935 and $1,204,560,000 by March 1, 1936. Of the latter amount $266,000,000 was forwarded to dependent families and $615,000,000 went for the purchase of materials and supplies. The average annual cost for each person enrolled was $1175. The personnel costs of the administration were exceedingly low, with only fifty-eight persons engaged. One million men passed through a period of service in the camps before June 30, 1935, and nearly two million before the service was discontinued in 1942, emerging into private employment with improved physique and new attitudes toward life. Funds for the maintenance of the camps came first from the $3,300,000,000 appropriation in 1933, no separate funds having been provided in the act establishing the corps. The Emergency Appropriation Act of 1935 ($4,880,000) designated $600,-000,000 for the continuation of the CCC until 1937. President Roosevelt desired to reduce the number of enrollees from 500,000 to 300,000 by July, 1936, as a part of the program to cut relief costs, but met strenuous opposition in Congress. A compromise was reached and instructions were issued to Administrator Fechner on March 23, 1936, gradually to reduce the number to 350,000 by March 31, 1937. There seemed to be little doubt at that time about the work continuing as a permanent part of the government's conservation program, but Congress abolished it in 1942.

During the last year of Hoover's Administration, Congress had authorized (July 17, 1932) the Reconstruction Finance Corporation to lend up to $300,000,000 to the states for relief purposes. Approximately $210,000,000 had been advanced by March 4, 1933. The sums were advanced as loans but the only security was a lien by the federal government against future appropriations for highway construction. State and local funds were so completely exhausted that 89 percent of the relief funds came from this federal money during January, 1933. Congress began discussion of the question of direct federal relief on March 27, and the Federal Emergency Relief Act was approved on May 12. Its purpose was "to provide for cooperation by the Federal Government with the states and territories and the District of Columbia in relieving hardship and suffering caused by unemployment and for other purposes." The Act authorized the Reconstruction Finance Corporation to borrow $500,000,000 which was to be made available to aid the states in carrying the relief load, but was to be dispensed through a special relief Administrator. The act stated the principle that federal aid was to constitute "⅓ of the public money expended by state and subdivisions" but left the way open for additional amounts if necessary. It provided that no one state should receive more than 15 percent of the total amount, and required a monthly report from the Administrator.

The Federal Emergency Relief Administration was placed under the direction of Harry L. Hopkins, former associate of Frances Perkins, Herbert Lehman, and Robert Wagner in social work in New York, Chairman of the Southern Division of the Red Cross during World War I, and Emergency Relief Administrator in New York under Governor Roosevelt. He directed the FERA, the Civil Works Administration (CWA), and the Works Progress Administration (WPA), and remained a confidential adviser and personal agent of President Roosevelt until his death in January, 1946. The Administrator had final power under the President to decide when state funds had been exhausted. From the first, the policy was followed of placing responsibility upon the state administrations. The Federal Emergency Relief Administration exercised no control except that of making or refusing to make grants-in-aid. Its authority ceased when grants were approved, and within the states the funds were dispensed in various ways. To obtain funds, the governor of a state was required to make application, stating the amount of money needed, the amount of available public and private funds, the standards of relief, and how the funds were to be administered. Both direct relief in the form of food, shelter, clothing, light and fuel, and work relief were furnished under the system. Surplus commodities were purchased, processed, and distributed to the needy. Destitute rural families were put to work, exchanging labor for food, tools, and livestock. Nursery schools, rural educational extension courses, and adult education classes were established. Money was used to continue schools which would have had to close for lack of funds. A student-aid program was set up to assist boys and girls in schools and colleges. As people found employment and dropped from relief, their places were taken by others whose savings had been exhausted, who chose aid from the government rather than from relatives as the depression continued, or who were thrown on public relief by the withdrawal of private charity. Hundreds of thousands who had been giving privately between 1929 and 1933 ceased to do so when the whole system was placed on a public expense basis. Allowances necessarily increased as prices rose, and reluctance to receive relief lessened. No doubt the local dispensing agencies continued to be more liberal with federal funds than they would have been with state and local funds.

More and more the relief rolls came to be made up of unemployables, those with larger-than-average families, the poorly educated, and the manual labor group. This fact determined the end of the Federal Emergency Relief Administration. In his message to Congress, January, 1935, President Roosevelt said:

The lessons of history confirmed by the evidence immediately before me show conclusively that continued dependence upon relief induces a spiritual and moral disintegration fundamentally destructive to the national fiber. To dole out relief in this way is to administer a narcotic, a subtle destroyer of the human spirit. . . . Local responsibility can and will be resumed for all unemployables, for common sense tells us that the wealth necessary for this task existed and still exists in the local community and the dictates of sound administration require that this responsibility be in the first instance a local one.

Final grants by the FERA were made in December, 1935, and states were given back the task of providing for all unemployables —persons, who because of illness, physical disability, or old age, were not able to work.

The case load carried by the FERA had varied as follows:

April, 1933	4,475,322
September, 1933	3,000,000
January, 1934	2,485,000
April, 1934	3,864,000
December, 1934	4,459,000
April, 1935	1,464,000
December, 1935	2,079,369

The low figures for January, 1934, were due to the operation of the Civil Works Administration and for December, 1935, to the existence of the new Works Progress Administration.

Congress had provided for indirect relief and recovery by creating a Public Works Administration (PWA) but the program was slow in getting started, and the winter of 1933–1934 approached with local relief funds exhausted and a minimum of 11,000,000 persons unemployed. The Civil Works Administration had been launched to carry some 4,000,000 men over the winter until the Public Works Administration could absorb them. The executive order creating it and naming Hopkins, already Federal Emergency Relief Administrator, Civil Works Administrator was issued on November 8, 1933. Four hundred million dollars were released by the FERA for the program and state and municipal officials were hurriedly called to Washington on November 15 to get it started. Four million men were to be put to work before December 1, one half to be taken from the relief rolls and the remainder selected from the self-sustaining unemployed by the local employment agencies. The entire machinery for the program was set up within one week. It was completely decentralized and consisted for the most part of existing relief agencies in all of the counties. This was a part of the Public Works provided for under the Recovery Act, but all work was done by day labor and no contracts were let. Local and state Civil Works Administrators supervised the work. Money was advanced only as needed to meet payrolls through the agency of the Veterans Administration Bureau. All employees were placed on a thirty-hour week and eight-hour day, with the same wage scale as other Public Works projects. No projects were undertaken which could not be completed within three months. They included work on streets, roads and highways; schools and universities; parks and playgrounds; public buildings and equipment; public lands; pest control; sanitation; waterways; utilities; and clerical work. All projects were approved by state and local authorities. Hundreds of different types of work were undertaken. A partial list would include: highway work, such as clearing right of way, grading, paving, resurfacing, eliminating curves, repairing ditches and traffic signals, and building parking spaces; school buildings, such as small construction work, painting, plastering and plumbing, building athletic fields, tennis courts, grading grounds and constructing paths, landscaping, constructing roadways and fencing; bathing beaches, golf courses, skating rinks, picnic grounds, etc.; waterways, such as flood control, soil erosion, building filter plants, and pumping stations; utilities, such as removing old car tracks, repairing gas lines, installing fire alarms and lighting bridges.

As has been said, the entire FERA program, including the CWA, was terminated following President Roosevelt's message of January, 1935. Unemployables were returned to the care of state and local governments and the federal government withdrew entirely from direct relief. It still assumed the responsibility of supplying work to all employables who wanted to work.

THE PUBLIC WORKS PROGRAM

The Public Works Program was authorized by Section II of the National Industrial Recovery Act, June 16, 1933. Secretary of the Interior, Harold I. Ickes, was made Public Works Administrator. The states were grouped into ten regions, each with a regional director. Each state had a non-partisan board of three members and an engineer administrator, all appointed by the President. The total personnel of the agency numbered 11,000, including 170 attorneys, 1000 engineers, 80 finance examiners, 800 accountants, and 225 special agents. There were legal, engineering, and financial departments of the Administrative Board at Washington, and a special Labor Board of Review and a Division of Investigations to iron out any labor troubles which might arise, and to prevent corruption and graft. The state boards sent their recommendations to Washington for approval until June, 1935, when the system was decentralized.

Three problems confronted the Public Works Administration from the first: labor, types of projects, and legal obstacles. It was decided that, before a project would be approved, it must be socially useful, sound from an engineering standpoint, an aid to the revival of industry, and provide immediate work for the unemployed. The difficult task was not to find projects which met these requirements but to overcome an inherent defect in the program of launching public work by providing financial aid to states and municipalities. Local governments were frequently restrained from borrowing money by charter provisions or state constitutions. In many cases, there was reluctance on the part of officials or of the voters in special elections to participate because it was felt that no further debt burdens should be incurred. Under Title II of the National Industrial Recovery Act, the Public Works Administration was permitted to make an outright contribution for non-federal public works of 30 percent of the labor and material costs and to lend, if the applicant desired, the remaining 70 percent on reasonable security. In 1934 Congress authorized the Reconstruction Finance Corporation to purchase such securities from the PWA, and authorized the PWA to use the money from such sales to make further loans. These rules applied only to funds made available from the 1933 relief appropriation of $3,300,000,000. The Emergency Relief Appropriation of 1935, amounting to $4,488,-000,000 and definitely allocating $446,000,000 to the PWA, allowed administrative determination of the federal percentage, which was fixed at 45 percent of the cost of the project. The final difficulty arose from the desire to keep wages low enough to encourage men to seek reemployment in private industry and reluctance of labor unions to consent to lower rates than those required by the rules of the craft. Title II of the National Industrial Recovery Act required a 30-hour week for all workers on PWA projects. By executive order of the President, the hours of work for all projects financed under the Emergency Relief Appropriation Act of 1935 were restricted to eight per day and 130 per month. In 1933, minimum hourly wages for skilled and unskilled labor were set at $1.20 and $.50, respectively, in the Northern Zone, $1.10 and $.45 in the Central Zone, and $1.00 and $.40 in the Southern Zone. On all contracts let after October 9, 1935, rates were to be equal to the prevailing wages in the locality where the project was located. It was estimated that for every person directly employed on PWA projects, indirect employment was provided for five persons. The 8010 non-federal projects undertaken under the Administration were estimated to have provided full time direct employment for one year to 720,000 persons and indirect employment to 3,500,000, at an annual average cost for those directly employed, in labor and material, of $2470. Of this amount $741 came from the federal government and the remainder from other sources. Before the end of the fiscal year 1935–1936, the Public Works Administration had carried out projects costing $2,410,828,000. Of this sum $711,337,000 came from the 1933 appropriation; $579,703,000 from the 1935 appropriation; $395,418,-000 from the sale of collateral securities; and $723,369,000 from the contributions of local governments. To this amount was added $300,000,000 by the Emergency Relief Appropriation Act of 1936. In spite of the inherent difficulties in the program and the steady decline in its prestige among administrative agencies, the Public Works Administration accomplished an amazing amount of construction work, including 883 sewer projects, 1497 waterworks, 23 garbage disposal plants, 263 hospitals, 741 street and highway projects, 166 bridges and viaducts, 32 railroad improvements, and 70 municipal power plants. In addition, $238,000,000 went for naval construction; $25,000,000 to the Coast Guard; $3,000,000 to the Bureau of Air Commerce; $15,000,000 to the Army and Navy Air Service; $8,000,000 to Public Health Work; $241,000,000 for sewage disposal and filtration plants; $125,000,000 to the Federal Housing Administration; $463,000,000 for secondary school, college, and university buildings; and $142,000,000 for slum clearance.

Congress had made an appropriation of $3,300,000,000 for relief work in 1933, and had delegated full authority to the President to allocate funds to various projects. In response to Roosevelt's message of January, 1935, Congress increased the new appropriation to $4,880,000,000 to make possible work relief instead of the dole. Roosevelt then (April 1) terminated the FERA and CWA, and turned all unemployables back to the states. It was impossible, however, to provide work for all unemployed under the Public Works Administration because the system was not flexible and too much of the money went into materials instead of wages. Roosevelt, therefore, set up a new agency under Hopkins, former director of FERA and CWA.

The Works Progress Administration was created by Executive Order on May 6, 1935, with Hopkins as Administrator to provide for "coordinated execution of the work relief program as a whole and for the execution of that program in such manner as to move from the relief rolls to work on such projects or into private employment the maximum number of persons in the shortest time possible." All existing work relief agencies were brought under his control. Local government units were to initiate plans for projects and these passed through the hands of the Works Progress Administrator and the Bureau of the Budget to the President. Projects were to be of two kinds: construction and non-construction. Construction projects, including highways, roads, streets, public buildings, parks, playgrounds, sewer systems and airports received 80 percent of the funds allotted before January 1, 1936. The remaining 20 percent went to non-construction projects including forestation, erosion control, sanitation, education, etc. All workers were required to be sixteen years of age, in good health and on relief during May, 1935. Placement of all workers was made by the United States Employment Service. Ninety percent of all workers had to be taken from the relief rolls and only one member of a family was to be employed. The maximum hours of work were eight per day and forty per week. The country was divided into four regions and within those regions wage scales were fixed for unskilled work, intermediate work, skilled work, and professional work and according to population centers.

By January 1, 1936, 69,152 projects had been approved at a cost of $947,732,727 to the federal government and $221,918,153 to local governments. Of these projects, 23,105 were for highways, roads and streets; 10,109 for educational work; 9,508 for public buildings; 6,256 for water supply and sewer systems; 4,892 for parks and playgrounds; 2,989 for conservation and flood control; 2,309 for sanitation and health; and 130 for electric utilities. In all, 8,500,000 persons received work at one time or another before the agency was discontinued in June, 1944.

The original FERA program had provided assistance to students in the public schools and colleges, and also education for unemployed women in camps similar to the CCC camps. In order that this form of relief might not cease when the FERA was discontinued, the National Youth Administration was established by Executive Order on June 26, 1935, as a division of the Public

Works Administration. Efforts to have it placed under the control
of the Commissioner of Education or the Department of Labor
were rejected and it was made an integral part of relief work with
Aubrey Williams, former Director of the Wisconsin Conference
for Social Work, as Executive Director. As in the case of FERA
work for students, responsibility was placed upon state and local
committees, including a personnel of 11,500 persons who served
without pay, for the administration of the work. The schools themselves were responsible for selecting students and assigning work.
In May, 1936, there was a total of 605,200 young people receiving
assistance: 6600 graduate students, 125,000 college students, 263,-
000 high school students, and 210,000 young men and women working on miscellaneous work projects. There were also 4500 young
women in camps for unemployed women. Maximum rates of pay
were $6 per month for high school students whose families were
on relief, $15 for college students, and $25 for graduate students.
Young people between the ages of sixteen and twenty-five from
relief families who were not in the above groups constituted the
210,000 on work projects under the supervision of a State Director.
These projects included community development, recreational
leadership, public service, and research. Women in camps for unemployed were receiving training for the most part in household
management. In addition, 2000 young people were apprenticed in
various crafts with the employer paying the wages. The organization cost $49,750,000 during its first year with an allocation of
$71,250,000 for the year 1936–1937. The program, from the date
of its inception under the FERA, kept thousands of young people
in school and prevented idleness and competition of young people
in the labor market.

RELIEF TO DEBTORS

The total mortgage debt of the nation in 1933 has been estimated
as high as $250,000,000,000. That part of it consisting of mortgages
on farms and city real estate and of bonded indebtedness of corporations and municipalities involved a common situation: debts con-
tracted at a time of appreciated values had to be paid with incomes

derived from depression prices and wages. One fifth of the national income in 1933 went to pay interest on debts. There was no legal escape for the debtor, no orderly procedure by which any portion of this indebtedness could be cancelled. There were the bankruptcy laws under which individuals and corporations surrendered all available assets to be liquidated at prevailing prices for the satisfaction of creditors. Corporations might go into receivership; but receiverships were, as a rule, only a more tedious route to the same destination. If there were a reorganization, the consent of all creditors must first be obtained. In such situations, real estate owners usually lost everything and the holders of mortgages frequently lost something. The same was true in the case of corporate bankruptcy. Always, however, the basis of other fortunes was laid by men who had available resources to acquire this real property at depression and forced sale prices. Municipal bondholders reaped a harvest because the real value of their interest returns rose by more than 50 percent. This inviolability of creditors' claims made it impossible to bring wages, prices, and values into proper balance at lower levels without terrific losses, and widespread injustice.

The government tried to prevent wholesale bankruptcies and loss of properties in three ways: by raising prices, by loans, and by new bankruptcy laws. Restoration of prices involved so many approaches aside from placing money in the hands of the unemployed, including devaluation of the dollar, the purchase of gold and silver, reduction of crop acreages, and limitations on industrial production, that it will be considered separately. Loans and bankruptcy laws were in the nature of direct relief to financially harassed individuals, corporations, and municipalities.

The Act creating the Reconstruction Finance Corporation had permitted it to make loans to financial institutions such as banks, trust companies, and building and loan companies, and to insurance companies and railroads. Industrial corporations could secure assistance only through the medium of a recognized, private lending agency. Something less than $4,000,000,000 thus found its way from the Reconstruction Finance Corporation to private borrowers before the end of the fiscal year 1933–1934. On June 19, 1934, a Loans-to-Industry Act was approved extending direct aid to the amount of $500,000 to any one corporation existing before January 1, 1934, and operating under the NRA codes. These loans were not to run for more than five years, the borrowing corporations must be financially sound and must show reasonable assurance of being able to bolster the labor market by virtue of the loans. The loans were to be made by the Reconstruction Finance Corporation from a revolving fund consisting of $300,000,000 of its own funds and $280,000,000 supplied by the Federal Reserve banks. First mortgages on real property, chattels, and accounts receivable were to constitute acceptable collateral.

The Agricultural Adjustment Act, approved on May 12, 1933, included an amendment to the original Farm Loan Act, authorizing the Federal Land Banks to issue 4 percent farm-loan bonds worth $2,000,000,000, and to use them in refinancing farm mortgages up to 50 percent of the value of the land and 20 percent of the value of permanent improvements. The government guaranteed the payment of interest on these bonds. Under the provisions of the law foreclosure proceedings could be suspended, by appeals to the Courts, while negotiations were pending.

A *Home Owners' Refinancing Act* (June 13, 1933) established a corporation with a capital of $200,000,000 and authority to issue bonds worth $2,000,000,000. The home owner might liquidate outstanding indebtedness, even if in default for two years, borrowing on a first mortgage from the corporation at 5 percent, the principal and interest to be amortized over a 15-year period. The act made it possible for banks, loaded with unsalable real estate, to exchange defaulted mortgages for government-guaranteed bonds. More than 1,000,000 homes were thus saved to their owners, and $225,000,000 in previously uncollectable taxes poured into the depleted treasuries of local government units. Since loans, secured by almost unlimited credit, could not entirely take care of liquidating excessively high debts, the government enacted three new bankruptcy laws in the spring of 1934. The Municipal Bankruptcy Act, May 24, 1934, made it possible for local government units to go into the federal courts on approval of the owners of 51 percent of their bonds with a petition for readjustment of their debts. The courts might approve any plan thus devised with the consent of only two-thirds of the bondholders, providing they held at least 75 percent of the outstanding obligations.

The Corporate Bankruptcy Act, June 7, 1934, permitted a corporation to go into court and petition for a reorganization under the jurisdiction of the court. Such reorganization could be completed with the consent of only two-thirds of the creditors. It eliminated costly receivers' fees by limiting them to the amount received by Federal Referees in Bankruptcy.

The Frazier-Lemke Farm Bankruptcy Act, June 28, 1934, was more detailed. A Federal District Judge could provide for an appraisal of a mortgaged farm. The owner of the farm then had to pay the principal of the newly appraised valuation within six years, meanwhile taking care of the taxes and making a one percent annual payment on the principal. If the creditors did not agree to this procedure, the court could order a five-year suspension of foreclosure proceedings, during which time the debtor was to pay a fair rental on the appraised valuation. This appraised valuation had to be liquidated within five years, otherwise a new appraisal could be demanded by any creditor. The purpose of the act was to stop foreclosures until government action or a return to normal conditions had provided a permanent solution of the mortgage problem.

DEVALUING THE DOLLAR

The government, recognizing that people could not be put back to work by private industry until prices had been restored to profit-making levels, not only bolstered consumers' purchasing power by aid to the unemployed, and extended long-term loans through the RFC to banks, home owners, corporations, and municipalities, but embarked upon an inflation of currency and credit. Recovery by deflation, government economy, wage cutting, and bankruptcy had failed. Deflation apparently had no bottom and all values were in danger of being swept away when the banking crisis forced drastic action upon the incoming administration. President Roosevelt issued his proclamation closing all banks within twenty-four hours after taking the oath of office. Four days later

(March 9), Congress passed the Banking and Gold Control Act sent to it by the President and, on March 16, the Agricultural Adjustment Act which included certain financial provisions. In his message submitting the Banking and Gold Control Act Roosevelt said:

In order that the first objective—the opening of banks for the resumption of business—may be accomplished, I ask of the Congress the immediate enactment of legislation giving to the executive branch of the government control over banks for the protection of depositors; authority forthwith to open such banks as rapidly as possible and authority to reorganize and re-open such banks as may be found to require reorganization to put them on a sound basis. I ask amendments to the Federal Reserve Act to provide for such additional currency, adequately secured, as it may become necessary to issue to meet all demands for currency and at the same time to achieve this end without increasing the unsecured indebtedness of the government of the United States.

The Emergency Banking and Gold Control Act provided that banks belonging to the Federal Reserve System could reopen when their condition had been determined and licenses had been issued by the Treasury Department. Those found to be insolvent were to be placed under "Conservators" for restricted operation or liquidation. The Treasury was authorized to capture all gold and gold certificates; the Reconstruction Finance Corporation to subscribe to the capital stock of banks and trust companies; and the Federal Reserve Banks to issue notes to member banks to a maximum of 100 percent on government bonds and 90 percent on other assets, and to make private loans on government bonds as collateral. Under this act many banks were allowed to open which later on were forced to close again. The reason was probably not one of haste or laxity in judging their financial condition, but rather leniency upon the assumption that the general price level could be raised by other anticipated measures—something which the Administration failed to accomplish.

By successive proclamations on March 10, April 5, and April 19, President Roosevelt took the country off the gold standard and ordered all private holdings of gold surrendered to the Federal Reserve banks. The Agricultural Adjustment Act of May 12 gave him discretionary power to do one or all of five things: (1) to replace government bonds worth $3,000,000,000 with paper currency having only the good faith of the government as security; (2) reduce the gold content of the dollar to a minimum of 50 percent; (3) accept a maximum of $200,000,000 worth of silver in war debt payments at not more than 50 cents an ounce; (4) re-establish bimetallism at whatever ratio seemed desirable; and (5) compel the Federal Reserve System to put $3,000,000,000 of government securities in the open market.

Congress thus placed discretionary power in the hands of the President instead of taking positive action for currency inflation. It enabled Roosevelt's financial advisers to try an entirely new experiment in government finance: that of raising prices by forcing down the value of the dollar in terms of gold and then keeping the dollar at a fixed exchange value by maintaining a fluctuating gold content. The government then devalued the dollar by decreeing a higher price for gold than the old $20.67 per ounce. The purpose was to allow all gold to flow into the Federal Reserve banks and to seize it under the right of eminent domain, thus giving to the government the profits accruing from revaluation.

23

An Experiment in Industrial Democracy

AGRICULTURE

HAVING considered the one really effective measure designed to rebuild the price structure and eventually to bring prices into proper balance by raising those which had not been artificially maintained, and the various measures which served to restore confidence and tide the unemployed over the period of distress, we must turn to those two measures which were designed to stabilize industry and restore the purchasing power of the farmers. The direct and immediate restoration of prices was attempted by the crop curtailment provisions of the Agricultural Adjustment Act and by certain provisions of the National Industrial Recovery Act. Both measures were intentionally limited in duration to a two-year period and quotas of production were subject to revision because over-production existed only in the sense of depleted consumer purchasing power. It is from the additional reform aspects of the two acts, however, that their proper place in history must be considered.

We must remember that the depression in agriculture began immediately after World War I and that during the 1920s relief was sought through the subsidy schemes of the McNary-Haugen bill. The next subsidy scheme to gain favor was the domestic allotment plan. This device originated with Walter J. Spillman of the Department of Agriculture. Professor John D. Black of Harvard University, Professor N. L. Wilson of Montana State College,

Secretary Henry A. Wallace of the Department of Agriculture and Chairman Henry I. Harriman of the United States Chamber of Commerce assisted in its development. It was first introduced into Congress as the Jones Bill and enacted, May 12, 1933, as an Act to Relieve the Existing National Emergency by Increasing Agricultural Purchasing Power, and is generally known as the Agricultural Adjustment Act. It had the endorsement of more than thirty leading farmers' organizations. The purpose of the act was to restore the exchange value of farm produce to its 1914 parity with other commodities. The farmers' purchasing power had fallen so far that the Department of Agriculture estimated it was responsible for the unemployment of 4,000,000 men in the cities, a fairly conservative statement in view of the fact that the rural market normally consumed one-fourth of the goods and services in the nation. This restoration of purchasing power was to be accomplished under the direction of the Secretary of Agriculture, a distinct departure from all previous schemes for solving the agricultural problem. An Agricultural Adjustment Administration was set up within the Department of Agriculture and divided into two divisions, one for production control and the other for regulation of processing and marketing. The act provided for voluntary reduction of crop acreage of basic agricultural commodities: wheat, cotton, corn, hogs, rice, tobacco, and milk, all of which had fallen to exceptionally low prices, had large exportable surpluses, and required processing before consumption. This reduction was to be accomplished by contracts, voluntarily agreed to, between the government and the individual farmer, the farmer reducing his acreage by a specified amount for a consideration or subsidy in cash from the government. The Secretary of Agriculture was given discretionary power to specify what use was to be made of land thus taken out of production. The money for such subsidies was to be raised through processing taxes and thus passed on to the consumer. This program aimed to do for the farmer what the manufacturers had already done for themselves by reducing production 48.7 percent in four years. The farmer meanwhile, by choice or by drought, had reduced production by less than five percent.

Under the administration of this act, state committees were created to assign quotas of production to the several counties and county committees to assign quotas to individual farmers, with no power except public opinion to force any farmer to join in the program. The quotas were based upon the average production over the preceding five years, and the individual farmer received from the government 42 cents per bushel of wheat to the amount of his quota, 5 cents per pound for cotton, 4 cents for tobacco and 2 cents for hogs. To meet these payments, a $1,000,000,000 processing tax —amounting to a sales tax—was imposed of 30 cents per bushel on wheat, 4.2 cents per pound on cotton, etc. The cotton agreements were entered into first with 1,000,000 growers, controlling 73 percent of the cotton acreage. They plowed under 10,000,000 acres, thus reducing the prospective crop by an estimated 4,400,-000 bales. In return, the government paid them $112,000,000 and the value of their cotton crop increased from $425,488,000 in 1932 to $857,000,000 in 1933. Contracts were also signed with 550,000 wheat growers, controlling 77 percent of the acreage. The government paid them $95,000,000 and the value of their crop increased from $169,000,000 in 1932 to $376,000,000 in 1933. In the case of hogs, the government purchased more than 7,000,000 pigs and brood sows, had them processed and either distributed the pork for emergency relief or destroyed it. The net result of the Agricultural Adjustment Administration's activities at the end of the first year was an increase in the farmer's total income of 38 percent and in his purchasing power of 25 percent. Not satisfied with results achieved in the control of cotton, Congress passed the Bankhead Cotton Control Act on April 21, 1934, which placed a prohibitive tax of one-half the prevailing market price upon all cotton offered for ginning by a grower in excess of his assigned quota. There was no mystery about the reason for doing this. Inspired by higher prices to return to independent production, about one-half the cotton growers indicated an intention to refrain from signing contracts for acreage reduction and to increase production. The Bankhead Act was designed to save the system from collapse.

It represented a radical departure from the principle of the original Agricultural Adjustment Act in that it introduced the element of compulsion into the system. The 1934 crop, therefore, was reduced to less than 10,000,000 bales and the price rose to 13 cents per pound, exactly double the price of 1932. This gave the farmer more money for his crops than he had previously received for 14,000,000 bales, plus $117,000,000 in benefit payments. The government also made direct loans to cotton growers, through the Commodity Credit Corporation of 10 cents per pound on the 1933–34 crop, 12 cents on the 1934–35 crop and 9 cents per pound on the 1935–36 crop. If the price advanced beyond the amount of the loan, the excess went to the farmer. If it did not rise, the government retained the cotton. This amounted to pegging the price of cotton above the world market price. The market price in 1933–34 was such that farmers were able to sell their crop and reimburse the government; but the 12-cent loan in 1934–35 left the government with a carry-over of nearly 4,000,000 bales. That and the belief by many that the South could compete in world markets with 10-cent cotton accounted for the reduction to loans of 9 cents per pound in 1935–36.

In spite of its widespread benefits to the agricultural producers, there was much opposition to the program and weighty arguments against its continuance. There was no question of its effectiveness with respect to crop reduction, and there was good reason for millions of acres of submarginal land being taken out of production. Moreover, it did not subsidize exports to further intensify the world trade war; and it made adequate provision for financing. But there was difficulty in effecting an equitable assignment of quotas and certain to be complications from the revision of quotas and from the increase in production by non-participating producers. It placed a heavy sales tax upon the consumer in urban communities for the benefit of the farmer. Between the tariffs on manufactured goods and the processing taxes, the consumer was in a difficult position. The reductions of crop acreage benefited some farmers but worked untold hardship upon the men who made their living on the railways, in the warehouses, on the wharves and upon the tenant farmers and agricultural laborers. In many sections of the South, the effect upon the cotton sharecropper was disastrous. There was normally a total of 1,500,000 sharecroppers whose position was little better than that of peons. The retirement of cotton acreage drove so many of them off the land as to add nearly 1,000,000 people to the relief rolls. The program likewise worked hardship upon those classes of agricultural producers who depended upon other crops for their raw materials. Poultry raisers and dairy men suffered most.

Moreover, as the United States reduced its acreage, particularly of wheat and cotton, other nations increased theirs to the highest levels in history. The Agricultural Adjustment program did not provide any methods by which foreign markets, lost through the international tariff and currency war, could be regained. The share of the United States in world trade had decreased from 14 to 10 percent, and Great Britain displaced the United States in 1933 as the leading nation for the first time since 1913. This decline in world trade was a major factor in the unemployment situation, Secretary Henry Wallace estimating that 7,000,000 persons were normally engaged in export services. Pegging the price of cotton above the world market price caused Brazil alone to increase her crop from 300,000 to 1,000,000 bales, to the particular injury of Texas which had been exporting 90 percent of her crop annually. Secretary Wallace, perfectly cognizant of that aspect of the situation, said: "Unless ways can be found to increase America's exports, the recovery of cotton exports on a permanent basis is doubtful." In his *America Must Choose*, he predicted that a program of self-containment would require the retirement from production of 50,000,000 acres of land. Finally, there existed considerable doubt, based upon scientific observation, whether there really was such a thing as over-production; whether surpluses had not accumulated because of improper distribution and a subnormal standard of living on the part of a considerable portion of the population. Certainly, the destruction of foodstuffs, including the dumping of more than $300,000 worth of pork into the Mississippi River at one time, was nothing but criminal waste; and, at a time when 15,000,000 families were dependent on public and private charity for the bare necessities of life, was not conducive to general approval of the scarcity theory.

In the midst of the trial period of the Agricultural Adjustment Administration's program, a drought of the first magnitude—the worst since 1894—occurred in the West. Millions of acres of crops were burned out completely and in some states benefit payments for acreage reduction were all the returns the farmers received for the year's income. Crop reduction and the drought combined added nearly 1,000,000 farm families to the relief rolls. The drought made the Administration's efforts at crop reduction appear feeble indeed. The hog reduction program had killed some 6,000,000 of the 82,000,000 unfattened pigs in 1933 and corn acreage was reduced 20 percent by contract agreements. The drought reduced the corn crop to less than 50 percent of the anticipated yield in 1934. It killed off by starvation 16 percent of the cattle and about 20,000,-000 swine, or 30 percent of the total, reducing the number in the country to nearly 8,000,000 less than the anticipated number under the AAA control program. There was not, and probably never will be, agreement as to whether acreage reduction, the drought, or inflation of currency and credit was most responsible for increasing the price of farm products. In view of the fact that the farmer's percentage of the national income had dropped from 18 in 1919 to 7 in 1932 and that the increase between 1933 and 1934 gave them an added 25 percent purchasing power, some credit must go to the acreage reduction program.

On January 6, 1936, the Supreme Court by a six to three decision declared the Agricultural Adjustment Act invalid (*United States v. Butler*). It was held to be an invasion of the reserved rights of the states. The Court said further: "Congress has no power to enforce its commands on the farmer to the ends sought by the Agricultural Adjustment Act. It must follow that it may not indirectly accomplish those ends by taxing and spending to purchase compliance." The minority opinion, written by Justice Harlan F. Stone, replied to this argument by saying, "It is a contradiction in terms to say that there is power to spend for the general welfare, while rejecting any power to impose conditions reasonably adapted to the attainment of the end which alone would justify the expenditure." The decision clearly pointed the way to invalidation of the Bankhead Act and Congress repealed it shortly afterward. It immediately put an end to the collection of processing taxes, but left the government obligated to fulfill its contracts with the farmers totalling an unpaid balance of about $500,000,000. It freed the Administration and the country from an institution which was devised as an emergency measure and which never had the full endorsement even of its Administrator, Secretary Wallace; one which had already created so much of a vested interest that there was extreme doubt of the ability of Congress ever to abolish it. The processing taxes had been regarded as a subsidy to agriculture for the purpose of equalizing the injustices of the tariff subsidies to manufacturers. Neither the tax nor the subsidy, according to the provisions of the law, were to go beyond the point of raising the exchange value of farm produce to 1909–1914 levels. It had accomplished about 85 percent of its objective before being invalidated, but only by reduction of crops and completely destroying the purchasing power of many people formerly a part of the agricultural industry. That the government would have encountered resistance to the abandonment of a measure which was clearly designed to meet an emergency, was shown by the haste with which a substitute program was devised.

The action of the Court left the farm problem exactly where it was in 1933, with the choice of reverting to cutthroat competition among 6,500,000 producers or devising a new formula for collective regimentation. A new law, known as the Soil Conservation and Domestic Allotment Act, was devised within a week and passed by Congress within two months after the Agricultural Adjustment Act was declared unconstitutional. It sought to regulate production indirectly through soil conservation, and by so doing to preserve and improve soil fertility, prevent erosion, and control floods. It also sought to re-establish the ratio between the purchasing power of farmers and non-farmers which prevailed between 1909 and 1914. It provided for state Agricultural Adjustment Administrations to be financed by federal subsidies. Until the several states established these administrative bodies, if ever, the federal government was to continue to subsidize the farmers from the general funds of the Treasury through payments for planting soil conservation crops. It was an application to agriculture of the established principle of grants to states for roads, schools, etc. It was intended to be a permanent institution, and gave the Secretary of Agriculture wide discretionary power in the spending of an authorized $500,-000,000 annually.

Once the Supreme Court had been reorganized, as will be revealed later, Congress enacted a new Agricultural Adjustment Act in February, 1938. This supplemented the Soil Conservation and Domestic Allotment Act and provided a comprehensive program under the Agricultural Adjustment Administration, including acreage allotments, soil conservation payments, parity payments to meet any differences between market and parity prices, an Ever-Normal Granary, and marketing quotas. The program was administered through county and community farmer committees, and farmers themselves had a voice in the formulation of policies. Cotton, corn, wheat, rice, and tobacco—staple crops which were sensitive to world price fluctuations—were included in the program. Acreage allotments were designed to control surpluses. If surpluses were produced, commodity loans were designed to keep them on the farms and off the market. Finally, two-thirds of the producers of any commodity could approve marketing quotas with a penalty attached to control surpluses which might develop in spite of acreage allotments and commodity loans. The program was to be financed by congressional appropriations. It not only raised the income of farmers by enormous amounts and stabilized agricultural economy, but provided, as of July, 1940, stored surpluses of 168,000,000 bushels of wheat, 447,000,000 bushels of corn, and 8,825,000 bales of cotton, all held under loans of 63 cents per bushel, 57 cents per bushel, and 9.3 cents per pound, respectively.

INDUSTRY

The National Industrial Recovery Act of June 16, 1933, may not be the most important single piece of legislation in Congressional history, but it is certainly one of the most interesting. In some respects, it was a legislative monstrosity. It combined two acts in one: (1) the Public Works program, which was a relief and recovery measure; and (2) the industrial control section, which was both a recovery measure and the most sweeping reform measure ever enacted in the nation's history. There was, and still remains, much confusion of thought about the act because the administration of the industrial control section was called incorrectly the National Recovery Administration. Neither the economic setting, the philosophy of its sponsors, nor the administration of the act justify any such limited interpretation as the name implies.

The National Industrial Recovery Act intended (1) to legalize those voluntary trade associations which President Hoover had encouraged by removing the restraints of the anti-trust laws; (2) to make them effective by bringing the recalcitrants into line through compulsion; but (3) to bestow these privileges upon trade and industry in return for an acknowledgment of their social responsibility in the form of concessions to labor and the consumer. In short, the act recognized the fact that competition had neither been preserved nor restored, repudiated the idea of organized cartels without control in the public interest, and sought to compose differences within the associations, bring them into harmony with the interests of society, and thus institute permanent economic stability. In doing this, it was intended to bring to a final settlement the two most vexing problems in modern economic history: that of the right of labor to organize and bargain collectively; and the efforts of the state government under the police powers and the federal government under the interstate commerce and taxing powers to end child labor, establish minimum wages, limit hours of labor, and control in the interest of social security the exploitation of women in industry.

The act was born in the midst of confusion. A dark pall of disaster had settled over the country. Fifteen million people were out of work and purchasing power had all but been destroyed by price and wage cutting, part-time employment, public and private economies. People who had money were hoarding it and people who had employment were living in daily fear of being discharged. Cities were facing complete bankruptcy, farms were being sold by the thousands, millions of people were being dispossessed of their homes, factories and banks were closed. Low wages, long hours, tragic waste, were the order of the day, particularly in industries like coal and oil. Steel plants, automobile factories, and innumerable other industries touched an all-time low in volume of production. Manufacturing and trade were in chaos as individual units sought to save themselves by cutthroat competition of the worst sort. Voluntary trade associations were helpless and labor was in danger of losing the gains of a half century of progress. Labor and industry both were clamoring for some sort of emergency relief and the National Industrial Recovery Act was the result.

The act was approved on June 16, 1933. The first section, dealing with industrial control, stated in its declaration of policy:

A national emergency productive of widespread unemployment and disorganization of industry, which burdens interstate and foreign commerce, affects the public welfare, and undermines the standards of living of the American people, is hereby declared to exist. It is hereby declared to be the policy of Congress to remove obstructions to the free flow of interstate and foreign commerce which tend to diminish the amount thereof; and to provide for the general welfare by promoting the organization of industry for the purpose of cooperative action among trade groups, to induce and maintain united action of labor and management under adequate governmental sanctions and supervision, to eliminate unfair competitive practices, to promote the fullest possible utilization of the present productive capacity of industries, to avoid undue restriction of production (except as may be temporarily required), to increase the consumption of industrial and agricultural products by increasing purchasing power, to reduce and relieve unemployment, to improve standards of labor, and otherwise to rehabilitate industry and to conserve natural resources.

The act provided (1) that codes of fair competition were to be written for each trade or industrial association, either by the President or such agents as he might designate, or by the association itself with presidential approval; (2) that no codes were to be approved which created monopolies or which failed to comply with the labor provisions of the act; (3) that the anti-trust laws were suspended with respect to any action taken in conformity with the codes; and (4) that the President might require licenses for producers in any industry where necessity demanded. This was the device for bringing recalcitrants into line, and it provided $500 fines and six months' imprisonment for each violation.

The significance of the first provision lay in the fact that the making of laws intimately affecting the lives and fortunes of the

people, and the violation of which was a criminal offense, was delegated by Congress to the President, by the President to Administrator General Hugh S. Johnson, and by Johnson to private citizens
sitting as members of the code authorities. The second provision
was already violated before it was written. It was humanly impossible for the Administrator, any other man or single group of
men, to have written the nearly 500 codes before the expiration
of the act. The mere detail of assembling representatives of the
several trades and industries would have been impossible had not
the associations fostered by Hoover's large staff of experts during
the twenties already been in existence. The codes were written by
associations themselves, by their legal talent which was well versed
in the art of evading the anti-trust laws, and the monopolistic
practices brought to light by the codes were already practised arts
before the law was written. In most cases the codes were little
more than the existing trade association agreements and, in some
cases, they were exact copies of such agreements.

The suspension of the anti-trust laws was equally interesting.
They had been enforced during the Harding-Coolidge-Hoover
regime only through the indirect force of advisory opinions from
the Attorney-General's office. They were to be enforced under the
NRA only by the opinion of the NRA Administrator as evidenced
by his willingness to approve the provisions of a particular code.
Nothing in the act, however, forbade appeals to the Federal Trade
Commission by aggrieved individuals and numerous appeals were
made. The licensing provision provided the teeth of the act. In
practice, the government exercised as little compulsion as possible.
Administrator Johnson conceived the idea of issuing to all firms
complying with the provisions of the codes an insignia consisting
of a blue eagle which they might display in their places of business
and on their products as evidence of cooperation. It had no legal
significance, but its absence was an invitation to the public to boycott the producer's goods. Public opinion never rallied to its support
and Henry Ford's refusal to display it led to its early disuse. In
addition to the right of prosecution under the licensing provisions
of the act and the power to deprive violators of their blue eagles,
the government might seek the assistance of the courts by apply-

ing for injunctions and it might institute proceedings through the agency of the Federal Trade Commission.

To administer the law, President Roosevelt established the National Recovery Administration with General Hugh S. Johnson the first Administrator and Donald Richberg his successor. He was provided with an assistant for industry, one for labor, a General Counsel and an Economic Advisor. There were eight divisional Administrators for preparing and administering the codes: (1) mining, utilities, automobiles, rubber and shipping; (2) lumber and machinery; (3) chemicals, leather and construction; (4) textiles; (5) amusements and services; (6) foodstuffs and agricultural products; (7) publishing and graphic arts; and (8) miscellaneous. There was an Industrial Advisory Board, a Consumer Advisory Board, a Labor Advisory Board, and a National Compliance Board. There were deputy administrators and code authorities for each trade and industry under the Divisional Administrators. There were state and local compliance boards, public relations boards and code review boards. Finally, the National Labor Board was created to enforce the right of collective bargaining. The system was made to function within a few months, partly because of the indefatigable labors of General Hugh S. Johnson, partly because too little time was allowed for hearings on the codes before they were put into force, but largely because associations already in existence drew up their own codes and merely submitted them for approval.

The original purpose of the act was to establish a tri-partite administration of the industrial system by management, labor, and the government. The anti-trust laws were suspended to enable cooperation, industrial coordination, and unified planning. Management, in return, was to recognize labor's right of collective bargaining, agree to certain minimum standards of wages, hours, and working conditions. Government, in turn, was to force compliance by all the units of industry and trade. Many Congressmen of both parties, who still professed belief in the ideal of competition under the anti-trust laws, denounced their suspension. Senator William E. Borah said: "We will have the steel industry, the drug industry and the different industries of the United States meeting and combining for the purpose of formulating a code, the great objective of which will be to fix prices." When President Roosevelt approved the act, he said:

The aim of this whole effort is to restore our rich domestic market by raising its vast consuming capacity. If we now inflate prices as fast and as far as we increase wages, the whole project will be set at naught. We cannot hope for the full effect of this plan unless, in these first critical months, and even at the expense of full initial profits, we defer price increases as long as possible.

It soon became apparent that the fears of Borah, President Roosevelt and others were well-founded. Congress, which had never been able to frame laws for the regulation of transportation and utilities in the interest of consumers, presumed too much on the sweet reasonableness of management and the strength of a liberal administration when it expected the whole of industry to sacrifice profits to a better balance between prices and wages. Industry was perfectly willing to shorten hours and increase wages, but it insisted upon raising prices too—and faster than it raised wages. It succeeded in doing so in writing the codes in spite of the fact that a Consumers Advisory Board was appointed, consisting of Mrs. Mary Rumsey of New York, President Frank Graham of the University of North Carolina, Mrs. Joseph J. Daniels of Indianapolis, and Mrs. Belle Sherwins, president of the National League of Women Voters. In many cases, too, labor was as intransigent as management. There were too many instances such as Harvey C. Fremming of the Oil Workers Union refusing to serve on the Labor Advisory Board for the oil industry unless the American Federation of Labor were empowered to name the other two labor representatives. Finally, the government not only went too far in attempting to place all industry under code authorities and in permitting price-fixing provisions to be written into the codes, but Administrator Johnson made the mistake of attempting to inspire boycotts against industrialists like Henry Ford who, for one reason or another, refused to display the blue eagle insignia.

The original intention of a tripartite administration was violated in the most important part of the program: the drawing up of the codes. Most of the code authorities consisted solely of representatives of the trade associations. They did agree to the establishment of a forty-hour week, to minimum wages of between 12 and 15 dollars per week and to the elimination of child labor. Those provisions were written into virtually all codes. They straightway violated the spirit of the law's collective bargaining provision, however, and sought to turn it to their own advantage by organizing company unions. The law specifically forbade "monopolies and monopolistic practices," but existing monopolies were retained and others were created. This was partly due to the physical impossibility of directing the mass of detail involved in organizing the codes; to the complex problems of policy involving an interpretation of the law; and to the existence of the system during such a short emergency period that decentralization of responsibility and of the several administrative functions was never carried out.

The lack of compliance was due largely, however, to giving voting control in the code authorities to the large producers, who concealed their war against independents behind fixed prices, wages, and production quotas. The steel industry, for instance, re-established in its code the basing point system by which shipping costs from distant factories were added to the price of steel produced and sold locally. This practice had been outlawed by the Federal Trade Commission in 1924. The Commission, after examining the code, reported that a complete monopoly had been re-established in violation of the Sherman Act, the Clayton Act, and previous orders of the Commission. Much difficulty was encountered from provisions prohibiting sales below cost. In determining costs, efficient and inefficient producers were lumped together to strike an average. It was impossible to average overhead costs at a time of depression or to determine a fair price for raw materials purchased at different times. In spite of these facts, open price-fixing provisions were written into more than one-half of the codes. Prices of commodities produced in these industries rose, in 1934, to 23 percent above 1929 levels. Many codes curtailed output by limiting the hours per week during which machinery could be kept in operation and by assigning quotas of production to particular plants. Others forbade the purchase of new machinery or the expansion of plant facilities. The rayon, hosiery and textile codes limited the working hours of machinery. The rayon, cement and ice codes forbade machine replacements. The oil and lumber codes assigned production quotas. All of these provisions gave new life to the old monopolies, increased living costs, and retarded consumption. Violations of the codes soon became so frequent that enforcement was not even attempted.

Before the end of 1933, it became apparent that the National Recovery Administration was a failure. An open forum was held in Washington to which any one was welcome who had a grievance. Price-fixing was denounced at these hearings by representatives of the chain stores and mail order houses, government purchasing agents, the Farm Bureau Federation, and the League of Women Voters. Trade association executives favored its retention; but, even among businessmen, price-fixing of products in other industries than their own was frowned upon. Reports by the Consumers Advisory Board, by the Federal Trade Commission and by the Brookings Institution further convinced the country that the system was a failure. The purpose of the act, as stated in the preamble, "to promote the fullest possible utilization of the present productive capacity of industries, to avoid undue restriction of production, to increase the consumption of industrial and agricultural products," had been defeated by price-fixing, the protection of monopolies, and restrictions upon production. The Brookings Institution report placed emphasis upon under-consumption rather than overproduction as the cause of the country's ills. A report by a committee headed by Clarence Darrow blamed the repeal of the anti-trust laws for the creation of monopolies and advocated a system of state socialism. The other reports placed emphasis upon the evils of price-fixing.

Liquidation of the NRA began in less than one year after the passage of the act. Its most complete failure had been in the service trades such as barbers, cleaners, and automobiles. President Roosevelt ordered abandonment of the codes in these trades in May, 1934. These industries were almost entirely local in nature and not a part of interstate commerce. They were given permission to establish local codes by retaining the provisions of their former codes relating to hours and wages. These local agreements could be arranged by 85 percent of the members of a particular industry.

Those who refused to join in the agreement were to be turned over to the mercies of an outraged public opinion by being deprived of their blue eagles. The next step in the liquidation process was taken by the Supreme Court. In the case of *Panama Refining Co. v. Ryan* (1933) it invalidated Section 9c of the National Industrial Recovery Act. This was a separate and distinct part of the act which gave the President, among other things, the power "to prohibit the transportation in interstate and foreign commerce of petroleum and the products thereof produced or withdrawn from storage in excess of the amount permitted to be produced or withdrawn from storage by any state law. . . ." The Supreme Court did not raise the fundamental question of whether Congress could regulate production under the Commerce Clause, but it denied the right of Congress to delegate unlimited legislative power to the Executive branch of the government. It condemned both branches of the government for failure to make declarations of policy and establish rules. On that point, it said: "Both Section 9c and the executive orders are in notable contrast with historic practice by which declarations of policy are made by the Congress and delegations are within the framework of that policy and have relation to facts and conditions to be formed and stated by the President in the appropriate exercise of the delegated authority." The third step was the resignation of Administrator Johnson and the elevation to that post of Donald Richberg from the position of General Counsel.

Meanwhile a sharp attack was made upon the system by the liberal forces in the 1934 Congress. Senators William E. Borah and Gerald P. Nye led in denouncing it as having retarded recovery, embittered relations between capital and labor, raised prices to the consumer, and failed to solve the problem of unemployment. They demanded that it be completely abandoned or drastically modified. The attack was not a partisan one, but came from liberals throughout the nation who recognized some virtue in the experiment. They believed that such achievements as minimum wages, abolition of child labor, etc., could be retained in some other way. This school of thought was that of Theodore Roosevelt, of Woodrow Wilson, and of Justice Brandeis. It believed that business and industry should be decentralized and kept that way by strict regulations; that competition could be restored. It was opposed to the new theory of a planned economy.

Administrator Richberg immediately declared for a radical change in policy which, if it had been carried through, would have eliminated price-fixing devices from all codes and placed codes on an entirely voluntary basis. It would have segregated the extractive industries into a special group and permitted cooperative planning to prevent waste of natural resources. All others would have been returned to a competitive basis under the anti-trust laws. It would have withdrawn the government from all participation in labor disputes. Finally, it would have sought some new way to prevent unsocial practices in business. President Roosevelt asked Congress, in February, 1935, to extend the National Industrial Recovery Act for another two years. His message contained a frank admission of its many failures and claimed for it many accomplishments. He admitted that it had fostered monopoly practices and sometimes worked hardships upon small producers; but insisted that these were more than outweighed by the elimination of child labor, and of unethical practices in competition, and by gains in wages, collective bargaining, and re-employment. He suggested that the system be placed on a voluntary basis and that price-fixing be abolished. His statement that "incorrigible minorities within an industry should not be allowed to write the rules of unfair play and compel all others to compete upon their low level" was a concise explanation of why trade and industrial associations had been formed originally. His further statement that "we must make certain that the privilege of cooperating to prevent unfair competition will not be transformed into license to strangle fair competition under the apparent sanction of law, or work to the oppression of small industries" explained equally well why the trade associations of the twenties were intolerable without government regulation.

In Congress, and in the nation at large, there was strong opposition to continuing even a revamped law. Sentiment in favor of its extension was equally strong. Business and industrial groups, of course, were heartily in favor of preserving code authorities rather than returning to the enforcement of the anti-trust laws by the

Federal Trade Commission. Self-regulation had been their own idea and the Chamber of Commerce reported 1508 of its members favored its continuation with only 420 opposed. The coal, oil, and textile industries had benefited so greatly that they viewed a return to competition with genuine alarm. The durable goods industries, hard-boiled to the last, wanted to continue price-fixing by code authorities with a minimum of representation for labor and consumer groups. In short, they clung to the theory of high prices and low wages which had been the country's undoing. Those liberals who supported the extension of the law had ample justification for their position. They felt that it had served a useful purpose as an emergency measure. Restriction of production had prevented those industries able to do so from piling up huge surpluses at depression wage and price levels, and thus had served to stabilize recovery when the banking and hoarding crisis had passed. It had given employment to at least 3,000,000 people. President Roosevelt placed the number at 4,000,000. It had increased the total annual returns to wage-earners by $3,000,000,000.

The psychological effect of the inauguration of the system had been good. The country at large was certainly better informed on social and economic questions than it had been previously; and people were more cognizant of economic ills which needed to be corrected. Child labor and sweat shops had been eradicated. Labor had made great gains in organization. Others denied that these things were true. They claimed that more than 40 percent of all employees in coded industries were working more than 40 hours per week and that 10 percent were working more than 48 hours. They denied that child labor had been eradicated and pointed to continued exploitation by newspapers and in agriculture as evidence. The Brookings Institution report went so far as to deny that the codes had stimulated employment or raised wages; and insisted that, on the contrary, they had retarded re-employment and lowered the aggregate returns of labor. About all that can be said, as between the two assumptions, is that the millions of statistics can can be used to prove anything.

The two questions before Congress were (1) whether the system could be simplified in such a way as to correct its weaknesses, and

(2) whether any action should be taken before the Supreme Court
had passed upon the disputed constitutionality of the original act.
Meanwhile, the Schechter Case was on its way through the courts.
Those constitutional lawyers who believed in the letter of the law
and the inflexibility of the Constitution, led by Congressman
James M. Beck of Philadelphia, had denounced the act as contrary
both to the letter and the spirit of the Constitution from the day
of its enactment. This group held the theory of emergency to be,
as Beck expressed it, "the most dangerous legal heresy that could
be invented." On the other hand, there was a not inconsiderable
school of thought, which regarded the Constitution as a living
charter and sufficiently flexible to permit emergency action. How
far the Supreme Court would go in the direction of constitutional
elasticity, no one knew. The lower courts were divided. When
Secretary Harold Ickes' control of oil shipments under Section 9c
had been challenged in the courts by F. W. Fischer of Tyler, Texas,
and the case had gone to District of Columbia Courts, Justice
Joseph Cox upheld the law with these words:

In the law, it is recognized that necessity confers many rights
and privileges that without the necessity might not be conferred.
It is said that self-preservation is the first law, and this principle,
in some degree at least, seems to extend to governments. . . . All
laws, including the Constitution, should be read in emergencies in
the light of the law of necessity.

The philosophy back of this decision was that legislative bodies
should be allowed wide latitude for experimentation in the solution
of social and economic questions; that judicial bodies could act
only in a negative capacity without power to make substitutions
for any legislative action they might invalidate; and that upon the
executive and legislative departments of government, both subject
to political control, should rest the responsibility for determining
economic policies. The Supreme Court, however, invalidated Section 9c of the act; and, then, in the case of *Schechter Poultry Corporation v. United States* (June 3, 1935) overthrew the whole
network of 750 code authorities by declaring the act to be an unconstitutional delegation of legislative power and an attempt to
invade intrastate commerce. It denied the theory that an emergency

justified an invasion by Congress of the jurisdiction of the states. The decision was by a unanimous Court. There can be no question about the sentiment of the country. It endorsed the decision. The system had failed and was already moribund before the Court's decision was rendered. Other recovery measures had taken effect, the emergency had passed, and the issue had lost its appeal. The decision of the Court had come mid-way between presidential elections, which made it impossible to present the questions of judicial review or constitutional amendment as campaign issues. There is no evidence that the people would have supported, even at that time, an amendment giving the federal government control over wages, hours, trade practices, or prices. President Roosevelt announced and Congress authorized continuation of a skeleton organization as a fact-finding agency. James L. O'Neill was appointed Administrator, and Leon C. Marshall was assigned to the task of compiling the organization's records. Their task was in reality that of writing a history of the organization and determining the results of its invalidation.

There were many offers of voluntary cooperation from industrialists, but there was much evidence, too, of immediate wage and price reductions and increases in the hours of labor. The National Association of Manufacturers urged its members "to take immediate steps to stabilize wages, hours, working conditions and competitive practices on a voluntary basis" through their trade associations. President Harper Sibley of the Chamber of Commerce of the United States took the same attitude, and recommended continuation of the cartels on a voluntary basis. Industry's chief concern was that the ten percent of business and industry not under the codes would introduce cutthroat competitive practices and thus destroy whatever gains had been made. Conservative newspapers and, particularly, political opponents of the Roosevelt Administration hailed the Supreme Court as the savior of the Constitution and the decision as returning the country to sound fundamentals.

Few people realized the complete significance of what had happened. Most people believed that their ideal of free competition in trade and industry was a fact. Actually, the invalidation of the

National Industrial Recovery Act, like all Supreme Court decisions, took the country back to where it started from when the act was passed. The only difference in this case was that free competition was less a fact than before and the government was in possession of a vast amount of information for use in finding some other solution to the problem. Responsibility was placed once more upon the Federal Trade Commission, the Department of Justice, and Congress to restore and preserve competition by reframing and effectually enforcing the anti-trust laws. It was not enough to say, as Senator Borah did, that there was power under the existing Constitution to do the things which needed to be done. That remained to be demonstrated. Congress still had its taxing and spending powers and its control over the tariff, all of which were regarded as effective weapons for the control of industry and trade if properly used.

Meanwhile, President Roosevelt adopted the practice of pressing through Congress acts of doubtful constitutionality. He was denounced most bitterly by partisan opponents for so doing. The problem of social and economic control, however, had become so insistent that the limits of the powers of Congress and of the state legislatures under the Constitution needed to be fully explored before the question of a constitutional amendment could be intelligently considered. Whether that idea was behind the Administration's action or political expediency as claimed by its critics, can be determined only from the perspective of time. The result will not be materially different whatever the motive may have been.

The first of these acts was the Bituminous Coal Conservation Act of 1935, generally known as the Guffey Coal Act. It was designed to take the place of the NRA code in the bituminous coal industry. The act established a national Bituminous Coal Commission in the Department of Interior, provided for limited amounts of production, and placed a 15 percent tax on the price at the mine, 90 percent of which was to be returned to producers who complied with the code. Minimum and maximum prices were to be established and a Labor Board was to settle all disputes between employers and employees. This was the first attempt to set up little NRA's in each of the basic industries. The act was quickly contested in the courts and, in *Carter v. Carter Coal Company* (May 19, 1936) the Supreme Court invalidated the act on the grounds (1) that the tax was not a revenue measure but a penalty to obtain compliance with regulatory provisions; (2) that Congress can regulate commerce but not production; (3) and that the federal government possesses no inherent powers.

LABOR

The labor provisions of the National Industrial Recovery Act embodied a sweeping repudiation of all that had gone before. The first and, in some ways, the most important part of the act with respect to labor was that which provided for codes in each industry. The long, unsuccessful battle against child labor by state legislation, required school attendance, and an unratified constitutional amendment was brushed aside. A provision was written into all codes, at the insistence of Secretary Frances Perkins, banning the labor of children under sixteen years of age. Minimum wages and maximum hours for labor were also established for the whole of every industry on the principle of protecting the efficient and well-intentioned producer against any who sought to profit by unrestrained exploitation. Nearly all codes limited the working week to 40 hours, with many exceptions for seasonal and unusual periods of production. Minimum wages were set at not less than $12 a week and, in some cases, were slightly above that amount.

Section 7a of the act dealt specifically with the question of collective bargaining. It said:

That employees shall have the right to organize and bargain collectively through representatives of their own choosing, and shall be free from the interference, restraint, or coercion of employers of labor, or their agents, in the designation of such representatives or in self-organization or in other concerted activities for the purpose of collective bargaining, or other mutual aid or protection; that no employee and no one seeking employment shall be required as a condition of employment to join any company union or to refrain from joining, organizing, or assisting a labor organization of his own choosing; and that employers shall comply with the maximum hours of labor, minimum rates of pay, and other conditions of employment approved or prescribed by the President.

The long controversy over the closed or open shop was thus thought to have been settled. The principle of cooperation was substituted for that of industrial warfare. The application of that principle, however, proved far more difficult than was anticipated. The governing boards of the NRA placed the following interpretation on Section 7a: (1) All provisions in the codes with respect to hours, wages, etc., were the minimum the government would recognize in any case. To that extent, the government dictated to both capital and labor; (2) employers and employees were at liberty to agree upon shorter hours, higher wages, etc., and to make any other arrangements which did not contravene code provisions; (3) employees might organize without interference from employers, but the government assumed no responsibility to promote labor organizations. Employers must recognize and bargain collectively with their employees through their chosen representatives; (4) workers might continue to deal individually with their employers if they chose to do so; (5) employers must not interfere with any employee's freedom to join any labor organization, and labor unions must not coerce a non-union employee.

The effort of the government to compel each side to respect the rights of the other met difficulty from the first. The dead weight of the past militated strongly against abandonment of the lockout, the blacklist, the strike, and the fight for the open and closed shop. The American Federation of Labor, having its local crafts already widely established, moved immediately to strengthen its position. Its membership rose to 4,500,000 within a few months, much of the increase being in new vertical unions chartered directly by the A. F. of L. and not a part of the craft organizations. The large industrialists, reluctant to abandon the principle of the open shop, met the challenge of the A. F. of L. by organizing company unions. The spirit of warfare, which was supposed to have been rendered obsolete by the new scheme, flared anew; and the conflict revealed several fundamental weaknesses in the new order. The steel industry, with its many subsidiaries, always had led the fight against new principles such as the eight-hour day and collective bargaining, and did not depart from its traditional role in this instance. The Weirton Steel plants at Clarksburg, West Virginia, and Steubenville, Ohio, were closed. The automobile accessory plants of the Budd Manufacturing Company at Philadelphia were purged of all striking employees. The organization of a company union by the H. C. Frick Coke Co. of Pennsylvania precipitated a strike of 15,000 coal miners. In a hundred localities, furious industrial strife threatened, and compelled the government to take its second step in the new program.

The National Recovery Administration, in line with its pronounced policy, requested strikers to resume operations during a period of settlement by negotiation. President Roosevelt made a personal appeal for peace, and then appointed Senator Robert F. Wagner head of a nationwide system of arbitration boards. The task undertaken by the National Labor Board was extremely difficult. It had no legal status other than Presidential fiat. The liberal press, including the *Nation* and the *New Republic*, was roundly criticizing the government for asking labor to forgo the use of the strike before it had outlawed the company union. The American Federation of Labor was striving for a dominant position in each industry in order to control the representatives for collective bargaining. The industrialists were contending for the open shop or, at most, company unions. The government was insisting that all laborers were free under the law to join any description of union or none at all as they saw fit, but that coercion of all kinds was forbidden. The workers of the Weirton Steel Company appealed directly to President Roosevelt against the company union, and he ordered a survey by the National Labor Board to determine whether workers in that company were being coerced into joining the company union. More important, however, was his direction to the Board to hold elections under its own auspices, where necessary, and to determine the wishes of the majority of the workers, which majority was then to speak for the whole. This principle of majority rule, a distinct departure from the first position of the government, played directly into the hands of the American Federation of Labor, and destroyed all rights of minority groups. It was specifically enunciated in the Denver Tramways Case (March 2, 1934) where the majority vote went to the Amalgamated Association of Street and Electric Railway Employees union.

This principle of elections under government supervision with the majority authorized to make agreements with the employers which would be binding upon all workers in the industry had a short life. It was incorporated in a bill introduced into Congress by Senator Wagner in February, 1934. The industrialists opposed the bill, of course, but so did the Civil Liberties Union and a large section of laboring men. It was directly contrary to the philosophy of Samuel Gompers who had repeatedly warned the workers against permitting government to interfere by compulsory unemployment insurance, etc. Here was a time when the national administration was distinctly friendly to labor. President Roosevelt himself, Secretary Frances Perkins, General Council of the NRA Donald Richberg, the members of the Labor Advisory Board: Leo Wolman, Sidney Hillman, William Green, John Frey and George L. Berry, made the Administration the most sympathetic to labor in history. Once the element of compulsion had been introduced, however, and organized labor became the creature of the government a struggle for its control was inevitable. Labor courts were the certain road to Fascism, when government fell into the hands of a less friendly administration. Farsighted friends of labor saw it and opposed the Wagner bill.

More important, however, from the standpoint of the individual laborer, was the provision which would have given to representatives of the majority the exclusive power to make agreements with their employers. Chairman Francis Biddle of the National Labor Relations Board defended it as an application of the democratic principle of majority rule which, of course, it was not because practically applied it would deny to all minorities in industry a voice in the determination of wages, hours, etc. It was a grave distortion of the principle of collective bargaining.

Meanwhile, a strike in the automobile industry which was leading the way to recovery again brought President Roosevelt's personal intervention. The settlement of March 25, 1934, repudiated this principle of majority rule and set up an industrial parliament established on the basis of proportional representation of all important groups of workers. Theoretically, it was the only correct application of the government's first interpretation of

Section 7a. It thwarted the plans both of the American Federation of Labor to dictate the working agreements of all labor and of the employers to compel membership in company-dictated unions. It laid the basis for the evolution of industrial unions. It abandoned the dangerous trend toward government-supported unions inherent in supervised elections and majority rule. It restored the government to its former position of neutral arbiter for voluntary mediation. It weakened the prestige of the National Labor Board, however, as it did that of the American Federation of Labor. That Board, meanwhile, had been refused permission to supervise an election in the Weirton Steel Company case. An appeal to the courts for an injunction was made and refused. Thus was the Norris-LaGuardia Act turned against a government agency in its first test in the courts.

The Wagner bill was then revised and passed as the Labor Disputes Joint Resolution of June 19, 1934. The act empowered the President to appoint boards for investigation and voluntary arbitration upon request by both sides to a dispute. These boards were to supervise elections for collective bargaining, and fines and imprisonment were to follow refusal to obey their orders. Their life was limited to the one year period remaining of the National Recovery Act.

The enactment of the Joint Resolution marked the end of the most significant year in all labor history. It began with an attempt by the government to induce capital and labor voluntarily to respect each other's rights and substitute cooperation for industrial warfare. The American Federation of Labor and employers each moved to secure a dominant position in the new program. The employers violated the spirit of the act by organizing company unions and labor retaliated with strikes. The government then moved to compel compliance and failed. Finally, it abandoned compulsion and set up machinery for voluntary arbitration at the moment when capital and labor were marshalling forces for a supreme test of strength all over the country. This abandonment of compulsion cannot be over emphasized. It meant that henceforth wages would be determined by the relative strength and skill of employer and employee and that labor would seek that form of organization best calculated to put its maximum strength and bargaining power into the contest. It meant, also, that in the test, government would offer its services for arbitration with both sides free to accept its findings or not as they chose, and with government free from suspicion of bias in the performance of its primary function of protecting the lives, property, and health of the people.

The test between capital and labor first introduced the country to the general strike. Strife began when a strike occurred in the Electric Auto-Lite Company of Toledo in February. Wages and recognition of the United Automobile Workers Federal Union were involved. Injunctions, company-paid deputies and, finally, state militia were brought into the struggle against the strikers. There was much destruction of property and several deaths. The strikers won their demands through *threat of a general strike* and the mediation efforts of the government, and the strike ended on June 5. A strike was threatened in the steel industry ten days later and was averted only through the influence of William Green, president of the American Federation of Labor.

On July 16, the first general strike was finally called in San Francisco. It began with a strike of 12,000 members of the International Longshoremen's Association and soon involved all marine workers. The American Federation of Labor was drawn in to protect its craft structure against the threat of industrial unions, and on July 16 all the San Francisco district was tied up. Again troops were brought into the contest, violent propaganda charging subversive communist activities was disseminated, and a wave of terrorism was begun by the employers with the active support of state and municipal administrations. More important than the injection of communistic charges into the dispute, however, was the general attitude of the public. The two cannot be entirely separated; but, however sympathetic people might have been to the cause of the union labor, they were unquestionably hostile to the principle of the general strike. A general strike is not an economic weapon but a revolutionary political weapon. It is not a strike against particular employers but against society and the state itself. It is so directly contrary to traditional public policy in the United States that it was the most impolitic and inexpedient action labor could have taken. Sensing the situation and seeking to save the face of the American Federation of Labor at the expense of the San Francisco laborers, President William Green disavowed any responsibility for it on behalf of his organization. The craft unionists went back to work and the longshoremen were forced to submit their grievances to arbitration.

The American Federation of Labor had failed to do more than increase its membership by 2,000,000 in the early days of a frankly friendly national administration. It failed to take advantage of its opportunity to organize along industrial lines and thus fortify itself against the day of a hostile administration. Instead, it supported the Wagner bill and the National Labor Board, thus actually seeking to make itself the ward of the government, surrendering its freedom of action at times of industrial strife, and laying itself open to destruction in event of hostile control. It had been frustrated in its attempt to establish a labor dictatorship, by the automobile code and the abandonment of the original Wagner bill. Its prestige was further weakened by the action of President Green in the San Francisco strike. Meanwhile, the solidarity of labor was proved in the Toledo strike. It was apparent that the next chapter in labor history would involve the question of who was to speak for labor in its controversies with capital, of the form of labor organization, rather than of contests between capital and labor.

The two principals in this contest were President Green of the American Federation of Labor and President John L. Lewis of the United Mine Workers of America. Miner's unions are essentially industrial unions, sometimes called vertical unions. The new federal unions chartered by the A. F. of L. in such industries as automobile, steel and rubber, were vertical unions within a single plant, but with the important exception that members of crafts (17 in the automobile industry), remained with their former organizations. Lewis contended that to deprive new unions of these skilled workers in an industry was to rob them of their skilled leadership and limit them to easily replaced, unskilled mass-production workers. The issue was joined at the San Francisco convention of 1933 where Lewis secured indorsement of the principle of industrial unions. The question of permitting them to have the skilled craftsmen was fought out at the Atlantic City convention in 1935 and, because federal unions were denied full voting strength, Lewis was defeated. A few weeks later the supporters of the industrial program met at Washington, D. C., and formed a Committee on Industrial Organization. President Green ordered the Committee disbanded. Lewis defied the order, resigned from the Executive Council of the A. F. of L. and was given authority to withhold his union's dues from that organization. The contest was no mere struggle for power. It was as broad as the labor movement itself. It was the difference between craft and industrial organization which meant a static labor movement or a vigorous labor movement in conformity with modern industrial conditions.

The government again entered the labor picture at this point. The National Industrial Recovery Act having been declared unconstitutional, Congress enacted the National Labor Relations Act, or Wagner-Connery Act, on July 5, 1935. The act created a National Labor Relations Board of three members, and reasserted the right of collective bargaining. It gave the Board the power to investigate complaints by labor or employer and to issue "cease and desist orders," after the manner of the Federal Trade Commission, where unfair practices affected interstate commerce. Certain practices were specified, the most important being interference with or refusal to recognize the right of collective bargaining and discrimination against union members. The act ranks with the Social Security Act as one of the two most important achievements of the New Deal. It outlawed once and for all every effort to prevent unionization. Workers could call an election whenever they wished to decide who should represent them in collective bargaining. The Board was to conduct these elections, and to certify the results. During the first seven years of its existence, it handled 49,986 cases. Thirty-five cases were taken on appeal to the Supreme Court of the United States, and the decisions of the Board were sustained in all but two of the cases. The Board conducted over 6000 elections in industrial plants during the same period. It had, in fact, become one of the most powerful and indispensable agencies of the government before our entry into World War II. The courts upheld the act, most employers thereafter cooperated in its enforcement, and unionization entered a period of tremendous power in the economic life of the nation. By 1940, there were 11,000,000 members of labor unions, and in many industries there was a new experiment in progress of cooperation between labor and management.

Meanwhile, however, the contest between the C.I.O. and the A. F. of L. reached a crisis. The ten unions which had joined the C.I.O. were suspended and nine of them were expelled from the A. F. of L. They met in convention, in November, 1938, and formally organized the Congress of Industrial Organization. The A. F. of L. continued to organize along craft lines, the C.I.O. to organize along industrial lines, and in some industries many men were members of both organizations (dual unionism). The A. F. of L. was conservative, the C.I.O. militant and progressive. Both organizations continued to grow until, by 1941, they each had about 4,000,000 members.

The C.I.O. began with several powerful unions such as the United Mine Workers, the Amalgamated Clothing Workers, and the International Ladies' Garment Workers. It revitalized the United Automobile Workers of America and introduced the country to the sit-down strike in a contest with General Motors Corporation. It won the strike, secured an agreement as the bargaining agency for all the corporation's employees, and then forced agreements from the other automobile companies. It then signed an agreement with the United States Steel Corporation; it organized the longshoremen and the rubber workers; and it organized thousands of men and women workers in the service and merchandising trades. All in all, it became the most militant trade union, and perhaps the most powerful, in the world.

24

Security as a Social Ideal

PROTECTING INVESTORS

THE year 1933 marked the resumption of the reform movement arrested by World War I. It differed from the reform period of Theodore Roosevelt and Woodrow Wilson only because reform measures were enacted almost before recovery had begun, whereas the reform legislation of the earlier period was passed after recovery had been completed. The country was passing through a social readjustment as well as a depression. The Roosevelt philosophy embraced the idea that people must somehow be sustained until they were able to find work and, afterward, should enjoy a decent standard of living. Men and women were seeking, not economic opportunity, but economic security. The reform measures enacted by Congress represent the demands of the people for new controls and adjustments for a greater degree of economic equality. It is not a question of their having emanated from the White House. The question is whether the measures sponsored by Roosevelt were more liberal or more conservative than Congress would have enacted had it been free from administrative restraint. Evidence indicates that they were more conservative; that the Roosevelt influence was a restraining influence at a time of social disintegration. Roosevelt was a conservative but his great popularity was due to his independence of vested interests and his sincere desire to restore recovery by bettering the condition of the average man. He restored the morale of the nation by the way in which he handled the monetary and banking situation. He boldly faced the

521

relief problem; eased the farmer's debts in the AAA; attacked child labor and the sweatshops in the NRA; and extended a helping hand to labor; but his program also included such items as the regulation of utility rates, security sales, and the stock exchange; home building; old-age and unemployment insurance; reciprocal tariffs; crime control; and neutrality legislation.

The first act of the Administration to provide for the financial security of the people was the Glass-Steagall Act of June 16, 1933. It sought to correct the weaknesses of the Federal Reserve System and to protect the deposits and investments of the people. It permitted national banks to engage in branch banking; divorced commercial and investment banking by forbidding commercial banks to sell securities directly or through affiliates and investment banks to accept deposits; gave the Federal Reserve Board power to prevent loans for speculation; and created a Federal Bank Deposit Insurance Corporation. The latter corporation was given $150,000,-000 capital stock, to which was to be added 50 percent of the surplus of Federal Reserve Banks, and ½ percent of the deposits of participating banks. Federal Reserve Banks were compelled to join the system, and non-member banks were permitted to participate until July 1, 1936. All deposits up to $10,000 were fully insured, those from $10,000 to $50,000 75 percent, and those over $50,000, 50 percent.

The regulation of stock exchanges and the marketing of securities grew out of the orgy of speculation after World War I, in which unscrupulous manipulators of the stock exchanges fleeced no less than a million investors out of an estimated $25,000,000,-000. No one, probably, will ever know the complete details of what happened; but there can be no question as to some of the contributing factors. Securities were sold to unsuspecting purchasers by false and incomplete statements of fact as to their real value. Many people bought securities for speculative purposes who were ignorant of everything except vague rumors of sudden wealth to be acquired by so doing; or who would have been incapable of sound investment or unwilling to heed sound advice even had all the facts been laid before them. Banks and investment trusts, which should have used scrupulous care in investing their clients' money and exerted every effort to advise their depositors against their own folly, too often did neither. Hundreds of men of prominence in business and public life, in whom the people had confidence, engaged in promoting speculative pools, accepted gratuities in the form of stocks at less than market price, and assisted in erecting nefarious holding companies which could accomplish no other purpose than increase consumers' costs, rob operating companies of legitimate revenues, and further the ends of financial chicanery. Officers of investment trusts, who were also directors of industrial corporations, used their dual position to unload worthless foreign and domestic stocks and bonds upon their investors. These things were possible because of the complete lack of regulation of the stock exchanges, the loose incorporation laws of the several states under which charters were secured, the interlocking directorates between commercial banks, investment banks, and industrial corporations, and the freedom from penalties under the law of the sellers of securities.

Concerning these things, Roosevelt said, in his inaugural address:

Practices of the unscrupulous money changers stand indicted in the court of public opinion, rejected in the hearts and minds of men. We require two safeguards against the return of the evils of the older order; there must be a strict supervision of all banking and credits and investments; there must be an end to speculation with other people's money.

Reform along these lines carried a wider appeal and the endorsement of more people in the country, liberal and conservative alike, than any other suggested by the Administration. Many economists agreed with the great British economist, John Maynard Keynes, that stock market speculation in the United States had robbed normal business all over the world of its legitimate capital and contributed heavily to the world depression. Some, no doubt, would have endorsed the statement of the iconoclastic John T. Flynn that not more than ten percent of the stock market transactions were made by legitimate investors or served any useful purpose to society. It was Professors Felix Frankfurter and James M. Landis, both of the Harvard Law School, who were responsible for the Truth-in-Securities Act. Chairman Richard Whitney of the New York Stock Exchange was in favor of reform. On the other hand, its opponents were the most powerful minority in the country.

Several types of legislation were proposed: (1) federal regulation of the stock markets; (2) the limitation of stock issues to equivalent capital investment and their sale to investors; (3) the fixing of responsibility upon the vendor of stocks and bonds; (4) prohibition of bonuses and management fees to directors of holding companies; and (5) federal charters for all corporations engaged in interstate commerce. One of the first acts of the special session of Congress in the spring of 1933 was passage of the Truth in Securities Act, which was approved by President Roosevelt on May 27. This act required that all security issues offered for sale must first be registered with and approved by the Federal Trade Commission, to which President Roosevelt appointed James M. Landis, one of the authors of the act. It also gave to the purchaser of a security the right to recover any losses incurred by misrepresentation and subjected the seller to a fine of $5000 and five years' imprisonment.

The following twelve months witnessed one of the historic dramas in the political history of the country. Wall Street, La Salle Street and all the lesser stock and brokerage communities throughout the country united forces to bring about a modification of the law at the next regular session of Congress. The same general indictment raised against all the reform measures of these years was again invoked: that it was delaying recovery—in this case, by retarding the re-financing essential to industrial expansion. The Investment Bankers Association of America adopted a resolution demanding a re-definition of "the indefinite liabilities imposed by the Securities Act, so as to make it possible for responsible enterprise to meet their requirements for new capital and to cooperate with the Recovery Program." For the most part, it was those financiers who had been responsible for the stock and bond swindles and those corporation directors and lawyers who had always opposed social legislation who led the attack and who, there is some reason to believe, delayed re-financing with the fixed

purpose of bringing pressure to bear upon Congress for modification of the act. Meanwhile, the Federal Trade Commission disavowed any intention to hamper legitimate refinancing, the Senate invited the presentation of all grievances substantiated with
facts, and Ferdinand Pecora was instructed to close up his investigation of banking practices and proceed with that of the stock
exchanges.

Early in the year, President Roosevelt appointed a committee,
under the chairmanship of Secretary of Commerce Daniel Roper,
to investigate the practices of the stock exchanges. This committee made its report in January, 1934. This report recommended
(1) that every exchange should be denied the use of the mails
and other channels of interstate commerce unless licensed by the
federal government; (2) that a federal administrative board be
established to regulate the exchanges to the end of fair business
practices; and (3) that definite rules be established by law, the
violation of which would subject an exchange to severe penalties.
President Roosevelt transmitted this report to Congress together
with recommendations for a regulatory law "for the protection
of investors, for the safe-guarding of values, and so far as it may be
possible, for the elimination of unnecessary, unwise and destructive speculation." The Fletcher-Rayburn bill was introduced the
following day. This bill was originally drawn up by Benjamin
Cohen, associate counsel for the Public Works Administration,
and Thomas Corcoran, associate counsel for the Reconstruction
Finance Corporation. Both were graduates of the Harvard Law
School and disciples of Felix Frankfurter. The bill was then revised
by Ferdinand Pecora's staff of experts and James M. Landis. It
placed all stock exchanges under the control of the Federal Trade
Commission; required a 60 percent margin on stock exchange
transactions; gave the Commission access to all records of the
brokerage houses; and prohibited short-selling and pools. It carried a fine of $25,000 and ten years' imprisonment for violations
by individuals and a fine of $500,000 for exchanges. Opponents of
the bill deluged the country with propaganda to defeat it. It was
charged that the margin required on brokers' transactions would
extend to bankers' loans; that these same requirements would

force banks to flood the market with securities; that business would languish and recovery stop. In Congress, every effort was made to keep regulation out of the hands of the Federal Trade Commission.

As finally passed on June 6, 1934, the act, variously known as the Securities Exchange Act and Stock Exchange Act, placed a limitation on bank credit for speculative purposes, established safeguards against the manipulation of the market, and insured full information to the buyer of securities. Specifically, it established the Securities and Exchange Commission and transferred to it the power over security sales formerly vested in the Federal Trade Commission. It gave the Federal Reserve Board discretionary power over credit facilities available for stock transactions. It prohibited pools, options, and other devices for the manipulation of prices, active trading by members of the exchange, and false information to purchasers. Shortly thereafter President Roosevelt appointed as the five members of the new commission: Joseph P. Kennedy, a financier and distinct friend of Wall Street who had rendered valuable service to the Roosevelt campaign; George C. Matthews, a former member of the Wisconsin Public Utilities Commission; Robert E. Healy, Counsel of the Federal Trade Commission; Ferdinand Pecora; and James Landis.

CURBING THE POWER INTERESTS

Congress then turned to the complicated question of electric power and light. The electric power industry had grown into a financial giant of $12,000,000,000 during the twenties. Great empires of producing, distributing, and holding companies had been created, with financial structures so complex that no one could say what were the actual costs of manufacturing and distributing electricity. Municipalities had erected publicly owned and operated plants in increasing numbers, but the power lobby prevented Congress from authorizing the operation of the great government owned plant at Muscle Shoals. The Roosevelt Administration insisted that electric power and light had become so essential to the comfort and health of the people and to the emancipation of women from the drudgery of house work—in short, that its availability to all the people was so pressing a problem of social reconstruction—that the authority and financial resources of the nation should be utilized to sweep away all obstructions to the fullest possible use of our resources for its manufacture and sale at reasonable rates. New Dealers also believed (1) that there were certain national geographical regions within the country, each with its own peculiar economic and social interests, resources, and problems; (2) that integration of social and economic life had reached the point where a deficiency of one region was a serious handicap to the entire nation; and (3) that the correction of these deficiencies could only be accomplished by a use of federal funds and a delegation of broad power by Congress to regional boards.

Therefore, on May 18, 1933, the Tennessee Valley Authority was created and the great power plant at Muscle Shoals once more became something more than a political football. The Tennessee Valley Authority was the largest and most comprehensive agency ever created in the United States for social service. It was to serve seven states—Tennessee, Virginia, North Carolina, Georgia, Alabama, Mississippi, and Kentucky—with electric power and agricultural fertilizers. Its work was to include reforestation, control of floods and soil erosion; and it had authority to resettle the population, establish subsistence homesteads, and provide vocational educational facilities. The funds were provided from the PWA. The power companies which had fought against the operation of the government-owned plant at Muscle Shoals for nearly two decades, once more threw their full strength against the whole adventure but without success. The right of the government to manufacture and dispose of power was upheld by the Supreme Court on February 17, 1936.

The New Dealers had in mind several of these regional authorities, but only the TVA received enough support in Congress to become a reality. Another, the Missouri Valley Authority has been discussed widely, and will become a major political issue in the future. Meanwhile, the TVA completely rehabilitated the population of the region. David E. Lilienthal, Chairman of the TVA after 1941, has said:

In that valley, the people and their institutions have in a decade completely changed the face of the region. The standard of living has materially increased for nearly all of the five million citizens. The productiveness of the area has grown many-fold. Opportunities for young men and women have mounted. There are new factories, new jobs, new professional opportunities. Standards of health and education have gone up. The soil and farm electricity have become the basis of attractive and prosperous living. With the modern tools they now have in their hands the people are fashioning a new valley.

The second act of the Administration which aroused bitter opposition from the utilities companies was the creation of the Public Works Administration with an immense sum of money to offer municipalities a 30 percent outright gift for the construction of water, gas, electric, and transportation projects. The utilities opposed it, as they had always opposed such public projects, on the ground that they destroyed private investments; but their strongest attack was an indirect one against the delegation of power to the Executive Department of the government. Here was a case where the allotment of funds was left to the discretion of the administrators of the Public Works Administration and the powerful lobby of the power interests was as helpless against them as it was effective against congressional action. The significance of the government action lay in its encouragement of publicly owned utilities designed to force private companies to reduce their rates to the basis of the fair return on an honest investment.

The third step was the creation by executive order of a subsidiary to the Tennessee Valley Authority known as the Electric Home and Farm Authority. Its purpose was to extend the use of electricity to the 220,000 farms in the Tennessee Valley. Producers of electric power had always defended high rates with the argument that they could not be reduced until consumption was increased and blamed the excessive cost of electrical appliances for its non-popularity. Manufacturers of electrical appliances, on the other hand, blamed high rates for the fact that so few people used the labor-saving devices they produced. The Tennessee Valley Authority was designed to test the validity of existing electric rates, and the Electric Farm and Home Authority was to provide appliances

528

of standard quality to the surrounding communities. Morris Lelwellyn Cooke, distinguished authority on public utilities, was appointed administrator of another agency known as the Rural Electrification Administration, with $100,000,000 to promote the building of transmission lines into rural areas as a beginning toward putting electricity into the 6,000,000 farm homes without it.

Finally, reform by regulation was added to reform by experimentation and competition. This was accomplished by the Wheeler-Rayburn Act of August, 1935. Every resource of the utility industry was marshaled against its passage, and, in the end, some important modifications were made in the bill as originally passed by the Senate. The act as passed gave to the Federal Power Commission the power to regulate interstate power transmission and to the Federal Trade Commission the power to regulate interstate gas. It compelled utility lobbyists to register with the Securities and Exchange Commission; forbade any officer of a bank, brokerage or investment house to serve as an officer or director of a utility company; and gave to the Securities and Exchange Commission authority to determine for utility companies the amounts which might be written off their books as depreciation and whether or not dividends might be allowed. The Act also gave the commission authority to liquidate all holding companies which it believed to be contrary to the public interest; in addition it forbade holding companies meanwhile to profit from transactions with their operating constituents.

HOUSING PROGRAM

Not only did the Roosevelt Administration seek to save homes to their owners by the Frazier-Lemke Farm Bankruptcy Act and the Home Owners Refinancing Act, but it undertook to revive the building industry by making funds available for building and repairs and to provide low-cost housing for the low income groups.

The construction industry had suffered an almost total collapse during the depression. Expenditures for all construction purposes had shrunk from $11,000,000,000 in 1928 to $3,000,000,000 in 1933. The construction of residential property had declined 95 percent. Normally, 2,500,000 men were engaged in construction work and as many more fabricating materials for construction projects. Recovery was impossible until the building industry revived. Houses had fallen into disrepair, with $500,000,000 spent for such purposes in 1928 and less than $50,000,000 in 1933.

The National Housing Act of June 28, 1934, created a Federal Housing Administration which, under the direction of James A. Moffett, operated along conservative lines in assisting private agencies to finance building, repairs, and improvements. It enabled home owners to borrow from banks, trust companies, building and loan associations, and finance companies, as much as $2000 for the improvement of homes, apartment buildings, stores, offices, factories, and farm buildings. A Home Credit Insurance Corporation was established to enable an individual to borrow 80 percent of the cost of building a new home from such companies at 5 percent interest for twenty years. The purpose of the plan was to loosen credit and to aid the builder by eliminating all mortgage fees and service charges for periodical refinancing. If payments were not made, the lending agency was authorized to take over the property and be guaranteed against loss by the government to 80 percent of its value. The act also created a Federal Savings and Loan Insurance Corporation to guarantee the deposits of Building and Loan Associations and authorized national mortgage associations under the supervision of the Federal Home Loan Bank Board. This attempt to attract private capital into the building industry and to lower the cost of credit to home builders was offset by the increased cost of building under the NRA codes and by the government's experimental housing program.

That part of the federal housing program which aroused the most heated controversy was under the direction of the Public Works Administration, and included projects (1) for the building of model homes with low rental value in the cities, and (2) the re-settling of farmers from sub-marginal lands in semi-rural villages known as subsistence homestead centers. In cities, money was made available to seven limited dividend corporations for the construction of low-rent apartment buildings. The Public Works Administration then undertook directly to eliminate twenty-seven slum districts; to construct model homes in these districts; and to build low-rent houses in twenty-three semi-urban districts. These fifty projects were located in thirty-five different cities. In all cases, the management of these new housing centers was to be placed in the hands of city housing authorities wherever they existed or were created. The sole interest of the Public Works Administration in the completed projects, representing an estimated investment of $208,000,000, was to be financial. Seventy-five percent of the cost of construction went into payrolls of men engaged in building or producing materials.

The purpose of providing low-cost housing cannot be said to have been entirely successful. The sum of $130,000,000 was spent to provide 25,000 dwellings for approximately 130,000 persons, making the rental values excessive for the lowest income groups. The high cost was due in part to the necessity of purchasing slum property directly from the 11,000 owners, ofttimes at excessive values. The type of construction, however, was modern in every detail, with fireproof materials, plumbing and sanitation, fresh air and sunlight.

It will be recalled that, under the Federal Emergency Relief Act, farm families were provided with funds to purchase needed livestock, feed, and supplies. In April, 1935, President Roosevelt, by executive order, created the Resettlement Administration under the Department of Agriculture, to remove destitute rural families from submarginal land and resettle them on subsistence homesteads. The agency undertook not only to create cooperative enterprises, but to encourage the development of a society in which industrial workers would derive subsistence from their own homestead farms by a program of part-time work in industry and part-time work on the soil. The Resettlement Administration undertook, under this plan, to construct four modern towns near industrial centers: Washington, Milwaukee, Cincinnati, and Bound Brook, New Jersey. They covered hundreds of acres and included homes, garden plots, small farms, and recreation centers.

The work of the Resettlement Administration was severely criticized as being an excessive expenditure of public funds in a field which belonged exclusively to private enterprise without going very far toward relieving the need for an estimated 16,000,-000 new home units. It was said to be an experiment in state socialism which caused private construction companies to hesitate to embark upon new building programs. Both observations were probably correct. The housing program must be regarded as an experimental reform, much the same as the Tennessee Valley Authority. Its purpose was to prove that the enormous slum areas of the industrial centers, with their unhealthful, immoral and depressing atmosphere, could be eliminated; that they could be supplanted by community centers embracing all the conveniences and conditions of life made possible by technology and boundless natural resources; and that exploitation of the urban masses by real estate speculators must give way, if necessary, before government competition in the housing industry.

Finally, the Administration enlarged its program and extended it to the whole of the rural population. A Farm Security Administration was created, September 1, 1937, to replace the Resettlement Administration. The general purpose of the FSA was to enable farm families to make a better living. Loans, for five years at 5 percent interest, were made to farmers who could not secure credit elsewhere, to purchase livestock, machinery, and fertilizers. County farm supervisors and home management supervisors were appointed to provide on-the-farm education. Burdensome debts were refinanced over long periods and at lower interest rates to permit improvements in farm operations. Long-term leases were encouraged to enable tenants to make improvements with security against loss by eviction. Cooperative marketing and group health insurance were promoted. Over a period of five years, the Administration lent $649,664,000 to 980,711 farmers. Debts of 117,000 farmers had been reduced by more than 75 percent. Eighty percent of the farmers with loans from the Administration had secured long-term leases. More than 600,000 persons were members of medical insurance groups sponsored by the Administration. Thirty thousand farmers had been given loans for the purchase of farms. Finally, camps were established to provide for 60,000 migratory families annually.

PERMANENT AID TO THE NEEDY

The Social Security Act was, after the National Industrial Recovery Act, the most interesting legislative experiment of the Roosevelt Administration and one of its greatest achievements. Most states already had provided against the hazards of industrial accidents with Workmen's Compensation laws, most of them had widows' and children's pension plans, and about half of them old-age pensions. Only Wisconsin, however, had ventured into the field of unemployment insurance. Society was no longer in a mood to tolerate an industrial system which reaped huge profits in good times and then cast the burden of supporting its laboring men upon society during depressions. This was the period of the Townsend Old Age Pension faith and an equally strong agitation for unemployment insurance, though the sentiment for either program was not universal. On July 8, 1934, President Roosevelt sent a social security message to Congress in which he stated his intention to appoint a Committee on Social Security to draw up a program for the consideration of the next Congress. He appointed the committee, consisting of Secretaries Frances Perkins, Henry Morgenthau, and Henry Wallace, Attorney-General Cummings and Relief Administrator Harry L. Hopkins; and it, in turn, called together one of the most able groups of technical advisors ever assembled to advise the government on a special problem, headed by Professor Edwin E. Witte of the University of Wisconsin. The report of this Commission was submitted to the President January 15, 1935. The Commission rejected health insurance from its recommendations and emphasized old-age annuities, dependency benefits, and unemployment insurance. The major problems in these were the relationship which should exist between the state and federal governments and who should pay the costs. The Commission suggested three possibilities: (1) a national system to be financed from the regular revenues of the Treasury; (2) a system of federal contributions to state devised programs; (3) a tax system previously presented in the Wagner-Lewis bill, of federal levies on payrolls, from which would be deducted any taxes to state unemployment insurance programs.

The recommendations of the Committee were incorporated into a bill and introduced into Congress by Senator Robert F. Wagner and Representative Davis L. Lewis on January 17. Hearings on the bill by committees in the two houses continued over a period of several months and it did not become a law until August 18. It provided for pensions to the aged, the blind, and dependent children; insurance annuities to the aged and unemployed; and services for maternity and child welfare, the physically infirm, and delinquents. The first provision of the act was so designed as to encourage state governments to enact old-age pension laws by providing federal contributions up to $15 per month for those over 65 years of age providing that the state (1) contributed at least an equal amount; (2) established state supervision of a state-wide system; (3) complied with the administrative requirements of the Federal Security Board; (4) set an age limit of not over 65; (5) admitted to benefits all who had resided in the state five of the preceding nine years. This part of the act carried an appropriation of $24,660,000 to finance the program until June 30, 1936.

The second provision, designed to lighten the burden upon the Treasury after January 1, 1942, provided for old-age annuities after that date for employees working some part of each of the five preceding years and earning a total during that time of not less than $2000. This did not apply to agricultural laborers, domestic servants, casual employees, public servants, nor employees of non-profit, religious, charitable, scientific, literary and educational institutions. The amount of the benefit payments each month was to be ½ percent of the first $3000 total wages received between 1936 and the date of eligibility, one-twelfth percent of all between $3000 and $45,000 and one-twenty-fourth of all over that amount. The maximum monthly benefit payment was to be $82.50 and the minimum $10. These benefits were to be paid from an Old Age Reserve Account in the United States Treasury; but the money was to be derived from an income tax on employees and an excise tax on employers. All employees coming under the annuity benefit plan were to pay 1 percent on their annual wage under $3000 during 1937–1939; 1½ percent during 1940–1942;

2 percent during 1943–1945; 2½ percent during 1946–1948 and 3 percent after January 1, 1949. Employers were to pay an equal amount on their total payrolls.

The third provision was for unemployment insurance. All employers of eight or more persons, except in agriculture, domestic service, merchant marine, and non-profit institutions, must pay a tax on total payrolls of 1 percent in 1936, 2 percent in 1937 and 3 percent thereafter. All funds paid into a state unemployment insurance fund were to be credited up to 90 percent of the federal tax providing the Social Security Board had approved the state system. Among the requirements were that compensation could not be denied any eligible individual for refusing to accept work (1) during a strike, lockout or labor dispute; (2) if the wages and hours were substantially less favorable than those prevailing in the community; (3) if the individual by accepting work would be required to join a company union or refrain from belonging to another labor organization. Otherwise, the states had considerable leeway although it was hoped that state plans would allow concessions to employers guaranteeing a minimum number of weeks' work to their employees during the year. The 10 percent nondeductible from the federal tax was to be returned to the states on the basis of need for administrative purposes.

The act further provided that each state was to be given $20,000 annually for maternal and child health services in rural areas, with $1,800,000 more to be distributed on the basis of need; each state to receive $20,000 annually for medical, surgical and corrective services to crippled children, with $1,830,000 more to be distributed on basis of need; $1,500,000 to be distributed annually for child welfare among delinquent, homeless, and dependent children in rural areas, no state to receive less than $10,000; and $15 per month federal grant to blind persons not in institutions or receiving old age pensions. Eight million dollars was to be available each year for public health work. The administration of the act was to be in the hands of a Social Security Board consisting of three members.

President Roosevelt spoke of the act, when he signed it, as being "a corner-stone in a structure which is being built which is by no means complete." It was certain that efforts would be made to repeal the act, that it would eventually be drastically revised, and that a test of its constitutionality would be made. It was variously criticized as being an incentive to further technological replacements, a hindrance to recovery, and wholly inadequate. The most serious indictments were (1) that the huge accumulations of reserves in the Treasury and the passing along of the costs to employees and consumers would decrease purchasing power; (2) that, at times of serious depression, funds would soon be exhausted and the system become a federal dole; (3) that no more than one-half of the wage-earners of the nation would benefit; and (4) that the large fund in the Treasury for investment would give that department tremendous additional powers for the stabilization of credit. Many men held that a well-planned public works program would be more adaptable to the needs of a depression. The act was not designed as a recovery measure, but for the purpose of easing employees over future short periods of unemployment and as an incentive to the establishment of an annual wage system in industry. By February 1, 1936, 32 states had set up old-age pension systems to share in the program and seven others already had laws that needed no change. Thirty-three states had complied with the requirement for benefits to the blind; 46 for dependent children; and 11 for unemployment insurance.

Meanwhile, Congress had passed and the President approved on June 27, 1934, the Railway Pension Act, providing for retirement annuities for railway employees. The funds for these annuities were to be contributed by the employer and employee and administered by a new agency known as the Railroad Retirement Board. Less than one year later (May 6, 1935) the act was invalidated by the Supreme Court in another five to four decision with Justices Hughes, Brandeis, Stone, and Cardozo dissenting. The majority held once more that Congress had no power to regulate hours and wages in industry under the commerce clause.

Finally Congress rounded out its security legislation with the Fair Labor Standards Act of June 25, 1938, popularly known as the Wage and Hour Law. The purpose of the act was to establish minimum standards of living necessary for health and efficiency and to eliminate child labor. It created a Wage and Hour Division in the Department of Labor, headed by an administrator, and gave administration of the child labor provisions to the Chief of the Children's Bureau in the same department. The act fixed minimum wage rates of 40 cents per hour after October 24, 1945, and a standard work week of 40 hours after October 24, 1940. All work in excess of 40 hours per week was to be paid for at not less than one and one-half the regular rate of pay. The act also forbade shipments in interstate or foreign commerce of goods produced in establishments where any person under 16 years of age is employed. The act is estimated to have shortened the hours of employment of more than 2,000,000 workers, and to have raised in substantial amounts the pay of an equal number.

PROHIBITION AND CRIME CONTROL

In some respects the most important reform measures of the Roosevelt Administration were those dealing with the liquor traffic and the control of crime. There was, all through the 1920s, a constant lowering of moral standards, increasing disrespect for law, and the growth of great crime syndicates in the cities with their activities reaching to all parts of the country. It was a period of widespread demoralization and lawlessness. World War I and prohibition were equally blamed. Home environment, education, and the churches were charged with responsibility. Whatever the cause, the age of criminals became steadily lower, particularly of those committing serious offenses, and it became increasingly apparent that the whole structure of society needed re-examination. It was equally apparent that national prohibition had failed to solve the problems of modern youth. Illicit liquor flowed as copiously as legal liquor ever had flowed. The hazards of getting a drink appealed to the craving for excitement of adventurous young people, and the liquor problem became an ever-present concern to parents and teachers. Slowly people rallied to the cause of repeal, reluctant to admit that the experiment had failed. The contest began in 1924 when the Smith and McAdoo forces waged a bitter battle in the Democratic National Convention. Smith was the

Democratic candidate in 1928 and openly favored repeal. In 1931, the Wickersham Commission reported that prohibition enforcement had completely broken down. In the spring of 1932, a *Literary Digest* poll showed widespread sentiment for repeal. The prohibition forces sought to discredit the poll by charging that it was being subsidized by anti-prohibitionists and that ballots were being improperly distributed. Actually, when the first half of the states had later voted, the *Digest* was shown to have been wrong by less than one-half of one percent. The poll was taken just previous to the party convention and the question could not be ignored. The Republican platform read:

We do not favor a submission limited to the issue of retention or repeal. We, therefore, believe that the people should have an opportunity to pass upon a proposed amendment, the provision of which, while retaining in the Federal Government power to preserve the gains already made in dealing with the evils inherent in the liquor traffic, shall allow the state to deal with the problem as their citizens may determine, but subject always to the power of the Federal Government to protect those states where prohibition may exist and safeguard our citizens everywhere from the return of the saloon and attendant abuses.

The Democratic platform declared:

We advocate the repeal of the Eighteenth Amendment. To effect such repeal we demand that Congress immediately propose a constitutional amendment to truly representative conventions in the states called to act solely on that proposal. We urge the enactment of such measures by the several states as will actually promote temperance, effectively prevent the return of the saloon, and bring liquor traffic into the open under complete supervision by the states.

Popular interest in the conventions centered on the prohibition question. There was a thorough discussion of the issue throughout the campaign, and the Democratic landslide was in part at least due to the desire for repeal. The short session of Congress passed, February 20, 1933, the Twenty-first Amendment to the Constitution and submitted it to conventions in the several states. The states themselves were allowed to arrange the time and method of holding the conventions and, although there was much diversity in methods chosen, the process marked the first popular referendum on a national issue. The amendment was ratified within a year and state legislatures faced the task of devising effective methods for the control of the liquor traffic, a task that was likely to cover many years. The desperate need for public revenues at the time led to heavy liquor taxes by state legislatures and Congress, and heavy taxation kept the price of beer, wines and liquors at such a high level that bootlegging gave promise of continuing to complicate the problem of law enforcement. On March 22, 1933, before the ratification of the Twenty-first Amendment, Congress legalized the sale of all beverages containing not more than 3.2 percent alcohol wherever state laws did not prohibit; levied a manufacturers' tax of five dollars a barrel on beer and wine; and rewrote the Webb-Kenyon Act for the protection of dry states.

Reform of the nation's criminal codes followed almost immediately after the disposal of the prohibition question. The cities of the United States had a homicide rate of 5.1 per 100,000 in 1900. The rate more than doubled by 1933. In the nation as a whole, it was 9.6 per 100,000 in that year with the total number of homicides exceeding 12,000. The annual property loss was estimated at $13,000,000,000. The consensus was that defective criminal laws were largely responsible. Ex-President William Howard Taft, in 1928, had maintained that the laws and not the courts were to blame. Specifically, he recommended (1) the improvement of jury personnel by making it impossible for criminal defense lawyers to challenge those best fitted for service; (2) that judges in state courts be given the right to comment on evidence; (3) that criminal procedure be expedited. To these may be added indictments of prevailing conditions by other observers, including (1) the influence of politics in local and state law enforcement; (2) the unethical practices of criminal lawyers; and (3) the sensationalism of the yellow press. The national emergency created by the growth of bootlegging, kidnapping and racketeering during the early years of the depression, accentuated as it was by poverty and unemployment and the almost complete collapse of public morality, forced the federal government to intervene. President Roosevelt had long been a member of the National Crime Commission and his private secretary, Colonel Louis M. Howe, had been Secretary to the Commission for many years. The President took the lead in a movement to strengthen the federal Criminal Code and encourage more active participation by the Department of Justice in curbing crime which had interstate ramifications. Raymond Moley, Assistant Secretary of State, was assigned the task of making a special study of criminal law and its relation to the federal government. A special division of the Department was created to deal with racketeering and kidnapping and seventeen new laws were placed on the statute books. These laws, passed in May and June, 1934, were designed (1) to prevent extortion and kidnapping by making it a federal offense to use telephones, telegraphs or radio to extort, and imposing a maximum penalty of death for transporting the victim of kidnapping across state lines; (2) to prevent any person from fleeing across state boundaries to escape from prosecution or from giving testimony in cases of murder, kidnapping, burglary, or robbery; (3) to simplify criminal procedure in federal courts; (4) to regulate the manufacture and sale of firearms; (5) to punish under federal law any offense against banks belonging to the Federal Reserve System; and (6) to permit the several states to enter into compacts for the suppression of crime.

25

Voices of Protest

NEW DEAL COSTS

EVERY item in the Roosevelt program was destined to be bitterly contested because each was of such a nature as sorely to trouble the minds and hearts of men. Human compassion and the generosity of a people distinguished for generosity were, from the first, confounded by real concern over justice, the security of their institutions, and of their basic social philosophy. Men who had no work, whose families lacked the barest necessities of food, shelter and clothing, were not much given to reflection on the blessings of decentralized government, the doctrine of judicial review, or of any other philosophical theory or institution. More than 15,000,000 men lived through the nightmare of unemployment during the depression. Their dependents numbered as many more. Liberty, to them, meant something quite different from what it meant to the men who later sponsored the American Liberty League. The latter might stoutly deny that liberty had changed its meaning; but the fact remained that it was given a new connotation by millions of people. Economic justice was as fundamental to liberty in 1932 as the Bill of Rights had been in 1787. Economic justice meant some relief for debtors at the expense of creditors. Existing law provided none. It meant that any man who was willing and able to work should not be denied the privilege. Tradition decreed that production would be resumed only when private capital was assured a return in the form of profits. Capital, unlike labor, did not work for wages. Both were essen-

541

tial to productive enterprise; but idle capital seldom meant distress in the owner's family as did idle labor. Economic justice meant, too, that none should suffer for lack of life's necessities. If the breadwinner of the family could find no labor, and the wells of private charity were dry, then government must supply the deficiency. If local and state governments were unable, unwilling or forbidden by state constitutions to do so, then the general government must assume the responsibility. None of this involved the demand for future security. That was a fundamental phase of the reform movement; but unemployment was a present fact—a condition and not a theory in 1933. The demand for future security would be a determining factor in politics; it might alter the nation's economic thought; it might even alter its political institutions; but relief was imperative, and upon the degree to which it was furnished and upon the ways and means by which it was financed might well depend the permanence of democratic institutions.

From first to last the Roosevelt Administration spent money lavishly, and much of it was deficit spending with a steady increase in the national debt. The government loaned money to banks, railroads, insurance companies, corporations, farmers, municipalities, and homeowners. It spent to rehabilitate the farmers, to build low-rent homes, to eradicate the city slums, to expand the forest areas, to create vast irrigation and water-power projects, to erect educational plants, and to build roads. Borrowing and spending on a large scale was defended as sound public policy, not only because it was necessary, but because it added to the country's social and economic assets, and raised the level of the national income, thus producing much larger tax revenues.

Actually, the deficit spending of the New Deal years was not excessive. The federal debt at the close of World War I had been $25,246,000,000. This had been reduced to $15,954,000,000 in 1930. This reduction during the twenties was the result of a government policy of balancing the budget every year and paying the public debt from the annual surpluses which flowed into the treasury. These surpluses ceased with the beginning of the depression in 1929; and, in spite of the Hoover policy of not spending federal funds for relief purposes, and of increasing taxes in an effort to balance the budget, the federal debt increased to $19,221,000,-000 in 1932. The annual surplus during the decade of the twenties had been about one billion dollars a year, and the annual deficit during Hoover's administration had averaged about one billion dollars a year.

During those last four years, the great burden of relief had fallen upon state and local governments, with state debts standing at $2,500,000,000 in 1932 and local debts at $16,500,000,000. New Deal spending increased the federal debt from $22,224,000,000 in 1933 to $27,876,000,000 in 1935, and to $42,585,000,000 in 1940. Thus the deficits for an eight year period were approximately $20,-000,000,000, of which about $12,000,000,000 were recoverable loans and expenditures for public construction. Non-recoverable annual deficits for relief of one sort or another, in short, beginning when 15,000,000 families were destitute and state and private funds were exhausted, and lasting through eight years, averaged about one billion dollars a year.

There was, however, a large increase in tax revenues during these years, as a result both of increased national income and of increased tax levies. Government revenues were $2,006,000,000 and government expenditures were $4,535,000,000 in 1932. Revenues were $5,387,000,000 and expenditures $8,998,000,000 in 1940.

It was this increase both in taxes and spending which sorely troubled so many men. That there should have been bitter accusations, misunderstanding, and fear was inevitable. Men who walked the streets in vain search for work with the cries of hungry children ringing in their ears could hardly have been expected to be philosophical about it. Men who had lost their savings and had seen the homes around which clustered the memories of a lifetime sold to satisfy the claims of distant creditors could not refrain from occasional violence. All of these people looked out of their barren lives in bitterness toward those who sat complacently with the nation's wealth in their grasp and condemned heavy governmental expenditures for the relief of human distress. They lent ready support to the EPIC plan of Upton Sinclair, to the Union for Social Justice of Father Charles E. Coughlin, to the Share the

Wealth clubs of Senator Huey Long, and to the Old Age Pension plan of Dr. Francis Townsend. Opposed to them was the rugged individualism of an earlier day: a philosophy which denied that the government could spend the nation into prosperity; which saw government budgets unbalanced, government debts accumulating, and wondered if they would be paid without a capital levy, repudiation, or worse. One can no more charge this group with insincerity, than one can pin the badge of demagoguery on their critics. That there was greed, selfishness, and deceit in all quarters is perfectly plain; but there was a respectable body of economic thought in the country which maintained that prolonged and excessive governmental spending would lead to the control of capital and labor by the state; and that higher taxes meant increased costs of production, lower returns to labor, and decreased consumption. This seems to have been apparent to the Roosevelt Administration and responsible for its efforts (1) to secure, by persuasion or compulsion, a greater return to labor at the expense of dividends, and (2) to finance recovery measures by borrowing instead of taxation that the immediate trend toward recovery might not be retarded.

POLITICS AND POLICIES

The most annoying aspect of the national situation in 1933 was the lack of a group devoted to a principle and strong enough to overawe the extremists and formulate a policy. The country was essentially conservative. The menace of the Technocrats, the Townsendites, the Share the Wealthers, the Communists, or any of the other minority groups was not in the programs they offered. Eventually, those programs would be analyzed, discussed, refined, and out of the ferment would come a modified national policy. The real danger was in the lack of an intelligent organized minority. The party in power was the traditional minority party faced with the task of consolidating its position. The Republican party was hopelessly disorganized and groping for issues. President Roosevelt attacked the problems which faced his administration in a way that cut squarely across party lines. The task which faced the Administration was both immense and complex. It was made more difficult by the great popularity of Roosevelt and the absence of a vocal opposition. Every one hesitated to criticize, partly from habit and partly through fear of hindering the process of recovery. No government can function properly without an intelligent minority and this was no exception. Every one wanted recovery, none wanted reform if reform invaded his own realm of privilege—yet sound recovery demanded drastic reform on many fronts. Liberalism requires experimentation, reason, and ofttimes compromise; but the open-mindedness President Roosevelt professed was difficult to maintain in the face of attack from both extremes. He turned out to be more of a liberal than was expected. The conservative forces of privilege and power, which had long been entrenched in both old parties to the despair of the independent voters, had not feared greatly the consequences of his nomination and election. The one exception had been the power interests which had deluged the convention with telegrams in an effort to prevent his nomination. The National Industrial Recovery Act, with its prohibition of child labor, the right of labor to organize, its minimum wage provisions and outlawing of unethical practices in competition, awakened them to a realization of what had happened. The laws regulating the sale of securities and the stock exchange struck dismay in the hearts of industrialists and financiers who had known no restraints other than their own conscience. The immediate disposition of the prohibition question alienated the die-hard drys. The inauguration of the Tennessee Valley Authority further incensed the already hostile power interests. The Agricultural Adjustment Act, designed to apply to agriculture the same control over volume of output which industry had always used, not only alienated the processors but touched the pockets of every consumer. These and every other act of the Administration added to the list of dissenters. In every case they cut across the unrealistic party alignments. People no longer thought of themselves as Democrats or Republicans. They were for the Roosevelt Administration or against it. Nothing showed the trend more clearly than one of the famous *Literary Digest* polls in which people were asked if they approved the policies of the Roosevelt Administration. The returns showed a slightly adverse sentiment; but in them were grouped all

545

degrees of opposition—Socialists, Wall Street conservatives, Free Silverites, Share the Wealthers, etc.—groups which were as far apart as the poles on any substitute program for the one they condemned.

Some of the opponents acted from purely partisan reasons and some from firm belief in a contrary economic philosophy or private-economic interests. The agricultural program was far from adequate, probably, as Secretary Wallace so frankly stated, because the fate of agriculture was dependent upon world conditions and foreign policy. That aside, however, the quota and price-pegging system had thrown marginal agricultural laborers upon relief; had benefited bankers, merchants, and landowners at the expense of the share-croppers; and had lost foreign markets to competing agricultural countries. The NRA had been launched on a much more extensive scale than was wise; had brought small business and service men (such as barbers and cleaners) in local communities under a bureaucracy; and had left a thousand small monopolies and price-fixing associations in every community. The Tennessee Valley Authority and Public Works loans for municipally owned utilities, not to mention the Securities and Exchange Acts, had angered those who had their savings invested in utility stocks, as well as the speculators and promoters. The Public Works Administration had embarked upon slum clearance and the building of low-rent housing. The Resettlement Administration had retired submarginal land and had tried to make rural life more attractive by promoting education and recreation facilities. It had built subsistence home-steads, camps for migratory laborers, and suburban towns. Critics insisted that its activities represented an excessive expenditure of public funds in a field which belonged exclusively to private enterprise; that it was accomplishing nothing toward relieving the need for 16,000,000 new home units; but, on the contrary, was trying an experiment in state socialism which caused private construction companies to hesitate to embark upon new building programs.

The second important aspect of the new situation was the lack of intelligent leadership in the opposition. Hoover remained the one opponent of the Administration with a respectable following. He waited two years before saying anything critical and then did so with the utmost dignity and propriety. His book *The Challenge to Liberty* included his first major indictment: that the policies of the Administration were totally and without reservation un-American, a repudiation of democratic institutions for a system of bureaucratic controls. From that point the same sensitiveness to personal criticism which had militated against his success as President destroyed his utmost usefulness as a minority leader. He made innumerable addresses in which he sought to prove that his Administration had succeeded in turning the tide against deflation and would have succeeded but for the lack of confidence growing out of Roosevelt's election. The second source of opposition centered in the activities of the financial and industrial leaders, Democrats as well as Republicans. Their tactics were not to discuss the merits of any particular measure, but rather to create fear of the whole. Personal liberty, the safeguards of the Constitution, all the beautiful and beneficent institutions of another day were being destroyed by an administration whose philosophy emanated from Russia rather than from the Fathers of the Constitution. In the whole of the millions of words which went out over the radio, through the press, and in private conversation there was little of practical value. It was the traditional tactics of a discredited leadership; but there was enough substance in the charges to cause most people to pass through a period of doubt at some time during the four years of bewildering activity by the federal government. Establishment of a vast bureaucracy, which was not under the civil service, had opened the way to graft. Reckless spending of public funds, derived from borrowing, was piling up a huge public debt which would eventually lower the standard of living by placing new burdens upon the taxpayers. The dole was not only destroying initiative and self-reliance, but was creating a political machine which would be self-perpetuating. The morale of an entire nation was being destroyed. The delegation of powers to the Executive Department would end in a dictatorship. Finally, constitutional government was in grave danger. This series of indictments was associated with the most bitter partisanship; they were the most difficult to prove or disprove; and they aroused the strongest emotions in the people. The important point is, however, that indictments, however strong, did not take the place of a substitute program. For seventy-five years, the Republican party had neglected the best interests of agriculture and labor, never consulting them and making concession grudgingly when forced to do so. The Roosevelt policies were dictated by the agrarians and labor, with strong support from an important group of industrialists. It was the first time such an alignment had materialized since before the Civil War. The Republican party was faced with the task of formulating a program which would regain for it the confidence of the people. It failed to do so for two years and, in the Congressional elections of 1934, party stalwarts such as David A. Reed of Pennsylvania and Simeon D. Fess of Ohio were retired to private life.

In the third place, there was an important issue involved in the question of emergency legislation. It centered in the delegation of power to the executive by Congress. This was done in practically all of the emergency laws. Pressure groups had almost destroyed the legislative process, and it was thought the Executive Department could better resist their demands. Senator William E. Borah led the attack against this departure from traditional procedure and the Supreme Court soon placed restraints upon it in the NRA and AAA decisions. There was a very real danger that emergency powers would be continued, at least sought, as permanent powers. Unless that tendency could be restrained and traditional limitations on the powers of government long considered an essential part of the American system restored, democratic government might well be lost. It was this phase of events which embodied the real promise of an opposition party, perhaps a realignment of parties on new and more realistic lines, but it failed to materialize.

THE SUPREME COURT

The controversy over the effect of New Deal policies upon constitutional government arose in part from the several decisions of the Supreme Court touching New Deal legislation. The Court, at first, had shown a disposition to give a liberal construction to the powers of the state legislatures. A Minnesota Moratorium Law, providing for the postponement of foreclosure sales, and challenged in the courts as impairment of the obligation of contracts, was upheld on January 8, 1934 (*Home Building and Loan Association v. Blaisdell et al.*). A New York Marketing Act, establishing a Milk Control Board with power to fix the retail price of milk, and challenged in the courts as a violation of the equal protection and due process clauses of the Fourteenth Amendment, was upheld on March 5, 1934 (*Nebbia v. New York*). Both decisions, however, had revealed a five to four division on the Court with a conservative bloc composed of Justices Willis Van Devanter, James C. McReynolds, George Sutherland, and Pierce Butler. Since Louis D. Brandeis, Harlan F. Stone, and Benjamin M. Cardozo were known to be consistent liberals, it was at once apparent that the fate of New Deal legislation of Congress would be determined by the attitude of Chief Justice Charles Evans Hughes and Justice Owen J. Roberts in any particular case.

An indication of the fate of the National Industrial Recovery Act was given on January 7, 1935. Section 9 (c) of that act gave the President discretionary power to prevent the movement in interstate commerce of oil produced in excess of the limits allowed by state authority. The act was challenged as an unconstitutional delegation of legislative power to the President, which the Court held was true, Justice Cardozo alone dissenting (*Panama Refining Company et al. v. Ryan et al.*). The Court, however, returned to its former alignment on February 18, in upholding the Joint Resolution of Congress eliminating the gold clause from all public and private contracts (*Norman v. Baltimore and Ohio Railroad Company*).

The first severe blows at the heart of the New Deal program came in May, 1935. On May 6, the Railroad Pensions Act, providing for the compulsory retirement of superannuated railroad employees, on pensions, which had been passed by Congress as an exercise of its authority over interstate commerce, was held not only to be contrary to the due process clause of the Constitution, but to be an unwarranted extension of the commerce power (*Railroad Retirement Board v. Alton Railroad Company*). Then, on May 27, three weeks before the power of the President to establish fair codes of competition in industry was to expire by limitation, the Court held that provision of the National Industrial Recovery Act to have been an unwarranted delegation of legislative power to the President, and an unwarranted attempt to reach beyond the limits of interstate commerce to regulate conditions in industry only indirectly affecting interstate commerce. It was a unanimous decision by the Court (*Schechter Poultry Corporation v. United States*). The Court, also on May 27, further emphasized the separation of powers by denying the authority of the President to remove a commissioner from the Federal Trade Commission (*Humphrey's Executor v. United States*); and invalidated the Frazier-Lemke Farm Bankruptcy Act.

The Supreme Court continued at its next term the trend begun in the spring of 1935. On January 6, 1936, the Agricultural Adjustment Act, designed to increase prices of agricultural products by paying to farmers bounties for crop reduction, the money to be derived from processing taxes, was held to be an unwarranted attempt by Congress to regulate conditions in agriculture and industry, and a discriminatory taxation of one class of citizens for the benefit of another class (*United States v. Butler et al.*). The right of the Tennessee Valley Authority, created by the Muscle Shoals Act of May 18, 1933, to dispose of surplus power, was upheld on February 17, 1936 (*Ashwander v. Tennessee Valley Authority*). Then came another series of adverse decisions. The Little NRA or National Bituminous Coal Commission, created by the Guffey Act after the *Schechter* decision, was declared unconstitutional on May 18, 1936 (*Carter v. Carter Coal Company et al.*). The Municipal Bankruptcy Act was declared unconstitutional on May 25, 1936 (*Ashton v. Cameron County Water Improvement District No. 1*). Finally, a New York State Minimum Wage Law was declared unconstitutional on June 1, 1936 (*Morehead v. New York ex. rel. Tipaldo*).

These decisions, taken together, stated certain constitutional principles which Congress might not disregard:

1. That Congress cannot delegate its law making powers to any other department of the government, nor to any administrative agency, nor to private individuals. It must formulate the nation's policies on a given subject and it must establish standards, although

it may leave to "selected instrumentalities the making of subordinate rules within prescribed limits" for the purpose of executing the law. Concerning Section 9c of the National Industrial Recovery Act, the Court said, in a unanimous decision: "(Congress) has declared no policy, has established no standard, has laid down no rule. There is no requirement, no definition of circumstances and conditions in which the transportation is to be allowed or prohibited."

2. Congress has no power to regulate conditions in industry under the Commerce Clause. Commerce does not begin until goods are placed in transit or in the hands of the agents who are to transport them, and manufacture for interstate commerce is not interstate commerce. Congress, therefore, may not exclude any article from interstate commerce because it disapproves of the manner of manufacture. Control over interstate commerce cannot be used to effect social reforms (Railway Pension Case, with Hughes, Stone, Cardozo and Brandeis dissenting).

3. Congress has no general powers "apart from the specific grants of the Constitution." Said Chief Justice Hughes: "If the people desire to give Congress the power to regulate industries within the states, and the relations of employers and employees in those industries, they are at liberty to declare their will in the appropriate manner, but it is not for the Court to amend the Constitution by judicial decision."

4. The power of Congress to tax does not include the power to accomplish indirectly by taxation a social reform which Congress has no constitutional power to accomplish directly. Nor may Congress levy taxes for the regulation of production.

5. Emergency conditions permit state governments to call upon reserved powers, but do not create or enlarge the Constitutional powers of the federal government. New York State was allowed to fix the price of milk, because "neither property rights nor contract rights are absolute; for government cannot exist if the citizen may at will use his property to the detriment of his fellows, or exercise his freedom of contract to work them harm." Minnesota was allowed to modify the obligations of contracts because "the question is no longer merely that of one party to a contract as against an-

other, but of the use of reasonable means to safeguard the economic structure upon which the good of all depends." Both decisions, however, were by a bare majority, with Justices Sutherland, Van Devanter, McReynolds, and Butler contending that an emergency does not overthrow the provisions of the Constitution designed to protect creditors from debtors relief laws. Finally, under no circumstances may either the federal government or the state governments impair the constitutional right of the individual to work for whatever wages he may desire. This principle was established in the New York Minimum Wage Case and, historically, may become one of the celebrated cases of the Court. The decision of the New York Court of Appeals was a 4 to 3 decision and based upon the Supreme Court's ruling in *Adkins v. Children's Hospital* (1923). Chief Justice Taft and Justice Holmes had dissented vigorously in this case and Justice Brandeis had taken no part in the decision. The Supreme Court's acceptance of the New York Court's decision was without a hearing of the case on its merits, with Chief Justice Hughes and Justices Stone, Cardozo and Brandeis contending that the Adkins Case was not applicable. Chief Justice Hughes said: "We have here a question of constitutional law of grave importance, applying to the statutes of several states in a matter of profound public interest. I think we should deal with that question upon its merits, without feeling that we are bound by a decision which on its facts is not strictly in point."

The legislation which these several decisions of the Court invalidated was passed at a time of grave economic emergency. It was customary, at the time, to speak of the legislation as constituting a program of economic planning. Nothing could be farther from the truth. It was true that the decade of the twenties had been a period of general governmental incompetence; that altered economic conditions had caused many to regard further concentration of power in the federal government as inevitable; and that the invalidation of many congressional acts by the Supreme Court caused many to believe that our constitutional form of government did not permit the measure of control essential to an ordered economic life under the new industrial scheme; but Congress had no plan, no policies; President Roosevelt had none; and the nation had none. The greatest achievement of the Roosevelt Administration was that it took a bewildered nation and, in a few short weeks, restored its morale and gave it renewed confidence. The Administration recognized the need for economic control, even though its methods failed; but its methods did not constitute a policy. If there was one single fact which reduced the charges of fascist or communistic tendencies to an absurdity, it was the conflict of purposes and division of counsels within the Administration from the first. What actually happened was that Congress, faced with the difficult task of legislating on modern social and economic questions in the crisis, and under extreme pressure from organized minorities, abandoned its legislative functions to the Administration. The decision of the Supreme Court invalidating the National Industrial Recovery Act may be considered, in one respect and in one only, one of the greatest decisions ever rendered. Here was a case where the sovereign powers of self-government were handed over to private businessmen, whose trade and industrial association regulations were clothed with the authority of federal statutes and, although they were written for private gain, without thought for the welfare of society as a whole, they were presented to the people as economic planning—the policies of the nation as determined by the considered judgment of Congress. There can be no question but that the Court's decision was in line with public sentiment. The enforcement of the law had completely broken down before the Court passed upon the question of its constitutionality. The public had awakened to the fact that it condoned price fixing, fostered monopolies, and led to rigidity in wages, hours, and prices. Why, then, did they criticize the Court's decision? Why did President Roosevelt speak impetuously of its having taken us back to horse and buggy days? First, because of the feeling that there must be social planning; that it must be translated into law for the control of economic life; and that legislative bodies, as constituted, were unfitted for the task. Second, because the several decisions of the Court eliminated all hope of controlling the conditions of production except by constitutional amendment. Third, because of the doubt that social-economic planning could be accomplished through the agencies of the forty-eight state governments.

There were circumstances connected with the constitutional test of the New Deal legislation which were of importance, but might well be overlooked. Opponents of the Administration had denounced the whole of the legislative program as unconstitutional and adopted a settled policy of overwhelming the Justice Department with appeals in the lower courts. The situation was such as to recall the words of former Chief Justice Edward D. White:

> There is great danger, it seems to me, to arise from the constant habit which prevails where anything is opposed or objected to, of referring without rhyme or reason to the Constitution as a means of preventing its accomplishment, thus creating the general impression that the Constitution is but a barrier to progress, instead of being the broad highway through which alone true progress may be enjoyed.

Added to this was the extraordinary spectacle of Chief Justice Hughes' denunciation of the majority opinion in the Railway Pension Case as reactionary; of Justice McReynolds' bitter words in the Gold Clause decision; and of the President's remarks following the NRA decision. The Court was divided on many cases, with Justice Cardozo representing the extreme liberal viewpoint, Justice McReynolds the extreme fundamentalist or State Rights viewpoint, and Justice Roberts holding the balance of power. These things being true, it was inevitable that the public should have thought in terms of what the Administration was seeking to accomplish (re-employment, increased purchasing power, elimination of child labor and vicious business practices), rather than in terms of methods; or that it should have regarded with some scepticism the statement of Justice Roberts in the AAA decision that "when an act of Congress is appropriately challenged in the Courts as not conforming to the Constitutional mandate, the judicial branch of the government has only one duty—to lay the Article of the Constitution which is invaded beside the statute which is challenged and to decide whether it squares with the former." On the other hand, there was remarkable unanimity in the Court on the important cases. A different decision in the Humphrey Case would have opened the way to executive raids on the personnel of the several administrative agencies. The Frazier-Lemke Act would eventually have destroyed the credit market of the farmers. The National Industrial Recovery Act would have given the President the power of life and death over all business and industry, with control of wages, hours of labor and prices, would have legalized cartels and trusts, and would have destroyed small business. All of these decisions, handed down on the same day, were by a unanimous Court. Section 7c of the NRA was held unconstitutional by an 8 to 1 decision; the Agricultural Adjustment Act by 6 to 3; and the Tennessee Valley Authority Act was upheld by 8 to 1. The Railway Pension Act and the New York Minimum Wage Law were invalidated by 5 to 4 decisions and these were the cases which promised to be of more than ordinary political significance. In the latter case, President Roosevelt criticized the decision because it created a sphere in which neither the state governments nor federal government could legislate. The question was, Did the Court correctly place statutory regulation of wages along with *ex post facto* laws, etc., as powers forbidden to both governments?

Several courses of action were suggested by those who felt that some way must be found to control modern social and economic conditions. The first impulse of many was either to deprive the Court of the power of review or to wait for an opportunity to appoint new and more liberal judges to the bench. These proposals were not new in American history, having been made many times in the past. One of the major items on the agenda of the Republican party when it came into power in 1861 had been to secure a reversal of the Court's attitude toward slavery and both of the above methods had been advocated on many occasions. The second suggestion was to secure the adoption of a constitutional amendment giving both the states and the federal government control over production, or for an amendment giving the states power to regulate wages, hours, and conditions of work in industry. The difficulty was that, while many people wanted a changed Constitution, no one could suggest the exact nature of the amendment desired. Neither party was willing to risk advocating such an amendment on the eve of a presidential election, but the issue was certain to be raised again after the election. The third course of procedure, and the one immediately adopted, was to attempt to do by means of interstate compacts what Congress had not been allowed to do by the Court. Finally, it was felt by some that the power of Congress over production was almost unlimited by a judicious use of the tariff and internal taxing powers.

The first of these courses of procedure was embodied in a Constitutional amendment introduced into Congress by Senator Norris. It read:

The Supreme Court shall have original and exclusive jurisdiction to render judgment declaring that any law enacted by Congress in whole or in part is invalid because it conflicts with some provision of the Constitution; but no such judgment shall be rendered unless concurred in by more than two-thirds of the members of the Court, and unless the action praying for such judgment shall have been commenced within six months after the enactment of the law.

This amendment, if it had been adopted, would have prevented the opponents of legislation from swamping the Justice Department with cases in the lower courts as was done in the case of certain legislation, but would have deprived the Supreme Court of the valuable opinions of the 142 Federal District Judges and 41 Circuit Judges and over-burdened it with work. It would have required the concurrence of seven members of the Court to invalidate an act of Congress and thus have lessened the number of dissenting opinions. Finally, it would have permitted the executive department to delay putting a law into effect until after six months had elapsed, and thus forestall any test whatever of an act's constitutionality. Josephus Daniels advocated a national convention to revise the Constitution to meet modern conditions. Governor Harold G. Hoffman of New Jersey favored a constitutional amendment requiring the Supreme Court to pass upon the constitutionality of acts of Congress before they went into effect. This, of course, would have made the Court a third house of Congress and have deprived them of the benefit of facts in the operation of the law before passing upon its constitutionality. Various measures of one kind or another were proposed by Representatives Dobbins of

Illinois, Monaghan of Montana, Marcantonio of New York, Maverick of Texas, and Senator Pope of Idaho.

The inauguration of interstate compacts was well under way before much of the federal legislation was invalidated. The several states had joined with the Department of Justice in supporting these laws before the Supreme Court. Illinois, Indiana, Ohio, Pennsylvania, Kentucky, Washington, and New Mexico were represented in the discussion of the Guffey Coal Act. Illinois, Massachusetts, Ohio, Connecticut, New Hampshire, New Jersey, and Rhode Island supported the New York Minimum Wage Law. Massachusetts created an Interstate Labor Compact Commission in 1933. New York called a six state conference on milk control. Virginia originated an Interstate Compact to limit the production of tobacco which was validated by Congress and embraced Pennsylvania, Ohio, Connecticut, and Wisconsin. Texas and Oklahoma took the lead in setting up control of oil production in the Southwest by Interstate Compact. Twenty-two states sent delegates to Chicago for a discussion of the whole range of activities in June, 1935, and definite movements were launched for agreements along the lines of crime control, traffic on highways, corporate taxation, marriage and divorce, hours of labor, health regulations, flood control, relief, and liquor licensing.

VOICE OF THE PEOPLE

The adjustment of political parties to social and economic realities having failed to materialize, the people were faced with the necessity in 1936 of choosing between the candidates and platforms of the two old-line parties. The Republicans met at Cleveland, June 9, 1936, and selected as their candidates Alfred M. Landon, depression governor of Kansas, and Colonel Frank Knox, owner of the Chicago *Daily News*. The Democrats met at Philadelphia on June 23, and renominated President Roosevelt and Vice-President Garner.

On the constitutional question which was much in the public mind, the Republicans denounced President Roosevelt for encroaching upon the powers of Congress and for adopting a hostile attitude toward the Supreme Court. The Democratic platform frankly endorsed the Roosevelt record, and said that such questions as unemployment relief, child labor, minimum wages, soil conservation, and agricultural production could not be "adequately handled exclusively by 48 separate state legislatures, 48 separate administrations, and 48 separate state courts." At the same time, it said: "We have sought and will continue to seek to meet these problems through legislation within the Constitution," and Senator Alben Barkley, in his keynote address, assured the country that "if, in the future, further amendments should become necessary to enable the people to work out their destiny and protect their fundamental rights or to govern some archaic interpretation never intended by its framers, I doubt not that the people will face that duty with the same calm intelligence which has guided them in the past." Roosevelt himself had left no doubt as to his attitude. He favored an enlargement of federal power for the control of wages, child labor, and industrial relations. His philosophy regarded unemployment relief, child labor, minimum wages, hours of labor, soil conservation, agricultural production, and flood control as national in scope and requiring control by the federal government; but he refused to say, during the campaign, whether he believed a constitutional amendment necessary to enable the federal government to control adequately industry and agriculture. Landon insisted it was a fundamental issue, as it certainly turned out to have been; but he failed to keep it alive by indirectly admitting that he was not certain whether such an amendment was necessary.

Republicans generally opposed any delegation of power over production to the federal government and endorsed the idea of state compacts as a solution to the problem, with Landon himself favoring an amendment giving the states additional legislative powers, if necessary. The issue, however, was not clear. Many men of both parties believed that government should be kept decentralized to avoid bureaucracy, to protect minority social and economic interests, and to preserve the experimental possibilities of state governments. But bankers and utility interests and the managers of transportation and industry had been in the past notorious champions of state rights or centralization, according as they believed one or the other department of government less likely to overcome the difficulty of bringing them under regulation. For all these interests suddenly to join forces in extolling the virtues of state rights raised some doubts as to their disinterestedness. President Hoover was a great centralizer of power. He championed prohibition to the last. He fostered industrial and trade cartels. He travelled far toward socialism by giving the federal government a tremendous financial stake in banks, railroads and insurance companies, and with his Farm Board program. But after Roosevelt's election, he suddenly emerged as the apostle of rugged individualism in economic life and state rights in constitutional theory. President Roosevelt, who had so fervently denounced boards and bureaus in 1932, and who had the solid support of the Bourbon, state-rights democracy of the South, had built up the greatest system of bureaucracy in the history of the nation and stood for an expansion of federal powers. The thing simply did not make sense to the independent voter.

The Republican platform vigorously denounced trusts and monopolies and Governor Landon said in Portland, September 12, "What the NRA really undertook to do in this country was to terminate our system of free competition, and to substitute for it a system of Government created and Government protected monopolies." This was another of the strange features of the campaign, because the trade and industrial association system was a relic of the Coolidge-Hoover regime, and the industrialists who were supporting the Republican candidate were trying to maintain the NRA on a voluntary basis. These associations, with their tendencies toward restraint of trade, price fixing, and other monopolistic practices, had been strong enough to dominate the government in writing the NRA codes, and they had emerged from the experience stronger than they were before. Newton D. Baker, L. W. Douglas, and Leo Wolman published a joint letter condemning the Harding, Coolidge, Hoover and Roosevelt Administrations as economically reactionary. On this point, they said: "We believe that the New Era and the New Deal are two streams from the same source. The one fostered private monopoly in the name of national prosperity. The other fostered state controlled monopolies in the name of national welfare." The Republicans made every effort to help the country forget, or rather keep them from understanding, the trade association movement of the Hoover regime. Their platform declared that "regulated monopoly has displaced free enterprise." It included the Democratic plank of 1912: "We favor the vigorous enforcement of the criminal laws, as well as the civil laws, against monopolies and trusts and their officials, and we demand the enactment of such additional legislation as is necessary to make it impossible for private monopoly to exist in the United States." The Republican candidate, Governor Landon, in his Portland speech, September 12, said: "We pledge ourselves to maintain a free competitive system, with a strict, impartial enforcement of Federal laws."

The issue here would seem to have been clearly drawn for and against the traditional American belief in the efficacy of free competition as written into the anti-trust laws and exemplified in the careers of Wilson and Brandeis. But the issue was not so clear. The two outstanding factors in the strangulation of the free competitive system were the protective tariff and the cartels. The Republican platform openly endorsed the high tariff policy, condemned the reciprocity tariff agreements of the Roosevelt Administration, and promised to repeal straightway the reciprocity trade agreement law "as futile and dangerous." Landon denounced these agreements as having "sold the farmer down the river," yet they were probably the soundest and least open to criticism of any of the Roosevelt policies. In the second place, the "stabilizers" among the manufacturing and financial interests were throwing their full support behind the Landon candidacy. What they wanted, and hoped to get, was a return to the conditions of the twenties, without government regulation of any sort.

The third issue before the country was the program of subsistence homesteads, the Tennessee Valley Authority, government generation and sale of power, and the program of work relief. Here was one of the most important issues facing the country. Flood control had passed the stage of debate. It was certain to occupy a prominent place in public works as road-building had in the past. Flood control, reforestation and checking of soil erosion were all part of a single problem. Engineers had already abandoned the old methods of operation for the newer system of controlling headwaters by drainage basins, reforestation, maintenance of grass lands, and small reservoirs. These things involved the erection of thousands of small power plants, recreation centers, the pollution of streams, internal navigation, and rural resettlement. The Tennessee Valley Authority, embracing the manufacture of fertilizers and electric power, soil erosion, reforestation, and flood control, was the largest single project along these lines. A shelter belt of trees one hundred miles wide and extending 1000 miles from Canada to the Texas Panhandle, embracing 64,000,000 acres, was the second largest. Land was being secured by cooperation with the farmers, through purchase or lease. The project was estimated to cost $75,000,000 and extend over a period of ten years. It was being carried out by the forestry service of the Department of Agriculture, which planned to plant a total of 2,000,000,000 trees. Construction projects were under way on the upper Mississippi and Missouri, the former including thirty-six projects; and similar work on the headwaters of the Ohio was contemplated.

The Republicans were silent as to what they intended with respect to this whole program. Nor did they differ radically from the Democrats with regard to continued subsidies to the farmers. The Republican platform promised to "protect and foster the family type of farm, traditional in American life"; to retire submarginal land; to balance "soil-building and soil-depleting"; and "to provide in the case of agricultural products of which there are exportable surpluses, the payment of reasonable benefits upon the domestically consumed portion of such crops in order to make the tariff effective." This meant an endorsement of the old McNary-Haugen equalization fee scheme, or of AAA benefit payments; and the continuation of the program by which the Roosevelt Administration had retired 3,000,000 acres of land at a cost of $100,000,-000. The idea of family type farms meant nothing. One of the chief indictments brought by Senator Vandenberg against the AAA benefit payments was that too much money was going to large industrial agricultural firms, and Congress had placed restrictions on large payments under the new soil conservation program.

The entire procedure was political. The disheartening thing about the revelations was the degree to which agriculture was being commercialized. Elimination of large farms from the conservation program simply fostered the process. A subsequent report of the Agricultural Department revealed that 100,000 farms were owned by 300 banks and insurance companies, one insurance company owning 2158 farms and another 4500 farms. Midwestern lands had fallen into the hands of the eastern financial interests through foreclosures during the depression. The consequence was an increase in the number of renters. It was this that the Frazier-Lemke Act had sought to prevent. Any attempt to subsidize with government funds the re-purchase of these lands would simply bail out the financial interests and shoulder a debt burden upon the taxpayer beside which the AAA benefit payments would appear small indeed. Yet so important was the farm vote in the election, and so eager were both parties to promise the farmers everything, that there was danger of one party or the other promising to do just that. There could be little choice between Republican promises of "adequate credit at reasonable rates" against Democratic promises of refinancing "at the lowest possible rates," the Landon plan of grain storage on farms against Secretary Wallace's "ever-normal granary" plan, or either party's flirtations with the idea of crop insurance against the other's.

The fourth issue before the country was that of labor organization and labor security. It is not necessary here to review the history of the labor movement. Industrial unionism was an established fact in 1933; but the industrial unionists were outside the ranks of the American Federation of Labor and leaning in the direction of communism. The NRA experiment swept them back into the American Federation of Labor and then out again, and resulted in the formation of many company unions. A three-cornered fight for domination of the ranks of labor loomed on the horizon. The Roosevelt Administration was favorable to industrial unions, which appeared to be labor's strongest form of organization. In many ways, the NRA had fostered industrial unions. The American Federation of Labor had long been friendly to the Republican party's principles, particularly to the protective tariff. William Hutcheson, President of the Carpenters and Joiners Union, was largely responsible for the expulsion of the Lewis group from the American Federation of Labor; and he became chairman of the Labor Campaign Committee for Landon. The United Mine Workers agreed to throw all their resources back of Roosevelt's re-election, and became a very significant aspect of the campaign in Pennsylvania, Ohio, West Virginia and Illinois. Sidney Hillman, President of the Amalgamated Clothing Workers, abandoned the Socialists and went to work for Lehman and Roosevelt. George L. Berry of the Pressman's Union organized leagues of labor voters in all the states for Roosevelt. David Dubinsky's support of Roosevelt was in part responsible for the charge by Chairman John D. Hamilton of the Republican National Committee and the Hearst newspapers that Roosevelt was courting the support of the communists. All of this in spite of the fact that John L. Lewis was a Republican, prominent in his support of Harding in 1920, Berry a Tennessee Democrat, and Hillman and Dubinsky right-wing socialists. Congressional investigating committees, meanwhile, conducted extensive inquiries into the use of private detective agencies to destroy labor organizations with some possibility that their findings might figure in the last stages of the campaign. Here again, however, the thoughtful voter was puzzled by the vagaries of politics, for back of the Administration's friendliness for labor—a fact recognized by friend and foe alike—loomed the dark shadow of peonage and fascist brutality in the share-cropping regions of the South.

A more important aspect of the campaign, with respect to labor, however, centered about the Social Security Act. This was one of the major items of the Roosevelt reform program. The Republican platform denounced the unemployment insurance and old age annuity provisions of the Social Security Act as unworkable, and inequitable because they made no provision for "two-thirds of our adult population." Both the platform and Landon's interpretation of it condemned the reserve fund features of the act and offered as a substitute (1) federal contributions to old-age pensions, the money to be derived from direct federal taxes; and (2) encouragement for the "adoption by states and territories of honest and practical measures for meeting the problems of unemployment insurance."

The final issue was that of government spending, the debt and taxation. It was the delegation of fiscal policies to the President, and the use he made of his power, that caused most disagreement. The Republican indictment, beginning with Senator Frederick Steiwer's keynote address, was that they had impaired credit, weakened confidence and retarded recovery, yet he himself had voted for the AAA, the TVA, the Thomas inflation amendment, the Frazier-Lemke Act, the proposal to pay the bonus with greenbacks and to override the bonus veto. But the debt in 1930 had stood at $15,954,000,000 and in 1936 at $33,393,000,000. The deficit for the six years of the depression stood at $19,386,000,000, for the Roosevelt Administration at $13,969,000,000. Expenses in 1934–1935 were $7,375,000,000 and in 1935–1936 they were $8,809,923,000, with estimated tax receipts for 1936–1937 at $4,917,000,000 and a tax system which might raise the amount to $6,000,000,000 with full recovery. The questions in every one's mind were: How long could the deficits continue without permanent damage? Were they necessary? Had value been received for the money spent? It was said that the WPA was an unplanned and haphazard undertaking with no lasting benefits; that industry, if relieved from uncertainty by a balanced budget, would speed up expansion and re-absorb the unemployed.

The Republicans were chary about promising to balance the budget immediately. An examination of the expenditures of the Seventy-fourth Congress explains the reason for their hesitancy. That Congress had appropriated $4,880,000,000 and $1,425,000,000 for emergency relief, plus $308,000,000 for the CCC. It had voted a $1,730,000,000 bonus bill; $296,185,000 for the AAA deficit; $440,000,000 for the Soil Conservation Act; $1,100,000,000 for national defense; $320,000,000 for floods in the East; $272,000,000 for flood control on the Mississippi; $50,000,000 for the first installment of a $410,000,000 rural electrification program; and $125,-000,000 for road building. The estimated cost of the most important items of government expense for 1936–1937, exclusive of relief, was $992,000,000 for ordinary expenditures; $585,000,000 for farm benefits; $1,160,000,000 for veterans; and $920,000,000 for national defense. It was inevitable, therefore, that when the opposition spoke of economizing, it should speak in general terms. Nevertheless, deficits of $3,989,000,000 in 1934, $3,500,000,000 in 1935, and $4,764,000,000 in 1936 were an encouragement for voters to support that party which gave most promise of reducing expenditures. The Democratic platform of 1932 had condemned extravagance in government and expansion of government bureaus and commissions; and the same indictment of their own administration was used effectively by the opposition in 1936. The country, incidentally, had finally come to believe that the Roosevelt policies of work relief had not provided adequate relief; had wasted funds on projects which were not regarded as socially useful; and had not given society full value for its enormous debt burden.

On the matter of taxes, however, there was great confusion of thought. Landon's financial views apparently included the idea that government revenue should be derived from direct taxes on incomes of individuals and corporations; that a continued large debt might find the country unable to meet a new emergency; that the tax on corporate surpluses should be repealed; that no further change should be made in the gold content of the dollar; and that dollars should be convertible in gold. The most important issue here was that of the income tax and corporation surplus tax. The Roosevelt Administration had not lowered the income tax base as far as many people thought socially desirable; but the Republicans refrained from stating what exemptions they favored. They denounced indirect and hidden taxes, but insisted upon retaining the most offensive of all such: the tariff duties. Finally, Landon denounced the undivided-profits tax on corporations as "the most cock-eyed piece of tax legislation ever imposed in a modern country." It happened that this tax measure was designed to eliminate the most flagrant method of evading income taxes. It was passed in the last days of the Seventy-fourth Congress and provided (1) for corporation income taxes of from 8 percent on the first $2000 to 15 percent on everything above $40,000; and (2) for a graduated tax, with a maximum of 27 percent on undivided profits.

The purpose of the tax was to prevent men whose income was derived from corporation profits from evading large personal income taxes by allowing the profits to be plowed back into the business without first being distributed as dividends and then re-invested. The principle of the tax was thoroughly in line with the attempt to revamp the income tax laws to prevent the evasions of the twenties, however much practical experience might prove the necessity for revision of rates. Landon denounced the tax as a measure which prevented expansion by the small businessman; but others denounced it on the broader indictment that it was a measure of social reform. This once more raised the issue, currently discussed since the first income tax of 1913, of how far reform should be the objective of taxation policies. An ascendancy of the negative view boded ill for the much discussed proposal of Nelson B. Gaskill, former chairman of the Federal Trade Commission, that the objectives of lower profits and higher wages be attained by a corporation profits tax with liberal exemptions for those corporations distributing a portion of their profits in the form of bonuses to employees.

Viewing these things in their broad perspective, there were two great and all-pervading issues before the people: (1) the relative merits of individual freedom under a government of limited powers versus the hope for economic security and economic stability through expansion of federal powers; and (2) economic and political isolation versus cooperation toward international stability. But the minority, which had failed to rise to the status of an intelligent opposition in Congress during the preceding four years, now faltered in the shadow of the election and blundered through the most hopelessly mismanaged campaign in many decades. The Republicans had small hope of winning the election from the first; but they did have a great opportunity to rehabilitate their party on sound and enduring principles with the aid of outstanding old-line Democrats, to inaugurate a re-alignment of parties along realistic lines, to give the nation an exhibition of statesmanship instead of partisanship and they failed to do so. On the contrary, they completely lost sight of principles in a desperate and, for the most part, stupid bid for votes.

The campaign entered the crucial October stage with labor, organized and unorganized, almost solidly behind Roosevelt's re-election. The Republican National Committee in conjunction with the American Manufacturers Association inaugurated, a few days before the election, an intense drive to break that support by reversion to the outmoded scheme of payroll intimidation. Workers received their pay in envelopes bearing a printed statement of the amounts to be deducted after January 1, as required by the Social Security Act which had been sponsored and approved by President Roosevelt. The effort failed to change labor's preference and reacted against the party among the millions of independent liberals who knew that men of both parties had supported the act as a non-partisan reform measure.

The charge of communism, upon which the Republican party had relied so heavily in all campaigns since World War I, and which was hurled at Roosevelt from the beginning of his Administration by Dr. Wirt, The Liberty League, Alfred E. Smith and others, was finally discredited by being overworked. It was an absurd charge in any case; but when it was leveled at such outstanding advisors of Roosevelt as Professor Felix Frankfurter of Harvard University, sometime visiting lecturer at Oxford University, it reached the heights of the ridiculous. Moreover, just as Prussianism had suddenly given way to communism in the minds of Americans as the great menace to democracy at the close of World War I, now communism had been replaced by fascism by events in Spain. Too many people felt that the Roosevelt Recovery Program had been exactly the sort of program required to save the country from radicalism of one sort or another to take the charge seriously. In short, many people believed that Roosevelt had saved both the capitalistic system of production and our democratic institutions.

The result was one of the most sweeping political endorsements ever given a presidential candidate. Roosevelt was returned to office by a popular majority of more than ten million and an electoral vote of 523 to 8. A hundred reasons could be given why various individuals cast their ballots as they did. Most of them probably because they, personally, and the country as a whole were economically more secure than four years before. Others, because they had seen government functioning for the welfare of the masses for the first time in their memory; because they believed the United States needed more men like Holmes, Brandeis, Stone and Cardozo in the Supreme Court and doubted if they would be appointed by those who denounced all liberals as communists; because they wanted the administration of the Securities and Exchange Acts, the Tennessee Valley Authority, and the Social Security Act to remain in the hands of their friends; because they believed the most important events of the ensuing four years would involve foreign relations and mistrusted Landon's ability to deal with such questions; because they believed that institutions survive or perish according as they meet the needs of human life, and that the government and the Constitution will live so long and only so long as they are made to function in the interests of the people. Above everything else, men refused to vote against a man who took a despairing and misgoverned nation, in one of the darkest hours of its history, and set its face toward the light, gave renewed hope and courage to its people, saved its homes and extended a helping hand to its young men and women. The talk about communism and fascism, debts and repudiation, and regimentation left them cold. The great endorsement given to Roosevelt in the election was not the result of bribes, or class hatreds, or yet of machine politics. It came from every class, from every economic group, from every nook and corner of the nation. It was an expression of faith, by a people who loved their institutions, in one who dared much that they might not perish.

THE CONSTITUTIONAL CRISIS

There had been indications during the presidential campaign that a supreme test of the scope and durability of New-Deal philosophy was about to be made. No one could say with certainty whether it would take the form of a new program of social legislation, carefully prepared and designed to satisfy the tests of constitutionality laid down by the Supreme Court; or of a Constitutional Amendment giving to the federal government the power to control economic processes, which the Supreme Court had declared was lacking; or of an attempt to circumvent the restraints of the fundamental law, as interpreted by the existing Court, by changing the Court's philosophy through its reorganization. The President, himself, may not have been certain until after the election. The party in power, however, was given such overwhelming majorities (328 to 107 in the House of Representatives, and 77 to 19 in the Senate) that the President was willing to risk, even if he had not previously planned, an unprecedented assault upon the independence of the judiciary.

No vacancies on the Supreme Bench had occurred during his first term. Six of the Justices were past seventy years of age, but apparently in good health and showing no signs of retiring. There were no indications that the President would have an early opportunity to nominate men to Supreme Court posts; and anyone who believed that the fruition of a great social revolution was being thwarted by a deliberate effort to keep the personnel of the Court intact until a more conservative Administration came into power, was justified in viewing the situation with alarm. Had the issue been made in the presidential canvass, the election might have been interpreted as a popular mandate. Had Congress been asked to pass resolutions submitting the question in the form of a constitutional amendment, a popular referendum could have been obtained as in the case of prohibition repeal. Instead, the President proposed to Congress, February 5, 1937, that the age for voluntary retirement of Supreme Court Justices be fixed at seventy; that the President be empowered to appoint one additional justice for each member of the Court who reached that age and failed to retire; and that the total membership of the Court should not exceed fifteen. Seldom has a proposal been supported by more carefully marshalled arguments; yet no other in modern times has aroused such widespread opposition.

The basic issue was the independence of the judiciary. This was a constitutional issue. Congress had the power to change the number of Justices on the Court. That had been done six times in the past. It had the power to fix an age for compulsory retirement, although the presidential proposal did not include that precise suggestion. Little concern would have been occasioned by such measures at a time of national tranquility, when no great social and economic issues were involved. This, however, was a moment of turmoil. A presidential election had just been concluded. Passions were running high. A combination of social, economic, and political issues confused the minds of men. What would have been, in ordinary times, a mere matter of governmental reorganization, now appeared to be an attempt to remove the restraints of the Constitution from the will of Congress; to appoint new Justices to the Supreme Court whose chief qualification would be a philosophy in harmony with that of the party in power; to establish a precedent by which a temporary majority in control of Congress and the Presidency could secure constitutional interpretations of permanent force; and to destroy the necessity of appeal by such a majority to the amending power. The President sought to evade rather than to deny this fundamental issue. Neither he, nor his supporters, appeared willing to make a frank denial of the efficacy of judicial review in a turbulent democracy.

The proposal accentuated the rift in the ranks of Democrats. In Congress, opposition to the reorganization of the Court was led by Senators Burton K. Wheeler of Montana, Royal S. Copeland of New York, Carter Glass of Virginia, and Edward R. Burke of Nebraska. They were supported by an imposing array of distinguished professional men, newspaper editors, and radio commentators. The opponents of the measure, however, showed no great willingness to defend the decisions of the Court on New Deal legislation. Indeed, they scarcely could have found common ground on this point, for many were outstanding liberals and many had been unalterably opposed to virtually all New Deal legislation. The debate, therefore, was far from satisfying to either the devotees of constitutional government or advocates of reform, although it was bitter and prolonged. Said the President: "A constant and systematic addition of younger blood will vitalize the courts and better equip them to recognize and apply the essential concepts of justice in the light of the needs and facts of an ever-changing world." Said the Judiciary Committee of the Senate, which finally reported adversely on the bill: "Let us of the 75th Congress declare that we would rather have an independent court, a fearless court, a court that will dare to announce its honest opinion in what it believes to be the defense of the liberties of the people, than a court that, out of fear, or sense of obligation to the appointing power, or factional passion, approves any measure we may enact."

The simple fact was that anyone who kept his attention focused upon the debate raging in Congress was missing the more important aspects of the contest. Out of the complexity and confusion of four years of New Dealing had emerged three major problems: social security, labor, and agriculture. If the New Deal program on these three questions could be made permanent, then all that had fallen by the wayside, either as unworkable or as unconstitutional, was of little significance over the long view. These were the issues which would determine elections, the ability of mankind to make progress by democratic processes, perhaps even the fate of democracy. The fate of the Social Security Act and the Wagner Labor Relations Act would soon come up for decision in the Supreme Court. The Soil Conservation Act of 1936 was admittedly a temporary expedient, and a new, more comprehensive program, eventually embraced in the Agricultural Adjustment Act of 1938, was being formulated. The C.I.O. was making a determined bid to organize the basic industries, with the new technique of sit-down strikes, and for a time there appeared to be danger of open warfare. The National Labor Relations Board seemed powerless to control either capital or labor, because everyone seemed to think that the Wagner Act was destined to go the way of the National Industrial Recovery Act. Not unimportant was the sharp and violent debate aroused by the charge that reactionary forces in the country had taken refuge in the Supreme Court. It was truly a critical period.

Then, in the midst of confusion and divided counsels in the country and in Congress, and of unyielding struggle for power between Congress and the Chief Executive, occurred a series of events which will long intrigue the student of government. The Supreme Court liberalized itself. Congress, on March 1, provided full pay for the Supreme Court Justices retiring after seventy years of age. The Supreme Court, on April 12, completely altered its previous position on the powers of Congress under the Commerce clause and sustained the Wagner-Connery Labor Relations Act (*National Labor Relations Board v. Jones and Laughlin Steel Corporation*). It was a five to four decision, Justice Roberts switching to the side of the former minority. The Senate Judiciary Committee reported adversely on the bill to reorganize the Court, on May 18. The Supreme Court, May 24, sustained the Social Securities Act (*Carmichael v. Southern Coal and Coke Co.*). In June, after the Senate Committee's adverse report, but before debate began in the Senate, Justice Van Devanter, the oldest of the members of the Court, resigned, probably at the suggestion of Chief Justice Hughes. These events thoroughly disorganized and weakened the case of the administrative forces. Then, on July 14, the administration leader, Senator Joseph Robinson of Arkansas, suddenly passed away, and a contest began between Senators Barkley of Kentucky and Harrison of Mississippi for the post of majority leader. The Court bill was now doomed to defeat and was returned to the committee on July 24, 1937. President Roosevelt subsequently had the opportunity to appoint several justices, including Senator Hugo Black of Alabama, Solicitor-General Stanley F. Reed of Kentucky, Professor Felix Frankfurter of Harvard Law School, Professor William O. Douglas of the Yale Law School, Attorney-General Frank Murphy, Attorney-General Robert Jackson, and James F. Byrnes of South Carolina.

The decision of the Supreme Court upholding the National Labor Relations Act had completely altered relations between capital and labor. The issue between the New Deal and big business from the beginning had been the right of labor to organize and to bargain collectively. Big business, as has been explained, had not objected to the principle of the National Industrial Recovery Act, but only to the collective bargaining provisions of Section 7A of the act. The decision in the *National Labor Relations Board* case robbed big business of the victory it thought it had won in the *Schechter* case, put a stop to the widespread violation of the Wagner Act, and gave to Congress broad powers to regulate practices in industry which bore directly upon interstate commerce.

26

International Anarchy

FAILURE OF COLLECTIVE SECURITY

THE Agricultural Adjustment Act and the Fair Labor Standards Act of 1938 substantially ended the legislative program of the New Deal in-so-far as its domestic policies were concerned. The revolt against the *laissez faire* philosophy of government and its relation to human rights and property rights, begun at the turn of the century, had been carried through to a successful conclusion. A Roosevelt had much to do with its beginning; and a Roosevelt had even more to do with its consummation. The responsibility of the state to provide social and economic security for its citizens; the responsibility of industry to society as well as to stockholders; the concept of labor as something more than a commodity to be bought in the open market; and the right and duty of the federal government to deal with all domestic problems which transcended state limits and state authority—these basic principles and innumerable collateral ones were now firmly established in the bedrock of public opinion and in the security of constitutional rectitude. The nation was free to turn to the second great problem of the century: the complete breakdown of international relations.

President Woodrow Wilson had enlisted the democratic peoples in a great crusade to create a new and better world order. The League of Nations had been established for that purpose, as a world security organization and a permanent agency for the expansion of a peaceful civilization. Its support had come from a passionate, almost world-wide desire to consolidate the gains of three centuries of expanding democratic institutions, and to make democracy the universal way of life throughout all the world. It had back of it a long history of arbitrations, alliances, and agreements formed to counteract the excesses of nationalism and promote peace. There was great expectation that it would make unnecessary all of the old forms of diplomatic arrangements and thus facilitate peaceful cooperation. The peace settlement created in Eastern Europe many small democracies whose people were not wholly conditioned to democratic processes. They needed, above everything else, an atmosphere of complete security in which to consolidate and stabilize their gains. Nor did the great and well-established democracies need it less to recover from the havoc of war. The peace settlement envisioned such an era with collective security based on cooperation, utter frankness, and wholesome morality in international relationships.

The United States, however, completely repudiated the Wilsonian idealism and retired into isolation. Other nations also repudiated Wilsonianism and endorsed the League Covenant with unexpressed, but none-the-less obvious, reservations. All of them followed a narrow, short-sighted policy, making a fetish of national self-interest. The offense of the United States was great because, having created the idealism and the hope for a better world order, its opportunity, indeed its responsibility, for world leadership was greatest. The offense of Great Britain was less because she did not retreat into complete isolation, but it was equally serious because of her far-flung empire and her close dependence upon the stability of continental Europe. The isolationism of Great Britain, Russia, and the United States left France unprotected, and enhanced her fear of future German aggression. She had suffered the devastation of her richest provinces, and an appalling depletion of her manpower. She doubted, perhaps rightly, that Germany would ever be other than a barbaric, revengeful neighbor. She sought to reduce Germany to economic and military impotence and keep her so. She sought to bolster the elusive collective security of the League by a system of treaties with Soviet Russia and with the lesser powers of Poland, Belgium, Czechoslovakia, Yugoslavia, and Rumania. Germany, it must be said, did not accept the totality of her defeat in 1918; nor did she express, much less feel, any contrition. Powerful forces began at once to create the fiction that her armies had never been defeated, and to prepare the way for a renewal of the contest.

Finally, little was said or done, either in the peace settlement or afterward, to provide a stable world economy. The League established various committees to deal with the international traffic in drugs, slavery, and women; to relieve distress from famine, flood, and earthquakes; to promote higher learning; and to improve the status of labor; but tariffs, reparations, and debts, raw materials and markets were too firmly entrenched in the sacred province of national self-interest to be touched. Whatever had been achieved in developing international political institutions rested, in 1929, on international economic chaos, and the depression opened the way to their disintegration.

There were then four factors to the ultimate emergence of international anarchy. First and most important, and most difficult to understand, was the loss of spiritual values and consequent decline of faith in democracy as a way of life. Far too many people lost their ability to respond to that system of ideas by which a modern humane society had been created. We have analyzed this regression in some detail in the United States. It took place also with varying degrees in the other democracies and led them down the road of appeasement. Second in importance was the economic war which followed cessation of conflict on the battlefront in 1919 and produced, not sudden death, but privation, hunger, disillusionment, and despair. In the third place was abandonment of the principle of collective security and return to intense nationalism, armaments, and secret diplomacy. Finally, there was the rise of totalitarianism, the causes of which still remain obscure.

RISE OF TOTALITARIANISM

Totalitarianism emerged after World War I as a counter-revolution against democracy. Its leaders scorned specific reform, endorsed radical and total revolution, and refused to countenance diversity or individualism. They sought to bring whole peoples into a uniform pattern of life; to regiment them politically into unquestioning obedience to themselves; to stamp out all opposition and dissent; to suppress freedom of religion; to prostitute science and education to their own selfish purposes; and to draw every phase of economic life under the control of the state. Specifically they repudiated the principles of international law and utterly disregarded the sanctity of treaties; were hostile to free enterprise; instituted government by men rather than by law; rejected freedom of enquiry and discussion; and ruthlessly trampled upon the rights and destroyed the lives of minorities. The peoples of Japan, Germany, and to some degree Italy embraced the doctrines of totalitarianism, subscribed to complete regimentation of their own cultural, economic, and political lives, and endorsed the principle of forceful division of the world into spheres of influence and exploitation.

The roots of totalitarianism lie deep in the past of these peoples, but the dictators emerged, consolidated their powers, and prepared for a campaign of international terrorism after the economic collapse of 1929, while the democracies were absorbed in the solution of their own internal problems. Once launched upon their careers, the dictators, whatever had been their original intentions, could not cease to promote racial and religious hatreds, could not abandon their programs of militarism, could not forego external aggression—because to have done so would have been to dissemble the entire psychological basis upon which their regimes rested. So it was, that while the people of the United States grappled with the problems of the great depression, and sought to provide permanent stability in their own economic life, a far greater threat to national security was emerging abroad.

Japan's conquest of Manchuria in 1931 and her invasion of Jehol in February, 1933, had evoked protests from the League of Nations and the Stimson declaration of non-recognition from the State Department of the United States; but nothing in the way of tangible opposition. Japanese militarists, therefore, felt free to embark upon their program of imperialism. Early in 1932, Premier Inukai and other civilian statesmen were assassinated to clear the way for their program. In March, 1933, Japan withdrew from the League of Nations; and in December, 1934, she denounced the naval limitations to which she had agreed at the Washington Conference. One year later her government gave full expression to her objective of creating a Greater East-Asia Co-prosperity Sphere in utter contradiction to the principles of the Open Door. This was followed by a new wave of assassinations, larger appropriations for the army, and the launching of a full scale war in China in July, 1937.

Adolf Hitler, appointed Chancellor of Germany by President von Hindenburg in 1933, inaugurated a reign of terrorism within his own country against political opponents, the Communists, and the Jewish minority. His party, the National Socialists, was led by a group of ruthless, crafty opportunists. They were, by all normal standards, psychopathic demagogues. Their philosophy was a philosophy of hate; their religion was a blind faith in German racial inheritance and their superior rights above those of all other peoples. They burned the Reichstag building and blamed the outrage upon the Communists to consolidate their power. They murdered a thousand men in their own party to consolidate their ranks. They crushed all opposition with ruthless cruelty by means of a secret police. They regimented the press, the radio, and the theater under a Ministry of Propaganda; education under a Ministry for Science, Education, and National Culture; religion under a Ministry for Ecclesiastical Affairs; and labor under a National Labor Front. They regimented the national economy and turned the energies of the whole people to rearmament. They initiated subversive activities in every country where a German minority existed.

Benito Mussolini of Italy, whose rise to power was no less crafty and barbarous than that of Hitler, poured troops and supplies into Africa all through the spring and summer of 1935, then launched a devastating assault upon Ethiopia in October. In the midst of the confusion created by the Ethiopian crisis Hitler moved quickly in defiance of the restraints placed upon Germany at Versailles. In March, 1935, he announced the creation of an air force and a conscript army. In June, 1935, he negotiated a naval treaty with

Great Britain which gave Germany parity in submarines. On March 7, 1936, he reoccupied the Rhineland.

The conflict of interests now shifted to Spain and became more intense. Civil War began in that country on July 17, 1936, with the Fascists in revolt against the presumed excesses of the Popular Front (liberal-radical) government. Mussolini and Hitler, eager to establish a Fascist regime back of France, furnished more than 100,000 veteran troops as well as many airplanes and much artillery to the rebel chieftain Franco. Russia, equally eager to promote communism in Spain and France, sent some aid to the Spanish government. Thus the ensuing Spanish Civil War was made a dress rehearsal for the conquest of all of Europe. In the midst of the European crisis, Japan pressed her conquest of China, launching an invasion at Peiping and then at Shanghai in July, 1937, with terrific destruction of life and property and inhuman treatment of non-combatants.

Mussolini and Hitler, in October, 1936, entered into close collaboration known as the Rome-Berlin Axis. Germany was given a free hand in Austria, Italy in Ethiopia, and all of Europe was notified that the price of peace was accommodation to the desires of the two dictators. Shortly thereafter, Germany, Japan, and Italy entered into the Anti-Comintern Pact giving Japan a free hand to subjugate East Asia. This pact was expanded in September, 1940, into a military alliance by which the three countries mutually agreed to support one another fully in event of attack by any power not then engaged in the conflict in Europe or the Far East. The alliance was obviously directed against the United States—the first of its kind in history. Thus were the three totalitarian states united in their campaign of international banditry. They were fully armed and ably led, and they faced a democratic world completely disorganized and confused.

APPEASEMENT

The democracies were incapable of arresting the progress of the dictators for several reasons. The League of Nations had promised security from aggression, but they had abandoned the League and lost the security from which a better world order might eventually have emerged. Not only had they failed to unite for collective security, but they had failed to provide, each for itself, adequate security by armament. They felt that armaments provoke war and so relied upon moral force. Compromise was inherent in the democratic process, so they would rely upon it in the solution of international problems. They had lost a generation of young men in World War I and did not propose to lose another. In 1939, therefore, it was unarmed democracies against well armed dictators, peaceful democracies against aggressive totalitarianism, moral force against absolute immorality, and compromise against masterful deception. Time after time the dictators were urged to return to moderation and reason, reminded of their moral obligations and economic interests, confronted with the principles of international law and their own treaty obligations. In return, the democracies received a medley of false assurances and professions of peaceful intentions, bombastic insults about the decadence of Democracy, a widespread infiltration of subversive agents in their midst, and finally the military alliances directed against their security.

When Germany, Italy, and Japan began their aggressions, world peace had been guaranteed, war had been outlawed, and maintenance of the *status quo* had been assured by four solemn agreements: the League Covenant, the Kellogg-Briand Pact, the Locarno Pacts, and the Nine-Power Treaty. The League of Nations was the principal peace structure, all other agreements resting upon the good faith of the signatory powers. The United States, however, was not a member of the League.

Neither the League, nor the United States, Great Britain, and France acting independently of the League had taken adequate steps to halt Japanese aggression in China. The United States had called Japan's attention to her violation of the Nine-Power Treaty and the Kellogg-Briand Pact, and announced that it would never recognize any new order established by force in the Far East. The League of Nations, nearly two years after Japan's invasion of Manchuria, declared her action in violation of the League Covenant. The United States, however, continued to trade with Japan, President Hoover resisting all demands for an economic boycott on the grounds that it would lead to war. The League did not impose economic sanctions as the smaller nations wished, because Great Britain and France, like the United States, feared the loss of trade and possible war. Japan, therefore, consolidated her gains in China, withdrew from the League, and kept the Pacific Islands assigned to her in 1919 as a mandate by the League.

Italy, seeing how helpless the League was to protect a weak nation against one of the great powers, proceeded with her long-planned conquest of Ethiopia in 1935. This time the League acted, though tardily and ineffectively. Economic sanctions were applied to Italy on November 18, 1935. Member states were not to ship arms or certain raw materials to Italy, to advance her credit or loans, or to import Italian goods. Sanctions, however, were ineffective because (1) Germany and the United States did not participate (the United States not being a member of the League and Germany having withdrawn on October 14, 1935), and (2) because the one essential to Italy's conduct of the war, oil, was not included. So long as Italy was able to get oil and to buy from the United States, the loss of imports from other countries was not disastrous. She triumphantly announced the annexation of Ethiopia and the existence of a new Roman Empire on May 9, 1936.

The Spanish Civil War was equal in sheer barbarism to the Italian conquest of Ethiopia. It also equally lowered the prestige of the democracies and enhanced that of Germany and Italy. Long after Italy and Russia had become actively engaged in the contest, Great Britain secured adherence by France, Italy, Germany, Russia, and Portugal to a Nonintervention Agreement. A nonintervention committee sat in London throughout the course of the war, but its labors diminished only slightly the aid of Italy and Germany to the Fascist revolutionaries. In April, 1939, three years after the conflict began, General Franco was undisputed ruler of Spain. France was almost surrounded by the armies of Hitler, Mussolini, and their Spanish protégé. The League of Nations was no longer a factor in international relationships. It remained for Prime Minister Neville Chamberlain of Great Britain to test the efficacy of compromise.

There had already begun the boldest attempt in history at world conquest while the democracies raced against time, internal dissension, and divided counsels to prepare for war. Hitler announced in February, 1938, that ten million Germans outside the boundaries of the Reich must be reunited with the Fatherland. Seven million of these were in Austria. In violation of earlier assurances that he had no intention to annex Austria, German armies poured across the border on March 11, and the union of Germany and Austria was proclaimed. The invasion of Austria was followed by a demand from Hitler for the Sudetenland of Czechoslovakia and by barbarous persecution of minorities in helpless Austria. Czechoslovakia was in many respects the most enlightened democracy of continental Europe, minority groups enjoying a wide latitude of local autonomy; but Hitler had followed his usual method of arousing internal strife through the agency of traitors and constant diatribes over the radio. First the traitor Konrad Henlein, leader of the Sudeten Germans, made impossible demands upon the government at Prague; then Hitler joined in violent denunciations and demands that the Sudetenland be ceded to Germany. Tension mounted during the summer. Great Britain mobilized her fleet. The French manned the Maginot Line. Germany rushed to completion her new defense line known as the West Wall.

Prime Minister Chamberlain, however, was ready to sacrifice Czechoslovakia for the sake of peace. Concession, compromise, adjustment of all differences, aims, and objectives between Germany and Italy on the one hand and France and Great Britain on the other was with him a fetish. German philosophy and methods being what they were, compromise was nothing less than complete surrender to the threat of force. Chamberlain himself went to Germany to see Hitler, as he had previously gone to Rome to appease Mussolini, each time making new concessions to new demands. Finally, at Munich, September 30, 1938, Hitler and Chamberlain signed an agreement to keep the peace by consultation on all questions that might arise. It meant, said Chamberlain, peace with honor for a generation. Actually there was little honor in the dismemberment of Czechoslovakia or in submission to the threat of force. Certainly, there was no guarantee of peace.

President Roosevelt had sent personal messages during the crisis to the governments of Czechoslovakia, France, Germany, and Great Britain (September 26) urging that negotiations not be supplanted by resort to force. The State Department, to its credit, made no claims that the settlement was based on sound principles or was an assurance of permanent peace. It was a diplomatic defeat of the first magnitude, suffered by Great Britain and France directly, but by the United States as well.

Hitler was now convinced of his invincibility. He was certain that the democracies would not fight on any issue; he was confident of his ability to plunder the continent of Europe by a mere threat of force. He invaded Czechoslovakia on March 14, 1939, in infamous violation of all his previous promises and to the complete chagrin of Chamberlain who, almost alone, had trusted his signature at Munich. The invasion, more than anything else, awakened the British people to the inevitability of war, and it shook the complacency of isolationists in the United States. The little country of Czechoslovakia was a model democracy, a veritable outpost of freedom in Europe. It was a symbol of the achievements of the great crusade to make the world safe for democracy. It had been launched upon its career of independent statehood by our insistence upon the principle of self-determination, with our money, and under the guiding genius of Thomas Masaryk who had been educated and had lived for 15 years in the United States. Its absorption by Nazi Germany was a severe blow to freedom everywhere.

Before the world could recover from the shock of his new adventure, Hitler had forced Lithuania to surrender Memel, had made demands upon Poland for the Polish Corridor, and had secured complete control of Rumanian economy. Mussolini invaded Albania on Good Friday (April 7, 1939) and quickly brought it under subjection. President Roosevelt asked both dictators, on April 14, for assurances that the remaining small nations of Europe would not be attacked; and promised, if such assurances were given, that the questions of disarmament and restoration of world trade on a basis of equality for all nations would be discussed immediately in international conference. Direct replies were not received; but Hitler, in a public statement, denied that such assurances were necessary. Meanwhile, Hitler continued his diplomatic and military pressure upon Poland for the return of the free city of Danzig and the Polish Corridor.

Great Britain now completely abandoned appeasement and joined in giving a joint Anglo-French pledge of military aid to Poland, Rumania, and Greece. The two countries made clear their full intention of going to war if Hitler pressed his demands for the Polish Corridor to the point of armed conflict. Yet, they were reluctant to face the prospect of war without the support of Russia. Russia, however, despite having joined the League of Nations in 1934, still feared aggression from the capitalistic countries and still sought safety in non-aggression pacts with her neighbors. British and French efforts to secure a mutual assistance pact with Russia failed. Russia feared the Democracies were trying to engineer a destructive Russo-German war which they might avoid. Conservatives in Britain and France distrusted the Communists more than they feared Germany. Russia asked territorial concessions in return for an alliance against Germany. Great Britain refused, on the grounds that to acquiesce in the absorption of Latvia, Estonia, and Lithuania by Russia would be a sacrifice of the principle the democracies were now seeking to uphold. Russia, therefore, signed a non-aggression pact with Germany on August 21, 1939. Free from the danger of prolonged war on two fronts, Hitler launched his invasion of Poland on September 1, 1939. Two days later, France and Great Britain declared war on Germany.

AMERICA'S QUEST FOR SECURITY

What of the United States while the dictators rose to power, the League died, and European democracies traveled the hard road of appeasement? The answer is, that the United States alternately sought international cooperation and retreated into haughty isolation in her quest for economic recovery and permanent peace. The United States did not want to go to war.

The first action of the Roosevelt Administration in foreign affairs was to send a delegation to the London Economic Conference, which met on June 12, 1933. The Conference was sponsored by the League of Nations and participation by the United States was approved by both the Hoover and Roosevelt Administrations, but with the understanding that tariffs, war debts, and reparations were not to be discussed. Roosevelt, during the presidential campaign, had condemned Republican tariff policies for bringing on economic chaos in the world, and had insisted that economic recovery must rest upon international cooperation. Certainly international cooperation was hopeless without American participation, and it was equally hopeless unless something drastic were done about tariffs and war debts. The Conference, therefore, was severely handicapped by the American limitations; and it was disrupted completely when the Roosevelt Administration refused to countenance international currency stabilization. Shortly thereafter the Administration embarked upon the self-containment program of the New Deal, which could not have been initiated except behind high tariff walls; and also upon recovery by currency inflation which could not have followed agreements on international currency stabilization. The Roosevelt Administration, therefore, must bear a large share of the blame for the failure of the London Conference.

On June 12, 1934, Congress took a realistic attitude toward tariff revision in passing the Trade Agreements Act, under which an effort was made to reduce tariff barriers by negotiation. The President was authorized to reduce rates by 50 percent on goods from nations willing to make similar concessions. Reductions were to be by treaty after scientific study, public hearings, and negotiation. Secretary Cordell Hull concluded 18 treaties before the end of Roosevelt's first term; and, while World War II prevented full exploration of the possibilities of the program, it increased enormously our foreign trade. It was a triumph for Hull's long fight against economic nationalism. It stopped the long, upward trend of tariff rates. It took tariff revision out of politics and placed it on a scientific basis. It clearly indicated that the long range policy of the New Deal was to modify curtailment of production as normal world trade could be restored. It did not, because it could not, repair the damage done by the retreat from international economic cooperation at the time of the London Conference.

On the question of war debts, isolationism again prevailed. European nations insisted at London on some adjustment of international debts as part of a general world stabilization program. The Roosevelt Administration, no doubt restrained by the fear of popular reaction as the Hoover Administration had been, refused to consider reduction or cancellation. France already had defaulted; Great Britain and Italy made only token payments in June, 1933. Congress then passed the Johnson Act, April 13, 1934, an isolationist measure, prohibiting any person under the jurisdiction of the United States to lend money to a government which had defaulted on its debts to the United States. The Attorney-General followed with a ruling that partial payment did not relieve a nation from the penalties of the act. It was then (June 15, 1934) that all nations except Finland entirely ceased payments. The Johnson Act also seriously interfered with the conclusion of sound agreements with Russia. The fifteen-year interlude in friendly relations with that country came to an end with the resumption of diplomatic relations on November 17, 1933. Each nation agreed to respect the territorial integrity of the other and to countenance no activity for the violent overthrow of the other's political and social order. Recognition was the result of the express promise of the U.S.S.R. in a letter of Maxim Litvinoff, November 16, 1933, "not to permit the formation or residence on its territory of any organization or group . . . which has as its aim the overthrow of . . . the political or social order of the whole or any part of the United States." Secretary Hull promptly protested, in August, 1935, against the action of the Third International Congress at Moscow in instructing Communist parties everywhere to encourage "revolutionary assumption of power" by the proletariat. Russia refused to admit that she had broken her pledge or to assume any responsibility for the action of the Communist International; but diplomatic relations were not broken off because of the incident. There can be no question, however, but that relations between the two countries would have been much closer during the trying period of world diplomacy had the Johnson Act not been passed. Russia needed credits to buy the enormous quantities of American goods she desired, and American firms stood ready to extend them, but she had refused to pay the debts of the Czarist regime. The renewal of friendly relations, therefore, was entirely political, without the strong bond of trade, and America's loss was Germany's gain.

With respect to Latin America, the renunciation of armed intervention announced in Hoover's Administration was continued as a permanent policy. The United States delegation to the Seventh International Conference of American States at Montevideo in 1933 supported a declaration against intervention and President Roosevelt definitely committed the country to the policy on December 28, 1933, by saying:

The maintenance of law and the orderly processes of government in this hemisphere is the concern of each individual nation within its own borders first of all. It is only if and when the failure of orderly processes of government affects the other nations of the continent that it becomes their concern; and the point to stress is that in such event it becomes the joint concern of a whole continent in which we are all neighbors.

The United States then refrained from intervention in Cuba during serious disorders under the regime of Gerardo Machado, and signed a treaty with Cuba, May 29, 1934, abrogating the Platt Amendment.

On June 15, 1934, the Senate ratified a Treaty of Non-Aggression and Conciliation, signed at Rio de Janeiro, October 10, 1933, binding the nations of the Western Hemisphere not to resort to war over boundary disputes, not to recognize any rearrangement of boundaries brought about by war, and not to interfere in the internal affairs of each other. The effect of this policy was very evident in the replies of the Latin-American nations to President Roosevelt's proposal, in 1936, for an Inter-American Conference for Peace at Buenos Aires. This conference, which Roosevelt himself attended, was the first step in a program for hemispheric solidarity against aggression, the American Republics pledging themselves to consultation in event of war, the threat of war, or intervention by any other nation.

Reciprocal trade agreements, recognition of Soviet Russia, and the promotion of hemispheric solidarity represented achievements of President Roosevelt and Secretary Hull while the country was engrossed in domestic problems and Congress was receptive to presidential leadership. The year 1935, however, marked a renewed interest by Congress and the nation at large in the conduct of foreign affairs. It was in 1935 that Hitler and Mussolini set out to plunder the world. The conquest of Ethiopia, the rearmament of Germany, reoccupation of the Rhineland, the Spanish Civil War, formation of the Rome-Berlin Axis, and signing of the Anti-Comintern Pact all occurred in little more than a year.

In the midst of Italian preparations for war on Ethiopia, Secretary Hull, in conversations with the Italian Ambassador, and Roosevelt, in direct communications to Mussolini, emphasized the deep concern of the United States that peace be preserved. A joint resolution, emanating from the State Department was introduced into Congress, giving the President discretionary power to impose an arms embargo on any one or all belligerent powers. Its purpose was to enable the United States to support the League of Nations in its application of sanctions against Italy.

The theory that cooperation with other nations was certain to thrust us into war had prevailed since 1920 and was still dominant when the dictators launched their program of aggression. A Senate committee, headed by the leading isolationist of the country, Gerald P. Nye of North Dakota, investigated the munitions industry between 1934 and 1936. It was made to appear that the arms traffic and financial transactions from 1914 to 1917 had been responsible for our entry into World War I. Now that the President had indicated his intention to support the League against aggressors, Congress reacted sharply, attempted to establish its own primacy in the conduct of foreign affairs, to circumscribe the power of the President in that field, and to base our foreign policy upon the determination that we must stay out of war. A Neutrality Act, August 31, 1935, forbade the selling or transporting of munitions to belligerents after the President had proclaimed a state of war to exist. The President might also withdraw the protection of the United States from citizens traveling on the ships of belligerents. This act deprived the State Department of the power to distinguish aggressor nations from those on the defensive, played into the hands of the totalitarian nations, which had been arming at a terrific rate for years, and renounced the principle of freedom of the seas which the nation had sought to uphold throughout its entire history. Congress added to these provisions of the Neutrality Act others in 1936, prohibiting loans to belligerents, extending the embargo to nations which joined a war already in progress, and exempted American republics which might engage in war against non-American nations. These amendments clearly warned members of the League that they could not purchase in the United States if economic sanctions led them into war. Finally, on May 1, 1937, Congress went still farther. It expressly prohibited travel on the vessels of belligerents, applied the provisions of the act to civil war as well as international conflicts, and gave the President power to enumerate articles which could be sold to belligerents only if they paid cash for them and carried them in their own ships. The cash and carry provision was limited to two years' duration.

Thus, by automatic embargoes, by prohibiting travel in war zones, and by forbidding trade and financial transactions with nations at war, did Congress seek to keep the nation out of war. This rigid formula deprived the President of a strong diplomatic weapon, placed small, peace-loving democracies in the same category with strongly-armed aggressor nations, added to the distress of Great Britain and France, and dealt a mortal blow to the League of Nations.

On July 7, 1937, Japan launched an invasion of China, first in North China at Peiping and then at Shanghai, with terrific destruction of life and property and barbarous treatment of noncombatants. It was the beginning of "total war" which was to carry the nations back to the customs of the Middle Ages. President Roosevelt refused to invoke the Neutrality Act, theoretically because no war had been declared, but actually because the sympathies of the people were with China and the provisions of the act would have worked to her disadvantage. But isolation sentiment was still strong and a suggestion of President Roosevelt, October 5, 1937, that aggressor nations should be "quarantined" evoked such bitter attacks from the isolationists that he did not return to the subject again. December 12, 1937, the Japanese bombed a United States gunboat, the *Panay*, which evoked strong protests and apologies, but still left the country far from a disposition to begin hostilities. Other incidents followed, with a firm declaration from Japan that a new order was in existence in the Far East. It was Japan's private domain into which other nations might enter only by sufferance. The Open Door and all treaties supporting it were obsolete. The United States served notice that it would adhere to the Hoover-Stimson policy of not recognizing new conditions achieved by conquest, continued to aid China *via* the Burma Road and later extended aid to Russia, and sought to avoid hostilities, as a matter of strategy, until naval forces adequate for operations in both the Atlantic and Pacific could be constructed.

27

Democracy's Lean Years

THE CONQUEST OF EUROPE

FORTY–EIGHT hours after Germany's invasion of Poland began the Polish air force of 1000 planes had virtually ceased to exist, and Warsaw was already a shambles. Four weeks exactly from the date of invasion military operations ceased. German and Russian armies had met at the River Bug. Poland was now divided between the two countries (September 29, 1939), with portions of the German Zone separately organized under a Nazi Administrator. The conquest of Poland revealed Germany's plan of operations. It included surprise attack; full use of armored offensive weapons; motorized infantry and artillery; destruction of airfields, communications, industries, and cities by bombing; airborne troops; traitors (fifth columnists) and spies; propaganda by radio and airborne pamphlets—surprise, speed, power, deception, ruthlessness, terrorism, and shocking cruelty—these, and more, were the tactics of total war; war that was destined to spread over all of Europe save Sweden, Switzerland, and Portugal in a few short months; war which was to carry civilization to the very brink of disaster.

The melancholy story of these early days cannot be fully told here. Suffice it to say that the conquest of Poland was followed by months of inactivity on the Western Front where French and German armies lay entrenched in the Maginot Line and the West Wall. Great Britain and France organized their blockade and their convoy system. They combed the seas for German surface raiders and submarines. They marshaled their resources and speeded production of the implements of war.

Then, on April 9, 1940, German troops invaded Denmark and Norway. Denmark offered no resistance; Norway was paralyzed by treachery; and both countries were soon organized under the Nazi tyranny. One month later (May 10) the neutrality of Belgium, Luxembourg, and the Netherlands was violated. The Dutch army surrendered on May 14, the Belgium army on May 28, both having suffered enormous casualties. The British army was driven from the continent, some 300,000 British and French soldiers without their armor being taken from the beaches at Dunkirk in an heroic rescue between May 28 and June 2. The Germans then turned South, and by June 10 were almost to Paris. Italy declared war upon Great Britain and France at that point, and France sued for an armistice on June 17. In October, the Italians extended the war to the Balkans by attacking Greece. Germany came to her assistance, overran Greece and Yugoslavia, and brought Hungary, Bulgaria, and Rumania under German control.

The power of the isolationist groups in the United States was great when World War II began; so great, indeed, that any thought of assuming responsibilities beyond the limits of the Americas was out of the question. The State Department could state principles, as Stimson had done when he said (1) that we would not recognize changes brought about by force; and (2) that war and recognition of war were now contrary to international law. The President could denounce Mussolini for disturbing the peace of the world, say that nations should abide by their pledges, and talk courageously about the necessity of quarantining aggressors. But, so long as Congress felt that we were secure in the Western Hemisphere behind our ocean barriers, and could continue to live in peace and plenty regardless of what happened in Europe and Asia, neither the State Department nor the President could assume the responsibility of upholding, by political commitments or otherwise, the principles they consistently expressed.

The rise of Hitler to power in Germany, accompanied by almost unbelievable barbarities against minority groups, the constant threat of force against the peaceful nations of Europe, and pernicious tirades against democratic institutions offended the finer sensibilities of the American people. The failure of European democracies, however, to stop the conquest of Ethiopia, Czechoslovakia, and Albania, and the overthrow of the Republican government in Spain, strengthened the conviction of many people that the United States should remain aloof from European affairs. The conquests of Hitler in 1939–1940, unequaled since the days of Napoleon, gave ascendancy in the United States to certain convictions:

1. That all of the things which were fundamental in the American way of life were under indictment by the totalitarian states; that the spiritual and cultural and economic freedom of the individual was being crushed to earth over three fourths of the world's surface; that the dictators had repudiated the principles of international law and utterly disregarded the sanctity of treaties; that they were hostile to free enterprise; that they believed in government by men and not by law; that they rejected freedom of enquiry and discussion; and that they had no respect for the rights of minorities.

2. That this was not just another war of imperialism; but that the Association of British Commonwealths was fighting to free the small nations of Europe, as well as themselves, from the constant threat of force; to preserve democratic institutions wherever they still existed and to restore the freedom of the individual in so far as possible where liberalism had been crushed; and to restore peace throughout the world by whatever means in the end might seem adequate, but with a minimum requirement of decency and respect for the law in international relationships.

3. That dictators, who were grinding their own people and those of neighboring states under the heel of tyranny, would not hesitate to destroy, by every means in their power, the greatest democracy of all time; that, having risen to power by crushing out the liberties of their own people, by playing upon racial and international hatreds, and by converting their nations into vast armament factories, they would not dissemble the psychological basis upon which their regimes rested, short of world conquest; and that they would not suddenly abandon their use of ideas as weapons, cease to carry

on subversive activities in the United States, and no longer try to confuse the democratic processes by stirring up racial, religious, and class hatred.

4. That the United States could not go on living under a war economy, as it would have to do in a hostile world, with any hope of solving its own economic problems; that it could not forever ignore its own stake in civilization; and that peace could never be restored in the world on a permanent basis without its active participation.

Congress had gone far beyond the prescriptions of international law in trying to isolate the United States from another war in Europe. Less than two years passed before it was apparent that the neutrality legislation would be swept away by an aroused public opinion, and that the United States would return to its traditional policy of trying to keep the sea lanes open in time of war. Public policy developed rapidly along four lines: (1) an unprecedented expansion of the army, navy, and air forces; (2) extension of all possible aid, short of war, to the nations which were fighting against aggression; (3) promotion of solidarity among the nations of the Western Hemisphere; and (4) construction of defense outposts in the Atlantic far distant from American shores. Congress, however, was always months behind public opinion during this transition period, partly because a presidential election was impending and Congress has ever been reluctant to define new public policies before an election.

A RELUCTANT CONGRESS

President Roosevelt, in compliance with the law, proclaimed the neutrality of the United States and imposed an embargo upon arms shipments to belligerents on September 5, 1939. To the people of the United States, he said:

This nation will remain a neutral nation, but I cannot ask that every American will remain neutral in thought as well. Even a neutral has a right to take account of facts. . . . I hope the United States will keep out of this war. I believe that it will. And I give you assurances that every effort of your government will be directed toward that end.

Public opinion, however, was strongly behind the Administration's desire to permit Great Britain and France to enjoy the benefits of their control of the seas. It was believed that purchases of airplanes, at least, by the democracies was absolutely essential to prevent a quick victory for the aggressor nations. It would also accelerate the expansion of aircraft manufacture for our own defense. Most people felt some doubts about the ability of France and Great Britain to survive; only the Nazi-minded and the ignorant could contemplate the possibility of their failure without deep concern not only for the safety of the United States, but for the fate of civilization.

President Roosevelt convened Congress in special session on September 21, 1939, and asked for a revision of the Neutrality Act. Congress complied to the extent of lifting the embargo from arms shipments; but the prohibition on loans to belligerents was retained; United States ships were barred from war zones; and citizens of the United States were forbidden to travel on the ships of belligerent nations. This act of November 4, 1939, meant that Great Britain must take title to goods before export, and it did nothing to relieve her from the strain upon her merchant marine and navy. How great that strain was is shown by the fact that approximately 3,000,000 tons of shipping were sunk during the first year of the war. More important, it meant that the United States, which insisted so strongly upon the necessity for preserving international law, was still unwilling to insist upon its rights as a neutral and the freedom of the seas for which it had fought since the founding of the Republic.

The Neutrality Act of 1939 was the last major effort to insulate the United States from the war in Europe. Henceforth, the Administration view that our stake in the war was as great as our stake in civilization gained ascendancy. The policy of the Administration was to gain as much time as possible for rearmament, particularly in naval building, to provide as deep à defense zone as possible from the American continent, and to strengthen the solidarity of the Americas. The 76th session of Congress, which convened on January 3, 1940, received from the President a request for immediate appropriation of $1,182,000,000 for defense. Congress delayed action. Then, on April 9, came the Nazi invasion of Norway and Denmark. By no stretch of the imagination could either nation be charged with having provoked attack. Neither wanted war; Denmark did not resist. Air power spanned a broad expanse of sea to conquer Norway. Greenland and Iceland belonged to Denmark and now were within the Nazi orbit. The way was open for the aggressor nations to carry the war to America. The President promptly recognized the independence of Greenland and Iceland and undertook to furnish them with needed supplies. Then Belgium and Holland fell victims to the German onslaught, and the assets of those countries in the United States were frozen to keep them out of the hands of Germany. Then the Germans approached Paris and Premier Reynaud sent a desperate plea to the United States for assistance. Unless France could have the assurance of early and active support from the United States, he said, she would "go under like a drowning man and disappear after having cast a last look toward the land of liberty from which she awaited salvation." President Roosevelt could only say that France could continue to purchase military supplies in the United States as long as she continued to resist, and that the United States would never recognize any infringement of the independence or territorial integrity of France; but that Congress alone had the power to make military commitments. He sought, and secured, assurances from the French government that the French fleet would not be surrendered to the Germans.

Then, and then only, with the British driven from the continent and France prostrate, did Congress act to strengthen the national defense. There followed a series of appropriations amounting to $13,000,000,000 within three months, and to $37,000,000,000 within twelve months after the invasion of Denmark and Norway. A new defense tax, designed to produce $994,000,000, and raising the national debt limit to $49,000,000,000 was adopted on June 22; and an act authorizing expenditures of $4,000,000,000 for a two-ocean navy was signed by the President on July 20.

On May 28, 1940, President Roosevelt appointed a National Defense Commission: Edward R. Stettinius, of the United States Steel Corporation, was placed in charge of the production of raw materials; William S. Knudsen, president of the General Motors Corporation, in charge of manufacturing; Sidney Hillman, vice-president of the C.I.O., in charge of labor and employment; Ralph Budd, chairman of the Chicago, Burlington, and Quincy Railroad, in charge of transportation; Chester C. Davis, of the Federal Reserve Board, in charge of production and export of agricultural products; Leon Henderson, of the Securities and Exchange Commission, in charge of price stabilization; and Harriet Elliott, dean of the Woman's College of the University of North Carolina, in charge of consumer interests. On June 20, he revamped his cabinet into a sort of coalition government by nominating Henry L. Stimson as Secretary of War and Frank Knox as Secretary of the Navy. Both were Republicans, and both favored increased aid to Great Britain. Stimson had been Secretary of War under Taft and Secretary of State under Hoover. Knox was publisher of the Chicago *Daily News* and had been the Republican candidate for Vice-President in 1936.

HEMISPHERIC DEFENSE

It was now that the good neighbor policy toward Latin America began to pay large dividends. Latin America should have been a fertile field for the activities of Axis agents, in view of the long record of armed intervention by the United States, the strong Spanish cultural ties, and the large numbers of Italian, German, and Japanese people in the population; but the repudiation of the Roosevelt Corollary by the State Department in the J. Reuben Clark Memorandum of 1928, abrogation of the Platt Amendment, withdrawal of marines from Nicaragua, the friendly visits of Presidents Hoover and Roosevelt, and the settlement of difficulties with Mexico had done much to obliterate the atmosphere of suspicion so prevalent in earlier days.

The Eighth International Conference of American States at Lima in 1938 reaffirmed continental solidarity; agreed to consultation in event the peace, security, or territorial integrity of any one of the Republics should be threatened; and provided for meetings of the foreign ministers of all the Republics at the request of any one of them. When war began in Europe, the Republic of Panama called such a meeting at Panama City on September 23, 1939. This conference approved a Declaration of Neutrality of the American Republics, established an Inter-American Economic and Advisory Committee, and declared, as an "inherent right," that there should be no hostile acts by belligerent nations within three hundred miles of the American shore. No provision was made to enforce the declaration, and of course Great Britain and Germany failed to respect it; but the few violations evoked sharply worded protests and talk of sanctions from the American Republics.

Finally, a meeting of foreign ministers, called by the United States, was held at Havana on June 21, 1940, to deal with the problem of American possessions of countries which had fallen under the control of Germany. This conference agreed to the principle of "collective trusteeship," and established an Inter-American Commission on Territorial Administration to intervene and govern any American possession of a non-American power in danger of a change of sovereignty. In substance, enforcement of the principles of the Monroe Doctrine was now the joint responsibility of the American Republics.

In order to ease the economic shock of the war upon those countries normally involved in heavy trade with European nations, President Roosevelt asked for an increase of $500,000,000 to the lending power of the Export-Import Bank, July 22, 1940. This was granted, together with authority to make liberal loans to Latin-American countries: $4,600,000 went to Costa Rica, September 24, for construction of the Pan-American highway; $30,000,000 to China, September 25, in return for that amount of tungsten; $20,000,000 to Brazil, September 26, to finance that country's steel industry. In addition, the United States made heavy purchases of defense materials, such as tungsten, graphite, bauxite, manganese, and quartz crystals, and assisted in stabilizing the prices of commodities of which these countries now had a surplus.

Drastic steps were also taken to help the hard-pressed British. They had lost most of their armament in the retreat from Dunkirk, and appeared helpless to ward off an invasion. Worse still, knowing that the Middle East must be held, they had sent all available forces from the British Isles to that area. All of the armament the United States could spare was collected and turned over to them. Then, on September 3, 1940, President Roosevelt announced that 50 "overage" destroyers had been exchanged for the right to build naval and air bases in British possessions in the Western Hemisphere. The sites secured by the United States were in Newfoundland, Bermuda, Jamaica, the Bahamas, St. Lucia, Trinidad, Antigua, and British Guiana. It was a history-making transaction in that it represented the first extension eastward of the frontiers of the United States. It was an acknowledgment of the changing problem of security created by air power. It served notice that the United States was prepared to run the risk of involvement in war to aid Great Britain. The trade was consummated by President Roosevelt without reference to Congress on advice of Attorney-General Jackson that such action was within his constitutional authority. There was, however, severe criticism of Roosevelt for this arbitrary action. The Republicans cited it as one more evidence of his disrespect for Congressional authority.

VERDICT OF THE PEOPLE

Congress authorized the President, August 27, 1940, to call the National Guard and reserve personnel into service. Then, on September 16, 1940, Congress passed the Selective Service and Training Act. This measure, known as the Burke-Wadsworth Act, inaugurated the first peacetime military draft in the history of the United States. All men between the ages of 21 and 35 were required to register for twelve months of military training. From the registrants (approximately 17,000,000) not more than 900,000 were to be selected for training in any one year; but those given training were to remain subject to recall into service for a 10-year period. Congress, by declaring an emergency, might retain the trainees in service longer than one year. The order of induction was to be determined by lot. The trainees were not to be employed beyond the limits of the Western Hemisphere, except in the territories and dependencies of the United States. Men engaged in essential occupations or having dependents were to be given deferred status. The National Guard had already been called out for intensive training, and the country soon had 1,500,000 men under arms.

Adoption of Selective Service in peacetime and in the midst of a presidential campaign was unprecedented in Congressional history. Few men familiar with the political history of the country would have believed it possible. It reveals both the gravity of the crisis and the degree to which interest in domestic problems had become subordinate to interest in foreign affairs. The trend toward a political realignment on the basis of foreign policy, begun by Roosevelt when he brought Stimson and Knox into his Cabinet, was continued in the party conventions. Republicans approached the campaign with confidence for many reasons. The Democrats had been in power for eight years, and their policies had aroused opposition from many classes of people. They did not believe any man could be elected to a third term in the Presidency; and Roosevelt had made no effort to groom another for the succession. Deep cleavages existed in Democratic ranks, as revealed by the battles to rejuvenate the Supreme Court and to prevent re-election of Senators who had opposed Roosevelt, and it was thought that only he possessed the political skill to maintain party solidarity. Roosevelt, however, had refrained from announcing his retirement, and most of the delegates to the Democratic convention at Chicago were pledged to vote for his renomination. In the convention, all other men and all issues other than foreign policy were subordinated and Roosevelt was nominated for a third term on the first ballot.

The Republicans met at Philadelphia, with the liberal young governor of Minnesota, Harold E. Stassen, as temporary Chairman. The leading candidates for the nomination were Thomas E. Dewey, Prosecuting Attorney of New York, and Senators Robert A. Taft of Ohio and Arthur H. Vandenberg of Michigan. The two Senators were staunch isolationists. Dewey was less so, but far from a supporter of the President's foreign policy. Early in 1939, however, there had appeared on the political horizon a new man in politics: Wendell L. Willkie, president of the Commonwealth and Southern Corporation, who had led the fight against establishment of the Tennessee Valley Authority. Willkie had a splendid record as an old-school liberal insofar as individual and minority rights were concerned. He was a champion of free enterprise and the philosophy of abundance. He insisted that the only way to give more people more of the good things of life was to produce more goods. Taxing and spending, governmental restraints upon free enterprise, and socialistic ventures would only destroy initiative and reduce every one to the level of poverty. Willkie's sincerity, winning personality, and courage caught the fancy of the people. A wave of enthusiasm for him swept the country and carried into the Republican convention. He was the only candidate for the nomination who believed that the nation should render all possible aid to Great Britain in her struggle against Germany. That was the determining factor in his nomination on the sixth ballot over the opposition of the Old Guard party bosses. Willkie had been a life-long Democrat. The vice-presidential candidate of the Democrats, Henry Wallace, had been a Republican until 1932.

The presidential election was determined by three fundamental issues: (1) the failure of the Republicans through eight years to formulate an intelligent alternative program for the social and economic reforms of the New Deal; (2) the effort of the Democrats to break the tradition of a two-term limitation for the Presidency; and (3) Roosevelt's foreign policy. There was a sharp cleavage in the Republican party between Willkie's young Republicans and the Old Guard. The former endorsed many of the domestic reforms of the New Deal, particularly the social security program and collective bargaining for labor. They also endorsed Roosevelt's foreign policy and the selective service act. Their single criticism on these questions was on the matter of method rather than principle. Their strongest talking point was to deny that any man was so indispensable that a tradition, which had come to have almost constitutional force, should be broken. The Old Guard, who hated Roosevelt and all his works, particularly collective bargaining—hated him so thoroughly that it made them passionate isolationists—and who resented the intrusion of Willkie into Republican circles, withheld their full support from the party's candidates.

It was difficult for the independent voter to distinguish between the philosophies of the two candidates. Both agreed to keep the country out of the war unless we were attacked, and to aid Great Britain in every way short of war. Both favored strengthening the national defense, including a system of selective service. Both promised to protect the interests of labor and the social security program. Willkie criticized the New Deal expenditures, the hostile attitude of the Administration toward private enterprise, and the slowness of the rearmament program. The second criticism was of doubtful validity, the last more of a criticism of Republican Congressmen than of Roosevelt. The election gave Roosevelt 27,241,000 popular votes and Willkie 22,327,000, with an electoral vote of 449 to 82.

War came ever closer as the United States worried through the presidential election. Preparedness measures continued, but not with the speed required by the crisis in world affairs. Willkie revealed high statesmanship in refraining from criticism of Roosevelt's foreign policies; but there was in the country a strong element of opposition. It arose in part from utter complacency toward events in Europe, in part from an inability of many people to view foreign affairs realistically because of their hatred of Roosevelt and the New Deal. An America First Committee was organized in September, 1940, which soon attained a membership of more than a million people. Some were honest pacifists; some believed the United States still had freedom of choice in the matter of peace or war; some were pro-Axis agents and Nazi sympathizers. They charged Roosevelt with dictatorial ambitions, predicted the death of American institutions in event of war, and appealed to every known prejudice in their efforts to obstruct the preparedness program and defeat Roosevelt. The presidential election, however, was correctly interpreted as an overwhelming endorsement of Roosevelt's foreign policy of giving all possible aid to the nations fighting the Axis powers.

EARTH–SHAKING EVENTS

Great Britain did not quit fighting when France fell as the Germans expected. They rallied from the disaster at Dunkirk; the United States sent them some arms; and they prepared grimly for an invasion. They had neither allies nor arms, only determination to fight on. Soon, they had Winston Churchill, of courageous heart and superb leadership, as Prime Minister. They had the nucleus of a resistance movement on the Continent in the form of governments-in-exile under the ruling sovereigns of Holland and Norway, de Gaulle of France, Beneš of Czechoslovakia, and Sikorski of Poland. They had the tremendous resources of their Empire and the Netherlands East Indies; and they still controlled the seas.

Germany was not prepared to launch an invasion. It was Hitler's first fatal error. The opportunity came but once. Instead of armies, they sent the Luftwaffe to bomb the Islands into submission. The Royal Air Force was still weak, but once again, as so often in the past, Britain called upon the individual courage and fighting qualities of her young men. With skill, and daring, and utter abandon, against overwhelming odds, they fought the invading air fleet. The Germans bombed docks, airfields, convoys, and factories by daylight until September. Then they shifted to a day and night bombing of London. Finally they resorted to mass raids upon industrial cities. Loss of life, property, and productive enterprises was appalling, but so was the loss to the Luftwaffe. In a few weeks' time, it lost 2375 planes, and from that loss its bomber command never recovered. The RAF, during those weeks, found strength to attack the coastal ports of the Nazis, thus forestalling every attempt to assemble an invading army. A handful of young men had saved England. Said Churchill: "Never in the field of human conflict was so much owed by so many to so few."

The Battle of Britain did not pass unnoticed in the United States. The people registered an unmistakable verdict of aid to Britain on election day. Her capacity to wage war had not been destroyed, but it had been seriously impaired, and the need for further aid was imperative. It was also very clear that only the

United States possessed industrial resources greater than those controlled by Germany on the Continent of Europe. President Roosevelt allotted one half of all production of implements of war to Great Britain on November 8, and spoke of the United States as the "arsenal of democracy" on December 29. Congress, after long and bitter debate, passed an Act to Promote the Defense of the United States, March 11, 1941. This Lend-Lease Act authorized the President to cause to be manufactured any defense article for the "government of any country whose defense the President deems vital to the defense of the United States," and to sell, exchange, lease, lend, or otherwise dispose of it to any such government, within the limits of Congressional appropriations. An original appropriation of $7,000,000,000 was made. Shipyards of the United States were thrown open for the repair and overhauling of British war vessels. The President was authorized to furnish defense information of all kinds to such nations, and to use his own discretion as to the terms and conditions on which supplies were furnished. The President was to make reports to Congress at least every 90 days; all contracts were to be concluded within a period of two years; and nothing in the act was to be construed as authorizing convoys or the entry of shipping into combat zones. The act was designed to make the United States the arsenal of the democratic nations which were fighting the Axis powers. It practically nullified the cash and carry provision of the Neutrality Act; and it did not in any way restrict the power of the President, as Commander-in-Chief of the army and navy, to defend the nation's merchant vessels on the high seas. By November, 1941, defense appropriations mounted to a total of more than $60,000,000,000, including $13,161,000,000 lease-lend commitments.

Adolf Hitler, in the late spring of 1941, made his second fatal error. With Western Europe securely in his control, and with Japan launched upon her career of expansion by the signing of the Anti-Comintern Pact (September 27, 1940), he violated his non-aggression pact and attacked the Soviet Union on June 22. The United States had warned Russia repeatedly of his intentions; and both the United States and Great Britain promptly extended the full benefits of the lend-lease program to Russia, exerting every effort to keep a steady stream of airplanes, tanks, and other supplies flowing into the port of Murmansk. Nine million men were soon locked in a death struggle along a 2000 mile front, the Russians fighting for national existence, the Germans for the rich food-producing Ukraine, the industrial Donets Basin, and the oil fields of the Caucasus.

This was a devastating war, in which the Russians followed a scorched-earth policy and "defense in depth," with the lines so fluid that commanders could scarcely keep in touch with their armies. Russia lost 500,000 square miles of territory before the German offensive was stopped 560 miles beyond the German border. Included in this area were the food, coal, and iron resources of the Ukraine, the extensive metallurgical industries of the Donets Basin and Crimea, and the large cities of Rostov, Kiev, and Kharkov. The Russians, however, had vast resources of men and industry beyond the Urals of which the Germans were not aware. They counterattacked at the end of November, saved Moscow, recaptured Rostov, and recovered about 100,000 square miles of territory. The Germans, unprepared for a winter campaign, and caught in a terrific snow storm, suffered heavy losses. An angry Hitler took personal control of army strategy, and prepared for another offensive toward the naval base of Sevastopol, the oil fields of the Caucasus, and Stalingrad.

Meanwhile, in the United States, events followed one another in rapid succession during the summer and autumn of 1941. Early in April, the government had received information that the crews of Italian vessels in the ports of the United States had been ordered to destroy them. Acting under the Espionage Act of June 15, 1917, which authorized seizure of foreign vessels "to prevent damage or injury to any harbor or waters of the United States," the government took into custody a total of 28 Italian, 2 German, and 36 Danish ships. Twenty of the Italian ships had already been damaged seriously. French vessels were placed under protective custody at a later date. Ten coast guard cutters were then placed at the disposal of the British for use in hunting submarines. An agreement was concluded with the Danish minister by which the United States was permitted to construct naval and air bases in Greenland. Finally, the President announced that the Red Sea was not closed to United States shipping by the provisions of the Neutrality Act, and a steady stream of tanks, airplanes, and other badly needed supplies began to flow to Britain's Middle Eastern armies.

President Roosevelt intimated, during the first week in June, that American naval and air patrols were keeping all shipping informed of the presence of submarine and surface raiders; and that strategic posts, such as the Azores and Dakar, would be occupied by the United States if necessary to prevent them from falling into the hands of the Axis powers. He issued a proclamation of an unlimited national emergency, subjecting all industry to priority control on a war basis. On May 21, the *Robin Moor*, a United States merchant vessel bound from New York to Capetown, was sunk by a German submarine without provisions being made for the crew and passengers. News of the outrage reached the people after the survivors had drifted for many days in open boats. The government then ordered all German consulates in the United States to close, and all Germans connected with the German Library of Information, German Railway and Tourist Agencies, and the German Transocean News Service to leave the country by July 10 because of activities wholly outside the scope of their legitimate duties. All Axis assets in the United States were frozen as a further blow to subversive activities.

Seventy-five percent of American supplies to Great Britain passed close to Iceland over the northern route. Informed by Great Britain that it would be necessary for her to withdraw her forces from the island, the United States sent marines into Reykjavík on July 7. The navy was ordered to "insure the safety of communications in the approaches between Iceland and the United States, as well as on the seas between the United States and all other strategic outposts." When Japan moved troops into Indo-China, the United States froze all Japanese credits and put all commercial transactions on a strict licensing basis, incorporated the Philippine defense forces in the United States army, and closed the Panama Canal to Japanese ships.

President Roosevelt and Prime Minister Winston Churchill

met in mid-Atlantic for a historic conference and promulgated the Atlantic Charter on August 14, 1941. There were eight points to this confession of faith. (1) It disavowed aggrandizement of every sort, with particular reference to territory, on the part of the United States and Great Britain. (2) It pledged the two nations to oppose territorial changes unless approved by the peoples concerned. (3) It endorsed the right of all peoples to determine the nature of their own particular forms of government. (4-8) It pledged the two nations to promote (a) the enjoyment by all states, large and small, victor and vanquished, of access on equal terms to trade and raw materials; (b) the collaboration of all nations for improvement in labor standards and social betterment; (c) peace in safety and economic security for all nations; (d) the freedom of the seas; and (e) compulsory disarmament of nations addicted to the use of force so that all might be freed from the burden of armaments. The charter was an epitome of what the peoples of the two nations had always stood for and sought to preserve, improve upon, and perpetuate. It was an invitation to other nations to cast their destiny with those whose foreign policy is conditioned by moral as well as political concepts and whose people insist upon maintaining good faith in their relations with other nations. On New Year's night, 1942, Great Britain, the United States, China, and Russia affixed their signatures to the principles of the Atlantic Charter and agreed to combine their resources to defeat the aggressor nations. Thus was born the United Nations.

The sinking of the *Robin Moor*, on May 21, was followed by the torpedoing of the *Sessa* (August 17), the *Steel Sea Farer* (September 7), the *Montana* (September 11), and the *I. C. White* (September 27). President Roosevelt issued an order to all naval vessels to fire at Axis submarines and surface raiders on sight, and agitation increased for the repeal of the Neutrality Act. The American Legion indicated the changing attitude of the people by passing a series of resolutions, at its 23rd annual convention, fully endorsing the government's foreign policy, demanding the repeal of the Neutrality Act, and endorsing another A.E.F., if necessary, and full aid to Russia in its fight against Germany.

War began, although undeclared, when a German submarine torpedoed, but did not sink, the U.S.S. *Kearney* on October 17, and sank the U.S.S. *Reuben James* on October 30. Congress repealed the more important provisions of the Neutrality Act early in November, permitting the arming of merchant ships and their entry into the ports of belligerent nations. Defense expenditures by that time had reached a total of $50,000,000 per day. Never before in its history had the nation been so well prepared for war before becoming engaged. It was not long in coming, though some people hoped to the end that it might be avoided.

Japan had sent an envoy extraordinary, Saburo Kurusu, to the United States, and he turned out to be a most extraordinary emissary indeed. He and the Japanese Ambassador, Kichisaburo Nomura, conducted long and serious negotiations with the State Department, beginning November 17, in what appeared to be a supreme effort to iron out differences between the two nations. Actually, they sought to lull the United States to sleep while preparations were completed for a surprise attack. It was a perfect example of the curious reasoning by which the dictators had for years been interpreting the humanitarianism and patience of the democracies as national decadence. The State Department did not relax its vigilance nor recede from its position. It called representatives of Great Britain, China, The Netherlands, and Australia into conference on November 24. Three days later it restated its basic principles for peace and security in the Pacific. These were (1) abandonment by Japan of her program of aggression; (2) withdrawal of her troops from China and French Indo-China; and (3) adherence to a peaceful economic policy. The Japanese envoys, acting out their dishonorable part of the drama to its bitter end, cabled for instructions.

On November 27, the same day that Secretary Hull restated our principles for peace in the Pacific, Premier Tojo of Japan declared that Japan was prepared and determined to drive Great Britain and the United States from Asia "for the honor and pride of mankind." Beginning on that day, as later revealed, a series of warnings were sent to the armed forces of the United States in the Pacific that war was believed to be imminent. All competent observers believed an early thrust by Japan at the Burma Road, China's life-line, perhaps at Singapore and the Dutch East Indies, was certain. The Japanese Cabinet, however, announced on December 1 that negotiations would be continued. The following day, the United States requested from Japan her reasons for continuing to mass troops in Indo-China. Japanese consulates began burning secret documents on December 3, and the State Department issued a severe denunciation of Japan's bad faith in continuing preparations for an assault upon the Burma Road while carrying on peace nego-tiations with the United States. The Japanese ambassadors made an urgent plea for an appointment at one o'clock in the afternoon, Sunday, December 7, and were received shortly after two o'clock by Secretary Hull. They presented a reply to the note of November 26, which he read before stating: "In all my 50 years of public service I have never seen a document that was more crowded with infamous falsehoods and distortions . . . on a scale so huge that I never imagined until today that any government on this planet was capable of uttering them."

The extreme bitterness of Hull's remarks was occasioned by the fact that some time previously, at dawn in Hawaii, the Japanese navy and air force had launched a surprise attack upon Pearl Harbor, and followed it with an attack upon American and British possessions throughout the Pacific area. The United States Ambassador to Japan, Joseph Grew, was not notified until three hours and 40 minutes after the attack had been made; and he had been informed 24 hours previously that Emperor Hirohito was instructing the government to continue its earnest efforts for peace. The wide and devastating scale on which the surprise attack was launched was in itself positive proof that preparations had been going on for many weeks and that it had been carefully timed long in advance. It was a repetition of the Nazi pattern of making war while professing peace.

The attack on Pearl Harbor cost the United States more than 3000 naval and air personnel, two battleships, three destroyers, many aircraft, and an unstated number of ships seriously damaged. Lieut.-Gen. Walter C. Short and Admiral Husband E. Kimmel were relieved of their commands. A presidential board of inquiry, headed by Associate Justice Owen J. Roberts of the Supreme Court, later charged that they had been properly informed that war was imminent, and had been ordered to prepare against an air raid; but that they had failed to confer upon proper measures to be taken and had been completely surprised. The United States declared war on Japan on Monday, December 8, with but one dissenting vote in Congress. Hitler and Mussolini declared war on the United States on December 11; and Congress accepted the challenge with a unanimous declaration of war on the same day.

One may search the pages of history in vain to find any previous period (scarcely more than a year) in which there occurred events of such grandeur and outrage, of such incredible loss and rich promise to mankind. We may record the losses of the Battle of Britain in terms of civilian casualties, planes destroyed, and property damaged; we may chart the course of armies across the vast Russian plains; we may calculate the products of American factories which flowed into the channels of lend-lease; we may state the principles agreed upon in the Atlantic Charter; and we may calculate the precise damage done at Pearl Harbor; but we can only speculate upon the terrible consequences to civilization had the defense of Britain and Russia failed; and we turn away helpless to understand either the evil power of men who sacrificed a nation of people like Japan or the tremendous moral reserves of democratic peoples.

In those hours Germany and Japan came so close to complete domination of the world that we do not yet realize how thin the thread of Allied survival had been stretched. In good conscience this nation can take little credit for its part in staving off disaster in those critical days. It is certain that the refusal of the British and Russian peoples to accept what appeared to be inevitable defeat was the great factor in the salvage of our civilization. Of almost equal importance was the failure of the enemy to make the most of the situation.

So spoke General George C. Marshall, Chief of Staff of the United States Army.

28

Preparing for Global War

POWER OF THE AXIS

THE power of the Axis was great indeed as the year 1942 opened. All of continental Europe except Sweden, Switzerland, and Portugal was prostrate beneath the heel of Nazi tyranny or subservient to the Führer's will. Even Italy, full-fledged partner of Germany in the program of world conquest, was little more than a vassal state. The Franco regime in Spain was indebted to Hitler and Mussolini, and was ever ready to do their bidding. The Vichy government of Marshal Pétain in unoccupied France was neither disposed nor able to maintain independent policies. Even Sweden, whose economy was closely bound to that of the Axis partners, had faltered in the hour of Germany's greatest triumphs, and had agreed to the transit of German troops to and from occupied Norway. German or Italian troops, German agents, and the dreaded Gestapo were everywhere from Norway to the Dardanelles, and in sufficient numbers to cope with all but sporadic and carefully executed resistance.

The Germans now had at their disposal the agriculture of Denmark, Holland, and France; the timber resources and fisheries of Norway; the iron of Sweden; the oil of Rumania; and the accumulated wealth and industries of an entire continent. They exploited these assets to the fullest extent, not hesitating to resort to forced labor, and eventually to compulsory military service, of non-German peoples. The Allied blockade of the continent, embracing the most efficient methods of economic warfare, gave promise of eventually exhausting Germany's supplies; but the full force of this war of attrition was certain to fall first upon the civilian population of the conquered countries rather than upon the common enemy, and the close collaboration of the French government under Marshal Pétain and Pierre Laval gave to Germany the vast resources of the French African empire. Sweden and Turkey also, struggling to remain neutral, provided some resources for Germany that were beyond the power of the Allied governments to touch. The greatest weakness of Germany, one which was to prove fatal in mechanized warfare, was lack of oil. Unless her armies could break through to the Caucasus and the Middle East, she must rely upon accumulated reserves, synthetics, and the minor production of subject regions such as Rumania.

In Africa, Algeria and French West Africa, with their great naval bases, were controlled by Vichy France. Libya was controlled by the Italians; but the British, under General Wavell, had advanced from Egypt, had captured Bardia, Tobruk, and Bengasi, had taken 133,000 prisoners, and had entrenched at El Agheila (December 9, 1940–February 7, 1941). In East Africa, they had driven the Italian forces from Eritrea, Ethiopia, and Somaliland. Then Crete had been lost to the Germans; and Egypt, with its great naval bases at Alexandria and Port Said, was again threatened from two directions when General Rommel came to the aid of the hard-pressed Italians and drove the British back to El Alamein, fifty miles from Alexandria (November, 1941, to January, 1942). Malta, Gibraltar, and Alexandria remained in British hands; but the Mediterranean was no longer a safe route for British convoys to the Near East; and the long route around Africa was endangered by the possibility of submarine sorties from the French port of Dakar.

In the Pacific, Japan met almost no resistance to her master stroke for what she called a Greater East Asia Co-Prosperity Sphere. The "Gibraltar of the Pacific" on Oahu Island, key to the United States defense system from the Panama Canal to Alaska, suffered a grievous blow on December 7, 1941, but did not fall. Guam, in the center of the Japanese Mandate, was lost (December 10), as was Wake (December 24); but Midway held and became the focal point of the first great victory over the Japanese at a later date. Thailand, already within the Japanese orbit, was overrun in a matter of hours by Japanese forces from Indo-China. Hong Kong surrendered on December 25. Japanese troops sifted down the coast of Malaya, meeting heroic, but futile, resistance from Australian contingents. Two powerful British battleships, *Prince of Wales* and *Repulse*, which ventured into the South China Sea without air support, were sunk. Singapore, $400,000,000 British naval base, was surrendered on February 15, 1942. Rangoon was occupied on March 7, and the Burma Road, lifeline to China, was cut by the capture of Lashio on April 29.

The islands of the Netherlands East Indies, stretching from British Malaya 4000 miles eastward to the Solomon Islands, were overrun in rapid succession before March 10. With them went the Dutch naval bases at Surabaya and Amboina. In the Philippines, a valiant army of United States infantry and Filipino Scouts retreated to Bataan Peninsula to fight a delaying action. Efforts to reinforce them from Australia proved unsuccessful, and their commander, General Douglas MacArthur, was transferred to Australia on orders from President Roosevelt. Manila fell on January 2, Bataan at the beginning of April, Corregidor on May 6. Only Australia remained, with Port Moresby to the north on New Guinea, and New Caledonia, as outposts from which to base future operations against Japan. India remained in British hands, but in a confused political condition, and thence were sent General Wavell to organize the military defenses and Sir Stafford Cripps to restore political solidarity. In the Aleutians, the islands of Attu, Agatu, and Kiska were occupied by the Japanese. China, weak from five years of war, fought on against overwhelming odds. She was shut off from the outside world, for Japan held her sea coast, most of her railroads, and her larger cities. Her capital had been removed to Chungking, and only through the indomitable courage of the young Chinese under the leadership of Chiang Kai-shek, and faith in future aid from America, was a portion of China preserved as a base for future offensive action against Japan proper.

The Allies lost heavily in strategic resources when Japan established control of the Southwest Pacific area, with its great stores of oil, tin, and rubber. A scorched-earth policy was applied by the retreating armies of the British and Netherlands East Indies, not too effectively, as it turned out; but the long distances from the British Isles and from the United States, over which supplies had to be carried before an offensive against Japan could be mounted, and the pressing necessity of consolidating every possible resource in the European and African areas, raised the serious question of whether important areas of production could be recovered before Japan had exploited them sufficiently to make herself a truly formidable adversary. Australia, though almost as large as continental United States, had a population of only about 7,000,000 people, few large-scale industries, no great naval bases, and few of the essential metals necessary for war production.

Warfare on the high seas had raged unabated from the beginning of the conflict. Britain had barely survived the three-month aerial blitzkrieg begun upon the Islands on August 8, 1940. Her small air force had added a glorious chapter to the history of British valor, destroying 2375 enemy planes and retaining control of the air over the homeland; but there had been untold loss of civilian lives and destruction of cities, factories, and port facilities. Then had come the desperate struggle to maintain the nation's lifelines to Canada, the United States and South America, to Africa, and to Australia. The convoy system had proved less satisfactory than in World War I. Longer-range submarines with new operating techniques extended the contest to every part of the high seas. Britain's navy and merchant marine were strained to the breaking point, and more than 7,000,000 tons of precious ships, mostly with cargoes, had been lost before the United States entered the war. Air patrol, begun previously, had proved helpful, but full protection in mid-Atlantic awaited the building of aircraft carriers and longer-range bombers. The vast area of the Pacific now also had to be controlled, temporarily at least, with a badly crippled United States fleet. The problem of maintaining the British lifelines to all parts of the empire, of maintaining a steady flow of lend-lease supplies to Russia, Britain, and the Near East, and of building up bases of future operations for the armies and fleets of the United States was a difficult one. Japan had naval superiority in the Pacific. Germany and Italy controlled the Mediterranean with combined sea and air power. The remnants of the French fleet, scattered through the ports of Southern France, North Africa, and French West Africa, held the balance of sea power at the moment, and they were precariously close to German control.

Turning from the matter of material assets to the more important question of prestige and moral power the balance sheet looked equally bad at the moment. Human freedom was now circumscribed within narrow limits and fighting for survival. We had created a number of little democracies in Eastern Europe, on the principle of self-determination; some, like Czechoslovakia, had shown great promise of releasing the rich culture and creative talents of minorities from oppressive restraints. They were now the battleground between millions who, on both sides, were regimented spiritually, culturally, and economically. In Western Europe the Nazis had ravaged every decent thing on which they could lay their hands. Young men had been hauled away to work in German factories, young women to serve as prostitutes to the German army; but worse still, about 250,000 liberals and many hundreds of thousands of Jews had been systematically murdered, and the most debased and traitorous elements in society raised to leadership and control. The great institutions of learning had been dispersed. Respect for law and treaty obligations in international relationships was at its lowest point in hundreds of years. Rule of law and independent judiciaries were things of the past. Millions of people had been killed; billions of dollars' worth of property had been destroyed.

Equally important was the situation in the great world of native peoples—the Philippines, the Netherlands East Indies, Burma, India, and Africa. We might not be able to win the war without their aid; we could not hope to keep the peace without their cooperation. Nature had given them an abundance of natural resources, but they had never known much more than sweat and toil, partly because they had been exploited by selfish interests from the white man's world; partly, too, because white men had never exerted their best efforts to elevate them and instruct them in the ways of industry and peace. They were becoming restless in the winter of 1941–1942, because day and night Axis agents had been spreading the gospel of hate against Anglo-Saxon civilization.

The war, therefore, was not a war between nations; nor a war of imperialism; nor a war for rubber, oil, and tin. It was a war for the survival of freedom among men against the most brutal and elemental passions. It was a war to preserve the possibility of progress. It was a war in which the triumph of Allied arms—remote as it seemed to be at first—must be followed at every stage by every effort to feed the hungry, to counteract hate and misery, to restore the social balance, and to start every people once more upon the quest for a richer and more abundant life.

ALLIED UNITY

Winston Churchill and Franklin D. Roosevelt had given to the democracies, in their darkest hours, their most important single asset: Allied unity. The first step in creating it was lend-lease, the second the Atlantic Charter. The United Nations might well turn out to be, as people variously hoped, a new world federation, a rejuvenated League of Nations, or a Union of Democracies. When the Atlantic Charter was promulgated, however, it was an expression of hope for a better world, and a promise of the two greatest democracies to devote their best intelligence to the details of a just and durable peace. Then came Pearl Harbor and entry of the United States into the war. At the historic ceremony in the White House, New Year's night, 1942, Great Britain and the United States signified their willingness to pool all resources in winning the war, and Russia and China joined them on the basis of the Atlantic Charter. In two important respects, the achievement of unity for collective security differed from the League of Nations: it came near the beginning of the war, and it was not rigid either as to objectives or methods. The nations were free to improvise procedure and develop their organization as the feeling of inter-dependence grew.

The close cooperation between Britain and the United States

was promptly re-affirmed after the entry of the United States into the war by the arrival in Washington of Prime Minister Churchill with his civilian and military aides. Churchill, in an historic address to Congress, referred pointedly to the matter by saying: "If we had kept together after the last war, if we had taken common measures for our safety, this renewal of the curse need never have fallen upon us." Close contact was kept throughout the conference with Britain's Foreign Secretary, Anthony Eden, then in Moscow; with Russia's Ambassador to the United States, Maxim Litvinoff; with China's Ambassador, Dr. Hu Shih; and with representatives of other nations. A combined Chiefs of Staff was created to unify the conduct of military and naval operations of the United States and Great Britain, and to guarantee the maximum utilization of manpower, to control the intelligence services and exchange of information, and to supervise the administration of conquered areas. Admiral William D. Leahy and Field Marshal Sir John Dill served as chief advisors to and representatives of President Roosevelt and Prime Minister Churchill respectively. General George C. Marshall was Chief-of-Staff of the United States Army. Admiral Ernest J. King was Commander-in-Chief of the United States Fleet. The three ranking members for Great Britain were Admiral Sir Charles Little, Lt. General Sir Colville Wemyss, and Air Chief Marshal A. T. Harris. Under the combined Chiefs of Staff was a Munitions Assignment Board headed by Harry Hopkins and Lord Beaverbrook, as well as a Raw Materials Board, a Shipping Adjustment Board, a Food Board, and a Production and Resources Board. Finally a Reverse Lend-Lease Agreement was signed making the unity of material resources, manpower, and operations complete. The importance of this action cannot be overestimated. The war could not have been won in any other way. The first result was in the development of a complete, over-all plan of strategy.

The grand strategy of the war, except for that of the Russian front, was also determined by President Roosevelt and Prime Minister Churchill at this conference, in consultation with their military and naval staffs. Their decision was first to concentrate upon the defeat of Germany. The risk of allowing Japan time in which to consolidate and exploit her conquests was more than balanced by the dire necessity, in January, 1942, of lending all possible assistance to Russia. Great Britain had to be protected at all costs. Military and air forces, concentrated there for that purpose, could also be readied for invasion thrusts into any of the European and African theaters of war. It was impossible to spread the existing naval forces and merchant marine enough to prepare an early offensive against Japan. Japan's defeat would inevitably follow that of Germany, although the reverse might not necessarily be true.

Once Allied strategy was revealed, there were loud murmurings from the Dutch, whose Far Eastern Empire was in the hands of the Japanese; mild protests from the Chinese, who still entertained doubts as to the future plans of white men for the Far East; and plain speaking from Australia, where Prime Minister John Curtin was so far provoked by Britain's feeble war effort in the Far East as curtly to remark that "Australia looks to America free from any pangs about our traditional links of friendship to Britain." A considerable segment of opinion in the United States believed the United States should turn its chief energies against the Japanese, thus challenging the basic allied strategy of the war. Its support was from those who had always feared the Yellow Peril, those who hated Russia, those who suspected Great Britain, and by some military strategists. They were effectively answered by Prime Minister Churchill in an address before Congress in May, 1943, to the effect that the British would fight to the end against Japan, if for no other reason than to retrieve their losses in the Far East and wipe out the disgrace of the Empire's greatest reverses. He also said that the major portion of the forces of the United States were in the Pacific.

The second major criticism of Allied strategy centered in the demand for an invasion of the European continent. Russia requested it on a scale large enough to draw at least one-fourth of the estimated 200 German divisions from the Eastern Front and thus relieve the pressure upon her hard-pressed armies. Substantial minorities in Great Britain and the United States urged it for a variety of reasons: because they were impatient to get on with the war, and thought an invasion essential to victory; because they feared a German victory in Russia would give her vast resources of oil and other raw materials, which would prolong the war indefinitely; because they felt that Great Britain and the United States were allowing Russia to bear an undue burden, either by design or by something less than the maximum war effort; or because they feared a negotiated peace between Germany and Russia which would give to the latter a free hand in Eastern Europe and to the former the power to force a stalemate in the West. Both Roosevelt and Churchill insisted that all possible aid was being given and would be continued to Russia, and promised by implication that a second front in Europe would be forthcoming. Where and when it would be established, of course, remained a closely guarded secret.

All of the combined resources of all the United Nations were available for use in the common task, and subject to disposal, not only where most needed, but instantly at critical periods. Ten million tons of shipping of nations controlled by the Axis (principally Norway, Holland, and Greece) were on the high seas or escaped from home ports at the time of German invasion. These ships were armed, repaired, and provisioned in British or American ports as most convenient, and were a powerful asset in the critical early days of the war. Ten thousand Polish airmen alone were equipped and trained in Great Britain and Canada by planes from the United States. Canada developed an air training program which included cadets from all of the United Nations. Cadets who escaped from the Netherlands East Indies were trained at Jackson, Mississippi. Chinese pilots and an entire Chinese army were equipped and trained in India by Britain and the United States. When the Trans-Iranian Railroad began carrying lend-lease supplies to Russia, it had new rails from the United States, freight cars from England, and locomotives from India. American forces were furnished food, hospitals, living quarters in Australia. They used the airfields, hospitals, storage depots, gasoline, and transportation available in Great Britain. When Pearl Harbor caught the United States unprepared for defense against air raids, antiaircraft guns and barrage balloons were rushed from Great Britain to the Panama Canal and the West Coast. When Russia needed tires, an entire tire factory was purchased from the Ford Motor Company and shipped. We stripped a Los Angeles power plant to send her electrical equipment. Following the surrender of Japan, our air force moved four Chinese armies from West and South China to Shanghai and Peiping, and the American army completely clothed the Chinese forces bound for Manchuria. Our ships were provisioned in the Russian ports of Murmansk and Archangel. We adopted the British 50 mm. Bofors gun for anti-aircraft defense; they adopted the American 105 mm. howitzer. Our scientists pooled resources to perfect radar and the atomic bomb. We got tin from Bolivia, copper from Chile, and both from the Belgian Congo. So one might continue indefinitely to list the advantages of combined resources of men, material, and ideas.

PRODUCTION AND LEND-LEASE

Everyone was aware of the time that must elapse before the full weight of American arms and productive capacity could be brought to bear in the worldwide contest. President Roosevelt left no doubt about the degree of effort required when on January 6, 1942, he issued a directive for production in 1942 of 60,000 planes, 45,000 tanks, 20,000 anti-aircraft guns, and 8,000,000 deadweight tons of merchant shipping. These were only the principal items, production of which would require a complete retooling of industrial plants, cessation of non-essential manufacturing, re-allocation of manpower, and vast expansion of the procurement program of raw material. People old enough to remember that, in World War I, the United States had produced only 80 tanks, and had failed completely to produce the airplanes, artillery, and ships needed by the armed services, were skeptical indeed.

Fortunately, British and French orders, our own defense program, and lend-lease had given us an advantageous start of many months. The British, before lend-lease was adopted, had requisitioned all the holdings, bank balances, and marketable investments of their citizens, and also had sent newly mined gold and exports, in order to buy war materials in this country. In all, about $4,500,000,000 in orders had been placed. The original $7,000,000,000 lend-lease appropriation had also made available a large sum for war contracts. A great deal of work had been done, therefore, in plant expansion and retooling. In 1939 we had produced no tanks and only 2100 planes; in 1941, we produced 900 tanks and 19,500 planes. We had an army of only 175,000 in 1939, an army of 1,500,000 in 1941. We were building new factories, shipyards, and processing plants. We had sent not only personnel to improve operations on the Burma Road from Lashio to Kunming but also trucks and gasoline. General Chennault, an American Reserve Officer, was serving as technical adviser to the Chinese Government and directing the activities of more than 100 veteran American fliers in the American Volunteer Group.

We were completing naval and air bases in Greenland and Iceland, and had established a new air route over the North Atlantic by way of Nova Scotia, Newfoundland, Labrador, Iceland, and Ireland. We had completed a second air route by way of Miami, the West Indies, and Brazil to Africa, and on across 2000 miles of deserts and jungles to Egypt, thence to Iran and India. We had an Air Transport Command organized to take planes and emergency supplies to American forces in every part of the world. The last British convoy had passed through the Mediterranean in January, 1941; but port facilities, railroads, air and naval bases, assembly plants, hospitals, and radio stations were nearing completion in the Red Sea and Persian Gulf areas. Supplies were flowing to Russia across the Pacific to Vladivostok, across the North Atlantic to Murmansk and Archangel, and across Iran to the Caspian Sea. A joint British and American railroad, 230 miles long, was carrying the supplies across the latter country. When the Japanese attack disrupted communications across the Pacific, supplies for General Chennault's airmen in China were promptly sent across the Atlantic to Africa and thence to China by way of India.

Much of lend-lease aid to Great Britain before Pearl Harbor had been in the form of food. Her food supplies had been cut drastically in three ways: by the Nazi conquest of Norway, Holland, Denmark, and France; by the need to save every inch of shipping space for raw materials and munitions; and by submarines. Before lend-lease, there was the added strain of saving scant financial resources for purchases of war supplies abroad. In the period between adoption of lend-lease and Pearl Harbor, we sent to Great Britain a million tons of food, largely evaporated milk, cheese, and eggs, together with millions of concentrated vitamins in tablet form. Early experiences in food shipments and the dearth of shipping space led to extensive development of new kinds of processing, particularly dehydrating of eggs, milk, vegetables, and soups. Dried egg production, for example, increased from 10,000,000 pounds in 1940 to 225,000,000 pounds in 1943. When the Russians were attacked by the Germans in the summer of 1941, Russia was promptly brought into the lend-lease system. The United States and Great Britain immediately sent supplies with every ship that could be spared. They had to go by the northern route, and were subject to attack by wolfpacks of submarines, by surface raiders, and by bombers based in northern Norway. They had to be carried in British and American ships, and convoyed by British and Canadian naval vessels. Of 107 ships sent during March, April, and May, 1942, one-fourth were lost; but 19 huge convoys had gone through by the end of 1942. From January 1 to November 1, 1942, supplies to Russia, largely over the northern route, included 3000 planes, 2400 tanks, 30,000 motor vehicles, 831,000 tons of machine tools, 42,000 tons of gasoline, 189,000 field telephones, 75,000 machine guns, 216,000 miles of barbed wire, and 1,500,000 pairs of army boots. The burden of shipping to Russia had shifted to the Persian Gulf by mid-summer of 1942, and all-American diesel powered freight trains were handling 100,000 tons a month across Iran by March of 1943. In the previous twelve months, 3,000,000 tons of supplies went through, plus hundreds of airplanes under their own power.

Total lend-lease shipments during the first year were $2,400,000,-000, of which Great Britain received 68 percent, mostly food. They amounted to $7,700,000,000 the second year, of which Great Britain received only 38 percent and Russia 29 percent, mostly munitions. They steadily increased to a maximum of $1,600,000,000 during the single month of March, 1944. Total lend-lease by the end of 1945 was $49,096,125,000, of which 54 percent was munitions and petroleum products, 21 percent was industrial products, 12 percent was food, and 11 percent was services. The principal amounts to the several countries were as follows:

British Empire (United Kingdom, Canada, Australia, South Africa, and India)	$30,753,000,000
Russia	11,141,000,000
France	2,377,000,000
China	1,335,000,000
Brazil	319,000,000
Netherlands	178,000,000
Belgium	82,000,000
Greece	76,000,000
Norway	37,000,000

In reverse lend-lease, we received $7,345,000,000, of which $6,306,-000,000 was from the British Empire and $760,000,000 was from France. We received little from Russia, having had no troops there during the war.

At the beginning of the war, the Office of Production Management under the direction of William S. Knudsen, was abolished. Knudsen was given the rank of Lieutenant-General, the first civilian ever to receive such an appointment, and placed in charge of Army production. A new War Production Board was created, and Donald M. Nelson, its head, was given greater powers over industry than those of Bernard M. Baruch in World War I. An Office of Price Administration, under Leon Henderson, was established, drawing its powers from the War Production Board, and specifically charged with the task of stabilizing rents and prices, preventing profiteering and speculation, and rationing of consumers' goods. A Board of Economic Warfare was created, under the chairmanship of Vice-President Henry Wallace, and including Knudsen, Henderson, and Nelson, to develop policies relative to the economic relations of the United States with other nations. A War Manpower Commission was created, under the chairmanship of Paul V. McNutt, to assure the most effective mobilization and utilization of manpower; but there was no resort to a universal draft of manpower for the national service. The nation chose, on the contrary, to force men by continuous pressure of the draft, and to induce them by high wages, into essential war industries.

In a period of four years, the United States proceeded to perform a miracle of production by the allocation of raw materials, the construction of new industrial plants, and the stopping of production of certain types of consumers' goods. Some entirely new industries were established. Loss of raw rubber supplies, for example, required the production of synthetic rubber, which was increased from 8283 tons in 1941 to 753,111 tons in 1944. Other industries so greatly expanded as to constitute new industries included aviation gasoline, explosives, ammunition, aircraft, and shipbuilding. The production of magnesium was increased from 10,000,000 pounds annually to 586,000,000 pounds; of copper from a prewar average of 250,000 tons to 786,000 tons; and of aluminum from 300,000 pounds to 2,257,000,000 pounds. Fifteen billion dollars were spent to build and equip new industrial plants, such as the Geneva Steel plant in Utah, the Basic Magnesium plant in Nevada, the Ford Bomber plant at Willow Run, the Chrysler Tank Arsenal in Detroit, and Kaiser's Permanent shipyard at Richmond, California. We built military camps, airfields, and housing for war workers. We increased electric power production from 161,000,000,000 kilowatt hours to 279,000,000,000 kilowatt hours. We installed power plants in naval vessels alone greater than the total electric power capacity of the United States. We greatly expanded agricultural production.

The greatest accomplishment was in shipbuilding. In 1940, the shipyards of the country had turned out only 53 cargo ships, totaling 634,000 deadweight tons; in 1941 they produced 95 ships, totaling 1,688,000 tons; but in the first seven months after Pearl Harbor, they built 367 ships for a total tonnage of 4,882,000. Production in the remaining five months brought the year's total to 8,090,800 tons. More remarkable still, building increased so rapidly, due to mass production methods which simplified the training of workers, that 8,818,622 tons were produced in the first six months of 1943. During this time shipbuilding yards had been increased from ten to sixty, and the time required to build a Liberty ship had been reduced from 242 to 41 days. In 1944, a total of 19,000,000 tons of ships were built. Meanwhile, the total tonnage of naval vessels was increased from 1,875,000 to 5,000,000, the number of combat ships from 380 to 1100, and the total number of all craft to 50,000. In three years, the country produced 44,000,000 tons of shipping, including a large number of fighting ships.

The production of airplanes was equally sensational. The country produced only 2100 military planes in the year 1939. During 1942, the first year of the war, we produced 48,000, with a monthly rate of 5400 at the close of the year. In 1943, production totaled 86,000, with a monthly rate of 7500 at the close of the year. We produced 96,359 planes, including 16,048 heavy bombers in 1944, a total of 170,000 from the time of Pearl Harbor to the invasion of France on June 6, 1944, and 297,000 between July 1, 1940 and July 31, 1945. During this same period of five years, American industry produced in addition 86,338 tanks, 17,400,000 rifles and side arms, 315,000 pieces of field artillery, 4,200,000 tons of artillery shells, 41,400,000,000 rounds of ammunition, 64,500 landing vessels, 6500 other naval vessels, and 5400 cargo ships.

In spite of all war production, however, only 40 percent of national production went into the war effort at any one time. War production was superimposed upon normal peacetime production, and total production of all goods increased from $88,000,-000,000 in 1939 to $198,000,000,000 in 1944. The output of manufacturing was tripled; and of raw material production was increased 60 percent. The American people had some inconveniences, as we shall see, but few, if any, real sacrifices to endure. There was, for example, little shortage in textiles until 1945, none whatever in amounts of food, and very little in services. This was accomplished by increasing the labor force from 54,000,000 workers to 64,000,000, and by increasing the average work week, in manufacturing, for example, from 37.7 hours to 45.2 hours.

There were 50,000,000 people gainfully employed when the war began, and about 4,000,000 able to work who were not employed. Of the gainfully employed, 13,000,000 worked in factories, 10,000,000 on farms, 11,000,000 in business and financial houses, 6,000,000 for the government, 3,000,000 in transportation and public utilities, 2,000,000 in construction work, 1,000,000 in mining, and 4,000,000 in a variety of other occupations. The government took 12,000,000 people into the armed services from all of these groups. It stopped private building construction to save for war purposes the 3,300,000 tons of steel used each year for that purpose. It rationed automobile tires. It stopped manufacturing of automobiles, leaving 44,000 dealers and their employees to the number of 400,000 without business or work. It rationed gasoline, and food. It forbade the manufacture of household appliances like radios, washing machines, and refrigerators. There was, in short, a great shifting of employed persons from various occupations into war industries. Other new workers were drawn from the 29,000,000 housewives, youngsters who otherwise would have been in school, men who had retired, and the physically handicapped. The number of female factory workers, for example, was doubled; some being housewives and some the wives of men in the armed services. In addition, thousands of men left the farms to enter the factories.

The war, of course, cost money; compared to World War I, the cost was staggering. World War I, which lasted less than two years, had cost about $35,000,000,000. Between Pearl Harbor and August 1, 1942, Congress authorized expenditures of $205,000,-000,000; between July 1, 1940 and July 1, 1943, $330,000,000,000. Actual spending was $4,500,000,000 per month by August 1942, and $8,000,000,000 per month by August 1943. The gross public debt at the end of 1939 was $69,900,000,000; at the end of 1941, it was $86,700,000,000; but, by April, 1946, it had reached $284,104,-000,000. Meanwhile, also, enormous amounts had been collected in taxes, and spent. Taxation during the war had the dual purpose of keeping down the public debt and preventing inflation. Individual and corporate income taxes were increased to the highest levels in the history of the country. The Treasury, in consequence, received from all sources during the war:

1941	$ 7,370,000,000
1942	13,047,000,000
1943	22,371,000,000
1944	40,121,000,000
1945	43,900,000,000

NATIONAL MORALE

The complete mobilization of manpower for war purposes created many problems for labor. Labor was not drafted into industry, as in Great Britain, nor were the standards established by the New Deal legislation abandoned. The forty-hour week, with higher rates of pay for all overtime, was retained. Ceilings on all prices of consumers' goods and rents were set by the Office of Price Administration under the Price Control Act of January, 1942. Price fixing was not easily administered, because it was opposed by everyone, including farmers, who had anything to sell; but, in spite of inequities, complaints, and some profiteering, the country was protected from ruinous inflation. Those people whose incomes were stationary, so called "white-collar workers" particularly, were able to maintain a decent standard of living.

Representatives of the A. F. of L. and the C.I.O. and industrial leaders met in conference with President Roosevelt soon after Pearl Harbor and agreed to refrain from all action which would retard maximum production, including strikes and lockouts. A National War Labor Board was established, representing labor, management and the government. As living costs increased, and it seemed impossible to keep them from doing so, the C.I.O. workers of the steel industry demanded a dollar a day increase in wages. The War Labor Board, July 16, 1942, granted them a 15 percent increase. This became known as the Little Steel Formula, and was applied in all wage controversies throughout the war period. Even so, the inability to keep wage and price increases uniform resulted in more than 3000 temporary work stoppages in the single year of 1942.

The most serious controversy was in the coal fields. John L. Lewis threatened to take his United Mine Workers out on strike in November, 1943, and President Roosevelt, acting under his war powers, caused the Secretary of Interior to take over the mines. This action was followed in April, 1944 by seizure of the mail-order firm of Montgomery, Ward, and Company because of a strike growing out of union recognition. Congress passed the Smith-Connally

Act imposing penalties on labor leaders who provoked strikes in plants working on government contracts; the government paid subsidies to farmers on important food crops; a 90 percent excess profits tax on corporations and the highest individual income taxes in history were imposed; and pressure was exerted to sell bonds to everyone to the limit of their ability to buy—all with the multiple objectives of maintaining production, financing the war, and preventing inflation of wages and prices. The effort was not 100 percent successful, but it was far more so than during World War I.

The same was true of the effort to marshal loyalty and regulate race relations. An Alien Registration Act of 1940 required all of the 5,000,000 people who were not citizens to register. The Federal Bureau of Investigation, and the Army and Navy intelligence services had performed a great deal of careful investigation previous to the outbreak of war. These services made careful investigations of all reports of disloyalty, always as careful to protect the innocent as to find the guilty, and to them belongs much of the credit for one of the nation's greatest achievements during the war: the avoidance of the hysteria of fear and widespread persecution of foreign-born so prevalent during and after World War I. Some Italians and a goodly number of Germans of questionable loyalty were interned. The German-American Bund, the Silver Shirts, and other organizations known to be Nazi-inspired were dissolved. The leaders of such organizations, and businessmen known to be Nazi controlled, were detained. Eight German agents, prepared for sabotage, who were landed by submarine on the East Coast, were apprehended. Six were electrocuted, and the other two were imprisoned. All of these things were done efficiently, quietly, and with judicial spirit in sharp contrast to the government procedures of 1918–1919.

The only really questionable action was the transfer of 110,000 Japanese descendants from the Pacific Coast area to other parts of the country. There was no evidence to show that they were other than loyal, and at least half of them were native-born Americans. The action was taken by the government because of (1) the danger, or at least fear, of invasion in the early days of the war; (2) the large concentration of vital war industries on the

Pacific Coast; (3) the constant movement of troops and ships through west coast ports; and (4) the difficulty of sorting the disloyal from the loyal members of so large a racial group. The action was, and must remain, arbitrary, regrettable, and of doubtful constitutionality; but it was thought necessary by those charged with national defense, and the people were not in a mood at that moment to weigh the rights of a few against the safety of the nation.

The most difficult problem of all the many in human relationships was the racial problem. No one acquainted with the disgraceful record of World War I period could fail to be apprehensive. Negroes were migrating in large numbers from rural to industrial centers. Cities like Norfolk, Los Angeles, Chicago, Detroit, and Indianapolis had to absorb large increases in their Negro populations at a time when there was a shortage of living quarters, recreational facilities, restaurants, etc.; when there was an equal migration of whites from the depressed areas of the South; and when the stress and strain of war made everyone short-tempered. Even in those cities where Negroes had developed their own economy there was grave danger of race conflicts.

The government met the possibility of discrimination against Negroes in industry and the armed services by creating a Fair Employment Practices Committee, a presidential order forbidding discrimination in war plants, and increased facilities for training Negro officers. The efforts of the government were counterbalanced by the subversive activities of Axis agents and fascist-minded demagogues, who fanned the smouldering embers of race conflict always present in the deeply ingrained prejudices of the people. A riot in Detroit, June 20, 1943, reached such proportions that federal troops were called to restore order. Hundreds of people were injured; 25 Negroes and 19 whites were killed. Race conflicts resulted in a paralyzing strike of transportation employees in Philadelphia, August 1, 1944, and again federal troops were called. New York experienced a riotous clash between Negroes and Jews in Harlem at a cost of five lives, 500 injured, and $5,000,000 property damage. Racial antipathy and juvenile delinquency combined to cause serious disturbances between Mexicans and service men in Los

Angeles. Finally, there was a medley of outbreaks in Boston and New York in which no one could distinguish who was against what, except that everyone involved was scornful of common decency.

Wars, of course, do awful things to people on the home front as well as on the battle front. Here was a case in which millions of families were separated, some of them forever. There was interminable moving about from one locality to another, living in cramped quarters, mothers working in factories, children earning fabulous wages; everyone free from the restraints of normal behavior; everyone seeking relaxation and companionship; no automobile travel for pleasure, but plenty of barrooms and dance halls of questionable character; child labor in restaurants and stores; child delinquency up 31 percent in the single year 1943. Admittedly, these things were disturbing; but underneath, society was stable and it came through the war as sound and strong as when the war began.

29

The Road to Victory

EUROPE AND AFRICA—1942

THE war in the Pacific against Japan was primarily a naval war, with support from ground and air forces. It could not be otherwise, in view of the immense distances between islands. It had to wait until naval superiority over Japan could be attained and longer-range bombers could be built. The war against Germany, on the other hand, was a ground and air war, with important supplemental support from the navy. In the end, Germany was defeated when her armies were annihilated; Japan ended the war with large armies intact, but with her navy at the bottom of the sea. During the war, Japan lost 11 battleships, 20 aircraft carriers, 38 cruisers, 132 destroyers, and 129 submarines. The United States lost in all theaters only 2 battleships, 5 aircraft carriers, 6 escort carriers, 10 cruisers, and 71 destroyers. The disparity in losses of the two nations is most significant because the United States was able to build and Japan was not able to do so. The United States commissioned during the war 8 battleships, 48 cruisers, 27 aircraft carriers, 110 escort carriers, 352 destroyers, 498 destroyer escorts, and 203 submarines. It ended the war with no less than five task forces each greater than any possible combination of enemy forces. Japan lost 3 battleships and 6 aircraft carriers early in the war, which more than counterbalanced losses of the United States at Pearl Harbor. By midsummer of 1944, the United States had commissioned so many vessels that the navy roamed the Pacific at will, sinking enemy vessels wherever it chanced to find them.

It is proper, therefore, to deal with the other theaters of war in the beginning, because Japan lost the war when she lost command of the sea—with that went her merchant fleet and her ability to supply her factories with raw materials, feed her people, and supply her distant armies.

There were six major fields of operations during the years 1942–1943: the Atlantic, Western Europe, Russia, North Africa, the Southwest Pacific, and China. The United States had no forces in Russia. General George C. Marshall was Chief-of-Staff of the Army, and the Army was divided into three agencies with Lieutenant-General Brehon B. Somervell in charge of Services of Supply, Lieutenant-General Leslie J. McNair in charge of Ground Forces, and Lieutenant-General Henry H. Arnold in charge of Air Forces. Admiral Ernest J. King was named Commander-in-Chief of the United States Fleet, with Admiral Harold S. Stark in command in Europe, Admiral Chester W. Nimitz in the Pacific, and Admiral William F. Halsey in the South Pacific. In the Southwest Pacific, General Sir Archibald Wavell was in general command of Allied forces until the Japanese captured Java. The Allies then split their unified command in that area. General Douglas MacArthur was withdrawn from the Philippines and placed in command in the Australian theater, where he and Admiral Halsey worked in close harmony. General Wavell was sent to prepare the defenses of India. Lieutenant-General Joseph W. Stilwell was placed in command of all United States forces in China, where Generalissimo Chiang Kai-shek was in supreme command. Lieutenant-General Dwight Eisenhower was later (November 16, 1942) made Commander-in-Chief of United Nations operations in North Africa, with Brigadier-General James H. Doolittle in command of Air Forces, Major-General George S. Patton in charge of United States Ground Forces, and General Montgomery in command of the British forces. Everywhere there was the closest harmony between the forces of the two nations and between the military, naval, and air commands.

The Battle of the Atlantic was not the most spectacular aspect of the war, but it was the most decisive. It was here that Germany almost won the war; and it was here that she lost it. German sub-

marine construction had been improved to the point where the
larger boats could travel 14,500 miles on a single load of fuel. They
could withstand depth charges to within 20 feet. They could crash
dive in a matter of seconds. They could submerge to a depth of
100 fathoms (600 feet). They could travel at a speed of 20 knots
on the surface. Admiral Karl Doenitz had introduced the technique of the wolf-pack, in which a large number of submarines
would rise to the surface or near-surface in the center of a convoy
and loose their torpedoes indiscriminately. He sent his boats to
prey upon the coastwise shipping of the United States, where there
were no convoys, and where ships were sharply silhouetted against
the lights of the mainland. He kept them in Mid-Atlantic beyond
the reach of land-based aircraft. He sent them into the South Atlantic to prey upon ships making the long, lonely haul around Africa.

The greatest losses of Allied shipping occurred in the first six
months of 1942 and along the Eastern seaboard of the United
States. Two hundred thirteen vessels engaged in coastal trade were
sunk, with insurance claims mounting to $73,000,000. Submarines
operated in the Gulf of Mexico, in the St. Lawrence, and in the
Caribbean. A serious oil shortage developed in the Eastern states,
and imports from South America were sharply curtailed. Losses
began to decline in July, 1942, with the convoying of coastal shipping; and, by January, 1943, submarines had largely abandoned
those areas where convoys operated. Allied losses, however, were
still nearly 1,000,000 tons per month, greater than the combined
building of the United States and Great Britain of 10,000,000 tons
for the year 1942. Moreover, Germany was still building submarines
faster than they were being sunk. Then there began a sharp decline
as more destroyer escorts, airplane carriers, and long-range flying
boats were brought into the battle. In April, 1943, sinkings were
less than half the total of 926,000 tons lost in March. In May, more
submarines were destroyed than probably were built. In May, June,
and July, 90 submarines were destroyed, for an average of one a
day; and it was revealed that construction of new ships during
1943 to August 1 had exceeded sinkings by 3,000,000 deadweight
tons.

Second in importance only to the Battle of the Atlantic was

that which raged over Western Europe. The Battle for Britain had marked the beginning of the decline of the Luftwaffe as compared to the relative strength of the Royal Air Force. R.A.F. attacks began at once on the Nazi bases from Le Havre to the Baltic. The former practice of dispersed raids was abandoned for that of concentrated bombing of industrial targets. Lübeck and Rostock suffered heavily in March, 1942. Late in May a 300-plane raid was launched against Mannheim. By June, the R.A.F. had embarked upon its avowed task of methodically destroying Germany. One thousand plane raids were launched against Cologne, Essen, Bremen, and Emden. Seven thousand bombers were sent over the continent in one week, with Lieutenant-General Henry H. Arnold of the United States Air Forces on hand to witness the performance. A small United States force first went over the continent on July 4, 1942. In August, our Eighth Air Force, under Major-General Carl Spaatz, began its first systematic raiding of Nazi arsenals in occupied France, at Brest, Lille, Le Havre, St. Nazaire. The R.A.F. hammered Cologne, Düsseldorf, Hamburg, and Saarbrücken in August; and, in November, it reached out to Genoa, Italy. All told, in 1942, it bombed 30 key cities, destroyed 2000 factories, made 86 raids with more than 100 planes, and dropped a total of 37,000 tons of bombs.

The Royal Air Force began the year 1943 with smashing attacks upon the industrial centers of the Ruhr Valley. By March the forces of Great Britain and the United States were engaged in round-the-clock bombing; the R.A.F. carrying maximum loads of bombs at night, and the United States Air Force carrying lighter loads for precision bombing in daylight while driving the Germans from the air with their heavier armaments. These tactics forced the Luftwaffe to keep their defenses on a 24-hour alert, to keep day as well as night fighter planes in Western Europe, and to draw heavily upon their air forces on the Russian Front. The list of factories, shipyards, railway centers, and power plants destroyed grew more impressive each day. Damage to civilian morale from the almost complete destruction of cities like Hamburg, Bremen, and Cologne must have been severe; and the continuous attacks upon submarine building centers and ports, such as Cologne, Wilhelmshaven, St. Nazaire, and Brest, contributed powerfully toward dissipating the U-boat menace.

In March alone Allied planes dumped 15,000 tons of bombs on Europe, 500 tons on Berlin in thirty minutes. In May the R.A.F. bombed the Möhne, Sorpe, and Eder dams, releasing great floods in the Ruhr and Eder valleys, damaging railway communications, destroying power stations, and seriously curtailing essential war industries. Concentrated bombings then began on Cuxhaven, Düsseldorf, Münster, Dortmund, Hannover, Kassel, Mannheim, and Stuttgart. Hamburg was almost completely destroyed in August and an all-out attack on Berlin was begun. United States air forces, between July 4, 1942, and the same date one year later, lost 265 bombers, destroyed 1200 German fighting planes, and dropped 12,000 tons of bombs in 75 raids.

The situation in Russia and North Africa was dark in the spring of 1942. German armies, seeking to fulfill a grand dream of Hitler's to conquer India and the Middle East, were moving toward the Caucasus and across North Africa toward Egypt, Palestine, and Arabia. In Russia, attack and counter-attack had slowly given way to a major German offensive as the plains and steppes dried. The attack was launched at the Black Sea naval base of Sevastopol; at Rostov; at Stalingrad; ultimately at the oil fields of the Caucasus. An estimated 1,500,000 Germans drove toward Stalingrad, supported by 2000 planes and thousands of tanks. In Africa, the British had pushed German and Italian forces under General Rommel back to El Agheila on the border of Tripolitania before Pearl Harbor; but Pearl Harbor had temporarily stopped the flow of reinforcements and supplies to British forces. Rommel counter-attacked on January 21, and was not stopped until he reached El Alamein on July 1—and then only with the greatest difficulty—seventy-five miles from the British naval base at Alexandria.

Immediate action was required to save the Suez Canal and the oil fields beyond, and to relieve the pressure on Russia. General Marshall and Harry Hopkins, personal representative of President Roosevelt, went to London in April, where plans were made for an invasion of Europe across the English Channel in 1943. It was agreed, also, to make an emergency invasion at an earlier date should the Russian situation require. The combined Chiefs of Staff met in London, when the African situation became serious, to discuss an immediate diversionary invasion of the continent; but diligent search of the United States and Great Britain for landing craft, including pleasure craft, revealed too few for the required six divisions. The decision was made, therefore, to delay the cross-channel invasion until 1944, and also operations against Japan, and to mount an invasion of North Africa. General Eisenhower, who was assembling supplies in Great Britain, was placed in command. The immediate contest became one of supply, in which the Germans enjoyed the short haul across the Mediterranean and the Allies traveled 12,000 miles around Africa to the Red Sea, a two months' trip.

Great Britain and the United States won the first phase of the battle. Seven hundred bombers went by air across the Atlantic and Africa. More than a thousand fighter planes went by carrier to the West Coast of Africa and then by air to Egypt or were shipped around Africa. Nine hundred tanks, many of the latest models taken from the training fields of the United States, were sent, as were 25,000 motor vehicles. Construction of airports, hospitals, warehouses, repair shops, and other installations were pushed to the limit. The Ninth Air Force was sent to Cairo to harass the German supply lines. The Russians got, during the first nine months of 1942, 3000 planes, 2400 tanks, 30,000 motor vehicles, and 42,000 tons of gasoline, plus great quantities of food, machine tools, machine guns, ammunition, and other items.

The Germans dissipated their strength recklessly before Stalingrad; but, after three months, the Russians not only were still in possession of the city, but were able to launch an offensive of their own. German transport lines broke down; the Russians held the rich oil fields of Grozny and Baku; and winter came with no advantage to the Germans for their terrific loss of men and supplies except that of having deprived Russia of vital war materials. That loss was more than counterbalanced by the Germans' own losses from bombings by the air fleets in Britain, and by the flood of supplies and food which poured into Russia from Britain and the United States.

A Russian counter-offensive began November 19, 1942. The siege of Stalingrad was lifted on February 2, 1943. The Germans had suffered a defeat of the first magnitude. In three months they were forced back as much as 350 miles at some points. Russia placed German casualties at 1,000,000 for the winter months. Rostov was retaken, and then Velikie Luki, Rzhev, and Vyazma, cities which had been in German hands since the early days of the war. German resistance finally stiffened, Kharkov was retaken, and spring rains immobilized the armies on the line of the Donets River.

The British Eighth Army, under General Bernard Montgomery, launched an offensive at El Alamein on October 24. Britain long since had lost control of the Mediterranean, and a constant stream of supplies had flowed to General Rommel from Greece and Crete, through Tobruk and Bengasi. Supplies for General Montgomery flowed from the United States and Great Britain over the much longer route around Africa. At that moment Germany, able to assemble a potential fleet of five battleships, two aircraft carriers, twelve cruisers, and twenty-five destroyers, and to call on the still undamaged part of the Italian fleet, needed only the French fleet at Toulon, the North African ports, and Dakar, in order to hold the balance of world naval power. This French fleet consisted of four battleships, fourteen cruisers, forty-two destroyers, and fifty-nine submarines. Great Britain and the United States had both exacted promises from the French that their fleet would never be turned over to the Germans. The State Department of the United States had maintained close relations with Vichy France to insure that the promise would be kept; and while doing so, had opened a friendly path into North Africa by delivering food to the French colonies.

The offensive of General Montgomery was destined to develop into a major operation. Rommel was pushed steadily back through Libya. On November 7, United States troops landed along the whole coastline of French Morocco and Algeria. Algiers, Oran, Casablanca, Rabat, keys to French North-African railway, highway, and airdrome systems, were soon in American hands. A part of the invading fleet of 850 ships came from Great Britain, a part from the United States, and only one ship was lost before landing operations began. Admiral Jean F. Darlan, Commander-in-Chief of all French sea, land, and air forces, was in Algiers, ostensibly to visit a sick son. Also there was General Henri Honoré Giraud, upon whom the Allied forces, under command of General Eisenhower, relied to win support of the French army of 400,000 and the French Civil Administration. Darlan was taken into protective custody; but, when it was discovered that he could deliver French collaboration and Giraud could not, because the French leaders remained loyal to the Vichy Government, an arrangement was made by which Darlan ordered the surrender of Algiers, promised to arrange for the surrender of Dakar, and took over civil administration of the colonies in the name of Marshal Pétain with the approval of General Eisenhower. Darlan's order to the French forces to cease firing reached Casablanca a few minutes before the American assault was to begin on November 11, and it undoubtedly saved many lives at this point alone. Giraud was named military commander of the French forces.

The Germans responded to Allied occupation of French Africa by occupying all of France and moving to seize the French fleet. The French faithfully carried out their agreement with the United States and blew up their ships with but few exceptions. Montgomery's forces advancing from the South, and both British and American forces advancing from the West, soon forced the Germans and Italians into the narrow promontory of Cap Bon, and to unconditional surrender. Thus in May, 1943, ended the dream of an Italian Empire, begun with the conquest of Ethiopia in 1935–1936. The Germans had lost 250,000 men in Africa, the Italians 470,000. In addition, the two Axis partners had lost 2000 tanks, 1500 guns, 5000 aircraft, and 3000 motor vehicles. British casualties (killed, wounded, prisoners) totaled 150,000; those of the United States, 12,000.

The conquest of North Africa was so momentous in its consequences as to defy analysis. It opened the Mediterranean once more to Allied shipping; and, by eliminating the long haul around Africa, did much to counterbalance the heavy losses to German U-boats. It opened the way to an invasion of Europe from the South, compelling Hitler to reconstitute completely his conception of a European Fortress. It forced the Germans to provide for the defense of Italy and the Balkans, thus further weakening their reserves in Western Europe and on the Russian Front. It gave new hope to the oppressed peoples of Europe, evidenced by an immediate increase in stories of sabotage and revolt. It reduced the area of rich hunting for the submarines. It ended the fiction of an independent, unoccupied France. It led directly to the invasion of Sicily, July 9, 1943, equivalent for all military purposes to an invasion of the mainland itself. The crushing defeats of the German armies before Stalingrad and at El Alamein ended Hitler's dream and placed the Germans on the defensive. Göring and Hitler began to talk about Germany's fighting for her life. The turning point of the war in Europe came in late summer of 1942.

FAR EAST, 1942–1943

Many factors entered into Allied strategy in the Far East. China, weak from five years of war, but fighting on under the leadership of Generalissimo Chiang Kai-shek, had to be preserved (1) as a matter of common decency; (2) as a base for future operations against Japan; and (3) to prevent the Japanese from retreating to the continent and continuing the war in the midst of a vast, rich area. The second factor was sea power. The road to Japan was by water, and the water provided a great highway for invasion only after the United States regained the naval superiority lost at Pearl Harbor. The third factor was a combination of immense distances, scarcity of landing craft for amphibious operations, and the prior claims of European forces to all kinds of supplies.

The supply line to China began at the Burmese port of Rangoon. A railroad carried supplies to Mandalay and thence to Lashio where the Burma Road to Kunming began. Japanese forces captured Rangoon on March 7, 1942, and swept north to Mandalay and Lashio in May. The supply line to China's armies and the American Volunteer Group of Flying Tigers was thus severed. Some supplies, which were piled up at Rangoon, including 2000 trucks, were moved northward into China ahead of the Japanese, but 1000 trucks and large quantities of machinery and raw materials were lost.

The threat to India was as serious as the dire plight of China. The Japanese were not stopped until they reached the Burma-Indian frontier. Here, there was a political as well as a military problem. India was in a most unhappy state of political turmoil. Two hundred fifty million Hindus, under the spiritual leadership of Mahatma Gandhi, were demanding complete independence from Britain, and non-resistance to Japanese invaders. Eighty million Moslems were unwilling for any change unless accorded a separate autonomy. Sixty million low caste peoples wanted Dominion status. Five hundred sixty-two native Princes were mostly satisfied with existing conditions. The country was a conglomerate of races and languages, with a 90 percent illiteracy. Gandhi, demanding full independence, no Moslem secession, and no war with Japan, fasted for 21 days. He lived; and he failed to get any concessions, or even to win a moral victory. General Wavell was appointed Viceroy of India in June, 1942, by which time any hopes Japan may have entertained that her easy victories in Burma and Malaya could be extended were dashed. Defense in depth, which had succeeded in Russia and China because the people were prepared for it, had failed in Burma, Malaya, and the Netherlands East Indies because the natives were not prepared for it. Some were openly hostile, most were passive, and only a few offered any opposition to the invader after the Allied armies were driven out. Britain had made certain of native cooperation in India and in the Middle East by not sacrificing the interests of the 80,000,000 Indian Mohammedans.

A Japanese naval task force swept the Bay of Bengal in April, sank three British warships, and destroyed a convoy bound for Calcutta. India's east coast ports, including Calcutta, now were closed. The west coast ports of Bombay, Karachi, and Cochin, already crowded with refugee shipping from Singapore and the Dutch East Indies, were the only ones left. Rommel was then at El Alamein. The German armies were advancing toward the Caucasus. The Japanese were at India's eastern border. Karachi promptly became the center of supply for all of India and China, terminal of the Trans-African air route and the shipping lanes around Africa. The British assured the safety of these sea lanes by seizing the French island of Madagascar off the east coast of Africa in May.

In India, already heavily engaged in manufacturing, the United States and British armies and supply forces constructed a veritable arsenal, including steel mills, ordnance plants, and shipbuilding yards. An air training school was established at Lahore in north-western India for training Chinese pilots. Chinese armies were flown to India for training. Supplies were flown to China for General Chennault, whose Flying Tigers were disbanded on July 4, and who remained to head the United States 14th Air Force. Everything to and from China went over the air route, popularly called the Himalayan Hump, which the United States Transport Command established in May, 1942.

In the Southwest Pacific, Japan's forces were moving ever closer to Australia, sole remaining base for operations against Japan. Australian troops were far away in Egypt, in the army of General Montgomery. United States, Dutch, and British naval forces had suffered severe losses in their effort to halt the Japanese advance through the Indies. The old shipping and air line from the United States to the Philippines and Java had been severed, and it was necessary to establish new lines over a much longer route to the South. Air power, and only air power, could stop the Japanese advance, and in that category the Japanese had great superiority. They established bases at Salamaua and Lae in Australia's outlying New Guinea, at Rabaul on New Britain, and in the Solomons; they destroyed the north Australian port of Darwin. An early invasion of Australia was expected.

The climax of defensive operations came in May and June, 1942. In the Coral Sea, off the Solomon Islands, a United States naval force under Rear Admiral Frank J. Fletcher, made contact with a Japanese force engaged in occupying Florida Island in the Solomons. The naval engagement which followed lasted three days and resulted in losses to the Japanese of one aircraft carrier sunk and another damaged, and one cruiser and two destroyers sunk; and to the United States of one aircraft carrier destroyed, one damaged, and one destroyer sunk. All damage was done by carrier-based planes, not a single shot being exchanged by naval vessels. It was this fact which made the results of the Battle of Midway, June 3–7, so significant.

The Japanese sent a full battle fleet against Midway, sole remaining outpost of the United States in the Central Pacific, including battleships, aircraft carriers, cruisers, destroyers, troop carriers, and submarines. The invading fleet was handed a crushing defeat, losing four aircraft carriers and one heavy cruiser. Once more the brunt of the battle was borne by aircraft, with Navy, Marine Corps, and Army planes participating. The battles of the Coral Sea and Midway stopped the Japanese advance in the Pacific, restored the balance of naval power, and removed all threat to Hawaii and the West Coast. To safeguard the southern shipping lane and to forestall an invasion of Australia, United States marines attacked the Islands of Guadalcanal and Tulagi on August 7. Japan made no less than five separate attempts to dislodge them, each developing into an important naval engagement. Four Allied cruisers and one transport were surprised and sunk on August 8, off Savo Island. Tables were reversed, and a Japanese naval force was severely mauled off the Eastern Solomons on August 24. Three Japanese cruisers and three destroyers were intercepted and sunk off Cape Esperance on October 11. Two Japanese destroyers were sunk and several carriers, cruisers, and at least one battleship were damaged off the Santa Cruz Islands on October 25. Finally, on November 13–15, a major battle developed in which Admiral Halsey's fleet sank one battleship, nine cruisers, six destroyers, and twelve transports. It was one of the most furious sea battles ever fought, the United States losing two cruisers and seven destroyers.

REDUCING THE OUTPOSTS

Expansion of Axis conquests having been stopped within twelve months after Pearl Harbor, there remained the task of marshaling resources for their total defeat. The Axis powers were now on the defensive. The British Isles, North Africa, India, Australia, and Hawaii were the principal staging areas for the conquest of Europe and Japan. The African campaign nearing completion, President

Roosevelt, Prime Minister Churchill, and the combined Chiefs of Staff met at Casablanca in January, 1943. The decision was made to continue preparation for the cross-Channel invasion, which General Marshall has called "one of the most tremendous logistical undertakings in military history," and "an operation unequaled in possibility for a major disaster." In Marshall's words:

It required provision for the transportation, shelter, hospitalization, supply, training, and general welfare of 1,200,000 men who had to be embarked in the United States and transported across the submarine infested Atlantic to the United Kingdom. The hospital plan alone, for example, called for 94,000 beds in existing installations, conversions, and new construction. . . . Living quarters had to be furnished for the assault forces and their supply troops. There had to be provision for 20,000,000 square feet of covering, storage, and shop space, and 44,000,000 square feet of open storage and hard landings. Parks for 50,000 military vehicles were planned; 270 miles of railroad had to be constructed. More than 20,000 railroad cars and 1000 locomotives were to be shipped to the United Kingdom. The Air Forces required 163 fields, seven centers for combat crews and replacements, accommodations for 450,000 men, and 8,500,000 square feet of storage and shop space.

It was decided at the Casablanca conference, therefore, to undertake a tremendous strategic bombardment of Germany, twenty-four hours each day, with special attention to submarine and aircraft industries, transportation, and oil refineries. It was further agreed to invade Sicily in July, 1943, and General Eisenhower was assigned the task. Another conference, at Washington, in May, approved a plan to bombard the Ploesti oil fields of Rumania from which Germany was receiving 3,000,000 tons of oil each year; to force Italy from the war; to increase the flow of airborne supplies from India to China; and to move against the Japanese in the Aleutians, the Marshalls, the Carolines, and New Guinea. In order not to become heavily involved in Italy, as Germany had been in North Africa, General Eisenhower was ordered to send seven veteran divisions from the Mediterranean area to Great Britain in November.

The attack on Sicily by combined British and American forces began on July 10, 1943. This was the largest amphibious operation yet undertaken, and it was marred by heavy fire from ships upon our own air transports which resulted in heavy losses among the paratroops. In spite of adverse weather conditions, 80,000 men, 7000 vehicles, and 300 tanks were landed within 48 hours. The battle continued for 39 days, with a loss of 167,000 men to the defenders as against 31,000 for the British and Americans. More serious to the Axis than loss of Sicily was the complete collapse of the Italian government. Mussolini was forced to resign on July 25, 1943, and the Italian king opened negotiations with General Eisenhower in an effort to surrender the Italian mainland without the knowledge of the Germans.

Another conference, at Quebec, was in progress at the time. General Eisenhower was directed to accept the Italian surrender and to occupy the Italian mainland. The decision was based upon the desire to draw German troops into Italy away from the Russian front and France, to establish air bases close to Germany's southern frontier; and to bring the entire Mediterranean under Allied control. Announcement was made of Italy's unconditional surrender on September 8, and the following day the Italian fleet put in at Allied harbors and invasion of the mainland began in the Gulf of Salerno. The landing operations again were successful, 108,000 tons of supplies, 30,000 motor vehicles, and 189,000 troops being landed on the beaches in eighteen days. The Germans elected to fight, increasing their strength to 24 divisions, and for several days the landing forces relied heavily upon the airforce and naval gunfire for survival. Thus began one of the most grueling campaigns of the war, with the invading forces scarcely equal to the defenders and little assistance from the Italians. The desire to reinforce General Clark was sacrificed to the necessity of hastening preparations for the invasion of France, and to the establishment of the Air Forces at Foggia. Ten airfields were completed, and 35,000 combat airmen were operating from Italy by the end of 1943. The armies drove slowly northward through mountainous country, and not until June 4, 1944, two days before the cross-Channel invasion began, did Rome come into the possession of the Allied armies.

Constant and serious consideration had been given by the combined Chiefs of Staff to the problem of aiding China. Supplies over the air route from India were increased to 10,000 tons per month after the Washington Conference of May, 1943; and to 20,000 per month after the Quebec Conference of July, 1943; but by no means could they ever be made adequate. It was decided at the Quebec Conference to reduce Japan by bombing, with the new superfortresses then coming off the assembly lines, and from bases in China and on islands in the Pacific. A Southeast Asia Command was established under the British Admiral, Lord Louis Mountbatten, with General Stilwell serving as his deputy in command of the China-Burma-India theater and as Chief of Staff to Generalissimo Chiang Kai-shek. The Royal Air Force and the United States Air Force were placed under Major-General George E. Stratemeyer. The Ledo Road from Assam, India, was to be extended by American engineers to the old Burma Road, and a pipe was to be built from Calcutta to Assam and then paralleling the Ledo Road to handle 54,000 tons of petroleum products per month. A campaign was to start at the end of the monsoon season to drive the Japanese out of Burma and safeguard the new road.

The Burma campaign will long remain one of the most unique in military history. Chinese troops, trained and equipped in India by General Stilwell, veteran American jungle fighters drawn from the entire Pacific area, under Brigadier-General Frank D. Merrill, and British and Indian jungle fighters under Major-General Orde C. Wingate, totaling 100,000 men, were moved into northern Burma and supplied through a lengthy campaign entirely by air. Below and around them at all times was an impassable country, jungle diseases of every kind, and a not-too-friendly native population. The Burma campaign began in February, 1944. The new road from India to China was opened in January, 1945, Mandalay was recaptured in March, and British forces re-entered Rangoon on May 3. The Japanese had lost 300,000 men; few escaped. Meanwhile supplies over the air route to China had increased to 46,000 tons per month, superfortresses of the Fourteenth Air Force were operating from ten large airfields in China, and 35 Chinese divisions had been trained and equipped.

The approach to Japan from the Pacific was of an entirely different character. General MacArthur, with headquarters in Australia, had 6 Australian and 4 American divisions. The troops in New Guinea were commanded by Lieutenant-General Walter Krueger; those in the Solomons by Admiral William F. Halsey. These forces were firmly established in the Solomons, all of Guadal-canal having come into our possession in February, 1943; and in eastern New Guinea, at Salamaua and Lae. The Kiruwina and Woodlark Islands between New Guinea and the Solomons were seized on June 23, 1943. Then began a pincers movement on the Japanese base at Rabaul on New Britain. In the Solomons, New Georgia was occupied on June 30, Vella Lavella on October 9, Bougainville on November 1. At the western end of New Britain, troops from Salamaua and Lae occupied Finchhafen on September 22 and Arawe on December 15, 1943. These operations brought the Japanese air and naval concentrations at Rabaul under con-stant attack by both carrier and land based planes. Then began a movement westward toward the Philippines along the northern shore of New Guinea. The Admiralty Islands were occupied Feb-ruary 29, 1944; Hollandia on April 22; and Sansapor on July 10. These operations represented the seizure of important air and naval sites by the combined operations of every branch of the services. American forces had complete superiority in the air and on the sea. They were able, therefore, to seize and hold strategic positions in the advance north and west, and to by-pass hundreds of thousands of Japanese, leaving them to die of starvation in the jungle. Operations now being 1300 miles closer to Japan than at the start of the offensive, headquarters were moved from Australia and the Solomons to Hollandia.

Full-scale operations began in the Central Pacific, where Admiral Nimitz was in command, with troops trained in the Hawaiian Islands. The Quebec Conference in August decided upon opera-tions against the Gilberts, the Marshalls, and the Marianas with the hope of somewhere forcing the Japanese navy into a decisive en-gagement. The Gilbert Islands were invaded on November 21, 1943, with terrible losses to the Second Marine Division on Tarawa. This operation opened a new type of warfare in which heavy enemy concentrations in small areas, fortified pill-boxes, and deadly beach obstacles had to be overcome. The lessons learned here were put to good account. More amphibious tractors were used thereafter to carry assault forces over outlying reefs and up onto the beaches; and the heavy fighting at Tarawa was not again equalled during the war.

The Marshall Islands, including Majuro, Wotje, and Kwajalein atolls were seized, beginning on January 31, and Einewetok on February 17, 1944. General MacArthur's forces seized the Admiralty Islands on February 29, 1944, and the great Japanese base at Truk was now within bombing range from two directions. Four Japanese destroyers and two cruisers were sunk there, February 16–18, and the base was thereafter of little value to the Japanese. Assaults on the Mariana Islands, north and west of Truk began on June 15, with heavy fighting on Saipan, Guam, and Tinian. Over 600 vessels, 2000 aircraft, and 300,000 personnel were used in the operations. Twenty-five days of extremely heavy fighting were required to get possession of Saipan, but the construction of airfields began almost from the first day of attack. The Navy had established construction battalions, "Seabees," at the outbreak of war, of men skilled in all types of construction and amphibious operations. These battalions landed with the first wave of assault troops in all Pacific operations to bring in equipment, repair airfields, and build bases of operation. Air bases were completed on Saipan for the huge superfortresses, and bombardment of the main Japanese Island of Honshu began on November 24, 1944. Meanwhile, Admiral Halsey's carrier planes had destroyed 2000 Japanese aircraft, the 14th Air Force in China had badly crippled Japan's supply lines in the China seas, and the Philippines were ripe for invasion.

Halsey's probing of Philippine defenses following operations in the Marianas led to a suggestion from Admiral Nimitz to the Quebec Conference of September, 1944, that projected operations against the intervening Islands of Yap and Mindanao be abandoned, and that invasion of the Philippines begin on October 20 instead of December 20 as previously scheduled. The Chiefs of Staff agreed and invasion of Leyte began on October 20, 1944, the landing force of General MacArthur being covered by planes from 18 escort carriers, and guarded by Admiral Halsey's naval task force. The first results of the invasion were a series of mighty sea battles in Surigao Strait, off Samar, and off Cape Engaño on the northern tip of Luzon, October 23–26. In this series of engagements, the Japanese lost 4 aircraft carriers, 3 battleships, 6 cruisers, and 5 destroyers. They also had severely damaged 7 battleships, 10 cruisers, and 10 destroyers. It was the worst defeat for Japan since the Battle of Midway; and it reduced her to the rank of a third rate naval power. It also raised Admiral Halsey to the ranks of the great naval heroes of the United States.

END OF THE ROAD

Assembly of army and air forces in Great Britain for the cross-Channel invasion began early in 1943. President Roosevelt and Prime Minister Churchill met at Cairo in November, and then with Marshal Stalin of Russia at Teheran. The determination to invade France in 1944 was re-affirmed; the shipyards were put under additional pressure to provide landing craft; the date of the invasion was postponed from May to June, 1944; and the invasion of Southern France was postponed until after the cross-Channel invasion to allow use of the same landing craft in both operations.

The air war against Germany, meanwhile, had continued with increasing fury. The first attack on the Ploesti airfields of Rumania was made on August 1, 1943, with a loss of 54 bombers; but they continued until the fields were destroyed. Radar bombings, providing precision attacks in all kinds of weather, began in the autumn. Shuttle flights from the new Italian bases, to Russia and to Great Britain began in June, 1944. American bombers alone dropped 1,550,000 tons of bombs on Germany and occupied countries between August, 1942, and June, 1944. Industries, bridges, and railroads were wrecked. More important, American bombers were accompanied by long range fighters in an effort to systematically deplete the German air power. By June 6, 1944, date of the invasion, the Allied air forces had complete command of the skies, and German air opposition was limited to sporadic night attacks. The invasion force, which included 1,533,000 men of the United States forces, was assisted by 3000 heavy bombers and 6500 other first line planes. The assault forces also had the support of 3 battleships, 2 cruisers, and 30 destroyers of the United States fleet alone, which reduced shore batteries and hindered enemy reinforcements until the line of battle passed beyond fire range.

The historic invasion over the beaches of Normandy began on June 6, in spite of high winds and rough seas. German defenses had been carefully prepared, including concealed gun emplacements, pill boxes, trenches, tank traps, and underwater obstacles connected by barbed wire and strewn with mines. German resistance was stubborn; losses were heavy; but five American divisions were put ashore the first day and the beachhead was secure. There was no port at which to land supplies. There had been constructed, therefore, in Great Britain two artificial harbors which were towed by tugs across the Channel and assembled by the Seabees, beginning on the second day of the invasion. In addition, five small boat shelters were provided by sinking old ships just off the beaches. The United States forces put 74,000 troops, 10,000 vehicles, and 17,000 tons of supplies on shore within a week; but a storm, June 18–22, destroyed the American harbor and severely damaged the British harbor. The port of Cherbourg was captured on June 27. It had been systematically destroyed by the Germans. Equipment for its complete replacement had been assembled in Great Britain before the invasion, but everything went in over the beaches for many days.

The battle for Normandy was intense. The weather was bad, making bombing operations ahead of the ground forces extremely hazardous. The terrain, interlaced by hedgerows and deep ditches, was admirably suited to defense. The Germans were determined to hold the invaders within the Peninsula. Nevertheless, a major offensive began on July 25. General Omar Bradley and Field Marshal Montgomery commanded the American and British Forces. The United States First Army was directly under Lieutenant-General Courtney H. Hodges and the Third Army under Lieutenant-General George S. Patton. General Patton's Army broke out of the Brittany Peninsula and isolated four German divisions. One hundred thousand Germans were captured and the remnants of their broken army were thrown back across the Seine River. The United States Seventh Army invaded France from the Mediterranean on August 15 and moved northward through the Rhone Valley. General Patton's advance was so swift, meanwhile, that supplies had to be forwarded by air. Paris was liberated on August 25, by which time the Germans had lost close to a half million men, including 200,000 prisoners. Two million Allied troops and 3,446,000 tons of supplies had been landed in France. Liége was captured on September 8, the Allied forces crossed the German frontier on September 11, and the German armies fell back to the safety of the old Hindenburg (Siegfried) Line. The British had swept northward through Belgium and the Netherlands, freeing Brussels on September 3, Antwerp on September 4, and capturing the launching sites of rocket bombs which had been causing such devastation in Great Britain. Antwerp, largest port in Western Europe, was undamaged. Toulon and Marseille on the Mediterranean were in operation before the end of September.

General Eisenhower sent his armies against the German defenses in the middle of November, on the eve of one of the most severe winters in many years. General von Rundstedt, under direct orders from Hitler, who was acting against the advice of his best generals, launched a counter offensive against a seventy-five mile sector of the American lines between Monschau and Trier on December 16. The lines were lightly held by 4 fresh American divisions. General von Rundstedt employed 24 divisions, including 8 armored divisions, in the assault, which developed into the battle of the Ardennes. This was one of the most brilliantly fought battles in all the annals of American warfare. The Germans advanced 50 miles, only to be contained and then hurled back with tremendous losses, including 220,000 men and 14,000 tanks and heavy artillery units.

General Patton's army reached the Rhine River at Cologne and Remagen on March 7, 1945. Finding the Ludendorff Bridge at Remagen intact and lightly held, a bridgehead was quickly established on the east bank of the Rhine. Germany's last defense line had been breached. Thereafter, the Allied advance was so swift and well executed that German armies ceased to exist as coordinated fighting forces. Three hundred fifty thousand prisoners were taken during March, as the Allied armies roamed almost at will, and the anticipated last stand of Hitler's legions in the mountain fastnesses of Austria and Bohemia never materialized. Russian forces, advancing from the East, captured Berlin, where Hitler had already committed suicide, and the German government surrendered all land, sea, and air forces to the Allies, May 7, 1945.

In the Pacific, meanwhile, the battle for the Philippines continued unabated. Philippine waters and the China seas became a graveyard for the remnants of the Japanese fleet and merchant marine as Admiral Halsey's fast striking task force roamed at will. Loss of their navy made it impossible for the Japanese to reinforce their troops from Japan or to transfer any part of the 260,000 in the Islands from one point to another. Leyte was in American hands by Christmas; Luzon was invaded at Lingayen Gulf on January 9. Between Lingayen and Manila lay a broad plain 100 miles long by 50 miles wide. As troops moved south toward Manila, another landing was made in Subic Bay (January 29); and at Nasugbu, south of Manila, on January 31. The City of Manila was recovered on February 23, 1945.

Japan had begun to feel the full force of American air power soon after the capture of the Marianas. Superfortress raids increased during December, 1944, and January, 1945, but with heavy losses due to the lack of fighter protection, and the long distance over which disabled planes had to fly to their home bases. The Volcano Islands were invaded in February to secure a closer base. Marines landed on Iwo Jima, only 775 miles from the Island of Honshu, on February 19. The island is only 5 miles long and 2 miles wide, but it was heavily fortified and defended with fanatical zeal. There were 60,000 marines in the assault force. In 26 days of fighting, they suffered 20,196 casualties, of whom 4305 were killed. It was a heavy price to pay for an air base; but, said Admiral King:

There was an increase in combat effectiveness of the B–29's due to the heightened morale of personnel, heavier bomb loads, and decrease in abortive flights . . . a substantial saving in valuable life in the number of B–29's which would have been shot down over Japan had there been no fighter cover, and in the number which would have been lost at sea had Iwo Jima not been available for emergency landings.

Operations now shifted to the chain of islands lying between Kyushu and Formosa. Okinawa, 350 miles from the industrial centers of Kyushu, containing naval anchorages and air bases from which all the sea lanes from Japan to the Chinese mainland could be controlled, was invaded on April 1, 1945. Okinawa was garrisoned by 120,000 Japanese troops, amply supplied with artillery and tanks, and was near enough to the main Japanese Islands to receive ample air protection. The assault force, including 548,000 army, navy, and marine corps personnel, 318 combat vessels, and 1139 auxiliary ships, was assembled from the United States, the Hawaiian Islands, Southwestern Pacific, and the Philippines. Landings were made without difficulty, 50,000 troops going ashore the first day. Then began a bitter battle which lasted for 82 days, during which 250 vessels were hit by suicide crashes of Japanese bombing planes and 34 vessels were sunk. Losses for the campaign were 109,000 for the Japanese, 39,000 for our own forces. During the Okinawa campaign, fast carrier task forces operated in Japanese waters, bombarding the coastal cities, bombing industrial areas, and systematically destroying Japanese naval and air power. More than 2300 Japanese planes were destroyed, and important fleet units, including a battleship, a cruiser, and 4 destroyers were sunk.

The Japanese had now lost their empire, their navy, their merchant marine, and a large part of their air force. Their industries were crumbling under the devastating attacks of the B–29's. General MacArthur and Admiral Nimitz had been directed by the Combined Chiefs of Staff, April 6, 1945, to prepare for an invasion of Japan. Plans were laid for an assault on the Island of Kyushu in the autumn of 1945 and upon Honshu in the spring of 1946. Admiral Halsey's Third Fleet, the greatest ever assembled in any waters, began its assaults on Japan on July 10. Numerous cities were shelled; fleet units and factories shelled and bombed. Three battleships were sunk at Kure, one at Yokosuka. Four cruisers were sunk at Kure; and, between July 10 and August 15,

2804 airplanes were destroyed, 1598 merchant vessels were sunk or damaged, and 195 railroad locomotives were destroyed.

The American forces were never called upon to make the sacrifice which invasion of the Japanese homeland would have entailed. A long and costly research project by British and American scientists for the secret of atomic fission had been successful. An atomic bomb had been tested in the desert of New Mexico, and General Spaatz of the air forces had been directed to drop one upon any one of four industrial centers after August 3, 1945. The bomb was dropped on Hiroshima on August 6 and another on Nagasaki three days later. Japan may well have been close to surrender in any case. Now her government hastened to avoid complete annihilation. Japan sued for peace on August 10, 1945. Japan was promptly occupied by American forces, and the formal surrender was carried out on the battleship *Missouri* in Tokyo Bay, September 2, 1945. World War II, which had cost the United States 201,367 killed, 570,783 wounded, and 56,867 missing had come to an end.

30

Unity in Peace

THE ELECTION OF 1944

INVASION of the continent of Europe had begun on the eve
of a presidential election campaign. Both national conventions
were held in Chicago, the Republicans meeting on June 26, the
Democrats on July 19; but national conventions were the least important part of the campaign. This was no ordinary election; it
was the first in wartime since 1864. Few people expected war in
the Pacific to end before 1946. There was widespread confidence
among the people, however, that victory over Germany would
come soon, perhaps before Christmas, 1944. Men were thinking
a great deal, and doing some talking, about the conditions of
peace: What terms would be imposed upon the conquered nations? What sort of organization of nations would be arranged
to keep the peace? What would be done to restore world trade
and stabilize currencies? What about demobilization of the vast
war machine, reconversion of industry, tax revision, jobs for veterans? What about social security and collective bargaining? Foreign and domestic problems, and the problems of both war and
peace, were of importance in the campaign. The independent voters
were concerned about winning the war, keeping the peace, and
attaining postwar economic security. Which candidate and which
party was best fitted to bring the war to an early, victorious conclusion, to establish an effective international organization to preserve the peace, and to handle the postwar economy of the nation?
Those were the three questions uppermost in men's minds.

The field of candidates for the Republican nomination narrowed down to three at an early date: Wendell Willkie, the Republican candidate of 1940; Governor John Bricker of Ohio; and Governor Thomas E. Dewey of New York. Willkie was a lonely soul in the Republican party. His efforts to liberalize the party and take control away from the Old Guard had been no more successful than that of La Follette at an earlier time. He advocated a strong centralized government; federal anti-lynching and anti-poll tax laws; extension of social security to include medical care; further reduction of tariff rates; acknowledgment of the permanence of collective bargaining; revision of taxes to encourage investments; and an effective international organization which would recognize the rights of small nations and adhere firmly to the objectives of the war being fought for freedom of men everywhere. Everything in his program, with the possible exception of tax revision, was anathema to large segments of the party. He chose to make his critical test of strength in Wisconsin—a most unhappy choice—and was hopelessly beaten in the primaries of that isolationist state. Knowing, then, that he could not win the party to his principles, and being too honorable and deadly earnest to surrender convictions for the sake of expediency, he announced his retirement from the race at Omaha early in April. He was not invited to speak at the convention and remained away.

Governor John Bricker, a personable, amiable man, and a splendid speaker, traveled widely, making friends everywhere, and treating the country to the best expositions of sound, stalwart Republicanism in many a year. His efforts were futile so far as the nomination was concerned, because party leaders had chosen Thomas E. Dewey at an early date. They worked carefully and efficiently to prevent a repetition of the 1940 episode in which the convention was stampeded into nominating a former independent Democrat. Governor Dewey, 42 years old, unbending, precise, efficient, lacking both the personal warmth of Bricker and the color of Willkie, remained steadfastly at his job in Albany. He refused to announce his candidacy for the nomination, seeking to create the impression that he was being drafted and having no part in the procedure. His official disinterestedness was overdone. He overplayed his part, and it cost him the valuable experience of a pre-convention campaign.

The Republican keynote address was given by Governor Earl Warren of California who refused to be considered for the vice-presidential nomination because he considered the postwar governorship of his state more important than the Vice-Presidency of the United States. The platform of the party was written under the supervision of Senator Robert Taft of Ohio. It meant little, since Dewey announced his own principles during the campaign, except that it revealed how bereft the party was of real, basic principles; how its leaders were still trimming, and hedging, and talking trivialities; and how much cynicism and fear were still relied upon to take the place of courageous leadership. Governor Bricker, seeing how hopeless his own chances were for the nomination, threw his support to Dewey and accepted the nomination for the vice-presidency. The young liberals, who had hoped to swing the convention for Lieutenant-Commander Harold E. Stassen, former Governor of Minnesota, never had the opportunity to enter the contest.

There was no contest in the Democratic party for the presidential nomination. Democrats correctly assumed that Roosevelt was the candidate of the party unless and until he should declare his unwillingness to serve. He made no such announcement, and his nomination on the first ballot was assured before the convention met. There were plenty of Democrats who disliked the idea of a fourth term for Roosevelt. The cleavage between New Deal Democrats and Southern Conservatives was deep. Senator Edwin C. Johnson summed up the opposition by saying: "Should the present running row between the Executive and Congress persist, America will find herself in a war crisis and a postwar crisis, and her government in a hopeless deadlock. Only a fool would close his eyes to this impending crisis. It overshadows all of the other political issues of the approaching campaign." Many more Democrats had grave misgivings about the President's health, and his ability to live through another four, grueling years in the White House. Reassuring statements from his personal physician did something to allay suspicions; but it made little difference in any case, since no one possessed the political stature to contest the nomination.

The vice-presidential nomination, however, presented difficulties. Vice-President Henry A. Wallace was more of a New Dealer than he was a Democrat. He believed as firmly in the necessity for continuing domestic reforms and responsible leadership in international affairs as Wendell Willkie. He was the leader of the progressives, both as to the functions of government in a modern industrial society and as to the desperate need for a consciously directed economic policy in the postwar period. He was opposed by the conservative elements in the country of both parties, and it was this contest over the vice-presidential nomination in the Democratic party which gave meaning to the statement in the Republican platform: "Four years more of New Deal policy would centralize all power in the President, and would daily subject every act of every citizen to regulation by his henchmen; and this country could remain a Republic only in name." Like Willkie, Wallace was in earnest, and he did not intend to be shelved at the behest of southern Bourbons. Moreover, he had the support of Sidney Hillman's Political Action Committee of the C.I.O. Domestic problems were not paramount with Roosevelt at the moment. The great task ahead was to cement international relations in such manner as to guarantee peace and stability in the postwar world. He had to have party harmony to guarantee support for his international program at any cost, and he did not demand Wallace's nomination. In the end, Senator Harry S. Truman of Missouri was nominated by a combination of Southerners and northern city bosses—nominated because he was not supported by anyone, nor opposed by anyone, came from a mid-western border state, and had a fine record in the Senate as the guardian of public funds against war graft and corruption.

In the campaign, Dewey was under the handicap of opposing a war President. It was a heavy handicap; but it was more than balanced by the fact that Roosevelt was a candidate for a *fourth* term and was known to be in poor health. The most important issue was foreign affairs, and here the Republicans tried valiantly to live down their long record of opposition to international cooperation, and their votes against rearmament appropriations, selective service, and lend lease. Governor Bricker, before the convention, said:

We were drawn in[to two world wars] because we had become of such great importance in world affairs, economically and politically, that we could not escape involvement. Neither Germany in the last war, nor Germany and Japan in this war, could hope to achieve world domination so long as the United States stood strong and free in this hemisphere. We have always had a tremendous stake in world order and stability.

Bricker favored a "cooperative organization of sovereign nations . . . to establish a reign of law among nations," but opposed an international police force or military alliance. Dewey favored "durable cohesion between Great Britain and ourselves, together, I hope, with Russia and China." There was nothing here, however, nor in the platform, from which the party could not escape at some future time as readily as President Harding had done from his pre-election pledge of support for an "association of nations." This fact was clearly understood by all.

During the campaign, delegates of the several United Nations met at Dumbarton Oaks, in a world security conference to prepare memoranda on the possible creation of a world organization to preserve peace. An exchange of statements by Dewey and Secretary Hull about the work of the conference raised the specter of another fight such as had occurred between Wilson and the irreconcilables. A conference was arranged between Dewey's confidential adviser, John Foster Dulles, and Secretary Hull; and, in an exchange of letters between Dewey and Hull, plans for post-war security were placed above party politics. Said Dewey: "Heretofore, war has been the only matter which has been lifted above partisanship during the presidential campaign. I recently said that if we are to have lasting peace, we must wage peace as we wage war." Hull replied: "These conversations and your letter constitute a heartening manifestation of national unity on the problem of the establishment of an international peace and security organization." This display of apparent national unity did much to remove foreign affairs from public discussions of the campaign; yet, not as a factor in the election. Both parties and both candidates were committed to American participation in a world organization to prevent another war. On the question of which man was best equipped to achieve this, there was wide variation. There was the record of Roosevelt's initiative in promoting and conciliation in achieving cooperation. The first famous conference in the Atlantic, and subsequent conferences at Washington, Casablanca, Quebec, Cairo, Teheran testified to intimate personal contacts with the heads of other governments. The appointment of bipartisan delegations to all conferences, the frequent consultations with Senators, and the initiation of postwar security plans during the war, showed how carefully Wilson's errors were being avoided. On the other hand, there was the vacillating record of Dewey, who had lacked both consistency and leadership on foreign policy. He had, for example, originally denounced lend-lease as "a grave blow, not only to national unity, but to all free government everywhere." He was sincere, but like his party, he had not formulated or stated a philosophy, a platform, or objectives.

In domestic policy, Dewey, like Willkie before him, accepted the reform measures of the New Deal and promised to carry them forward. He was not opposed to bank deposit insurance; nor collective bargaining; nor regulation of child labor, wages, and hours; nor old-age pensions and unemployment insurance; nor the Civilian Conservation Corps; nor the Tennessee Valley Authority; nor the Security and Exchange Acts; nor public works; but, whether endorsement meant approval or fear to condemn, the Republicans had nothing to offer but an acceptance of New Deal measures and a promise to administer them better. The party was still looking backward. Tennessee Valley Authority was a fact. They favored it, but they did not endorse an extension of it to the Missouri Valley. They would keep the Social Security Act; but they remained impressively silent about the Second Bill of Rights which President Roosevelt had sent to Congress the preceding January:

The right to a useful and remunerative job in the industries or shops or farms or mines of the nation;

The right to earn enough to provide adequate food and clothing and recreation;

The right of every farmer to raise and sell his products at a return which will give him and his family a decent living;

The right of every business man, large and small, to trade in an atmosphere of freedom from unfair competition and domination by monopolies at home or abroad;

The right of every family to a decent home;

The right to adequate medical care and the opportunity to achieve and enjoy good health;

The right to adequate protection from the economic fears of old age, sickness and accident and unemployment;

The right to a good education;

All of these rights spell security. And after this war is won we must be prepared to move forward, in the implementation of these rights, to new goals of human happiness and well-being.

It was a bitter campaign—that was unavoidable in the tenseness of global war—in which Roosevelt was re-elected for three reasons. The first was the great faith of the masses in his leadership. He had brought the country through a domestic crisis and a foreign crisis, each unprecedented, and probably could have had the votes of millions for a fifth or even a sixth term. The second was the belief that it would be foolish and dangerous to change chief executives when both the war and the program for world security were progressing satisfactorily. Everyone knew that the myriad threads of global war and postwar organization, from every battlefront, every lend-lease agency, and every conference, led to Roosevelt, and to destroy this nerve center, as a minimum for three months between the election and the inauguration, might well be disastrous. The third was the inability of the Republicans to realize that the United States had become an industrial nation and organized labor a power to be respected in political campaigns. Sidney Hillman and his PAC could not be brushed off with charges of communism. The popular vote was 25,603,000 to 22,006,000 but the electoral vote was another Roosevelt landslide, 432 to 99.

AGENDA FOR PEACE

The vote in the presidential election was a mandate for the continuation of the Roosevelt plan for international security organizations to maintain world peace and economic stability. Two important international conferences looking toward these objectives were held during the campaign. The first was the United Nations Monetary and Financial Conference at Bretton Woods, New Hampshire, in July; and the second was the World Security Conference at Dumbarton Oaks in August.

Representatives of 44 nations, including all of the powers engaged in war against Germany, were represented at Bretton Woods. The conference agreed to establish an International Bank for Reconstruction and Development, and an International Monetary Fund. The purpose was to provide long term loans to restore economies destroyed by the war; to finance reconversion of war economies to peacetime economies; and to assist in the development of previously unexplored resources of backward nations. Loans could be made to national governments or to individuals for use outside their own countries. The Bank was to be capitalized at $10,000,-000,000 of which the United States was to provide $3,175,000,000. Other major contributions were to be as follows: Great Britain (not including the Dominions), $1,300,000,000; Russia, $1,200,000,000; France, $450,000,000; China, $600,000,000; and Canada, $325,000,-000. Nations were to share in control in proportion to their financial contributions, the United States controlling 28 percent of the voting strength. The purpose of this international monetary fund was to restore and expand world trade by removing exchange restrictions, curbing currency depreciations, and stabilizing currency exchange rates. It was hoped in this way to eliminate the worst features of the disastrous trade warfare which followed World War I.

At Dumbarton Oaks, a skeleton plan of organization for the United Nations was designed. There were to be (1) a General Assembly consisting of representatives of all member nations; (2) a Security Council of eleven members, five to represent the United States, Great Britain, Russia, China, and eventually France, the remaining six to be elected by the General Assembly; (3) an International Court of Justice; (4) a Secretariat; (5) an Economic and Social Council to deal with food, agriculture, finance, civil aviation, public health, etc.; and (6) a Military Staff Committee, consisting of the Chiefs of Staff of the five permanent members of the Security Council. The principles of equality for all nations, renunciation of all force or threat of force, and full cooperation to prevent aggression were embraced in the Charter. Here was the nucleus for an organization which would provide both the atmosphere of security so essential to progress and assistance in achieving it. The heart of the plan was the Security Council which, at its own initiative or by request, could investigate disputes between nations or conditions which might lead to disputes and take all necessary measures to maintain the peace. It might do this, after full investigation, by cutting off all communications with the offending nation, by severing diplomatic and economic relations, and ultimately by the use of force. Member nations were required to provide armed forces promptly upon request.

The public was invited by the State Department to discuss these two achievements, and President Roosevelt, soon after his fourth inauguration, urged Congress to approve them. The Dumbarton Oaks agreement was only the basic framework of a United Nations organization which was to be discussed, perhaps amended, and embraced within a charter by a later conference. Secretary Hull had previously held a series of precedent-breaking conferences with the members of the Senate Foreign Relations Committee in April and May, 1944, in an effort to keep all political influences and jealousies over Senate prerogatives out of the debates. There had been the understanding by which foreign affairs were not dragged through the mud of a presidential campaign. Then, on January 10, Senator Arthur Vandenberg of Michigan delivered a history-making speech in the Senate in which he advocated a treaty between the principal allied powers to keep Germany disarmed by force if necessary. Vandenberg had belonged to the group of isolationists along with Burton K. Wheeler, Bennett Clark, and Hiram Johnson, and could well have followed the Henry Cabot Lodge tradition. Instead, he took a statesmanlike position, scorned all political chicanery, and assured cooperation between the executive and legislative branches of the government.

President Roosevelt, Prime Minister Churchill, and Marshal Stalin, with their foreign secretaries and Chiefs of Staff then met at Yalta, on the shores of the Black Sea in February. The two most fateful decisions of this conference dealt with Germany and the United Nations. It was agreed "to destroy German militarism and to insure that Germany will never again be able to disturb the peace of the world." This was to be done by disarming and disbanding all armed forces; breaking up the German General Staff; removing or destroying all German military equipment; controlling all German industry usable for military production; punishing all war criminals; exacting reparations in kind; wiping out the Nazi party; and military occupation for an indefinite period. It was also agreed to hold a United Nations conference at San Francisco on April 25, 1945, to prepare a charter for the organization along the lines of the Dumbarton Oaks agreement. President Roosevelt went before Congress immediately after his return from Yalta, and gave to that body an informal report of the conference and the many obstacles still to be overcome in achieving complete international unity. He then appointed, as delegates to the San Francisco Conference, Senator Arthur H. Vandenberg, Commander Harold E. Stassen, Representative Charles Eaton of New Jersey, and Dean Virginia C. Gildersleeve of Barnard College—all Republicans; and Democrats Edward Stettinius, Cordell Hull, Senator Tom Connally, and Representative Sol Bloom. Both branches of Congress, both parties, and the Senate Foreign Relations Committee were ably represented. Connally assured the Senate that there would be no partisanship in the delegation at San Francisco; and that the Dumbarton Oaks agreement would be liberalized. Said Vandenberg: "I have no illusions that the San Francisco conference can chart the millennium. . . . But I have faith that we may perfect this charter of peace and justice so that reasonable men of good will shall find in it so much good and so much emancipation for human hopes that all lesser doubts and disagreements may be resolved in its favor." Commander Stassen published a statement of his own views in which he emphasized the importance (1) of a continuing international organization "based on justice and law and insured by force"; (2) of delegating "a limited portion of our national sovereignty to the United Nations organization"; (3) of recognizing the interrelationship of the peace and happiness of the American people and those of other nations; (4) of promoting free enquiry and discussion throughout the world; (5) of reducing the aggressor nations to military impotence; and (6) of recognizing the right of every people to determine the nature of its own institutional development "so long as they do not trample on basic human rights or threaten the peace of the world."

Had the same degree of national unity been achieved in a program of domestic policy, the progress of the nation might indeed have seemed secure. Such was not to be. There were in the country two tremendous, conflicting forces. The one embraced the ideal of a postwar economy in which the government would promote the utilization of all the nation's resources for full production, full employment, and ever-increasing prosperity for all. The other was opposed to a continuing New Deal or a Second New Deal, and embraced a return to complete reliance upon individualism and private enterprise in economic life. President Roosevelt was the architect of the progressive domestic policies as he was of the new international policies. The two, in fact, were inseparable in contemplating the shape of things to come, because of the tremendous power of the United States in world economy. The Second Bill of Rights he had sent to Congress in January, 1944, embraced his social and economic objectives. It was his program of security and prosperity for all "regardless of station, race, or creed." He believed firmly that "individual freedom cannot exist without economic security and independence"; and equally that "unless there is security at home there cannot be lasting peace in the world." It is important for the student of history to ponder the fate of this program in those days of earth-shaking events in the spring of 1945.

Roosevelt sacrificed a great deal when he bought party unity at the expense of dropping Henry Wallace from the Vice-Presidency; and only the terrible urgency of his foreign policies probably could have reconciled him to it; but he sought to do more than recover the loss by nominating Wallace to succeed Jesse Jones as Director of the Reconstruction Finance Corporation. This multi-billion dollar government lending agency had been the key to the recovery program and the war production program. It owned outright 950 war plants which had cost the government $6,000,000,000. It had large holdings in as many more. The Director had power to loan any amount, to anyone, on any terms he might choose without congressional approval. The agency had the power of life and death over small business enterprises; and it had tremendous potential power to direct the future of the nation's economy. Roosevelt had nominated the one man in the country whose vision of full employment, increased production, guaranteed annual wages, higher standards of living, extension of social security, more Tennessee Valley Authorities, and a multitude of other social and economic gains equalled his own. Once more Republicans and Southern Democrats combined to stop New Dealing, and once more the President had no choice but to accept defeat on domestic policy for the sake of saving his international program. Vice-President Truman, Speaker Sam Rayburn, and Senate Majority Leader Alben Barkley applied the rules of practical politics and secured the confirmation of Wallace as Secretary of Commerce, but only by taking away from that Department all control over the Reconstruction Finance Corporation. The trend was continued when the President nominated another New Dealer, Aubrey Williams, for the post of Rural Electrification Administrator. Williams had been one-time director of the National Youth Administration, and what was worse in the eyes of Southern Bourbons, organizer for the National Farmers' Union. His appointment was not confirmed.

More devastating to the cause of liberalism than the attacks of reactionary congressmen were the ravages of illness and death. Wendell Willkie, courageous, democratic liberal of the Republican party, and one of the foremost champions of individual freedom and international cooperation in the world, died suddenly in mid-October, 1944. Both Wallace and Willkie believed firmly in free enterprise, and worked to keep it free from abuses and a vital force in the modern world; both thought in terms of the United States as a part of a larger economic and political world; both were repudiated by the reactionaries of their parties, who feared change. George Norris, whose career of public service linked the New Freedom of Woodrow Wilson to the New Deal of Roosevelt, preceded Willkie in death by only a few weeks. Cordell Hull, father of reciprocal trade agreements, whose career in the government service was as long and distinguished as that of Norris, resigned from his post as Secretary of State because of ill health late in November, 1944.

The greatest blow to liberalism came on April 12, 1945, with the death of President Roosevelt at Warm Springs, Georgia. He died a few weeks before the Nazi surrender, a few days before the San Francisco conference. The war was ending—the task of world organization and reconstruction was just beginning. It was he who had given to the war some meaning other than self-defense. The Atlantic Charter, with its freedom of thought, freedom of worship, freedom from want, freedom from fear, was a pledge of fair play for all. Almost single-handed, he had rallied the moral forces of the world from the lethargy, the retreat, the defeatist attitude of two decades. Almost in the shadow of death, he had journeyed to Yalta to smooth the clash of interests and personalities between Churchill and Stalin and thus preserve the possibility of a working United Nations organization.

In 1933, Roosevelt had taken a depressed, fearful people and turned their faces toward the light with his famous rallying call: "the only thing we have to fear is fear itself." He had placed the vast resources of the nation to relieving the distress and sorrow which had crept into millions of homes. He had made the government function in the interest of the people, perhaps to a greater degree than ever before in the nation's history as regards the simple essentials of work, food, clothing, and shelter. He had saved the country from civil strife, and in doing so, had preserved the vital forces needed to carry it through the period of international chaos. It is a significant fact that a much higher percentage of young people than of any other class supported the Roosevelt Administration in elections; it is also a fact that, when the foreign crisis came, the young people met it more courageously than any generation of young people before them, and with more unity and understanding of purpose than their elders. The nation they served so nobly had been, during practically all their years of understanding, under the government of Roosevelt and the New Deal. It was he who clearly saw the menace of aggression and prepared the country to meet it; who marshaled the productive resources of the nation for its role as the arsenal of democracy; who united the nation behind a program of international cooperation.

Roosevelt was a man of vision, of great personal charm, of unusual intellectual attainments. He was recognized everywhere on earth as the greatest statesman of his time. His death brought a feeling of intense personal loss to hundreds of millions of people, far distant from our shores, who did not even speak our language, because he was to them the symbol of a great, humane, and generous America. He was a humanitarian, who went beyond the pressing duty of relief to fashion a reform program into an enduring part of our governmental structure. He was the Thomas Jefferson of the twentieth century, and his stature will grow through the years. When he died the most cohesive force among the peoples of the world was lost; the bright hopes for world solidarity and the resumption of expanding democratic institutions were greatly dimmed; and the liberals were left once more, as in 1919, confused, bewildered, and without leadership.

A NEW AGE

The death of Roosevelt more than ever focused the hopes of all humanity, with its eternal yearning for peace, upon the conference at San Francisco. Once more, as so frequently in past history, the nations were seeking a formula by which war would not only be placed beyond the pale of law but beyond the realm of possibility. There was reason for hope in the fact that the conference was meeting on the soil of the most powerful nation and greatest democracy of its time. There was reason for hope in the fact that since 1919 we had learned the futility of trying to create a modern utopia out of the wreckage of war by the fiat of a peace conference. There was reason for hope in the knowledge that politicians were not going to sacrifice world welfare again for the sordid sake of party advantage. But there were deep, underlying causes for misgiving. The movement for a world security organization in 1918 had been based upon a passionate worldwide desire to consolidate the gains of three centuries of expanding democratic institutions. The movement in 1945 arose from a realization that the horrors of war had become intolerable—in short from fear. The world atmosphere in 1918 was congenial to sympathy, understanding, and tolerance between nations; in 1945, it was such as to promote rigid patterns of political, social, and economic orders. Finally, it was perfectly plain throughout the course of the war, and more so throughout Roosevelt's painstaking efforts to construct the basis for postwar cooperation, that the test of success in the conduct of every aspect of international relationships was the ability of Russia and the democracies to live in peace. Harold E. Stassen had outlined a program of bold idealism, embracing a partial surrender of national sovereignty, the dedication of American productive genius and financial resources to the improvement of living standards elsewhere, the emancipation of men everywhere from cultural and spiritual restraints by inclusion of the principles of our Bill of Rights in the World Charter, and the implementation of world unity by giving to the international organization the power of legislation over such matters as communications, utilization of natural resources, and the maintenance of health, education, and public morality. His program gave new hope for leadership to the liberal forces of the nation, but it did not erase two stubborn facts. The first was that millions of people in the United States and elsewhere seemed to have lost completely the capacity to respond to the system of liberal ideas through which a generous and humane society had been built and maintained. The second was that, however much the five great powers might give lip service to the freedom of man, some of them were not willing to have it extended in any such fashion as Stassen proposed to their own people or to those they controlled. The San Francisco Conference had scarcely begun its work, when Secretary Stettinius announced that an agreement had been reached by the four great powers that "enumeration of individual and collective human rights and fundamental freedoms in the charter could not be attempted at this conference." Thus at one stroke the whole question of freedom and civil rights, for the preservation of which millions of men had died was postponed to some future time.

The San Francisco Conference made no fundamental change in the structural framework of the United Nations organization as agreed upon at Dumbarton Oaks. The Charter contained no Bill of Rights but there was a recognition of human rights in the Preamble, in Chapter IV (General Assembly), and in Chapter IX (Economic and Social Council). One purpose of the organization, as stated in the Preamble, was "to employ international machinery for the promotion of the economic and social advancement of all peoples." The General Assembly was given power to "initiate studies and make recommendations for the purpose of promoting international cooperation in the economic, social, cultural, educational and health fields and assisting in the realization of human rights and basic freedoms for all without distinction as to race, sex, language or religion." The Economic and Social Council was authorized to "make recommendations for the purpose of promoting respect for, and observance of human rights and fundamental freedoms." Thus the absence of a specific Bill of Rights for the individual was in part compensated by the wide latitude given to these two agencies by the language of the Charter.

The second important feature of the Charter was recognition that force may be necessary to the maintenance of peace, and that only the combined strength and unity of the great powers can preserve peace. Thus the strength of the United Nations organization, in fact its entire future existence, depended upon the degree of unity among the five great powers: United States, Great Britain, Russia, China, and France. If they could not live in peace with each other, then the United Nations would perish in the horrors of another war, for there was no authority for the use of force against any one of the big five.

Scarcely had the new world organization been perfected at San Francisco, when the atomic bomb was dropped on Hiroshima. Thus almost at the same time mankind was given its one best hope for peace and the certainty of complete annihilation if it failed to keep the peace. Whatever isolationists' doubts remained as to the wisdom of international cooperation, or perfectionists' objections to the imperfections of the United Nations Charter, were swept away in the dust of Japanese cities. The United States Senate ratified the Charter with but two dissenting votes. A new age—the age of atomic energy—and a new epoch in history—that of international cooperation—had begun. One world had become a reality.

THE UNITED NATIONS

Secretary of State Edward R. Stettinius had said at San Francisco: "The sovereignty of no nation, not even the most powerful, is absolute. There is no such thing as complete freedom of decision for any nation." Nevertheless, no nation wanted to surrender any part of its sovereignty to the United Nations. The small nations were disposed to surrender more sovereign powers than the large nations, because their one hope in the new world even more than in the old one lay in collective security. The large nations were in a strong position to weigh the relative advantages of reliance upon their own strength and collective security. This was particularly true of the United States and Russia, the only two nations really capable of fighting a modern war against any possible combination of nations. Fortunately, these two nations, neither of which had been a member of the League of Nations in its early years, were both members of the United Nations. Unfortunately, the Yalta Conference had agreed that any one of the large powers—Russia, United States, Great Britain, France, China—could prevent the Security Council from acting on any matter, and Russia insisted upon retaining this precious right of the veto. It was later agreed that no one power could veto *discussions* of any question in the Security Council, but that any five of the eleven members could do so; and, of course, any one member could still veto any *action* by the Security Council. Since the real power of the United Nations to preserve the peace lay in the Security Council, actually in the hands of the permanent "Big Five" members, the power of the veto was a serious obstacle to the achievement of collective security. Equally questionable was the provision that only when international peace is broken or immediately threatened can the United Nations intervene in matters "essentially within the domestic jurisdiction" of a member nation. The Assembly was composed of one representative from each of the 51 member nations. Its power lay in its ability to discuss any question not already before the Security Council, and thus to marshal public opinion throughout the free portions of the world, and in its control of the Economic and Social Council.

A Preparatory Commission met in London in August, 1945, to choose a permanent site for the United Nations, and to arrange for the incorporation of the affairs of the League of Nations in the new organization. Among the assets of the League were a $30,000,-000 palace at Geneva, a treasury of $15,000,000, and a library of incalculable value. All of the 51 member nations having ratified the United Nations Organization Charter by the end of 1945, the first session of the Assembly met in London on January 10, 1946. Six non-permanent members were elected to the Security Council: Australia, Brazil, and Poland for two years; The Netherlands, Egypt, and Mexico for one year. Trygvie Lie was elected Secretary-General. New York City was selected as a temporary site for the United Nations. Franco Spain was barred from membership. Fifteen judges were elected to the International Court of Justice, and the Court was given its first case, involving a British-Guatemalan dispute over British Honduras. Finally, the Assembly created an Atomic Control Commission, and adjourned to meet in New York in September.

The United Nations Atomic Energy Commission, consisting of the 11 member nations of the Security Council and Canada, held a total of 82 discussions extending over a period of 28 weeks, and finally sent a report to the Security Council. The report was adopted by a vote of 10–0, Russia and Poland abstaining from voting. It was significant that by this action they registered their disapproval of the report, but did not prevent by the veto the report from coming before the Council for discussion. Atomic control and the veto were definitely linked together.

President Truman had appointed James F. Byrnes to the post of Secretary of State in July, 1945. Byrnes had been a former United States Senator from South Carolina, a Supreme Court Justice, and Director of Economic Stabilization under President Roosevelt. To Byrnes had fallen the task of protecting the interests of the United States and promoting world cooperation through the

United Nations organization. From the very first, the United States and Russia had emerged as representatives of two worlds of economics, politics, and morality. Byrnes, representing the Western Democratic World, had first sought to curb Russian expansion in China, Eastern Europe, and the Balkans by patience and concessions, only to discover that each concession led to new demands. Finally, he accepted the policy of firmness advocated by Senator Arthur H. Vandenberg, and stood inflexibly for certain principles at the United Nations Conference in London. He insisted that small nations had a right to be heard, that Germany must be restored economically as a basis for the reconstruction of Europe, and that the United States must continue permanently its interest in European affairs.

President Truman and Prime Ministers Attlee of Great Britain and King of Canada had agreed in November, 1945, to ask for a special commission under the United Nations to (1) arrange for free exchange of basic information on atomic energy, (2) establish controls to see that it be used only for peaceful purposes, (3) draw up a convention to outlaw its use in war, and (4) set up international inspection to enforce the convention. Russia insisted upon procedure in that order, but the United States refused to reveal any secrets about atomic energy or the atomic bomb until the right of the veto should be surrendered. Otherwise any one of the Big Five nations could arm herself with the weapons, and *do it not only effectively but legally* under the protection of the veto of all discussion, investigation, or punitive action. Control would require for the "control authority," in the words of the Atomic Energy Commission, "broad privileges of movement and inspection, including rights to conduct surveys by ground and air," and this Russia, hidden behind an "iron curtain," refused to accede. It remained to be seen, in January, 1947, whether the deadlock which emerged in the A.E.C. could be broken in the Security Council. The advantage was with the United States so long, and only so long, as scientists of other nations failed to solve the problem of nuclear fission.

VICTOR AND VANQUISHED

When Secretary Stimson stated in August, 1932, that the Kellogg-Briand pact had altered the entire concept of international law respecting war, and that thenceforth war was illegal, aggressive war a crime, he expressed what was to become the underlying principle of the world's most sensational trial, that of the Nazi war criminals.

In November, 1943, Roosevelt, Stalin, and Churchill had announced that the Nazi leaders would be punished. Later, the question arose whether the matter should be handled politically or judicially. The British argued for the former; they had so dealt with Napoleon. The United States demanded a judicial process, and so it was finally agreed. An International Tribunal was created in August, 1945. The trial was held at Nürnberg, Germany, over a period of nearly a year, with Justice Robert H. Jackson of the United States Supreme Court as Chief Prosecutor.

One purpose of a trial, rather than summary punishment, was the desire to educate the German people to the Nazi record of infamy, and discredit both the leaders and the cause. Another was to clarify the record by obtaining, perhaps, much information as to objectives and methods which would otherwise be lost. The main purpose, however, was to fill the gaps of international law, so that henceforth it would be a crime of first magnitude for heads of states to wage aggressive war or to persecute subject peoples.

The trial was in every respect a judicial process, not a star chamber. In the end, the Court weighed the evidence, measured the degree of guilt, and assessed the penalties on each defendant. The motive was justice, applied under law. Many able men in the United States denied that aggressive war was criminal between 1933 and 1945. The German defendants, of course, said their acts were not crimes when committed, and that they were, in effect, being tried under ex post facto law. Whatever the verdict of history may be on that point, Justice Jackson showed that Germany had pledged herself not to engage in aggressive war, and that she had accepted the Geneva Convention. The trial itself revealed a long and melancholy record of crimes unequaled since the Christian Era began. Not only had the defendants conspired to enslave the world by aggressive war, they had plundered occupied countries, deported civilian populations, subjected whole peoples to slave labor, gathered opponents into concentration camps, systematically exterminated Jews and Christians, and violated all the rules of war by their cruel and inhuman treatment of Allied prisoners. Twelve of the defendants were sentenced to death: Herman Goering, Joachim von Ribbentrop, Field Marshal Wilhelm Keitel, Ernst Kaltenbrunner, Alfred Rosenberg, Hans Frank, Wilhelm Frick, Julius Streicher, Fritz Sauckel, General Alfred Jodl, Arthur Seyss-Inquart, and Martin Bormann. Three were sentenced to life imprisonment: Rudolf Hess, Walter Funk, and Admiral Erich Raeder. Lesser sentences were given to others: Albert Speer and Baldur von Shirack, twenty years; Constantin von Neurath, fifteen years; and Admiral Karl Doenitz, ten years. Three were acquitted: Hjalmar Schacht, Hans Fritzsche, and Franz von Papen.

The merit of individual sentences, like the legal basis for the indictments, may be argued for many years. The reason for not bringing to trial the German General Staff and the industrialists, who would seem to have been equally guilty, may also become a matter of controversy. The one certainty was that the long-suffering peoples of the world who have borne the cost of wars for centuries approved the verdict, hoping, perhaps, that it might serve to restrain future aggressors. Few would dispute the statement of Justice Jackson that "in the long perspective of history, the present century will not hold an admirable position, unless its second half is to redeem its first. . . . If we cannot eliminate the causes and prevent the repetition of these barbaric events, it is not an irresponsible prophecy to say that this twentieth century may yet succeed in bringing the doom of civilization."

The problem of what to do with the conquered peoples was much more difficult than the disposition of their former leaders. In Japan, where the United States had practically a free hand, General Douglas MacArthur continued to carry out a bold experiment of trying to democratize the nation, ruling through the former Emperor. In Europe, the United States did not have a free hand. Long before the War's end an agreement had been reached for the division of Germany into three zones of occupation, the military forces of Great Britain, Russia, and the United States each having one zone. Then, in September, 1945, the Foreign Ministers of the five great powers met in London to begin writing the terms of the peace settlement for Germany, Italy, and the Balkans.

Both in the administration of Germany and in the discussions of the peace settlement, as in the operations of the United Nations, the conflict between Russia and the Western Democracies emerged at once. Russia, eager to compensate herself for her vast war losses, was waging a bold offensive to exploit the conquered nations to her own economic advantage and the spread of communism; seeking the oil of Iran, access to the Mediterranean, a belt of satellite nations from the Baltic to the Black Sea; taking what she wanted without consulting other nations, in Germany, in Manchuria, in the Balkans. In her ambition to regain territory lost after World War I she obtained control of desired areas by force and by infiltration. By these methods, she gained 273,000 square miles of territory and 23,000,000 people, stripped Manchuria and East Germany of their industries, and exacted heavy indemnities from the conquered nations. Peace treaties were long delayed, but when the first were ready for signatures in January, 1947, it was revealed that Russia was to receive $100,000,000 from Italy, $200,000,-000 from Hungary, $300,000,000 from Rumania, and $300,000,000 from Finland. She fomented revolution in Iran, closed the Danube river to free trade, and withheld her support from the International Monetary Fund, the International Bank for Reconstruction, and the United Nations Educational, Scientific, and Cultural Organization. She controlled the richest food-producing area of Germany but refused to allow any food to move from that area to western Germany.

Eventually, Secretary Byrnes announced a firm policy both with regard to Germany and to Russia's intransigence. In New York, February 28, 1946, he announced that the United States would support the one-world principle of the United Nations with all its power and influence. Disputes between nations must be settled through the machinery of that organization, not by unilateral action of any nation, by aggression, or by wars of nerves or threats of force. The United States must maintain the power, through such agencies as universal military training and a large amphibious striking force, to support its convictions. In Stuttgart, Germany, September 5, 1946, he stated the over-all policy of the United States toward Germany to be one of helping "the German people to win their way back to an honorable place among the free and peace-loving nations of the world." Germany must be kept peaceful by long-term military occupation or inspection, not by the destruction of German industry. The unity of Germany must be restored; she must not be permanently dismembered. All boundary settlements must be acceptable to the German people. A federal government must be established. Germany must assist in restoring the Europe she had devastated; and the United States must and would assist in restoring Germany to self-sufficiency.

Such was to be our objective in a Germany which had become an arena of power politics, with Russia, and to a degree Great Britain, seeking to revive a strong Germany as an ally against the other in some future war; with Russia trying to extend communism and the Western Democracies trying to extend representative government; with Russia cooperating with seeming reluctance, and the United States making an earnest effort to establish peace on a permanent basis through the United Nations. The test of strength would come when the Foreign Ministers meet in Moscow, March 10, 1947, to work out the peace settlement for Germany.

Bibliography

BOOKS FOR SUPPLEMENTARY READING AND REFERENCE

CHAPTERS 1–4

SOCIAL AND ECONOMIC TRENDS, BEFORE WORLD WAR I

Abbott, Edith, *Women in Industry*. New York, 1910.

Addams, Jane, *Twenty Years at Hull House*. New York, 1923.

Barrett, Don Carlos, *The Greenbacks and Resumption of Specie Payments, 1862–1879* (Harvard Economic Studies, XXXVI). Cambridge, 1931.

Beard, Charles A. and Beard, Mary R., *Rise of American Civilization*. New York, 1927.

Beer, Thomas, *The Mauve Decade*. New York, 1926.

Blanshard, Paul, *Labor in Southern Cotton Mills*. New York, 1927.

Botkin, Benjamin A., *Lay My Burden Down*. Chicago, 1945.

Bryce, James, *The American Commonwealth*. 2 vols. New York, 1922–23.

Buck, Paul H., *The Road to Reunion*. Boston, 1937.

Buck, Solon Justus, *The Agrarian Crusade* (The Chronicles of America Series, XLV). New Haven, 1921.

——, *The Granger Movement* (Harvard Historical Studies, XIX). Cambridge, 1913.

Byrn, Edward W., *The Progress of Invention in the Nineteenth Century*. New York, 1900.

Calhoun, Arthur Wallace, *A Social History of the American Family*. 3 vols. Cleveland, 1917–1919.

677

Carpenter, Niles, *Immigrants and Their Children*, 1920. Washington, 1927.

Chapin, Francis Stuart, *Cultural Change*. New York, 1928.

Cleveland, F. A. and Powell, F. W., *Railway Promotion and Capitalization in the United States*. New York, 1909.

Commons, John R., *Races and Immigrants in America*. New York, 1920.

——, *Social Reform and the Church*. New York, 1894.

Couch, William Terry, ed., *Culture in the South*. Chapel Hill, 1934.

Cubberly, E. P., *Public Education in the United States*. Boston, 1919.

Dabney, Charles W., *Universal Education in the South*. 2 vols. Chapel Hill, 1936.

Dabney, Virginius, *Liberalism in the South*. Chapel Hill, 1932.

David, Henry, *The History of the Haymarket Affair*. New York, 1936.

Dewey, Davis R., *Financial History of the United States*. New York, 1934.

Dick, Everett, *The Sod-House Frontier*. New York, 1937.

——, *Vanguards of the Frontier*. New York, 1941.

Douglas, Paul H., *Real Wages in the United States, 1890–1926*. Boston, 1930.

Dutcher, Dean, *The Negro in Modern Industrial Society*. Lancaster, Pa., 1930.

Embree, Edwin R., *American Negroes*. New York, 1942.

Emerson, Guy, *The New Frontier*. New York, 1920.

Epstein, R. C., *The Automobile Industry*. Chicago, 1928.

Feldman, Herman, *Racial Factors in American Industry*. New York, 1931.

Fine, Nathan, *Labor and Farmer Parties in the United States, 1828–1928*. New York, 1928.

Fish, Carl Russell, *The Civil Service and the Patronage* (Harvard Historical Studies, XI). New York, 1905.

Garis, Roy Lawrence, *Immigration Restriction*. New York, 1929.

Geiger, George R., *The Philosophy of Henry George*. Grand Forks, S. D., 1931.

George, Henry, Jr., *The Life of Henry George*. New York, 1905.

Gildersleeve, Basil Lanneau, *The Creed of the Old South, 1865–1915*. Baltimore, 1915.

Glasson, William Henry, *Federal Military Pensions in the United States*. New York, 1918.

Gompers, Samuel, *Seventy Years of Life and Labor*. 2 vols. London, 1925.

Hafen, Leroy R. and Rister, Carl C., *Western America*. New York, 1941.

Hall, Thomas Cuming, *Religious Background of American Culture*. Boston, 1930.

Harris, Herbert, *American Labor*. New Haven, 1939.

Harvey, Rowland H., *Samuel Gompers*. Stanford, 1935.

Haynes, Frederick E., *Third Party Movements Since the Civil War*. Iowa City, 1916.

Hendrick, Burton J., *The Age of Big Business* (The Chronicles of America Series, XXXIX). New Haven, 1919.

Hepburn, Alonzo B., *A History of Currency in the United States*. New York, 1915.

Hibbard, Benjamin H., *History of the Public Land Policies*. New York, 1924.

Hicks, John D., *The Populist Revolt*. Minneapolis, 1931.

Hough, Emerson, *The Passing of the Frontier*. New Haven, 1918.

Hourwich, Isaac A., *Immigration and Labor*. New York, 1912.

Ise, John, *The United States Forest Policy*. New Haven, 1920.

Jenks, Jeremiah W. and Lauck, W. Jett, *The Immigration Problem*. New York, 1926.

Johnson, Charles S., *The Negro in American Civilization*. New York, 1930.

Kendrick, Benjamin B. and Arnett, Alex M., *The South Looks at Its Past*. Chapel Hill, 1935.

Kennedy, Louise V., *The Negro Peasant Turns Cityward*. New York, 1930.

Kirkland, Edward C., *A History of American Economic Life*. New York, 1934.

Kirkpatrick, Clifford, *Religion in Human Affairs*. New York, 1929.

Lewinson, Paul, *Race, Class and Party*. London, 1932.

Lindquist, Ruth, *The Family in the Present Social Order*. Chapel Hill, 1931.

Logan, Rayford W., *What the Negro Wants*. Chapel Hill, 1944.

Lynd, Robert S. and Helen M., *Middletown*. New York, 1929.

MacDonald, Austin F., *Federal Aid: A Study of the American Subsidy System*. New York, 1928.

McGiffert, Arthur C., *The Rise of Modern Religious Ideas*. New York, 1915.

Mangum, Charles S., *The Legal Status of the Negro*. Chapel Hill, 1940.

Mears, Eliot G., *Resident Orientals on the American Pacific Coast*. New York, 1928.

Mitchell, Broadus and Mitchell, George S., *Industrial Revolution in the South*. Baltimore, 1930.

Mitchell, John, *Organized Labor*. Philadelphia, 1903.

Moody, John, *The Railroad Builders* (The Chronicles of America Series, XXXVIII). New Haven, 1919.

——, *The Masters of Capital* (The Chronicles of America Series, XLI). New Haven, 1919.

Moton, Robert, *What the Negro Thinks*. Garden City, 1929.

Mumford, Lewis, *Technics and Civilization*. New York, 1934.

Myers, Gustavus, *History of the Great American Fortunes*. 3 vols. Chicago, 1909–1911.

——, *The Masters of Capital* (The Chronicles of America Series, XLI). New Haven, 1919.

Nevins, Allan, *The Emergence of Modern America* (A History of American Life, VIII). New York, 1927.

——, *Grover Cleveland: A Study in Courage*. New York, 1932.

Nixon, Herman C., *Forty Acres and Steel Mules*. Chapel Hill, 1938.

Odum, Howard W., *An American Epoch*. New York, 1930.

——, *Southern Regions of the United States*. Chapel Hill, 1936.

Oliver, John W., *History of Civil War Military Pensions, 1861–1885* (University of Wisconsin, Bulletin No. 884). Madison, 1917.

Orth, Samuel P., *Our Foreigners* (The Chronicles of America Series, XXXV). New Haven, 1921.

Parrington, Vernon Louis, "The Beginnings of Critical Realism in America" (*Main Currents in American Thought*, III). New York, 1930.

Paxson, Frederic L., *History of the American Frontier, 1763–1893*. Boston, 1924.

Peck, Harry Thurston, *Twenty Years of the Republic, 1885–1905*. New York, 1920.

Potwin, Marjorie A., *Cotton Mill People of the Piedmont*. New York, 1927.

Powderly, Terence V., *Thirty Years of Labor*. Columbus, 1889.

President's Research Committee on Social Trends, *Recent Social Trends in the United States*. New York, 1933.

Raushenbusch, Walter, *Christianity and the Social Crisis*. New York, 1907.

Riegel, Robert E., *The Story of the Western Railroads*. New York, 1926.

Ripley, William Z., *Trusts, Pools and Corporations*. Boston, 1916.

Robertson, William J., *The Changing South*. New York, 1927.

Rugg, Harold O., *Culture and Education in America*. New York, 1931.

Schlesinger, Arthur M., *The Rise of the City* (A History of American Life, X). New York, 1933.

Slosson, Edwin E., *American Spirit in Education* (The Chronicles of America Series, XXXIII). New Haven, 1921.

Sullivan, Mark, *Our Times, The Turn of the Century*. New York, 1926.

Thomas, Norman M., *Human Exploitation in the United States*. New York, 1934.

Thompson, Holland, *The New South* (The Chronicles of America Series, XLII). New Haven, 1919.

——, *The Age of Inventions* (The Chronicles of America Series, XXXVII). New Haven, 1921.

Thompson, Walter, *Federal Centralization*. New York, 1923.

Turner, Frederick Jackson, *The Frontier in American History*. New York, 1920.

Vance, Rupert B., *Human Factors in Cotton Culture*. Chapel Hill, 1929.

——, *Human Geography of the South*. Chapel Hill, 1932.

Van Hise, Charles R., *Concentration and Control*. New York, 1914.

Villard, Oswald G., *Fighting Years*. New York, 1939.

Ward, Harry F., *The Social Creed and the Churches*. Cincinnati, 1914.

Webb, Walter P., *The Great Plains*. Boston, 1931.

Wesley, Charles H., *Negro Labor in the United States, 1850–1925*. New York, 1927.

Wittke, Carl, *We Who Built America*. New York, 1940.

Woodson, Carter G., *The Negro in Our History*. Washington, 1922.

CHAPTERS 5–10

GOVERNMENT AND FOREIGN POLICY BEFORE WORLD WAR I

Adamic, Louis, Dynamite: The Story of Class Violence in America. London, 1931.

Baker, Ray Stannard, Life and Letters of Woodrow Wilson. 4 vols. Garden City, 1927–1931.

Bau, Minchien J., The Open Door Doctrine in Relation to China. New York, 1923.

Beard, Charles A., The Supreme Court and the Constitution. New York, 1931.

Bemis, Samuel Flagg, ed., The American Secretaries of State and Their Diplomacy. 10 vols. New York, 1927–1929.

Berman, Edward, Labor and the Sherman Act. New York, 1930.

Blakeslee, George H., The Recent Foreign Policy of the United States. New York, 1925.

Boudin, Louis B., Government by Judiciary. New York, 1932.

Bowers, Claude G., Beveridge and the Progressive Era. Boston, 1932.

Brandeis, Louis D., Other People's Money. New York, 1914.

Browne, W. R., Altgeld of Illinois, 1847–1902. New York, 1924.

Buell, Raymond Leslie, International Relations. New York, 1929.

Callahan, James Morton, American Foreign Policy in Mexican Relations. New York, 1932.

——, American Relations in the Pacific. Baltimore, 1901.

Cardozo, Benjamin N., The Nature of the Judicial Process. New Haven, 1925.

Carpenter, E. J., America in Hawaii. Boston, 1899.

Chadbourn, James H., Lynching and the Law. Chapel Hill, 1933.

Chamberlain, John, Farewell to Reform. New York, 1933.

Chapman, Charles E., A History of the Cuban Republic. New York, 1927.

Chase, Stuart, The Tragedy of Waste. New York, 1925.

Clark, Champ, My Quarter Century of American Politics. New York, 1920.

Clark, J. D., The Federal Trust Policy. Baltimore, 1931.

Clark, Victor S., Porto Rico and Its Problems. Washington, 1930.

Colvin, David Leigh, Prohibition in the United States. New York, 1926.

Comer, John P., *Legislative Functions of National Administrative Authorities*. New York, 1927.

Commons, John R. and others, *History of Labor in the United States*. 4 vols. New York, 1918–1936.

Commons, John R. and Andrews, John B., *Principles of Labor Legislation*. New York, 1920.

Coolidge, Archibald C., *The United States as a World Power*. New York, 1908.

Corwin, E. S., *The Twilight of the Supreme Court*. New Haven, 1934.

Cox, Isaac J., *Nicaragua and the United States, 1909–1927* (World Peace Foundation, Pamphlet X, No. 7). Boston, 1927.

Croly, Herbert D., *Marcus Alonzo Hanna*. New York, 1912.

——, *The Promise of American Life*. New York, 1909.

Daniels, Josephus, *The Wilson Era*. Chapel Hill, 1944.

Dennett, Tyler, *Americans in Eastern Asia*. New York, 1922.

——, *John Hay*. New York, 1933.

——, *Theodore Roosevelt and the Russo-Japanese War*. Garden City, 1925.

De Witt, Benjamin P., *The Progressive Movement*. New York, 1915.

Dickinson, John, *Administrative Justice and the Supremacy of the Law in the United States*. Cambridge, 1927.

Dodd, William E., *Woodrow Wilson and His Work*. New York, 1920.

Dreier, Thomas, *Heroes of Insurgency*. Boston, 1910.

Duffy, Herbert S., *William Howard Taft*. New York, 1930.

Dunn, Robert W., *American Foreign Investments*. New York, 1926.

Faulkner, Harold U., *The Quest for Social Justice, 1898–1914* (A History of American Life, XI). New York, 1931.

——, *American Economic History*. New York, 1924.

Forbes, William C., *The Philippine Islands*. 2 vols. Boston, 1928.

Frankfurter, Felix and Greene, Nathan, *The Labor Injunction*. New York, 1930.

Frankfurter, Felix, ed., *Mr. Justice Brandeis*. New Haven, 1932.

——, *Mr. Justice Holmes and the Constitution*. Cambridge, 1927.

Frankfurter, Felix and Landis, James M., *The Business of the Supreme Court*. New York, 1928.

Fuller, Raymond G., *Child Labor and the Constitution*. New York, 1923.

Glass, Carter, *An Adventure in Constructive Finance*. Garden City, 1927.

Gosnell, Harold F., *Boss Platt and the New York Machine*. Chicago, 1924.

Groat, George G., *Attitude of American Courts in Labor Cases* (Columbia University, Studies in History, Economics and Public Law, XLII). New York, 1911.

Hackett, Charles W., *The Mexican Revolution and the United States, 1910–1926* (World Peace Foundation, Pamphlet IX, No. 5). Boston, 1926.

Haines, C. Grove, *The American Doctrine of Judicial Supremacy*. Berkeley, Cal., 1932.

Haynes, Frederick E., *Third Party Movements Since the Civil War*. Iowa City, 1916.

——, *Social Politics in the United States*. Boston, 1924.

Henderson, Gerard Carl, *The Federal Trade Commission*. New Haven, 1924.

Hibben, Paxton, *The Peerless Leader: William Jennings Bryan*. New York, 1929.

Hill, Howard C., *Roosevelt and the Caribbean*. Chicago, 1927.

Hillquit, Morris, *History of Socialism in the United States*. New York, 1910.

Hockett, John A., *A Determination of the Major Social Problems*. New York, 1927.

Howe, Frederic C., *Wisconsin, An Experiment in Democracy*. New York, 1912.

Holt, William S., *Federal Farm Loan Bureau*. Baltimore, 1924.

Hoxie, Robert F., *Trade Unionism in the United States*. New York, 1917.

Hughes, Charles Evans, *The Supreme Court of the United States*. New York, 1928.

Jenks, L. H., *Our Cuban Colony*. New York, 1928.

Jones, Chester Lloyd, *Caribbean Backgrounds and Prospects*. New York, 1931.

Jones, Eliot, *Trust Problem in the United States*. New York, 1921.

Kerney, James, *The Political Education of Woodrow Wilson*. New York, 1926.

King, W. I., *Wealth and Income of the People of the United States*. New York, 1915.

Kohlsaat, H. H., *From McKinley to Harding*. New York, 1923.

La Follette, Robert M., Autobiography: A Personal Narrative of Political Experience. Madison, Wis., 1913.

Laidler, Harry W., Concentration of Control in American Industry. New York, 1931.

Latané, John H., America as a World Power, 1897–1907 (American Nation Series). New York, 1907.

——, A History of American Foreign Policy. Garden City, 1927.

Lief, Alfred, ed., The Dissenting Opinions of Mr. Justice Holmes. New York, 1929.

——, The Social and Economic Views of Mr. Justice Brandeis. New York, 1930.

——, Democracy's Norris. New York, 1939.

Lippmann, Walter. A Preface to Politics. New York, 1914.

Lloyd, Henry Demarest, Wealth Against Commonwealth. New York, 1894.

Lorwin, Lewis L., The American Federation of Labor: History, Policies and Prospects. Washington, 1933.

McBain, Howard Lee, The Living Constitution. New York, 1927.

McCaleb, Walter F., Theodore Roosevelt. New York, 1931.

McCarthy, Charles, The Wisconsin Idea. New York, 1912.

McConnell, Francis J., Humanism and Christianity. New York, 1928.

Madison, Charles A., Critics and Crusaders. New York, 1947.

Mason, Alpheus T., Brandeis, Lawyer and Judge in the Modern State. Princeton, 1933.

Merriam, Charles E., American Political Ideas, 1867–1917. New York, 1920.

——, Four American Party Leaders. New York, 1926.

——, The Written Constitution and the Unwritten Attitude. New York, 1931.

Miller, Hugh Gordon, The Isthmian Highway. New York, 1929.

Millspaugh, Arthur C., Haiti under American Control, 1915–1930. Boston, 1931.

Moody, John, The Truth About the Trusts. New York, 1904.

Moore, Blaine F., The Supreme Court and Unconstitutional Legislation. New York, 1913.

Munro, William B., The Initiative, Referendum and Recall. New York, 1912.

Myers, Gustavus, History of the Supreme Court of the United States. Chicago, 1912.

Odegard, Peter H., *Pressure Politics: The Story of the Anti-Saloon League*. New York, 1928.

Olcott, Charles S., *The Life of William McKinley*. 2 vols. Boston, 1916.

Perkins, Dexter, *The Monroe Doctrine, 1826–1867*. Baltimore, 1933.

Perlman, Selig, *History of Trade Unionism in the United States*. New York, 1923.

Pinchot, Gifford, *The Fight for Conservation*. New York, 1910.

Pollard, Joseph P., *Mr. Justice Cardozo*. New York, 1935.

Powell, Thomas Reed, *The Supreme Court and State Police Power, 1922–1930*. Charlottesville, Va., 1932.

Pringle, Henry F., *Theodore Roosevelt*. New York, 1931.

——, *The Life and Times of William Howard Taft*. 2 vols. New York, 1939.

Ransom, William L., *Majority Rule and the Judiciary*. New York, 1912.

Raper, Arthur F., *The Tragedy of Lynching*. Chapel Hill, 1933.

Remer, Charles F., *Foreign Investments in China*. New York, 1933.

Regier, Cornelius C., *The Era of the Muckrakers*. Chapel Hill, 1932.

Richardson, Dorsey, *Constitutional Doctrines of Justice Holmes*. Baltimore, 1924.

Ripley, William Z., *Railroads: Rates and Regulation*. New York, 1912.

Rippy, James F., *The Capitalists and Colombia*. New York, 1931.

——, *The United States and Mexico*. New York, 1931.

Robertson, William S., *Hispanic-American Relations with the United States*. New York, 1923.

Robinson, Edgar E. and West, Victor J., *The Foreign Policy of Woodrow Wilson*. New York, 1917.

Robinson, Edgar E., *Evolution of American Political Parties*. New York, 1924.

Roosevelt, Theodore, *The New Nationalism*. New York, 1910.

Seager, Henry R. and Gulick, Charles A., *Trust and Corporation Problems*. New York, 1929.

Seligman, E. R. A., *Economics of Farm Relief*. New York, 1929.

Sharfman, I. L., *The Interstate Commerce Commission: A Study in Administrative Law and Procedure*. 4 vols. New York, 1931–1935.

Smyth, William E., The Conquest of Arid America. New York, 1900.

Spahr, E. S., History and Theory of Agricultural Credit in the United States. New York, 1932.

Stanton, S. B., The Behring Sea Controversy. New York, 1892.

Stanwood, Edward, A History of the Presidency. 2 vols. Boston, 1916–1924.

Steffens, Lincoln, Autobiography of Lincoln Steffens. 2 vols. New York, 1931.

Stephenson, Nathaniel W., Nelson W. Aldrich: A Leader in American Politics. New York, 1930.

Stimson, Henry L., American Policy in Nicaragua. New York, 1927.

Storey, Moorfield and Lichauco, Marcial P., Conquest of the Philippines by the United States, 1898–1925. New York, 1926.

Taft, William Howard, The Anti-Trust Act and the Supreme Court. New York, 1914.

Tarbell, Ida M., The Tariff in Our Times. New York, 1931.

Taussig, Frank W., The Tariff History of the United States. New York, 1931.

Teele, Ray P., Irrigation in the United States. New York, 1915.

Treat, P. J., Japan and the United States, 1853–1921. Boston, 1921.

Tumulty, Joseph P., Woodrow Wilson as I Knew Him. Garden City, 1921.

Van Hise, Charles R. and Havemeyer, Loomis, The Conservation of Our Natural Resources. New York, 1930.

Walker, Albert H., History of the Sherman Law. New York, 1910.

Warburg, Paul M., The Federal Reserve System. 2 vols. New York, 1930.

Ware, Norman J., The Labor Movement in the United States, 1860–1895. New York, 1929.

Warren, Charles, Congress, the Constitution, and the Supreme Court. Boston, 1930.

——, The Supreme Court in United States History. 2 vols. Boston, 1932.

Weyl, Walter E., The New Democracy. New York, 1912.

White, William Allen, Masks in a Pageant. New York, 1928.

Willis, H. Parker, The Federal Reserve System. New York, 1923.

Willoughby, W. F., Territories and Dependencies of the United States. New York, 1905.

——, *Principles of Judicial Administration*. Washington, 1929.

Willoughby, W. W., *Principles of the Constitutional Law of the United States*. New York, 1930.

——, *The Constitutional Law of the United States*. New York, 1910.

——, *Foreign Rights and Interests in China*. 2 vols. Baltimore, 1920.

Winkler, Max, *Investments of United States Capital in Latin America* (World Peace Foundation, Pamphlet XII, No. 6). Boston, 1928.

Wilson, Woodrow, *The New Democracy*. New York, 1916.

——, *The New Freedom*. New York, 1913.

Wright, Quincey, ed., *Interpretations of American Foreign Policy*. Chicago, 1930.

CHAPTERS 11–16

WORLD WAR I AND ITS AFTERMATH

Allen, Devere, *The Fight for Peace*. New York, 1930.

American Civil Liberties Union. The Attempted Deportation of John Strachey (1935).

Bills in Congress for Freedom of the Air (1936).

Civil Liberties in American Colonies (1933).

Free Speech in 1924 (1924).

Free Speech, 1926: The Work of the Union (1926).

Fight for Civil Liberty, 1930–1931 (1931).

Gags on Teaching, New York (1933).

How Goes the Bill of Rights? (1936).

Land of the Free (1935).

Land of Pilgrims' Pride, 1932–1933 (1933).

Liberty Under the New Deal (1934).

So This Is Free Speech! (1935).

So This Is Liberty! (1924).

State Laws Against Free Speech (1926).

State Police in Relation to Labor and Civil Liberties (1924).

Strike Is Criminal Syndicalism—in California (1932).

Sweet Land of Liberty (1932).

War-Time Prosecution and Mob Violence (1920).

What Shocked the Censors (1933).

Who's Un-American? An Answer to the "Patriots" (1935).

Anonymous, *Arbitration and the United States* (World Peace Foundation, Pamphlet IX, Nos. 6–7). Boston, 1926.

Bailey, Thomas A., *Woodrow Wilson and the Lost Peace*. New York, 1944.

——, *A Diplomatic History of the American People*. New York, 1942.

——, *Woodrow Wilson and the Great Betrayal*. New York, 1945.

Baker, Newton D., *Why We Went to War*. New York, 1936.

Baker, Ray Stannard, *Woodrow Wilson, Life and Letters*. 8 vols. Garden City, 1927–1939.

——, *What Wilson Did at Paris*. New York, 1919.

Baruch, Bernard M., *American Industry in the War*. Washington, 1921.

——, *The Making of the Reparation and Economic Sections of the Treaty*. New York, 1920.

Bassett, John S., *Our War with Germany*. New York, 1919.

——, *The League of Nations*. New York, 1928.

Bates, Ernest Sutherland, *This Land of Liberty*. New York, 1930.

Beales, A. C. F., *The History of Peace*. New York, 1931.

Beard, Mary R., *A Short History of the American Labor Movement*. New York, 1925.

Benns, F. Lee, *Europe Since 1914*. New York, 1934.

Bergmann, Karl, *The History of Reparations*. London, 1927.

Berman, Edward, *Labor Disputes and the President of the United States* (Columbia University, Studies in History, Economics and Public Law, CXI, No. 2). New York, 1924.

Bing, Alexander M., *War-time Strikes and Their Adjustment*. New York, 1921.

Bogart, Ernest L., *War Costs and Their Financing*. New York, 1921.

Brissenden, Paul F., *The I.W.W.: A Study of American Syndicalism* (Columbia University Studies, LXXXIII). New York, 1919.

Brookings Institution, *United States Shipping Board*. Washington, 1931.

Carlton, Frank T., *The History and Problems of Organized Labor*. Boston, 1920.

Chafee, Zechariah, Jr., *The Inquiring Mind*. New York, 1928.

——, *Freedom of Speech*. New York, 1920.

Chambrun, Colonel de and Marenches, Captain de, *The American Army in the European Conflict*. New York, 1919.

Clarkson, Grosvenor B., *Industrial America in the World War.* Boston, 1923.

Cole, Stewart G., *The History of Fundamentalism.* New York, 1931.

Coleman, McAlister, *Eugene V. Debs: A Man Unafraid.* New York, 1930.

Counts, George S., *Soviet Challenge to America.* New York, 1931.

Creel, George, *How We Advertised America.* New York, 1920.

Curti, Merle E., *The American Peace Crusade.* Durham, 1929.

——, *Bryan and World Peace* (Smith College, Studies in History, Nos. 3–4). Northampton, 1931.

——, *Peace or War: The American Struggle, 1636–1936.* New York, 1936.

Dunn, Robert W., *Company Unions.* New York, 1927.

Ellingwood, Albert R. and Coombs, Whitney, *The Government and Railroad Transportation.* Boston, 1930.

Fay, S. B., *The Origins of the World War.* 2 vols. New York, 1928.

Fine, Nathan, *Labor and Farmer Parties in the United States, 1828–1928.* New York, 1928.

Fisher, Irving, *Prohibition at Its Worst.* New York, 1926.

Fleming, Denna F., *The Treaty Veto of the American Senate.* New York, 1930.

——, *The United States and the League of Nations, 1918–1920.* New York, 1932.

Frankfurter, Felix, *The Case of Sacco and Vanzetti.* Boston, 1927.

Frankfurter, Felix and Greene, N., *The Labor Injunction.* New York, 1930.

Gambs, John S., *The Decline of the I.W.W.* New York, 1932.

Garrison, Winfred E., *Intolerance.* New York, 1934.

Gibson, R. H. and Prendergast, M., *German Submarine War, 1914–1918.* New York, 1931.

Gompers, Samuel, *Seventy Years of Life and Labor.* 2 vols. New York, 1925.

Harbord, James G., *America in the World War.* Boston, 1933.

Harris, Abram L. and Spero, Sterling D., *Black Worker: The Negro and the Labor Movement.* New York, 1931.

Hayes, Arthur Garfield, *Let Freedom Ring.* New York, 1928.

——, *Trial by Prejudice.* New York, 1933.

Haynes, Frederick E., *Social Politics in the United States.* Boston, 1924.

Hillquit, Morris, *History of Socialism in the United States*. New York, 1910.

Hines, Walker D., *War History of American Railroads* (Economic and Social History of the World War, J. T. Shotwell, ed.). New Haven, 1928.

Holt, William S., *Treaties Defeated by the Senate*. Baltimore, 1933.

House, Edward M. and Seymour, Charles, eds. *What Really Happened at Paris*. New York, 1921.

Hoxie, Robert F., *Trade Unionism in the United States*. New York, 1920.

Hudson, Manley O., *Permanent Court of International Justice and the Question of American Participation*. Cambridge, 1925.

Huidekoper, Frederic L., *The Military Unpreparedness of the United States*. New York, 1915.

Irwin, William H., *How Red Is America?* New York, 1927.

Jessup, Philip C., *The United States and the World Court* (World Peace Foundation, Pamphlet XII, No. 4). Boston, 1929.

Joad, C. E. M., *Liberty Today*. New York, 1935.

Kent, Frank R., *The Great Game of Politics*. New York, 1928.

Kenworthy, J. M. and Young, G., *Freedom of the Seas*. New York, 1928.

Keynes, John M., *Economic Consequences of the Peace*. London, 1919.

Lansing, Robert, *The Big Four and Others of the Peace Conference*. Boston, 1921.

Lasswell, Harold D., *Propaganda Technique in the World War*. London, 1927.

Lippmann, Walter, *American Inquisitors*. New York, 1928.

Lodge, Henry Cabot, *Senate and the League of Nations*. New York, 1925.

Macy, John A., *Socialism in America*. Garden City, 1916.

Mason, Alpheus T., *Organized Labor and the Law*. Durham, 1925.

Mayo, Katherine, *Soldiers What Next!* Boston, 1934.

Mecklin, John M., *The Ku Klux Klan: A Study of the American Mind*. New York, 1924.

Merz, Charles, *The Dry Decade*. Garden City, 1931.

Moulton, Harold G. and Pasvolsky, Leo, *War Debts and World Prosperity*. New York, 1932.

National Industrial Conference Board. *The American Merchant Marine Problem*. New York, 1929.

——, *The Inter-Ally Debts and the United States*. New York, 1925.

Noble, George B., *Policies and Opinions at Paris, 1919*. New York, 1935.

Noyes, A. D., *The War Period in American Finance, 1908–1925*. New York, 1926.

Oneal, James, *American Communism*. New York, 1927.

Paxson, Frederick L., *America at War, 1917–1918*. Boston, 1939.

——, *Pre-War Years, 1913–1917*. Boston, 1936.

Perkins, Dexter, *America and Two Wars*. Boston, 1944.

Perlman, Selig, *A History of Trade Unionism in the United States*. New York, 1922.

Pierce, Bessie L., *Public Opinion and the Teaching of History in the United States*. New York, 1926.

——, *Citizens Organizations and the Civic Training of Youth*. New York, 1933.

Ponsonby, Arthur, *Falsehood in War Time*. London, 1928.

Powell, Edward A., *The Army behind the Army*. New York, 1919.

Raup, Bruce, *Education and Organized Interests in America*. New York, 1936.

Saposs, David J., *Left-Wing Unionism*. New York, 1926.

Schmitt, Bernadotte E., *The Coming of the War*. 2 vols. New York, 1930.

Scott, James B., *A Survey of International Relations Between the United States and Germany, 1914–1917*. New York, 1917.

Seldes, George, *Freedom of the Press*. New York, 1935.

——, *Iron, Blood and Profits*. New York, 1934.

Seymour, Charles, *Woodrow Wilson and the World War* (Chronicles of America Series, XLVIII). New Haven, 1921.

——, ed., *The Intimate Papers of Colonel House*. 4 vols. Boston, 1928.

——, *American Neutrality, 1914–1917*. New Haven, 1935.

——, *American Diplomacy During the World War*. Baltimore, 1934.

Shipley, Maynard, *The War on Modern Science*. New York, 1927.

Shotwell, James T., *War as an Instrument of National Policy*. New York, 1929.

Siegfried, André, *America Comes of Age*. New York, 1927.

Surface, Frank M., *The Grain Trade during the World War*. New York, 1928.

Temperley, H. W. V., ed., *A History of the Peace Conference of Paris*. 6 vols. London, 1920–1924.

Thomas, Norman M., *The Conscientious Objector in America*. New York, 1923.

——, *Is Conscience a Crime?* New York, 1927.

Tuttle, Florence G., *Alternatives to War*. New York, 1931.

Van Hise, Charles R., *Conservation and Regulation in the United States during the World War*. Washington, 1917.

Ware, Norman, *The Labor Movement in the United States, 1860–1895*. New York, 1929.

Wesley, C. H., *Negro Labor in the United States, 1850–1925*. New York, 1927.

Whipple, Leon, *The Story of Civil Liberty in the United States*. New York, 1927.

Whitney, Edson L., *The American Peace Society: A Centennial History*. Washington, 1928.

Willoughby, William F., *Government Organization in War Time and After*. New York, 1919.

Witte, Edwin E., *The Government in Labor Disputes*. New York, 1932.

Wolf, Harry D., *The Railroad Labor Board*. Chicago, 1927.

Wolman, Leo, *The Growth of American Trade Unions*. New York, 1924.

Slosson, Preston W., *Great Crusade and After, 1914–1928* (A History of American Life, XII). New York, 1930.

CHAPTERS 17–20

BETWEEN TWO WARS

Adams, James Truslow, *Our Business Civilization*. New York, 1929.

Adams, Samuel H., *The Incredible Era*. Boston, 1939.

Allen, Frederick L., *Only Yesterday, an Informal History of the 1920's*. New York, 1931.

——, *The Lords of Creation*. New York, 1935.

Allen, Robert S., *Washington Merry-Go-Round*. New York, 1931.

Beard, Charles A., ed., *Whither Mankind*. New York, 1928.

Berle, Adolf A. and Means, G. C., *The Modern Corporation and Private Property*. New York, 1932.

Black, John D., *Agricultural Reform in the United States*. New York, 1929.

Bonbright, James C. and Means, Gardiner C., *The Holding Company*. New York, 1932.

Borsodi, Ralph, *This Ugly Civilization*. New York, 1929.

Brooks, Robert R., *Unions of Their Own Choosing*. New Haven, 1939.

Capper, Arthur, *The Agricultural Bloc*. New York, 1922.

Carver, Thomas N., *The Present Economic Revolution in the United States*. Boston, 1925.

Chase, Stuart, *Men and Machines*. New York, 1929.

——, *Prosperity: Fact or Myth*. New York, 1929.

——, *A New Deal*. New York, 1932.

Childs, Harwood L., *Labor and Capital in National Politics*. Columbus, 1930.

Clark, Evans, ed., *The Internal Debts of the United States*. New York, 1933.

Clark, John M., *Social Control of Business*. Chicago, 1926.

Committee on Recent Economic Changes, *Recent Economic Changes in the United States*. 2 vols. New York, 1929.

Coolidge, Calvin, *Autobiography*. New York, 1929.

Corey, Lewis, *The Decline of American Capitalism*. New York, 1934.

Crecraft, Earl W., *Government and Business*. Yonkers-on-Hudson, 1928.

Dixon, Frank H., *Railroads and Government, 1910–1921*. New York, 1922.

Donald, W. J. A., *Trade Associations*. New York, 1933.

Donham, Wallace B., *Business Adrift*. New York, 1931.

Douglas, Paul H., *Real Wages in the United States, 1890–1926*. Boston, 1930.

Dunn, R. W., *Company Unions*. New York, 1927.

Elsbree, Hugh L., *Interstate Transmission of Electric Power*. Cambridge, 1931.

Fetter, Frank A., *The Masquerade of Monopoly*. New York, 1931.

Forrester, Robert B., *Report on Large Scale Cooperative Marketing in the United States*. London, 1925.

Foth, Joseph H., *Trade Associations, Their Services to Industry*. New York, 1930.

Frankfurter, Felix and Greene, Nathan, *The Labor Injunction*. New York, 1930.

Gambs, John S., *The Decline of the I.W.W*. New York, 1932.

Gamio, Manuel, Mexican Immigration to the United States. Chicago, 1930.

Garis, Roy L., Immigration Restriction. New York, 1927.

Gee, Wilson, The Place of Agriculture in American Life. New York, 1930.

Hadley, Arthur T., Railroad Transportation, Its History and Its Law. New York, 1903.

Hallgren, Mauritz A., Seeds of Revolt. New York, 1933.

Harris, Seymour, Economics of Social Security. New York, 1941.

Hardy, Charles O., Recent Growth of the Electric Light and Power Industry. Washington, 1929.

Heer, Clarence, The Post-war Expansion of State Expenditures. New York, 1926.

Heermance, Edgar L., The Ethics of Business: A Study of Current Methods. New York, 1926.

Hexter, Maurice B., Social Consequences of Business Cycles. Boston, 1925.

Hill, Edwin C., The American Scene. New York, 1933.

Hoover, Herbert C., American Individualism. New York, 1923.

——, The Challenge to Liberty. New York, 1934.

——, The New Day. Stanford University, 1929.

Jones, Eliot, The Anthracite Coal Combination in the United States (Harvard Economic Studies, XI). Cambridge, 1914.

Jones, Joseph M., Tariff Retaliation. Philadelphia, 1934.

Josephson, Matthew, The President Makers. New York, 1940.

King, W. I., The National Income and Its Purchasing Power. New York, 1930.

Kirsh, Benjamin S., Trade Associations: The Legal Aspects. New York, 1928.

Kuznets, Simon S., Seasonal Variations in Industry and Trade. New York, 1933.

Laidler, Harry W., Concentration of Control in American Industry. New York, 1931.

Lippincott, Isaac, What the Farmer Needs. New York, 1928.

Lynd, Robert S. and Lynd, Helen M., Middletown: A Study in Contemporary American Culture. New York, 1929.

MacVeagh, Rogers, The Transportation Act, 1920: Its Sources, History and Text. New York, 1923.

Malin, James C., The United States after the World War. Boston, 1930.

Marquand, H. A., *Dynamics of Industrial Combination*. New York, 1931.

Mazur, Paul M., *American Prosperity*. New York, 1928.

Merz, Charles, *The Great American Band Wagon*. New York, 1928.

Mitchell, George S., *Textile Unionism in the South*. Chapel Hill, 1931.

Myers, James, *Representative Government in Industry*. New York, 1924.

National Industrial Conference Board, *Cost of Government in the United States, 1928–1929*. New York, 1931.

——, *The Agricultural Problem in the United States*. New York, 1926.

——, *Mergers and the Law*. New York, 1929.

——, *Trade Associations: Their Economic Significance and Legal Status*. New York, 1925.

Nourse, Edwin G., *American Agriculture and the European Market*. New York, 1924.

Peel, Roy V. and Donnelly, Thomas C., *The 1928 Campaign*. New York, 1931.

Pringle, Henry F., *Alfred E. Smith: A Critical Study*. New York, 1927.

Raushenbush, H. S. and Laidler, Harry W., *Power Control*. New York, 1928.

Ravage, M. E., *The Story of Teapot Dome*. New York, 1924.

Ripley, William Z., *Main Street and Wall Street*. Boston, 1927.

Schuman, Frederick L., *American Policy Toward Russia Since 1917*. New York, 1928.

Seager, Henry R. and Gulick, Charles A., *Trust and Corporation Problems*. New York, 1929.

Seldes, Gilbert V., *The Years of the Locust* (America, 1929–1932). Boston, 1933.

Shannon, Fred A., *Economic History of the People of the United States*. New York, 1934.

Slosson, Preston W., *The Great Crusade and After, 1914–1928* (A History of American Life, XII). New York, 1931.

Smith, Alfred E., *Progressive Democracy*. New York, 1928.

Soule, George H., *The Coming American Revolution*. New York, 1934.

——, *A Planned Society*. New York, 1932.

Southard, F. A., American Industry in Europe. Boston, 1931.

Stephenson, George M., A History of American Immigration, 1820–1924. Boston, 1926.

Tippetts, Charles S. and Livermore, Shaw, Business Organization and Control. New York, 1932.

Tugwell, Rexford G., Industrial Discipline and the Governmental Acts. New York, 1933.

——, Industry's Coming of Age. New York, 1927.

Twelve Southerners, I'll Take My Stand. New York, 1930.

United States Federal Trade Commission, Open-Price Trade Associations. Washington, 1929.

Walsh, John R., C.I.O.; Industrial Unionism in Action. New York, 1937.

Waters, Walter W., B.E.F.: The Whole Story of the Bonus Army. New York, 1933.

White, William Allen, A Puritan in Babylon. New York, 1938.

——, Masks in a Pageant. New York, 1928.

Wilbur, Ray L. and Hyde, Arthur M., The Hoover Policies. New York, 1937.

CHAPTERS 21–25

THE NEW DEAL

Adamic, Louis, Dynamite. Revised edition, New York, 1934.

Allen, Frederick L., Since Yesterday: The Nineteen Thirties in America. New York, 1940.

Arkright, Frank, The ABC of Technocracy. New York, 1933.

Ayres, Leonard P., Economics of Recovery. New York, 1934.

Bates, Ernest S., American Faith: Its Religious, Political, and Economic Foundations. New York, 1940.

Beard, Charles A., The Future Comes. New York, 1933.

Beard, Charles A., America Faces the Future. Boston, 1932.

Beard, Charles A. and Beard, Mary R., America in Midpassage. New York, 1939.

Becker, Carl L. and others, Safeguarding Civil Liberty Today. Ithaca, N. Y., 1945.

Berle, Adolf A., America's Recovery Program. London, 1934.

Brown, Douglass V. and others, The Economics of the Recovery Program. New York, 1934.

Burns, Eveline M., Toward Social Security. New York, 1936.

Cahill, Marion C., *Shorter Hours: A Study of the Movement Since the Civil War*. New York, 1932.

Casgill, Oscar, *Intellectual America: Ideas on the March*. New York, 1941.

Chase, Stuart, *The Economy of Abundance*. New York, 1934.

——, *Technocracy: An Interpretation*. New York, 1933.

Clark, John M., *Social Control of Business*. New York, 1939.

Coughlin, Charles E., *A Series of Lectures on Social Justice*. Royal Oak, Mich., 1935.

Crowell, Chester T., "The Townsend Plan: a Challenge to Congress," in *American Mercury*, XXXIV, 456–460.

Daniell, F. Raymond, "Gentleman from Louisiana," in *Current History*, XLI, 172–178.

Daugherty, Carroll R., *Labor Under the NRA*. Boston, 1934.

Deane, Albert, *The Deane Plan for Mutual Security*. New York, 1936.

Dearing, Charles L., *The ABC of the NRA*. Washington, 1934.

Douglas, Paul H., *Social Security in the United States*. New York, 1936.

Epstein, Abraham, *The Challenge of the Aged*. New York, 1928.

Eriksson, Erik McK., *The Supreme Court and the New Deal*. Rosemead, Calif., 1940.

Ezekiel, Mordecai, *$2500 a Year, from Scarcity to Abundance*. New York, 1936.

Fay, Bernard, *Roosevelt and His America*. Boston, 1933.

Fechner, Robert, *Report of the Director of Emergency Conservation Work, April 5, 1933–June 30, 1935*. Washington, 1936.

Federal Emergency Relief Administration, *Report on Education Camps for Unemployed Women, 1934–1935*. Washington, 1936.

Feldman, Herman, *Prohibition, Its Economic and Industrial Aspects*. New York, 1930.

Filene, Edward A., *The Way Out*. Garden City, 1924.

Filler, Louis, *Crusaders for American Liberalism*. New York, 1939.

Gee, Wilson, *American Farm Policy*. New York, 1934.

Gordon, M. S., *Barriers to World Trade*. New York, 1941.

Hall, John Raymond, *Tomorrow's Route*. New York, 1932.

Holcombe, Arthur N., *The New Party Politics*. New York, 1933.

Hoover, Herbert C., *Addresses upon the American Road, 1933–1938*. New York, 1938.

Hopkins, Harry L., *United States Federal Emergency Relief Ad-*

ministration, Monthly Reports, May, 1933–December, 1935. Washington, 1936.

Hutton, David G., *Midwest at Noon*. Chicago, 1946.

Ickes, Harold L., *Accomplishments of the Federal Emergency Administration of Public Works, July 8, 1933–May 18, 1936*. Washington, 1936.

Johnson, Hugh S., *The Blue Eagle from Egg to Earth*. Garden City, N. Y., 1935.

Kelly, Fred J. and McNeely, John H., *Federal Student Aid Program* (United States Department of Interior, Bulletin No. 14, 1935). Washington, 1935.

Kirsh, Benjamin S. and Shapiro, Harold R., *The National Industrial Recovery Act*. New York, 1933.

Lambert, A. B., *In Reply to Technocracy, a 100% Profit Tax*. St. Louis, 1933.

Landis, James M., *The Administrative Process*. New Haven, 1938.

Lief, Alfred, ed., *Dissenting Opinions of Mr. Justice Holmes*. New York, 1929.

——, *Social and Economic Views of Mr. Justice Brandeis*. New York, 1930.

Lindley, Ernest K., *The Roosevelt Revolution, First Phase*. New York, 1933.

——, *Halfway with Roosevelt*. New York, 1937.

——, *A New Deal for Youth*. New York, 1938.

Lippmann, Walter, "Is the Townsend Plan for Old-Age Revolving Pensions Sound?" in *The Congressional Digest*, XIV, 92–94.

Long, Huey P., *My First Days in the White House*. Harrisburg, 1935.

Looker, Earle, *This Man Roosevelt*. New York, 1932.

MacDonald, Austin F., *Federal Aid, A Study of the American Subsidy System*. New York, 1928.

MacDonald, William, *The Menace of Recovery*. New York, 1934.

Odum, Howard W. and Willard, D. W., *Systems of Public Welfare*. Chapel Hill, 1925.

Ogburn, William F., ed., *Social Change and the New Deal*. Chicago, 1934.

Oxley, Howard W., *Education in Civilian Conservation Corps Camps* (Civilian Conservation Corps). Washington, 1936.

Peterson, Frank, "Concerning the Townsend Plan," in *The New Republic*, LXXXI, 305–306.

Pritchett, Charles H., *The Tennessee Valley Authority*. Chapel Hill, 1943.

Ryan, John A., *A Better Economic Order*. New York, 1935.

——, *Distributive Justice*. New York, 1916.

——, *A Living Wage*. New York, 1906.

Roosevelt, Franklin D., *Looking Forward*. New York, 1933.

——, *On Our Way*. New York, 1934.

Samson, Leon, *The American Mind; A Study in Socio-Analysis*. New York, 1932.

Schafer, Joseph, *A Social History of American Agriculture*. New York, 1936.

Schlesinger, Arthur M., *The New Deal in Action, 1933–1939*. New York, 1940.

Schuman, Frederick L., *American Policy Toward Russia Since 1917*. New York, 1928.

Schmeckebier, Laurence F., *New Federal Organizations* (Brookings Institution). Washington, 1934.

Scott, Howard, *An Introduction to Technocracy*. New York, 1933.

Sinclair, Upton B., *The Way Out, What Lies Ahead for America*. New York, 1933.

Smith, Webster, *The Kingfish*. New York, 1933.

Stearns, H. E., ed., *America Now*. New York, 1938.

Stevenson, Marietta and Spear, Ralph E., *The Social Security Program*. Chicago, 1936.

Stein, Emanuel, *Labor and the New Deal*. New York, 1934.

Strachey, John, *The Coming Struggle for Power*. New York, 1934.

Swing, Raymond G., "Dr. Townsend Solves It All," in *The Nation*, CXL, 268–270.

Swope, Gerard, *The Swope Plan: Details, Criticisms, Analysis*. New York, 1931.

Terborgh, George W., *Price Control Devices in NRA Codes*. Washington, 1934.

Thomas, Norman M., *The Choice Before Us*. New York, 1934.

Tugwell, Rexford G., *Mr. Hoover's Economic Policy*. New York, 1932.

University of Chicago, "The Economic Meaning of the Townsend Plan" (Public Policy, Pamphlet No. 20). Chicago, 1936.

United States Bureau of the Census, *Relief Expenditures by Governmental and Private Organizations*. Washington, 1932.

United States Superintendent of Documents, Catalogue of the

Public Documents of Congress and of All Departments of the Government, 1933–1935.

Unofficial Observer, *The New Dealers*. New York, 1934.

Valenstein, Lawrence and Weiss, E. B., *Business under the Recovery Act*. New York, 1933.

Vance, Rupert B., *All These People*. Chapel Hill, 1945.

Wallace, Henry A., *America Must Choose*. New York, 1934.

——, *New Frontiers*. New York, 1934.

——, *Democracy Reborn*. New York, 1944.

——, *Whose Constitution?* New York, 1936.

Webb, Walter P., *Divided We Stand; The Crisis of a Frontierless Democracy*. New York, 1937.

Whitney, Simon N., *Trade Associations and Industrial Control; A Critique of the NRA*. New York, 1934.

Willkie, Wendell L., *This Is Wendell Willkie*. New York, 1940.

Wolman, Leo, *Labor and the State*. New York, 1940.

CHAPTERS 26–30

WORLD WAR II

Beard, Charles A., *A Foreign Policy for America*. New York, 1936.

Berle, Adolf A., *New Directions in the New World*. New York, 1940.

Buell, Raymond L., *Isolated America*. New York, 1940.

Churchill, Winston, *Step by Step, 1936–1939*. Toronto, 1939.

——, *While England Slept: A Survey of World Affairs, 1932–1938*. New York, 1938.

Colby, Charles C., *Geographic Aspects of International Relations*. Chicago, 1938.

Dulles, John Foster, *War, Peace, and Change*. New York, 1939.

Earle, Edward M., *Against This Torrent*. Princeton, N. J., 1941.

Emeny, Brooks, *The Strategy of Raw Materials*. New York, 1934.

Foreman, Clark and Raushenbush, Stephen, *Total Defense*. New York, 1940.

Grew, Joseph C., *Ten Years in Japan*. New York, 1944.

Ichihashi, Yamato, *The Washington Conference and After*. Stanford, 1928.

Jessup, Philip C., ed., *Neutrality: Its History, Economics, and Law*. 4 vols. New York, 1936.

Johnson, Walter, *The Battle Against Isolation*. Chicago, 1944.

Lerner, Max, *Ideas Are Weapons*. New York, 1939.

Marshall, S. L. A., *Blitzkrieg*. New York, 1940.

Moulton, Harold G. and Pasvolsky, Leo, *War Debts and World Prosperity*. Washington, 1932.

Myrdal, Gunnar, *An American Dilemma*. 2 vols. New York, 1944.

Ogburn, William F., *American Society in Wartime*. Chicago, 1943.

Perkins, Dexter, *Hands Off: A History of the Monroe Doctrine*. Boston, 1941.

Pyle, Ernie, *Here Is Your War*. New York, 1943.

Raushenbush, Hilmar S., *The March of Fascism*. New Haven, 1940.

Robinson, Henry M., *Fantastic Interim*. New York, 1943.

Schuman, Frederick L., *Night Over Europe*. New York, 1941.

Speier, Hans and Kahler, A., eds., *War in Our Time*. New York, 1939.

Stettinius, Edward R., *Lend-Lease, Weapon for Victory*. New York, 1944.

Thompson, Warren S., *Population and Peace in the Pacific*. Chicago, 1946.

Tobin, Harold J. and Bidwell, Percy W., *Mobilizing Civilian America*. New York, 1940.

Wallace, Henry A., *The Century of the Common Man*. New York, 1943.

Welles, Sumner, *The Time for Decision*. New York, 1944.

Whittlesey, Derwent, *The Earth and the State*. New York, 1941.

Willkie, Wendell L., *One World*. New York, 1943.

Index

5277